Classics of Western Political Thought

Short Course Edition

Michael Julius, Editor

CONTENTS

* denotes complete text

PLATO

The writings of Plato (428-348 BC) are considered foundation to our entire cannon of knowledge, covering not only philosophy and politics but also the physical sciences science, mathematics, religion, and beyond. Born to a wealthy family and taught by Socrates, Plato came of age of age during the zenith of Athenian power and culture, only to suffer through the execution of his teacher in the aftermath of Sparta's victory in the Peloponnesian War. He would go on to be a teacher himself—notably to Aristotle—and later in life founded one of the world's most influential schools: The Academy.

A curious thing about most Platonic writings is that they are not written in his own voice, but rather presented as 'Socratic Dialogues', with Socrates as the narrator. These dialogues represent the use of the elenchus (ἔλεγχος)—the Socratic method of dialectic that he employed to show the ignorance his interlocutors. This method of disputation can be seen in the *Apology* and the *Crito* which, while discussing the nature of citizenship in a democracy, show the ultimate resort of the Socratic method: Socrates forces to drink the hemlock for crimes against the public.

The *Republic* is also a Socratic dialogue, and is perhaps Plato's most important and influential political work. Presented as a conversation between Socrates and a group of others about the nature of justice, it acts as a vehicle for Plato to present his vision of the perfect city: Kallipolis. Touching on a wide range of social and political issues, it would not be hyperbole to suggest that *Republic* is the starting point for political philosophy, and the birthplace of the vexing discussions we still have today.

APOLOGY
PLATO

I know not, O Athenians! how far you have been influenced by my accusers for my part, in listening to them I almost forgot myself, so plausible were their arguments however, so to speak, they have said nothing true. But of the many falsehoods which they uttered I wondered at one of them especially, that in which they said that you ought to be on your guard lest you should be deceived by me, as being eloquent in speech. For that they are not ashamed of being forthwith convicted by me in fact, when I shall show that I am not by any means eloquent, this seemed to me the most shameless thing in them, unless indeed they call him eloquent who speaks the truth. For, if they mean this, then I would allow that I am an orator, but not after their fashion for they, as I affirm, have said nothing true, but from me you shall hear the whole truth. Not indeed, Athenians, arguments highly wrought, as theirs were, with choice phrases and expressions, nor adorned, but you shall hear a speech uttered without premeditation in such words as first present themselves. For I am confident that what I say will be just, and let none of you expect otherwise, for surely it would not become my time of life to come before you like a youth with a got up speech. Above all things, therefore, I beg and implore this of you, O Athenians! if you hear me defending myself in the same language as that in which I am accustomed to speak both in the forum at the counters, where many of you have heard me, and elsewhere, not to be surprised or disturbed on this account. For the case is this: I now for the first time come before a court of justice, though more than seventy years old; I am therefore utterly a stranger to the language here. As, then, if I were really a stranger, you would have pardoned me if I spoke in the language and the manner in which I had been educated, so now I ask this of you as an act of justice, as it appears to me, to disregard the manner of my speech, for perhaps it may be somewhat worse, and perhaps better, and to consider this only, and to give your attention to this, whether I speak what is just or not; for this is the virtue of a judge, but of an orator to speak the truth.

First, then, O Athenians! I am right in defending myself against the first false accusations alleged against me, and my first accusers, and then against the latest accusations, and the latest accusers. For many have been accusers of me to you, and for many years, who have asserted nothing true, of whom I am more afraid than of Anytus and his party, although they too are formidable; but those are still more formidable, Athenians, who, laying hold of many of you from childhood, have persuaded you, and accused me of what is not true: "that there is one Socrates, a wise man, who occupies himself about celestial matters, and has explored every thing under the earth, and makes the worse appear the better reason." Those, O Athenians! who have spread abroad this report are my formidable accusers; for they who hear them think that such as search into these things do not believe that there are gods. In the next place, these accusers are numerous, and have accused me now

Text based off the Benjamin Jowett translation, with adjustments for modern spellings.

for a long time; moreover, they said these things to you at that time of life in which you were most credulous, when you were boys and some of you youths, and they accused me al-
5 together in my absence, when there was no one to defend me. But the most unreasonable thing of all is, that it is not possible to learn and mention their names, except that one of them happens to be a comic poet. Such, how-
10 ever, as, influenced by envy and calumny, have persuaded you, and those who, being them-selves persuaded, have persuaded others, all these are most difficult to deal with; for it is not possible to bring any of them forward
15 here, nor to confute any; but it is altogether necessary to fight, as it were with a shadow, in making my defense, and to convict when there is no one to answer. Consider, therefore, as I have said, that my accusers are twofold, some
20 who have lately accused me, and others long since, whom I have made mention of; and believe that I ought to defend myself against these first; for you heard them accusing me first, and much more than these last.
25

Well. I must make my defense, then, O Athe-nians! and endeavor in this so short a space of time to remove from your minds the calumny which you have long entertained. I wish, in-
30 deed, it might be so, if it were at all better both for you and me, and that in making my defense I could effect something more advan-tageous still: I think, however, that it will be difficult, and I am not entirely ignorant what
35 the difficulty is. Nevertheless, let this turn out as may be pleasing to God, I must obey the law and make my defense.

Let us, then, repeat from the beginning what
40 the accusation is from which the calumny against me has arisen, and relying on which Melitus has preferred this indictment against me. Well. What, then, do they who charge me say in their charge? For it is necessary to read
45 their deposition as of public accusers. "Socra-tes acts wickedly, and is criminally curious in searching into things under the earth, and in the heavens, and in making the worse appear the better cause, and in teaching these same
50 things to others." Such is the accusation: for such things you have yourselves seen in the comedy of Aristophanes, one Socrates there carried about, saying that he walks in the air, and acting many other buffooneries, of which
55 I understand nothing whatever. Nor do I say this as disparaging such a science, if there be any one skilled in such things, only let me not be prosecuted by Melitus on a charge of this kind; but I say it, O Athenians! because I have
60 nothing to do with such matters. And I call upon most of you as witnesses of this, and require you to inform and tell each other, as many of you as have ever heard me convers-ing; and there are many such among you.
65 Therefore tell each other, if any one of you has ever heard me conversing little or much on such subjects. And from this you will know that other things also, which the multitude assert of me, are of a similar nature.
70

However not one of these things is true; nor, if you have heard from any one that I attempt to teach men, and require payment, is this true. Though this, indeed, appears to me to be
75 an honorable thing, if one should be able to instruct men, like Gorgias the Leontine, Prodicus the Cean, and Hippias the Elean. For each of these, O Athenians! is able, by going through the several cities, to persuade the
80 young men, who can attach themselves gratui-tously to such of their own fellow-citizens as they please, to abandon their fellow-citizens and associate with them, giving them money and thanks besides. There is also another wise
85 man here, a Parian, who, I hear, is staying in the city. For I happened to visit a person who

7

spends more money on the sophists than all others together: I mean Callias, son of Hipponicus. I therefore asked him, for he has two sons, "Callias," I said, "if your two sons were
5 colts or calves, we should have had to choose a master for them, and hire a person who would make them excel in such qualities as belong to their nature; and he would have been a groom or an agricultural laborer. But
10 now, since your sons are men, what master do you intend to choose for them? Who is there skilled in the qualities that become a man and a citizen? For I suppose you must have considered this, since you have sons. Is there any
15 one," I said, "or not?" "Certainly," he answered. "Who is he?" said I, "and whence does he come? and on what terms does he teach?" He replied, "Evenus the Parian, Socrates, for five minæ." And I deemed Evenus
20 happy, if he really possesses this art, and teaches admirably. And I too should think highly of myself, and be very proud, if I possessed this knowledge, but I possess it not, O Athenians.

25 Perhaps, one of you may now object: "But, Socrates, what have you done, then? Whence have these calumnies against you arisen? For surely if you had not busied yourself more
30 than others, such a report and story would never have got abroad, unless you had done something different from what most men do. Tell us, therefore, what it is, that we may not pass a hasty judgment on you." He who
35 speaks thus appears to me to speak justly, and I will endeavor to show you what it is that has occasioned me this character and imputation. Listen, then: to some of you perhaps I shall appear to jest, yet be assured that I shall tell
40 you the whole truth. For I, O Athenians! have acquired this character through nothing else than a certain wisdom. Of what kind, then, is this wisdom? Perhaps it is merely human wis-

dom. For in this, in truth, I appear to be wise.
45 They probably, whom I have just now mentioned, possessed a wisdom more than human, otherwise I know not what to say about it; for I am not acquainted with it, and whosoever says I am, speaks falsely, and for the purpose
50 of calumniating me. But, O Athenians! do not cry out against me, even though I should seem to you to speak somewhat arrogantly. For the account which I am going to give you is not my own; but I shall refer to an authority
55 whom you will deem worthy of credit. For I shall adduce to you the god at Delphi as a witness of my wisdom, if I have any, and of what it is. You doubtless know Chærepho: he was my associate from youth, and the associate of
60 most of you; he accompanied you in your late exile, and returned with you. You know, then, what kind of a man Chærepho was, how earnest in whatever he undertook. Having once gone to Delphi, he ventured to make the fol-
65 lowing inquiry of the oracle (and, as I said, O Athenians! do not cry out), for he asked if there was any one wiser than I. The Pythian thereupon answered that there was not one wiser; and of this, his brother here will give
70 you proofs, since he himself is dead.

Consider, then, why I mention these things: it is because I am going to show you whence the calumny against me arose. For when I heard
75 this, I reasoned thus with myself, What does the god mean? What enigma is this? For I am not conscious to myself that I am wise, either much or little. What, then, does he mean by saying that I am the wisest? For assuredly he
80 does not speak falsely: that he could not do. And for a long time I was in doubt what he meant; afterward, with considerable difficulty, I had recourse to the following method of searching out his meaning. I went to one of
85 those who have the character of being wise, thinking that there, if anywhere, I should con-

fute the oracle, and show in answer to the response that This man is wiser than I, though you affirmed that I was the wisest. Having, then, examined this man (for there is no occa-
5 sion to mention his name; he was, however, one of our great politicians, in examining whom I felt as I proceed to describe, O Athenians!), having fallen into conversation with him, this man appeared to be wise in the opin-
10 ion of most other men, and especially in his own opinion, though in fact he was not so. I thereupon endeavored to show him that he fancied himself to be wise, but really was not. Hence I became odious, both to him and to
15 many others who were present. When I left him, I reasoned thus with myself: I am wiser than this man, for neither of us appears to know anything great and good; but he fancies he knows something, although he knows
20 nothing; whereas I, as I do not know anything, so I do not fancy I do. In this trifling particu-lar, then, I appear to be wiser than he, because I do not fancy I know what I do not know. After that I went to another who was thought
25 to be wiser than the former, and formed the very same opinion. Hence I became odious to him and to many others.

After this I went to others in turn, perceiving
30 indeed, and grieving and alarmed, that I was making myself odious; however, it appeared necessary to regard the oracle of the god as of the greatest moment, and that, in order to discover its meaning, I must go to all who had
35 the reputation of possessing any knowledge. And by the dog, O Athenians! for I must tell you the truth, I came to some such conclusion as this: those who bore the highest reputation appeared to me to be most deficient, in my
40 researches in obedience to the god, and others who were considered inferior more nearly approaching to the possession of understand-ing. But I must relate to you my wandering,

and the labors which I underwent, in order
45 that the oracle might prove incontrovertible. For after the politicians I went to the poets, as well the tragic as the dithyrambic and others, expecting that here I should in very fact find myself more ignorant than they. Taking up,
50 therefore, some of their poems, which ap-peared to me most elaborately finished, I questioned them as to their meaning, that at the same time I might learn something from them. I am ashamed, O Athenians! to tell you
55 the truth; however, it must be told. For, in a word, almost all who were present could have given a better account of them than those by whom they had been composed. I soon dis-covered this, therefore, with regard to the po-
60 ets, that they do not effect their object by wis-dom, but by a certain natural inspiration, and under the influence of enthusiasm, like proph-ets and seers; for these also say many fine things, but they understand nothing that they
65 say. The poets appeared to me to be affected in a similar manner; and at the same time I perceived that they considered themselves, on account of their poetry, to be the wisest of men in other things, in which they were not. I
70 left them, therefore, under the persuasion that I was superior to them, in the same way that I was to the politicians.

At last, therefore, I went to the artisans. For I
75 was conscious to myself that I knew scarcely anything, but I was sure that I should find them possessed of much beautiful knowledge. And in this I was not deceived; for they knew things which I did not, and in this respect they
80 were wiser than I. But, O Athenians! even the best workmen appeared to me to have fallen into the same error as the poets; for each, be-cause he excelled in the practice of his art, thought that he was very wise in other most
85 important matters, and this mistake of theirs obscured the wisdom that they really pos-

sessed. I therefore asked myself, in behalf of the oracle, whether I should prefer to continue as I am, possessing none, either of their wisdom or their ignorance, or to have both as they have. I answered, therefore, to myself and to the oracle, that it was better for me to continue as I am.

From this investigation, then, O Athenians! many enmities have arisen against me, and those the most grievous and severe, so that many calumnies have sprung from them, and among them this appellation of being wise; for those who are from time to time present think that I am wise in those things, with respect to which I expose the ignorance of others. The god, however, O Athenians! appears to be really wise, and to mean this by his oracle: that human wisdom is worth little or nothing; and it is clear that he did not say this to Socrates, but made use of my name, putting me forward as an example, as if he had said, that man is the wisest among you, who, like Socrates, knows that he is in reality worth nothing with respect to wisdom. Still, therefore, I go about and search and inquire into these things, in obedience to the god, both among citizens and strangers, if I think any one of them is wise; and when he appears to me not to be so, I take the part of the god, and show that he is not wise. And, in consequence of this occupation, I have no leisure to attend in any considerable degree to the affairs of the state or my own; but I am in the greatest poverty through my devotion to the service of the god.

10. In addition to this, young men, who have much leisure and belong to the wealthiest families, following me of their own accord, take great delight in hearing men put to the test, and often imitate me, and themselves attempt to put others to the test; and then, I think, they find a great abundance of men who fancy they know something, although they know little or nothing. Hence those who are put to the test by them are angry with me, and not with them, and say that "there is one Socrates, a most pestilent fellow, who corrupts the youth." And when any one asks them by doing or teaching what, they have nothing to say, for they do not know; but, that they may not seem to be at a loss, they say such things as are ready at hand against all philosophers; "that he searches into things in heaven and things under the earth, that he does not believe there are gods, and that he makes the worse appear the better reason." For they would not, I think, be willing to tell the truth that they have been detected in pretending to possess knowledge, whereas they know nothing. Therefore, I think, being ambitions and vehement and numerous, and speaking systematically and persuasively about me, they have filled your ears, for a long time and diligently calumniating me. From among these, Melitus, Anytus and Lycon have attacked me; Melitus being angry on account of the poets, Anytus on account of the artisans and politicians, and Lycon on account of the rhetoricians. So that, as I said in the beginning, I should wonder if I were able in so short a time to remove from your minds a calumny that has prevailed so long. This, O Athenians! is the truth; and I speak it without concealing or disguising anything from you, much or little; though I very well know that by so doing I shall expose myself to odium. This, however, is a proof that I speak the truth, and that this is the nature of the calumny against me, and that these are its causes. And if you will investigate the matter, either now or hereafter, you will find it to be so.

With respect, then, to the charges which my first accusers have alleged against me, let this be a sufficient apology to you. To Melitus, that

good and patriotic man, as he says, and to my later accusers, I will next endeavor to give an answer; and here, again, as there are different accusers, let us take up their deposition. It is
5 pretty much as follows: "Socrates," it says, "acts unjustly in corrupting the youth, and in not believing in those gods in whom the city believes, but in other strange divinities." Such is the accusation; let us examine each particu-
10 lar of it. It says that I act unjustly in corrupting the youth. But I, O Athenians! say that Melitus acts unjustly, because he jests on serious subjects, rashly putting men upon trial, under pretense of being zealous and solicitous about
15 things in which he never at any time took any concern. But that this is the case I will endeavor to prove to you.

Come, then, Melitus, tell me, do you not con-
20 sider it of the greatest importance that the youth should be made as virtuous as possible?

Mel. I do.

25 *Socr.* Well, now, tell the judges who it is that makes them better, for it is evident that you know, since it concerns you so much; for, having detected me in corrupting them, as you say, you have cited me here, and accused me:
30 come, then, say, and inform the judges who it is that makes them better. Do you see, Melitus, that you are silent, and have nothing to say? But does it not appear to you to be disgraceful, and a sufficient proof of what I say,
35 that you never took any concern about the matter? But tell me, friend, who makes them better?
Mel. The laws.

40 *Socr.* I do not ask this, most excellent sir, but what man, who surely must first know this very thing, the laws?

45 *Mel.* These, Socrates, the judges.

Socr. How say you, Melitus? Are these able to instruct the youth, and make them better?

50 *Mel.* Certainly.

Socr. Whether all, or some of them, and others not?

55 *Mel.* All.

Socr. You say well, by Juno! and have found a great abundance of those that confer benefit. But what further? Can these hearers make them better, or not?
60
Mel. They, too, can.

Socr. And what of the senators?

65 *Mel.* The senators, also.

Socr. But, Melitus, do those who attend the public assemblies corrupt the younger men? or do they all make them better?
70
Mel. They too.

Socr. All the Athenians, therefore, as it seems, make them honorable and good, except me;
75 but I alone corrupt them. Do you say so?

Mel. I do assert this very thing.

Socr. You charge me with great ill-fortune. But
80 answer me: does it appear to you to be the same, with respect to horses? Do all men make them better, and is there only some one that spoils them? or does quite the contrary of this take place? Is there some one person who
85 can make them better, or very few; that is, the trainers? But if the generality of men should

meddle with and make use of horses, do they spoil them? Is not this the case, Melitus, both with respect to horses and all other animals? It certainly is so, whether you and Anytus deny it or not. For it would be a great good-fortune for the youth if only one person corrupted, and the rest benefited them. However, Melitus, you have sufficiently shown that you never bestowed any care upon youth; and you clearly evince your own negligence, in that you have never paid any attention to the things with respect to which you accuse me.

Tell us further, Melitus, in the name of Jupiter, whether is it better to dwell with good or bad citizens? Answer, my friend; for I ask you nothing difficult. Do not the bad work some evil to those that are continually near them, but the good some good?

Mel. Certainly.

Socr. Is there any one that wishes to be injured rather than benefited by his associates? Answer, good man; for the law requires you to answer. Is there any one who wishes to be injured?

Mel. No, surely.

Socr. Come, then, whether do you accuse me here, as one that corrupts the youth, and makes them more depraved, designedly or undesignedly?

Mel. Designedly, I say.

Socr. What, then, Melitus, are you at your time of life so much wiser than I at my time of life, as to know that the evil are always working some evil to those that are most near to them, and the good some good; but I have arrived at such a pitch of ignorance as not to know that

if I make any one of my associates depraved, I shall be in danger of receiving some evil from him; and yet I designedly bring about this so great evil, as you say? In this I can not believe you, Melitus, nor do I think would any other man in the world. But either I do not corrupt the youth, or, if I do corrupt them, I do it undesignedly: so that in both cases you speak falsely. But if I corrupt them undesignedly, for such involuntary offenses it is not usual to accuse one here, but to take one apart, and teach and admonish one. For it is evident that if I am taught, I shall cease doing what I do undesignedly. But you shunned me, and were not willing to associate with and instruct me; but you accuse me here, where it is usual to accuse those who need punishment, and not instruction.

Thus, then, O Athenians! this now is clear that I have said; that Melitus never paid any attention to these matters, much or little. However, tell us, Melitus, how you say I corrupt the youth? Is it not evidently, according to the indictment which you have preferred, by teaching them not to believe in the gods in whom the city believes, but in other strange deities? Do you not say that, by teaching these things, I corrupt the youth?

Mel. Certainly I do say so.

Socr. By those very gods, therefore, Melitus, of whom the discussion now is, speak still more clearly both to me and to these men. For I can not understand whether you say that I teach them to believe that there are certain gods (and in that case I do believe that there are gods, and am not altogether an atheist, nor in this respect to blame), not, however, those which the city believes in, but others; and this it is that you accuse me of, that I introduce others. Or do you say outright that I do not myself believe that there are gods, and that I teach others the same?

Mel. I say this: that you do not believe in any gods at all.

Socr. O wonderful Melitus, how come you to say this? Do I not, then, like the rest of mankind, believe that the sun and moon are gods?

Mel. No, by Jupiter, O judges! for he says that the sun is a stone, and the moon an earth.

Socr. You fancy that you are accusing Anaxagoras, my dear Melitus, and thus you put a slight on these men, and suppose them to be so illiterate as not to know that the books of Anaxagoras of Clazomene are full of such assertions. And the young, moreover, learn these things from me, which they might purchase for a drachma, at most, in the orchestra, and so ridicule Socrates, if he pretended they were his own, especially since they are so absurd? I ask then, by Jupiter, do I appear to you to believe that there is no god?

Mel. No, by Jupiter, none whatever.

Socr. You say what is incredible, Melitus, and that, as appears to me, even to yourself. For this man, O Athenians! appears to me to be very insolent and intemperate and to have preferred this indictment through downright insolence, intemperance, and wantonness. For he seems, as it were, to have composed an enigma for the purpose of making an experiment. Whether will Socrates the wise know that I am jesting, and contradict myself, or shall I deceive him and all who hear me? For, in my opinion, he clearly contradicts himself in the indictment, as if he should say, Socrates is guilty of wrong in not believing that there are gods, and in believing that there are gods. And

this, surely, is the act of one who is trifling.

Consider with me now, Athenians, in what respect he appears to me to say so. And do you, Melitus, answer me; and do ye, as I besought you at the outset, remember not to make an uproar if I speak after my usual manner.

Is there any man, Melitus, who believes that there are human affairs, but does not believe that there are men? Let him answer, judges, and not make so much noise. Is there any one who does not believe that there are horses, but that there are things pertaining to horses? or who does not believe that there are pipers, but that there are things pertaining to pipes? There is not, O best of men! for since you are not willing to answer, I say it to you and to all here present. But answer to this at least: is there any one who believes that there are things relating to demons, but does not believe that there are demons?

Mel. There is not.

Socr. How obliging you are in having hardly answered; though compelled by these judges! You assert, then, that I do believe and teach things relating to demons, whether they be new or old; therefore, according to your admission, I do believe in things relating to demons, and this you have sworn in the bill of indictment. If, then, I believe in things relating to demons, there is surely an absolute necessity that I should believe that there are demons. Is it not so? It is. For I suppose you to assent, since you do not answer. But with respect to demons, do we not allow that they are gods, or the children of gods? Do you admit this or not?

Mel. Certainly.

Socr. Since, then, I allow that there are de- mons, as you admit, if demons are a kind of gods, this is the point in which I say you speak enigmatically and divert yourself in saying that
5 I do not allow there are gods, and again that I do allow there are, since I allow that there are demons? But if demons are the children of gods, spurious ones, either from nymphs or any others, of whom they are reported to be,
10 what man can think that there are sons of gods, and yet that there are not gods? For it would be just as absurd as if any one should think that there are mules, the offspring of horses and asses, but should not think there
15 are horses and asses. However, Melitus, it can not be otherwise than that you have preferred this indictment for the purpose of trying me, or because you were at a loss what real crime to allege against me; for that you should per-
20 suade any man who has the smallest degree of sense that the same person can think that there are things relating to demons and to gods, and yet that there are neither demons, nor gods, not heroes, is utterly impossible.
25

That I am not guilty, then, O Athenians! ac- cording to the indictment of Melitus, appears to me not to require a lengthened defense; but what I have said is sufficient. And as to what I
30 said at the beginning, that there is a great en- mity toward me among the multitude, be as- sured it is true. And this it is which will con- demn me, if I am condemned, not Melitus, nor Anytus, but the calumny and envy of the
35 multitude, which have already condemned many others, and those good men, and will, I think, condemn others also; for there is no danger that it will stop with me.

40 Perhaps, however, some one may say, "Are you not ashamed, Socrates, to have pursued a study from which you are now in danger of dying?" To such a person I should answer

with good reason, You do not say well, friend,
45 if you think that a man, who is even of the least value, ought to take into the account the risk of life or death, and ought not to consider that alone when be performs any action, whether he is acting justly or unjustly, and the
50 part of a good man or bad man. For, accord- ing to your reasoning, all those demi-gods that died at Troy would be vile characters, as well all the rest as the son of Thetis, who so far despised danger in comparison of submitting
55 to disgrace, that when his mother, who was a goddess, spoke to him, in his impatience to kill Hector, something to this effect, as I think, "My son, if you revenge the death of your friend Patroclus, and slay Hector, you will
60 yourself die, for," she said, "death awaits you immediately after Hector;" but he, on hearing this, despised death and danger, and dreading much more to live as a coward, and not avenge his friend, said, "May I die immediately
65 when I have inflicted punishment on the guilty, that I may not stay here an object of ridicule, by the curved ships, a burden to the ground?"—do you think that he cared for death and danger? For thus it is, O Athenians!
70 in truth: wherever any one has posted himself, either thinking it to be better, or has been posted by his chief, there, as it appears to me, he ought to remain and meet danger, taking no account either of death or anything else in
75 comparison with disgrace.

I then should be acting strangely, O Atheni- ans! if, when the generals whom you chose to command me assigned me my post at Potidæa,
80 at Amphipolis, and at Delium, I then remained where they posted me, like any other person, and encountered the danger of death; but when the deity, as I thought and believed, as- signed it as my duty to pass my life in the
85 study of philosophy, and examining myself and others, I should on that occasion, through

fear of death or any thing else whatsoever, desert my post, strange indeed would it be; and then, in truth, any one might justly bring me to trial, and accuse me of not believing in

5 the gods, from disobeying the oracle, fearing death, and thinking myself to be wise when I am not. For to fear death, O Athenians! is nothing else than to appear to be wise, without being so; for it is to appear to know what

10 one does not know. For no one knows but that death is the greatest of all good to man; but men fear it, as if they well knew that it is the greatest of evils. And how is not this the most reprehensible ignorance, to think that

15 one knows what one does not know? But I, O Athenians! in this, perhaps, differ from most men; and if I should say that I am in any thing wiser than another, it would be in this, that not having a competent knowledge of the

20 things in Hades, I also think that I have not such knowledge. But to act unjustly, and to disobey my superior, whether God or man, I know is evil and base. I shall never, therefore, fear or shun things which, for aught I know,

25 maybe good, before evils which I know to be evils. So that, even if you should now dismiss me, not yielding to the instances of Anytus, who said that either I should not appear here at all, or that, if I did appear, it was impossible

30 not to put me to death, telling you that if I escaped, your sons, studying what Socrates teaches, would all be utterly corrupted; if you should address me thus, "Socrates, we shall not now yield to Anytus, but dismiss you, on

35 this condition, however, that you no longer persevere in your researches nor study philosophy; and if hereafter you are detected in so doing, you shall die"—if, as I said, you should dismiss, me on these terms, I should say to

40 you, "O Athenians! I honor and love you; but I shall obey God rather than you; and so long as I breathe and am able, I shall not cease studying philosophy, and exhorting you and

45 warning any one of you I may happen to meet, saying, as I have been accustomed to do: 'O best of men! seeing you are an Athenian, of a city the most powerful and most renowned for wisdom and strength, are you not ashamed of being careful for riches, how you may acquire

50 them in greatest abundance, and for glory, and honor, but care not nor take any thought for wisdom and truth, and for your soul, how it maybe made most perfect?'" And if any one of you should question my assertion, and affirm

55 that he does care for these things, I shall not at once let him go, nor depart, but I shall question him, sift and prove him. And if he should appear to me not to possess virtue, but to pretend that he does, I shall reproach him for that

60 he sets the least value on things of the greatest worth, but the highest on things that are worthless. Thus I shall act to all whom I meet, both young and old, stranger and citizen, but rather to you, my fellow-citizens, because ye

65 are more nearly allied to me. For be well assured, this the deity commands. And I think that no greater good has ever befallen you in the city than my zeal for the service of the god. For I go about doing nothing else than

70 persuading you, both young and old, to take no care either for the body, or for riches, prior to or so much as for the soul, how it may be made most perfect, telling you that virtue does not spring from riches, but riches and all other

75 human blessings, both private and public, from virtue. If, then, by saying these things, I corrupt the youth, these things must be mischievous; but if any one says that I speak other things than these, he misleads you.[4] Therefore

80 I must say, O Athenians! either yield to Anytus, or do not, either dismiss me or not, since I shall not act otherwise, even though I must die many deaths.

85 Murmur not, O Athenians! but continue to attend to my request, not to murmur at what I

say, but to listen, for, as I think, you will derive benefit from listening. For I am going to say other things to you, at which, perhaps, you will raise a clamor; but on no account do so.

5 Be well assured, then, if you put me to death, being such a man as I say I am, you will not injure me more than yourselves. For neither will Melitus nor Anytus harm me; nor have they the power; for I do not think that it is

10 possible for a better man to be injured by a worse. He may perhaps have me condemned to death, or banished, or deprived of civil rights; and he or others may perhaps consider these as mighty evils; I, how ever, do not con-

15 sider them so, but that it is much more so to do what he is now doing, to endeavor to put a man to death unjustly. Now, therefore, O Athenians! I am far from making a defense on my behalf, as any one might think, but I do so

20 on your own behalf, lest by condemning me you should offend at all with respect to the gift of the deity to you. For, if you should put me to death, you will not easily find such another, though it may be ridiculous to say so,

25 altogether attached by the deity to this city as to a powerful and generous horse, somewhat sluggish from his size, and requiring to be roused by a gad-fly; so the deity appears to have united me, being such a person as I am,

30 to the city, that I may rouse you, and persuade and reprove every one of you, nor ever cease besetting you throughout the whole day. Such another man, O Athenians! will not easily be found; therefore, if you will take my advice,

35 you will spare me. But you, perhaps, being irritated like drowsy persons who are roused from sleep, will strike me, and, yielding to Anytus, will unthinkingly condemn me to death; and then you will pass the rest of your life in

40 sleep, unless the deity, caring for you, should send some one else to you. But that I am a person who has been given by the deity to this city, you may discern from hence; for it is not

like the ordinary conduct of men, that I
45 should have neglected all my own affairs, and suffered my private interest to be neglected for so many years, and that I should constantly attend to your concerns, addressing myself to each of you separately, like a father, or elder

50 brother, persuading you to the pursuit of virtue. And if I had derived any profit from this course, and had received pay for my exhortations, there would have been some reason for my conduct; but now you see yourselves that

55 my accusers, who have so shamelessly calumniated me in everything else, have not had the impudence to charge me with this, and to bring witnesses to prove that I ever either exacted or demanded any reward. And I think I

60 produce a sufficient proof that I speak the truth, namely, my poverty.

Perhaps, however, it may appear absurd that I, going about, thus advise you in private and
65 make myself busy, but never venture to present myself in public before your assemblies and give advice to the city. The cause of this is that which you have often and in many places heard me mention; because I am moved by a

70 certain divine and spiritual influence, which also Melitus, through mockery, has set out in the indictment. This began with me from childhood, being a kind of voice which, when present, always diverts me from what I am

75 about to do, but never urges me on. This it is which opposed my meddling in public politics; and it appears to me to have opposed me very properly. For be well assured, O Athenians! if I had long since attempted to intermeddle

80 with politics, I should have perished long ago, and should not have at all benefited you or myself. And be not angry with me for speaking the truth. For it is not possible that any man should be safe who sincerely opposes

85 either you, or any other multitude, and who prevents many unjust and illegal actions from

being committed in a city; but it is necessary that he who in earnest contends for justice, if he will be safe for but a short time, should live privately, and take no part in public affairs.

5

I will give you strong proofs of this, not words, but what you value, facts. Hear, then, what has happened to me, that you may know that I would not yield to any one contrary to what is just, through fear of death, at the same time by not yielding I must perish. I shall tell you what will be displeasing and wearisome, yet true. For I, O Athenians! never bore any other magisterial office in the city, but have been a senator: and our Antiochean tribe happened to supply the Prytanes when you chose to condemn in a body the ten generals who had not taken off those that perished in the sea-fight, in violation of the law, as you afterward all thought. At that time I alone of the Prytanes opposed your doing anything contrary to the laws, and I voted against you; and when the orators were ready to denounce me, and to carry me before a magistrate, and you urged and cheered them on, I thought I ought rather to meet the danger with law and justice on my side, than through fear of imprisonment or death, to take part with you in your unjust designs. And this happened while the city was governed by a democracy. But when it became an oligarchy, the Thirty, having sent for me with four others to the Tholus, ordered us to bring Leon the Salaminian from Salamis, that he might be put to death; and they gave many similar orders to many others, wishing to involve as many as they could in guilt. Then, however, I showed, not in word but in deed, that I did not care for death, if the expression be not too rude, in the smallest degree; but that all my care was to do nothing unjust or unholy. For that government, strong as it was, did not so overawe me as to make me commit an unjust action; but when we

came out from the Tholus, the four went to Salamis, and brought back Leon; but I went away home. And perhaps for this I should have been put to death, if that government had not been speedily broken up. And of this you can have many witnesses.

Do you think, then, that I should have survived so many years if I had engaged in public affairs, and, acting as becomes a good man, had aided the cause of justice, and, as I ought, had deemed this of the highest importance? Far from it, O Athenians! nor would any other man have done so. But I, through the whole of my life, if I have done anything in public, shall be found to be a man, and the very same in private, who has never made a concession to any one contrary to justice, neither to any other, nor to any one of these whom my calumniators say are my disciples. I, however, was never the preceptor of any one; but if any one desired to hear me speaking, and to see me busied about my own mission, whether he were young or old, I never refused him. Nor do I discourse when I receive money, and not when I do not receive any, but I allow both rich and poor alike to question me, and, if any one wishes it, to answer me and hear what I have to say. And for these, whether any one proves to be a good man or not, I cannot justly be responsible, because I never either promised them any instruction or taught them at all. But if any one says that he has ever learned or heard anything from me in private which all others have not, be well assured that he does not speak the truth.

But why do some delight to spend so long a time with me? Ye have heard, O Athenians! I have told you the whole truth, that they delight to hear those closely questioned who think that they are wise but are not; for this is by no means disagreeable. But this duty, as I

17

say, has been enjoined me by the deity, by oracles, by dreams, and by every mode by which any other divine decree has ever enjoined anything to man to do. These things, O

5 Athenians! are both true, and easily confuted if not true. For if I am now corrupting some of the youths, and have already corrupted others, it were fitting, surely, that if any of them, having become advanced in life, had discovered

10 that I gave them bad advice when they were young, they should now rise up against me, accuse me, and have me punished; or if they were themselves unwilling to do this, some of their kindred, their fathers, or brothers, or

15 other relatives, if their kinsman have ever sustained any damage from me, should now call it to mind. Many of them, however, are here present, whom I see: first, Crito, my contemporary and fellow-burgher, father of this

20 Critobulus; then Lysanias of Sphettus, father of this Æschines; again, Antiphon of Cephisus, father of Epigenes. There are those others, too, whose brothers maintained the same intimacy with me, namely, Nicostratus,

25 son of Theodotus, brother of Theodotus— Theodotus indeed is dead, so that he could not deprecate his brother's proceedings—and Paralus here, son of Demodocus, whose brother was Theages; and Adimantus, son of

30 Ariston, whose brother is this Plato; and Æantodorus, whose brother is this Apollodorus. I could also mention many others to you, some one of whom certainly Melitus ought to have adduced in his speech as a witness. If, howev-

35 er, he then forgot to do so, let him now adduce them; I give him leave to do so, and let him say it, if he has anything of the kind to allege. But, quite contrary to this, you will find, O Athenians! all ready to assist me, who have

40 corrupted and injured their relatives, as Melitus and Anytus say. For those who have been themselves corrupted might perhaps have some reason for assisting me; but those who

45 have not been corrupted, men now advanced in life, their relatives, what other reason can they have for assisting me, except that right and just one, that they know that Melitus speaks falsely, and that I speak the truth.

50 Well, then, Athenians, these are pretty much the things I have to say in my defense, and others perhaps of the same kind. Perhaps, however, some among you will be indignant on recollecting his own case, if he, when en-

55 gaged in a cause far less than this, implored and besought the judges with many tears, bringing forward his children in order that he might excite their utmost compassion, and many others of his relatives and friends,

60 whereas I do none of these things, although I may appear to be incurring the extremity of danger. Perhaps, therefore, some one, taking notice of this, may become more determined against me, and, being enraged at this very

65 conduct of mine, may give his vote under the influence of anger. If, then, any one of you is thus affected—I do not, however, suppose that there is—but if there should be, I think I may reasonably say to him: "I, too, O best of

70 men, have relatives; for, to make use of that saying of Homer, I am not sprung from an oak, nor from a rock, but from men, so that I, too, O Athenians! have relatives, and three sons, one now grown up, and two boys: I shall

75 not, however, bring any one of them forward and implore you to acquit me." Why, then, shall I not do this? Not from contumacy, O Athenians! nor disrespect toward you. Whether or not I am undaunted at the prospect of

80 death is another question; but, out of regard to my own character, and yours, and that of the whole city, it does not appear to me to be honorable that I should do any thing of this kind at my age, and with the reputation I have,

85 whether true or false. For it is commonly agreed that Socrates in some respects excels

the generality of men. If, then, those among you who appear to excel either in wisdom, or fortitude, or any other virtue whatsoever, should act in such a manner as I have often seen some when they have been brought to trial, it would be shameful, who appearing indeed to be something, have conducted themselves in a surprising manner, as thinking they should suffer something dreadful by dying, and as if they would be immortal if you did not put them to death. Such men appear to me to bring disgrace on the city, so that any stranger might suppose that such of the Athenians as excel in virtue, and whom they themselves choose in preference to themselves for magistracies and other honors, are in no respect superior to women. For these things, O Athenians! neither ought we to do who have attained to any height of reputation, nor, should we do them, ought you to suffer us; but you should make this manifest, that you will much rather condemn him who introduces these piteous dramas, and makes the city ridiculous, than him who quietly awaits your decision.

But, reputation apart, O Athenians! it does not appear to me to be right to entreat a judge, or to escape by entreaty; but one ought to inform and persuade him. For a judge does not sit for the purpose of administering justice out of favor, but that he may judge rightly, and he is sworn not to show favor to whom he pleases, but that he will decide according to the laws. It is, therefore, right that neither should we accustom you, nor should you accustom yourselves, to violate your oaths; for in so doing neither of us would act righteously. Think not then, O Athenians! that I ought to adopt such a course toward you as I neither consider honorable, nor just, nor holy, as well, by Jupiter! on any other occasion, and now especially when I am accused of impiety by this Melitus.

For clearly, if I should persuade you, and by my entreaties should put a constraint on you who are bound by an oath, I should teach you to think that there are no gods, and in reality, while making my defense, should accuse myself of not believing in the gods. This, however, is far from being the case; for I believe, O Athenians! as none of my accusers do, and I leave it to you and to the deity to judge concerning me in such way as will be best both for me and for you.

[Socrates here concludes his defense, and, the votes being taken, he is declared guilty by a majority of voices. He thereupon resumes his address.]

That I should not be grieved, O Athenians! at what has happened—namely, that you have condemned me—as well many other circumstances concur in bringing to pass; and, moreover this, that what has happened has not happened contrary to my expectation; but I much rather wonder at the number of votes on either side. For I did not expect that I should be condemned by so small a number, but by a large majority; but now, as it seems, if only three more votes had changed sides, I should have been acquitted. So far as Melitus is concerned, as it appears to me, I have been already acquitted; and not only have I been acquitted, but it is clear to every one that had not Anytus and Lycon come forward to accuse me, he would have been fined a thousand drachmas, for not having obtained a fifth part of the votes.

The man, then, awards me the penalty of death. Well. But what shall I, on my part, O Athenians! award myself? Is it not clear that it will be such as I deserve? What, then, is that? Do I deserve to suffer, or to pay a fine? for that I have purposely during my life not remained quiet, but neglecting what most men seek after, money-making, domestic concerns, military command, popular oratory, and, moreover, all the magistracies, conspiracies,

5 and cabals that are met with in the city, thinking that I was in reality too upright a man to be safe if I took part in such things, I therefore did not apply myself to those pursuits, by attending to which I should have been of no

10 service either to you or to myself; but in order to confer the greatest benefit on each of you privately, as I affirm, I thereupon applied myself to that object, endeavoring to persuade every one of you not to take any care of his

15 own affairs before he had taken care of himself in what way he may become the best and wisest, nor of the affairs of the city before he took care of the city itself; and that he should attend to other things in the same manner.

20 What treatment, then, do I deserve, seeing I am such a man? Some reward, O Athenians! if, at least, I am to be estimated according to my real deserts; and, moreover, such a reward as would be suitable to me. What, then, is suit-

25 able to a poor man, a benefactor, and who has need of leisure in order to give you good advice? There is nothing so suitable, O Athenians! as that such a man should be maintained in the Prytaneum, and this much more than if

30 one of you had been victorious at the Olympic games in a horserace, or in the two or four horsed chariot race: for such a one makes you appear to be happy, but I, to be so; and he does not need support, but I do. If, therefore,

35 I must award a sentence according to my just deserts, I award this, maintenance in the Prytaneum.

Perhaps, however, in speaking to you thus, I

40 appear to you to speak in the same presumptuous manner as I did respecting commiseration and entreaties; but such is not the case, O Athenians! it is rather this: I am persuaded that

I never designedly injured any man, though I

45 can not persuade you of this, for we have conversed with each other but for a short time. For if there were the same law with you as with other men, that in capital cases the trial should list not only one day, but many, I think

50 you would be persuaded; but it is not easy in a short time to do away with, great calumnies. Being persuaded, then, that I have injured no one, I am far from intending to injure myself, and of pronouncing against myself that I am

55 deserving of punishment, and from awarding myself any thing of the kind. Through fear of what? lest I should suffer that which Melitus awards me, of which I say I know not whether it he good or evil? Instead of this, shall I

60 choose what I well know to be evil, and award that? Shall I choose imprisonment? And why should I live in prison, a slave to the established magistracy, the Eleven? Shall I choose a fine, and to be imprisoned until I have paid it?

65 But this is the same as that which I just now mentioned, for I have not money to pay it. Shall I, then, award myself exile? For perhaps you would consent to this award. I should indeed be very fond of life, O Athenians! if I

70 were so devoid of reason as not to be able to reflect that you, who are my fellow-citizens, have been unable to endure my manner of life and discourses, but they have become so burdensome and odious to you that you now seek

75 to be rid of them: others, however, will easily bear them. Far from it, O Athenians! A fine life it would be for me at my age to go out wandering, and driven from city to city, and so to live. For I well know that, wherever I may

80 go, the youth will listen to me when I speak, as they do here. And if I repulse them, they will themselves drive me out, persuading the elders; and if I do not repulse them, their fathers and kindred will banish me on their account.

85

Perhaps, however, some one will say, Can you

not, Socrates, when you have gone from us, live a silent and quiet life? This is the most difficult thing of all to persuade some of you. For if I say that that would be to disobey the deity, and that, therefore, it is impossible for me to live quietly, you would not believe me, thinking I spoke ironically. If, on the other hand, I say that this is the greatest good to man, to discourse daily on virtue, and other things which you have heard me discussing, examining both myself and others, but that the unexamined life is not worth living for, still less would you believe me if I said this. Such, however, is the case, as I affirm, O Athenians! though it is not easy to persuade you. And at the same time I am not accustomed to think myself deserving of any ill. If, indeed, I were rich, I would amerce myself in such a sum as I should be able to pay; for then I should have suffered no harm, but now—for I can not, unless you are willing to amerce me in such a sum as I am able to pay. But perhaps I could pay you a mina of silver: in that sum, then, I amerce myself. But Plato here, O Athenians! and Crito Critobulus, and Apollodorus bid me amerce myself in thirty minæ, and they offer to be sureties. I amerce myself, then, to you in that sum; and they will be sufficient sureties for the money.

[The judges now proceeded to pass the sentence, and condemned Socrates to death; whereupon he continued:]

For the sake of no long space of time, O Athenians! you will incur the character and reproach at the hands of those who wish to defame the city, of having put that wise man, Socrates, to death. For those who wish to defame you will assert that I am wise, though I am not. If, then, you had waited for a short time, this would have happened of its own accord; for observe my age, that it is far advanced in life, and near death. But I say this not to you all, but to those only who have condemned me to die. And I say this, too, to the same persons. Perhaps you think, O Athenians! that I have been convicted through the want of arguments, by which I might have persuaded you, had I thought it right to do and say any thing, so that I might escape punishment. Far otherwise: I have been convicted through want indeed, yet not of arguments, but of audacity and impudence, and of the inclination to say such things to you as would have been most agreeable for you to hear, had I lamented and bewailed and done and said many other things unworthy of me, as I affirm, but such as you are accustomed to hear from others. But neither did I then think that I ought, for the sake of avoiding danger, to do any thing unworthy of a freeman, nor do I now repent of having so defended myself; but I should much rather choose to die, having so defended myself, than to live in that way. For neither in a trial nor in battle is it right that I or any one else should employ every possible means whereby he may avoid death; for in battle it is frequently evident that a man might escape death by laying down his arms, and throwing himself on the mercy of his pursuers. And there are many other devices in every danger, by which to avoid death, if a man dares to do and say every thing. But this is not difficult, O Athenians! to escape death; but it is much more difficult to avoid depravity, for it runs swifter than death. And now I, being slow and aged, am overtaken by the slower of the two; but my accusers, being strong and active, have been overtaken by the swifter, wickedness. And now I depart, condemned by you to death; but they condemned by truth, as guilty of iniquity and injustice: and I abide my sentence, and so do they. These things, perhaps, ought so to be, and I think that they are for the best.

In the next place, I desire to predict to you who have condemned me, what will be your fate; for I am now in that condition in which men most frequently prophesy—namely,

5 when they are about to die. I say, then, to you, O Athenians! who have condemned me to death, that immediately after my death a punishment will overtake you, far more severe, by Jupiter! than that which you have inflicted on

10 me. For you have done this, thinking you should be freed from the necessity of giving an account of your lives. The very contrary, however, as I affirm, will happen to you. Your accusers will be more numerous, whom I have

15 now restrained, though you did not perceive it; and they will be more severe, inasmuch as they are younger, and you will be more indignant. For if you think that by putting men to death you will restrain any one from upbraiding you

20 because you do not live well, you are much mistaken; for this method of escape is neither possible nor honorable; but that other is most honorable and most easy, not to put a check upon others, but for a man to take heed to

25 himself how he may be most perfect. Having predicted thus much to those of you who have condemned me, I take my leave of you.

But with you who have voted for my acquittal
30 I would gladly hold converse on what has now taken place, while the magistrates are busy, and I am not yet carried to the place where I must die. Stay with me, then, so long, O Athenians! for nothing hinders our conversing

35 with each other, while we are permitted to do so; for I wish to make known to you, as being my friends, the meaning of that which has just now befallen me. To me, then, O my judges! and in calling you judges I call you rightly—a

40 strange thing has happened. For the wonted prophetic voice of my guardian deity on every former occasion, even in the most trifling affairs, opposed me if I was about to do any

thing wrong; but now that has befallen me
45 which ye yourselves behold, and which any one would think, and which is supposed to be the extremity of evil; yet neither when I departed from home in the morning did the warning of the god oppose me, nor when I

50 came up here to the place of trial, nor in my address when I was about to say any thing; yet on other occasions it has frequently restrained me in the midst of speaking. But now it has never, throughout this proceeding, opposed

55 me, either in what I did or said. What, then, do I suppose to be the cause of this? I will tell you: what has befallen me appears to be a blessing; and it is impossible that we think rightly who suppose that death is an evil. A

60 great proof of this to me is the fact that it is impossible but that the accustomed signal should have opposed me, unless I had been about to meet with some good.

65 Moreover, we may hence conclude that there is great hope that death is a blessing. For to die is one of two things: for either the dead may be annihilated, and have no sensation of any thing whatever; or, as it is said, there are a

70 certain change and passage of the soul from one place to another. And if it is a privation of all sensation, as it were a sleep in which the sleeper has no dream, death would be a wonderful gain. For I think that if any one, having

75 selected a night in which he slept so soundly as not to have had a dream, and having compared this night with all the other nights and days of his life, should be required, on consideration, to say how many days and nights he

80 had passed better and more pleasantly than this night throughout his life, I think that not only a private person, but even the great king himself, would find them easy to number, in comparison with other days and nights. If,

85 therefore, death is a thing of this kind, I say it is a gain; for thus all futurity appears to be

nothing more than one night. But if, on the other hand, death is a removal from hence to another place, and what is said be true, that all the dead are there, what greater blessing can
5   there be than this, my judges? For if, on arriving at Hades, released from these who pretend to be judges, one shall find those who are true judges, and who are said to judge there, Minos and Rhadamanthus, Æacus and Triptolemus,
10   and such others of the demi-gods as were just during their own life, would this be a sad removal? At what price would you not estimate a conference with Orpheus and Musæus, Hesiod and Homer? I indeed should be willing to
15   die often, if this be true. For to me the sojourn there would be admirable, when I should meet with Palamedes, and Ajax, son of Telamon, and any other of the ancients who has died by an unjust sentence. The comparing my suffer-
20   ings with theirs would, I think, be no unpleasing occupation. But the greatest pleasure would be to spend my time in questioning and examining the people there as I have done those here, and discovering who among them
25   is wise, and who fancies himself to be so, but is not. At what price, my judges, would not any one estimate the opportunity of questioning him who led that mighty army against Troy, or Ulysses, or Sisyphus, or ten thousand
30   others whom one might mention both men and women—with whom to converse and associate, and to question them, would be an inconceivable happiness? Surely for that the judges there do not condemn to death; for in
35   other respects those who live there are more

happy than those who are here, and are henceforth immortal, if, at least, what is said be true.

You, therefore, O my judges! ought to enter-
40   tain good hopes with respect to death, and to meditate on this one truth, that to a good man nothing is evil, neither while living nor when dead, nor are his concerns neglected by the gods. And what has befallen me is not the
45   effect of chance; but this is clear to me, that now to die, and be freed from my cares is better for me On this account the warning in no way turned me aside; and I bear no resentment toward those who condemned me, or against
50   my accusers, although they did not condemn and accuse me with this intention, but thinking to injure me: in this they deserve to be blamed.

55   Thus much, however, I beg of them. Punish my sons when they grow up, O judges! paining them as I have pained you, if they appear to you to care for riches or anything else before virtue; and if they think themselves to be
60   something when they are nothing, reproach them as I have done you, for not attending to what they ought, and for conceiving themselves to be something when they are worth nothing. If ye do this, both I and my sons shall
65   have met with just treatment at your hands.

But it is now time to depart—for me to die, for you to live. But which of us is going to a better state is unknown to every one but God.
70

CRITO
PLATO

SOCRATES: Why have you come at this hour, Crito? it must be quite early.

CRITO: Yes, certainly.

5 SOCRATES: What is the exact time?

CRITO: The dawn is breaking.

10 SOCRATES: I wonder that the keeper of the prison would let you in.

CRITO: He knows me because I often come, Socrates; moreover. I have done him a kind-
15 ness.

SOCRATES: And are you only just arrived?

CRITO: No, I came some time ago.

20 SOCRATES: Then why did you sit and say nothing, instead of at once awakening me?

CRITO: I should not have liked myself, Soc-
25 rates, to be in such great trouble and unrest as you are--indeed I should not: I have been watching with amazement your peaceful slumbers; and for that reason I did not awake you, because I wished to minimize the pain. I
30 have always thought you to be of a happy dis-position; but never did I see anything like the easy, tranquil manner in which you bear this calamity.

35 SOCRATES: Why, Crito, when a man has

Text based of the Benjamin Jowett translation, with adjustments for modern spellings.

reached my age he ought not to be repining at the approach of death.

CRITO: And yet other old men find them-
40 selves in similar misfortunes, and age does not prevent them from repining.

SOCRATES: That is true. But you have not told me why you come at this early hour.

45

CRITO: I come to bring you a message which is sad and painful; not, as I believe, to yourself, but to all of us who are your friends, and sad-dest of all to me.

50

SOCRATES: What? Has the ship come from Delos, on the arrival of which I am to die?

CRITO: No, the ship has not actually arrived,
55 but she will probably be here to-day, as per-sons who have come from Sunium tell me that they have left her there; and therefore to-morrow, Socrates, will be the last day of your life.
60

SOCRATES: Very well, Crito; if such is the will of God, I am willing; but my belief is that there will be a delay of a day.

65 CRITO: Why do you think so?

SOCRATES: I will tell you. I am to die on the day after the arrival of the ship?

70 CRITO: Yes; that is what the authorities say.

SOCRATES: But I do not think that the ship

will be here until to-morrow; this I infer from a vision which I had last night, or rather only just now, when you fortunately allowed me to sleep.

CRITO: And what was the nature of the vision?

SOCRATES: There appeared to me the likeness of a woman, fair and comely, clothed in bright raiment, who called to me and said: O Socrates,

'The third day hence to fertile Phthia shalt thou go.' (Homer, Il.)

CRITO: What a singular dream, Socrates!

SOCRATES: There can be no doubt about the meaning, Crito, I think.

CRITO: Yes; the meaning is only too clear. But, oh! my beloved Socrates, let me entreat you once more to take my advice and escape. For if you die I shall not only lose a friend who can never be replaced, but there is another evil: people who do not know you and me will believe that I might have saved you if I had been willing to give money, but that I did not care. Now, can there be a worse disgrace than this--that I should be thought to value money more than the life of a friend? For the many will not be persuaded that I wanted you to escape, and that you refused.

SOCRATES: But why, my dear Crito, should we care about the opinion of the many? Good men, and they are the only persons who are worth considering, will think of these things truly as they occurred.

CRITO: But you see, Socrates, that the opinion of the many must be regarded, for what is now happening shows that they can do the greatest evil to any one who has lost their good opinion.

SOCRATES: I only wish it were so, Crito; and that the many could do the greatest evil; for then they would also be able to do the greatest good--and what a fine thing this would be! But in reality they can do neither; for they cannot make a man either wise or foolish; and whatever they do is the result of chance.

CRITO: Well, I will not dispute with you; but please to tell me, Socrates, whether you are not acting out of regard to me and your other friends: are you not afraid that if you escape from prison we may get into trouble with the informers for having stolen you away, and lose either the whole or a great part of our property; or that even a worse evil may happen to us?

Now, if you fear on our account, be at ease; for in order to save you, we ought surely to run this, or even a greater risk; be persuaded, then, and do as I say.

SOCRATES: Yes, Crito, that is one fear which you mention, but by no means the only one.

CRITO: Fear not--there are persons who are willing to get you out of prison at no great cost; and as for the informers they are far from being exorbitant in their demands--a little money will satisfy them. My means, which are certainly ample, are at your service, and if you have a scruple about spending all mine, here are strangers who will give you the use of theirs; and one of them, Simmias the Theban, has brought a large sum of money for this very purpose; and Cebes and many others are prepared to spend their money in helping

you to escape. I say, therefore, do not hesitate on our account, and do not say, as you did in the court (compare Apol.), that you will have a difficulty in knowing what to do with yourself
5 anywhere else. For men will love you in other places to which you may go, and not in Athens only; there are friends of mine in Thessaly, if you like to go to them, who will value and protect you, and no Thessalian will give you
10 any trouble. Nor can I think that you are at all justified, Socrates, in betraying your own life when you might be saved; in acting thus you are playing into the hands of your enemies, who are hurrying on your destruction. And
15 further I should say that you are deserting your own children; for you might bring them up and educate them; instead of which you go away and leave them, and they will have to take their chance; and if they do not meet with
20 the usual fate of orphans, there will be small thanks to you. No man should bring children into the world who is unwilling to persevere to the end in their nurture and education. But you appear to be choosing the easier part, not
25 the better and manlier, which would have been more becoming in one who professes to care for virtue in all his actions, like yourself. And indeed, I am ashamed not only of you, but of us who are your friends, when I reflect
30 that the whole business will be attributed entirely to our want of courage. The trial need never have come on, or might have been managed differently; and this last act, or crowning folly, will seem to have occurred
35 through our negligence and cowardice, who might have saved you, if we had been good for anything; and you might have saved yourself, for there was no difficulty at all. See now, Socrates, how sad and discreditable are the
40 consequences, both to us and you. Make up your mind then, or rather have your mind already made up, for the time of deliberation is over, and there is only one thing to be done,

which must be done this very night, and if we
45 delay at all will be no longer practicable or possible; I beseech you therefore, Socrates, be persuaded by me, and do as I say.

SOCRATES: Dear Crito, your zeal is invalua-
50 ble, if a right one; but if wrong, the greater the zeal the greater the danger; and therefore we ought to consider whether I shall or shall not do as you say. For I am and always have been one of those natures who must be guided by
55 reason, whatever the reason may be which upon reflection appears to me to be the best; and now that this chance has befallen me, I cannot repudiate my own words: the principles which I have hitherto honored and
60 revered I still honor, and unless we can at once find other and better principles, I am certain not to agree with you; no, not even if the power of the multitude could inflict many more imprisonments, confiscations, deaths,
65 frightening us like children with hobgoblin terrors. What will be the fairest way of considering the question? Shall I return to your old argument about the opinions of men?--we were saying that some of them are to be re-
70 garded, and others not. Now were we right in maintaining this before I was condemned? And has the argument which was once good now proved to be talk for the sake of talking-- mere childish nonsense? That is what I want
75 to consider with your help, Crito:--whether, under my present circumstances, the argument appears to be in any way different or not; and is to be allowed by me or disallowed. That argument, which, as I believe, is maintained by
80 many persons of authority, was to the effect, as I was saying, that the opinions of some men are to be regarded, and of other men not to be regarded. Now you, Crito, are not going to die to-morrow—at least, there is no human
85 probability of this, and therefore you are disinterested and not liable to be deceived by the

circumstances in which you are placed. Tell me then, whether I am right in saying that some opinions, and the opinions of some men only, are to be valued, and that other opinions,
5 and the opinions of other men, are not to be valued. I ask you whether I was right in maintaining this?

CRITO: Certainly.
10
SOCRATES: The good are to be regarded, and not the bad?

CRITO: Yes.
15
SOCRATES: And the opinions of the wise are good, and the opinions of the unwise are evil?

20 CRITO: Certainly.

SOCRATES: And what was said about another matter? Is the pupil who devotes himself to the practice of gymnastics supposed to
25 attend to the praise and blame and opinion of every man, or of one man only—his physician or trainer, whoever he may be?

CRITO: Of one man only.
30
SOCRATES: And he ought to fear the censure and welcome the praise of that one only, and not of the many?

35 CRITO: Clearly so.

SOCRATES: And he ought to act and train, and eat and drink in the way which seems good to his single master who has understand-
40 ing, rather than according to the opinion of all other men put together?

CRITO: True.

45 SOCRATES: And if he disobeys and disregards the opinion and approval of the one, and regards the opinion of the many who have no understanding, will he not suffer evil?

50 CRITO: Certainly he will.

SOCRATES: And what will the evil be, whither tending and what affecting, in the disobedient person?
55
CRITO: Clearly, affecting the body; that is what is destroyed by the evil.

SOCRATES: Very good; and is not this true,
60 Crito, of other things which we need not separately enumerate? In questions of just and unjust, fair and foul, good and evil, which are the subjects of our present consultation, ought we to follow the opinion of the many and to
65 fear them; or the opinion of the one man who has understanding? ought we not to fear and reverence him more than all the rest of the world: and if we desert him shall we not destroy and injure that principle in us which may
70 be assumed to be improved by justice and deteriorated by injustice;--there is such a principle?

CRITO: Certainly there is, Socrates.
75
SOCRATES: Take a parallel instance:--if, acting under the advice of those who have no understanding, we destroy that which is improved by health and is deteriorated by dis-
80 ease, would life be worth having? And that which has been destroyed is--the body?

CRITO: Yes.

85 SOCRATES: Could we live, having an evil and corrupted body?

CRITO: Certainly not.

SOCRATES: And will life be worth having, if that higher part of man be destroyed, which is improved by justice and depraved by injustice? Do we suppose that principle, whatever it may be in man, which has to do with justice and injustice, to be inferior to the body?

CRITO: Certainly not.

SOCRATES: More honorable than the body?

CRITO: Far more.

SOCRATES: Then, my friend, we must not regard what the many say of us: but what he, the one man who has understanding of just and unjust, will say, and what the truth will say. And therefore you begin in error when you advise that we should regard the opinion of the many about just and unjust, good and evil, honorable and dishonorable.--'Well,' some one will say, 'but the many can kill us.'

CRITO: Yes, Socrates; that will clearly be the answer.

SOCRATES: And it is true; but still I find with surprise that the old argument is unshaken as ever. And I should like to know whether I may say the same of another proposition-- that not life, but a good life, is to be chiefly valued?

CRITO: Yes, that also remains unshaken.

SOCRATES: And a good life is equivalent to a just and honorable one—that holds also?

CRITO: Yes, it does.

SOCRATES: From these premises I proceed to argue the question whether I ought or ought not to try and escape without the consent of the Athenians: and if I am clearly right in escaping, then I will make the attempt; but if not, I will abstain. The other considerations which you mention, of money and loss of character and the duty of educating one's children, are, I fear, only the doctrines of the multitude, who would be as ready to restore people to life, if they were able, as they are to put them to death—and with as little reason. But now, since the argument has thus far prevailed, the only question which remains to be considered is, whether we shall do rightly either in escaping or in suffering others to aid in our escape and paying them in money and thanks, or whether in reality we shall not do rightly; and if the latter, then death or any other calamity which may ensue on my remaining here must not be allowed to enter into the calculation.

CRITO: I think that you are right, Socrates; how then shall we proceed?

SOCRATES: Let us consider the matter together, and do you either refute me if you can, and I will be convinced; or else cease, my dear friend, from repeating to me that I ought to escape against the wishes of the Athenians: for I highly value your attempts to persuade me to do so, but I may not be persuaded against my own better judgment. And now please to consider my first position, and try how you can best answer me.

CRITO: I will.

SOCRATES: Are we to say that we are never intentionally to do wrong, or that in one way we ought and in another way we ought not to do wrong, or is doing wrong always evil and dishonorable, as I was just now saying, and as has been already acknowledged by us? Are all our former admissions which were made within a few days to be thrown away? And have

5 we, at our age, been earnestly discoursing with one another all our life long only to discover that we are no better than children? Or, in spite of the opinion of the many, and in spite of consequences whether better or worse,

10 shall we insist on the truth of what was then said, that injustice is always an evil and dishonor to him who acts unjustly? Shall we say so or not?

15 CRITO: Yes.

SOCRATES: Then we must do no wrong?

CRITO: Certainly not.

20
SOCRATES: Nor when injured injure in return, as the many imagine; for we must injure no one at all?

25 CRITO: Clearly not.

SOCRATES: Again, Crito, may we do evil?

CRITO: Surely not, Socrates.

30
SOCRATES: And what of doing evil in return for evil, which is the morality of the many--is that just or not?

35 CRITO: Not just.

SOCRATES: For doing evil to another is the same as injuring him?

40 CRITO: Very true.
SOCRATES: Then we ought not to retaliate or render evil for evil to any one, whatever evil we may have suffered from him. But I would

45 have you consider, Crito, whether you really mean what you are saying. For this opinion has never been held, and never will be held, by any considerable number of persons; and those who are agreed and those who are not agreed upon this point have no common

50 ground, and can only despise one another when they see how widely they differ. Tell me, then, whether you agree with and assent to my first principle, that neither injury nor retaliation nor warding off evil by evil is ever

55 right. And shall that be the premise of our argument? Or do you decline and dissent from this? For so I have ever thought, and continue to think; but, if you are of another opinion, let me hear what you have to say. If,

60 however, you remain of the same mind as formerly, I will proceed to the next step.

CRITO: You may proceed, for I have not changed my mind.

65
SOCRATES: Then I will go on to the next point, which may be put in the form of a question:--Ought a man to do what he admits to be right, or ought he to betray the right?

70
CRITO: He ought to do what he thinks right.

SOCRATES: But if this is true, what is the application? In leaving the prison against the

75 will of the Athenians, do I wrong any? or rather do I not wrong those whom I ought least to wrong? Do I not desert the principles which were acknowledged by us to be just— what do you say?

80
CRITO: I cannot tell, Socrates, for I do not know.

SOCRATES: Then consider the matter in this

85 way:--Imagine that I am about to play truant (you may call the proceeding by any name

which you like), and the laws and the government come and interrogate me: 'Tell us, Socrates,' they say; 'what are you about? are you
not going by an act of yours to overturn us--
5   the laws, and the whole state, as far as in you
lies?

Do you imagine that a state can subsist and
not be overthrown, in which the decisions of
10 law have no power, but are set aside and
trampled upon by individuals?' What will be
our answer, Crito, to these and the like words?
Any one, and especially a rhetorician, will have
a good deal to say on behalf of the law which
15 requires a sentence to be carried out. He will
argue that this law should not be set aside; and
shall we reply, 'Yes; but the state has injured
us and given an unjust sentence.' Suppose I
say that?

20

CRITO: Very good, Socrates.

SOCRATES: 'And was that our agreement
with you?' the law would answer; 'or were you
25 to abide by the sentence of the state?' And if I
were to express my astonishment at their
words, the law would probably add: 'Answer,
Socrates, instead of opening your eyes--you
are in the habit of asking and answering ques-
30 tions. Tell us,--What complaint have you to
make against us which justifies you in attempting to destroy us and the state? In the first
place did we not bring you into existence?
Your father married your mother by our aid
35 and begat you. Say whether you have any objection to urge against those of us who regulate marriage?' None, I should reply. 'Or
against those of us who after birth regulate the
nurture and education of children, in which
40 you also were trained? Were not the laws,
which have the charge of education, right in
commanding your father to train you in music
and gymnastic?' Right, I should reply. 'Well

then, since you were brought into the world
45 and nurtured and educated by us, can you deny in the first place that you are our child and
slave, as your fathers were before you? And if
this is true you are not on equal terms with us;
nor can you think that you have a right to do
50 to us what we are doing to you. Would you
have any right to strike or revile or do any
other evil to your father or your master, if you
had one, because you have been struck or reviled by him, or received some other evil at his
55 hands?--you would not say this? And because
we think right to destroy you, do you think
that you have any right to destroy us in return,
and your country as far as in you lies? Will
you, O professor of true virtue, pretend that
60 you are justified in this? Has a philosopher
like you failed to discover that our country is
more to be valued and higher and holier far
than mother or father or any ancestor, and
more to be regarded in the eyes of the gods
65 and of men of understanding? also to be
soothed, and gently and reverently entreated
when angry, even more than a father, and either to be persuaded, or if not persuaded, to
be obeyed? And when we are punished by
70 her, whether with imprisonment or stripes, the
punishment is to be endured in silence; and if
she lead us to wounds or death in battle, thither we follow as is right; neither may any one
yield or retreat or leave his rank, but whether
75 in battle or in a court of law, or in any other
place, he must do what his city and his country
order him; or he must change their view of
what is just: and if he may do no violence to
his father or mother, much less may he do
80 violence to his country.' What answer shall we
make to this, Crito? Do the laws speak truly,
or do they not?

CRITO: I think that they do.

85

SOCRATES: Then the laws will say: 'Consider, Socrates, if we are speaking truly that in your present attempt you are going to do us an injury. For, having brought you into the world, and nurtured and educated you, and given you and every other citizen a share in every good which we had to give, we further proclaim to any Athenian by the liberty which we allow him, that if he does not like us when he has become of age and has seen the ways of the city, and made our acquaintance, he may go where he pleases and take his goods with him. None of us laws will forbid him or interfere with him. Anyone who does not like us and the city, and who wants to emigrate to a colony or to any other city, may go where he likes, retaining his property. But he who has experience of the manner in which we order justice and administer the state, and still remains, has entered into an implied contract that he will do as we command him. And he who disobeys us is, as we maintain, thrice wrong: first, because in disobeying us he is disobeying his parents; secondly, because we are the authors of his education; thirdly, because he has made an agreement with us that he will duly obey our commands; and he neither obeys them nor convinces us that our commands are unjust; and we do not rudely impose them, but give him the alternative of obeying or convincing us;--that is what we offer, and he does neither.

'These are the sort of accusations to which, as we were saying, you, Socrates, will be exposed if you accomplish your intentions; you, above all other Athenians.' Suppose now I ask, why I rather than anybody else? They will justly retort upon me that I above all other men have acknowledged the agreement. 'There is clear proof,' they will say, 'Socrates, that we and the city were not displeasing to you. Of all Athenians you have been the most constant resident in the city, which, as you never leave, you may be supposed to love. For you never went out of the city either to see the games, except once when you went to the Isthmus, or to any other place unless when you were on military service; nor did you travel as other men do. Nor had you any curiosity to know other states or their laws: your affections did not go beyond us and our state; we were your especial favorites, and you acquiesced in our government of you; and here in this city you begat your children, which is a proof of your satisfaction. Moreover, you might in the course of the trial, if you had liked, have fixed the penalty at banishment; the state which refuses to let you go now would have let you go then. But you pretended that you preferred death to exile, and that you were not unwilling to die. And now you have forgotten these fine sentiments, and pay no respect to us the laws, of whom you are the destroyer; and are doing what only a miserable slave would do, running away and turning your back upon the compacts and agreements which you made as a citizen. And first of all answer this very question: Are we right in saying that you agreed to be governed according to us in deed, and not in word only? Is that true or not?' How shall we answer, Crito? Must we not assent?

CRITO: We cannot help it, Socrates.

SOCRATES: Then will they not say: 'You, Socrates, are breaking the covenants and agreements which you made with us at your leisure, not in any haste or under any compulsion or deception, but after you have had seventy years to think of them, during which time you were at liberty to leave the city, if we were not to your mind, or if our covenants appeared to you to be unfair. You had your choice, and might have gone either to Lacedaemon or Crete, both which states are often praised by you for their good government, or to some other Hellenic or foreign state. Whereas you, above all other Athenians, seemed to be so fond of the state, or, in other words, of us her laws (and who would care about a state which has no laws?), that you never stirred out of her; the halt, the blind, the maimed, were not more stationary in her than you were. And now you run away and forsake your agreements. Not so, Socrates, if you will take our advice; do not make yourself ridiculous by escaping out of the city.

'For just consider, if you transgress and err in this sort of way, what good will you do either to yourself or to your friends? That your friends will be driven into exile and deprived of citizenship, or will lose their property, is tolerably certain; and you yourself, if you fly to one of the neighboring cities, as, for example, Thebes or Megara, both of which are well governed, will come to them as an enemy, Socrates, and their government will be against you, and all patriotic citizens will cast an evil eye upon you as a subverter of the laws, and you will confirm in the minds of the judges the justice of their own condemnation of you. For he who is a corrupter of the laws is more than likely to be a corrupter of the young and foolish portion of mankind. Will you then flee from well-ordered cities and virtuous men? and is existence worth having on these terms? Or will you go to them without shame, and talk to them, Socrates? And what will you say to them? What you say here about virtue and justice and institutions and laws being the best things among men? Would that be decent of you? Surely not. But if you go away from well-governed states to Crito's friends in Thessaly, where there is great disorder and license, they will be charmed to hear the tale of your escape from prison, set off with ludicrous particulars of the manner in which you were wrapped in a goatskin or some other disguise, and metamorphosed as the manner is of runaways; but will there be no one to remind you that in your old age you were not ashamed to violate the most sacred laws from a miserable desire of a little more life? Perhaps not, if you keep them in a good temper; but if they are out of temper you will hear many degrading things; you will live, but how?--as the flatterer of all men, and the servant of all men; and doing what?--eating and drinking in Thessaly, having gone abroad in order that you may get a dinner. And where will be your fine sentiments about justice and virtue? Say that you wish to live for the sake of your children--you want to bring them up and educate them--will you take them into Thessaly and deprive them of Athenian citizenship? Is this the benefit which you will confer upon them? Or are you under the impression that they will be better cared for and educated here if you are still alive, although absent from them; for your friends will take care of them?

Do you fancy that if you are an inhabitant of Thessaly they will take care of them, and if you are an inhabitant of the other world that they will not take care of them? Nay; but if they who call themselves friends are good for anything, they will--to be sure they will.

'Listen, then, Socrates, to us who have brought you up. Think not of life and children first, and of justice afterwards, but of justice first, that you may be justified before the princes of the world below. For neither will you nor any that belong to you be happier or holier or juster in this life, or happier in another, if you do as Crito bids. Now you depart in innocence, a sufferer and not a doer of evil; a victim, not of the laws, but of men. But if you go forth, returning evil for evil, and injury for injury, breaking the covenants and agreements which you have made with us, and

wronging those whom you ought least of all to
wrong, that is to say, yourself, your friends,
your country, and us, we shall be angry with
you while you live, and our brethren, the laws
5   in the world below, will receive you as an enemy; for they will know that you have done
your best to destroy us. Listen, then, to us
and not to Crito.'

10   This, dear Crito, is the voice which I seem to
hear murmuring in my ears, like the sound of
the flute in the ears of the mystic; that voice, I
say, is humming in my ears, and prevents me
from hearing any other. And I know that any-
15   thing more which you may say will be vain.
Yet speak, if you have anything to say.

CRITO: I have nothing to say, Socrates.

20   SOCRATES: Leave me then, Crito, to fulfill
the will of God, and to follow whither he
leads.

REPUBLIC
PLATO

The scene is laid in the house of Cephalus at
the Piraeus; and the whole dialogue is narrated
by Socrates the day after it actually took place
to Timaeus, Hermocrates, Critias, and a name-
5 less person, who are introduced in the Timaeus.

BOOK I

10 I went down yesterday to the Piraeus with
Glaucon the son of Ariston, that I might offer
up my prayers to the goddess (Bendis, the
Thracian Artemis.); and also because I wanted
to see in what manner they would celebrate
15 the festival, which was a new thing. I was delighted with the procession of the inhabitants;
but that of the Thracians was equally, if not
more, beautiful. When we had finished our
prayers and viewed the spectacle, we turned in
20 the direction of the city; and at that instant
Polemarchus the son of Cephalus chanced to
catch sight of us from a distance as we were
starting on our way home, and told his servant
to run and bid us wait for him. The servant
25 took hold of me by the cloak behind, and said:
Polemarchus desires you to wait.

I turned round, and asked him where his master was.

30

There he is, said the youth, coming after you,
if you will only wait.

Certainly we will, said Glaucon; and in a few
35 minutes Polemarchus appeared, and with him

Text based off the Benjamin Jowett translation,
with adjustments for modern spellings.

Adeimantus, Glaucon's brother, Niceratus the
son of Nicias, and several others who had
been at the procession.

40 Polemarchus said to me: I perceive, Socrates,
that you and your companion are already on
your way to the city.

You are not far wrong, I said.
45

But do you see, he rejoined, how many we
are?

Of course.
50

And are you stronger than all these? for if not,
you will have to remain where you are.

May there not be the alternative, I said, that
55 we may persuade you to let us go?

But can you persuade us, if we refuse to listen
to you? he said.

60 Certainly not, replied Glaucon.

Then we are not going to listen; of that you
may be assured.

65 Adeimantus added: Has no one told you of
the torch-race on horseback in honor of the
goddess which will take place in the evening?

With horses! I replied: That is a novelty. Will
70 horsemen carry torches and pass them one to
another during the race?
Yes, said Polemarchus, and not only so, but a

festival will be celebrated at night, which you certainly ought to see. Let us rise soon after supper and see this festival; there will be a gathering of young men, and we will have a
5 good talk. Stay then, and do not be perverse.

Glaucon said: I suppose, since you insist, that we must.

10 Very good, I replied.

Accordingly we went with Polemarchus to his house; and there we found his brothers Lysias and Euthydemus, and with them Thra-
15 symachus the Chalcedonian, Charmantides the Paeanian, and Cleitophon the son of Aris- tonymus. There too was Cephalus the father of Polemarchus, whom I had not seen for a long time, and I thought him very much aged.
20 He was seated on a cushioned chair, and had a garland on his head, for he had been sacrific- ing in the court; and there were some other chairs in the room arranged in a semicircle, upon which we sat down by him. He saluted
25 me eagerly, and then he said:--

You don't come to see me, Socrates, as often as you ought: If I were still able to go and see you I would not ask you to come to me. But at
30 my age I can hardly get to the city, and there- fore you should come oftener to the Piraeus. For let me tell you, that the more the pleasures of the body fade away, the greater to me is the pleasure and charm of conversation. Do not
35 then deny my request, but make our house your resort and keep company with these young men; we are old friends, and you will be quite at home with us.

40 I replied: There is nothing which for my part I like better, Cephalus, than conversing with aged men; for I regard them as travellers who have gone a journey which I too may have to

go, and of whom I ought to enquire, whether
45 the way is smooth and easy, or rugged and difficult. And this is a question which I should like to ask of you who have arrived at that time which the poets call the 'threshold of old age'—Is life harder towards the end, or what
50 report do you give of it?

I will tell you, Socrates, he said, what my own feeling is. Men of my age flock together; we are birds of a feather, as the old proverb says;
55 and at our meetings the tale of my acquaint- ance commonly is--I cannot eat, I cannot drink; the pleasures of youth and love are fled away: there was a good time once, but now that is gone, and life is no longer life. Some
60 complain of the slights which are put upon them by relations, and they will tell you sadly of how many evils their old age is the cause. But to me, Socrates, these complainers seem to blame that which is not really in fault. For if
65 old age were the cause, I too being old, and every other old man, would have felt as they do. But this is not my own experience, nor that of others whom I have known. How well I remember the aged poet Sophocles, when in
70 answer to the question, How does love suit with age, Sophocles,--are you still the man you were?

Peace, he replied; most gladly have I escaped
75 the thing of which you speak; I feel as if I had escaped from a mad and furious master. His words have often occurred to my mind since, and they seem as good to me now as at the time when he uttered them. For certainly old
80 age has a great sense of calm and freedom; when the passions relax their hold, then, as Sophocles says, we are freed from the grasp not of one mad master only, but of many. The truth is, Socrates, that these regrets, and also
85 the complaints about relations, are to be at- tributed to the same cause, which is not old

age, but men's characters and tempers; for he who is of a calm and happy nature will hardly feel the pressure of age, but to him who is of an opposite disposition youth and age are equally a burden.

I listened in admiration, and wanting to draw him out, that he might go on--Yes, Cephalus, I said: but I rather suspect that people in general are not convinced by you when you speak thus; they think that old age sits lightly upon you, not because of your happy disposition, but because you are rich, and wealth is well known to be a great comforter.

You are right, he replied; they are not convinced: and there is something in what they say; not, however, so much as they imagine. I might answer them as Themistocles answered the Seriphian who was abusing him and saying that he was famous, not for his own merits but because he was an Athenian: 'If you had been a native of my country or I of yours, neither of us would have been famous.' And to those who are not rich and are impatient of old age, the same reply may be made; for to the good poor man old age cannot be a light burden, nor can a bad rich man ever have peace with himself.

May I ask, Cephalus, whether your fortune was for the most part inherited or acquired by you?

Acquired! Socrates; do you want to know how much I acquired? In the art of making money I have been midway between my father and grandfather: for my grandfather, whose name I bear, doubled and trebled the value of his patrimony, that which he inherited being much what I possess now; but my father Lysanias reduced the property below what it is at present: and I shall be satisfied if I leave to these my sons not less but a little more than I received.

That was why I asked you the question, I replied, because I see that you are indifferent about money, which is a characteristic rather of those who have inherited their fortunes than of those who have acquired them; the makers of fortunes have a second love of money as a creation of their own, resembling the affection of authors for their own poems, or of parents for their children, besides that natural love of it for the sake of use and profit which is common to them and all men. And hence they are very bad company, for they can talk about nothing but the praises of wealth.

That is true, he said.

Yes, that is very true, but may I ask another question?--What do you consider to be the greatest blessing which you have reaped from your wealth?

One, he said, of which I could not expect easily to convince others. For let me tell you, Socrates, that when a man thinks himself to be near death, fears and cares enter into his mind which he never had before; the tales of a world below and the punishment which is exacted there of deeds done here were once a laughing matter to him, but now he is tormented with the thought that they may be true: either from the weakness of age, or because he is now drawing nearer to that other place, he has a clearer view of these things; suspicions and alarms crowd thickly upon him, and he begins to reflect and consider what wrongs he has done to others. And when he finds that the sum of his transgressions is great he will many a time like a child start up in his sleep for fear, and he is filled with dark forebodings. But to him who is conscious of no sin, sweet hope, as Pindar charmingly says, is the kind nurse of his age:

'Hope,' he says, 'cherishes the soul of him who
5 lives in justice and holiness, and is the nurse of his age and the companion of his journey;-- hope which is mightiest to sway the restless soul of man.'

10 How admirable are his words! And the great blessing of riches, I do not say to every man, but to a good man, is, that he has had no oc- casion to deceive or to defraud others, either intentionally or unintentionally; and when he
15 departs to the world below he is not in any apprehension about offerings due to the gods or debts which he owes to men. Now to this peace of mind the possession of wealth greatly contributes; and therefore I say, that, setting
20 one thing against another, of the many ad- vantages which wealth has to give, to a man of sense this is in my opinion the greatest.

Well said, Cephalus, I replied; but as concern-
25 ing justice, what is it?--to speak the truth and to pay your debts--no more than this? And even to this are there not exceptions? Suppose that a friend when in his right mind has depos- ited arms with me and he asks for them when
30 he is not in his right mind, ought I to give them back to him? No one would say that I ought or that I should be right in doing so, any more than they would say that I ought always to speak the truth to one who is in his
35 condition.

You are quite right, he replied.

But then, I said, speaking the truth and paying
40 your debts is not a correct definition of justice.

Quite correct, Socrates, if Simonides is to be believed, said Polemarchus interposing.

I fear, said Cephalus, that I must go now, for I
45 have to look after the sacrifices, and I hand over the argument to Polemarchus and the company…

[Polemarchus suggests that justice is 'repayment of
50 *debt'—i.e. fulfilling obligations. Socrates shows that he is wrong… - MJ]*

Several times in the course of the discussion Thrasymachus had made an attempt to get the
55 argument into his own hands, and had been put down by the rest of the company, who wanted to hear the end. But when Pole- marchus and I had done speaking and there was a pause, he could no longer hold his
60 peace; and, gathering himself up, he came at us like a wild beast, seeking to devour us. We were quite panic-stricken at the sight of him.

He roared out to the whole company: What
65 folly, Socrates, has taken possession of you all? And why, sillybillies, do you knock under to one another? I say that if you want really to know what justice is, you should not only ask but answer, and you should not seek honor to
70 yourself from the refutation of an opponent, but have your own answer; for there is many a one who can ask and cannot answer. And now I will not have you say that justice is duty or advantage or profit or gain or interest, for this
75 sort of nonsense will not do for me; I must have clearness and accuracy.

I was panic-stricken at his words, and could not look at him without trembling. Indeed I
80 believe that if I had not fixed my eye upon him, I should have been struck dumb: but when I saw his fury rising, I looked at him first, and was therefore able to reply to him.

85 Thrasymachus, I said, with a quiver, don't be hard upon us. Polemarchus and I may have

been guilty of a little mistake in the argument, but I can assure you that the error was not intentional. If we were seeking for a piece of gold, you would not imagine that we were 'knocking under to one another,' and so losing our chance of finding it. And why, when we are seeking for justice, a thing more precious than many pieces of gold, do you say that we are weakly yielding to one another and not doing our utmost to get at the truth? Nay, my good friend, we are most willing and anxious to do so, but the fact is that we cannot. And if so, you people who know all things should pity us and not be angry with us.

How characteristic of Socrates! he replied, with a bitter laugh;--that's your ironical style! Did I not foresee--have I not already told you, that whatever he was asked he would refuse to answer, and try irony or any other shuffle, in order that he might avoid answering?

You are a philosopher, Thrasymachus, I replied, and well know that if you ask a person what numbers make up twelve, taking care to prohibit him whom you ask from answering twice six, or three times four, or six times two, or four times three, 'for this sort of nonsense will not do for me,'--then obviously, if that is your way of putting the question, no one can answer you. But suppose that he were to retort, 'Thrasymachus, what do you mean? If one of these numbers which you interdict be the true answer to the question, am I falsely to say some other number which is not the right one?--is that your meaning?'—How would you answer him?

Just as if the two cases were at all alike! he said.

Why should they not be? I replied; and even if they are not, but only appear to be so to the person who is asked, ought he not to say what he thinks, whether you and I forbid him or not?

I presume then that you are going to make one of the interdicted answers?

I dare say that I may, notwithstanding the danger, if upon reflection I approve of any of them.

But what if I give you an answer about justice other and better, he said, than any of these? What do you deserve to have done to you?

Done to me!--as becomes the ignorant, I must learn from the wise—that is what I deserve to have done to me.

What, and no payment! a pleasant notion!

I will pay when I have the money, I replied.

But you have, Socrates, said Glaucon: and you, Thrasymachus, need be under no anxiety about money, for we will all make a contribution for Socrates.

Yes, he replied, and then Socrates will do as he always does--refuse to answer himself, but take and pull to pieces the answer of some one else.

Why, my good friend, I said, how can any one answer who knows, and says that he knows, just nothing; and who, even if he has some faint notions of his own, is told by a man of authority not to utter them? The natural thing is, that the speaker should be some one like yourself who professes to know and can tell what he knows. Will you then kindly answer, for the edification of the company and of myself?

Glaucon and the rest of the company joined in
my request, and Thrasymachus, as any one
might see, was in reality eager to speak; for he
thought that he had an excellent answer, and
5 would distinguish himself. But at first he affected to insist on my answering; at length he
consented to begin. Behold, he said, the wisdom of Socrates; he refuses to teach himself,
and goes about learning of others, to whom he
10 never even says Thank you.

That I learn of others, I replied, is quite true;
but that I am ungrateful I wholly deny. Money
I have none, and therefore I pay in praise,
15 which is all I have; and how ready I am to
praise any one who appears to me to speak
well you will very soon find out when you
answer; for I expect that you will answer well.

20 Listen, then, he said; I proclaim that justice is
nothing else than the interest of the stronger.
And now why do you not praise me? But of
course you won't.

25 Let me first understand you, I replied. Justice,
as you say, is the interest of the stronger.
What, Thrasymachus, is the meaning of this?
You cannot mean to say that because Polyga-
las, the pancratiast, is stronger than we are,
30 and finds the eating of beef conducive to his
bodily strength, that to eat beef is therefore
equally for our good who are weaker than he
is, and right and just for us?

35 That's abominable of you, Socrates; you take
the words in the sense which is most damag-
ing to the argument.

Not at all, my good sir, I said; I am trying to
40 understand them; and I wish that you would
be a little clearer.

Well, he said, have you never heard that forms

of government differ; there are tyrannies, and
45 there are democracies, and there are aristocracies?

Yes, I know.

50 And the government is the ruling power in
each state?

Certainly.

55 And the different forms of government make
laws democratical, aristocratical, tyrannical,
with a view to their several interests; and these
laws, which are made by them for their own
interests, are the justice which they deliver to
60 their subjects, and him who transgresses them
they punish as a breaker of the law, and unjust. And that is what I mean when I say that
in all states there is the same principle of justice, which is the interest of the government;
65 and as the government must be supposed to
have power, the only reasonable conclusion is,
that everywhere there is one principle of justice, which is the interest of the stronger.

70 Now I understand you, I said; and whether
you are right or not I will try to discover. But
let me remark, that in defining justice you have
yourself used the word 'interest' which you
forbade me to use. It is true, however, that in
75 your definition the words 'of the stronger' are
added.

A small addition, you must allow, he said.

80 Great or small, never mind about that: we
must first enquire whether what you are saying
is the truth. Now we are both agreed that justice is interest of some sort, but you go on to
say 'of the stronger'; about this addition I am
85 not so sure, and must therefore consider further.

Proceed.

I will; and first tell me, Do you admit that it is just for subjects to obey their rulers?

I do.

But are the rulers of states absolutely infallible, or are they sometimes liable to err?

To be sure, he replied, they are liable to err.

Then in making their laws they may sometimes make them rightly, and sometimes not?

True.

When they make them rightly, they make them agreeably to their interest; when they are mistaken, contrary to their interest; you admit that?

Yes.

And the laws which they make must be obeyed by their subjects,--and that is what you call justice?

Doubtless.

Then justice, according to your argument, is not only obedience to the interest of the stronger but the reverse?

What is that you are saying? he asked.

I am only repeating what you are saying, I believe. But let us consider: Have we not admitted that the rulers may be mistaken about their own interest in what they command, and also that to obey them is justice? Has not that been admitted?

Yes.

Then you must also have acknowledged justice not to be for the interest of the stronger, when the rulers unintentionally command things to be done which are to their own injury. For if, as you say, justice is the obedience which the subject renders to their commands, in that case, O wisest of men, is there any escape from the conclusion that the weaker are commanded to do, not what is for the interest, but what is for the injury of the stronger?

Nothing can be clearer, Socrates, said Polemarchus.

Yes, said Cleitophon, interposing, if you are allowed to be his witness.

But there is no need of any witness, said Polemarchus, for Thrasymachus himself acknowledges that rulers may sometimes command what is not for their own interest, and that for subjects to obey them is justice.

Yes, Polemarchus,--Thrasymachus said that for subjects to do what was commanded by their rulers is just.

Yes, Cleitophon, but he also said that justice is the interest of the stronger, and, while admitting both these propositions, he further acknowledged that the stronger may command the weaker who are his subjects to do what is not for his own interest; whence follows that justice is the injury quite as much as the interest of the stronger.

But, said Cleitophon, he meant by the interest of the stronger what the stronger thought to be his interest,--this was what the weaker had to do; and this was affirmed by him to be justice.

Those were not his words, rejoined Pole-marchus.

Never mind, I replied, if he now says that they
5 are, let us accept his statement. Tell me, Thra-symachus, I said, did you mean by justice what the stronger thought to be his interest, wheth-er really so or not?

10 Certainly not, he said. Do you suppose that I call him who is mistaken the stronger at the time when he is mistaken?

Yes, I said, my impression was that you did so,
15 when you admitted that the ruler was not in-fallible but might be sometimes mistaken.

You argue like an informer, Socrates. Do you mean, for example, that he who is mistaken
20 about the sick is a physician in that he is mis-taken? or that he who errs in arithmetic or grammar is an arithmetician or grammarian at the time when he is making the mistake, in respect of the mistake? True, we say that the
25 physician or arithmetician or grammarian has made a mistake, but this is only a way of speaking; for the fact is that neither the grammarian nor any other person of skill ever makes a mistake in so far as he is what his
30 name implies; they none of them err unless their skill fails them, and then they cease to be skilled artists. No artist or sage or ruler errs at the time when he is what his name implies; though he is commonly said to err, and I
35 adopted the common mode of speaking. But to be perfectly accurate, since you are such a lover of accuracy, we should say that the ruler, in so far as he is a ruler, is unerring, and, being unerring, always commands that which is for
40 his own interest; and the subject is required to execute his commands; and therefore, as I said at first and now repeat, justice is the interest of the stronger.

Indeed, Thrasymachus, and do I really appear
45 to you to argue like an informer?

Certainly, he replied.

And do you suppose that I ask these questions
50 with any design of injuring you in the argu-ment?

Nay, he replied, 'suppose' is not the word--I know it; but you will be found out, and by
55 sheer force of argument you will never prevail.

I shall not make the attempt, my dear man; but to avoid any misunderstanding occurring between us in future, let me ask, in what sense
60 do you speak of a ruler or stronger whose in-terest, as you were saying, he being the superi-or, it is just that the inferior should execute--is he a ruler in the popular or in the strict sense of the term?
65

In the strictest of all senses, he said. And now cheat and play the informer if you can; I ask no quarter at your hands. But you never will be able, never.
70

And do you imagine, I said, that I am such a madman as to try and cheat, Thrasymachus? I might as well shave a lion.

75 Why, he said, you made the attempt a minute ago, and you failed.

Enough, I said, of these civilities. It will be better that I should ask you a question: Is the
80 physician, taken in that strict sense of which you are speaking, a healer of the sick or a maker of money? And remember that I am now speaking of the true physician.

85 A healer of the sick, he replied.

And the pilot--that is to say, the true pilot--is he a captain of sailors or a mere sailor?

A captain of sailors.

5

The circumstance that he sails in the ship is not to be taken into account; neither is he to be called a sailor; the name pilot by which he is distinguished has nothing to do with sailing,
10 but is significant of his skill and of his authority over the sailors.

Very true, he said.

15 Now, I said, every art has an interest?

Certainly.

For which the art has to consider and provide?
20 Yes, that is the aim of art.

And the interest of any art is the perfection of it--this and nothing else?
25 What do you mean?

I mean what I may illustrate negatively by the example of the body. Suppose you were to ask
30 me whether the body is self-sufficing or has wants, I should reply: Certainly the body has wants; for the body may be ill and require to be cured, and has therefore interests to which the art of medicine ministers; and this is the
35 origin and intention of medicine, as you will acknowledge. Am I not right?

Quite right, he replied.

40 But is the art of medicine or any other art faulty or deficient in any quality in the same way that the eye may be deficient in sight or the ear fail of hearing, and therefore requires

another art to provide for the interests of see-
45 ing and hearing--has art in itself, I say, any similar liability to fault or defect, and does every art require another supplementary art to provide for its interests, and that another and another without end? Or have the arts to look
50 only after their own interests? Or have they no need either of themselves or of another?-- having no faults or defects, they have no need to correct them, either by the exercise of their own art or of any other; they have only to
55 consider the interest of their subject-matter. For every art remains pure and faultless while remaining true--that is to say, while perfect and unimpaired. Take the words in your precise sense, and tell me whether I am not right.
60

Yes, clearly.

Then medicine does not consider the interest of medicine, but the interest of the body?
65

True, he said.

Nor does the art of horsemanship consider the interests of the art of horsemanship, but
70 the interests of the horse; neither do any other arts care for themselves, for they have no needs; they care only for that which is the subject of their art?

75 True, he said.

But surely, Thrasymachus, the arts are the superiors and rulers of their own subjects?

80 To this he assented with a good deal of reluctance.

Then, I said, no science or art considers or enjoins the interest of the stronger or superior,
85 but only the interest of the subject and weaker?

He made an attempt to contest this proposition also, but finally acquiesced.

Then, I continued, no physician, in so far as he is a physician, considers his own good in what he prescribes, but the good of his patient; for the true physician is also a ruler having the human body as a subject, and is not a mere money-maker; that has been admitted?

Yes.

And the pilot likewise, in the strict sense of the term, is a ruler of sailors and not a mere sailor?

That has been admitted.

And such a pilot and ruler will provide and prescribe for the interest of the sailor who is under him, and not for his own or the ruler's interest?

He gave a reluctant 'Yes.'

Then, I said, Thrasymachus, there is no one in any rule who, in so far as he is a ruler, considers or enjoins what is for his own interest, but always what is for the interest of his subject or suitable to his art; to that he looks, and that alone he considers in everything which he says and does.

When we had got to this point in the argument, and every one saw that the definition of justice had been completely upset, Thrasymachus, instead of replying to me, said: Tell me, Socrates, have you got a nurse?

Why do you ask such a question, I said, when you ought rather to be answering?

Because she leaves you to snivel, and never wipes your nose: she has not even taught you to know the shepherd from the sheep.

What makes you say that? I replied.

Because you fancy that the shepherd or neatherd fattens or tends the sheep or oxen with a view to their own good and not to the good of himself or his master; and you further imagine that the rulers of states, if they are true rulers, never think of their subjects as sheep, and that they are not studying their own advantage day and night. Oh, no; and so entirely astray are you in your ideas about the just and unjust as not even to know that justice and the just are in reality another's good; that is to say, the interest of the ruler and stronger, and the loss of the subject and servant; and injustice the opposite; for the unjust is lord over the truly simple and just: he is the stronger, and his subjects do what is for his interest, and minister to his happiness, which is very far from being their own. Consider further, most foolish Socrates, that the just is always a loser in comparison with the unjust. First of all, in private contracts: wherever the unjust is the partner of the just you will find that, when the partnership is dissolved, the unjust man has always more and the just less. Secondly, in their dealings with the State: when there is an income-tax, the just man will pay more and the unjust less on the same amount of income; and when there is anything to be received the one gains nothing and the other much. Observe also what happens when they take an office; there is the just man neglecting his affairs and perhaps suffering other losses, and getting nothing out of the public, because he is just; moreover he is hated by his friends and acquaintance for refusing to serve them in unlawful ways. But all this is reversed in the case of the unjust man.

I am speaking, as before, of injustice on a large
scale in which the advantage of the unjust is
most apparent; and my meaning will be most
clearly seen if we turn to that highest form of
5 injustice in which the criminal is the happiest
of men, and the sufferers or those who refuse
to do injustice are the most miserable--that is
to say tyranny, which by fraud and force takes
away the property of others, not little by little
10 but wholesale; comprehending in one, things
sacred as well as profane, private and public;
for which acts of wrong, if he were detected
perpetrating any one of them singly, he would
be punished and incur great disgrace--they
15 who do such wrong in particular cases are
called robbers of temples, and man-stealers
and burglars and swindlers and thieves. But
when a man besides taking away the money of
the citizens has made slaves of them, then,
20 instead of these names of reproach, he is
termed happy and blessed, not only by the
citizens but by all who hear of his having
achieved the consummation of injustice. For
mankind censure injustice, fearing that they
25 may be the victims of it and not because they
shrink from committing it. And thus, as I have
shown, Socrates, injustice, when on a sufficient scale, has more strength and freedom
and mastery than justice; and, as I said at first,
30 justice is the interest of the stronger, whereas
injustice is a man's own profit and interest.

Thrasymachus, when he had thus spoken,
having, like a bath-man, deluged our ears with
35 his words, had a mind to go away. But the
company would not let him; they insisted that
he should remain and defend his position; and
I myself added my own humble request that
he would not leave us. Thrasymachus, I said to
40 him, excellent man, how suggestive are your
remarks! And are you going to run away before you have fairly taught or learned whether
they are true or not? Is the attempt to deter-

mine the way of man's life so small a matter in
45 your eyes—to determine how life may be
passed by each one of us to the greatest advantage?

And do I differ from you, he said, as to the
50 importance of the enquiry?

You appear rather, I replied, to have no care
or thought about us, Thrasymachus--whether
we live better or worse from not knowing
55 what you say you know, is to you a matter of
indifference. Prithee, friend, do not keep your
knowledge to yourself; we are a large party;
and any benefit which you confer upon us will
be amply rewarded. For my own part I openly
60 declare that I am not convinced, and that I do
not believe injustice to be more gainful than
justice, even if uncontrolled and allowed to
have free play. For, granting that there may be
an unjust man who is able to commit injustice
65 either by fraud or force, still this does not
convince me of the superior advantage of injustice, and there may be others who are in the
same predicament with myself. Perhaps we
may be wrong; if so, you in your wisdom
70 should convince us that we are mistaken in
preferring justice to injustice.

And how am I to convince you, he said, if you
are not already convinced by what I have just
75 said; what more can I do for you? Would you
have me put the proof bodily into your souls?
Heaven forbid! I said; I would only ask you to
be consistent; or, if you change, change openly
and let there be no deception. For I must re-
80 mark, Thrasymachus, if you will recall what
was previously said, that although you began
by defining the true physician in an exact
sense, you did not observe a like exactness
when speaking of the shepherd; you thought
85 that the shepherd as a shepherd tends the
sheep not with a view to their own good, but

like a mere diner or banqueter with a view to
the pleasures of the table; or, again, as a trader
for sale in the market, and not as a shepherd.
Yet surely the art of the shepherd is concerned
5   only with the good of his subjects; he has only
to provide the best for them, since the perfection of the art is already ensured whenever all
the requirements of it are satisfied. And that
was what I was saying just now about the rul-
10   er. I conceived that the art of the ruler, considered as ruler, whether in a state or in private
life, could only regard the good of his flock or
subjects; whereas you seem to think that the
rulers in states, that is to say, the true rulers,
15   like being in authority.

Think! Nay, I am sure of it.

Then why in the case of lesser offices do men
20   never take them willingly without payment,
unless under the idea that they govern for the
advantage not of themselves but of others?
Let me ask you a question:

25   Are not the several arts different, by reason of
their each having a separate function? And,
my dear illustrious friend, do say what you
think, that we may make a little progress.

30   Yes, that is the difference, he replied.

And each art gives us a particular good and
not merely a general one--medicine, for example, gives us health; navigation, safety at sea,
35   and so on?

Yes, he said.

And the art of payment has the special func-
40   tion of giving pay: but we do not confuse this
with other arts, any more than the art of the
pilot is to be confused with the art of medicine, because the health of the pilot may be
improved by a sea voyage. You would not be
45   inclined to say, would you, that navigation is
the art of medicine, at least if we are to adopt
your exact use of language?

Certainly not.
50

Or because a man is in good health when he
receives pay you would not say that the art of
payment is medicine?

55   I should not.
Nor would you say that medicine is the art of
receiving pay because a man takes fees when
he is engaged in healing?

60   Certainly not.

And we have admitted, I said, that the good of
each art is specially confined to the art?

65   Yes.

Then, if there be any good which all artists
have in common, that is to be attributed to
something of which they all have the common
70   use?

True, he replied.

And when the artist is benefited by receiving
75   pay the advantage is gained by an additional
use of the art of pay, which is not the art professed by him?

He gave a reluctant assent to this.
80

Then the pay is not derived by the several artists from their respective arts. But the truth is,
that while the art of medicine gives health, and
the art of the builder builds a house, another
85   art attends them which is the art of pay. The
various arts may be doing their own business

and benefiting that over which they preside, but would the artist receive any benefit from his art unless he were paid as well?

5 I suppose not.

But does he therefore confer no benefit when he works for nothing?

10 Certainly, he confers a benefit.

Then now, Thrasymachus, there is no longer any doubt that neither arts nor governments provide for their own interests; but, as we 15 were before saying, they rule and provide for the interests of their subjects who are the weaker and not the stronger--to their good they attend and not to the good of the superior. And this is the reason, my dear Thra- 20 symachus, why, as I was just now saying, no one is willing to govern; because no one likes to take in hand the reformation of evils which are not his concern without remuneration. For, in the execution of his work, and in giv- 25 ing his orders to another, the true artist does not regard his own interest, but always that of his subjects; and therefore in order that rulers may be willing to rule, they must be paid in one of three modes of payment, money, or 30 honor, or a penalty for refusing.

What do you mean, Socrates? said Glaucon. The first two modes of payment are intelligible enough, but what the penalty is I do not 35 understand, or how a penalty can be a payment.

You mean that you do not understand the nature of this payment which to the best men 40 is the great inducement to rule? Of course you know that ambition and avarice are held to be, as indeed they are, a disgrace?

45 Very true.

And for this reason, I said, money and honor have no attraction for them; good men do not wish to be openly demanding payment for governing and so to get the name of hirelings, 50 nor by secretly helping themselves out of the public revenues to get the name of thieves. And not being ambitious they do not care about honor. Wherefore necessity must be laid upon them, and they must be induced to serve 55 from the fear of punishment. And this, as I imagine, is the reason why the forwardness to take office, instead of waiting to be compelled, has been deemed dishonorable. Now the worst part of the punishment is that he who 60 refuses to rule is liable to be ruled by one who is worse than himself.

And the fear of this, as I conceive, induces the good to take office, not because they would, 65 but because they cannot help--not under the idea that they are going to have any benefit or enjoyment themselves, but as a necessity, and because they are not able to commit the task of ruling to any one who is better than them- 70 selves, or indeed as good. For there is reason to think that if a city were composed entirely of good men, then to avoid office would be as much an object of contention as to obtain office is at present; then we should have plain 75 proof that the true ruler is not meant by nature to regard his own interest, but that of his subjects; and every one who knew this would choose rather to receive a benefit from another than to have the trouble of conferring one. 80 So far am I from agreeing with Thrasymachus that justice is the interest of the stronger. This latter question need not be further discussed at present; but when Thrasymachus says that the life of the unjust is more advantageous 85 than that of the just, his new statement appears to me to be of a far more serious character. Which of us has spoken truly? And which sort of life, Glaucon, do you prefer?

I for my part deem the life of the just to be
5 the more advantageous, he answered.

Did you hear all the advantages of the unjust which Thrasymachus was rehearsing?

10 Yes, I heard him, he replied, but he has not convinced me.

Then shall we try to find some way of convincing him, if we can, that he is saying what is
15 not true?

Most certainly, he replied.

If, I said, he makes a set speech and we make
20 another recounting all the advantages of being just, and he answers and we rejoin, there must be a numbering and measuring of the goods which are claimed on either side, and in the end we shall want judges to decide; but if we
25 proceed in our enquiry as we lately did, by making admissions to one another, we shall unite the offices of judge and advocate in our own persons.

30 Very good, he said.

And which method do I understand you to prefer? I said.

35 That which you propose.

Well, then, Thrasymachus, I said, suppose you begin at the beginning and answer me. You say that perfect injustice is more gainful than
40 perfect justice?

Yes, that is what I say, and I have given you my reasons.

And what is your view about them? Would
45 you call one of them virtue and the other vice?

Certainly.

I suppose that you would call justice virtue
50 and injustice vice?

What a charming notion! So likely too, seeing that I affirm injustice to be profitable and justice not.

55
What else then would you say?

The opposite, he replied.

60 And would you call justice vice?

No, I would rather say sublime simplicity.

Then would you call injustice malignity?

65
No; I would rather say discretion.

And do the unjust appear to you to be wise and good?

70
Yes, he said; at any rate those of them who are able to be perfectly unjust, and who have the power of subduing states and nations; but perhaps you imagine me to be talking of cut-
75 purses. Even this profession if undetected has advantages, though they are not to be compared with those of which I was just now speaking.

80 I do not think that I misapprehend your meaning, Thrasymachus, I replied; but still I cannot hear without amazement that you class injustice with wisdom and virtue, and justice with the opposite.

85
Certainly I do so class them.

Now, I said, you are on more substantial and almost unanswerable ground; for if the injustice which you were maintaining to be profitable had been admitted by you as by others to be vice and deformity, an answer might have been given to you on received principles; but now I perceive that you will call injustice honorable and strong, and to the unjust you will attribute all the qualities which were attributed by us before to the just, seeing that you do not hesitate to rank injustice with wisdom and virtue.

You have guessed most infallibly, he replied.

Then I certainly ought not to shrink from going through with the argument so long as I have reason to think that you, Thrasymachus, are speaking your real mind; for I do believe that you are now in earnest and are not amusing yourself at our expense.

I may be in earnest or not, but what is that to you?--to refute the argument is your business.

Very true, I said; that is what I have to do: But will you be so good as answer yet one more question? Does the just man try to gain any advantage over the just?

Far otherwise; if he did he would not be the simple amusing creature which he is.

And would he try to go beyond just action?

He would not.

And how would he regard the attempt to gain an advantage over the unjust; would that be considered by him as just or unjust?

He would think it just, and would try to gain the advantage; but he would not be able.

Whether he would or would not be able, I said, is not to the point. My question is only whether the just man, while refusing to have more than another just man, would wish and claim to have more than the unjust?

Yes, he would.

And what of the unjust--does he claim to have more than the just man and to do more than is just?

Of course, he said, for he claims to have more than all men.

And the unjust man will strive and struggle to obtain more than the unjust man or action, in order that he may have more than all?

True.

We may put the matter thus, I said--the just does not desire more than his like but more than his unlike, whereas the unjust desires more than both his like and his unlike?

Nothing, he said, can be better than that statement.

And the unjust is good and wise, and the just is neither?

Good again, he said.

And is not the unjust like the wise and good and the just unlike them?

Of course, he said, he who is of a certain nature, is like those who are of a certain nature; he who is not, not.

Each of them, I said, is such as his like is?

Certainly, he replied.

Very good, Thrasymachus, I said; and now to take the case of the arts: you would admit that one man is a musician and another not a musician?

Yes.

And which is wise and which is foolish? Clearly the musician is wise, and he who is not a musician is foolish.

And he is good in as far as he is wise, and bad in as far as he is foolish?

Yes.

And you would say the same sort of thing of the physician?

Yes.

And do you think, my excellent friend, that a musician when he adjusts the lyre would desire or claim to exceed or go beyond a musician in the tightening and loosening the strings?

I do not think that he would.

But he would claim to exceed the non-musician?

Of course.

And what would you say of the physician? In prescribing meats and drinks would he wish to go beyond another physician or beyond the practice of medicine?

He would not.

But he would wish to go beyond the non-physician?

Yes.

And about knowledge and ignorance in general; see whether you think that any man who has knowledge ever would wish to have the choice of saying or doing more than another man who has knowledge. Would he not rather say or do the same as his like in the same case? That, I suppose, can hardly be denied.

And what of the ignorant? would he not desire to have more than either the knowing or the ignorant?

I dare say.

And the knowing is wise?

Yes.

And the wise is good?

True.

Then the wise and good will not desire to gain more than his like, but more than his unlike and opposite?

I suppose so.

Whereas the bad and ignorant will desire to gain more than both?

Yes.

But did we not say, Thrasymachus, that the unjust goes beyond both his like and unlike? Were not these your words?

They were.

And you also said that the just will not go beyond his like but his unlike?

Yes.

Then the just is like the wise and good, and the unjust like the evil and ignorant?

That is the inference.

And each of them is such as his like is?

That was admitted.

Then the just has turned out to be wise and good and the unjust evil and ignorant.

Thrasymachus made all these admissions, not fluently, as I repeat them, but with extreme reluctance; it was a hot summer's day, and the perspiration poured from him in torrents; and then I saw what I had never seen before, Thrasymachus blushing. As we were now agreed that justice was virtue and wisdom, and injustice vice and ignorance, I proceeded to another point:

Well, I said, Thrasymachus, that matter is now settled; but were we not also saying that injustice had strength; do you remember?

Yes, I remember, he said, but do not suppose that I approve of what you are saying or have no answer; if however I were to answer, you would be quite certain to accuse me of haranguing; therefore either permit me to have my say out, or if you would rather ask, do so, and I will answer 'Very good,' as they say to story-telling old women, and will nod 'Yes' and 'No.'

Certainly not, I said, if contrary to your real opinion.

Yes, he said, I will, to please you, since you will not let me speak. What else would you have?

Nothing in the world, I said; and if you are so disposed I will ask and you shall answer.

Proceed.

Then I will repeat the question which I asked before, in order that our examination of the relative nature of justice and injustice may be carried on regularly. A statement was made that injustice is stronger and more powerful than justice, but now justice, having been identified with wisdom and virtue, is easily shown to be stronger than injustice, if injustice is ignorance; this can no longer be questioned by any one. But I want to view the matter, Thrasymachus, in a different way: You would not deny that a state may be unjust and may be unjustly attempting to enslave other states, or may have already enslaved them, and may be holding many of them in subjection?

True, he replied; and I will add that the best and most perfectly unjust state will be most likely to do so.

I know, I said, that such was your position; but what I would further consider is, whether this power which is possessed by the superior state can exist or be exercised without justice or only with justice.

If you are right in your view, and justice is wisdom, then only with justice; but if I am right, then without justice.

I am delighted, Thrasymachus, to see you not only nodding assent and dissent, but making answers which are quite excellent.

That is out of civility to you, he replied.

You are very kind, I said; and would you have the goodness also to inform me, whether you
5 think that a state, or an army, or a band of robbers and thieves, or any other gang of evil-doers could act at all if they injured one another?

10 No indeed, he said, they could not.

But if they abstained from injuring one another, then they might act together better?

15 Yes.

And this is because injustice creates divisions and hatreds and fighting, and justice imparts harmony and friendship; is not that true,
20 Thrasymachus?

I agree, he said, because I do not wish to quarrel with you.

25 How good of you, I said; but I should like to know also whether injustice, having this tendency to arouse hatred, wherever existing, among slaves or among freemen, will not make them hate one another and set them at
30 variance and render them incapable of common action?

Certainly.

35 And even if injustice be found in two only, will they not quarrel and fight, and become enemies to one another and to the just?

They will.
40

And suppose injustice abiding in a single person, would your wisdom say that she loses or that she retains her natural power?

45 Let us assume that she retains her power.

Yet is not the power which injustice exercises of such a nature that wherever she takes up her abode, whether in a city, in an army, in a
50 family, or in any other body, that body is, to begin with, rendered incapable of united action by reason of sedition and distraction; and does it not become its own enemy and at variance with all that opposes it, and with the just?
55 Is not this the case?

Yes, certainly.

And is not injustice equally fatal when existing
60 in a single person; in the first place rendering him incapable of action because he is notmat unity with himself, and in the second place making him an enemy to himself and the just? Is not that true, Thrasymachus?
65

Yes.

And O my friend, I said, surely the gods are just?
70

Granted that they are.

But if so, the unjust will be the enemy of the gods, and the just will be their friend?
75

Feast away in triumph, and take your fill of the argument; I will not oppose you, lest I should displease the company.

80 Well then, proceed with your answers, and let me have the remainder of my repast. For we have already shown that the just are clearly wiser and better and abler than the unjust, and that the unjust are incapable of common ac-
85 tion; nay more, that to speak as we did of men who are evil acting at any time vigorously to-

gether, is not strictly true, for if they had been perfectly evil, they would have laid hands up-on one another; but it is evident that there must have been some remnant of justice in
5 them, which enabled them to combine; if there had not been they would have injured one another as well as their victims; they were but half-villains in their enterprises; for had they been whole villains, and utterly unjust,
10 they would have been utterly incapable of action. That, as I believe, is the truth of the matter, and not what you said at first. But whether the just have a better and happier life than the unjust is a further question which we also
15 proposed to consider. I think that they have, and for the reasons which I have given; but still I should like to examine further, for no light matter is at stake, nothing less than the rule of human life.

20

Proceed.

I will proceed by asking a question: Would you not say that a horse has some end?

25

I should.

And the end or use of a horse or of anything would be that which could not be accom-
30 plished, or not so well accomplished, by any other thing?

I do not understand, he said.

35 Let me explain: Can you see, except with the eye?

Certainly not.

40 Or hear, except with the ear?

No.

These then may be truly said to be the ends of
45 these organs?

They may.

But you can cut off a vine-branch with a dag-
50 ger or with a chisel, and in many other ways?

Of course.

And yet not so well as with a pruning-hook
55 made for the purpose?

True.

May we not say that this is the end of a prun-
60 ing-hook?

We may.

Then now I think you will have no difficulty in
65 understanding my meaning when I asked the question whether the end of anything would be that which could not be accomplished, or not so well accomplished, by any other thing?

70 I understand your meaning, he said, and assent.

And that to which an end is appointed has also an excellence? Need I ask again whether
75 the eye has an end?

It has.

And has not the eye an excellence?
80
Yes.

And the ear has an end and an excellence also?

85 True.

And the same is true of all other things; they have each of them an end and a special excellence?

5 That is so.

Well, and can the eyes fulfill their end if they are wanting in their own proper excellence and have a defect instead?

10 How can they, he said, if they are blind and cannot see?

You mean to say, if they have lost their proper 15 excellence, which is sight; but I have not arrived at that point yet. I would rather ask the question more generally, and only enquire whether the things which fulfill their ends fulfill them by their own proper excellence, and 20 fail of fulfilling them by their own defect?

Certainly, he replied.

I might say the same of the ears; when de-25 prived of their own proper excellence they cannot fulfill their end?

True.

30 And the same observation will apply to all other things?

I agree.

35 Well; and has not the soul an end which nothing else can fulfill? For example, to superintend and command and deliberate and the like. Are not these functions proper to the soul, and can they rightly be assigned to any other?

40 To no other.

And is not life to be reckoned among the ends of the soul?

45 Assuredly, he said.

And has not the soul an excellence also?

50 Yes.

And can she or can she not fulfill her own ends when deprived of that excellence?

55 She cannot.

Then an evil soul must necessarily be an evil ruler and superintendent, and the good soul a good ruler?

60 Yes, necessarily.

And we have admitted that justice is the excellence of the soul, and injustice the defect of 65 the soul?

That has been admitted.

Then the just soul and the just man will live 70 well, and the unjust man will live ill?

That is what your argument proves.

And he who lives well is blessed and happy, 75 and he who lives ill the reverse of happy?

Certainly.

Then the just is happy, and the unjust misera-80 ble?

So be it.

But happiness and not misery is profitable.

85 Of course.

Then, my blessed Thrasymachus, injustice can never be more profitable than justice.

Let this, Socrates, he said, be your entertain-
5 ment at the Bendidea.

For which I am indebted to you, I said, now that you have grown gentle towards me and have left off scolding. Nevertheless, I have not
10 been well entertained; but that was my own fault and not yours. As an epicure snatches a taste of every dish which is successively brought to table, he not having allowed him-self time to enjoy the one before, so have I
15 gone from one subject to another without having discovered what I sought at first, the nature of justice. I left that enquiry and turned away to consider whether justice is virtue and wisdom or evil and folly; and when there arose
20 a further question about the comparative ad-vantages of justice and injustice, I could not refrain from passing on to that. And the result of the whole discussion has been that I know nothing at all. For I know not what justice is,
25 and therefore I am not likely to know whether it is or is not a virtue, nor can I say whether the just man is happy or unhappy.

[In Books II and III Socrates begins a full investiga-
30 *tion of the nature of justice by starting the 'construc-*
tion' of the perfect city—the city in which justice will
exist. He argues that for justice to exist their must be
a governing class ('the Guardians') who will look after
the affairs of the city. In the close of Book III he ar-
35 *gues that while the common people will need to own*
property we must restrict it from the Guardians… -
MJ)

BOOK IV

40

Here Adeimantus interposed a question: How would you answer, Socrates, said he, if a per-son were to say that you are making these

people miserable, and that they are the cause
45 of their own unhappiness; the city in fact be-longs to them, but they are none the better for it; whereas other men acquire lands, and build large and handsome houses, and have every-thing handsome about them, offering sacrific-
50 es to the gods on their own account, and prac-ticing hospitality; moreover, as you were say-ing just now, they have gold and silver, and all that is usual among the favorites of fortune; but our poor citizens are no better than mer-
55 cenaries who are quartered in the city and are always mounting guard?

Yes, I said; and you may add that they are only fed, and not paid in addition to their food, like
60 other men; and therefore they cannot, if they would, take a journey of pleasure; they have no money to spend on a mistress or any other luxurious fancy, which, as the world goes, is thought to be happiness; and many other ac-
65 cusations of the same nature might be added.

But, said he, let us suppose all this to be in-cluded in the charge.

70 You mean to ask, I said, what will be our an-swer?

Yes.

75 If we proceed along the old path, my belief, I said, is that we shall find the answer. And our answer will be that, even as they are, our guardians may very likely be the happiest of men; but that our aim in founding the State
80 was not the disproportionate happiness of any one class, but the greatest happiness of the whole; we thought that in a State which is or-dered with a view to the good of the whole we should be most likely to find justice, and in the
85 ill-ordered State injustice: and, having found them, we might then decide which of the two

is the happier. At present, I take it, we are fashioning the happy State, not piecemeal, or with a view of making a few happy citizens, but as a whole; and by-and-by we will proceed
5 to view the opposite kind of State.

Suppose that we were painting a statue, and some one came up to us and said, Why do you not put the most beautiful colors on the most
10 beautiful parts of the body--the eyes ought to be purple, but you have made them black--to him we might fairly answer, Sir, you would not surely have us beautify the eyes to such a degree that they are no longer eyes; consider
15 rather whether, by giving this and the other features their due proportion, we make the whole beautiful. And so I say to you, do not compel us to assign to the guardians a sort of happiness which will make them anything but
20 guardians; for we too can clothe our husbandmen in royal apparel, and set crowns of gold on their heads, and bid them till the ground as much as they like, and no more. Our potters also might be allowed to repose
25 on couches, and feast by the fireside, passing round the winecup, while their wheel is conveniently at hand, and working at pottery only as much as they like; in this way we might make every class happy--and then, as you im-
30 agine, the whole State would be happy. But do not put this idea into our heads; for, if we listen to you, the husbandman will be no longer a husbandman, the potter will cease to be a potter, and no one will have the character of
35 any distinct class in the State. Now this is not of much consequence where the corruption of society, and pretension to be what you are not, is confined to cobblers; but when the guardians of the laws and of the government are
40 only seeming and not real guardians, then see how they turn the State upside down; and on the other hand they alone have the power of giving order and happiness to the State. We

mean our guardians to be true saviors and not
45 the destroyers of the State, whereas our opponent is thinking of peasants at a festival, who are enjoying a life of revelry, not of citizens who are doing their duty to the State. But, if so, we mean different things, and he is speak-
50 ing of something which is not a State. And therefore we must consider whether in appointing our guardians we would look to their greatest happiness individually, or whether this principle of happiness does not rather reside
55 in the State as a whole. But if the latter be the truth, then the guardians and auxiliaries, and all others equally with them, must be compelled or induced to do their own work in the best way. And thus the whole State will grow
60 up in a noble order, and the several classes will receive the proportion of happiness which nature assigns to them.

I think that you are quite right.
65

I wonder whether you will agree with another remark which occurs to me.

What may that be?
70

There seem to be two causes of the deterioration of the arts.

What are they?
75

Wealth, I said, and poverty.

How do they act?

80 The process is as follows: When a potter becomes rich, will he, think you, any longer take the same pains with his art?

Certainly not.
85

He will grow more and more indolent and

careless?

Very true.

5 And the result will be that he becomes a worse potter?

Yes; he greatly deteriorates.

10 But, on the other hand, if he has no money, and cannot provide himself with tools or instruments, he will not work equally well himself, nor will he teach his sons or apprentices to work equally well.

15

Certainly not.

Then, under the influence either of poverty or of wealth, workmen and their work are equally 20 liable to degenerate?

That is evident.

Here, then, is a discovery of new evils, I said, 25 against which the guardians will have to watch, or they will creep into the city unobserved.

What evils?

30 Wealth, I said, and poverty; the one is the parent of luxury and indolence, and the other of meanness and viciousness, and both of discontent.

35 That is very true, he replied; but still I should like to know, Socrates, how our city will be able to go to war, especially against an enemy who is rich and powerful, if deprived of the sinews of war.

40

There would certainly be a difficulty, I replied, in going to war with one such enemy; but there is no difficulty where there are two of them.

45

How so? he asked.

In the first place, I said, if we have to fight, our side will be trained warriors fighting 50 against an army of rich men.

That is true, he said.

And do you not suppose, Adeimantus, that a 55 single boxer who was perfect in his art would easily be a match for two stout and well-to-do gentlemen who were not boxers?

Hardly, if they came upon him at once.
60 What, now, I said, if he were able to run away and then turn and strike at the one who first came up? And supposing he were to do this several times under the heat of a scorching sun, might he not, being an expert, overturn 65 more than one stout personage?

Certainly, he said, there would be nothing wonderful in that.

70 And yet rich men probably have a greater superiority in the science and practice of boxing than they have in military qualities.

Likely enough.

75

Then we may assume that our athletes will be able to fight with two or three times their own number?

80 I agree with you, for I think you right.

And suppose that, before engaging, our citizens send an embassy to one of the two cities, telling them what is the truth: Silver and gold 85 we neither have nor are permitted to have, but you may; do you therefore come and help us

in war, and take the spoils of the other city: Who, on hearing these words, would choose to fight against lean wiry dogs, rather than, with the dogs on their side, against fat and
5 tender sheep?

That is not likely; and yet there might be a danger to the poor State if the wealth of many States were to be gathered into one.
10

But how simple of you to use the term State at all of any but our own!

Why so?
15

You ought to speak of other States in the plural number; not one of them is a city, but many cities, as they say in the game. For indeed any city, however small, is in fact divided
20 into two, one the city of the poor, the other of the rich; these are at war with one another; and in either there are many smaller divisions, and you would be altogether beside the mark if you treated them all as a single State. But if
25 you deal with them as many, and give the wealth or power or persons of the one to the others, you will always have a great many friends and not many enemies. And your State, while the wise order which has now
30 been prescribed continues to prevail in her, will be the greatest of States, I do not mean to say in reputation or appearance, but in deed and truth, though she number not more than a thousand defenders. A single State which is
35 her equal you will hardly find, either among Hellenes or barbarians, though many that appear to be as great and many times greater.

That is most true, he said.
40

And what, I said, will be the best limit for our rulers to fix when they are considering the size of the State and the amount of territory which

they are to include, and beyond which they
45 will not go?

What limit would you propose?

I would allow the State to increase so far as is
50 consistent with unity; that, I think, is the proper limit.

Very good, he said.

55 Here then, I said, is another order which will have to be conveyed to our guardians: Let our city be accounted neither large nor small, but one and self-sufficing.

60 And surely, said he, this is not a very severe order which we impose upon them.

And the other, said I, of which we were speaking before is lighter still,--I mean the duty of
65 degrading the offspring of the guardians when inferior, and of elevating into the rank of guardians the offspring of the lower classes, when naturally superior. The intention was, that, in the case of the citizens generally, each
70 individual should be put to the use for which nature intended him, one to one work, and then every man would do his own business, and be one and not many; and so the whole city would be one and not many.
75

Yes, he said; that is not so difficult.

The regulations which we are prescribing, my good Adeimantus, are not, as might be supposed, a number of great principles, but trifles
80 all, if care be taken, as the saying is, of the one great thing,--a thing, however, which I would rather call, not great, but sufficient for our purpose.
85

What may that be? he asked.

Education, I said, and nurture: If our citizens are well educated, and grow into sensible men, they will easily see their way through all these, as well as other matters which I omit; such,

5 for example, as marriage, the possession of women and the procreation of children, which will all follow the general principle that friends have all things in common, as the proverb says.

10

That will be the best way of settling them.

Also, I said, the State, if once started well, moves with accumulating force like a wheel.

15 For good nurture and education implant good constitutions, and these good constitutions taking root in a good education improve more and more, and this improvement affects the breed in man as in other animals.

20

Very possibly, he said.

Then to sum up: This is the point to which, above all, the attention of our rulers should be

25 directed,--that music and gymnastic be pre-served in their original form, and no innova-tion made. They must do their utmost to maintain them intact. And when any one says that mankind most regard

30

'The newest song which the singers have,'

they will be afraid that he may be praising, not new songs, but a new kind of song; and this

35 ought not to be praised, or conceived to be the meaning of the poet; for any musical in-novation is full of danger to the whole State, and ought to be prohibited. So Damon tells me, and I can quite believe him;--he says that

40 when modes of music change, the fundamen-tal laws of the State always change with them.

Yes, said Adeimantus; and you may add my

suffrage to Damon's and your own.

45

Then, I said, our guardians must lay the foun-dations of their fortress in music?

Yes, he said; the lawlessness of which you

50 speak too easily steals in.

Yes, I replied, in the form of amusement; and at first sight it appears harmless.

55 Why, yes, he said, and there is no harm; were it not that little by little this spirit of licence, finding a home, imperceptibly penetrates into manners and customs; whence, issuing with greater force, it invades contracts between

60 man and man, and from contracts goes on to laws and constitutions, in utter recklessness, ending at last, Socrates, by an overthrow of all rights, private as well as public.

65 Is that true? I said.

That is my belief, he replied.

Then, as I was saying, our youth should be

70 trained from the first in a stricter system, for if amusements become lawless, and the youths themselves become lawless, they can never grow up into well-conducted and virtuous citizens.

75

Very true, he said.
And when they have made a good beginning in play, and by the help of music have gained the habit of good order, then this habit of

80 order, in a manner how unlike the lawless play of the others! will accompany them in all their actions and be a principle of growth to them, and if there be any fallen places in the State will raise them up again.

85

Very true, he said.

Thus educated, they will invent for themselves any lesser rules which their predecessors have altogether neglected.

5 What do you mean?

I mean such things as these:--when the young are to be silent before their elders; how they are to show respect to them by standing and
10 making them sit; what honor is due to parents; what garments or shoes are to be worn; the mode of dressing the hair; deportment and manners in general. You would agree with me?

15 Yes.

But there is, I think, small wisdom in legislating about such matters,--I doubt if it is ever done; nor are any precise written enactments
20 about them likely to be lasting.

Impossible.

It would seem, Adeimantus, that the direction
25 in which education starts a man, will determine his future life. Does not like always attract like?

To be sure.
30

Until some one rare and grand result is reached which may be good, and may be the reverse of good?
That is not to be denied.
35

And for this reason, I said, I shall not attempt to legislate further about them.

Naturally enough, he replied.
40

Well, and about the business of the agora, and the ordinary dealings between man and man, or again about agreements with artisans; about
45 insult and injury, or the commencement of actions, and the appointment of juries, what would you say? there may also arise questions about any impositions and exactions of market and harbor dues which may be required, and
50 in general about the regulations of markets, police, harbors, and the like. But, oh heavens! shall we condescend to legislate on any of these particulars?

I think, he said, that there is no need to im-
55 pose laws about them on good men; what regulations are necessary they will find out soon enough for themselves.

Yes, I said, my friend, if God will only pre-
60 serve to them the laws which we have given them.

And without divine help, said Adeimantus, they will go on for ever making and mending
65 their laws and their lives in the hope of attaining perfection.

You would compare them, I said, to those invalids who, having no self-restraint, will not
70 leave off their habits of intemperance?

Exactly.

Yes, I said; and what a delightful life they lead!
75 they are always doctoring and increasing and complicating their disorders, and always fancying that they will be cured by any nostrum which anybody advises them to try.

80 Such cases are very common, he said, with invalids of this sort.

Yes, I replied; and the charming thing is that they deem him their worst enemy who tells
85 them the truth, which is simply that, unless they give up eating and drinking and wenching

and idling, neither drug nor cautery nor spell nor amulet nor any other remedy will avail.

Charming! he replied. I see nothing charming
5 in going into a passion with a man who tells you what is right.

These gentlemen, I said, do not seem to be in your good graces.
10
Assuredly not.

Nor would you praise the behavior of States which act like the men whom I was just now
15 describing. For are there not ill-ordered States in which the citizens are forbidden under pain of death to alter the constitution; and yet he who most sweetly courts those who live under this regime and indulges them and fawns upon
20 them and is skillful in anticipating and gratifying their humors is held to be a great and good statesman--do not these States resemble the persons whom I was describing?

25 Yes, he said; the States are as bad as the men; and I am very far from praising them.

But do you not admire, I said, the coolness and dexterity of these ready ministers of polit-
30 ical corruption?

Yes, he said, I do; but not of all of them, for there are some whom the applause of the multitude has deluded into the belief that they are
35 really statesmen, and these are not much to be admired.

What do you mean? I said; you should have more feeling for them. When a man cannot
40 measure, and a great many others who cannot measure declare that he is four cubits high, can he help believing what they say?

Nay, he said, certainly not in that case.
45
Well, then, do not be angry with them; for are they not as good as a play, trying their hand at paltry reforms such as I was describing; they are always fancying that by legislation they will
50 make an end of frauds in contracts, and the other rascalities which I was mentioning, not knowing that they are in reality cutting off the heads of a hydra?

55 Yes, he said; that is just what they are doing.

I conceive, I said, that the true legislator will not trouble himself with this class of enactments whether concerning laws or the consti-
60 tution either in an ill-ordered or in a well-ordered State; for in the former they are quite useless, and in the latter there will be no difficulty in devising them; and many of them will naturally flow out of our previous regulations.
65
What, then, he said, is still remaining to us of the work of legislation?

Nothing to us, I replied; but to Apollo, the
70 God of Delphi, there remains the ordering of the greatest and noblest and chiefest things of all.

Which are they? he said.
75
The institution of temples and sacrifices, and the entire service of gods, demigods, and heroes; also the ordering of the repositories of the dead, and the rites which have to be ob-
80 served by him who would propitiate the inhabitants of the world below. These are matters of which we are ignorant ourselves, and as founders of a city we should be unwise in trusting them to any interpreter but our ances-
85 tral deity. He is the god who sits in the center, on the navel of the earth, and he is the inter-

preter of religion to all mankind.

You are right, and we will do as you propose.

5 But where, amid all this, is justice? son of Ariston, tell me where. Now that our city has been
made habitable, light a candle and search, and
get your brother and Polemarchus and the rest
of our friends to help, and let us see where in
10 it we can discover justice and where injustice,
and in what they differ from one another, and
which of them the man who would be happy
should have for his portion, whether seen or
unseen by gods and men.

15
Nonsense, said Glaucon: did you not promise
to search yourself, saying that for you not to
help justice in her need would be an impiety?
I do not deny that I said so, and as you remind
20 me, I will be as good as my word; but you
must join.

We will, he replied.

25 Well, then, I hope to make the discovery in
this way: I mean to begin with the assumption
that our State, if rightly ordered, is perfect.

That is most certain.
30
And being perfect, is therefore wise and valiant and temperate and just.

That is likewise clear.
35
And whichever of these qualities we find in
the State, the one which is not found will be
the residue?

40 Very good.

If there were four things, and we were searching for one of them, wherever it might be, the

45 one sought for might be known to us from the
first, and there would be no further trouble; or
we might know the other three first, and then
the fourth would clearly be the one left.

Very true, he said.
50
And is not a similar method to be pursued
about the virtues, which are also four in number?

55 Clearly.

First among the virtues found in the State,
wisdom comes into view, and in this I detect a
certain peculiarity.
60
What is that?

The State which we have been describing is
said to be wise as being good in counsel?
65
Very true.

And good counsel is clearly a kind of
knowledge, for not by ignorance, but by
70 knowledge, do men counsel well?

Clearly.

And the kinds of knowledge in a State are
75 many and diverse?
Of course.

There is the knowledge of the carpenter; but is
that the sort of knowledge which gives a city
80 the title of wise and good in counsel?

Certainly not; that would only give a city the
reputation of skill in carpentering.

85 Then a city is not to be called wise because
possessing a knowledge which counsels for

the best about wooden implements?

Certainly not.

5 Nor by reason of a knowledge which advises about brazen pots, I said, nor as possessing any other similar knowledge?

Not by reason of any of them, he said.

10

Nor yet by reason of a knowledge which cultivates the earth; that would give the city the name of agricultural?

15 Yes.

Well, I said, and is there any knowledge in our recently-founded State among any of the citizens which advises, not about any particular
20 thing in the State, but about the whole, and considers how a State can best deal with itself and with other States?

There certainly is.

25

And what is this knowledge, and among whom is it found? I asked.

It is the knowledge of the guardians, he re-
30 plied, and is found among those whom we were just now describing as perfect guardians.

And what is the name which the city derives from the possession of this sort of
35 knowledge?

The name of good in counsel and truly wise.

And will there be in our city more of these
40 true guardians or more smiths?

The smiths, he replied, will be far more numerous.

Will not the guardians be the smallest of all
45 the classes who receive a name from the profession of some kind of knowledge?

Much the smallest.

50 And so by reason of the smallest part or class, and of the knowledge which resides in this presiding and ruling part of itself, the whole State, being thus constituted according to nature, will be wise; and this, which has the only
55 knowledge worthy to be called wisdom, has been ordained by nature to be of all classes the least.

Most true.

60

Thus, then, I said, the nature and place in the State of one of the four virtues has somehow or other been discovered.

65 And, in my humble opinion, very satisfactorily discovered, he replied.
Again, I said, there is no difficulty in seeing the nature of courage, and in what part that quality resides which gives the name of coura-
70 geous to the State.

How do you mean?

Why, I said, every one who calls any State
75 courageous or cowardly, will be thinking of the part which fights and goes out to war on the State's behalf.

No one, he replied, would ever think of any
80 other.

The rest of the citizens may be courageous or may be cowardly, but their courage or coward-ice will not, as I conceive, have the effect of
85 making the city either the one or the other.

Certainly not.

The city will be courageous in virtue of a portion of herself which preserves under all circumstances that opinion about the nature of things to be feared and not to be feared in which our legislator educated them; and this is what you term courage.

I should like to hear what you are saying once more, for I do not think that I perfectly understand you.

I mean that courage is a kind of salvation.

Salvation of what?

Of the opinion respecting things to be feared, what they are and of what nature, which the law implants through education; and I mean by the words 'under all circumstances' to intimate that in pleasure or in pain, or under the influence of desire or fear, a man preserves, and does not lose this opinion. Shall I give you an illustration?

If you please.

You know, I said, that dyers, when they want to dye wool for making the true sea-purple, begin by selecting their white color first; this they prepare and dress with much care and pains, in order that the white ground may take the purple hue in full perfection. The dyeing then proceeds; and whatever is dyed in this manner becomes a fast color, and no washing either with lyes or without them can take away the bloom. But, when the ground has not been duly prepared, you will have noticed how poor is the look either of purple or of any other color.

Yes, he said; I know that they have a washed-out and ridiculous appearance.

Then now, I said, you will understand what our object was in selecting our soldiers, and educating them in music and gymnastic; we were contriving influences which would prepare them to take the dye of the laws in perfection, and the color of their opinion about dangers and of every other opinion was to be indelibly fixed by their nurture and training, not to be washed away by such potent lyes as pleasure--mightier agent far in washing the soul than any soda or lye; or by sorrow, fear, and desire, the mightiest of all other solvents. And this sort of universal saving power of true opinion in conformity with law about real and false dangers I call and maintain to be courage, unless you disagree.

But I agree, he replied; for I suppose that you mean to exclude mere uninstructed courage, such as that of a wild beast or of a slave--this, in your opinion, is not the courage which the law ordains, and ought to have another name.

Most certainly.

Then I may infer courage to be such as you describe?

Why, yes, said I, you may, and if you add the words 'of a citizen, you will not be far wrong;--hereafter, if you like, we will carry the examination further, but at present we are seeking not for courage but justice; and for the purpose of our enquiry we have said enough.

You are right, he replied.

Two virtues remain to be discovered in the State--first, temperance, and then justice which is the end of our search.

Very true.

Now, can we find justice without troubling ourselves about temperance?

I do not know how that can be accomplished, he said, nor do I desire that justice should be brought to light and temperance lost sight of; and therefore I wish that you would do me the favor of considering temperance first.

Certainly, I replied, I should not be justified in refusing your request.

Then consider, he said.

Yes, I replied; I will; and as far as I can at present see, the virtue of temperance has more of the nature of harmony and symphony than the preceding.

How so? he asked.

Temperance, I replied, is the ordering or controlling of certain pleasures and desires; this is curiously enough implied in the saying of 'a man being his own master;' and other traces of the same notion may be found in language.

No doubt, he said.

There is something ridiculous in the expression 'master of himself;' for the master is also the servant and the servant the master; and in all these modes of speaking the same person is denoted.

Certainly.

The meaning is, I believe, that in the human soul there is a better and also a worse principle; and when the better has the worse under control, then a man is said to be master of himself; and this is a term of praise: but when, owing to evil education or association, the better principle, which is also the smaller, is overwhelmed by the greater mass of the worse--in this case he is blamed and is called the slave of self and unprincipled.

Yes, there is reason in that.

And now, I said, look at our newly-created State, and there you will find one of these two conditions realized; for the State, as you will acknowledge, may be justly called master of itself, if the words 'temperance' and 'self-mastery' truly express the rule of the better part over the worse.

Yes, he said, I see that what you say is true.

Let me further note that the manifold and complex pleasures and desires and pains are generally found in children and women and servants, and in the freemen so called who are of the lowest and more numerous class.

Certainly, he said.

Whereas the simple and moderate desires which follow reason, and are under the guidance of mind and true opinion, are to be found only in a few, and those the best born and best educated.

Very true.

These two, as you may perceive, have a place in our State; and the meaner desires of the many are held down by the virtuous desires and wisdom of the few.

That I perceive, he said.

Then if there be any city which may be described as master of its own pleasures and desires, and master of itself, ours may claim such a designation?

5 Certainly, he replied.

It may also be called temperate, and for the same reasons?

10 Yes.

And if there be any State in which rulers and subjects will be agreed as to the question who are to rule, that again will be our State?

15

Undoubtedly.

And the citizens being thus agreed among themselves, in which class will temperance be
20 found--in the rulers or in the subjects?

In both, as I should imagine, he replied.

Do you observe that we were not far wrong in
25 our guess that temperance was a sort of harmony?

Why so?

30 Why, because temperance is unlike courage and wisdom, each of which resides in a part only, the one making the State wise and the other valiant; not so temperance, which extends to the whole, and runs through all the
35 notes of the scale, and produces a harmony of the weaker and the stronger and the middle class, whether you suppose them to be stronger or weaker in wisdom or power or numbers or wealth, or anything else. Most truly then
40 may we deem temperance to be the agreement of the naturally superior and inferior, as to the right to rule of either, both in states and individuals.

I entirely agree with you.
45

And so, I said, we may consider three out of the four virtues to have been discovered in our State. The last of those qualities which make a state virtuous must be justice, if we
50 only knew what that was.

The inference is obvious.

The time then has arrived, Glaucon, when, like
55 huntsmen, we should surround the cover, and look sharp that justice does not steal away, and pass out of sight and escape us; for beyond a doubt she is somewhere in this country: watch therefore and strive to catch a sight of her,
60 and if you see her first, let me know.

Would that I could! but you should regard me rather as a follower who has just eyes enough to see what you show him--that is about as
65 much as I am good for.

Offer up a prayer with me and follow.

I will, but you must show me the way.
70

Here is no path, I said, and the wood is dark and perplexing; still we must push on.

Let us push on.
75

Here I saw something: Halloo! I said, I begin to perceive a track, and I believe that the quarry will not escape.

80 Good news, he said.

Truly, I said, we are stupid fellows.

Why so?
85

Why, my good sir, at the beginning of our

enquiry, ages ago, there was justice tumbling
out at our feet, and we never saw her; nothing
could be more ridiculous. Like people who go
about looking for what they have in their
5 hands--that was the way with us--we looked
not at what we were seeking, but at what was
far off in the distance; and therefore, I suppose, we missed her.

10 What do you mean?

I mean to say that in reality for a long time
past we have been talking of justice, and have
failed to recognize her.

15

I grow impatient at the length of your exordi-
um.

Well then, tell me, I said, whether I am right
20 or not: You remember the original principle
which we were always laying down at the
foundation of the State, that one man should
practice one thing only, the thing to which his
nature was best adapted;--now justice is this
25 principle or a part of it.

Yes, we often said that one man should do
one thing only.

Further, we affirmed that justice was doing
30 one's own business, and not being a busybody;
we said so again and again, and many others
have said the same to us.

35 Yes, we said so.

Then to do one's own business in a certain
way may be assumed to be justice. Can you tell
me whence I derive this inference?

40

I cannot, but I should like to be told.

Because I think that this is the only virtue

which remains in the State when the other
45 virtues of temperance and courage and wisdom are abstracted; and, that this is the ultimate cause and condition of the existence of
all of them, and while remaining in them is
also their preservative; and we were saying that
50 if the three were discovered by us, justice
would be the fourth or remaining one.

That follows of necessity.

55 If we are asked to determine which of these
four qualities by its presence contributes most
to the excellence of the State, whether the
agreement of rulers and subjects, or the
preservation in the soldiers of the opinion
60 which the law ordains about the true nature of
dangers, or wisdom and watchfulness in the
rulers, or whether this other which I am mentioning, and which is found in children and
women, slave and freeman, artisan, ruler, sub-
65 ject,--the quality, I mean, of every one doing
his own work, and not being a busybody,
would claim the palm--the question is not so
easily answered.

70 Certainly, he replied, there would be a difficulty in saying which.

Then the power of each individual in the State
to do his own work appears to compete with
75 the other political virtues, wisdom, temperance, courage.

Yes, he said.

80 And the virtue which enters into this competition is justice?

Exactly.

85 Let us look at the question from another point
of view: Are not the rulers in a State those to

whom you would entrust the office of determining suits at law?

Certainly.

And are suits decided on any other ground but
that a man may neither take what is another's,
nor be deprived of what is his own?

Yes; that is their principle.

Which is a just principle?

Yes.

Then on this view also justice will be admitted
to be the having and doing what is a man's
own, and belongs to him?

Very true.

Think, now, and say whether you agree with
me or not. Suppose a carpenter to be doing
the business of a cobbler, or a cobbler of a
carpenter; and suppose them to exchange their
implements or their duties, or the same person
to be doing the work of both, or whatever be
the change; do you think that any great harm
would result to the State?

Not much.

But when the cobbler or any other man whom
nature designed to be a trader, having his heart
lifted up by wealth or strength or the number
of his followers, or any like advantage, attempts to force his way into the class of warriors, or a warrior into that of legislators and
guardians, for which he is unfitted, and either
to take the implements or the duties of the
other; or when one man is trader, legislator,
and warrior all in one, then I think you will
agree with me in saying that this interchange

and this meddling of one with another is the
ruin of the State.

Most true.

Seeing then, I said, that there are three distinct
classes, any meddling of one with another, or
the change of one into another, is the greatest
harm to the State, and may be most justly
termed evil-doing?

Precisely.

And the greatest degree of evil-doing to one's
own city would be termed by you injustice?

Certainly.

This then is injustice; and on the other hand
when the trader, the auxiliary, and the guardian each do their own business, that is justice,
and will make the city just.

I agree with you.

We will not, I said, be over-positive as yet; but
if, on trial, this conception of justice be verified in the individual as well as in the State,
there will be no longer any room for doubt; if
it be not verified, we must have a fresh enquiry. First let us complete the old investigation, which we began, as you remember, under
the impression that, if we could previously
examine justice on the larger scale, there
would be less difficulty in discerning her in the
individual. That larger example appeared to be
the State, and accordingly we constructed as
good a one as we could, knowing well that in
the good State justice would be found. Let the
discovery which we made be now applied to
the individual--if they agree, we shall be satisfied; or, if there be a difference in the individual, we will come back to the State and have

another trial of the theory. The friction of the two when rubbed together may possibly strike a light in which justice will shine forth, and the vision which is then revealed we will fix in our souls.

That will be in regular course; let us do as you say.

I proceeded to ask: When two things, a greater and less, are called by the same name, are they like or unlike in so far as they are called the same?

Like, he replied.

The just man then, if we regard the idea of justice only, will be like the just State?

He will.

And a State was thought by us to be just when the three classes in the State severally did their own business; and also thought to be temperate and valiant and wise by reason of certain other affections and qualities of these same classes?

True, he said.

And so of the individual; we may assume that he has the same three principles in his own soul which are found in the State; and he may be rightly described in the same terms, because he is affected in the same manner?

Certainly, he said.

Once more then, O my friend, we have alighted upon an easy question--whether the soul has these three principles or not?

An easy question! Nay, rather, Socrates, the proverb holds that hard is the good.

Very true, I said; and I do not think that the method which we are employing is at all adequate to the accurate solution of this question; the true method is another and a longer one. Still we may arrive at a solution not below the level of the previous enquiry.

May we not be satisfied with that? he said;-- under the circumstances, I am quite content.

I too, I replied, shall be extremely well satisfied.

Then faint not in pursuing the speculation, he said.

Must we not acknowledge, I said, that in each of us there are the same principles and habits which there are in the State; and that from the individual they pass into the State?--how else can they come there? Take the quality of passion or spirit;--it would be ridiculous to imagine that this quality, when found in States, is not derived from the individuals who are supposed to possess it, e.g. the Thracians, Scythians, and in general the northern nations; and the same may be said of the love of knowledge, which is the special characteristic of our part of the world, or of the love of money, which may, with equal truth, be attributed to the Phoenicians and Egyptians.

Exactly so, he said.

There is no difficulty in understanding this.

None whatever.

But the question is not quite so easy when we proceed to ask whether these principles are three or one; whether, that is to say, we learn with one part of our nature, are angry with another, and with a third part desire the satisfaction of our natural appetites; or whether the whole soul comes into play in each sort of action--to determine that is the difficulty.

Yes, he said; there lies the difficulty.

Then let us now try and determine whether they are the same or different.

How can we? he asked.

I replied as follows: The same thing clearly cannot act or be acted upon in the same part or in relation to the same thing at the same time, in contrary ways; and therefore whenever this contradiction occurs in things apparently the same, we know that they are really not the same, but different.

Good.

For example, I said, can the same thing be at rest and in motion at the same time in the same part?

Impossible.

Still, I said, let us have a more precise statement of terms, lest we should hereafter fall out by the way. Imagine the case of a man who is standing and also moving his hands and his head, and suppose a person to say that one and the same person is in motion and at rest at the same moment--to such a mode of speech we should object, and should rather say that one part of him is in motion while another is at rest.

Very true.

And suppose the objector to refine still fur-ther, and to draw the nice distinction that not only parts of tops, but whole tops, when they spin round with their pegs fixed on the spot, are at rest and in motion at the same time (and he may say the same of anything which revolves in the same spot), his objection would not be admitted by us, because in such cases things are not at rest and in motion in the same parts of themselves; we should rather say that they have both an axis and a circumference, and that the axis stands still, for there is no deviation from the perpendicular; and that the circumference goes round. But if, while revolving, the axis inclines either to the right or left, forwards or backwards, then in no point of view can they be at rest.

That is the correct mode of describing them, he replied.

Then none of these objections will confuse us, or incline us to believe that the same thing at the same time, in the same part or in relation to the same thing, can act or be acted upon in contrary ways.

Certainly not, according to my way of thinking.

Yet, I said, that we may not be compelled to examine all such objections, and prove at length that they are untrue, let us assume their absurdity, and go forward on the understanding that hereafter, if this assumption turn out to be untrue, all the consequences which follow shall be withdrawn.

Yes, he said, that will be the best way.

Well, I said, would you not allow that assent and dissent, desire and aversion, attraction and repulsion, are all of them opposites, whether they are regarded as active or passive (for that makes no difference in the fact of their opposition)?

Yes, he said, they are opposites.

Well, I said, and hunger and thirst, and the desires in general, and again willing and wishing,--all these you would refer to the classes already mentioned. You would say--would you not?--that the soul of him who desires is seeking after the object of his desire; or that he is drawing to himself the thing which he wishes to possess: or again, when a person wants anything to be given him, his mind, longing for the realization of his desire, intimates his wish to have it by a nod of assent, as if he had been asked a question?

Very true.

And what would you say of unwillingness and dislike and the absence of desire; should not these be referred to the opposite class of repulsion and rejection?

Certainly.

Admitting this to be true of desire generally, let us suppose a particular class of desires, and out of these we will select hunger and thirst, as they are termed, which are the most obvious of them?

Let us take that class, he said.

The object of one is food, and of the other drink?

Yes.

And here comes the point: is not thirst the desire which the soul has of drink, and of drink only; not of drink qualified by anything else; for example, warm or cold, or much or little, or, in a word, drink of any particular sort: but if the thirst be accompanied by heat, then the desire is of cold drink; or, if accompanied by cold, then of warm drink; or, if the thirst be excessive, then the drink which is desired will be excessive; or, if not great, the quantity of drink will also be small: but thirst pure and simple will desire drink pure and simple, which is the natural satisfaction of thirst, as food is of hunger?

Yes, he said; the simple desire is, as you say, in every case of the simple object, and the qualified desire of the qualified object.

But here a confusion may arise; and I should wish to guard against an opponent starting up and saying that no man desires drink only, but good drink, or food only, but good food; for good is the universal object of desire, and thirst being a desire, will necessarily be thirst after good drink; and the same is true of every other desire.

Yes, he replied, the opponent might have something to say.

Nevertheless I should still maintain, that of relatives some have a quality attached to either term of the relation; others are simple and have their correlatives simple.

I do not know what you mean.

Well, you know of course that the greater is relative to the less?

Certainly.

And the much greater to the much less?

Yes.

And the sometime greater to the sometime less, and the greater that is to be to the less that is to be?

5 Certainly, he said.

And so of more and less, and of other correlative terms, such as the double and the half, or again, the heavier and the lighter, the swifter
10 and the slower; and of hot and cold, and of any other relatives;--is not this true of all of them?

Yes.
15

And does not the same principle hold in the sciences? The object of science is knowledge (assuming that to be the true definition), but the object of a particular science is a particular
20 kind of knowledge; I mean, for example, that the science of house-building is a kind of knowledge which is defined and distinguished from other kinds and is therefore termed architecture.
25

Certainly.

Because it has a particular quality which no other has?
30

Yes.

And it has this particular quality because it has an object of a particular kind; and this is true
35 of the other arts and sciences?

Yes.

Now, then, if I have made myself clear, you
40 will understand my original meaning in what I said about relatives. My meaning was, that if one term of a relation is taken alone, the other is taken alone; if one term is qualified, the oth-

er is also qualified. I do not mean to say that
45 relatives may not be disparate, or that the science of health is healthy, or of disease necessarily diseased, or that the sciences of good and evil are therefore good and evil; but only that, when the term science is no longer used
50 absolutely, but has a qualified object which in this case is the nature of health and disease, it becomes defined, and is hence called not merely science, but the science of medicine.

55 I quite understand, and I think as you do.

Would you not say that thirst is one of these essentially relative terms, having clearly a relation--
60

Yes, thirst is relative to drink.

And a certain kind of thirst is relative to a certain kind of drink; but thirst taken alone is
65 neither of much nor little, nor of good nor bad, nor of any particular kind of drink, but of drink only?

Certainly.
70

Then the soul of the thirsty one, in so far as he is thirsty, desires only drink; for this he yearns and tries to obtain it?

75 That is plain.

And if you suppose something which pulls a thirsty soul away from drink, that must be different from the thirsty principle which
80 draws him like a beast to drink; for, as we were saying, the same thing cannot at the same time with the same part of itself act in contrary ways about the same.

85 Impossible.

No more than you can say that the hands of
the archer push and pull the bow at the same
time, but what you say is that one hand pushes
and the other pulls.

5

Exactly so, he replied.

And might a man be thirsty, and yet unwilling
to drink?

10

Yes, he said, it constantly happens.

And in such a case what is one to say? Would
you not say that there was something in the
15 soul bidding a man to drink, and something
else forbidding him, which is other and
stronger than the principle which bids him?

I should say so.

20

And the forbidding principle is derived from
reason, and that which bids and attracts proceeds from passion and disease?

25 Clearly.

Then we may fairly assume that they are two,
and that they differ from one another; the one
with which a man reasons, we may call the
30 rational principle of the soul, the other, with
which he loves and hungers and thirsts and
feels the flutterings of any other desire, may be
termed the irrational or appetitive, the ally of
sundry pleasures and satisfactions?

35

Yes, he said, we may fairly assume them to be
different.

Then let us finally determine that there are
40 two principles existing in the soul. And what
of passion, or spirit? Is it a third, or akin to
one of the preceding?

45 I should be inclined to say--akin to desire.

Well, I said, there is a story which I remember
to have heard, and in which I put faith. The
story is, that Leontius, the son of Aglaion,
coming up one day from the Piraeus, under
50 the north wall on the outside, observed some
dead bodies lying on the ground at the place
of execution. He felt a desire to see them, and
also a dread and abhorrence of them; for a
time he struggled and covered his eyes, but at
55 length the desire got the better of him; and
forcing them open, he ran up to the dead bodies, saying, Look, ye wretches, take your fill of
the fair sight.

60 I have heard the story myself, he said.

The moral of the tale is, that anger at times
goes to war with desire, as though they were
two distinct things.

65

Yes; that is the meaning, he said.

And are there not many other cases in which
we observe that when a man's desires violently
70 prevail over his reason, he reviles himself, and
is angry at the violence within him, and that in
this struggle, which is like the struggle of factions in a State, his spirit is on the side of his
reason;--but for the passionate or spirited ele-
75 ment to take part with the desires when reason
decides that she should not be opposed, is a
sort of thing which I believe that you never
observed occurring in yourself, nor, as I
should imagine, in any one else?

80

Certainly not.

Suppose that a man thinks he has done a
wrong to another, the nobler he is the less able
85 is he to feel indignant at any suffering, such as
hunger, or cold, or any other pain which the

injured person may inflict upon him--these he deems to be just, and, as I say, his anger refuses to be excited by them.

5 True, he said.

But when he thinks that he is the sufferer of the wrong, then he boils and chafes, and is on the side of what he believes to be justice; and
10 because he suffers hunger or cold or other pain he is only the more determined to persevere and conquer. His noble spirit will not be quelled until he either slays or is slain; or until he hears the voice of the shepherd, that is,
15 reason, bidding his dog bark no more.

The illustration is perfect, he replied; and in our State, as we were saying, the auxiliaries were to be dogs, and to hear the voice of the
20 rulers, who are their shepherds.

I perceive, I said, that you quite understand me; there is, however, a further point which I wish you to consider.

25

What point?

You remember that passion or spirit appeared at first sight to be a kind of desire, but now we
30 should say quite the contrary; for in the conflict of the soul spirit is arrayed on the side of the rational principle.

Most assuredly.

35

But a further question arises: Is passion different from reason also, or only a kind of reason; in which latter case, instead of three principles in the soul, there will only be two, the rational
40 and the concupiscent; or rather, as the State was composed of three classes, traders, auxiliaries, counselors, so may there not be in the individual soul a third element which is pas-

sion or spirit, and when not corrupted by bad
45 education is the natural auxiliary of reason?

Yes, he said, there must be a third.

Yes, I replied, if passion, which has already
50 been shown to be different from desire, turn out also to be different from reason.

But that is easily proved:--We may observe even in young children that they are full of
55 spirit almost as soon as they are born, whereas some of them never seem to attain to the use of reason, and most of them late enough.

Excellent, I said, and you may see passion
60 equally in brute animals, which is a further proof of the truth of what you are saying. And we may once more appeal to the words of Homer, which have been already quoted by us,
65

'He smote his breast, and thus rebuked his soul,'

for in this verse Homer has clearly supposed
70 the power which reasons about the better and worse to be different from the unreasoning anger which is rebuked by it.
Very true, he said.

75 And so, after much tossing, we have reached land, and are fairly agreed that the same principles which exist in the State exist also in the individual, and that they are three in number.

80 Exactly.

Must we not then infer that the individual is wise in the same way, and in virtue of the same quality which makes the State wise?

85

Certainly.

Also that the same quality which constitutes
courage in the State constitutes courage in the
individual, and that both the State and the
individual bear the same relation to all the
5   other virtues?

Assuredly.

And the individual will be acknowledged by us
10 to be just in the same way in which the State is
just?

That follows, of course.

15 We cannot but remember that the justice of
the State consisted in each of the three classes
doing the work of its own class?

We are not very likely to have forgotten, he
20 said.

We must recollect that the individual in whom
the several qualities of his nature do their own
work will be just, and will do his own work?
25

Yes, he said, we must remember that too.

And ought not the rational principle, which is
wise, and has the care of the whole soul, to
30 rule, and the passionate or spirited principle to
be the subject and ally?

Certainly.

35 And, as we were saying, the united influence
of music and gymnastic will bring them into
accord, nerving and sustaining the reason with
noble words and lessons, and moderating and
soothing and civilizing the wildness of passion
40 by harmony and rhythm?

Quite true, he said.

45 And these two, thus nurtured and educated,
and having learned truly to know their own
functions, will rule over the concupiscent,
which in each of us is the largest part of the
soul and by nature most insatiable of gain;
over this they will keep guard, lest, waxing
50 great and strong with the fullness of bodily
pleasures, as they are termed, the concupiscent
soul, no longer confined to her own sphere,
should attempt to enslave and rule those who
are not her natural-born subjects, and over-
55 turn the whole life of man?

Very true, he said.

Both together will they not be the best de-
60 fenders of the whole soul and the whole body
against attacks from without; the one counsel-
ing, and the other fighting under his leader,
and courageously executing his commands
and counsels?
65

True.

And he is to be deemed courageous whose
spirit retains in pleasure and in pain the com-
70 mands of reason about what he ought or
ought not to fear?

Right, he replied.

75 And him we call wise who has in him that
little part which rules, and which proclaims
these commands; that part too being supposed
to have a knowledge of what is for the interest
of each of the three parts and of the whole?
80

Assuredly.

And would you not say that he is temperate
who has these same elements in friendly har-
85 mony, in whom the one ruling principle of
reason, and the two subject ones of spirit and

desire are equally agreed that reason ought to
rule, and do not rebel?

Certainly, he said, that is the true account of
temperance whether in the State or individual.

And surely, I said, we have explained again
and again how and by virtue of what quality a
man will be just.

That is very certain.

And is justice dimmer in the individual, and is
her form different, or is she the same which
we found her to be in the State?

There is no difference in my opinion, he said.

Because, if any doubt is still lingering in our
minds, a few commonplace instances will satisfy us of the truth of what I am saying.

What sort of instances do you mean?

If the case is put to us, must we not admit that
the just State, or the man who is trained in the
principles of such a State, will be less likely
than the unjust to make away with a deposit of
gold or silver? Would any one deny this?

No one, he replied.

Will the just man or citizen ever be guilty of
sacrilege or theft, or treachery either to his
friends or to his country?

Never.

Neither will he ever break faith where there
have been oaths or agreements?

Impossible.

No one will be less likely to commit adultery,
or to dishonor his father and mother, or to fail
in his religious duties?

No one.

And the reason is that each part of him is doing its own business, whether in ruling or being ruled?

Exactly so.

Are you satisfied then that the quality which
makes such men and such states is justice, or
do you hope to discover some other?

Not I, indeed.

Then our dream has been realized; and the
suspicion which we entertained at the beginning of our work of construction, that some
divine power must have conducted us to a
primary form of justice, has now been verified?

Yes, certainly.

And the division of labor which required the
carpenter and the shoemaker and the rest of
the citizens to be doing each his own business,
and not another's, was a shadow of justice,
and for that reason it was of use?

Clearly.

But in reality justice was such as we were describing, being concerned however, not with
the outward man, but with the inward, which
is the true self and concernment of man: for
the just man does not permit the several elements within him to interfere with one another, or any of them to do the work of others,--
he sets in order his own inner life, and is his
own master and his own law, and at peace

with himself; and when he has bound together the three principles within him, which may be compared to the higher, lower, and middle notes of the scale, and the intermediate intervals--when he has bound all these together, and is no longer many, but has become one entirely temperate and perfectly adjusted nature, then he proceeds to act, if he has to act, whether in a matter of property, or in the treatment of the body, or in some affair of politics or private business; always thinking and calling that which preserves and co-operates with this harmonious condition, just and good action, and the knowledge which presides over it, wisdom, and that which at any time impairs this condition, he will call unjust action, and the opinion which presides over it ignorance.

You have said the exact truth, Socrates.

Very good; and if we were to affirm that we had discovered the just man and the just State, and the nature of justice in each of them, we should not be telling a falsehood?

Most certainly not.

May we say so, then?

Let us say so.

And now, I said, injustice has to be considered.

Clearly.

Must not injustice be a strife which arises among the three principles--a meddlesome-ness, and interference, and rising up of a part of the soul against the whole, an assertion of unlawful authority, which is made by a rebellious subject against a true prince, of whom he is the natural vassal,--what is all this confusion and delusion but injustice, and intemperance and cowardice and ignorance, and every form of vice?

Exactly so.

And if the nature of justice and injustice be known, then the meaning of acting unjustly and being unjust, or, again, of acting justly, will also be perfectly clear?

What do you mean? he said.

Why, I said, they are like disease and health; being in the soul just what disease and health are in the body.

How so? he said.

Why, I said, that which is healthy causes health, and that which is unhealthy causes disease.

Yes.

And just actions cause justice, and unjust actions cause injustice?
That is certain.

And the creation of health is the institution of a natural order and government of one by another in the parts of the body; and the creation of disease is the production of a state of things at variance with this natural order?

True.

And is not the creation of justice the institution of a natural order and government of one by another in the parts of the soul, and the creation of injustice the production of a state of things at variance with the natural order?

Exactly so, he said.

Then virtue is the health and beauty and well-being of the soul, and vice the disease and weakness and deformity of the same?

True.

And do not good practices lead to virtue, and evil practices to vice?

Assuredly.

Still our old question of the comparative advantage of justice and injustice has not been answered: Which is the more profitable, to be just and act justly and practice virtue, whether seen or unseen of gods and men, or to be unjust and act unjustly, if only unpunished and unreformed?

In my judgment, Socrates, the question has now become ridiculous. We know that, when the bodily constitution is gone, life is no longer endurable, though pampered with all kinds of meats and drinks, and having all wealth and all power; and shall we be told that when the very essence of the vital principle is undermined and corrupted, life is still worth having to a man, if only he be allowed to do whatever he likes with the single exception that he is not to acquire justice and virtue, or to escape from injustice and vice; assuming them both to be such as we have described?

Yes, I said, the question is, as you say, ridiculous. Still, as we are near the spot at which we may see the truth in the clearest manner with our own eyes, let us not faint by the way.

Certainly not, he replied.

Come up hither, I said, and behold the various forms of vice, those of them, I mean, which are worth looking at.

I am following you, he replied: proceed.

I said, The argument seems to have reached a height from which, as from some tower of speculation, a man may look down and see that virtue is one, but that the forms of vice are innumerable; there being four special ones which are deserving of note.

What do you mean? he said.

I mean, I replied, that there appear to be as many forms of the soul as there are distinct forms of the State.

How many?

There are five of the State, and five of the soul, I said.

What are they?

The first, I said, is that which we have been describing, and which may be said to have two names, monarchy and aristocracy, accordingly as rule is exercised by one distinguished man or by many.

True, he replied.

But I regard the two names as describing one form only; for whether the government is in the hands of one or many, if the governors have been trained in the manner which we have supposed, the fundamental laws of the State will be maintained.

That is true, he replied.

(Having defined justice Socrates uses Book V to refute

a series of arguments by Adiemantus and Polemarchus concerning the regulation of the perfect city. In particular Socrates defends the idea that the male an female guardians ought to be educated in the same way and

5 *that children ought to be raised collectively—and in such a manner that they never know their parents. In Book VI he discusses the idea of the philosopher-king, the ideal rule (i.e the perfected Gaurdian). The P-K will possess the knowledge of the good, which he elabo-*

10 *rates on in Book VII's Allegory of the Cave... - MJ)*

BOOK VII

And now, I said, let me show in a figure how
15 far our nature is enlightened or unenlightened:--Behold! human beings living in a underground den, which has a mouth open towards the light and reaching all along the den;
here they have been from their childhood, and
20 have their legs and necks chained so that they
cannot move, and can only see before them,
being prevented by the chains from turning
round their heads. Above and behind them a
fire is blazing at a distance, and between the
25 fire and the prisoners there is a raised way; and
you will see, if you look, a low wall built along
the way, like the screen which marionette
players have in front of them, over which they
show the puppets.

30

I see.

And do you see, I said, men passing along the
wall carrying all sorts of vessels, and statues
35 and figures of animals made of wood and
stone and various materials, which appear over
the wall? Some of them are talking, others
silent.

40 You have shown me a strange image, and they
are strange prisoners.

Like ourselves, I replied; and they see only

their own shadows, or the shadows of one
45 another, which the fire throws on the opposite
wall of the cave?

True, he said; how could they see anything but
the shadows if they were never allowed to
50 move their heads?

And of the objects which are being carried in
like manner they would only see the shadows?

55 Yes, he said.

And if they were able to converse with one
another, would they not suppose that they
were naming what was actually before them?
60

Very true.

And suppose further that the prison had an
echo which came from the other side, would
65 they not be sure to fancy when one of the
passers-by spoke that the voice which they
heard came from the passing shadow?
No question, he replied.

70 To them, I said, the truth would be literally
nothing but the shadows of the images.

That is certain.

75 And now look again, and see what will naturally follow if the prisoners are released and disa-
bused of their error. At first, when any of
them is liberated and compelled suddenly to
stand up and turn his neck round and walk
80 and look towards the light, he will suffer sharp
pains; the glare will distress him, and he will be
unable to see the realities of which in his former state he had seen the shadows; and then
conceive some one saying to him, that what he
85 saw before was an illusion, but that now, when
he is approaching nearer to being and his eye

is turned towards more real existence, he has a
clearer vision,--what will be his reply? And you
may further imagine that his instructor is
pointing to the objects as they pass and requiring him to name them,--will he not be perplexed? Will he not fancy that the shadows
which he formerly saw are truer than the objects which are now shown to him?

Far truer.

And if he is compelled to look straight at the
light, will he not have a pain in his eyes which
will make him turn away to take refuge in the
objects of vision which he can see, and which
he will conceive to be in reality clearer than
the things which are now being shown to him?

True, he said.

And suppose once more, that he is reluctantly
dragged up a steep and rugged ascent, and
held fast until he is forced into the presence of
the sun himself, is he not likely to be pained
and irritated? When he approaches the light
his eyes will be dazzled, and he will not be able
to see anything at all of what are now called
realities.

Not all in a moment, he said.

He will require to grow accustomed to the
sight of the upper world. And first he will see
the shadows best, next the reflections of men
and other objects in the water, and then the
objects themselves; then he will gaze upon the
light of the moon and the stars and the spangled heaven; and he will see the sky and the
stars by night better than the sun or the light
of the sun by day?

Certainly.

Last of all he will be able to see the sun, and
not mere reflections of him in the water, but
he will see him in his own proper place, and
not in another; and he will contemplate him as
he is.

Certainly.

He will then proceed to argue that this is he
who gives the season and the years, and is the
guardian of all that is in the visible world, and
in a certain way the cause of all things which
he and his fellows have been accustomed to
behold?

Clearly, he said, he would first see the sun and
then reason about him.

And when he remembered his old habitation,
and the wisdom of the den and his fellow-
prisoners, do you not suppose that he would
felicitate himself on the change, and pity
them?

Certainly, he would.

And if they were in the habit of conferring
honors among themselves on those who were
quickest to observe the passing shadows and
to remark which of them went before, and
which followed after, and which were together; and who were therefore best able to draw
conclusions as to the future, do you think that
he would care for such honors and glories, or
envy the possessors of them? Would he not
say with Homer,

'Better to be the poor servant of a poor master,'

and to endure anything, rather than think as
they do and live after their manner?

Yes, he said, I think that he would rather suffer anything than entertain these false notions and live in this miserable manner.

5   Imagine once more, I said, such an one coming suddenly out of the sun to be replaced in his old situation; would he not be certain to have his eyes full of darkness?

10   To be sure, he said.

And if there were a contest, and he had to compete in measuring the shadows with the prisoners who had never moved out of the 15 den, while his sight was still weak, and before his eyes had become steady (and the time which would be needed to acquire this new habit of sight might be very considerable), would he not be ridiculous? Men would say of 20 him that up he went and down he came without his eyes; and that it was better not even to think of ascending; and if any one tried to loose another and lead him up to the light, let them only catch the offender, and they would 25 put him to death.

No question, he said.

This entire allegory, I said, you may now ap-30 pend, dear Glaucon, to the previous argument; the prison-house is the world of sight, the light of the fire is the sun, and you will not misapprehend me if you interpret the journey upwards to be the ascent of the soul into the 35 intellectual world according to my poor belief, which, at your desire, I have expressed-- whether rightly or wrongly God knows. But, whether true or false, my opinion is that in the world of knowledge the idea of good appears 40 last of all, and is seen only with an effort; and, when seen, is also inferred to be the universal author of all things beautiful and right, parent of light and of the lord of light in this visible

world, and the immediate source of reason 45 and truth in the intellectual; and that this is the power upon which he who would act rationally either in public or private life must have his eye fixed.

50   I agree, he said, as far as I am able to understand you.

Moreover, I said, you must not wonder that those who attain to this beatific vision are un-55 willing to descend to human affairs; for their souls are ever hastening into the upper world where they desire to dwell; which desire of theirs is very natural, if our allegory may be trusted.

60

Yes, very natural.

And is there anything surprising in one who passes from divine contemplations to the evil 65 state of man, misbehaving himself in a ridiculous manner; if, while his eyes are blinking and before he has become accustomed to the surrounding darkness, he is compelled to fight in courts of law, or in other places, about the 70 images or the shadows of images of justice, and is endeavoring to meet the conceptions of those who have never yet seen absolute justice?

75   Anything but surprising, he replied.

Any one who has common sense will remember that the bewilderments of the eyes are of two kinds, and arise from two causes, either 80 from coming out of the light or from going into the light, which is true of the mind's eye, quite as much as of the bodily eye; and he who remembers this when he sees any one whose vision is perplexed and weak, will not be too 85 ready to laugh; he will first ask whether that soul of man has come out of the brighter life,

and is unable to see because unaccustomed to
the dark, or having turned from darkness to
the day is dazzled by excess of light. And he
will count the one happy in his condition and
5 state of being, and he will pity the other; or, if
he have a mind to laugh at the soul which
comes from below into the light, there will be
more reason in this than in the laugh which
greets him who returns from above out of the
10 light into the den.

That, he said, is a very just distinction.

But then, if I am right, certain professors of
15 education must be wrong when they say that
they can put a knowledge into the soul which
was not there before, like sight into blind eyes.

They undoubtedly say this, he replied.
20

Whereas, our argument shows that the power
and capacity of learning exists in the soul already; and that just as the eye was unable to
turn from darkness to light without the whole
25 body, so too the instrument of knowledge can
only by the movement of the whole soul be
turned from the world of becoming into that
of being, and learn by degrees to endure the
sight of being, and of the brightest and best of
30 being, or in other words, of the good.

Very true.

And must there not be some art which will
35 effect conversion in the easiest and quickest
manner; not implanting the faculty of sight,
for that exists already, but has been turned in
the wrong direction, and is looking away from
the truth?
40

Yes, he said, such an art may be presumed.

And whereas the other so-called virtues of the
soul seem to be akin to bodily qualities, for
45 even when they are not originally innate they
can be implanted later by habit and exercise,
the virtue of wisdom more than anything else
contains a divine element which always remains, and by this conversion is rendered use-
50 ful and profitable; or, on the other hand, hurtful and useless. Did you never observe the
narrow intelligence flashing from the keen eye
of a clever rogue--how eager he is, how clearly
his paltry soul sees the way to his end; he is
55 the reverse of blind, but his keen eye-sight is
forced into the service of evil, and he is mischievous in proportion to his cleverness?

Very true, he said.
60

But what if there had been a circumcision of
such natures in the days of their youth; and
they had been severed from those sensual
pleasures, such as eating and drinking, which,
65 like leaden weights, were attached to them at
their birth, and which drag them down and
turn the vision of their souls upon the things
that are below--if, I say, they had been released
from these impediments and turned in the
70 opposite direction, the very same faculty in
them would have seen the truth as keenly as
they see what their eyes are turned to now.

Very likely.
75

Yes, I said; and there is another thing which is
likely, or rather a necessary inference from
what has preceded, that neither the uneducat-
ed and uninformed of the truth, nor yet those
80 who never make an end of their education,
will be able ministers of State; not the former,
because they have no single aim of duty which
is the rule of all their actions, private as well as
public; nor the latter, because they will not act
85 at all except upon compulsion, fancying that
they are already dwelling apart in the islands of

the blest.

Very true, he replied.

Then, I said, the business of us who are the
founders of the State will be to compel the
best minds to attain that knowledge which we
have already shown to be the greatest of all--
they must continue to ascend until they arrive
at the good; but when they have ascended and
seen enough we must not allow them to do as
they do now.

What do you mean?

I mean that they remain in the upper world:
but this must not be allowed; they must be
made to descend again among the prisoners in
the den, and partake of their labors and honors, whether they are worth having or not.

But is not this unjust? he said; ought we to
give them a worse life, when they might have a
better?

You have again forgotten, my friend, I said,
the intention of the legislator, who did not aim
at making any one class in the State happy
above the rest; the happiness was to be in the
whole State, and he held the citizens together
by persuasion and necessity, making them
benefactors of the State, and therefore benefactors of one another; to this end he created
them, not to please themselves, but to be his
instruments in binding up the State.

True, he said, I had forgotten.

Observe, Glaucon, that there will be no injustice in compelling our philosophers to have a
care and providence of others; we shall explain
to them that in other States, men of their class
are not obliged to share in the toils of politics:

and this is reasonable, for they grow up at
their own sweet will, and the government
would rather not have them.

Being self-taught, they cannot be expected to
show any gratitude for a culture which they
have never received. But we have brought you
into the world to be rulers of the hive, kings
of yourselves and of the other citizens, and
have educated you far better and more perfectly than they have been educated, and you
are better able to share in the double duty.
Wherefore each of you, when his turn comes,
must go down to the general underground
abode, and get the habit of seeing in the dark.
When you have acquired the habit, you will
see ten thousand times better than the inhabitants of the den, and you will know what the
several images are, and what they represent,
because you have seen the beautiful and just
and good in their truth. And thus our State,
which is also yours, will be a reality, and not a
dream only, and will be administered in a spirit
unlike that of other States, in which men fight
with one another about shadows only and are
distracted in the struggle for power, which in
their eyes is a great good. Whereas the truth is
that the State in which the rulers are most reluctant to govern is always the best and most
quietly governed, and the State in which they
are most eager, the worst.

Quite true, he replied.

And will our pupils, when they hear this, refuse to take their turn at the toils of State,
when they are allowed to spend the greater
part of their time with one another in the
heavenly light?

Impossible, he answered; for they are just
men, and the commands which we impose
upon them are just; there can be no doubt that

every one of them will take office as a stern necessity, and not after the fashion of our present rulers of State.

5 Yes, my friend, I said; and there lies the point. You must contrive for your future rulers another and a better life than that of a ruler, and then you may have a well-ordered State; for only in the State which offers this, will they
10 rule who are truly rich, not in silver and gold, but in virtue and wisdom, which are the true blessings of life. Whereas if they go to the administration of public affairs, poor and hungering after their own private advantage,
15 thinking that hence they are to snatch the chief good, order there can never be; for they will be fighting about office, and the civil and domestic broils which thus arise will be the ruin of the rulers themselves and of the whole
20 State.

Most true, he replied.

And the only life which looks down upon the
25 life of political ambition is that of true philosophy. Do you know of any other?
Indeed, I do not, he said.

And those who govern ought not to be lovers
30 of the task? For, if they are, there will be rival lovers, and they will fight.

No question.

35 Who then are those whom we shall compel to be guardians? Surely they will be the men who are wisest about affairs of State, and by whom the State is best administered, and who at the same time have other honors and another and
40 a better life than that of politics?
They are the men, and I will choose them, he replied.

And now shall we consider in what way such
45 guardians will be produced, and how they are to be brought from darkness to light,--as some are said to have ascended from the world below to the gods?

50 By all means, he replied.

The process, I said, is not the turning over of an oyster-shell (In allusion to a game in which two parties fled or pursued according as an
55 oyster-shell which was thrown into the air fell with the dark or light side uppermost.), but the turning round of a soul passing from a day which is little better than night to the true day of being, that is, the ascent from below, which
60 we affirm to be true philosophy?

Quite so.

And should we not enquire what sort of
65 knowledge has the power of effecting such a change?

Certainly.
What sort of knowledge is there which would
70 draw the soul from becoming to being? And another consideration has just occurred to me: You will remember that our young men are to be warrior athletes?

75 Yes, that was said.

Then this new kind of knowledge must have an additional quality?

80 What quality?

Usefulness in war.

Yes, if possible.
85

There were two parts in our former scheme of

education, were there not?

Just so.

5 There was gymnastic which presided over the growth and decay of the body, and may therefore be regarded as having to do with generation and corruption?

10 True.

Then that is not the knowledge which we are seeking to discover?

15 No.

But what do you say of music, which also entered to a certain extent into our former scheme?

20

Music, he said, as you will remember, was the counterpart of gymnastic, and trained the guardians by the influences of habit, by harmony making them harmonious, by rhythm

25 rhythmical, but not giving them science; and the words, whether fabulous or possibly true, had kindred elements of rhythm and harmony in them. But in music there was nothing which tended to that good which you are now seek-

30 ing.

You are most accurate, I said, in your recollection; in music there certainly was nothing of the kind. But what branch of knowledge is

35 there, my dear Glaucon, which is of the desired nature; since all the useful arts were reckoned mean by us?

Undoubtedly; and yet if music and gymnastic

40 are excluded, and the arts are also excluded, what remains?

Well, I said, there may be nothing left of our

special subjects; and then we shall have to take

45 something which is not special, but of universal application.

What may that be?

50 A something which all arts and sciences and intelligences use in common, and which every one first has to learn among the elements of education.

55 What is that?

The little matter of distinguishing one, two, and three--in a word, number and calculation:--do not all arts and sciences necessarily partake

60 of them?

Yes.

Then the art of war partakes of them?

65

To be sure.

Then Palamedes, whenever he appears in tragedy, proves Agamemnon ridiculously unfit to

70 be a general. Did you never remark how he declares that he had invented number, and had numbered the ships and set in array the ranks of the army at Troy; which implies that they had never been numbered before, and Aga-

75 memnon must be supposed literally to have been incapable of counting his own feet--how could he if he was ignorant of number? And if that is true, what sort of general must he have been?

80

I should say a very strange one, if this was as you say.

Can we deny that a warrior should have a

85 knowledge of arithmetic?

Certainly he should, if he is to have the smallest understanding of military tactics, or indeed, I should rather say, if he is to be a man at all.

5 I should like to know whether you have the same notion which I have of this study?

What is your notion?

10 It appears to me to be a study of the kind which we are seeking, and which leads naturally to reflection, but never to have been rightly used; for the true use of it is simply to draw the soul towards being.

15

Will you explain your meaning? he said.

I will try, I said; and I wish you would share the enquiry with me, and say 'yes' or 'no' when 20 I attempt to distinguish in my own mind what branches of knowledge have this attracting power, in order that we may have clearer proof that arithmetic is, as I suspect, one of them.

25

Explain, he said.

I mean to say that objects of sense are of two kinds; some of them do not invite thought 30 because the sense is an adequate judge of them; while in the case of other objects sense is so untrustworthy that further enquiry is imperatively demanded.

35 You are clearly referring, he said, to the manner in which the senses are imposed upon by distance, and by painting in light and shade.

No, I said, that is not at all my meaning.

40

Then what is your meaning?

When speaking of uninviting objects, I mean

those which do not pass from one sensation 45 to the opposite; inviting objects are those which do; in this latter case the sense coming upon the object, whether at a distance or near, gives no more vivid idea of anything in particular than of its opposite. An illustration will 50 make my meaning clearer:--here are three fingers--a little finger, a second finger, and a middle finger.

Very good.

55

You may suppose that they are seen quite close: And here comes the point.

What is it?

60

Each of them equally appears a finger, whether seen in the middle or at the extremity, whether white or black, or thick or thin--it makes no difference; a finger is a finger all the 65 same. In these cases a man is not compelled to ask of thought the question what is a finger? for the sight never intimates to the mind that a finger is other than a finger.

70 True.

And therefore, I said, as we might expect, there is nothing here which invites or excites intelligence.

75

There is not, he said.

But is this equally true of the greatness and smallness of the fingers? Can sight adequately 80 perceive them? and is no difference made by the circumstance that one of the fingers is in the middle and another at the extremity? And in like manner does the touch adequately perceive the qualities of thickness or thinness, of 85 softness or hardness? And so of the other senses; do they give perfect intimations of

such matters? Is not their mode of operation on this wise--the sense which is concerned with the quality of hardness is necessarily concerned also with the quality of softness, and
5 only intimates to the soul that the same thing is felt to be both hard and soft?

You are quite right, he said.

10 And must not the soul be perplexed at this intimation which the sense gives of a hard which is also soft? What, again, is the meaning of light and heavy, if that which is light is also heavy, and that which is heavy, light?
15

Yes, he said, these intimations which the soul receives are very curious and require to be explained.

20 Yes, I said, and in these perplexities the soul naturally summons to her aid calculation and intelligence, that she may see whether the several objects announced to her are one or two.

25 True.

And if they turn out to be two, is not each of them one and different?
Certainly.
30

And if each is one, and both are two, she will conceive the two as in a state of division, for if there were undivided they could only be conceived of as one?
35

True.

The eye certainly did see both small and great, but only in a confused manner; they were not
40 distinguished.

Yes.

Whereas the thinking mind, intending to light
45 up the chaos, was compelled to reverse the process, and look at small and great as separate and not confused.

Very true.
50

Was not this the beginning of the enquiry 'What is great?' and 'What is small?'

Exactly so.
55

And thus arose the distinction of the visible and the intelligible.

Most true.
60

This was what I meant when I spoke of impressions which invited the intellect, or the reverse--those which are simultaneous with opposite impressions, invite thought; those
65 which are not simultaneous do not.

I understand, he said, and agree with you.

And to which class do unity and number be-
70 long?

I do not know, he replied.

Think a little and you will see that what has
75 preceded will supply the answer; for if simple unity could be adequately perceived by the sight or by any other sense, then, as we were saying in the case of the finger, there would be nothing to attract towards being; but when
80 there is some contradiction always present, and one is the reverse of one and involves the conception of plurality, then thought begins to be aroused within us, and the soul perplexed and wanting to arrive at a decision asks 'What
85 is absolute unity?' This is the way in which the study of the one has a power of drawing and

converting the mind to the contemplation of true being.

And surely, he said, this occurs notably in the case of one; for we see the same thing to be both one and infinite in multitude?

Yes, I said; and this being true of one must be equally true of all number?

Certainly.

And all arithmetic and calculation have to do with number?

Yes.

And they appear to lead the mind towards truth?

Yes, in a very remarkable manner.

Then this is knowledge of the kind for which we are seeking, having a double use, military and philosophical; for the man of war must learn the art of number or he will not know how to array his troops, and the philosopher also, because he has to rise out of the sea of change and lay hold of true being, and therefore he must be an arithmetician.

That is true.

And our guardian is both warrior and philosopher?

Certainly.

Then this is a kind of knowledge which legislation may fitly prescribe; and we must endeavor to persuade those who are to be the principal men of our State to go and learn arithmetic, not as amateurs, but they must carry on the study until they see the nature of numbers with the mind only; nor again, like merchants or retail-traders, with a view to buying or selling, but for the sake of their military use, and of the soul herself; and because this will be the easiest way for her to pass from becoming to truth and being.

That is excellent, he said.

Yes, I said, and now having spoken of it, I must add how charming the science is! and in how many ways it conduces to our desired end, if pursued in the spirit of a philosopher, and not of a shopkeeper!

How do you mean?

I mean, as I was saying, that arithmetic has a very great and elevating effect, compelling the soul to reason about abstract number, and rebelling against the introduction of visible or tangible objects into the argument. You know how steadily the masters of the art repel and ridicule any one who attempts to divide absolute unity when he is calculating, and if you divide, they multiply (Meaning either (1) that they integrate the number because they deny the possibility of fractions; or (2) that division is regarded by them as a process of multiplication, for the fractions of one continue to be units.), taking care that one shall continue one and not become lost in fractions.

That is very true.

Now, suppose a person were to say to them: O my friends, what are these wonderful numbers about which you are reasoning, in which, as you say, there is a unity such as you demand, and each unit is equal, invariable, indivisible,--what would they answer?

They would answer, as I should conceive, that they were speaking of those numbers which can only be realized in thought.

5 Then you see that this knowledge may be truly called necessary, necessitating as it clearly does the use of the pure intelligence in the attainment of pure truth?

10 Yes; that is a marked characteristic of it.

And have you further observed, that those who have a natural talent for calculation are generally quick at every other kind of 15 knowledge; and even the dull, if they have had an arithmetical training, although they may derive no other advantage from it, always become much quicker than they would otherwise have been.

20

Very true, he said.

And indeed, you will not easily find a more difficult study, and not many as difficult.

25

You will not.

And, for all these reasons, arithmetic is a kind of knowledge in which the best natures should 30 be trained, and which must not be given up.

I agree.

Let this then be made one of our subjects of 35 education. And next, shall we enquire whether the kindred science also concerns us?

You mean geometry?

40 Exactly so.

Clearly, he said, we are concerned with that part of geometry which relates to war; for in pitching a camp, or taking up a position, or 45 closing or extending the lines of an army, or any other military maneuver, whether in actual battle or on a march, it will make all the difference whether a general is or is not a geometrician.

50

Yes, I said, but for that purpose a very little of either geometry or calculation will be enough; the question relates rather to the greater and more advanced part of geometry--whether 55 that tends in any degree to make more easy the vision of the idea of good; and thither, as I was saying, all things tend which compel the soul to turn her gaze towards that place, where is the full perfection of being, which she 60 ought, by all means, to behold.
True, he said.

Then if geometry compels us to view being, it concerns us; if becoming only, it does not 65 concern us?

Yes, that is what we assert.

Yet anybody who has the least acquaintance 70 with geometry will not deny that such a conception of the science is in flat contradiction to the ordinary language of geometricians.

How so?

75

They have in view practice only, and are always speaking, in a narrow and ridiculous manner, of squaring and extending and applying and the like--they confuse the necessities 80 of geometry with those of daily life; whereas knowledge is the real object of the whole science.

Certainly, he said.

85

Then must not a further admission be made?

What admission?

That the knowledge at which geometry aims is knowledge of the eternal, and not of aught perishing and transient.

That, he replied, may be readily allowed, and is true.

Then, my noble friend, geometry will draw the soul towards truth, and create the spirit of philosophy, and raise up that which is now unhappily allowed to fall down.

Nothing will be more likely to have such an effect.

Then nothing should be more sternly laid down than that the inhabitants of your fair city should by all means learn geometry. Moreover the science has indirect effects, which are not small.

Of what kind? he said.

There are the military advantages of which you spoke, I said; and in all departments of knowledge, as experience proves, any one who has studied geometry is infinitely quicker of apprehension than one who has not.

Yes indeed, he said, there is an infinite difference between them.

Then shall we propose this as a second branch of knowledge which our youth will study?

Let us do so, he replied.

And suppose we make astronomy the third--what do you say?

I am strongly inclined to it, he said; the observation of the seasons and of months and years is as essential to the general as it is to the farmer or sailor.

I am amused, I said, at your fear of the world, which makes you guard against the appearance of insisting upon useless studies; and I quite admit the difficulty of believing that in every man there is an eye of the soul which, when by other pursuits lost and dimmed, is by these purified and re-illumined; and is more precious far than ten thousand bodily eyes, for by it alone is truth seen. Now there are two classes of persons: one class of those who will agree with you and will take your words as a revelation; another class to whom they will be utterly unmeaning, and who will naturally deem them to be idle tales, for they see no sort of profit which is to be obtained from them. And therefore you had better decide at once with which of the two you are proposing to argue. You will very likely say with neither, and that your chief aim in carrying on the argument is your own improvement; at the same time you do not grudge to others any benefit which they may receive.

I think that I should prefer to carry on the argument mainly on my own behalf.

Then take a step backward, for we have gone wrong in the order of the sciences.

What was the mistake? he said.

After plane geometry, I said, we proceeded at once to solids in revolution, instead of taking solids in themselves; whereas after the second dimension the third, which is concerned with cubes and dimensions of depth, ought to have followed.

That is true, Socrates; but so little seems to be known as yet about these subjects.

Why, yes, I said, and for two reasons:--in the first place, no government patronizes them; this leads to a want of energy in the pursuit of them, and they are difficult; in the second

5 place, students cannot learn them unless they have a director. But then a director can hardly be found, and even if he could, as matters now stand, the students, who are very conceited, would not attend to him. That, however,

10 would be otherwise if the whole State became the director of these studies and gave honor to them; then disciples would want to come, and there would be continuous and earnest search, and discoveries would be made; since even

15 now, disregarded as they are by the world, and maimed of their fair proportions, and although none of their votaries can tell the use of them, still these studies force their way by their natural charm, and very likely, if they had

20 the help of the State, they would some day emerge into light.

Yes, he said, there is a remarkable charm in them. But I do not clearly understand the

25 change in the order. First you began with a geometry of plane surfaces?

Yes, I said.

30 And you placed astronomy next, and then you made a step backward?

Yes, and I have delayed you by my hurry; the ludicrous state of solid geometry, which, in

35 natural order, should have followed, made me pass over this branch and go on to astronomy, or motion of solids.

True, he said.

40

Then assuming that the science now omitted would come into existence if encouraged by the State, let us go on to astronomy, which

will be fourth.

45

The right order, he replied. And now, Socrates, as you rebuked the vulgar manner in which I praised astronomy before, my praise shall be given in your own spirit. For every

50 one, as I think, must see that astronomy compels the soul to look upwards and leads us from this world to another.

Every one but myself, I said; to every one else

55 this may be clear, but not to me.

And what then would you say?

I should rather say that those who elevate as-

60 tronomy into philosophy appear to me to make us look downwards and not upwards.

What do you mean? he asked.

65 You, I replied, have in your mind a truly sublime conception of our knowledge of the things above. And I dare say that if a person were to throw his head back and study the fretted ceiling, you would still think that his

70 mind was the percipient, and not his eyes. And you are very likely right, and I may be a simpleton: but, in my opinion, that knowledge only which is of being and of the unseen can make the soul look upwards, and whether a

75 man gapes at the heavens or blinks on the ground, seeking to learn some particular of sense, I would deny that he can learn, for nothing of that sort is matter of science; his soul is looking downwards, not upwards,

80 whether his way to knowledge is by water or by land, whether he floats, or only lies on his back.

I acknowledge, he said, the justice of your

85 rebuke. Still, I should like to ascertain how astronomy can be learned in any manner more

conducive to that knowledge of which we are speaking?

I will tell you, I said: The starry heaven which we behold is wrought upon a visible ground, and therefore, although the fairest and most perfect of visible things, must necessarily be deemed inferior far to the true motions of absolute swiftness and absolute slowness, which are relative to each other, and carry with them that which is contained in them, in the true number and in every true figure. Now, these are to be apprehended by reason and intelligence, but not by sight.

True, he replied.

The spangled heavens should be used as a pattern and with a view to that higher knowledge; their beauty is like the beauty of figures or pictures excellently wrought by the hand of Daedalus, or some other great artist, which we may chance to behold; any geometrician who saw them would appreciate the exquisiteness of their workmanship, but he would never dream of thinking that in them he could find the true equal or the true double, or the truth of any other proportion.

No, he replied, such an idea would be ridiculous.

And will not a true astronomer have the same feeling when he looks at the movements of the stars? Will he not think that heaven and the things in heaven are framed by the Creator of them in the most perfect manner? But he will never imagine that the proportions of night and day, or of both to the month, or of the month to the year, or of the stars to these and to one another, and any other things that are material and visible can also be eternal and subject to no deviation--that would be absurd; and it is equally absurd to take so much pains in investigating their exact truth.

I quite agree, though I never thought of this before.

Then, I said, in astronomy, as in geometry, we should employ problems, and let the heavens alone if we would approach the subject in the right way and so make the natural gift of reason to be of any real use.

That, he said, is a work infinitely beyond our present astronomers.

Yes, I said; and there are many other things which must also have a similar extension given to them, if our legislation is to be of any value. But can you tell me of any other suitable study?

No, he said, not without thinking.

Motion, I said, has many forms, and not one only; two of them are obvious enough even to wits no better than ours; and there are others, as I imagine, which may be left to wiser persons.

But where are the two?

There is a second, I said, which is the counterpart of the one already named.

And what may that be?

The second, I said, would seem relatively to the ears to be what the first is to the eyes; for I conceive that as the eyes are designed to look up at the stars, so are the ears to hear harmonious motions; and these are sister sciences--as the Pythagoreans say, and we, Glaucon, agree with them?

Yes, he replied.

But this, I said, is a laborious study, and therefore we had better go and learn of them; and
5 they will tell us whether there are any other
applications of these sciences. At the same
time, we must not lose sight

of our own higher object.
10
What is that?

There is a perfection which all knowledge
ought to reach, and which our pupils ought
15 also to attain, and not to fall short of, as I was
saying that they did in astronomy. For in the
science of harmony, as you probably know,
the same thing happens. The teachers of harmony compare the sounds and consonances
20 which are heard only, and their labor, like that
of the astronomers, is in vain.

Yes, by heaven! he said; and 'tis as good as a
play to hear them talking about their con-
25 densed notes, as they call them; they put their
ears close alongside of the strings like persons
catching a sound from their neighbor's wall--
one set of them declaring that they distinguish
an intermediate note and have found the least
30 interval which should be the unit of measure-
ment; the others insisting that the two sounds
have passed into the same--either party setting
their ears before their understanding.

35 You mean, I said, those gentlemen who tease
and torture the strings and rack them on the
pegs of the instrument: I might carry on the
metaphor and speak after their manner of the
blows which the plectrum gives, and make
40 accusations against the strings, both of back-
wardness and forwardness to sound; but this
would be tedious, and therefore I will only say
that these are not the men, and that I am re-

ferring to the Pythagoreans, of whom I was
45 just now proposing to enquire about harmony.
For they too are in error, like the astronomers;
they investigate the numbers of the harmonies
which are heard, but they never attain to prob-
lems--that is to say, they never reach the natu-
50 ral harmonies of number, or reflect why some
numbers are harmonious and others not.

That, he said, is a thing of more than mortal
knowledge.
55
A thing, I replied, which I would rather call
useful; that is, if sought after with a view to
the beautiful and good; but if pursued in any
other spirit, useless.
60
Very true, he said.

Now, when all these studies reach the point of
inter-communion and connection with one
65 another, and come to be considered in their
mutual affinities, then, I think, but not till
then, will the pursuit of them have a value for
our objects; otherwise there is no profit in
them.
70
I suspect so; but you are speaking, Socrates, of
a vast work.

What do you mean? I said; the prelude or
75 what? Do you not know that all this is but the
prelude to the actual strain which we have to
learn? For you surely would not regard the
skilled mathematician as a dialectician?

80 Assuredly not, he said; I have hardly ever
known a mathematician who was capable of
reasoning.

But do you imagine that men who are unable
85 to give and take a reason will have the
knowledge which we require of them?

Neither can this be supposed.

And so, Glaucon, I said, we have at last arrived at the hymn of dialectic. This is that
5 strain which is of the intellect only, but which the faculty of sight will nevertheless be found to imitate; for sight, as you may remember, was imagined by us after a while to behold the real animals and stars, and last of all the sun
10 himself. And so with dialectic; when a person starts on the discovery of the absolute by the light of reason only, and without any assistance of sense, and perseveres until by pure intelligence he arrives at the perception of the
15 absolute good, he at last finds himself at the end of the intellectual world, as in the case of sight at the end of the visible.

Exactly, he said.

20

Then this is the progress which you call dialectic?

True.

25

But the release of the prisoners from chains, and their translation from the shadows to the images and to the light, and the ascent from the underground den to the sun, while in his
30 presence they are vainly trying to look on animals and plants and the light of the sun, but are able to perceive even with their weak eyes the images in the water (which are divine), and are the shadows of true existence (not shad-
35 ows of images cast by a light of fire, which compared with the sun is only an image)--this power of elevating the highest principle in the soul to the contemplation of that which is best in existence, with which we may compare the
40 raising of that faculty which is the very light of the body to the sight of that which is brightest in the material and visible world--this power is given, as I was saying, by all that study and

45 pursuit of the arts which has been described.

I agree in what you are saying, he replied, which may be hard to believe, yet, from another point of view, is harder still to deny. This, however, is not a theme to be treated of
50 in passing only, but will have to be discussed again and again. And so, whether our conclusion be true or false, let us assume all this, and proceed at once from the prelude or preamble to the chief strain (A play upon the Greek
55 word, which means both 'law' and 'strain.'), and describe that in like manner. Say, then, what is the nature and what are the divisions of dialectic, and what are the paths which lead thither; for these paths will also lead to our
60 final rest.

Dear Glaucon, I said, you will not be able to follow me here, though I would do my best, and you should behold not an image only but
65 the absolute truth, according to my notion. Whether what I told you would or would not have been a reality I cannot venture to say; but you would have seen something like reality; of that I am confident.

70

Doubtless, he replied.

But I must also remind you, that the power of dialectic alone can reveal this, and only to one
75 who is a disciple of the previous sciences.

Of that assertion you may be as confident as of the last.

80 And assuredly no one will argue that there is any other method of comprehending by any regular process all true existence or of ascertaining what each thing is in its own nature; for the arts in general are concerned with the
85 desires or opinions of men, or are cultivated with a view to production and construction, or

for the preservation of such productions and constructions; and as to the mathematical sciences which, as we were saying, have some apprehension of true being--geometry and the like--they only dream about being, but never can they behold the waking reality so long as they leave the hypotheses which they use unexamined, and are unable to give an account of them. For when a man knows not his own first principle, and when the conclusion and intermediate steps are also constructed out of he knows not what, how can he imagine that such a fabric of convention can ever become science?

Impossible, he said.

Then dialectic, and dialectic alone, goes directly to the first principle and is the only science which does away with hypotheses in order to make her ground secure; the eye of the soul, which is literally buried in an outlandish slough, is by her gentle aid lifted upwards; and she uses as handmaids and helpers in the work of conversion, the sciences which we have been discussing. Custom terms them sciences, but they ought to have some other name, implying greater clearness than opinion and less clearness than science: and this, in our previous sketch, was called understanding. But why should we dispute about names when we have realities of such importance to consider?

Why indeed, he said, when any name will do which expresses the thought of the mind with clearness?

At any rate, we are satisfied, as before, to have four divisions; two for intellect and two for opinion, and to call the first division science, the second understanding, the third belief, and the fourth perception of shadows, opinion being concerned with becoming, and intellect with being; and so to make a proportion:--

As being is to becoming, so is pure intellect to opinion. And as intellect is to opinion, so is science to belief, and understanding to the perception of shadows.

But let us defer the further correlation and subdivision of the subjects of opinion and of intellect, for it will be a long enquiry, many times longer than this has been.

As far as I understand, he said, I agree.

And do you also agree, I said, in describing the dialectician as one who attains a conception of the essence of each thing? And he who does not possess and is therefore unable to impart this conception, in whatever degree he fails, may in that degree also be said to fail in intelligence? Will you admit so much?

Yes, he said; how can I deny it?

And you would say the same of the conception of the good? Until the person is able to abstract and define rationally the idea of good, and unless he can run the gauntlet of all objections, and is ready to disprove them, not by appeals to opinion, but to absolute truth, never faltering at any step of the argument--unless he can do all this, you would say that he knows neither the idea of good nor any other good; he apprehends only a shadow, if anything at all, which is given by opinion and not by science;--dreaming and slumbering in this life, before he is well awake here, he arrives at the world below, and has his final quietus.

In all that I should most certainly agree with you.

And surely you would not have the children of

your ideal State, whom you are nurturing and educating--if the ideal ever becomes a reality—you would not allow the future rulers to be like posts (Literally 'lines,' probably the starting-point of a race-course.), having no reason in them, and yet to be set in authority over the highest matters?

Certainly not.

Then you will make a law that they shall have such an education as will enable them to attain the greatest skill in asking and answering questions?

Yes, he said, you and I together will make it.

Dialectic, then, as you will agree, is the coping-stone of the sciences, and is set over them; no other science can be placed higher--the nature of knowledge can no further go?
I agree, he said.

But to whom we are to assign these studies, and in what way they are to be assigned, are questions which remain to be considered.

Yes, clearly.

You remember, I said, how the rulers were chosen before?

Certainly, he said.

The same natures must still be chosen, and the preference again given to the surest and the bravest, and, if possible, to the fairest; and, having noble and generous tempers, they should also have the natural gifts which will facilitate their education.

And what are these?

Such gifts as keenness and ready powers of acquisition; for the mind more often faints from the severity of study than from the severity of gymnastics: the toil is more entirely the mind's own, and is not shared with the body.

Very true, he replied.

Further, he of whom we are in search should have a good memory, and be an unwearied solid man who is a lover of labor in any line; or he will never be able to endure the great amount of bodily exercise and to go through all the intellectual discipline and study which we require of him.

Certainly, he said; he must have natural gifts.

The mistake at present is, that those who study philosophy have no vocation, and this, as I was before saying, is the reason why she has fallen into disrepute: her true sons should take her by the hand and not bastards.

What do you mean?

In the first place, her votary should not have a lame or halting industry--I mean, that he should not be half industrious and half idle: as, for example, when a man is a lover of gymnastic and hunting, and all other bodily exercises, but a hater rather than a lover of the labor of learning or listening or enquiring. Or the occupation to which he devotes himself may be of an opposite kind, and he may have the other sort of lameness.

Certainly, he said.

And as to truth, I said, is not a soul equally to be deemed halt and lame which hates voluntary falsehood and is extremely indignant at herself and others when they tell lies, but is patient of involuntary falsehood, and does not mind wallowing like a swinish beast in the mire of ignorance, and has no shame at being detected?

To be sure.

And, again, in respect of temperance, courage, magnificence, and every other virtue, should we not carefully distinguish between the true son and the bastard? for where there is no discernment of such qualities states and individuals unconsciously err; and the state makes a ruler, and the individual a friend, of one who, being defective in some part of virtue, is in a figure lame or a bastard.

That is very true, he said.

All these things, then, will have to be carefully considered by us; and if only those whom we introduce to this vast system of education and training are sound in body and mind, justice herself will have nothing to say against us, and we shall be the saviors of the constitution and of the State; but, if our pupils are men of another stamp, the reverse will happen, and we shall pour a still greater flood of ridicule on philosophy than she has to endure at present.

That would not be creditable.

Certainly not, I said; and yet perhaps, in thus turning jest into earnest I am equally ridiculous.

In what respect?

I had forgotten, I said, that we were not serious, and spoke with too much excitement. For when I saw philosophy so undeservedly trampled under foot of men I could not help feeling a sort of indignation at the authors of her disgrace: and my anger made me too vehement.

Indeed! I was listening, and did not think so.

But I, who am the speaker, felt that I was. And now let me remind you that, although in our former selection we chose old men, we must not do so in this. Solon was under a delusion when he said that a man when he grows old may learn many things--for he can no more learn much than he can run much; youth is the time for any extraordinary toil.

Of course.

And, therefore, calculation and geometry and all the other elements of instruction, which are a preparation for dialectic, should be presented to the mind in childhood; not, however, under any notion of forcing our system of education.

Why not?

Because a freeman ought not to be a slave in the acquisition of knowledge of any kind. Bodily exercise, when compulsory, does no harm to the body; but knowledge which is acquired under compulsion obtains no hold on the mind.

Very true.

Then, my good friend, I said, do not use compulsion, but let early education be a sort of amusement; you will then be better able to find out the natural bent.

That is a very rational notion, he said.

Do you remember that the children, too, were

to be taken to see the battle on horseback; and
that if there were no danger they were to be
brought close up and, like young hounds, have
a taste of blood given them?

5

Yes, I remember.

The same practice may be followed, I said, in
all these things--labors, lessons, dangers--and
10 he who is most at home in all of them ought
to be enrolled in a select number.
At what age?

At the age when the necessary gymnastics are
15 over: the period whether of two or three years
which passes in this sort of training is useless
for any other purpose; for sleep and exercise
are unpropitious to learning; and the trial of
who is first in gymnastic exercises is one of
20 the most important tests to which our youth
are subjected.

Certainly, he replied.

25 After that time those who are selected from
the class of twenty years old will be promoted
to higher honor, and the sciences which they
learned without any order in their early education will now be brought together, and they
30 will be able to see the natural relationship of
them to one another and to true being.

Yes, he said, that is the only kind of
knowledge which takes lasting root.
35

Yes, I said; and the capacity for such
knowledge is the great criterion of dialectical
talent: the comprehensive mind is always the
dialectical.
40

I agree with you, he said.

These, I said, are the points which you must
consider; and those who have most of this
45 comprehension, and who are most steadfast in
their learning, and in their military and other
appointed duties, when they have arrived at
the age of thirty have to be chosen by you out
of the select class, and elevated to higher hon-
50 or; and you will have to prove them by the
help of dialectic, in order to learn which of
them is able to give up the use of sight and the
other senses, and in company with truth to
attain absolute being: And here, my friend,
55 great caution is required.

Why great caution?

Do you not remark, I said, how great is the
60 evil which dialectic has introduced?

What evil? he said.

The students of the art are filled with lawless-
65 ness.
Quite true, he said.

Do you think that there is anything so very
unnatural or inexcusable in their case? or will
70 you make allowance for them?

In what way make allowance?

I want you, I said, by way of parallel, to imag-
75 ine a supposititious son who is brought up in
great wealth; he is one of a great and numerous family, and has many flatterers. When he
grows up to manhood, he learns that his alleged are not his real parents; but who the real
80 are he is unable to discover. Can you guess
how he will be likely to behave towards his
flatterers and his supposed parents, first of all
during the period when he is ignorant of the
false relation, and then again when he knows?
85 Or shall I guess for you?

If you please.

Then I should say, that while he is ignorant of the truth he will be likely to honor his father and his mother and his supposed relations more than the flatterers; he will be less inclined to neglect them when in need, or to do or say anything against them; and he will be less willing to disobey them in any important matter.

He will.

But when he has made the discovery, I should imagine that he would diminish his honor and regard for them, and would become more devoted to the flatterers; their influence over him would greatly increase; he would now live after their ways, and openly associate with them, and, unless he were of an unusually good disposition, he would trouble himself no more about his supposed parents or other relations.
Well, all that is very probable. But how is the image applicable to the disciples of philosophy?

In this way: you know that there are certain principles about justice and honor, which were taught us in childhood, and under their parental authority we have been brought up, obeying and honoring them.

That is true.

There are also opposite maxims and habits of pleasure which flatter and attract the soul, but do not influence those of us who have any sense of right, and they continue to obey and honor the maxims of their fathers.

True.

Now, when a man is in this state, and the questioning spirit asks what is fair or honorable, and he answers as the legislator has taught him, and then arguments many and diverse refute his words, until he is driven into believing that nothing is honorable any more than dishonorable, or just and good any more than the reverse, and so of all the notions which he most valued, do you think that he will still honor and obey them as before?
Impossible.

And when he ceases to think them honorable and natural as heretofore, and he fails to discover the true, can he be expected to pursue any life other than that which flatters his desires?

He cannot.

And from being a keeper of the law he is converted into a breaker of it?

Unquestionably.

Now all this is very natural in students of philosophy such as I have described, and also, as I was just now saying, most excusable.

Yes, he said; and, I may add, pitiable.

Therefore, that your feelings may not be moved to pity about our citizens who are now thirty years of age, every care must be taken in introducing them to dialectic.

Certainly.

There is a danger lest they should taste the dear delight too early; for youngsters, as you may have observed, when they first get the taste in their mouths, argue for amusement, and are always contradicting and refuting others in imitation of those who refute them; like puppy-dogs, they rejoice in pulling and tearing at all who come near them.

5 Yes, he said, there is nothing which they like better.

And when they have made many conquests and received defeats at the hands of many, 10 they violently and speedily get into a way of not believing anything which they believed before, and hence, not only they, but philosophy and all that relates to it is apt to have a bad name with the rest of the world.

15

Too true, he said.

But when a man begins to get older, he will no longer be guilty of such insanity; he will imi-20 tate the dialectician who is seeking for truth, and not the eristic, who is contradicting for the sake of amusement; and the greater moderation of his character will increase instead of diminishing the honor of the pursuit.

25

Very true, he said.

And did we not make special provision for this, when we said that the disciples of philos-30 ophy were to be orderly and steadfast, not, as now, any chance aspirant or intruder?

Very true.

35 Suppose, I said, the study of philosophy to take the place of gymnastics and to be continued diligently and earnestly and exclusively for twice the number of years which were passed in bodily exercise--will that be enough?

40

Would you say six or four years? he asked.

Say five years, I replied; at the end of the time

they must be sent down again into the den and 45 compelled to hold any military or other office which young men are qualified to hold: in this way they will get their experience of life, and there will be an opportunity of trying whether, when they are drawn all manner of ways by 50 temptation, they will stand firm or flinch.

And how long is this stage of their lives to last?

55 Fifteen years, I answered; and when they have reached fifty years of age, then let those who still survive and have distinguished themselves in every action of their lives and in every branch of knowledge come at last to their 60 consummation: the time has now arrived at which they must raise the eye of the soul to the universal light which lightens all things, and behold the absolute good; for that is the pattern according to which they are to order 65 the State and the lives of individuals, and the remainder of their own lives also; making philosophy their chief pursuit, but, when their turn comes, toiling also at politics and ruling for the public good, not as though they were 70 performing some heroic action, but simply as a matter of duty; and when they have brought up in each generation others like themselves and left them in their place to be governors of the State, then they will depart to the Islands 75 of the Blest and dwell there; and the city will give them public memorials and sacrifices and honor them, if the Pythian oracle consent, as demigods, but if not, as in any case blessed and divine.

80

You are a sculptor, Socrates, and have made statues of our governors faultless in beauty.

Yes, I said, Glaucon, and of our governesses 85 too; for you must not suppose that what I have been saying applies to men only and not to women as far as their natures can go.

There you are right, he said, since we have made them to share in all things like the men.

Well, I said, and you would agree (would you not?) that what has been said about the State and the government is not a mere dream, and although difficult not impossible, but only possible in the way which has been supposed; that is to say, when the true philosopher kings are born in a State, one or more of them, despising the honors of this present world which they deem mean and worthless, esteeming above all things right and the honor that springs from right, and regarding justice as the greatest and most necessary of all things, whose ministers they are, and whose principles will be exalted by them when they set in order their own city?

How will they proceed?

They will begin by sending out into the coun-
try all the inhabitants of the city who are more than ten years old, and will take possession of their children, who will be unaffected by the habits of their parents; these they will train in their own habits and laws, I mean in the laws which we have given them: and in this way the State and constitution of which we were speaking will soonest and most easily attain happiness, and the nation which has such a constitution will gain most.

Yes, that will be the best way. And I think, Socrates, that you have very well described how, if ever, such a constitution might come into being.

Enough then of the perfect State, and of the man who bears its image--there is no difficulty in seeing how we shall describe him.

There is no difficulty, he replied; and I agree with you in thinking that nothing more need be said.

ARISTOTLE

Plato may have been the father of Western philosophy and science, but Aristotle (382-322 BC) was the individual to bring those studies—and many others—into full bloom. Called 'The First Teacher' in medieval Islamic scholarship and 'The Philosopher' in the medieval Christian world, Aristotle was the originator of what we now call the scientific method and his writings serve and his writings served as the basis for fields as disparate as physics and poetry. It might not be hyperbole to suggest that Aristotle is the most significant single individual in the intellectual history of the world.

Aristotle was born in what is now northern Greece, but what was then the independent and only moderately Hellenic kingdom of Macedon. As a young man Aristotle traveled to Athens where he studied under Plato at the Academy. Having been passed over for leadership of the Academy at the death of Plato and likely fearing persecution following the defeat of Athens by Macedon, Aristotle returned to his homeland in the 340s to become the personal tutor of the future Alexander the Great. He would later go on to found his own school in Athens known as the Lyceum, but would have to flee the city again in the years preceding this death.

Aristotle was in many ways the first political scientist—the first scholar to attack the question of politics in a 'scientific' fashion. He did this is a pair of works—*Ethics* and *Politics*—which look at the study of human affairs. While *Ethics* is more a discussion of political society, *Politics* is a rigorous attempt to scientifically explain the proper forms of social structure. It attempts a similar task to Plato's *Republic*, but is most fundamentally scientific—it wants to treat with the world as it is. Thus, it deals less with abstractions—'what is justice'—and most with concrete issues such as the relationship between government and society, citizen and state, and insider and outsider. His writings, though following in the footsteps of Plato and Socrates, and no less original and no less important in shaping the world in which we live.

POLITICS
ARISTOTLE

BOOK I
CHAPTER I

As we see that every city is a society, and every
society is established for some good purpose;
for an apparent [1252a] good is the spring of
all human actions; it is evident that this is the
principle upon which they are every one
founded, and this is more especially true of
that which has for its object the best possible,
and is itself the most excellent, and compre-
hends all the rest.

Now this is called a city, and the society thereof a political society; for those who think that
the principles of a political, a regal, a family,
and a herile government are the same are mistaken, while they suppose that each of these
differ in the numbers to whom their power
extends, but not in their constitution: so that
with them a herile government is one composed of a very few, a domestic of more, a
civil and a regal of still more, as if there was
no difference between a large family and a
small city, or that a regal government and a
political one are the same, only that in the one
a single person is continually at the head of
public affairs; in the other, that each member
of the state has in his turn a share in the government, and is at one time a magistrate, at
another a private person, according to the
rules of political science. But now this is not
true, as will be evident to any one who will
consider this question in the most approved
method. As, in an inquiry into every other

subject, it is necessary to separate the different
parts of which it is compounded, till we arrive
at their first elements, which are the most minute parts thereof; so by the same proceeding
we shall acquire a knowledge of the primary
parts of a city and see wherein they differ
from each other, and whether the rules of art
will give us any assistance in examining into
each of these things which are mentioned.

CHAPTER II

Now if in this particular science any one
would attend to its original seeds, and their
first shoot, he would then as in others have
the subject perfectly before him; and perceive,
in the first place, that it is requisite that those
should be joined together whose species cannot exist without each other, as the male and
the female, for the business of propagation;
and this not through choice, but by that natural impulse which acts both upon plants and
animals also, for the purpose of their leaving
behind them others like themselves. It is also
from natural causes that some beings command and others obey, that each may obtain
their mutual safety; for a being who is endowed with a mind capable of reflection and
forethought is by nature the superior and governor, whereas he whose excellence is merely
corporeal is formect to be a slave; whence it
follows that the different state of master
[1252b] and slave is equally advantageous to
both. But there is a natural difference between
a female and a slave: for nature is not like the
artists who make the Delphic swords for the
use of the poor, but for every particular pur-

Text based off the William Ellis translation, with
adjustments for modern spellings.

pose she has her separate instruments, and
thus her ends are most complete, for whatsoever is employed on one subject only, brings
that one to much greater perfection than when
5 employed on many; and yet among the barbarians, a female and a slave are upon a level in
the community, the reason for which is, that
amongst them there are none qualified by nature to govern, therefore their society can be
10 nothing but between slaves of different sexes.
For which reason the poets say, it is proper
for the Greeks to govern the barbarians, as if a
barbarian and a slave were by nature one.

Now of these two societies the domestic is the
15 first, and Hesiod is right when he says, "First a
house, then a wife, then an ox for the plough,"
for the poor man has always an ox before a
household slave. That society then which nature has established for daily support is the
20 domestic, and those who compose it are called
by Charondas *homosipuoi*, and by Epimenides
the Cretan *homokapnoi*; but the society of many
families, which was first instituted for their
lasting, mutual advantage, is called a village,
25 and a village is most naturally composed of
the descendants of one family, whom some
persons call *homogalaktes*, the children and the
children's children thereof: for which reason
cities were originally governed by kings, as the
30 barbarian states now are, which are composed
of those who had before submitted to kingly
government; for every family is governed by
the elder, as are the branches thereof, on account of their relationship thereunto, which is
35 what Homer says, "Each one ruled his wife
and child;" and in this scattered manner they
formerly lived. And the opinion which universally prevails, that the gods themselves are
subject to kingly government, arises from
40 hence, that all men formerly were, and many
are so now; and as they imagined themselves
to be made in the likeness of the gods, so they
supposed their manner of life must needs be
45 the same.

And when many villages so entirely join themselves together as in every respect to form but
one society, that society is a city, and contains
in itself, if I may so speak, the end and perfec-
50 tion of government: first founded that we
might live, but continued that we may live
happily. For which reason every city must be
allowed to be the work of nature, if we admit
that the original society between male and
55 female is; for to this as their end all subordinate societies tend, and the end of everything
is the nature of it. For what every being is in
its most perfect state, that certainly is the na-
60 ture of that being, whether it be a man, a
horse, or a house: besides, whatsoever produces the final cause and the end which we
[1253a] desire, must be best; but a government
complete in itself is that final cause and what
65 is best.

Hence it is evident that a city is a natural production, and that man is naturally a political
animal, and that whosoever is naturally and
70 not accidentally unfit for society, must be either inferior or superior to man: thus the man
in Homer, who is reviled for being "without
society, without law, without family." Such a
one must naturally be of a quarrelsome dispo-
75 sition, and as solitary as the birds.

The gift of speech also evidently proves that
man is a more social animal than the bees, or
any of the herding cattle: for nature, as we say,
80 does nothing in vain, and man is the only animal who enjoys it. Voice indeed, as being the
token of pleasure and pain, is imparted to others also, and thus much their nature is capable
of, to perceive pleasure and pain, and to im-
85 part these sensations to others; but it is by
speech that we are enabled to express what is

useful for us, and what is hurtful, and of course what is just and what is unjust: for in this particular man differs from other animals, that he alone has a perception of good and
5 evil, of just and unjust, and it is a participation of these common sentiments which forms a family and a city.

Besides, the notion of a city naturally precedes
10 that of a family or an individual, for the whole must necessarily be prior to the parts, for if you take away the whole man, you cannot say a foot or a hand remains, unless by equivocation, as supposing a hand of stone to be made,
15 but that would only be a dead one; but everything is understood to be this or that by its energic qualities and powers, so that when these no longer remain, neither can that be said to be the same, but something of the
20 same name. That a city then precedes an individual is plain, for if an individual is not in himself sufficient to compose a perfect government, he is to a city as other parts are to a whole; but he that is incapable of society, or
25 so complete in himself as not to want it, makes no part of a city, as a beast or a god. There is then in all persons a natural impetus to associate with each other in this manner, and he who first founded civil society was the
30 cause of the greatest good; for as by the completion of it man is the most excellent of all living beings, so without law and justice he would be the worst of all, for nothing is so difficult to subdue as injustice in arms: but
35 these arms man is born with, namely, prudence and valor, which he may apply to the most opposite purposes, for he who abuses them will be the most wicked, the most cruel, the most lustful, and most gluttonous being
40 imaginable; for justice is a political virtue, by the rules of it the state is regulated, and these rules are the criterion of what is right.

CHAPTER III

45 Since it is now evident of what parts a city is composed, it will be necessary to treat first of family government, for every city is made up of families, and every family [1253b] has again
50 its separate parts of which it is composed. When a family is complete, it consists of freemen and slaves; but as in every subject we should begin with examining into the smallest parts of which it consists, and as the first and
55 smallest parts of a family are the master and slave, the husband and wife, the father and child, let us first inquire into these three, what each of them may be, and what they ought to be; that is to say, the herile, the nuptial, and
60 the paternal. Let these then be considered as the three distinct parts of a family: some think that the providing what is necessary for the family is something different from the government of it, others that this is the greatest
65 part of it; it shall be considered separately; but we will first speak of a master and a slave, that we may both understand the nature of those things which are absolutely necessary, and also try if we can learn anything better on this sub-
70 ject than what is already known. Some persons have thought that the power of the master over his slave originates from his superior knowledge, and that this knowledge is the same in the master, the magistrate, and the
75 king, as we have already said; but others think that herile government is contrary to nature, and that it is the law which makes one man a slave and another free, but that in nature there is no difference; for which reason that power
80 cannot be founded in justice, but in force.

CHAPTER IV

Since then a subsistence is necessary in every
85 family, the means of procuring it certainly makes up part of the management of a family,

for without necessaries it is impossible to live, and to live well. As in all arts which are brought to perfection it is necessary that they should have their proper instruments if they would complete their works, so is it in the art of managing a family: now of instruments some of them are alive, others inanimate; thus with respect to the pilot of the ship, the tiller is without life, the sailor is alive; for a servant is as an instrument in many arts. Thus property is as an instrument to living; an estate is a multitude of instruments; so a slave is an animated instrument, but every one that can minister of himself is more valuable than any other instrument; for if every instrument, at command, or from a preconception of its master's will, could accomplish its work (as the story goes of the statues of Daedalus; or what the poet tells us of the tripods of Vulcan, "that they moved of their own accord into the assembly of the gods "), the shuttle would then weave, and the lyre play of itself; nor would the architect want servants, or the [1254a] master slaves. Now what are generally called instruments are the efficients of something else, but possessions are what we simply use: thus with a shuttle we make something else for our use; but we only use a coat, or a bed: since then making and using differ from each other in species, and they both require their instruments, it is necessary that these should be different from each other. Now life is itself what we use, and not what we employ as the efficient of something else; for which reason the services of a slave are for use. A possession may be considered in the same nature as a part of anything; now a part is not only a part of something, but also is nothing else; so is a possession; therefore a master is only the master of the slave, but no part of him; but the slave is not only the slave of the master, but nothing else but that. This fully explains what is the nature of a slave, and what are his capac-

ities; for that being who by nature is nothing of himself, but totally another's, and is a man, is a slave by nature; and that man who is the property of another, is his mere chattel, though he continues a man; but a chattel is an instrument for use, separate from the body.

CHAPTER V

But whether any person is such by nature, and whether it is advantageous and just for any one to be a slave or no, or whether all slavery is contrary to nature, shall be considered hereafter; not that it is difficult to determine it upon general principles, or to understand it from matters of fact; for that some should govern, and others be governed, is not only necessary but useful, and from the hour of their birth some are marked out for those purposes, and others for the other, and there are many species of both sorts.

And the better those are who are governed the better also is the government, as for instance of man, rather than the brute creation: for the more excellent the materials are with which the work is finished, the more excellent certainly is the work; and wherever there is a governor and a governed, there certainly is some work produced; for whatsoever is composed of many parts, which jointly become one, whether conjunct or separate, evidently show the marks of governing and governed; and this is true of every living thing in all nature; nay, even in some things which partake not of life, as in music; but this probably would be a disquisition too foreign to our present purpose. Every living thing in the first place is composed of soul and body, of these the one is by nature the governor, the other the governed; now if we would know what is natural, we ought to search for it in those subjects in which nature appears most perfect, and not in

those which are corrupted; we should therefore examine into a man who is most perfectly
formed both in soul and body, in whom this is
evident, for in the depraved and vicious the
5 body seems [1254b] to rule rather than the
soul, on account of their being corrupt and
contrary to nature. We may then, as we affirm,
perceive in an animal the first principles of
herile and political government; for the soul
10 governs the body as the master governs his
slave; the mind governs the appetite with a
political or a kingly power, which shows that it
is both natural and advantageous that the body
should be governed by the soul, and the pa-
15 thetic part by the mind, and that part which is
possessed of reason; but to have no ruling
power, or an improper one, is hurtful to all;
and this holds true not only of man, but of
other animals also, for tame animals are natu-
20 rally better than wild ones, and it is advantageous that both should be under subjection to
man; for this is productive of their common
safety: so is it naturally with the male and the
female; the one is superior, the other inferior;
25 the one governs, the other is governed; and
the same rule must necessarily hold good with
respect to all mankind. Those men therefore
who are as much inferior to others as the body
is to the soul, are to be thus disposed of, as
30 the proper use of them is their bodies, in
which their excellence consists; and if what I
have said be true, they are slaves by nature,
and it is advantageous to them to be always
under government. He then is by nature
35 formed a slave who is qualified to become the
chattel of another person, and on that account
is so, and who has just reason enough to know
that there is such a faculty, without being in-
dued with the use of it; for other animals have
40 no perception of reason, but are entirely guided by appetite, and indeed they vary very little
in their use from each other; for the advantage
which we receive, both from slaves and tame

animals, arises from their bodily strength ad-
45 ministering to our necessities; for it is the intention of nature to make the bodies of slaves
and freemen different from each other, that
the one should be robust for their necessary
purposes, the others erect, useless indeed for
50 what slaves are employed in, but fit for civil
life, which is divided into the duties of war
and peace; though these rules do not always
take place, for slaves have sometimes the bodies of freemen, sometimes the souls; if then it
55 is evident that if some bodies are as much
more excellent than others as the statues of
the gods excel the human form, every one will
allow that the inferior ought to be slaves to
the superior; and if this is true with respect to
60 the body, it is still juster to determine in the
same manner, when we consider the soul;
though it is not so easy to perceive the beauty
of [1255a] the soul as it is of the body. Since
then some men are slaves by nature, and oth-
65 ers are freemen, it is clear that where slavery is
advantageous to any one, then it is just to
make him a slave.

CHAPTER VI

70

But it is not difficult to perceive that those
who maintain the contrary opinion have some
reason on their side; for a man may become a
slave two different ways; for he may be so by
75 law also, and this law is a certain compact, by
which whatsoever is taken in battle is adjudged
to be the property of the conquerors: but
many persons who are conversant in law call
in question this pretended right, and say that it
80 would be hard that a man should be compelled by violence to be the slave and subject
of another who had the power to compel him,
and was his superior in strength; and upon this
subject, even of those who are wise, some
85 think one way and some another; but the
cause of this doubt and variety of opinions

arises from hence, that great abilities, when
accompanied with proper means, are generally
able to succeed by force: for victory is always
owing to a superiority in some advantageous
5 circumstances; so that it seems that force never prevails but in consequence of great abilities. But still the dispute concerning the justice
of it remains; for some persons think, that
justice consists in benevolence, others think it
10 just that the powerful should govern: in the
midst of these contrary opinions, there are no
reasons sufficient to convince us, that the right
of being master and governor ought not to be
placed with those who have the greatest abili-
15 ties. Some persons, entirely resting upon the
right which the law gives (for that which is
legal is in some respects just), insist upon it
that slavery occasioned by war is just, not that
they say it is wholly so, for it may happen that
20 the principle upon which the wars were commenced is unjust; moreover no one will say
that a man who is unworthily in slavery is
therefore a slave; for if so, men of the noblest
families might happen to be slaves, and the
25 descendants of slaves, if they should chance to
be taken prisoners in war and sold: to avoid
this difficulty they say that such persons
should not be called slaves, but barbarians
only should; but when they say this, they do
30 nothing more than inquire who is a slave by
nature, which was what we at first said; for we
must acknowledge that there are some persons
who, wherever they are, must necessarily be
slaves, but others in no situation; thus also it is
35 with those of noble descent: it is not only in
their own country that they are Esteemed as
such, but everywhere, but the barbarians are
respected on this account at home only; as if
nobility and freedom were of two sorts, the
40 one universal, the other not so. Thus says the
Helen of Theodectes:

"Who dares reproach me with the name of

slave? When from the immortal gods, on ei-
45 ther side, I draw my lineage."

Those who express sentiments like these,
show only that they distinguish the slave and
the freeman, the noble and the ignoble from
50 each other by their virtues and their [1255b]
vices; for they think it reasonable, that as a
man begets a man, and a beast a beast, so
from a good man, a good man should be descended; and this is what nature desires to do,
55 but frequently cannot accomplish it.

It is evident then that this doubt has some
reason in it, and that these persons are not
slaves, and those freemen, by the appointment
60 of nature; and also that in some instances it is
sufficiently clear, that it is advantageous to
both parties for this man to be a slave, and
that to be a master, and that it is right and just,
that some should be governed, and others
65 govern, in the manner that nature intended; of
which sort of government is that which a master exercises over a slave. But to govern ill is
disadvantageous to both; for the same thing is
useful to the part and to the whole, to the
70 body and to the soul; but the slave is as it were
a part of the master, as if he were an animated
part of his body, though separate. For which
reason a mutual utility and friendship may
subsist between the master and the slave, I
75 mean when they are placed by nature in that
relation to each other, for the contrary takes
place amongst those who are reduced to slavery by the law, or by conquest.

CHAPTER VII

80

It is evident from what has been said, that a
herile and a political government are not the
same, or that all governments are alike to each
85 other, as some affirm; for one is adapted to
the nature of freemen, the other to that of

slaves. Domestic government is a monarchy, for that is what prevails in every house; but a political state is the government of free men and equals. The master is not so called from

5 his knowing how to manage his slave, but because he is so; for the same reason a slave and a freeman have their respective appellations. There is also one sort of knowledge proper for a master, another for a slave; the slave's is of

10 the nature of that which was taught by a slave at Syracuse; for he for a stipulated sum instructed the boys in all the business of a household slave, of which there are various sorts to be learnt, as the art of cookery, and

15 other such-like services, of which some are allotted to some, and others to others; some employments being more honorable, others more necessary; according to the proverb, "One slave excels another, one master excels

20 another:" in such-like things the knowledge of a slave consists. The knowledge of the master is to be able properly to employ his slaves, for the mastership of slaves is the employment, not the mere possession of them; not that this

25 knowledge contains anything great or respectable; for what a slave ought to know how to do, that a master ought to know how to order; for which reason, those who have it in their power to be free from these low attentions,

30 employ a steward for this business, and apply themselves either to public affairs or philosophy: the knowledge of procuring what is necessary for a family is different from that which belongs either to the master or the slave: and

35 to do this justly must be either by war or hunting. And thus much of the difference between a master and a slave.

CHAPTER VIII

40

[1256a] As a slave is a particular species of property, let us by all means inquire into the nature of property in general, and the acquisi-

tion of money, according to the manner we

45 have proposed. In the first place then, some one may doubt whether the getting of money is the same thing as economy, or whether it is a part of it, or something subservient to it; and if so, whether it is as the art of making shuttles

50 is to the art of weaving, or the art of making brass to that of statue founding, for they are not of the same service; for the one supplies the tools, the other the matter: by the matter I mean the subject out of which the work is

55 finished, as wool for the cloth and brass for the statue. It is evident then that the getting of money is not the same thing as economy, for the business of the one is to furnish the means of the other to use them; and what art is there

60 employed in the management of a family but economy, but whether this is a part of it, or something of a different species, is a doubt; for if it is the business of him who is to get money to find out how riches and possessions

65 may be procured, and both these arise from various causes, we must first inquire whether the art of husbandry is part of money-getting or something different, and in general, whether the same is not true of every acquisition and

70 every attention which relates to provision. But as there are many sorts of provision, so are the methods of living both of man and the brute creation very various; and as it is impossible to live without food, the difference in that par-

75 ticular makes the lives of animals so different from each other. Of beasts, some live in herds, others separate, as is most convenient for procuring themselves food; as some of them live upon flesh, others on fruit, and others on

80 whatsoever they light on, nature having so distinguished their course of life, that they can very easily procure themselves subsistence; and as the same things are not agreeable to all, but one animal likes one thing and another

85 another, it follows that the lives of those beasts who live upon flesh must be different

from the lives of those who live on fruits; so is it with men, their lives differ greatly from each other; and of all these the shepherd's is the idlest, for they live upon the flesh of tame 5 animals, without any trouble, while they are obliged to change their habitations on account of their flocks, which they are compelled to follow, cultivating, as it were, a living farm. Others live exercising violence over living 10 creatures, one pursuing this thing, another that, these preying upon men; those who live near lakes and marshes and rivers, or the sea itself, on fishing, while others are fowlers, or hunters of wild beasts; but the greater part of 15 mankind live upon the produce of the earth and its cultivated fruits; and the manner in which all those live who follow the direction of nature, and labor for their own subsistence, is nearly the same, without ever thinking to 20 procure any provision by way of exchange or merchandise, such are shepherds, husbandmen, [1256b] robbers, fishermen, and hunters: some join different employments together, and thus live very agreeably; supplying those 25 deficiencies which were wanting to make their subsistence depend upon themselves only: thus, for instance, the same person shall be a shepherd and a robber, or a husbandman and a hunter; and so with respect to the rest, they 30 pursue that mode of life which necessity points out. This provision then nature herself seems to have furnished all animals with, as well immediately upon their first origin as also when they are arrived at a state of maturity; 35 for at the first of these periods some of them are provided in the womb with proper nourishment, which continues till that which is born can get food for itself, as is the case with worms and birds; and as to those which bring 40 forth their young alive, they have the means for their subsistence for a certain time within themselves, namely milk. It is evident then that we may conclude of those things that are,

that plants are created for the sake of animals, 45 and animals for the sake of men; the tame for our use and provision; the wild, at least the greater part, for our provision also, or for some other advantageous purpose, as furnishing us with clothes, and the like. As nature 50 therefore makes nothing either imperfect or in vain, it necessarily follows that she has made all these things for men: for which reason what we gain in war is in a certain degree a natural acquisition; for hunting is a part of it, 55 which it is necessary for us to employ against wild beasts; and those men who being intended by nature for slavery are unwilling to submit to it, on which occasion such a. war is by nature just: that species of acquisition then 60 only which is according to nature is part of economy; and this ought to be at hand, or if not, immediately procured, namely, what is necessary to be kept in store to live upon, and which are useful as well for the state as the 65 family. And true riches seem to consist in these; and the acquisition of those possessions which are necessary for a happy life is not infinite; though Solon says otherwise in this verse:

70

"No bounds to riches can be fixed for man;"

for they may be fixed as in other arts; for the instruments of no art whatsoever are infinite, 75 either in their number or their magnitude; but riches are a number of instruments in domestic and civil economy; it is therefore evident that the acquisition of certain things according to nature is a part both of domestic and civil 80 economy, and for what reason.

CHAPTER IX

There is also another species of acquisition 85 which they [1257a] particularly call pecuniary, and with great propriety; and by this indeed it

seems that there are no bounds to riches and wealth. Now many persons suppose, from their near relation to each other, that this is one and the same with that we have just men-
5 tioned, but it is not the same as that, though not very different; one of these is natural, the other is not, but rather owing to some art and skill; we will enter into a particular examination of this subject.
10

The uses of every possession are two, both dependent upon the thing itself, but not in the same manner, the one supposing an inseparable connection with it, the other not; as a
15 shoe, for instance, which may be either worn, or exchanged for something else, both these are the uses of the shoe; for he who exchanges a shoe with some man who wants one, for money or provisions, uses the shoe as a shoe,
20 but not according to the original intention, for shoes were not at first made to be exchanged. The same thing holds true of all other possessions; for barter, in general, had its original beginning in nature, some men having a sur-
25 plus, others too little of what was necessary for them: hence it is evident, that the selling provisions for money is not according to the natural use of things; for they were obliged to use barter for those things which they wanted;
30 but it is plain that barter could have no place in the first, that is to say, in family society; but must have begun when the number of those who composed the community was enlarged: for the first of these had all things in common;
35 but when they came to be separated they were obliged to exchange with each other many different things which both parties wanted. Which custom of barter is still preserved amongst many barbarous nations, who pro-
40 cure one necessary with another, but never sell anything; as giving and receiving wine for corn and the like. This sort of barter is not contradictory to nature, nor is it any species of mon-

ey-getting; but is necessary in procuring that
45 subsistence which is so consonant thereunto. But this barter introduced the use of money, as might be expected; for a convenient place from whence to import what you wanted, or to export what you had a surplus of, being
50 often at a great distance, money necessarily made its way into commerce; for it is not everything which is naturally most useful that is easiest of carriage; for which reason they invented something to exchange with each other
55 which they should mutually give and take, that being really valuable itself, should have the additional advantage of being of easy conveyance, for the purposes of life, as iron and silver, or anything else of the same nature: and
60 this at first passed in value simply according to its weight or size; but in process of time it had a certain stamp, to save the trouble of weighing, which stamp expressed its value. [1257b]

65 Money then being established as the necessary medium of exchange, another species of money-getting soon took place, namely, by buying and selling, at probably first in a simple manner, afterwards with more skill and experience,
70 where and how the greatest profits might be made. For which reason the art of money-getting seems to be chiefly conversant about trade, and the business of it to be able to tell where the greatest profits can be made, being
75 the means of procuring abundance of wealth and possessions: and thus wealth is very often supposed to consist in the quantity of money which any one possesses, as this is the medium by which all trade is conducted and a for-
80 tune made, others again regard it as of no value, as being of none by nature, but arbitrarily made so by compact; so that if those who use it should alter their sentiments, it would be worth nothing, as being of no service for any
85 necessary purpose. Besides, he who abounds in money often wants necessary food; and it is

impossible to say that any person is in good circumstances when with all his possessions he may perish with hunger.

5 Like Midas in the fable, who from his insatiable wish had everything he touched turned into gold. For which reason others endeavor to procure other riches and other property, and rightly, for there are other riches and
10 property in nature; and these are the proper objects of economy: while trade only procures money, not by all means, but by the exchange of it, and for that purpose it is this which it is chiefly employed about, for money is the first
15 principle and the end of trade; nor are there any bounds to be set to what is thereby acquired. Thus also there are no limits to the art of medicine, with respect to the health which it attempts to procure; the same also is true of
20 all other arts; no line can be drawn to terminate their bounds, the several professors of them being desirous to extend them as far as possible. (But still the means to be employed for that purpose are limited; and these are the
25 limits beyond which the art cannot proceed.) Thus in the art of acquiring riches there are no limits, for the object of that is money and possessions; but economy has a boundary, though this has not: for acquiring riches is not the
30 business of that, for which reason it should seem that some boundary should be set to riches, though we see the contrary to this is what is practiced; for all those who get riches add to their money without end; the cause of
35 which is the near connection of these two arts with each other, which sometimes occasions the one to change employments with the other, as getting of money is their common object: for economy requires the possession of
40 wealth, but not on its own account but with another view, to purchase things necessary therewith; but the other procures it merely to increase it: so that some persons are con-

firmed in their belief, that this is the proper
45 object of economy, and think that for this purpose money should be saved and hoarded up without end; the reason for which disposition is, that they are intent upon living, but not upon living well; and this desire being bound-
50 less in its extent, the means which they aim at for that purpose are boundless also; and those who propose to live well, often confine that to the enjoyment of the pleasures of sense; so that as this also seems to depend upon what a
55 man has, all their care is to get money, and hence arises the other cause for this art; for as this enjoyment is excessive in its degree, they endeavor to procure means proportionate to supply it; and if they cannot do this merely by
60 the art of dealing in money, they will endeavor to do it by other ways, and apply all their powers to a purpose they were not by nature intended for. Thus, for instance, courage was intended to inspire fortitude, not to get money
65 by; neither is this the end of the soldier's or the physician's art, but victory and health. But such persons make everything subservient to money-getting, as if this was the only end; and to the end everything ought to refer.
70

We have now considered that art of money-getting which is not necessary, and have seen in what manner we became in want of it; and also that which is necessary, which is different
75 from it; for that economy which is natural, and whose object is to provide food, is not like this unlimited in its extent, but has its bounds.

CHAPTER X

80

We have now determined what was before doubtful, whether or no the art of getting money is his business who is at the head of a family or a state, and though not strictly so, it
85 is however very necessary; for as a politician does not make men, but receiving them from

the hand of nature employs them to proper purposes; thus the earth, or the sea, or something else ought to supply them with provisions, and this it is the business of the master of the family to manage properly; for it is not the weaver's business to make yarn, but to use it, and to distinguish what is good and useful from what is bad and of no service; and indeed some one may inquire why getting money should be a part of economy when the art of healing is not, as it is as requisite that the family should be in health as that they should eat, or have anything else which is necessary; and as it is indeed in some particulars the business both of the master of the family, and he to whom the government of the state is entrusted, to see after the health of those under their care, but in others not, but the physician's; so also as to money; in some respects it is the business of the master of the family, in others not, but of the servant; but as we have already said, it is chiefly nature's, for it is her part to supply her offspring with food; for everything finds nourishment left for it in what produced it; for which reason the natural riches of all men arise from fruits and animals. Now money-making, as we say, being twofold, it may be applied to two purposes, the service of the house or retail trade; of which the first is necessary and commendable, the other justly censurable; for it has not its origin in [1258b] nature, but by it men gain from each other; for usury is most reasonably detested, as it is increasing our fortune by money itself, and not employing it for the purpose it was originally intended, namely exchange.

And this is the explanation of the name (TOKOS), which means the breeding of money. For as offspring resemble their parents, so usury is money bred of money. Whence of all forms of money-making it is most against nature.

CHAPTER XI

Having already sufficiently considered the general principles of this subject, let us now go into the practical part thereof; the one is a liberal employment for the mind, the other necessary. These things are useful in the management of one's affairs; to be skillful in the nature of cattle, which are most profitable, and where, and how; as for instance, what advantage will arise from keeping horses, or oxen, or sheep, or any other live stock; it is also necessary to be acquainted with the comparative value of these things, and which of them in particular places are worth most; for some do better in one place, some in another. Agriculture also should be understood, and the management of arable grounds and orchards; and also the care of bees, and fish, and birds, from whence any profit may arise; these are the first and most proper parts of domestic management.

With respect to gaining money by exchange, the principal method of doing this is by merchandise, which is carried on in three different ways, either by sending the commodity for sale by sea or by land, or else selling it on the place where it grows; and these differ from each other in this, that the one is more profitable, the other safer. The second method is by usury. The third by receiving wages for work done, and this either by being employed in some mean art, or else in mere bodily labor. There is also a third species of improving a fortune, that is something between this and the first; for it partly depends upon nature, partly upon exchange; the subject of which is, things that are immediately from the earth, or their produce, which, though they bear no fruit, are yet useful, such as selling of timber and the whole art of metallurgy, which includes many different species, for there are various sorts of things dug out of the earth.

These we have now mentioned in general, but to enter into particulars concerning each of them, though it might be useful to the artist, would be tiresome to dwell on. Now of all the works of art, those are the most excellent wherein chance has the least to do, and those are the meanest which deprave the body, those the most servile in which bodily strength alone is chiefly wanted, those most illiberal which require least skill; but as there are books written on these subjects by some persons, as by Chares the Panian, and Apollodorus the Lemnian, upon husbandry and planting; and by others on other matters, [1259b] let those who have occasion consult them thereon; besides, every person should collect together whatsoever he hears occasionally mentioned, by means of which many of those who aimed at making a fortune have succeeded in their intentions; for all these are useful to those who make a point of getting money, as in the contrivance of Thales the Milesian (which was certainly a gainful one, but as it was his it was attributed to his wisdom, though the method he used was a general one, and would universally succeed), when they reviled him for his poverty, as if the study of philosophy was useless: for they say that he, perceiving by his skill in astrology that there would be great plenty of olives that year, while it was yet winter, having got a little money, he gave earnest for all the oil works that were in Miletus and Chios, which he hired at a low price, there being no one to bid against him; but when the season came for making oil, many persons wanting them, he all at once let them upon what terms he pleased; and raising a large sum of money by that means, convinced them that it was easy for philosophers to be rich if they chose it, but that that was not what they aimed at; in this manner is Thales said to have shown his

wisdom. It indeed is, as we have said, generally gainful for a person to contrive to make a monopoly of anything; for which reason some cities also take this method when they want money, and monopolize their commodities.

There was a certain person in Sicily who laid out a sum of money which was deposited in his hand in buying up all the iron from the iron merchants; so that when the dealers came from the markets to purchase, there was no one had any to sell but himself; and though he put no great advance upon it, yet by laying out fifty talents he made an hundred. When Dionysius heard this he permitted him to take his money with him, but forbid him to continue any longer in Sicily, as being one who contrived means for getting money inconsistent with his affairs. This man's view and Thales's was exactly the same; both of them contrived to procure a monopoly for themselves: it is useful also for politicians to understand these things, for many states want to raise money and by such means, as well as private families, nay more so; for which reason some persons who are employed in the management of public affairs confine themselves to this province only.

CHAPTER XII

There are then three parts of domestic government, the masters, of which we have already treated, the fathers, and the husbands; now the government of the wife and children should both be that of free persons, but not the [1259b] same; for the wife should be treated as a citizen of a free state, the children should be under kingly power; for the male is by nature superior to the female, except when something happens contrary to the usual course of nature, as is the elder and perfect to the younger and imperfect. Now in the gener-

ality of free states, the governors and the governed alternately change place; for an equality without any preference is what nature chooses; however, when one governs and another is
5 governed, she endeavors that there should be a distinction between them in forms, expressions, and honors; according to what Amasis said of his laver. This then should be the established rule between the man and the wom-
10 an. The government of children should be kingly; for the power of the father over the child is founded in affection and seniority, which is a species of kingly government; for which reason Homer very properly calls Jupi-
15 ter "the father of gods and men," who was king of both these; for nature requires that a king should be of the same species with those whom he governs, though superior in some particulars, as is the case between the elder
20 and the younger, the father and the son.

CHAPTER XIII

It is evident then that in the due government
25 of a family, greater attention should be paid to the several members of it and their virtues than to the possessions or riches of it; and greater to the freemen than the slaves: but here some one may doubt whether there is any
30 other virtue in a slave than his organic services, and of higher estimation than these, as temperance, fortitude, justice, and such-like habits, or whether they possess only bodily qualities: each side of the question has its dif-
35 ficulties; for if they possess these virtues, wherein do they differ from freemen? and that they do not, since they are men, and partakers of reason, is absurd. Nearly the same inquiry may be made concerning a woman and a child,
40 whether these also have their proper virtues; whether a woman ought to be temperate, brave, and just, and whether a child is temperate or no; and indeed this inquiry ought to be

general, whether the virtues of those who, by
45 nature, either govern or are governed, are the same or different; for if it is necessary that both of them should partake of the fair and good, why is it also necessary that, without exception, the one should govern, the other
50 always be governed? for this cannot arise from their possessing these qualities in different degrees; for to govern, and to be governed, are things different in species, but more or less are not. And yet it is wonderful that one party
55 ought to have them, and the other not; for if he who is to govern should not be temperate and just, how can he govern well? or if he is to be governed, how can he be governed well? for he who is intemperate [1260a] and a cow-
60 ard will never do what he ought: it is evident then that both parties ought to be virtuous; but there is a difference between them, as there is between those who by nature command and who by nature obey, and this origi-
65 nates in the soul; for in this nature has planted the governing and submitting principle, the virtues of which we say are different, as are those of a rational and an irrational being. It is plain then that the same principle may be ex-
70 tended farther, and that there are in nature a variety of things which govern and are governed; for a freeman is governed in a different manner from a slave, a male from a female, and a man from a child: and all these have
75 parts of mind within them, but in a different manner. Thus a slave can have no power of determination, a woman but a weak one, a child an imperfect one. Thus also must it necessarily be with respect to moral virtues; all
80 must be supposed to possess them, but not in the same manner, but as is best suited to every one's employment; on which account he who is to govern ought to be perfect in moral virtue, for his business is entirely that of an archi-
85 tect, and reason is the architect; while others want only that portion of it which may be suf-

ficient for their station; from whence it is evident, that although moral virtue is common to all those we have spoken of, yet the temperance of a man and a woman are not the same,
5 nor their courage, nor their justice, though Socrates thought otherwise; for the courage of the man consists in commanding, the woman's in obeying; and the same is true in other particulars: and this will be evident to those who
10 will examine different virtues separately; for those who use general terms deceive themselves when they say, that virtue consists in a good disposition of mind, or doing what is right, or something of this sort. They do much
15 better who enumerate the different virtues as Georgias did, than those who thus define them; and as Sophocles speaks of a woman, we think of all persons, that their 'virtues should be applicable to their
20 characters, for says he,

"Silence is a woman's ornament,"

but it is not a man's; and as a child is incom-
25 plete, it is evident that his virtue is not to be referred to himself in his present situation, but to that in which he will be complete, and his preceptor. In like manner the virtue of a slave is to be referred to his master; for we laid it
30 down as a maxim, that the use of a slave was to employ him in what you wanted; so that it is clear enough that few virtues are wanted in his station, only that he may not neglect his work through idleness or fear: some person
35 may question if what I have said is true, whether virtue is not necessary for artificers in their calling, for they often through idleness neglect their work, but the difference between them is very great; for a slave is connected
40 with you for life, but the artificer not so nearly: as near therefore as the artificer approaches to the situation of a slave, just so much ought he to have of the virtues of one; for a mean

artificer is to a certain point a slave; but then a
45 slave is one of those things which are by nature what they are, but this is not true [1260b] of a shoemaker, or any other artist. It is evident then that a slave ought to be trained to those virtues which are proper for his situation
50 by his master; and not by him who has the power of a master, to teach him any particular art. Those therefore are in the wrong who would deprive slaves of reason, and say that they have only to follow their orders; for
55 slaves want more instruction than children, and thus we determine this matter.

It is necessary, I am sensible, for every one who treats upon government, to enter particu-
60 larly into the relations of husband and wife, and of parent and child, and to show what are the virtues of each and their respective connections with each other; what is right and what is wrong; and how the one ought to be
65 followed, and the other avoided. Since then every family is part of a city, and each of those individuals is part of a family, and the virtue of the parts ought to correspond to the virtue of the whole; it is necessary, that both the wives
70 and children of the community should be instructed correspondent to the nature thereof, if it is of consequence to the virtue of the state, that the wives and children therein should be virtuous, and of consequence it cer-
75 tainly is, for the wives are one half of the free persons; and of the children the succeeding citizens are to be formed. As then we have determined these points, we will leave the rest to be spoken to in another place, as if the sub-
80 ject was now finished; and beginning again anew, first consider the sentiments of those who have treated of the most perfect forms of government.

85 *(In Book II Aristotle examines the ideal common-wealths put forward by others—such as in Plato's*

115

Republic—and looks at the best existing polities… -MJ)

BOOK III
CHAPTER I

Every one who inquires into the nature of government, and what are its different forms, should make this almost his first question, What is a city? For upon this there is a dispute: for some persons say the city did this or that, while others say, not the city, but the oligarchy, or the tyranny. We see that the city is the only object which both the politician and legislator have in view in all they do: but government is a certain ordering of those who inhabit a city. As a city is a collective body, and, like other wholes, composed of many parts, it is evident our first inquiry must be, what a citizen is: for a city is a certain number of citizens. So that we must consider whom we ought to call citizen, and who is one; for this is often doubtful: for every one will not allow that this character is applicable to the same person; for that man who would be a citizen in a republic would very often not be one in an oligarchy. We do not include in this inquiry many of those who acquire this appellation out of the ordinary way, as honorary persons, for instance, but those only who have a natural right to it.

Now it is not residence which constitutes a man a citizen; for in this sojourners and slaves are upon an equality with him; nor will it be sufficient for this purpose, that you have the privilege of the laws, and may plead or be impleaded, for this all those of different nations, between whom there is a mutual agreement for that purpose, are allowed; although it very often happens, that sojourners have not a perfect right therein without the protection of a patron, to whom they are obliged to apply, which shows that their share in the community is incomplete. In like manner, with respect to boys who are not yet enrolled, or old men who are past war, we admit that they are in some respects citizens, but not completely so, but with some exceptions, for these are not yet arrived to years of maturity, and those are past service; nor is there any difference between them. But what we mean is sufficiently intelligible and clear, we want a complete citizen, one in whom there is no deficiency to be corrected to make him so. As to those who are banished, or infamous, there may be the same objections made and the same answer given. There is nothing that more characterizes a complete citizen than having a share in the judicial and executive part of the government.

With respect to offices, some are fixed to a particular time, so that no person is, on any account, permitted to fill them twice; or else not till some certain period has intervened; others are not fixed, as a juryman's, and a member of the general assembly: but probably some one may say these are not offices, nor have the citizens in these capacities any share in the government; though surely it is ridiculous to say that those who have the principal power in the state bear no office in it. But this objection is of no weight, for it is only a dispute about words; as there is no general term which can be applied both to the office of a juryman and a member of the assembly. For the sake of distinction, suppose we call it an indeterminate office: but I lay it down as a maxim, that those are citizens who could exercise it. Such then is the description of a citizen who comes nearest to what all those who are called citizens are. Every one also should know, that of the component parts of those things which differ from each other in species, after the first or second remove, those which follow have either nothing at all or very little common to each.

Now we see that governments differ from each other in their form, and that some of them are defective, others [1275b] as excellent as possible: for it is evident, that those which have many deficiencies and degeneracies in them must be far inferior to those which are without such faults. What I mean by degeneracies will be hereafter explained. Hence it is clear that the office of a citizen must differ as governments do from each other: for which reason he who is called a citizen has, in a democracy, every privilege which that station supposes. In other forms of government he may enjoy them; but not necessarily: for in some states the people have no power; nor have they any general assembly, but a few select men.

The trial also of different causes is allotted to different persons; as at Lacedaemon all disputes concerning contracts are brought before some of the ephori: the senate are the judges in cases of murder, and so on; some being to be heard by one magistrate, others by another: and thus at Carthage certain magistrates determine all causes. But our former description of a citizen will admit of correction; for in some governments the office of a juryman and a member of the general assembly is not an indeterminate one; but there are particular persons appointed for these purposes, some or all of the citizens being appointed jurymen or members of the general assembly, and this either for all causes and all public business whatsoever, or else for some particular one: and this may be sufficient to show what a citizen is; for he who has a right to a share in the judicial and executive part of government in any city, him we call a citizen of that place; and a city, in one word, is a collective body of such persons sufficient in themselves to all the purposes of life.

CHAPTER II

In common use they define a citizen to be one who is sprung from citizens on both sides, not on the father's or the mother's only. Others carry the matter still further, and inquire how many of his ancestors have been citizens, as his grandfather, great-grandfather, etc., but some persons have questioned how the first of the family could prove themselves citizens, according to this popular and careless definition. Gorgias of Leontium, partly entertaining the same doubt, and partly in jest, says, that as a mortar is made by a mortar-maker, so a citizen is made by a citizen-maker, and a Larisssean by a Larissean-maker. This is indeed a very simple account of the matter; for if citizens are so, according to this definition, it will be impossible to apply it to the first founders or first inhabitants of states, who cannot possibly claim in right either of their father or mother. It is probably a matter of still more difficulty to determine their rights as citizens who are admitted to their freedom after any revolution in the state. As, for instance, at Athens, after the expulsion of the tyrants, when Clisthenes enrolled many foreigners and city-slaves amongst the tribes; and the doubt with respect to them was, not whether they were citizens or no, but whether they were legally so or not. Though indeed some persons may have this further [1276a] doubt, whether a citizen can be a citizen when he is illegally made; as if an illegal citizen, and one who is no citizen at all, were in the same predicament: but since we see some persons govern unjustly, whom yet we admit to govern, though not justly, and the definition of a citizen is one who exercises certain offices, for such a one we have defined a citizen to be, it is evident, that a citizen illegally created yet continues to be a citizen, but whether justly or unjustly so belongs to the former inquiry.

CHAPTER III

5

It has also been doubted what was and what was not the act of the city; as, for instance, when a democracy arises out of an aristocracy or a tyranny; for some persons then refuse to
10 fulfill their contracts; as if the right to receive the money was in the tyrant and not in the state, and many other things of the same nature; as if any covenant was founded for violence and not for the common good. So in like
15 manner, if anything is done by those who have the management of public affairs where a democracy is established, their actions are to be considered as the actions of the state, as well as in the oligarchy or tyranny.

20

And here it seems very proper to consider this question, When shall we say that a city is the same, and when shall we say that it is different?

25

It is but a superficial mode of examining into this question to begin with the place and the people; for it may happen that these may be divided from that, or that some one of them
30 may live in one place, and some in another (but this question may be regarded as no very knotty one; for, as a city may acquire that appellation on many accounts, it may be solved many ways); and in like manner, when men
35 inhabit one common place, when shall we say that they inhabit the same city, or that the city is the same? for it does not depend upon the walls; for I can suppose Peloponnesus itself surrounded with a wall, as Babylon was, and
40 every other place, which rather encircles many nations than one city, and that they say was taken three days when some of the inhabitants knew nothing of it: but we shall find a proper

time to determine this question; for the extent
45 of a city, how large it should be, and whether it should consist of more than one people, these are particulars that the politician should by no means be unacquainted with. This, too, is a matter of inquiry, whether we shall say
50 that a city is the same while it is inhabited by the same race of men, though some of them are perpetually dying, others coming into the world, as we say that a river or a fountain is the same, though the waters are continually
55 changing; or when a revolution takes place shall we [1276b] say the men are the same, but the city is different: for if a city is a community, it is a community of citizens; but if the mode of government should alter, and be-
60 come of another sort, it would seem a necessary consequence that the city is not the same; as we regard the tragic chorus as different from the comic, though it may probably consist of the same performers: thus every other
65 community or composition is said to be different if the species of composition is different; as in music the same hands produce different harmony, as the Doric and Phrygian. If this is true, it is evident, that when we speak of
70 a city as being the same we refer to the government there established; and this, whether it is called by the same name or any other, or inhabited by the same men or different. But whether or not it is right to dissolve the com-
75 munity when the constitution is altered is another question.

CHAPTER IV

80 What has been said, it follows that we should consider whether the same virtues which constitute a good man make a valuable citizen, or different; and if a particular inquiry is necessary for this matter we must first give a general
85 description of the virtues of a good citizen; for as a sailor is one of those who make up a

118

community, so is a citizen, although the province of one sailor may be different from another's (for one is a rower, another a steersman, a third a boatswain, and so on, each having their several appointments), it is evident that the most accurate description of any one good sailor must refer to his peculiar abilities, yet there are some things in which the same description may be applied to the whole crew, as the safety of the ship is the common business of all of them, for this is the general center of all their cares: so also with respect to citizens, although they may in a few particulars be very different, yet there is one care common to them all, the safety of the community, for the community of the citizens composes the state; for which reason the virtue of a citizen has necessarily a reference to the state. But if there are different sorts of governments, it is evident that those actions which constitute the virtue of an excellent citizen in one community will not constitute it in another; wherefore the virtue of such a one cannot be perfect: but we say, a man is good when his virtues are perfect; from whence it follows, that an excellent citizen does not possess that virtue which constitutes a good man.

Those who are any ways doubtful concerning this question may be convinced of the truth of it by examining into the best formed states: for, if it is impossible that a city should consist entirely of excellent citizens (while it is necessary that every one should do well in his calling, in which consists his excellence, as it is impossible that all the citizens should have the same [1277a] qualifications) it is impossible that the virtue of a citizen and a good man should be the same; for all should possess the virtue of an excellent citizen: for from hence necessarily arise the perfection of the city: but that every one should possess the virtue of a good man is impossible without all the citizens

in a well-regulated state were necessarily virtuous.

Besides, as a city is composed of dissimilar parts, as an animal is of life and body; the soul of reason and appetite; a family of a man and his wife--property of a master and a slave; in the same manner, as a city is composed of all these and many other very different parts, it necessarily follows that the virtue of all the citizens cannot be the same; as the business of him who leads the band is different from the other dancers. From all which proofs it is evident that the virtues of a citizen cannot be one and the same.

But do we never find those virtues united which constitute a good man and excellent citizen? for we say, such a one is an excellent magistrate and a prudent and good man; but prudence is a necessary qualification for all those who engage in public affairs. Nay, some persons affirm that the education of those who are intended to command should, from the beginning, be different from other citizens, as the children of kings are generally instructed in riding and warlike exercises; and thus Euripides says:

"... No showy arts Be mine, but teach me what the state requires."

As if those who are to rule were to have an education peculiar to themselves. But if we allow, that the virtues of a good man and a good magistrate may be the same, and a citizen is one who obeys the magistrate, it follows that the virtue of the one cannot in general be the same as the virtue of the other, although it may be true of some particular citizen; for the virtue of the magistrate must be different from the virtue of the citizen. For which reason Jason declared that was he deprived of his kingdom he should pine away with regret, as not knowing how to live a private man. But it is a great recommendation to know how to command as well as to obey; and to do both

5 these things well is the virtue of an accomplished citizen. If then the virtue of a good man consists only in being able to command, but the virtue of a good citizen renders him equally fit for the one as well as the other, the

10 commendation of both of them is not the same. It appears, then, that both he who commands and he who obeys should each of them learn their separate business: but that the citizen should be master of and take part in

15 both these, as any one may easily perceive; in a family government there is no occasion for the master to know how to perform the necessary offices, but rather to enjoy the labor of others; for to do the other is a servile part. I mean by

20 the other, the common family business of the slave.

There are many sorts of slaves; for their employments are various: of these the handi-

25 craftsmen are one, who, as their name imports, get their living by the labor of their hands, and amongst these all mechanics are included; [1277b] for which reasons such workmen, in some states, were not formerly

30 admitted into any share in the government; till at length democracies were established: it is not therefore proper for any man of honor, or any citizen, or any one who engages in public affairs, to learn these servile employments

35 without they have occasion for them for their own use; for without this was observed the distinction between a master and a slave would be lost.

40 But there is a government of another sort, in which men govern those who are their equals in rank, and freemen, which we call a political government, in which men learn to command

by first submitting to obey, as a good general

45 of horse, or a commander-in-chief, must acquire a knowledge of their duty by having been long under the command of another, and the like in every appointment in the army: for well is it said, no one knows how to command

50 who has not himself been under command of another. The virtues of those are indeed different, but a good citizen must necessarily be endowed with them; he ought also to know in what manner freemen ought to govern, as well

55 as be governed: and this, too, is the duty of a good man. And if the temperance and justice of him who commands is different from his who, though a freeman, is under command, it is evident that the virtues of a good citizen

60 cannot be the same as justice, for instance but must be of a different species in these two different situations, as the temperance and courage of a man and a woman are different from each other; for a man would appear a

65 coward who had only that courage which would be graceful in a woman, and a woman would be thought a talker who should take as large a part in the conversation as would become a man of consequence.

70

The domestic employments of each of them are also different; it is the man's business to acquire subsistence, the woman's to take care of it. But direction and knowledge of public

75 affairs is a virtue peculiar to those who govern, while all others seem to be equally requisite for both parties; but with this the governed have no concern, it is theirs to entertain just notions: they indeed are like flute-makers,

80 while those who govern are the musicians who play on them. And thus much to show whether the virtue of a good man and an excellent citizen is the same, or if it is different, and also how far it is the same, and how far different.

85

CHAPTER V

But with respect to citizens there is a doubt
remaining, whether those only are truly so
5 who are allowed to share in the government,
or whether the mechanics also are to be considered as such? for if those who are not permitted to rule are to be reckoned among them,
it is impossible that the virtue of all the citi-
10 zens should be the same, for these also are
citizens; and if none of them are admitted to
be citizens, where shall they be ranked? for
they are neither [1278a] sojourners nor foreigners? or shall we say that there will no in-
15 convenience arise from their not being citizens, as they are neither slaves nor freedmen:
for this is certainly true, that all those are not
citizens who are necessary to the existence of
a city, as boys are not citizens in the same
20 manner that men are, for those are perfectly
so, the others under some conditions; for they
are citizens, though imperfect ones: for in
former times among some people the mechanics were either slaves or foreigners, for which
25 reason many of them are so now: and indeed
the best regulated states will not permit a mechanic to be a citizen; but if it be allowed
them, we cannot then attribute the virtue we
have described to every citizen or freeman,
30 but to those only who are disengaged from
servile offices. Now those who are employed
by one person in them are slaves; those who
do them for money are mechanics and hired
servants: hence it is evident on the least reflec-
35 tion what is their situation, for what I have
said is fully explained by appearances. Since
the number of communities is very great, it
follows necessarily that there will be many
different sorts of citizens, particularly of those
40 who are governed by others, so that in one
state it may be necessary to admit mechanics
and hired servants to be citizens, but in others
it may be impossible; as particularly in an aris-

tocracy, where honors are bestowed on virtue
45 and dignity: for it is impossible for one who
lives the life of a mechanic or hired servant to
acquire the practice of virtue. In an oligarchy
also hired servants are not admitted to be citizens; because there a man's right to bear any
50 office is regulated by his fortune; but mechanics are, for many citizens are very rich.

There was a law at Thebes that no one could
have a share in the government till he had
55 been ten years out of trade. In many states the
law invites strangers to accept the freedom of
the city; and in some democracies the son of a
free-woman is himself free. The same is also
observed in many others with respect to natu-
60 ral children; but it is through want of citizens
regularly born that they admit such: for these
laws are always made in consequence of a
scarcity of inhabitants; so, as their numbers
increase, they first deprive the children of a
65 male or female slave of this privilege, next the
child of a free-woman, and last of all they will
admit none but those whose fathers and
mothers were both free.

70 That there are many sorts of citizens, and that
he may be said to be as completely who shares
the honors of the state, is evident from what
has been already said. Thus Achilles, in
Homer, complains of Agamemnon's treating
75 him like an unhonored stranger; for a stranger
or sojourner is one who does not partake of
the honors of the state: and whenever the
right to the freedom of the city is kept obscure, it is for the sake of the inhabitants.
80 [1278b] From what has been said it is plain
whether the virtue of a good man and an excellent citizen is the same or different: and we
find that in some states it is the same, in others not; and also that this is not true of each
85 citizen, but of those only who take the lead, or
are capable of taking the lead, in public affairs,

either alone or in conjunction with others.

CHAPTER VI

5 Having established these points, we proceed next to consider whether one form of government only should be established, or more than one; and if more, how many, and of what sort, and what are the differences between

10 them. The form of government is the ordering and regulating of the city, and all the offices in it, particularly those wherein the supreme power is lodged; and this power is always possessed by the administration; but the admin-

15 istration itself is that particular form of government which is established in any state: thus in a democracy the supreme power is lodged in the whole people; on the contrary, in an oligarchy it is in the hands of a few. We say

20 then, that the form of government in these states is different, and we shall find the same thing hold good in others. Let us first determine for whose sake a city is established; and point out the different species of rule which

25 man may submit to in social life.

I have already mentioned in my treatise on the management of a family, and the power of the master, that man is an animal naturally formed

30 for society, and that therefore, when he does not want any foreign assistance, he will of his own accord desire to live with others; not but that mutual advantage induces them to it, as far as it enables each person to live more

35 agreeably; and this is indeed the great object not only to all in general, but also to each individual: but it is not merely matter of choice, but they join in society also, even that they may be able to live, which probably is not

40 without some share of merit, and they also support civil society, even for the sake of preserving life, without they are grievously overwhelmed with the miseries of it: for it is very

45 evident that men will endure many calamities for the sake of living, as being something naturally sweet and desirable.

It is easy to point out the different modes of government, and we have already settled them

50 in our exoteric discourses. The power of the master, though by nature equally serviceable, both to the master and to the slave, yet nevertheless has for its object the benefit of the master, while the benefit of the slave arises

55 accidentally; for if the slave is destroyed, the power of the master is at an end: but the authority which a man has over his wife, and children, and his family, which we call domestic government, is either for the benefit of

60 those who are under subjection, or else for the common benefit of the whole: but its particular object is the benefit of the governed, as we see in other arts; in physic, for instance, and the gymnastic exercises, wherein, if any benefit

65 [1279a] arise to the master, it is accidental; for nothing forbids the master of the exercises from sometimes being himself one of those who exercises, as the steersman is always one of the sailors; but both the master of the exer-

70 cises and the steersman consider the good of those who are under their government. Whatever good may happen to the steersman when he is a sailor, or to the master of the exercises when he himself makes one at the games, is

75 not intentional, or the object of their power; thus in all political governments which are established to preserve and defend the equality of the citizens it is held right to rule by turns. Formerly, as was natural, every one expected

80 that each of his fellow-citizens should in his turn serve the public, and thus administer to his private good, as he himself when in office had done for others; but now every one is desirous of being continually in power, that he

85 may enjoy the advantage which he makes of public business and being in office; as if places

were a never-failing remedy for every complaint, and were on that account so eagerly sought after.

5 It is evident, then, that all those governments which have a common good in view are rightly established and strictly just, but those who have in view only the good of the rulers are all founded on wrong principles, and are widely 10 different from what a government ought to be, for they are tyranny over slaves, whereas a city is a community of freemen.

CHAPTER VII

15

Having established these particulars, we come to consider next the different number of governments which there are, and what they are; and first, what are their excellences: for when 20 we have determined this, their defects will be evident enough.

It is evident that every form of government or administration, for the words are of the same 25 import, must contain a supreme power over the whole state, and this supreme power must necessarily be in the hands of one person, or a few, or many; and when either of these apply their power for the common good, such states 30 are well governed; but when the interest of the one, the few, or the many who enjoy this power is alone consulted, then ill; for you must either affirm that those who make up the community are not citizens, or else let these 35 share in the advantages of government. We usually call a state which is governed by one person for the common good, a kingdom; one that is governed by more than one, but by a few only, an aristocracy; either because the 40 government is in the hands of the most worthy citizens, or because it is the best form for the city and its inhabitants. When the citizens at large govern for the public good, it is called

a state; which is also a common name for all 45 other governments, and these distinctions are consonant to reason; for it will not be difficult to find one person, or a very few, of very distinguished abilities, but almost impossible to meet with the majority [1279b] of a people 50 eminent for every virtue; but if there is one common to a whole nation it is valor; for this is created and supported by numbers: for which reason in such a state the profession of arms will always have the greatest share in the 55 government.

Now the corruptions attending each of these governments are these; a kingdom may degenerate into a tyranny, an aristocracy into an oli- 60 garchy, and a state into a democracy. Now a tyranny is a monarchy where the good of one man only is the object of government, an oligarchy considers only the rich, and a democracy only the poor; but neither of them have a 65 common good in view.

CHAPTER VIII

It will be necessary to enlarge a little more 70 upon the nature of each of these states, which is not without some difficulty, for he who would enter into a philosophical inquiry into the principles of them, and not content himself with a superficial view of their outward 75 conduct, must pass over and omit nothing, but explain the true spirit of each of them.

A tyranny then is, as has been said, a monarchy, where one person has an absolute and 80 despotic power over the whole community and every member therein: an oligarchy, where the supreme power of the state is lodged with the rich: a democracy, on the contrary, is where those have it who are worth little or 85 nothing. But the first difficulty that arises from the distinctions which we have laid down is this, should it happen that the majority of the inhabitants who possess the power of the state (for this is a democracy) should be rich, the question is, how does this agree with what we have said? The same difficulty occurs, should it ever happen that the poor compose a smaller part of the people than the rich, but from their superior abilities acquire the supreme power; for this is what they call an oligarchy; it should seem then that our definition of the different states was not correct: nay, moreover, could any one suppose that the majority of the people were poor, and the minority rich, and then describe the state in this manner, that an oligarchy was a government in which the rich, being few in number, possessed the supreme power, and that a democracy was a state in which the poor, being many in number, possessed it, still there will be another difficulty; for what name shall we give to those states we have been describing? I mean, that in which the greater number are rich, and that in which the lesser number are poor (where each of these possess the supreme power), if there are no other states than those we have described.

It seems therefore evident to reason, that whether the supreme power is vested in the hands of many or few may be a matter of accident; but that it is clear enough, that when it is in the hands of the few, it will be a government of the rich; when in the hands of the many, it will be a government of the poor; since in all countries there are many poor and few rich: it is not therefore the cause that has been already assigned (namely, the number of people in power) that makes the difference between the two governments; but an oligarchy and democracy differ in this from each other, in the poverty of those who govern in the one, and the riches 1280a of those who govern in the other; for when the government

is in the hands of the rich, be they few or be they more, it is an oligarchy; when it is in the hands of the poor, it is a democracy: but, as we have already said, the one will be always few, the other numerous, but both will enjoy liberty; and from the claims of wealth and liberty will arise continual disputes with each other for the lead in public affairs.

CHAPTER IX

Let us first determine what are the proper limits of an oligarchy and a democracy, and what is just in each of these states; for all men have some natural inclination to justice; but they proceed therein only to a certain degree; nor can they universally point out what is absolutely just; as, for instance, what is equal appears just, and is so; but not to all; only among those who are equals: and what is unequal appears just, and is so; but not to all, only amongst those who are unequals; which circumstance some people neglect, and therefore judge ill; the reason for which is, they judge for themselves, and every one almost is the worst judge in his own cause. Since then justice has reference to persons, the same distinctions must be made with respect to persons which are made with respect to things, in the manner that I have already described in my Ethics.

As to the equality of the things, these they agree in; but their dispute is concerning the equality of the persons, and chiefly for the reason above assigned; because they judge ill in their own cause; and also because each party thinks, that if they admit what is right in some particulars, they have done justice on the whole: thus, for instance, if some persons are unequal in riches, they suppose them unequal in the whole; or, on the contrary, if they are equal in liberty, they suppose them equal in the whole: but what is absolutely just they omit; for if civil society was founded for the sake of preserving and increasing property, every one's right in the city would be equal to

5 his fortune; and then the reasoning of those who insist upon an oligarchy would be valid; for it would not be right that he who contributed one mina should have an equal share in the hundred along with him who brought in

10 all the rest, either of the original money or what was afterwards acquired.

Nor was civil society founded merely to preserve the lives of its members; but that they

15 might live well: for otherwise a state might be composed of slaves, or the animal creation: but this is not so; for these have no share in the happiness of it; nor do they live after their own choice; nor is it an alliance mutually to

20 defend each other from injuries, or for a commercial intercourse: for then the Tyrrhenians and Carthaginians, and all other nations between whom treaties of commerce subsist, would be citizens of one city; for they have

25 articles to regulate their exports and imports, and engagements for mutual protection, and alliances for mutual defense; but [1280b] yet they have not all the same magistrates established among them, but they are different

30 among the different people; nor does the one take any care, that the morals of the other should be as they ought, or that none of those who have entered into the common agreements should be unjust, or in any degree vi-

35 cious, only that they do not injure any member of the confederacy. But whosoever endeavors to establish wholesome laws in a state, attends to the virtues and the vices of each individual who composes it; from whence it is evident,

40 that the first care of him who would found a city, truly deserving that name, and not nominally so, must be to have his citizens virtuous; for otherwise it is merely an alliance for self-

defense; differing from those of the same cast

45 which are made between different people only in place: for law is an agreement and a pledge, as the sophist Lycophron says, between the citizens of their intending to do justice to each other, though not sufficient to make all the

50 citizens just and good.

And that this is fact is evident, for could any one bring different places together, as, for instance, enclose Megara and Corinth in a

55 wall, yet they would not be one city, not even if the inhabitants intermarried with each other, though this inter-community contributes much to make a place one city. Besides, could we suppose a set of people to live separate

60 from each other, but within such a distance as would admit of an intercourse, and that there were laws subsisting between each party, to prevent their injuring one another in their mutual dealings, supposing one a carpenter, an-

65 other a husbandman, shoemaker, and the like, and that their numbers were ten thousand, still all that they would have together in common would be a tariff for trade, or an alliance for mutual defense, but not the same city. And

70 why? not because their mutual intercourse is not near enough, for even if persons so situated should come to one place, and every one should live in his own house as in his native city, and there should be alliances subsisting

75 between each party to mutually assist and prevent any injury being done to the other, still they would not be admitted to be a city by those who think correctly, if they preserved the same customs when they were together as

80 when they were separate.

It is evident, then, that a city is not a community of place; nor established for the sake of mutual safety or traffic with each other; but

85 that these things are the necessary consequences of a city, although they may all exist

125

where there is no city: but a city is a society of people joining together with their families and their children to live agreeably for the sake of having their lives as happy and as independent as possible: and for this purpose it is necessary that they should live in one place and inter-marry with each other: hence in all cities there are family-meetings, clubs, sacrifices, and pub-lic entertainments to promote friendship; for a love of sociability is friendship itself; so that the end then for which a city is established is, that the inhabitants of it may live happy, and these things are conducive to that end: for it is a community of families and villages for the sake of a perfect independent life; that is, as we have already said, for the sake of living well and happily. It is not therefore founded for the purpose of men's merely [1281a] living together, but for their living as men ought; for which reason those who contribute most to this end deserve to have greater power in the city than those who are their equals in family and freedom, but their inferiors in civil virtue, or those who excel them in wealth but are below them in worth. It is evident from what has been said, that in all disputes upon gov-ernment each party says something that is just.

CHAPTER X

It may also be a doubt where the supreme power ought to be lodged. Shall it be with the majority, or the wealthy, with a number of proper persons, or one better than the rest, or with a tyrant? But whichever of these we pre-fer some difficulty will arise. For what? shall the poor have it because they are the majority? they may then divide among themselves, what belongs to the rich: nor is this unjust; because truly it has been so judged by the supreme power. But what avails it to point out what is the height of injustice if this is not? Again, if the many seize into their own hands every-

thing which belongs to the few, it is evident that the city will be at an end. But virtue will never destroy what is virtuous; nor can what is right be the ruin of the state: therefore such a law can never be right, nor can the acts of a tyrant ever be wrong, for of necessity they must all be just; for he, from his unlimited power, compels every one to obey his com-mand, as the multitude oppress the rich. Is it right then that the rich, the few, should have the supreme power? and what if they be guilty of the same rapine and plunder the posses-sions of the majority, that will be as right as the other: but that all things of this sort are wrong and unjust is evident.

Well then, these of the better sort shall have it: but must not then all the other citizens live unhonored, without sharing the offices of the city; for the offices of a city are its honors, and if one set of men are always in power, it is evident that the rest must be without honor. Well then, let it be with one person of all oth-ers the fittest for it: but by this means the power will be still more contracted, and a greater number than before continue unhon-ored. But some one may say, that it is wrong to let man have the supreme power and not the law, as his soul is subject to so many pas-sions. But if this law appoints an aristocracy, or a democracy, how will it help us in our pre-sent doubts? for those things will happen which we have already mentioned.

CHAPTER XI

Other particulars we will consider separately; but it seems proper to prove, that the supreme power ought to be lodged with the many, ra-ther than with those of the better sort, who are few; and also to explain what doubts (and probably just ones) may arise: now, though not one individual of the many may himself be

fit for the supreme power, yet when these many are joined together, it does not follow but they may be better qualified for it than those; and this not separately, but as a collec-
5 tive body; as the public suppers exceed those which are given at one person's private ex-pense: for, as they are many, each person brings in his share of virtue and wisdom; and thus, coming together, they are like one man
10 made up of a multitude, with many feet, many hands, and many intelligences: thus is it with respect to the manners and understandings of the multitude taken together; for which reason the public are the best judges of music and
15 poetry; for some understand one part, some another, and all collectively the whole; and in this particular men of consequence differ from each of the many; as they say those who are beautiful do from those who are not so, and as
20 fine pictures excel any natural objects, by col-lecting the several beautiful parts which were dispersed among different originals into one, although the separate parts, as the eye or any other, might be handsomer than in the picture.
25

But if this distinction is to be made between every people and every general assembly, and some few men of consequence, it may be doubtful whether it is true; nay, it is clear
30 enough that, with respect to a few, it is not; since the same conclusion might be applied even to brutes: and indeed wherein do some men differ from brutes? Not but that nothing prevents what I have said being true of the
35 people in some states. The doubt then which we have lately proposed, with all its conse-quences, may be settled in this manner; it is necessary that the freemen who compose the bulk of the people should have absolute pow-
40 er in some things; but as they are neither men of property, nor act uniformly upon principles of virtue, it is not safe to trust them with the first offices in the state, both on account of

their iniquity and their ignorance; from the
45 one of which they will do what is wrong, from the other they will mistake: and yet it is dan-gerous to allow them no power or share in the government; for when there are many poor people who are incapable of acquiring the
50 honors of their country, the state must neces-sarily have many enemies in it; let them then be permitted to vote in the public assemblies and to determine causes; for which reason Socrates, and some other legislators, gave
55 them the power of electing the officers of the state, and also of inquiring into their conduct when they came out of office, and only pre-vented their being magistrates by themselves; for the multitude when they are collected to-
60 gether have all of them sufficient understand-ing for these purposes, and, mixing among those of higher rank, are serviceable to the city, as some things, which alone are improper for food, when mixed with others make the
65 whole more wholesome than a few of them would be.

But there is a difficulty attending this form of government, for it seems, that the person who
70 himself was capable of curing any one who was then sick, must be the best judge whom to employ as a physician; but such a one must be himself a physician; and the same holds true in every other practice and art: and as a physician
75 ought [1282a] to give an account of his prac-tice to a physician, so ought it to be in other arts: those whose business is physic may be divided into three sorts, the first of these is he who makes up the medicines; the second pre-
80 scribes, and is to the other as the architect is to the mason; the third is he who understands the science, but never practices it: now these three distinctions may be found in those who understand all other arts; nor have we less
85 opinion of their judgment who are only in-structed in the principles of the art than of

127

those who practice it: and with respect to elections the same method of proceeding seems right; for to elect a proper person in any science is the business of those who are skillful

5 therein; as in geometry, of geometricians; in steering, of steersmen: but if some individuals should know something of particular arts and works, they do not know more than the professors of them: so that even upon this princi-

10 ple neither the election of magistrates, nor the censure of their conduct, should be entrusted to the many.

But probably all that has been here said may

15 not be right; for, to resume the argument I lately used, if the people are not very brutal indeed, although we allow that each individual knows less of these affairs than those who have given particular attention to them, yet

20 when they come together they will know them better, or at least not worse; besides, in some particular arts it is not the workman only who is the best judge; namely, in those the works of which are understood by those who do not

25 profess them: thus he who builds a house is not the only judge of it, for the master of the family who inhabits it is a better; thus also a steersman is a better judge of a tiller than he who made it; and he who gives an entertain-

30 ment than the cook. What has been said seems a sufficient solution of this difficulty; but there is another that follows: for it seems absurd that the power of the state should be lodged with those who are but of indifferent morals,

35 instead of those who are of excellent characters. Now the power of election and censure are of the utmost consequence, and this, as has been said, in some states they entrust to the people; for the general assembly is the

40 supreme court of all, and they have a voice in this, and deliberate in all public affairs, and try all causes, without any objection to the meanness of their circumstances, and at any age:

45 but their treasurers, generals, and other great officers of state are taken from men of great fortune and worth. This difficulty also may be solved upon the same principle; and here too they may be right, for the power is not in the man who is member of the assembly, or coun-

50 cil, but the assembly itself, and the council, and the people, of which each individual of the whole community are the parts, I mean as senator, adviser, or judge; for which reason it is very right, that the many should have the

55 greatest powers in their own hands; for the people, the council, and the judges are composed of them, and the property of all these collectively is more than the property of any person or a few who fill the great offices of

60 the state: and thus I determine these points.

The first question that we stated shows plainly, that the supreme power should be lodged in laws duly made and that the magistrate or

65 magistrates, either one or more, should be authorized to determine those cases which the laws cannot particularly speak to, as it is impossible for them, in general language, to explain themselves upon everything that may

70 arise: but what these laws are which are established upon the best foundations has not been yet explained, but still remains a matter of some question: but the laws of every state will necessarily be like every state, either trifling or

75 excellent, just or unjust; for it is evident, that the laws must be framed correspondent to the constitution of the government; and, if so, it is plain, that a well-formed government will have good laws, a bad one, bad ones.

80

CHAPTER XII

Since in every art and science the end aimed at is always good, so particularly in this, which is

85 the most excellent of all, the founding of civil society, the good wherein aimed at is justice;

for it is this which is for the benefit of all. Now, it is the common opinion, that justice is a certain equality; and in this point all the philosophers are agreed when they treat of mor-
5 als: for they say what is just, and to whom; and that equals ought to receive equal: but we should know how we are to determine what things are equal and what unequal; and in this there is some difficulty, which calls for the
10 philosophy of the politician. Some persons will probably say, that the employments of the state ought to be given according to every particular excellence of each citizen, if there is no other difference between them and the rest
15 of the community, but they are in every respect else alike: for justice attributes different things to persons differing from each other in their character, according to their respective merits. But if this is admitted to be true, com-
20 plexion, or height, or any such advantage will be a claim for a greater share of the public rights. But that this is evidently absurd is clear from other arts and sciences; for with respect to musicians who play on the flute together,
25 the best flute is not given to him who is of the best family, for he will play never the better for that, but the best instrument ought to be given to him who is the best artist.

30 If what is now said does not make this clear, we will explain it still further: if there should be any one, a very excellent player on the flute, but very deficient in family and beauty, though each of them are more valuable endowments
35 than a skill in music, and excel this art in a higher degree than that player excels others, yet the best flutes ought to be given to him; for the superiority [1283a] in beauty and fortune should have a reference to the business in
40 hand; but these have none. Moreover, according to this reasoning, every possible excellence might come in comparison with every other; for if bodily strength might dispute the point

45 with riches or liberty, even any bodily strength might do it; so that if one person excelled in size more than another did in virtue, and his size was to qualify him to take place of the other's virtue, everything must then admit of a
50 comparison with each other; for if such a size is greater than virtue by so much, it is evident another must be equal to it: but, since this is impossible, it is plain that it would be contrary to common sense to dispute a right to any office in the state from every superiority what-
55 soever: for if one person is slow and the other swift, neither is the one better qualified nor the other worse on that account, though in the gymnastic races a difference in these particulars would gain the prize; but a pretension to
60 the offices of the state should be founded on a superiority in those qualifications which are useful to it: for which reason those of family, independency, and fortune, with great propriety, contend with each other for them; for these
65 are the fit persons to fill them: for a city can no more consist of all poor men than it can of all slaves But if such persons are requisite, it is evident that those also who are just and valiant are equally so; for without justice and valor no
70 state can be supported, the former being necessary for its existence, the latter for its happiness.

CHAPTER XIII
75

It seems, then, requisite for the establishment of a state, that all, or at least many of these particulars should be well canvassed and inquired into; and that virtue and education may
80 most justly claim the right of being considered as the necessary means of making the citizens happy, as we have already said. As those who are equal in one particular are not therefore equal in all, and those who are unequal in one
85 particular are not therefore unequal in all, it follows that all those governments which are

established upon a principle which supposes they are, are erroneous.

We have already said, that all the members of the community will dispute with each other for the offices of the state; and in some particulars justly, but not so in general; the rich, for instance, because they have the greatest landed property, and the ultimate right to the soil is vested in the community; and also because their fidelity is in general most to be depended on. The freemen and men of family will dispute the point with each other, as nearly on an equality; for these latter have a right to a higher regard as citizens than obscure persons, for honorable descent is everywhere of great esteem: nor is it an improper conclusion, that the descendants of men of worth will be men of worth themselves; for noble birth is the fountain of virtue to men of family: for the same reason also we justly say, that virtue has a right to put in her pretensions. Justice, for instance, is a virtue, and so necessary to society, that all others must yield her the precedence.

Let us now see what the many have to urge on their side against the few; and they may say, that if, when collectively taken, they are compared with them, they are stronger, richer, and better than they are. But should it ever happen that all these should inhabit the [1283b] same city, I mean the good, the rich, the noble, as well as the many, such as usually make up the community, I ask, will there then be any reason to dispute concerning who shall govern, or will there not? for in every community which we have mentioned there is no dispute where the supreme power should be placed; for as these differ from each other, so do those in whom that is placed; for in one state the rich enjoy it, in others the meritorious, and thus each according to their separate manners.

Let us however consider what is to be done when all these happen at the same time to inhabit the same city. If the virtuous should be very few in number, how then shall we act? shall we prefer the virtuous on account of their abilities, if they are capable of governing the city? or should they be so many as almost entirely to compose the state?

There is also a doubt concerning the pretensions of all those who claim the honors of government: for those who found them either on fortune or family have nothing which they can justly say in their defense; since it is evident upon their principle, that if any one person can be found richer than all the rest, the right of governing all these will be justly vested in this one person. In the same manner, one man who is of the best family will claim it from those who dispute the point upon family merit: and probably in an aristocracy the same dispute might arise on the score of virtue, if there is one man better than all the other men of worth who are in the same community; it seems just, by the same reasoning, that he should enjoy the supreme power. And upon this principle also, while the many suppose they ought to have the supreme command, as being more powerful than the few, if one or more than one, though a small number should be found stronger than themselves, these ought rather to have it than they.

All these things seem to make it plain, that none of these principles are justly founded on which these persons would establish their right to the supreme power; and that all men whatsoever ought to obey them: for with respect to those who claim it as due to their virtue or their fortune, they might have justly some objection to make; for nothing hinders but that it may sometimes happen, that the many may be better or richer than the few, not as individuals, but in their collective capacity.

As to the doubt which some persons have
proposed and objected, we may answer it in
5 this manner; it is this, whether a legislator,
who would establish the most perfect system
of laws, should calculate them for the use of
the better part of the citizens, or the many, in
the circumstances we have already mentioned?
10 The rectitude of anything consists in its equality; that therefore which is equally right will be
advantageous to the whole state, and to every
member of it in common.

15 Now, in general, a citizen is one who both
shares in the government and also in his turn
submits to be governed; [1284a] their condition, it is true, is different in different states:
the best is that in which a man is enabled to
20 choose and to persevere in a course of virtue
during his whole life, both in his public and
private state. But should there be one person,
or a very few, eminent for an uncommon degree of virtue, though not enough to make up
25 a civil state, so that the virtue of the many, or
their political abilities, should be too inferior
to come in comparison with theirs, if more
than one; or if but one, with his only; such are
not to be considered as part of the city; for it
30 would be doing them injustice to rate them on
a level with those who are so far their inferiors
in virtue and political abilities, that they appear
to them like a god amongst men. From
whence it is evident, that a system of laws
35 must be calculated for those who are equal to
each other in nature and power. Such men,
therefore, are not the object of law; for they
are themselves a law: and it would be ridiculous in any one to endeavor to include them in
40 the penalties of a law: for probably they might
say what Antisthenes tells us the lions did to
the hares when they demanded to be admitted
to an equal share with them in the government. And it is on this account that democrat-
45 ic states have established the ostracism; for an
equality seems the principal object of their
government. For which reason they compel all
those who are very eminent for their power,
their fortune, their friendships, or any other
50 cause which may give them too great weight in
the government, to submit to the ostracism,
and leave the city for a stated time; as the fabulous histories relate the Argonauts served
Hercules, for they refused to take him with
55 them in the ship Argo on account of his superior valor. For which reason those who hate a
tyranny and find fault with the advice which
Periander gave to Thrasybulus, must not think
there was nothing to be said in its defense; for
60 the story goes, that Periander said nothing to
the messenger in answer to the business he
was consulted about, but striking off those
ears of corn which were higher than the rest,
reduced the whole crop to a level; so that the
65 messenger, without knowing the cause of what
was done, related the fact to Thrasybulus, who
understood by it that he must take off all the
principal men in the city. Nor is this serviceas-
ble to tyrants only; nor is it tyrants only who
70 do it; for the same thing is practiced both in
oligarchies and democracies: for the ostracism
has in a manner nearly the same power, by
restraining and banishing those who are too
great; and what is done in one city is done also
75 by those who have the supreme power in separate states; as the Athenians with respect to
the Samians, the Chians, and the Lesbians; for
when they suddenly acquired the superiority
over all Greece, they brought the other states
80 into subjection, contrary to the treaties which
subsisted between them. The King of Persia
also very often reduces the Medes and Baby-
lonians when they assume upon their former
power: [1284b] and this is a principle which all
85 governments whatsoever keep in their eye;
even those which are best administered, as

well as those which are not, do it; these for the sake of private utility, the others for the public good.

5 The same thing is to be perceived in the other arts and sciences; for a painter would not represent an animal with a foot disproportionally large, though he had drawn it remarkably beautiful; nor would the shipwright make the
10 prow or any other part of the vessel larger than it ought to be; nor will the master of the band permit any who sings louder and better than the rest to sing in concert with them. There is therefore no reason that a monarch
15 should not act in agreement with free states, to support his own power, if they do the same thing for the benefit of their respective communities; upon which account when there is any acknowledged difference in the power of
20 the citizens, the reason upon which the ostracism is founded will be politically just; but it is better for the legislator so to establish his state at the beginning as not to want this remedy: but if in course of time such an inconvenience
25 should arise, to endeavor to amend it by some such correction. Not that this was the use it was put to: for many did not regard the benefit of their respective communities, but made the ostracism a weapon in the hand of sedi-
30 tion.

It is evident, then, that in corrupt governments it is partly just and useful to the individual, though probably it is as clear that it is
35 not entirely just: for in a well-governed state there may be great doubts about the use of it, not on account of the pre-eminence which one may have in strength, riches, or connection: but when the pre-eminence is virtue,
40 what then is to be done? for it seems not right to turn out and banish such a one; neither does it seem right to govern him, for that would be like desiring to share the power with

Jupiter and to govern him: nothing then re-
45 mains but what indeed seems natural, and that is for all persons quietly to submit to the government of those who are thus eminently virtuous, and let them be perpetually kings in the separate states.
50

CHAPTER XIV

What has been now said, it seems proper to change our subject and to inquire into the
55 nature of monarchies; for we have already admitted them to be one of those species of government which are properly founded. And here let us consider whether a kingly government is proper for a city or a country whose
60 principal object is the happiness of the inhabitants, or rather some other. But let us first determine whether this is of one kind only, or more; [1285a] and it is easy to know that it consists of many different species, and that
65 the forms of government are not the same in all: for at Sparta the kingly power seems chiefly regulated by the laws; for it is not supreme in all circumstances; but when the king quits the territories of the state he is their general in
70 war; and all religious affairs are entrusted to him: indeed the kingly power with them is chiefly that of a general who cannot be called to an account for his conduct, and whose command is for life: for he has not the power
75 of life and death, except as a general; as they frequently had in their expeditions by martial law, which we learn from Homer; for when Agamemnon is affronted in council, he restrains his resentment, but when he is in the
80 field and armed with this power, he tells the Greeks:

"Whoe'er I know shall shun th' impending fight,
85 To dogs and vultures soon shall be a prey; For death is mine...."

This, then, is one species of monarchical government in which the kingly power is in a general for life; and is sometimes hereditary, sometimes elective: besides, there is also another, which is to be met with among some of the barbarians, in which the kings are invested with powers nearly equal to a tyranny, yet are, in some respects, bound by the laws and the customs of their country; for as the barbarians are by nature more prone to slavery than the Greeks, and those in Asia more than those in Europe, they endure without murmuring a despotic government; for this reason their governments are tyrannies; but yet not liable to be overthrown, as being customary and according to law. Their guards also are such as are used in a kingly government, not a despotic one; for the guards of their kings are his citizens, but a tyrant's are foreigners. The one commands, in the manner the law directs, those who willingly obey; the other, arbitrarily, those who consent not. The one, therefore, is guarded by the citizens, the other against them.

These, then, are the two different sorts of these monarchies, and another is that which in ancient Greece they called _aesumnetes_; which is nothing more than an elective tyranny; and its difference from that which is to be found amongst the barbarians consists not in its not being according to law, but only in its not being according to the ancient customs of the country. Some persons possessed this power for life, others only for a particular time or particular purpose, as the people of Mitylene elected Pittacus to oppose the exiles, who were headed by Antimenides and Alcaeus the poet, as we learn from a poem of his; for he upbraids the Mitylenians for having chosen Pittacus for their tyrant, and with one [1285b] voice extolling him to the skies who was the ruin of a rash and devoted people. These sorts of government then are, and ever were, despotic, on account of their being tyrannies; but inasmuch as they are elective, and over a free people, they are also kingly.

A fourth species of kingly government is that which was in use in the heroic times, when a free people submitted to a kingly government, according to the laws and customs of their country. For those who were at first of benefit to mankind, either in arts or arms, or by collecting them into civil society, or procuring them an establishment, became the kings of a willing people, and established an hereditary monarchy. They were particularly their generals in war, and presided over their sacrifices, excepting such only as belonged to the priests: they were also the supreme judges over the people; and in this case some of them took an oath, others did not; they did, the form of swearing was by their scepter held out.

In ancient times the power of the kings extended to everything whatsoever, both civil, domestic, and foreign; but in after-times they relinquished some of their privileges, and others the people assumed, so that, in some states, they left their kings only the right of presiding over the sacrifices; and even those whom it were worth while to call by that name had only the right of being commander-in-chief in their foreign wars.

These, then, are the four sorts of kingdoms: the first is that of the heroic times; which was a government over a free people, with its rights in some particulars marked out; for the king was their general, their judge, and their high priest. The second, that of the barbarians; which is an hereditary despotic government regulated by laws: the third is that which they call aesumnetic, which is an elective tyranny. The fourth is the Lacedaemonian; and this, in few words, is nothing more than an hereditary generalship: and in these particulars they differ from each other. There is a fifth species of kingly government, which is when one person has a supreme power over all things whatsoever, in the manner that every state and every city has over those things which belong to the public: for as the master of a family is king in his own house, so such a king is master of a family in his own city or state.

CHAPTER XV

But the different sorts of kingly governments may, if I may so say, be reduced to two; which we will consider more particularly. The last spoken of, and the Lacedaemonian, for the chief of the others are placed between these, which are as it were at the extremities, they having less power than an absolute government, and yet more than the Lacedaemonians; so that the whole matter in question may be reduced to these two points; the one is, whether it is advantageous to the citizens to have the office of general continue in one person for life, and whether it should be confined to any particular families or whether every one should be eligible: the other, whether [1286a] it is advantageous for one person to have the supreme power over everything or not. But to enter into the particulars concerning the office of a Lacedaemonian general would be rather to frame laws for a state than to consider the nature and utility of its constitution, since we know that the appointing of a general is what is done in every state. Passing over this question then, we will proceed to consider the other part of their government, which is the polity of the state; and this it will be necessary to examine particularly into, and to go through such questions as may arise.

Now the first thing which presents itself to our consideration is this, whether it is best to be governed by a good man, or by good laws? Those who prefer a kingly government think that laws can only speak a general language, but cannot adapt themselves to particular circumstances; for which reason it is absurd in any science to follow written rule; and even in Egypt the physician was allowed to alter the mode of cure which the law prescribed to him, after the fourth day; but if he did it sooner it was at his own peril: from whence it is evident, on the very same account, that a government of written laws is not the best; and yet general reasoning is necessary to all those who are to govern, and it will be much more perfect in those who are entirely free from passions than in those to whom they are natural. But now this is a quality which laws possess; while the other is natural to the human soul. But some one will say in answer to this, that man will be a better judge of particulars. It will be necessary, then, for a king to be a lawgiver, and that his laws should be published, but that those should have no authority which are absurd, as those which are not, should. But whether is it better for the community that those things which cannot possibly come under the cognizance of the law either at all or properly should be under the government of every worthy citizen, as the present method is, when the public community, in their general assemblies, act as judges and counselors, where all their determinations are upon particular cases, for one individual, be he who he will, will be found, upon comparison, inferior to a whole people taken collectively: but this is what a city is, as a public entertainment is better than one man's portion: for this reason the multitude judge of many things better than any one single person. They are also less liable to corruption from their numbers, as water is from its quantity: besides, the judgment of an individual must necessarily be perverted if he is overcome by anger or any other passion; but it would be hard indeed if the whole community should be misled by anger. Moreover, let the people be free, and they will do nothing but in conformity to the law, except only in those cases which the law cannot speak to. But though what I am going to propose may not easily be met with, yet if the majority of the state should happen to be good men, should they prefer one uncorrupt governor or many equally good, is it not evident that they should choose the many? But there may be divisions among [1286b] these which cannot happen when there is but one. In answer to this it may be replied that all their souls will be as much animated with virtue as this one man's.

If then a government of many, and all of them good men, compose an aristocracy, and the government of one a kingly power, it is evident that the people should rather choose the first than the last; and this whether the state is powerful or not, if many such persons so alike can be met with: and for this reason probable it was, that the first governments were generally monarchies; because it was difficult to find a number of persons eminently virtuous, more particularly as the world was then divided into small communities; besides, kings were appointed in return for the benefits they had conferred on mankind; but such actions are peculiar to good men: but when many persons equal in virtue appeared at the time, they brooked not a superiority, but sought after an equality and established a free state; but after this, when they degenerated, they made a property of the public; which probably gave rise to oligarchies; for they made wealth meritorious, and the honors of government were reserved for the rich: and these afterwards turned to tyrannies and these in their turn gave rise to democracies; for the power of the ty-rants continually decreasing, on account of their rapacious avarice, the people grew powerful enough to frame and establish democracies: and as cities after that happened to increase, probably it was not easy for them to be under any other government than a democracy. But if any person prefers a kingly government in a state, what is to be done with the king's children? Is the family also to reign? But should they have such children as some persons usually have, it will be very detrimental. It may be said, that then the king who has it in his power will never permit such children to succeed to his kingdom. But it is not easy to trust to that; for it is very hard and requires greater virtue than is to be met with in human nature. There is also a doubt concerning the power with which a king should be entrusted: whether he should be allowed force sufficient to compel those who do not choose to be obedient to the laws, and how he is to support his government? for if he is to govern according to law and do nothing of his own will which is contrary thereunto, at the same time it will be necessary to protect that power with which he guards the law, This matter however may not be very difficult to determine; for he ought to have a proper power, and such a one is that which will be sufficient to make the king superior to any one person or even a large part of the community, but inferior to the whole, as the ancients always appointed guards for that person whom they created aesumnetes or tyrant; and some one advised the Syracusians, when Dionysius asked for guards, to allow him such.

CHAPTER XVI

[1287a] We will next consider the absolute monarch that we have just mentioned, who does everything according to his own will: for a king governing under the direction of laws

which he is obliged to follow does not of himself create any particular species of government, as we have already said: for in every
state whatsoever, either aristocracy or democracy, it is easy to appoint a general for life; and
there are many who entrust the administration
of affairs to one person only; such is the government at Dyrrachium, and nearly the same
at Opus. As for an absolute monarchy as it is
called, that is to say, when the whole state is
wholly subject to the will of one person,
namely the king, it seems to many that it is
unnatural that one man should have the entire
rule over his fellow-citizens when the state
consists of equals: for nature requires that the
same right and the same rank should necessarily take place amongst all those who are
equal by nature: for as it would be hurtful to
the body for those who are of different constitutions to observe the same regimen, either of
diet or clothing, so is it with respect to the
honors of the state as hurtful, that those who
are equal in merit should be unequal in rank;
for which reason it is as much a man's duty to
submit to command as to assume it, and this
also by rotation; for this is law, for order is
law; and it is more proper that law should
govern than any one of the citizens: upon the
same principle, if it is advantageous to place
the supreme power in some particular persons,
they should be appointed to be only guardians,
and the servants of the laws, for the supreme
power must be placed somewhere; but they
say, that it is unjust that where all are equal
one person should continually enjoy it. But it
seems unlikely that man should be able to ad-
just that which the law cannot determine; it
may be replied, that the law having laid down
the best rules possible, leaves the adjustment
and application of particulars to the discretion
of the magistrate; besides, it allows anything to
be altered which experience proves may be
better established. Moreover, he who would

place the supreme power in mind, would place
it in God and the laws; but he who entrusts
man with it, gives it to a wild beast, for such
his appetites sometimes make him; for passion
influences those who are in power, even the
very best of men: for which reason law is reason without desire.

The instance taken from the arts seems fallacious: wherein it is said to be wrong for a sick
person to apply for a remedy to books, but
that it would be far more eligible to employ
those who are skillful in physic; for these do
nothing contrary to reason from motives of
friendship but earn their money by curing the
sick, whereas those who have the management
of public affairs do many things through hatred or favor. And, as a proof of what we have
advanced, it may be observed, that whenever a
sick person suspects that his physician has
been persuaded by his enemies to be guilty of
any foul practice to him in his profession, he
then rather chooses to apply to books for his
cure: and not only this [1287b] but even physicians themselves when they are ill call in other physicians: and those who teach others the
gymnastic exercises, exercise with those of the
same profession, as being incapable from self-
partiality to form a proper judgment of what
concerns themselves. From whence it is evident, that those who seek for what is just, seek
for a mean; now law is a mean. Moreover; the
moral law is far superior and conversant with
far superior objects than the written law; for
the supreme magistrate is safer to be trusted to
than the one, though he is inferior to the other. But as it is impossible that one person
should have an eye to everything himself, it
will be necessary that the supreme magistrate
should employ several subordinate ones under
him; why then should not this be done at first,
instead of appointing one person in this manner? Besides, if, according to what has been

already said, the man of worth is on that account fit to govern, two men of worth are
certainly better than one: as, for instance, in
Homer, "Let two together go:" and also Aga-
5 memnon's wish; "Were ten such faithful counsel mine!" Not but that there are even now
some particular magistrates invested with supreme power to decide, as judges, those things
which the law cannot, as being one of those
10 cases which comes not properly under its jurisdiction; for of those which can there is no
doubt: since then laws comprehend some
things, but not all, it is necessary to enquire
and consider which of the two is preferable,
15 that the best man or the best law should govern; for to reduce every subject which can
come under the deliberation of man into a law
is impossible.

20 No one then denies, that it is necessary that
there should be some person to decide those
cases which cannot come under the cognizance of a written law: but we say, that it is
better to have many than one; for though eve-
25 ry one who decides according to the principles
of the law decides justly; yet surely it seems
absurd to suppose, that one person can see
better with two eyes, and hear better with two
ears, or do better with two hands and two feet,
30 than many can do with many: for we see that
absolute monarchs now furnish themselves
with many eyes and ears and hands and feet;
for they entrust those who are friends to them
and their government with part of their power;
35 for if they are not friends to the monarch, they
will not do what he chooses; but if they are
friends to him, they are friends also to his
government: but a friend is an equal and like
his friend: if then he thinks that such should
40 govern, he thinks that his equal also should
govern. These are nearly the objections which
are usually made to a kingly power.

CHAPTER XVII

Probably what we have said may be true of
45 some persons, but not of others; for some
men are by nature formed to be under the
government of a master; others, of a king;
others, to be the citizens of a free state, just
and useful; but a tyranny is not according to
50 nature, nor the other perverted forms of government; for they are contrary to it. But it is
evident from what has been said, that among
equals it is neither advantageous nor [1288a]
right that one person should be lord over all
55 where there are no established laws, but his
will is the law; or where there are; nor is it
right that one who is good should have it over
those who are good; or one who is not good
over those who are not good; nor one who is
60 superior to the rest in worth, except in a particular manner, which shall be described,
though indeed it has been already mentioned.
But let us next determine what people are best
qualified for a kingly government, what for an
65 aristocratic, and what for a democratic. And,
first, for a kingly; and it should be those who
are accustomed by nature to submit the civil
government of themselves to a family eminent
for virtue: for an aristocracy, those who are
70 naturally framed to bear the rule of free men,
whose superior virtue makes them worthy of
the management of others: for a free state, a
war-like people, formed by nature both to
govern and be governed by laws which admit
75 the poorest citizen to share the honors of the
commonwealth according to his worth. But
whenever a whole family or any one of another shall happen so far to excel in virtue as to
exceed all other persons in the community,
80 then it is right that the kingly power should be
in them, or if it is an individual who does so,
that he should be king and lord of all; for this,
as we have just mentioned, is not only correspondent to that principle of right which all
85 founders of all states, whether aristocracies,
oligarchies, or democracies, have a regard to

(for in placing the supreme power they all think it right to fix it to excellence, though not the same); but it is also agreeable to what has been already said; as it would not be right to

5 kill, or banish, or ostracize such a one for his superior merit. Nor would it be proper to let him have the supreme power only in turn; for it is contrary to nature that what is highest should ever be lowest: but this would be the

10 case should such a one ever be governed by others. So that there can nothing else be done but to submit, and permit him continually to enjoy the supreme power. And thus much with respect to kingly power in different

15 states, and whether it is or is not advantageous to them, and to what, and in what manner.

CHAPTER XVIII

20 Since then we have said that there are three sorts of regular governments, and of these the best must necessarily be that which is administered by the best men (and this must be that which happens to have one man, or one fami-

25 ly, or a number of persons excelling all the rest in virtue, who are able to govern and be governed in such a manner as will make life most agreeable, and we have already shown that the virtue of a good man and of a citizen in the

30 most perfect government will be the same), it is evident, that in the same manner, and for those very qualities which would procure a man the character of good, any one would say, that the government of a state was a well-

35 established aristocracy or kingdom; so that it will be found to be education and [1288b] morals that are almost the whole which go to make a good man, and the same qualities will make a good citizen or good king.

40 These particulars being treated of, we will now proceed to consider what sort of government is best, how it naturally arises, and how it is established; for it is necessary to make a prop-

er inquiry concerning this.

45

BOOK IV
CHAPTER XI

We proceed now to inquire what form of gov-
50 ernment and what manner of life is best for communities in general, not adapting it to that superior virtue which is above the reach of the vulgar, or that education which every advantage of nature and fortune only can fur-
55 nish, nor to those imaginary plans which may be formed at pleasure; but to that mode of life which the greater part of mankind can attain to, and that government which most cities may establish: for as to those aristocracies
60 which we have now mentioned, they are either too perfect for a state to support, or one so nearly alike to that state we now going to inquire into, that we shall treat of them both as one.

65

The opinions which we form upon these subjects must depend upon one common principle: for if what I have said in my treatise on Morals is true, a happy life must arise from an
70 uninterrupted course of virtue; and if virtue consists in a certain medium, the middle life must certainly be the happiest; which medium is attainable [1295b] by every one. The boundaries of virtue and vice in the state must also
75 necessarily be the same as in a private person; for the form of government is the life of the city. In every city the people are divided into three sorts; the very rich, the very poor, and those who are between them. If this is univer-
80 sally admitted, that the mean is best, it is evident that even in point of fortune mediocrity is to be preferred; for that state is most submissive to reason; for those who are very handsome, or very strong, or very noble, or
85 very rich; or, on the contrary; those who are very poor, or very weak, or very mean, with

difficulty obey it; for the one are capricious and greatly flagitious, the other rascally and mean, the crimes of each arising from their different excesses: nor will they go through
5 the different offices of the state; which is detrimental to it: besides, those who excel in strength, in riches, or friends, or the like, neither know how nor are willing to submit to command: and this begins at home when they
10 are boys; for there they are brought up too delicately to be accustomed to obey their preceptors: as for the very poor, their general and excessive want of what the rich enjoy reduces them to a state too mean: so that the one
15 know not how to command, but to be commanded as slaves, the others know not how to submit to any command, nor to command themselves but with despotic power.

20 A city composed of such men must therefore consist of slaves and masters, not freemen; where one party must hate, and the other despise, where there could be no possibility of friendship or political community: for com-
25 munity supposes affection; for we do not even on the road associate with our enemies. It is also the genius of a city to be composed as much as possible of equals; which will be most so when the inhabitants are in the middle
30 state: from whence it follows, that that city must be best framed which is composed of those whom we say are naturally its proper members. It is men of this station also who will be best assured of safety and protection;
35 for they will neither covet what belongs to others, as the poor do; nor will others covet what is theirs, as the poor do what belongs to the rich; and thus, without plotting against any one, or having any one plot against them, they
40 will live free from danger: for which reason Phocylides wisely wishes for the middle state, as being most productive of happiness. It is plain, then, that the most perfect political

45 community must be amongst those who are in the middle rank, and those states are best instituted wherein these are a larger and more respectable part, if possible, than both the other; or, if that cannot be, at least than either of them separate; so that being thrown into the
50 balance it may prevent either scale from preponderating.

It is therefore the greatest happiness which the citizens can enjoy to possess a moderate and
55 convenient fortune; for when some possess too much, and others nothing at [1296a] all, the government must either be in the hands of the meanest rabble or else a pure oligarchy; or, from the excesses of both, a tyranny; for this
60 arises from a headstrong democracy or an oligarchy, but very seldom when the members of the community are nearly on an equality with each other. We will assign a reason for this when we come to treat of the alterations
65 which different states are likely to undergo. The middle state is therefore best, as being least liable to those seditions and insurrections which disturb the community; and for the same reason extensive governments are least
70 liable to these inconveniences; for there those in a middle state are very numerous, whereas in small ones it is easy to pass to the two extremes, so as hardly to have any in a medium remaining, but the one half rich, the other
75 poor: and from the same principle it is that democracies are more firmly established and of longer continuance than oligarchies; but even in those when there is a want of a proper number of men of middling fortune, the poor
80 extend their power too far, abuses arise, and the government is soon at an end. We ought to consider as a proof of what I now advance, that the best lawgivers themselves were those in the middle rank of life,
85 amongst whom was Solon, as is evident from his poems, and Lycurgus, for he was not a

king, and Charondas, and indeed most others. What has been said will show us why of so many free states some have changed to democracies, others to oligarchies: for whenever the number of those in the middle state has been too small, those who were the more numerous, whether the rich or the poor, always overpowered them and assumed to themselves the administration of public affairs; from hence arose either a democracy or an oligarchy. Moreover, when in consequence of their disputes and quarrels with each other, either the rich get the better of the poor, or the poor of the rich, neither of them will establish a free state; but, as the record of their victory, one which inclines to their own principles, and form either a democracy or an oligarchy.

Those who made conquests in Greece, having all of them an eye to the respective forms of government in their own cities, established either democracies or oligarchies, not considering what was serviceable to the state, but what was similar to their own; for which reason a government has never been established where the supreme power has been placed amongst those of the middling rank, or very seldom; and, amongst a few, one man only of those who have yet been conquerors has been persuaded to give the preference to this order of [1296b] men: it is indeed an established custom with the inhabitants of most cities not to desire an equality, but either to aspire to govern, or when they are conquered, to submit.

Thus we have shown what the best state is, and why. It will not be difficult to perceive of the many states which there are, for we have seen that there are various forms both of democracies and oligarchies, to which we should give the first place, to which the second, and in the same manner the next also; and to observe what are the particular excellences and defects of each, after we have first described the best possible; for that must be the best which is nearest to this, that worst which is most distant from the medium, without any one has a particular plan of his own which he judges by. I mean by this, that it may happen, that although one form of government may be better than another, yet there is no reason to prevent another from being preferable thereunto in particular circumstances and for particular purposes.

CHAPTER XII

After what has been said, it follows that we should now show what particular form of government is most suitable for particular persons; first laying this down as a general maxim, that that party which desires to support the actual administration of the state ought always to be superior to that which would alter it. Every city is made up of quality and quantity: by quality I mean liberty, riches, education, and family, and by quantity its relative populousness: now it may happen that quality may exist in one of those parts of which the city is composed, and quantity in another; thus the number of the ignoble may be greater than the number of those of family, the number of the poor than that of the rich; but not so that the quantity of the one shall overbalance the quality of the other; those must be properly adjusted to each other; for where the number of the poor exceeds the proportion we have mentioned, there a democracy will rise up, and if the husbandry should have more power than others, it will be a democracy of husbandmen; and the democracy will be a particular species according to that class of men which may happen to be most numerous: thus, should these be the husbandmen, it will be of these, and the best;

if of mechanics and those who hire themselves out, the worst possible: in the same manner it may be of any other set between these two. But when the rich and the noble prevail more by their quality than they are deficient in quantity, there an oligarchy ensues; and this oligarchy may be of different species, according to the nature of the prevailing party. Every legislator in framing his constitution ought to have a particular regard to those in the middle rank of life; and if he intends an oligarchy, these should be the object of his laws; if a democracy, to these they should be entrusted; and whenever their number exceeds that of the two others, or at least one of them, they give [1297a] stability to the constitution; for there is no fear that the rich and the poor should agree to conspire together against them, for neither of these will choose to serve the other. If any one would choose to fix the administration on the widest basis, he will find none preferable to this; for to rule by turns is what the rich and the poor will not submit to, on account of their hatred to each other. It is, moreover, allowed that an arbitrator is the most proper person for both parties to trust to; now this arbitrator is the middle rank.

Those who would establish aristocratical governments are mistaken not only in giving too much power to the rich, but also in deceiving the common people; for at last, instead of an imaginary good, they must feel a real evil, for the encroachments of the rich are more destructive to the state than those of the poor.

CHAPTER XIII

There are five particulars in which, under fair pretenses, the rich craftily endeavor to undermine the rights of the people, these are their public assemblies, their offices of state, their courts of justice, their military power, and their gymnastic exercises. With respect to their public assemblies, in having them open to all, but in fining the rich only, or others very little, for not attending; with respect to offices, in permitting the poor to swear off, but not granting this indulgence to those who are within the census; with respect to their courts of justice, in fining the rich for non-attendance, but the poor not at all, or those a great deal, and these very little, as was done by the laws of Charondas. In some places every citizen who was enrolled had a right to attend the public assemblies and to try causes; which if they did not do, a very heavy fine was laid upon them; that through fear of the fine they might avoid being enrolled, as they were then obliged to do neither the one nor the other. The same spirit of legislation prevailed with respect to their bearing arms and their gymnastic exercises; for the poor are excused if they have no arms, but the rich are fined; the same method takes place if they do not attend their gymnastic exercises, there is no penalty on one, but there is on the other: the consequence of which is, that the fear of this penalty induces the rich to keep the one and attend the other, while the poor do neither. These are the deceitful contrivances of oligarchical legislators.

The contrary prevails in a democracy; for there they make the poor a proper allowance for attending the assemblies and the courts, but give the rich nothing for doing it: whence it is evident, that if any one would properly blend these customs together, they must extend both the pay and the fine to every member of the community, and then every one would share in it, whereas part only now do. The citizens of a free state ought to [1297b] consist of those only who bear arms: with respect to their census it is not easy to determine exactly what it ought to be, but the rule that should direct upon this subject should be to make it as extensive as possible, so that those who are enrolled in it make up a greater part of the people than those who are not; for those who are poor, although they partake not of the offices of the state, are willing to live quiet, provided that no one disturbs them in their property: but this is not an easy matter; for it may not always happen, that those who are at the head of public affairs are of a humane behavior. In time of war the poor are accustomed to show no alacrity without they have provisions found them; when they have, then indeed they are willing to fight.

In some governments the power is vested not only in those who bear arms, but also in those who have borne them. Among the Malienses the state was composed of these latter only, for all the officers were soldiers who had served their time. And the first states in Greece which succeeded those where kingly power was established, were governed by the military. First of all the horse, for at that time the strength and excellence of the army depended on the horse, for as to the heavy-armed foot they were useless without proper discipline; but the art of tactics was not known to the ancients, for which reason their strength lay in their horse: but when cities grew larger, and they depended more on their foot, greater numbers partook of the freedom of the city; for which reason what we call republics were formerly called democracies. The ancient governments were properly oligarchies or kingdoms; for on account of the few persons in each state, it would have been impossible to have found a sufficient number of the middle rank; so these being but few, and those used to subordination, they more easily submitted to be governed.

We have now shown why there are many sorts of governments, and others different from those we have treated of: for there are more species of democracies than one, and the like is true of other forms, and what are their differences, and whence they arise; and also of all others which is the best, at least in general; and which is best suited for particular people.

CHAPTER XIV

We will now proceed to make some general reflections upon the governments next in order, and also to consider each of them in particular; beginning with those principles which appertain to each: now there are three things in all states which a careful legislator ought well to consider, which are of great consequence to all, and which properly attended to the state must necessarily be happy; and according to the variation of which the one will differ from the other. The first of these is the [1298a] public assembly; the second the officers of the state, that is, who they ought to be, and with what power they should be entrusted, and in what manner they should be appointed; the third, the judicial department.

Now it is the proper business of the public assembly to determine concerning war and peace, making or breaking off alliances, to enact laws, to sentence to death, banishment, or confiscation of goods, and to call the magistrates to account for their behavior when in office. Now these powers must necessarily be entrusted to the citizens in general, or all of them to some; either to one magistrate or more; or some to one, and some to another, or some to all, but others to some: to entrust all to all is in the spirit of a democracy, for the people aim at equality. There are many methods of delegating these powers to the citizens at large, one of which is to let them execute them by turn, and not altogether, as was done by Tellecles, the Milesian, in his state. In others the supreme council is composed of the different magistrates, and they succeed to the offices of the community by proper divisions

5 of tribes, wards, and other very small proportions, till every one in his turn goes through them: nor does the whole community ever meet together, without it is when new laws are enacted, or some national affair is debated, or

10 to hear what the magistrates have to propose to them. Another method is for the people to meet in a collective body, but only for the purpose of holding the comitia, making laws, determining concerning war or peace, and

15 inquiring into the conduct of their magistrates, while the remaining part of the public business is conducted by the magistrates, who have their separate departments, and are chosen out of the whole community either by vote or

20 ballot. Another method is for the people in general to meet for the choice of the magistrates, and to examine into their conduct; and also to deliberate concerning war and alliances, and to leave other things to the magistrates,

25 whoever happen to be chosen, whose particular employments are such as necessarily require persons well skilled therein. A fourth method is for every person to deliberate upon every subject in public assembly, where the

30 magistrates can determine nothing of themselves, and have only the privilege of giving their opinions first; and this is the method of the most pure democracy, which is analogous to the proceedings in a dynastic oligarchy and

35 a tyrannic monarchy.

These, then, are the methods in which public business is conducted in a democracy. When the power is in the hands of part of the com-

40 munity only, it is an oligarchy and this also admits of different customs; for whenever the officers of the state are chosen out of those who have a moderate fortune, and these from

that circumstance are many, and when they

45 depart not from that line which the law has laid down, but carefully follow it, and when all within the census are eligible, certainly it is then an oligarchy, but founded on true principles of government [1298b] from its modera-

50 tion. When the people in general do not partake of the deliberative power, but certain persons chosen for that purpose, who govern according to law; this also, like the first, is an oligarchy. When those who have the delibera-

55 tive power elect each other, and the son succeeds to the father, and when they can supersede the laws, such a government is of necessity a strict oligarchy. When some persons determine on one thing, and others on another,

60 as war and peace, and when all inquire into the conduct of their magistrates, and other things are left to different officers, elected either by vote or lot, then the government is an aristocracy or a free state. When some are chosen by

65 vote and others by lot, and these either from the people in general, or from a certain number elected for that purpose, or if both the votes and the lots are open to all, such a state is partly an aristocracy, partly a free govern-

70 ment itself. These are the different methods in which the deliberative power is vested in different states, all of whom follow some regulation here laid down. It is advantageous to a democracy, in the present sense of the word,

75 by which I mean a state wherein the people at large have a supreme power, even over the laws, to hold frequent public assemblies; and it will be best in this particular to imitate the example of oligarchies in their courts of jus-

80 tice; for they fine those who are appointed to try causes if they do not attend, so should they reward the poor for coming to the public assemblies: and their counsels will be best when all advise with each other, the citizens with the

85 nobles, the nobles with the citizens. It is also advisable when the council is to be composed

of part of the citizens, to elect, either by vote or lot, an equal number of both ranks. It is also proper, if the common people in the state are very numerous, either not to pay every one 5 for his attendance, but such a number only as will make them equal to the nobles, or to reject many of them by lot.

In an oligarchy they should either call up some 10 of the common people to the council, or else establish a court, as is done in some other states, whom they call pre-advisers or guardians of the laws, whose business should be to propose first what they should afterwards en- 15 act. By this means the people would have a place in the administration of public affairs, without having it in their power to occasion any disorder in the government. Moreover, the people may be allowed to have a vote in what- 20 ever bill is proposed, but may not themselves propose anything contrary thereto; or they may give their advice, while the power of determining may be with the magistrates only. It is also necessary to follow a contrary practice 25 to what is established in democracies, for the people should be allowed the power of pardoning, but not of condemning, for the cause should be referred back again to the magistrates: whereas the contrary takes place in re- 30 publics; for the power of pardoning is with the few, but not of condemning, which is always referred [1299a] to the people at large. And thus we determine concerning the deliberative power in any state, and in whose hands it shall 35 be.

CHAPTER XV

We now proceed to consider the choice of 40 magistrates; for this branch of public business contains many different Parts, as how many there shall be, what shall be their particular office, and with respect to time how long each

of them shall continue in place; for some 45 make it six months, others shorter, others for a year, others for a much longer time; or whether they should be perpetual or for a long time, or neither; for the same person may fill the same office several times, or he may not 50 be allowed to enjoy it even twice, but only once: and also with respect to the appointment of magistrates, who are to be eligible, who is to choose them, and in what manner; for in all these particulars we ought properly 55 to distinguish the different ways which may be followed; and then to show which of these is best suited to such and such governments.

Now it is not easy to determine to whom we 60 ought properly to give the name of magistrate, for a government requires many persons in office; but every one of those who is either chosen by vote or lot is not to be reckoned a magistrate. The priests, for instance, in the 65 first place; for these are to be considered as very different from civil magistrates: to these we may add the choregi and heralds; nay, even ambassadors are elected: there are some civil employments which belong to the citizens; 70 and these are either when they are all engaged in one thing, as when as soldiers they obey their general, or when part of them only are, as in governing the women or educating the youth; and also some economic, for they often 75 elect corn-meters: others are servile, and in which, if they are rich, they employ slaves. But indeed they are most properly called magistrates, who are members of the deliberative council, or decide causes, or are in some 80 command, the last more especially, for to command is peculiar to magistrates. But to speak truth, this question is of no great consequence, nor is it the province of the judges to decide between those who dispute about 85 words; it may indeed be an object of speculative inquiry; but to inquire what officers are

necessary in a state, and how many, and what, though not most necessary, may yet be advantageous in a well-established government, is a much more useful employment, and this with
5 respect to all states in general, as well as to small cities.

In extensive governments it is proper to allot one employment to one person, as there are
10 many to serve the public in so numerous a society, where some may be passed over for a long time, and others never be in office but once; and indeed everything is better done which has the whole attention of one person,
15 than when that [1299b] attention is divided amongst many; but in small states it is necessary that a few of the citizens should execute many employments; for their numbers are so small it will not be convenient to have many
20 of them in office at the same time; for where shall we find others to succeed them in turn? Small states will sometimes want the same magistrates and the same laws as large ones; but the one will not want to employ them so
25 often as the other; so that different charges may be entrusted to the same person without any inconvenience, for they will not interfere with each other, and for want of sufficient members in the community it will be neces-
30 sary. If we could tell how many magistrates are necessary in every city, and how many, though not necessary, it is yet proper to have, we could then the better know how many different offices one might assign to one magistrate.
35 It is also necessary to know what tribunals in different places should have different things under their jurisdiction, and also what things should always come under the cognizance of the same magistrate; as, for instance, decency
40 of manners, shall the clerk of the market take cognizance of that if the cause arises in the market, and another magistrate in another place, or the same magistrate everywhere: or

shall there be a distinction made of the fact, or
45 the parties? as, for instance, in decency of manners, shall it be one cause when it relates to a man, another when it relates to a woman?

In different states shall the magistrates be dif-
50 ferent or the same? I mean, whether in a democracy, an oligarchy, an aristocracy, and a monarchy, the same persons shall have the same power? or shall it vary according to the different formation of the government? as in
55 an aristocracy the offices of the state are allotted to those who are well educated; in an oligarchy to those who are rich; in a democracy to the freemen? Or shall the magistrates differ as the communities differ? For it may happen
60 that the very same may be sometimes proper, sometimes otherwise: in this state it may be necessary that the magistrate have great powers, in that but small. There are also certain magistrates peculiar to certain states--as the
65 pre-advisers are not proper in a democracy, but a senate is; for one such order is necessary, whose business shall be to consider beforehand and prepare those bills which shall be brought before the people that they may have
70 leisure to attend to their own affairs; and when these are few in number the state inclines to an oligarchy. The pre-advisers indeed must always be few for they are peculiar to an oligarchy: and where there are both these offices
75 in the same state, the pre-adviser's is superior to the senator's, the one having only a democratical power, the other an oligarchical: and indeed the [1300a] power of the senate is lost in those democracies, in which the people,
80 meeting in one public assembly, take all the business into their own hands; and this is likely to happen either when the community in general are in easy circumstances, or when they are paid for their attendance; for they are
85 then at leisure often to meet together and determine everything for themselves. A magis-

trate whose business is to control the manners of the boys, or women, or who takes any department similar to this, is to be found in an aristocracy, not in a democracy; for who can

5 forbid the wives of the poor from appearing in public? neither is such a one to be met with in an oligarchy; for the women there are too delicate to bear control.

10 And thus much for this subject. Let us endeavor to treat at large of the establishment of magistrates, beginning from first principles. Now, they differ from each other in three ways, from which, blended together, all the

15 varieties which can be imagined arise. The first of these differences is in those who appoint the magistrates, the second consists in those who are appointed, the third in the mode of appointment; and each of these three differ in

20 three manners; for either all the citizens may appoint collectively, or some out of their whole body, or some out of a particular order in it, according to fortune, family, or virtue, or some other rule (as at Megara, where the right

25 of election was amongst those who had returned together to their country, and had reinstated themselves by force of arms) and this either by vote or lot. Again, these several modes may be differently formed together, as

30 some magistrates may be chosen by part of the community, others by the whole; some out of part, others out of the whole; some by vote, others by lot: and each of these different modes admit of a four-fold subdivision; for

35 either all may elect all by vote or by lot; and when all elect, they may either proceed without any distinction, or they may elect by a certain division of tribes, wards, or companies, till they have gone through the whole community:

40 and some magistrates may be elected one way, and others another. Again, if some magistrates are elected either by vote or lot of all the citizens, or by the vote of some and the lot of

some, or some one way and some another;

45 that is to say, some by the vote of all, others by the lot of all, there will then be twelve different methods of electing the magistrates, without blending the two together. Of these there are two adapted to a democracy; namely,

50 to have all the magistrates chosen out of all the people, either by vote or lot, or both; that is to say, some of them by lot, some by vote. In a free state the whole community should not elect at the same time, but some out of the

55 whole, or out of some particular rank; and this either by lot, or vote, or both: and they should elect either out of the whole community, or out of some particular persons in it, and this both by lot and vote. In an oligarchy it is

60 proper to choose some magistrates out of the whole body of the citizens, some by vote, some by lot, others by both: by lot is most correspondent to that form of government. In a free aristocracy, some magistrates [1300b]

65 should be chosen out of the community in general, others out of a particular rank, or these by choice, those by lot. In a pure oligarchy, the magistrates should be chosen out of certain ranks, and by certain persons, and some

70 of those by lot, others by both methods; but to choose them out of the whole community is not correspondent to the nature of this government. It is proper in an aristocracy for the whole community to elect their magistrates

75 out of particular persons, and this by vote.

These then are all the different ways of electing of magistrates; and they have been allotted according to the nature of the different com-

80 munities; but what mode of proceeding is proper for different communities, or how the offices ought to be established, or with what powers shall be particularly explained. I mean by the powers of a magistrate, what should be

85 his particular province, as the management of the finances or the laws of the state; for differ-

ent magistrates have different powers, as that of the general of the army differs from the clerk of the market.

CHAPTER XVI

Of the three parts of which a government is formed, we now come to consider the judicial; and this also we shall divide in the same manner as we did the magisterial, into three parts. Of whom the judges shall consist, and for what causes, and how. When I say of whom, I mean whether they shall be the whole people, or some particulars; by for what causes I mean, how many different courts shall be appointed; by how, whether they shall be elected by vote or lot.

Let us first determine how many different courts there ought to be. Now these are eight. The first of these is the court of inspection over the behavior of the magistrats when they have quitted their office; the second is to punish those who have injured the public; the third is to take cognizance of those causes in which the state is a party; the fourth is to decide between magistrates and private persons, who appeal from a fine laid upon them; the fifth is to determine disputes which may arise concerning contracts of great value; the sixth is to judge between foreigners, and of murders, of which there are different species; and these may all be tried by the same judges or by different ones; for there are murders of malice prepense and of chance-medley; there is also justifiable homicide, where the fact is admitted, and the legality of it disputed.

There is also another court called at Athens the Court of Phreattae, which determines points relating to a murder committed by one who has run away, to decide whether he shall return; though such an affair happens but seldom, and in very large cities; the seventh, to determine causes wherein strangers are concerned, and this whether they are between stranger and stranger or between a stranger and a citizen. The eighth and last is for small actions, from one to five drachma's, or a little more; for these ought also to be legally determined, but not to be brought before the whole body of the judges. But without entering into any particulars concerning actions for murder, and those wherein strangers are the parties, let us particularly treat of those courts which have the jurisdiction of those matters which more particularly relate to the affairs of the community and which if not well conducted occasion seditions and commotions in the state. Now, of necessity, either all persons must have a right to judge of all these different causes, appointed for that purpose, either by vote or lot, or all of all, some of them by vote, and others by lot, or in some causes by vote, in others by lot. Thus there will be four sorts of judges. There [1301a] will be just the same number also if they are chosen out of part of the people only; for either all the judges must be chosen out of that part either by vote or lot, or some by lot and some by vote, or the judges in particular causes must be chosen some by vote, others by lot; by which means there will be the same number of them also as was mentioned. Besides, different judges may be joined together; I mean those who are chosen out of the whole people or part of them or both; so that all three may sit together in the same court, and this either by vote, lot, or both. And thus much for the different sorts of judges. Of these appointments that which admits all the community to be judges in all causes is most suitable to a democracy; the second, which appoints that certain persons shall judge all causes, to an oligarchy; the third, which appoints the whole community to be judges in some causes, but particular persons in others, to an aristocracy or free state.

(In Book V Aristotle discusses revolutions, and how they bring about changes to government. In large part, he argues that good types of governments become bad— monarchies become tyrannies, aristocracies oligarchies, and 'states' democracies... -MJ)

BOOK VI
CHAPTER I

We have already shown what is the nature of the supreme council in the state, and wherein one may differ from another, and how the different magistrates should be regulated; and also the judicial department, and what is best suited to what state; and also to what causes both the destruction and preservation of governments are owing.

As there are very many species of democracies, as well as of other states, it will not be amiss to consider at the same time anything which we may have omitted to mention concerning either of them, and to allot to each that mode of conduct which is peculiar to and advantageous for them; and also to inquire into the combinations of all these different modes of government which we [1317a] have mentioned; for as these are blended together the government is altered, as from an aristocracy to be an oligarchy, and from a free state to be a democracy. Now, I mean by those combinations of government (which I ought to examine into, but have not yet done), namely, whether the deliberative department and the election of magistrates is regulated in a manner correspondent to an oligarchy, or the judicial to an aristocracy, or the deliberative part only to an oligarchy, and the election of magistrates to an aristocracy, or whether, in any other manner, everything is not regulated according to the nature of the government.

But we will first consider what particular sort of democracy is fitted to a particular city, and also what particular oligarchy to a particular people; and of other states, what is advantageous to what. It is also necessary to show clearly, not only which of these governments is best for a state, but also how it ought to be established there, and other things we will treat of briefly.

And first, we will speak of a democracy; and this will at the same time show clearly the nature of its opposite which some persons call an oligarchy; and in doing this we must examine into all the parts of a democracy, and everything that is connected therewith; for from the manner in which these are compounded together different species of democracies arise: and hence it is that they are more than one, and of various natures. Now, there are two causes which occasion there being so many democracies; one of which is that which we have already mentioned; namely, there being different sorts of people; for in one country the majority are husbandmen, in another mechanics, and hired servants; if the first of these is added to the second, and the third to both of them, the democracy will not only differ in the particular of better or worse, but in this, that it will be no longer the same government; the other is that which we will now speak of. The different things which are connected with democracies and seem to make part of these states, do, from their being joined to them, render them different from others: this attending a few, that more, and another all. It is necessary that he who would found any state which he may happen to approve of, or correct one, should be acquainted with all these particulars. All founders of states endeavor to comprehend within their own plan everything of nearly the same kind with it; but in doing this they err, in the manner I have already described in treating of the preservation and destruction of governments. I will now speak of these first principles and manners, and whatever else a democratical state requires.

CHAPTER II

Now the foundation of a democratical state is liberty, and people have been accustomed to say this as if here only liberty was to be found; for they affirm that this is the end proposed by every democracy. But one part of liberty is to govern and be governed alternately; for, according to democratical justice, equality is measured by numbers, and not by worth: and this being just, it is necessary that the supreme power should be vested in the people at large; and that what the majority determine should be final: so that in a democracy the poor ought to have more power than the rich, as being the greater number; for this is one mark of liberty which all framers of a democracy lay down as a criterion of that state; another is, to live as every one likes; for this, they say, is a right which liberty gives, since he is a slave who must live as he likes not. This, then, is another criterion of a democracy. Hence arises the claim to be under no command whatsoever to any one, upon any account, any otherwise than by rotation, and that just as far only as that person is, in his turn, under his also. This also is conducive to that equality which liberty demands. These things being premised, and such being the government, it follows that such rules as the following should be observed in it, that all the magistrates should be chosen out of all the people, and all to command each, and each in his turn all: that all the magistrates should be chosen by lot, except to those offices only which required some particular knowledge and skill: that no census, or a very small one, should be required to qualify a man for any office: that none should be in the same employment twice, or very few, and very seldom, except in the army: that all their appointments should be limited to a very short time, or at least as many as possible: that the whole community should be qualified to judge in all causes whatsoever, let the object be ever so extensive, ever so interesting, or of ever so high a nature; as at Athens, where the people at large judge the magistrates when they come out of office, and decide concerning public affairs as well as private contracts: that the supreme power should be in the public assembly; and that no magistrate should be allowed any discretionary power but in a few instances, and of no consequence to public business. Of all magistrates a senate is best suited to a democracy, where the whole community is not paid for giving their attendance; for in that case it loses its power; for then the people will bring all causes before them, by appeal, as we have already mentioned in a former book. In the next place, there should, if possible, be a fund to pay all the citizens-- who have any share in the management of public affairs, either as members of the assembly, judges, and magistrates; but if this cannot be done, at least the magistrates, the judges the senators, and members of the supreme assembly, and also those officers who are obliged to eat at a common table ought to be paid. Moreover, as an oligarchy is said to be a government of men of family, fortune, and education; so, on the contrary, a democracy is a government in the hands of men of no birth, indigent circumstances, and mechanical employments. In this state also no office [1318a] should be for life; and, if any such should remain after the government has been long changed into a democracy, they should endeavor by degrees to diminish the power; and also elect by lot instead of vote. These things, then, appertain to all democracies; namely, to be established on that principle of justice

which is homogeneous to those governments; that is, that all the members of the state, by number, should enjoy an equality, which seems chiefly to constitute a democracy, or
5 government of the people: for it seems perfectly equal that the rich should have no more share in the government than the poor, nor be alone in power; but that all should be equal, according to number; for thus, they think, the
10 equality and liberty of the state best preserved.

CHAPTER III

In the next place we must inquire how this
15 equality is to be procured. Shall the qualifications be divided so that five hundred rich should be equal to a thousand poor, or shall the thousand have equal power with the five hundred? or shall we not establish our equality
20 in this manner? but divide indeed thus, and afterwards taking an equal number both out of the five hundred and the thousand, invest them with the power of creating the magistrates and judges. Is this state then established
25 according to perfect democratical justice, or rather that which is guided by numbers only? For the defenders of a democracy say, that that is just which the majority approve of: but the favorers of an oligarchy say, that that is
30 just which those who have most approve of; and that we ought to be directed by the value of property. Both the propositions are unjust; for if we agree with what the few propose we erect a tyranny: for if it should happen that an
35 individual should have more than the rest who are rich, according to oligarchical justice, this man alone has a right to the supreme power; but if superiority of numbers is to prevail, injustice will then be done by confiscating the
40 property of the rich, who are few, as we have already said. What then that equality is, which both parties will admit, must be collected from the definition of right which is common to

them both; for they both say that what the
45 majority of the state approves of ought to be established. Be it so; but not entirely: but since a city happens to be made up of two different ranks of people, the rich and the poor, let that be established which is approved of by both
50 these, or the greater part: but should there be opposite sentiments, let that be established which shall be approved of by the greater part: but let this be according to the census; for instance, if there should be ten of the rich and
55 twenty of the poor, and six of the first and fifteen of the last should agree upon any measure, and the remaining four of the rich should join with the remaining five of the poor in opposing it, that party whose census
60 when added together should determine which opinion should be law, and should these happen to be equal, it should be regarded as a case similar to an assembly or court of justice dividing equally upon any question that comes
65 before them, who either determine it by lot or some such method. But although, with [1318b] respect to what is equal and just, it may be very difficult to establish the truth, yet it is much easier to do than to persuade those
70 who have it in their power to encroach upon others to be guided thereby; for the weak always desire what is equal and just, but the powerful pay no regard thereunto.

75 ## CHAPTER IV

There are four kinds of democracies. The best is that which is composed of those first in order, as we have already said, and this also is
80 the most ancient of any. I call that the first which every one would place so, was he to divide the people; for the best part of these are the husbandmen. We see, then, that a democracy may be framed where the majority live by
85 tillage or pasturage; for, as their property is but small, they will not be at leisure perpetually to

hold public assemblies, but will be continually employed in following their own business, not having otherwise the means of living; nor will they be desirous of what another enjoys, but
5 will rather like to follow their own business than meddle with state affairs and accept the offices of government, which will be attended with no great profit; for the major part of mankind are rather desirous of riches than
10 honor (a proof of this is, that they submitted to the tyrannies in ancient times, and do now submit to the oligarchies, if no one hinders them in their usual occupations, or deprives them of their property; for some of them soon
15 get rich, others are removed from poverty); besides, their having the right of election and calling their magistrates to account for their conduct when they come out of office, will satisfy their desire of honors, if any of them
20 entertain that passion: for in some states, though the commonalty have not the right of electing the magistrates, yet it is vested in part of that body chosen to represent them: and it is sufficient for the people at large to possess
25 the deliberative power: and this ought to be considered as a species of democracy; such was that formerly at Mantinsea: for which reason it is proper for the democracy we have been now treating of to have a power (and it
30 has been usual for them to have it) of censuring their magistrates when out of office, and sitting in judgment upon all causes: but that the chief magistrates should be elected, and according to a certain census, which should
35 vary with the rank of their office, or else not by a census, but according to their abilities for their respective appointments. A state thus constituted must be well constituted; for the magistracies will be always filled with the best
40 men with the approbation of the people; who will not envy their superiors: and these and the nobles should be content with this part in the administration; for they will not be governed

by their inferiors. They will be also careful to
45 use their power with moderation, as there are others to whom full power is delegated to censure their conduct; for it is very serviceable to the state to have them dependent upon others, and not to be permitted to do whatsoever they
50 choose; for with such a liberty there would be no check to that evil particle there is in every one: therefore it is [1319a] necessary and most for the benefit of the state that the offices thereof should be filled by the principal per-
55 sons in it, whose characters are unblemished, and that the people are not oppressed. It is now evident that this is the best species of democracy, and on what account; because the people are such and have such powers as they
60 ought to have. To establish a democracy of husbandmen some of those laws which were observed in many ancient states are universally useful; as, for instance, on no account to permit any one to possess more than a certain
65 quantity of land, or within a certain distance from the city. Formerly also, in some states, no one was allowed to sell their original lot of land. They also mention a law of one Oxylus, which forbade any one to add to their patri-
70 mony by usury. We ought also to follow the law of the Aphutaeans, as useful to direct us in this particular we are now speaking of; for they having but very little ground, while they were a numerous people, and at the same time
75 were all husbandmen, did not include all their lands within the census, but divided them in such a manner that, according to the census, the poor had more power than the rich.

80 Next to the commonalty of husbandmen is one of shepherds and herdsmen; for they have many things in common with them, and, by their way of life, are excellently qualified to make good soldiers, stout in body, and able to
85 continue in the open air all night. The general-ity of the people of whom other democracies

are composed are much worse than these; for their lives are wretched nor have they any business with virtue in anything they do; these are your mechanics, your exchange-men, and hired servants; as all these sorts of men frequent the exchange and the citadel, they can readily attend the public assembly; whereas the husbandmen, being more dispersed in the country, cannot so easily meet together; nor are they equally desirous of doing it with these others! When a country happens to be so situated that a great part of the land lies at a distance from the city, there it is easy to establish a good democracy or a free state for the people in general will be obliged to live in the country; so that it will be necessary in such a democracy, though there may be an exchange-mob at hand, never to allow a legal assembly without the inhabitants of the country attend. We have shown in what manner the first and best democracy ought to be established, and it will be equally evident as to the rest, for from these we [1319b] should proceed as a guide, and always separate the meanest of the people from the rest.

But the last and worst, which gives to every citizen without distinction a share in every part of the administration, is what few citizens can bear, nor is it easy to preserve for any long time, unless well supported by laws and manners. We have already noticed almost every cause that can destroy either this or any other state. Those who have taken the lead in such a democracy have endeavored to support it, and make the people powerful by collecting together as many persons as they could and giving them their freedom, not only legitimately but naturally born, and also if either of their parents were citizens, that is to say, if either their father or mother; and this method is better suited to this state than any other: and thus the demagogues have usually managed. They

ought, however, to take care, and do this no longer than the common people are superior to the nobles and those of the middle rank, and then stop; for, if they proceed still further, they will make the state disorderly, and the nobles will ill brook the power of the common people, and be full of resentment against it; which was the cause of an insurrection at Cyrene: for a little evil is overlooked, but when it becomes a great one it strikes the eye. It is, moreover, very-useful in such a state to do as Clisthenes did at Athens, when he was desirous of increasing the power of the people, and as those did who established the democracy in Cyrene; that is, to institute many tribes and fraternities, and to make the religious rites of private persons few, and those common; and every means is to be contrived to associate and blend the people together as much as possible; and that all former customs be broken through. Moreover, whatsoever is practiced in a tyranny seems adapted to a democracy of this species; as, for instance, the licentiousness of the slaves, the women, and the children; for this to a certain degree is useful in such a state; and also to overlook every one's living as they choose; for many will support such a government: for it is more agreeable to many to live without any control than as prudence would direct.

CHAPTER V

It is also the business of the legislator and all those who would support a government of this sort not to make it too great a work, or too perfect; but to aim only to render it stable: for, let a state be constituted ever so badly, there is no difficulty in its continuing a few days: they should therefore endeavor to procure its safety by all those ways which we have described in assigning the causes of the preservation and destruction of governments;

avoiding what is hurtful, and by framing such laws, written and unwritten, as contain those things which chiefly tend to the preservation of the state; nor to suppose that that is useful

5 either for a democratic or [1320a] an oligarchic form of government which contributes to make them more purely so, but what will contribute to their duration: but our demagogues at present, to flatter the people, occasion fre-

10 quent confiscations in the courts; for which reason those who have the welfare of the state really at heart should act directly opposite to what they do, and enact a law to prevent forfeitures from being divided amongst the peo-

15 ple or paid into the treasury, but to have them set apart for sacred uses: for those who are of a bad disposition would not then be the less cautious, as their punishment would be the same; and the community would not be so

20 ready to condemn those whom they sat in judgment on when they were to get nothing by it: they should also take care that the causes which are brought before the public should be as few as possible, and punish with the utmost

25 severity those who rashly brought an action against any one; for it is not the commons but the nobles who are generally prosecuted: for in all things the citizens of the same state ought to be affectionate to each other, at least not to

30 treat those who have the chief power in it as their enemies.

Now, as the democracies which have been lately established are very numerous, and it is

35 difficult to get the common people to attend the public assemblies without they are paid for it, this, when there is not a sufficient public revenue, is fatal to the nobles; for the deficiencies therein must be necessarily made up

40 by taxes, confiscations, and fines imposed by corrupt courts of justice: which things have already destroyed many democracies. Whenever, then, the revenues of the state are small,

there should be but few public assemblies and

45 but few courts of justice: these, however, should have very extensive jurisdictions, but should continue sitting a few days only, for by this means the rich would not fear the expense, although they should receive nothing

50 for their attendance, though the poor did; and judgment also would be given much better; for the rich will not choose to be long absent from their own affairs, but will willingly be so for a short time: and, when there are sufficient

55 revenues, a different conduct ought to be pursued from what the demagogues at present follow; for now they divide the surplus of the public money amongst the poor; these receive it and again want the same supply, while the

60 giving it is like pouring water into a sieve: but the true patriot in a democracy ought to take care that the majority of the community are not too poor, for this is the cause of rapacity in that government; he therefore should en-

65 deavor that they may enjoy perpetual plenty; and as this also is advantageous to the rich, what can be saved out of the public money should be put by, and then divided at once amongst the poor, if possible, in such a quan-

70 tity as may enable every one of them to purchase a little field, and, if that cannot be done, at least to give each of them enough to procure the implements [1320b] of trade and husbandry; and if there is not enough for all to

75 receive so much at once, then to divide it according to tribes or any other allotment. In the meantime let the rich pay them for necessary services, but not be obliged to find them in useless amusements. And something like this

80 was the manner in which they managed at Carthage, and preserved the affections of the people; for by continually sending some of their community into colonies they procured plenty. It is also worthy of a sensible and gen-

85 erous nobility to divide the poor amongst them, and supplying them with what is neces-

sary, induce them to work; or to imitate the conduct of the people at Tarentum: for they, permitting the poor to partake in common of everything which is needful for them, gain the affections of the commonalty. They have also two different ways of electing their magistrates; for some are chosen by vote, others by lot; by the last, that the people at large may have some share in the administration; by the former, that the state may be well governed: the same may be accomplished if of the same magistrates you choose some by vote, others by lot. And thus much for the manner in which democracies ought to be established.

CHAPTER VI

What has been already said will almost of itself sufficiently show how an oligarchy ought to be founded; for he who would frame such a state should have in his view a democracy to oppose it; for every species of oligarchy should be founded on principles diametrically opposite to some species of democracy.

The first and best-framed oligarchy is that which approaches near to what we call a free state; in which there ought to be two different census, the one high, the other low: from those who are within the latter the ordinary officers of the state ought to be chosen; from the former the supreme magistrates: nor should any one be excluded from a part of the administration who was within the census; which should be so regulated that the commonalty who are included in it should by means thereof be superior to those who have no share in the government; for those who are to have the management of public affairs ought always to be chosen out of the better sort of the people. Much in the same manner ought that oligarchy to be established which is next in order: but as to that which is most opposite to a pure democracy, and approaches nearest to a dynasty and a tyranny, as it is of all others the worst, so it requires the greatest care and caution to preserve it: for as bodies of sound and healthy constitutions and ships which are well manned and well found for sailing can bear many injuries without perishing, while a diseased body or a leaky ship with an indifferent crew cannot support the [1321a] least shock; so the worst-established governments want most looking after. A number of citizens is the preservation of a democracy; for these are opposed to those rights which are founded in rank: on the contrary, the preservation of an oligarchy depends upon the due regulation of the different orders in the society.

CHAPTER VII

As the greater part of the community are divided into four sorts of people; husbandmen, mechanics, traders, and hired servants; and as those who are employed in war may likewise be divided into four; the horsemen, the heavy-armed soldier, the light-armed, and the sailor, where the nature of the country can admit a great number of horse; there a powerful oligarchy may be easily established: for the safety of the inhabitants depends upon a force of that sort; but those who can support the expense of horsemen must be persons of some considerable fortune. Where the troops are chiefly heavy-armed, there an oligarchy, inferior in power to the other, may be established; for the heavy-armed are rather made up of men of substance than the poor: but the light-armed and the sailors always contribute to support a democracy: but where the number of these is very great and a sedition arises, the other parts of the community fight at a disadvantage; but a remedy for this evil is to be learned from skillful generals, who always mix a proper number of light-armed soldiers with their horse and heavy-armed: for it is with those that the populace get the better of the men of fortune in an insurrection; for these

5 being lighter are easily a match for the horse and the heavy-armed: so that for an oligarchy to form a body of troops from these is to form it against itself: but as a city is composed of persons of different ages, some young and

10 some old, the fathers should teach their sons, while they were very young, a light and easy exercise; but, when they are grown up, they should be perfect in every warlike exercise. Now, the admission of the people to any share

15 in the government should either be (as I said before) regulated by a census, or else, as at Thebes, allowed to those who for a certain time have ceased from any mechanic employment, or as at Massalia, where they are chosen

20 according to their worth, whether citizens or foreigners. With respect to the magistrates of the highest rank which it may be necessary to have in a state, the services they are bound to do the public should be expressly laid down,

25 to prevent the common people from being desirous of accepting their employments, and also to induce them to regard their magistrates with favor when they know what a price they pay for their honors. It is also necessary that

30 the magistrates, upon entering into their offices, should make magnificent sacrifices and erect some public structure, that the people partaking of the entertainment, and seeing the city ornamented with votive gifts in their tem-

35 ples and public structures, may see with pleasure the stability of the government: add to this also, that the nobles will have their generosity recorded: but now this is not the conduct which those who are at present at the head of

40 an oligarchy pursue, but the contrary; for they are not more desirous of honor than of gain; for which reason such oligarchies may more properly be called little democracies. Thus [1321b] we have explained on what principles

45 a democracy and an oligarchy ought to be established…

155

MACHIAVELLI

Niccolo Machiavelli (1469-1527) is considered by many to be the first 'modern' political philosopher, and is so different than anyone else that he has become an adjective: Machiavellian means duplicitous or tricky. Born in Florence during the era of her Republic, Machiavelli grew to become a mid-level government official, primarily responsible for foreign affairs. However, when the resurgent Medici family crushed the Florentine Republic in 1512, Machiavelli was tortured by the new government and eventually exiled. It is in this exile that Machiavelli's two great works, *The Discourses* (on republics) and *The Prince* (on principalities), were constructed.

The Prince is, at minimum, an enigmatic work. Though constructed in the classical style of a 'mirror for princes' it differs rather sharply for other examples of the style: it purports to tell the reinstalled Medici how to successfully govern—not through kindness, honesty, and love, but through measure brutality and calculated fear. *The Prince* strips bare the philosophy (and religion) than often imbued the study of politics—so much so that the book has been frequently banned since its publication. This is the mystery of *The Prince*: is Machiavelli honestly professing that this radically different understanding of virtue and this targeted cruelty is, in fact the best way to govern? Or, is he trying bring down his enemies—those who tortured and exiled him—from within?

THE PRINCE
NICOLLO MACHIAVELLI

DEDICATION

To the Magnificent Lorenzo Di Piero De'
Medici:

5

Those who strive to obtain the good graces of
a prince are accustomed to come before him
with such things as they hold most precious,
or in which they see him take most delight;
10 whence one often sees horses, arms, cloth of
gold, precious stones, and similar ornaments
presented to princes, worthy of their greatness.

15 Desiring therefore to present myself to your
Magnificence with some testimony of my devotion towards you, I have not found among
my possessions anything which I hold more
dear than, or value so much as, the knowledge
20 of the actions of great men, acquired by
long experience in contemporary affairs, and a
continual study of antiquity; which, having
reflected upon it with great and prolonged
diligence, I now send, digested into a little
25 volume, to your Magnificence.

And although I may consider this work unworthy of your countenance, nevertheless I
trust much to your benignity that it may be
30 acceptable, seeing that it is not possible for me
to make a better gift than to offer you the opportunity of understanding in the shortest
time all that I have learnt in so many years,
and with so many troubles and dangers; which

35 work I have not embellished with swelling or
magnificent words, nor stuffed with rounded
periods, nor with any extrinsic allurements or
adornments whatever, with which so many are
accustomed to embellish their works; for I
40 have wished either that no honor should be
given it, or else that the truth of the matter
and the weightiness of the theme shall make it
acceptable.

45 Nor do I hold with those who regard it as a
presumption if a man of low and humble condition dare to discuss and settle the concerns
of princes; because, just as those who draw
landscapes place themselves below in the plain
50 to contemplate the nature of the mountains
and of lofty places, and in order to contemplate the plains place themselves upon high
mountains, even so to understand the nature
of the people it needs to be a prince, and to
55 understand that of princes it needs to be of
the people.

Take then, your Magnificence, this little gift in
the spirit in which I send it; wherein, if it be
60 diligently read and considered by you, you will
learn my extreme desire that you should attain
that greatness which fortune and your other
attributes promise. And if your Magnificence
from the summit of your greatness will some-
65 times turn your eyes to these lower regions,
you will see how unmeritedly I suffer a great
and continued malignity of fortune.

70

Text based off the W.K. Marriott translation,
with adjustments for modern spellings.

CHAPTER I

HOW MANY KINDS OF PRINCIPALITIES THERE ARE, AND BY WHAT MEANS THEY ARE ACQUIRED

5

All states, all powers, that have held and hold rule over men have been and are either republics or principalities.

10 Principalities are either hereditary, in which the family has been long established; or they are new.

The new are either entirely new, as was Milan
15 to Francesco Sforza, or they are, as it were, members annexed to the hereditary state of the prince who has acquired them, as was the kingdom of Naples to that of the King of Spain.

20

Such dominions thus acquired are either accustomed to live under a prince, or to live in freedom; and are acquired either by the arms of the prince himself, or of others, or else by
25 fortune or by ability.

CHAPTER II

CONCERNING HEREDITARY PRINCIPALITIES

30

I will leave out all discussion on republics, inasmuch as in another place I have written of them at length, and will address myself only to principalities. In doing so I will keep to the
35 order indicated above, and discuss how such principalities are to be ruled and preserved.

I say at once there are fewer difficulties in holding hereditary states, and those long accustomed to the family of their prince, than
40 new ones; for it is sufficient only not to transgress the customs of his ancestors, and to deal prudently with circumstances as they arise, for

a prince of average powers to maintain himself
45 in his state, unless he be deprived of it by some extraordinary and excessive force; and if he should be so deprived of it, whenever anything sinister happens to the usurper, he will regain it.

50

We have in Italy, for example, the Duke of Ferrara, who could not have withstood the attacks of the Venetians in '84, nor those of Pope Julius in '10, unless he had been long
55 established in his dominions. For the hereditary prince has less cause and less necessity to offend; hence it happens that he will be more loved; and unless extraordinary vices cause him to be hated, it is reasonable to expect that
60 his subjects will be naturally well disposed towards him; and in the antiquity and duration of his rule the memories and motives that make for change are lost, for one change always leaves the toothing for another.

65

CHAPTER III

CONCERNING MIXED PRINCIPALITIES

70 But the difficulties occur in a new principality. And firstly, if it be not entirely new, but is, as it were, a member of a state which, taken collectively, may be called composite, the changes arise chiefly from an inherent difficulty which
75 there is in all new principalities; for men change their rulers willingly, hoping to better themselves, and this hope induces them to take up arms against him who rules: wherein they are deceived, because they afterwards find
80 by experience they have gone from bad to worse. This follows also on another natural and common necessity, which always causes a new prince to burden those who have submitted to him with his soldiery and with infinite
85 other hardships which he must put upon his new acquisition.

In this way you have enemies in all those whom you have injured in seizing that principality, and you are not able to keep those friends who put you there because of your not 5 being able to satisfy them in the way they expected, and you cannot take strong measures against them, feeling bound to them. For, although one may be very strong in armed forces, yet in entering a province one has always 10 need of the goodwill of the natives.

For these reasons Louis the Twelfth, King of France, quickly occupied Milan, and as quickly lost it; and to turn him out the first time it 15 only needed Lodovico's own forces; because those who had opened the gates to him, finding themselves deceived in their hopes of future benefit, would not endure the ill-treatment of the new prince. It is very true 20 that, after acquiring rebellious provinces a second time, they are not so lightly lost afterwards, because the prince, with little reluctance, takes the opportunity of the rebellion to punish the delinquents, to clear out the sus-25 pects, and to strengthen himself in the weakest places. Thus to cause France to lose Milan the first time it was enough for the Duke Lodovico to raise insurrections on the borders; but to cause him to lose it a second time it was nec-30 essary to bring the whole world against him, and that his armies should be defeated and driven out of Italy; which followed from the causes above mentioned.

35 Nevertheless Milan was taken from France both the first and the second time. The general reasons for the first have been discussed; it remains to name those for the second, and to see what resources he had, and what any 40 one in his situation would have had for maintaining himself more securely in his acquisition than did the King of France.

Now I say that those dominions which, when 45 acquired, are added to an ancient state by him who acquires them, are either of the same country and language, or they are not. When they are, it is easier to hold them, especially when they have not been accustomed to self-50 government; and to hold them securely it is enough to have destroyed the family of the prince who was ruling them; because the two peoples, preserving in other things the old conditions, and not being unlike in customs, 55 will live quietly together, as one has seen in Brittany, Burgundy, Gascony, and Normandy, which have been bound to France for so long a time: and, although there may be some difference in language, nevertheless the customs 60 are alike, and the people will easily be able to get on amongst themselves. He who has annexed them, if he wishes to hold them, has only to bear in mind two considerations: the one, that the family of their former lord is 65 extinguished; the other, that neither their laws nor their taxes are altered, so that in a very short time they will become entirely one body with the old principality.

70 But when states are acquired in a country differing in language, customs, or laws, there are difficulties, and good fortune and great energy are needed to hold them, and one of the greatest and most real helps would be that he 75 who has acquired them should go and reside there. This would make his position more secure and durable, as it has made that of the Turk in Greece, who, notwithstanding all the other measures taken by him for holding that 80 state, if he had not settled there, would not have been able to keep it. Because, if one is on the spot, disorders are seen as they spring up, and one can quickly remedy them; but if one is not at hand, they are heard of only when they 85 are great, and then one can no longer remedy them. Besides this, the country is not pillaged

by your officials; the subjects are satisfied by prompt recourse to the prince; thus, wishing to be good, they have more cause to love him, and wishing to be otherwise, to fear him. He who would attack that state from the outside must have the utmost caution; as long as the prince resides there it can only be wrested from him with the greatest difficulty.

The other and better course is to send colonies to one or two places, which may be as keys to that state, for it is necessary either to do this or else to keep there a great number of cavalry and infantry. A prince does not spend much on colonies, for with little or no expense he can send them out and keep them there, and he offends a minority only of the citizens from whom he takes lands and houses to give them to the new inhabitants; and those whom he offends, remaining poor and scattered, are never able to injure him; whilst the rest being uninjured are easily kept quiet, and at the same time are anxious not to err for fear it should happen to them as it has to those who have been despoiled. In conclusion, I say that these colonies are not costly, they are more faithful, they injure less, and the injured, as has been said, being poor and scattered, cannot hurt. Upon this, one has to remark that men ought either to be well treated or crushed, because they can avenge themselves of lighter injuries, of more serious ones they cannot; therefore the injury that is to be done to a man ought to be of such a kind that one does not stand in fear of revenge.

But in maintaining armed men there in place of colonies one spends much more, having to consume on the garrison all the income from the state, so that the acquisition turns into a loss, and many more are exasperated, because the whole state is injured; through the shifting of the garrison up and down all become ac-quainted with hardship, and all become hostile, and they are enemies who, whilst beaten on their own ground, are yet able to do hurt. For every reason, therefore, such guards are as useless as a colony is useful.

Again, the prince who holds a country differing in the above respects ought to make himself the head and defender of his less powerful neighbors, and to weaken the more powerful amongst them, taking care that no foreigner as powerful as himself shall, by any accident, get a footing there; for it will always happen that such a one will be introduced by those who are discontented, either through excess of ambition or through fear, as one has seen already. The Romans were brought into Greece by the Aetolians; and in every other country where they obtained a footing they were brought in by the inhabitants. And the usual course of affairs is that, as soon as a powerful foreigner enters a country, all the subject states are drawn to him, moved by the hatred which they feel against the ruling power. So that in respect to those subject states he has not to take any trouble to gain them over to himself, for the whole of them quickly rally to the state which he has acquired there. He has only to take care that they do not get hold of too much power and too much authority, and then with his own forces, and with their goodwill, he can easily keep down the more powerful of them, so as to remain entirely master in the country. And he who does not properly manage this business will soon lose what he has acquired, and whilst he does hold it he will have endless difficulties and troubles.

The Romans, in the countries which they annexed, observed closely these measures; they sent colonies and maintained friendly relations with the minor powers, without increasing their strength; they kept down the greater, and did not allow any strong foreign powers to gain authority. Greece appears to me sufficient for an example. The Achaeans and Aetolians were kept friendly by them, the kingdom of

5 Macedonia was humbled, Antiochus was driven out; yet the merits of the Achaeans and Aetolians never secured for them permission to increase their power, nor did the persuasions of Philip ever induce the Romans to be

10 his friends without first humbling him, nor did the influence of Antiochus make them agree that he should retain any lordship over the country. Because the Romans did in these instances what all prudent princes ought to do,

15 who have to regard not only present troubles, but also future ones, for which they must prepare with every energy, because, when foreseen, it is easy to remedy them; but if you wait until they approach, the medicine is no longer

20 in time because the malady has become incurable; for it happens in this, as the physicians say it happens in hectic fever, that in the beginning of the malady it is easy to cure but difficult to detect, but in the course of time,

25 not having been either detected or treated in the beginning, it becomes easy to detect but difficult to cure. This it happens in affairs of state, for when the evils that arise have been foreseen (which it is only given to a wise man

30 to see), they can be quickly redressed, but when, through not having been foreseen, they have been permitted to grow in a way that every one can see them, there is no longer a remedy. Therefore, the Romans, foreseeing

35 troubles, dealt with them at once, and, even to avoid a war, would not let them come to a head, for they knew that war is not to be avoided, but is only to be put off to the advantage of others; moreover they wished to

40 fight with Philip and Antiochus in Greece so as not to have to do it in Italy; they could have avoided both, but this they did not wish; nor did that ever please them which is for ever in

45 the mouths of the wise ones of our time:--Let us enjoy the benefits of the time--but rather the benefits of their own valor and prudence, for time drives everything before it, and is able to bring with it good as well as evil, and evil as well as good.

50

But let us turn to France and inquire whether she has done any of the things mentioned. I will speak of Louis (and not of Charles) as the one whose conduct is the better to be ob-

55 served, he having held possession of Italy for the longest period; and you will see that he has done the opposite to those things which ought to be done to retain a state composed of divers elements.

60

King Louis was brought into Italy by the ambition of the Venetians, who desired to obtain half the state of Lombardy by his intervention. I will not blame the course taken by the king,

65 because, wishing to get a foothold in Italy, and having no friends there--seeing rather that every door was shut to him owing to the conduct of Charles--he was forced to accept those friendships which he could get, and he would

70 have succeeded very quickly in his design if in other matters he had not made some mistakes. The king, however, having acquired Lombardy, regained at once the authority which Charles had lost: Genoa yielded; the Floren-

75 tines became his friends; the Marquess of Mantua, the Duke of Ferrara, the Bentivogli, my lady of Forli, the Lords of Faenza, of Pesaro, of Rimini, of Camerino, of Piombino, the Lucchese, the Pisans, the Sienese--everybody

80 made advances to him to become his friend. Then could the Venetians realize the rashness of the course taken by them, which, in order that they might secure two towns in Lombardy, had made the king master of two-thirds

85 of Italy.

Let any one now consider with what little difficulty the king could have maintained his position in Italy had he observed the rules above laid down, and kept all his friends secure and protected; for although they were numerous they were both weak and timid, some afraid of the Church, some of the Venetians, and thus they would always have been forced to stand in with him, and by their means he could easily have made himself secure against those who remained powerful. But he was no sooner in Milan than he did the contrary by assisting Pope Alexander to occupy the Romagna. It never occurred to him that by this action he was weakening himself, depriving himself of friends and of those who had thrown themselves into his lap, whilst he aggrandized the Church by adding much temporal power to the spiritual, thus giving it greater authority. And having committed this prime error, he was obliged to follow it up, so much so that, to put an end to the ambition of Alexander, and to prevent his becoming the master of Tuscany, he was himself forced to come into Italy.

And as if it were not enough to have aggrandized the Church, and deprived himself of friends, he, wishing to have the kingdom of Naples, divides it with the King of Spain, and where he was the prime arbiter in Italy he takes an associate, so that the ambitious of that country and the malcontents of his own should have somewhere to shelter; and whereas he could have left in the kingdom his own pensioner as king, he drove him out, to put one there who was able to drive him, Louis, out in turn.

The wish to acquire is in truth very natural and common, and men always do so when they can, and for this they will be praised not blamed; but when they cannot do so, yet wish to do so by any means, then there is folly and blame. Therefore, if France could have attacked Naples with her own forces she ought to have done so; if she could not, then she ought not to have divided it. And if the partition which she made with the Venetians in Lombardy was justified by the excuse that by it she got a foothold in Italy, this other partition merited blame, for it had not the excuse of that necessity.

Therefore Louis made these five errors: he destroyed the minor powers, he increased the strength of one of the greater powers in Italy, he brought in a foreign power, he did not settle in the country, he did not send colonies. Which errors, had he lived, were not enough to injure him had he not made a sixth by taking away their dominions from the Venetians; because, had he not aggrandized the Church, nor brought Spain into Italy, it would have been very reasonable and necessary to humble them; but having first taken these steps, he ought never to have consented to their ruin, for they, being powerful, would always have kept off others from designs on Lombardy, to which the Venetians would never have consented except to become masters themselves there; also because the others would not wish to take Lombardy from France in order to give it to the Venetians, and to run counter to both they would not have had the courage.

And if any one should say: "King Louis yielded the Romagna to Alexander and the kingdom to Spain to avoid war," I answer for the reasons given above that a blunder ought never to be perpetrated to avoid war, because it is not to be avoided, but is only deferred to your disadvantage. And if another should allege the pledge which the king had given to the Pope that he would assist him in the enterprise, in exchange for the dissolution of his marriage and for the cap to Rouen, to that I reply what I shall write later on concerning the faith of princes, and how it ought to be kept.

5 Thus King Louis lost Lombardy by not having followed any of the conditions observed by those who have taken possession of countries and wished to retain them. Nor is there any miracle in this, but much that is reasonable
10 and quite natural. And on these matters I spoke at Nantes with Rouen, when Valentino, as Cesare Borgia, the son of Pope Alexander, was usually called, occupied the Romagna, and on Cardinal Rouen observing to me that the
15 Italians did not understand war, I replied to him that the French did not understand state-craft, meaning that otherwise they would not have allowed the Church to reach such great-ness. And in fact it has been seen that the
20 greatness of the Church and of Spain in Italy has been caused by France, and her ruin may be attributed to them. From this a general rule is drawn which never or rarely fails: that he who is the cause of another becoming power-
25 ful is ruined; because that predominancy has been brought about either by astuteness or else by force, and both are distrusted by him who has been raised to power.

30 **CHAPTER IV**

WHY THE KINGDOM OF DARIUS,
CONQUERED BY ALEXANDER, DID
NOT REBEL AGAINST THE SUCCES-
SORS OF ALEXANDER AT HIS DEATH

35

Considering the difficulties which men have had to hold to a newly acquired state, some might wonder how, seeing that Alexander the Great became the master of Asia in a few
40 years, and died whilst it was scarcely settled (whence it might appear reasonable that the whole empire would have rebelled), neverthe-less his successors maintained themselves, and

had to meet no other difficulty than that
45 which arose among themselves from their own ambitions.

I answer that the principalities of which one has record are found to be governed in two
50 different ways; either by a prince, with a body of servants, who assist him to govern the kingdom as ministers by his favor and permis-sion; or by a prince and barons, who hold that dignity by antiquity of blood and not by the
55 grace of the prince. Such barons have states and their own subjects, who recognize them as lords and hold them in natural affection. Those states that are governed by a prince and his servants hold their prince in more consid-
60 eration, because in all the country there is no one who is recognized as superior to him, and if they yield obedience to another they do it as to a minister and official, and they do not bear him any particular affection.

65

The examples of these two governments in our time are the Turk and the King of France. The entire monarchy of the Turk is governed by one lord, the others are his servants; and,
70 dividing his kingdom into sanjaks, he sends there different administrators, and shifts and changes them as he chooses. But the King of France is placed in the midst of an ancient body of lords, acknowledged by their own
75 subjects, and beloved by them; they have their own prerogatives, nor can the king take these away except at his peril. Therefore, he who considers both of these states will recognize great difficulties in seizing the state of the
80 Turk, but, once it is conquered, great ease in holding it. The causes of the difficulties in seizing the kingdom of the Turk are that the usurper cannot be called in by the princes of the kingdom, nor can he hope to be assisted in
85 his designs by the revolt of those whom the lord has around him. This arises from the rea-

sons given above; for his ministers, being all slaves and bondmen, can only be corrupted with great difficulty, and one can expect little advantage from them when they have been
5   corrupted, as they cannot carry the people with them, for the reasons assigned. Hence, he who attacks the Turk must bear in mind that he will find him united, and he will have to rely more on his own strength than on the
10 revolt of others; but, if once the Turk has been conquered, and routed in the field in such a way that he cannot replace his armies, there is nothing to fear but the family of this prince, and, this being exterminated, there
15 remains no one to fear, the others having no credit with the people; and as the conqueror did not rely on them before his victory, so he ought not to fear them after it.

20 The contrary happens in kingdoms governed like that of France, because one can easily en-ter there by gaining over some baron of the kingdom, for one always finds malcontents and such as desire a change. Such men, for the
25 reasons given, can open the way into the state and render the victory easy; but if you wish to hold it afterwards, you meet with infinite diffi-culties, both from those who have assisted you and from those you have crushed. Nor is it
30 enough for you to have exterminated the fami-ly of the prince, because the lords that remain make themselves the heads of fresh move-ments against you, and as you are unable ei-ther to satisfy or exterminate them, that state
35 is lost whenever time brings the opportunity. Now if you will consider what was the nature of the government of Darius, you will find it similar to the kingdom of the Turk, and there-fore it was only necessary for Alexander, first
40 to overthrow him in the field, and then to take the country from him. After which victory, Darius being killed, the state remained secure to Alexander, for the above reasons. And if his

successors had been united they would have
45 enjoyed it securely and at their ease, for there were no tumults raised in the kingdom except those they provoked themselves.

But it is impossible to hold with such tranquil-
50 ity states constituted like that of France. Hence arose those frequent rebellions against the Romans in Spain, France, and Greece, owing to the many principalities there were in these states, of which, as long as the memory
55 of them endured, the Romans always held an insecure possession; but with the power and long continuance of the empire the memory of them passed away, and the Romans then became secure possessors. And when fighting
60 afterwards amongst themselves, each one was able to attach to himself his own parts of the country, according to the authority he had assumed there; and the family of the former lord being exterminated, none other than the
65 Romans were acknowledged.

When these things are remembered no one will marvel at the ease with which Alexander held the Empire of Asia, or at the difficulties
70 which others have had to keep an acquisition, such as Pyrrhus and many more; this is not occasioned by the little or abundance of ability in the conqueror, but by the want of uniformi-ty in the subject state.
75

CHAPTER V
CONCERNING THE WAY TO GOVERN CITIES OR PRINCIPALITIES WHICH LIVED UNDER THEIR OWN LAWS BE-
80   FORE THEY WERE ANNEXED

Whenever those states which have been ac-quired as stated have been accustomed to live under their own laws and in freedom, there
85 are three courses for those who wish to hold them: the first is to ruin them, the next is to

reside there in person, the third is to permit them to live under their own laws, drawing a tribute, and establishing within it an oligarchy which will keep it friendly to you. Because such a government, being created by the prince, knows that it cannot stand without his friendship and interest, and does it utmost to support him; and therefore he who would keep a city accustomed to freedom will hold it more easily by the means of its own citizens than in any other way.

There are, for example, the Spartans and the Romans. The Spartans held Athens and Thebes, establishing there an oligarchy, nevertheless they lost them. The Romans, in order to hold Capua, Carthage, and Numantia, dismantled them, and did not lose them. They wished to hold Greece as the Spartans held it, making it free and permitting its laws, and did not succeed. So to hold it they were compelled to dismantle many cities in the country, for in truth there is no safe way to retain them otherwise than by ruining them. And he who becomes master of a city accustomed to freedom and does not destroy it, may expect to be destroyed by it, for in rebellion it has always the watchword of liberty and its ancient privileges as a rallying point, which neither time nor benefits will ever cause it to forget. And whatever you may do or provide against, they never forget that name or their privileges unless they are disunited or dispersed, but at every chance they immediately rally to them, as Pisa after the hundred years she had been held in bondage by the Florentines.

But when cities or countries are accustomed to live under a prince, and his family is exterminated, they, being on the one hand accustomed to obey and on the other hand not having the old prince, cannot agree in making one from amongst themselves, and they do not know how to govern themselves. For this reason they are very slow to take up arms, and a prince can gain them to himself and secure them much more easily. But in republics there is more vitality, greater hatred, and more desire for vengeance, which will never permit them to allow the memory of their former liberty to rest; so that the safest way is to destroy them or to reside there.

CHAPTER VI
CONCERNING NEW PRINCIPALITIES WHICH ARE ACQUIRED BY ONE'S OWN ARMS AND ABILITY

Let no one be surprised if, in speaking of entirely new principalities as I shall do, I adduce the highest examples both of prince and of state; because men, walking almost always in paths beaten by others, and following by imitation their deeds, are yet unable to keep entirely to the ways of others or attain to the power of those they imitate. A wise man ought always to follow the paths beaten by great men, and to imitate those who have been supreme, so that if his ability does not equal theirs, at least it will savor of it. Let him act like the clever archers who, designing to hit the mark which yet appears too far distant, and knowing the limits to which the strength of their bow attains, take aim much higher than the mark, not to reach by their strength or arrow to so great a height, but to be able with the aid of so high an aim to hit the mark they wish to reach.

I say, therefore, that in entirely new principalities, where there is a new prince, more or less difficulty is found in keeping them, accordingly as there is more or less ability in him who has acquired the state. Now, as the fact of becoming a prince from a private station presupposes either ability or fortune, it is clear

that one or other of these things will mitigate in some degree many difficulties. Nevertheless, he who has relied least on fortune is established the strongest. Further, it facilitates
5 matters when the prince, having no other state, is compelled to reside there in person.

But to come to those who, by their own ability and not through fortune, have risen to be
10 princes, I say that Moses, Cyrus, Romulus, Theseus, and such like are the most excellent examples. And although one may not discuss Moses, he having been a mere executor of the will of God, yet he ought to be admired, if
15 only for that favor which made him worthy to speak with God. But in considering Cyrus and others who have acquired or founded kingdoms, all will be found admirable; and if their particular deeds and conduct shall be consid-
20 ered, they will not be found inferior to those of Moses, although he had so great a preceptor. And in examining their actions and lives one cannot see that they owed anything to fortune beyond opportunity, which brought
25 them the material to mold into the form which seemed best to them. Without that opportunity their powers of mind would have been extinguished, and without those powers the opportunity would have come in vain.
30
It was necessary, therefore, to Moses that he should find the people of Israel in Egypt enslaved and oppressed by the Egyptians, in order that they should be disposed to follow him
35 so as to be delivered out of bondage. It was necessary that Romulus should not remain in Alba, and that he should be abandoned at his birth, in order that he should become King of Rome and founder of the fatherland. It was
40 necessary that Cyrus should find the Persians discontented with the government of the Medes, and the Medes soft and effeminate through their long peace. Theseus could not

45 have shown his ability had he not found the Athenians dispersed. These opportunities, therefore, made those men fortunate, and their high ability enabled them to recognize the opportunity whereby their country was ennobled and made famous.
50
Those who by valorous ways become princes, like these men, acquire a principality with difficulty, but they keep it with ease. The difficul-
55 ties they have in acquiring it rise in part from the new rules and methods which they are forced to introduce to establish their government and its security. And it ought to be remembered that there is nothing more difficult to take in hand, more perilous to conduct, or
60 more uncertain in its success, than to take the lead in the introduction of a new order of things, because the innovator has for enemies all those who have done well under the old conditions, and lukewarm defenders in those
65 who may do well under the new. This coolness arises partly from fear of the opponents, who have the laws on their side, and partly from the incredulity of men, who do not readily believe in new things until they have
70 had a long experience of them. Thus it happens that whenever those who are hostile have the opportunity to attack they do it like partisans, whilst the others defend lukewarmly, in such wise that the prince is endangered along
75 with them.

It is necessary, therefore, if we desire to discuss this matter thoroughly, to inquire whether these innovators can rely on themselves or
80 have to depend on others: that is to say, whether, to consummate their enterprise, have they to use prayers or can they use force? In the first instance they always succeed badly, and never compass anything; but when they
85 can rely on themselves and use force, then they are rarely endangered. Hence it is that all

armed prophets have conquered, and the unarmed ones have been destroyed. Besides the
reasons mentioned, the nature of the people is
variable, and whilst it is easy to persuade them,
5 it is difficult to fix them in that persuasion.
And thus it is necessary to take such measures
that, when they believe no longer, it may be
possible to make them believe by force.

10 If Moses, Cyrus, Theseus, and Romulus had
been unarmed they could not have enforced
their constitutions for long--as happened in
our time to Fra Girolamo Savonarola, who
was ruined with his new order of things im-
15 mediately the multitude believed in him no
longer, and he had no means of keeping steadfast those who believed or of making the unbelievers to believe. Therefore such as these
have great difficulties in consummating their
20 enterprise, for all their dangers are in the ascent, yet with ability they will overcome them;
but when these are overcome, and those who
envied them their success are exterminated,
they will begin to be respected, and they will
25 continue afterwards powerful, secure, honored, and happy.

To these great examples I wish to add a lesser
one; still it bears some resemblance to them,
and I wish it to suffice me for all of a like
30 kind: it is Hiero the Syracusan. This man rose
from a private station to be Prince of Syracuse, nor did he, either, owe anything to fortune but opportunity; for the Syracusans, be-
35 ing oppressed, chose him for their captain,
afterwards he was rewarded by being made
their prince. He was of so great ability, even as
a private citizen, that one who writes of him
says he wanted nothing but a kingdom to be a
40 king. This man abolished the old soldiery, organized the new, gave up old alliances, made
new ones; and as he had his own soldiers and
allies, on such foundations he was able to

45 build any edifice: thus, whilst he had endured
much trouble in acquiring, he had but little in
keeping.

CHAPTER VII
CONCERNING NEW PRINCIPALITIES
50 WHICH ARE ACQUIRED EITHER BY
THE ARMS OF OTHERS OR BY GOOD
FORTUNE

Those who solely by good fortune become
55 princes from being private citizens have little
trouble in rising, but much in keeping atop;
they have not any difficulties on the way up,
because they fly, but they have many when
they reach the summit. Such are those to
60 whom some state is given either for money or
by the favor of him who bestows it; as happened to many in Greece, in the cities of Ionia
and of the Hellespont, where princes were
made by Darius, in order that they might hold
65 the cities both for his security and his glory; as
also were those emperors who, by the corruption of the soldiers, from being citizens came
to empire. Such stand simply elevated upon
the goodwill and the fortune of him who has
70 elevated them--two most inconstant and unstable things. Neither have they the knowledge
requisite for the position; because, unless they
are men of great worth and ability, it is not
reasonable to expect that they should know
75 how to command, having always lived in a
private condition; besides, they cannot hold it
because they have not forces which they can
keep friendly and faithful.

80 States that rise unexpectedly, then, like all other things in nature which are born and grow
rapidly, cannot leave their foundations and
correspondencies fixed in such a way that the
first storm will not overthrow them; unless, as
85 is said, those who unexpectedly become princes are men of so much ability that they know

they have to be prepared at once to hold that which fortune has thrown into their laps, and that those foundations, which others have laid BEFORE they became princes, they must lay

5 AFTERWARDS.

Concerning these two methods of rising to be a prince by ability or fortune, I wish to adduce two examples within our own recollection,

10 and these are Francesco Sforza and Cesare Borgia. Francesco, by proper means and with great ability, from being a private person rose to be Duke of Milan, and that which he had acquired with a thousand

15 anxieties he kept with little trouble. On the other hand, Cesare Borgia, called by the people Duke Valentino, acquired his state during the ascendancy of his father, and on its decline he lost it, notwithstanding that he had taken

20 every measure and done all that ought to be done by a wise and able man to fix firmly his roots in the states which the arms and fortunes of others had bestowed on him.

25 Because, as is stated above, he who has not first laid his foundations may be able with great ability to lay them afterwards, but they will be laid with trouble to the architect and danger to the building. If, therefore, all the

30 steps taken by the duke be considered, it will be seen that he laid solid foundations for his future power, and I do not consider it superfluous to discuss them, because I do not know what better precepts to give a new prince than

35 the example of his actions; and if his dispositions were of no avail, that was not his fault, but the extraordinary and extreme malignity of fortune.

40 Alexander the Sixth, in wishing to aggrandize the duke, his son, had many immediate and prospective difficulties. Firstly, he did not see his way to make him master of any state that

was not a state of the Church; and if he was

45 willing to rob the Church he knew that the Duke of Milan and the Venetians would not consent, because Faenza and Rimini were already under the protection of the Venetians. Besides this, he saw the arms of Italy, especial-

50 ly those by which he might have been assisted, in hands that would fear the aggrandizement of the Pope, namely, the Orsini and the Colonnesi and their following. It behooved him, therefore, to upset this state of affairs and

55 embroil the powers, so as to make himself securely master of part of their states. This was easy for him to do, because he found the Venetians, moved by other reasons, inclined to bring back the French into Italy; he would

60 not only not oppose this, but he would render it more easy by dissolving the former marriage of King Louis. Therefore the king came into Italy with the assistance of the Venetians and the consent of Alexander. He was no sooner

65 in Milan than the Pope had soldiers from him for the attempt on the Romagna, which yielded to him on the reputation of the king. The duke, therefore, having acquired the Romagna and beaten the Colonnesi, while wishing to

70 hold that and to advance further, was hindered by two things: the one, his forces did not appear loyal to him, the other, the goodwill of France: that is to say, he feared that the forces of the Orsini, which he was using, would not

75 stand to him, that not only might they hinder him from winning more, but might themselves seize what he had won, and that the king might also do the same. Of the Orsini he had a warning when, after taking Faenza and at-

80 tacking Bologna, he saw them go very unwillingly to that attack. And as to the king, he learned his mind when he himself, after taking the Duchy of Urbino, attacked Tuscany, and the king made him desist from that undertak-

85 ing; hence the duke decided to depend no more upon the arms and the luck of others.

For the first thing he weakened the Orsini and Colonnesi parties in Rome, by gaining to himself all their adherents who were gentlemen, making them his gentlemen, giving them good pay, and, according to their rank, honoring them with office and command in such a way that in a few months all attachment to the factions was destroyed and turned entirely to the duke. After this he awaited an opportunity to crush the Orsini, having scattered the adherents of the Colonna house. This came to him soon and he used it well; for the Orsini, perceiving at length that the aggrandizement of the duke and the Church was ruin to them, called a meeting of the Magione in Perugia. From this sprung the rebellion at Urbino and the tumults in the Romagna, with endless dangers to the duke, all of which he overcame with the help of the French. Having restored his authority, not to leave it at risk by trusting either to the French or other outside forces, he had recourse to his wiles, and he knew so well how to conceal his mind that, by the mediation of Signor Pagolo--whom the duke did not fail to secure with all kinds of attention, giving him money, apparel, and horses--the Orsini were reconciled, so that their simplicity brought them into his power at Sinigalia. Having exterminated the leaders, and turned their partisans into his friends, the duke laid sufficiently good foundations to his power, having all the Romagna and the Duchy of Urbino; and the people now beginning to appreciate their prosperity, he gained them all over to himself. And as this point is worthy of notice, and to be imitated by others, I am not willing to leave it out.

When the duke occupied the Romagna he found it under the rule of weak masters, who rather plundered their subjects than ruled them, and gave them more cause for disunion than for union, so that the country was full of robbery, quarrels, and every kind of violence; and so, wishing to bring back peace and obedience to authority, he considered it necessary to give it a good governor. Thereupon he promoted Messer Ramiro d'Orco, a swift and cruel man, to whom he gave the fullest power. This man in a short time restored peace and unity with the greatest success. Afterwards the duke considered that it was not advisable to confer such excessive authority, for he had no doubt but that he would become odious, so he set up a court of judgment in the country, under a most excellent president, wherein all cities had their advocates. And because he knew that the past severity had caused some hatred against himself, so, to clear himself in the minds of the people, and gain them entirely to himself, he desired to show that, if any cruelty had been practiced, it had not originated with him, but in the natural sternness of the minister. Under this pretense he took Ramiro, and one morning caused him to be executed and left on the piazza at Cesena with the block and a bloody knife at his side. The barbarity of this spectacle caused the people to be at once satisfied and dismayed.

But let us return whence we started. I say that the duke, finding himself now sufficiently powerful and partly secured from immediate dangers by having armed himself in his own way, and having in a great measure crushed those forces in his vicinity that could injure him if he wished to proceed with his conquest, had next to consider France, for he knew that the king, who too late was aware of his mistake, would not support him. And from this time he began to seek new alliances and to temporize with France in the expedition which she was making towards the kingdom of Naples against the Spaniards who were besieging Gaeta. It was his intention to secure himself against them, and this he would have quickly accomplished had Alexander lived.

Such was his line of action as to present affairs. But as to the future he had to fear, in the
first place, that a new successor to the Church
might not be friendly to him and might seek
to take from him that which Alexander had
given him, so he decided to act in four ways.
Firstly, by exterminating the families of those
lords whom he had despoiled, so as to take
away that pretext from the Pope. Secondly, by
winning to himself all the gentlemen of Rome,
so as to be able to curb the Pope with their
aid, as has been observed. Thirdly, by converting the college more to himself. Fourthly, by
acquiring so much power before the Pope
should die that he could by his own measures
resist the first shock. Of these four things, at
the death of Alexander, he had accomplished
three. For he had killed as many of the dispos-
sessed lords as he could lay hands on, and few
had escaped; he had won over the Roman
gentlemen, and he had the most numerous
party in the college. And as to any fresh acquisition, he intended to become master of Tuscany, for he already possessed Perugia and
Piombino, and Pisa was under his protection.
And as he had no longer to study France (for
the French were already driven out of the
kingdom of Naples by the Spaniards, and in
this way both were compelled to buy his
goodwill), he pounced down upon Pisa. After
this, Lucca and Siena yielded at once, partly
through hatred and partly through fear of the
Florentines; and the Florentines would have
had no remedy had he continued to prosper,
as he was prospering the year that Alexander
died, for he had acquired so much power and
reputation that he would have stood by himself, and no longer have depended on the luck
and the forces of others, but solely on his own
power and ability.

But Alexander died five years after he had first
drawn the sword. He left the duke with the
state of Romagna alone consolidated, with the
rest in the air, between two most powerful
hostile armies, and sick unto death. Yet there
were in the duke such boldness and ability,
and he knew so well how men are to be won
or lost, and so firm were the foundations
which in so short a time he had laid, that if he
had not had those armies on his back, or if he
had been in good health, he would have overcome all difficulties. And it is seen that his
foundations were good, for the Romagna
awaited him for more than a month. In Rome,
although but half alive, he remained secure;
and whilst the Baglioni, the Vitelli, and the
Orsini might come to Rome, they could not
effect anything against him. If he could not
have made Pope him whom he wished, at least
the one whom he did not wish would not have
been elected. But if he had been in sound
health at the death of Alexander, everything
would have been different to him. On the day
that Julius the Second was elected, he told me
that he had thought of everything that might
occur at the death of his father, and had provided a remedy for all, except that he had never anticipated that, when the death did happen, he himself would be on the point to die.

When all the actions of the duke are recalled, I
do not know how to blame him, but rather it
appears to be, as I have said, that I ought to
offer him for imitation to all those who, by the
fortune or the arms of others, are raised to
government. Because he, having a lofty spirit
and far-reaching aims, could not have regulated his conduct otherwise, and only the shortness of the life of Alexander and his own sickness frustrated his designs. Therefore, he who
considers it necessary to secure himself in his
new principality, to win friends, to overcome
either by force or fraud, to make himself be-

loved and feared by the people, to be followed
and revered by the soldiers, to exterminate
those who have power or reason to hurt him,
to change the old order of things for new, to
5   be severe and gracious, magnanimous and
liberal, to destroy a disloyal soldiery and to
create new, to maintain friendship with kings
and princes in such a way that they must help
him with zeal and offend with caution, cannot
10 find a more lively example than the actions of
this man.

Only can he be blamed for the election of
Julius the Second, in whom he made a bad
15 choice, because, as is said, not being able to
elect a Pope to his own mind, he could have
hindered any other from being elected Pope;
and he ought never to have consented to the
election of any cardinal whom he had injured
20 or who had cause to fear him if they became
pontiffs. For men injure either from fear or
hatred. Those whom he had injured, amongst
others, were San Pietro ad Vincula, Colonna,
San Giorgio, and Ascanio. The rest, in be-
25 coming Pope, had to fear him, Rouen and the
Spaniards excepted; the latter from their relationship and obligations, the former from his
influence, the kingdom of France having relations with him. Therefore, above everything,
30 the duke ought to have created a Spaniard
Pope, and, failing him, he ought to have consented to Rouen and not San Pietro ad Vincula. He who believes that new benefits will
cause great personages to forget old injuries is
35 deceived. Therefore, the duke erred in his
choice, and it was the cause of his ultimate
ruin.

CHAPTER VIII
40 CONCERNING THOSE WHO HAVE
OBTAINED A PRINCIPALITY BY
WICKEDNESS

Although a prince may rise from a private
45 station in two ways, neither of which can be
entirely attributed to fortune or genius, yet it is
manifest to me that I must not be silent on
them, although one could be more copiously
treated when I discuss republics. These meth-
50 ods are when, either by some wicked or nefar-
ious ways, one ascends to the principality, or
when by the favor of his fellow-citizens a private person becomes the prince of his country. And speaking of the first method, it will
55 be illustrated by two examples--one ancient,
the other modern--and without entering further into the subject, I consider these two examples will suffice those who may be compelled to follow them.
60

Agathocles, the Sicilian, became King of Syracuse not only from a private but from a low
and abject position. This man, the son of a
potter, through all the changes in his fortunes
65 always led an infamous life. Nevertheless, he
accompanied his infamies with so much ability
of mind and body that, having devoted himself to the military profession, he rose through
its ranks to be Praetor of Syracuse. Being es-
70 tablished in that position, and having deliberately resolved to make himself prince and to
seize by violence, without obligation to others,
that which had been conceded to him by assent, he came to an understanding for this
75 purpose with Amilcar, the Carthaginian, who,
with his army, was fighting in Sicily. One
morning he assembled the people and the senate of Syracuse, as if he had to discuss with
them things relating to the Republic, and at a
80 given signal the soldiers killed all the senators
and the richest of the people; these dead, he
seized and held the princedom of that city
without any civil commotion. And although
he was twice routed by the Carthaginians, and
85 ultimately besieged, yet not only was he able to
defend his city, but leaving part of his men for

its defense, with the others he attacked Africa, and in a short time raised the siege of Syracuse. The Carthaginians, reduced to extreme necessity, were compelled to come to terms

5 with Agathocles, and, leaving Sicily to him, had to be content with the possession of Africa.

Therefore, he who considers the actions and

10 the genius of this man will see nothing, or little, which can be attributed to fortune, inasmuch as he attained pre-eminence, as is shown above, not by the favor of any one, but step by step in the military profession, which

15 steps were gained with a thousand troubles and perils, and were afterwards boldly held by him with many hazardous dangers. Yet it cannot be called talent to slay fellow-citizens, to deceive friends, to be without faith, without

20 mercy, without religion; such methods may gain empire, but not glory. Still, if the courage of Agathocles in entering into and extricating himself from dangers be considered, together with his greatness of mind in enduring and

25 overcoming hardships, it cannot be seen why he should be esteemed less than the most notable captain. Nevertheless, his barbarous cruelty and inhumanity with infinite wickedness do not permit him to be celebrated among the

30 most excellent men. What he achieved cannot be attributed either to fortune or genius.

In our times, during the rule of Alexander the Sixth, Oliverotto da Fermo, having been left

35 an orphan many years before, was brought up by his maternal uncle, Giovanni Fogliani, and in the early days of his youth sent to fight under Pagolo Vitelli, that, being trained under his discipline, he might attain some high position

40 in the military profession. After Pagolo died, he fought under his brother Vitellozzo, and in a very short time, being endowed with wit and a vigorous body and mind, he became the first

man in his profession. But it appearing a paltry

45 thing to serve under others, he resolved, with the aid of some citizens of Fermo, to whom the slavery of their country was dearer than its liberty, and with the help of the Vitelleschi, to seize Fermo. So he wrote to Giovanni Fogliani

50 that, having been away from home for many years, he wished to visit him and his city, and in some measure to look upon his patrimony; and although he had not labored to acquire anything except honor, yet, in order that the

55 citizens should see he had not spent his time in vain, he desired to come honorably, so would be accompanied by one hundred horsemen, his friends and retainers; and he entreated Giovanni to arrange that he should

60 be received honorably by the Fermians, all of which would be not only to his honor, but also to that of Giovanni himself, who had brought him up.

65 Giovanni, therefore, did not fail in any attentions due to his nephew, and he caused him to be honorably received by the Fermians, and he lodged him in his own house, where, having passed some days, and having arranged what

70 was necessary for his wicked designs, Oliverotto gave a solemn banquet to which he invited Giovanni Fogliani and the chiefs of Fermo. When the viands and all the other entertainments that are usual in such banquets

75 were finished, Oliverotto artfully began certain grave discourses, speaking of the greatness of Pope Alexander and his son Cesare, and of their enterprises, to which discourse Giovanni and others answered; but he rose at once, say-

80 ing that such matters ought to be discussed in a more private place, and he betook himself to a chamber, whither Giovanni and the rest of the citizens went in after him. No sooner were they seated than soldiers issued from secret

85 places and slaughtered Giovanni and the rest. After these murders Oliverotto, mounted on

horseback, rode up and down the town and
besieged the chief magistrate in the palace, so
that in fear the people were forced to obey
him, and to form a government, of which he
5 made himself the prince. He killed all the malcontents who were able to injure him, and
strengthened himself with new civil and military ordinances, in such a way that, in the year
during which he held the principality, not only
10 was he secure in the city of Fermo, but he had
become formidable to all his neighbors. And
his destruction would have been as difficult as
that of Agathocles if he had not allowed himself to be overreached by Cesare Borgia, who
15 took him with the Orsini and Vitelli at Sinigalia, as was stated above. Thus one year
after he had committed this parricide, he was
strangled, together with Vitellozzo, whom he
had made his leader in valor and wickedness.
20

Some may wonder how it can happen that
Agathocles, and his like, after infinite treacher-
ies and cruelties, should live for long secure in
his country, and defend himself from external
25 enemies, and never be conspired against by his
own citizens; seeing that many others, by
means of cruelty, have never been able even in
peaceful times to hold the state, still less in the
doubtful times of war. I believe that this fol-
30 lows from severities being badly or properly
used. Those may be called properly used, if of
evil it is possible to speak well, that are applied
at one blow and are necessary to one's security, and that are not persisted in afterwards
35 unless they can be turned to the advantage of
the subjects. The badly employed are those
which, notwithstanding they may be few in the
commencement, multiply with time rather
than decrease. Those who practice the first
40 system are able, by aid of God or man, to mitigate in some degree their rule, as Agathocles
did. It is impossible for those who follow the
other to maintain themselves.

Hence it is to be remarked that, in seizing a
45 state, the usurper ought to examine closely
into all those injuries which it is necessary for
him to inflict, and to do them all at one stroke
so as not to have to repeat them daily; and
thus by not unsettling men he will be able to
50 reassure them, and win them to himself by
benefits. He who does otherwise, either from
timidity or evil advice, is always compelled to
keep the knife in his hand; neither can he rely
on his subjects, nor can they attach themselves
55 to him, owing to their continued and repeated
wrongs. For injuries ought to be done all at
one time, so that, being tasted less, they offend less; benefits ought to be given little by
little, so that the flavor of them may last long-
60 er.

And above all things, a prince ought to live
amongst his people in such a way that no unexpected circumstances, whether of good or
65 evil, shall make him change; because if the
necessity for this comes in troubled times, you
are too late for harsh measures; and mild ones
will not help you, for they will be considered
as forced from you, and no one will be under
70 any obligation to you for them.

CHAPTER IX
CONCERNING A CIVIL PRINCIPALITY

75 But coming to the other point--where a leading citizen becomes the prince of his country,
not by wickedness or any intolerable violence,
but by the favor of his fellow citizens--this
may be called a civil principality: nor is genius
80 or fortune altogether necessary to attain to it,
but rather a happy shrewdness. I say then that
such a principality is obtained either by the
favor of the people or by the favor of the nobles. Because in all cities these two distinct
85 parties are found, and from this it arises that
the people do not wish to be ruled nor op-

pressed by the nobles, and the nobles wish to rule and oppress the people; and from these two opposite desires there arises in cities one of three results, either a principality, self-government, or anarchy.

A principality is created either by the people or by the nobles, accordingly as one or other of them has the opportunity; for the nobles, seeing they cannot withstand the people, begin to cry up the reputation of one of themselves, and they make him a prince, so that under his shadow they can give vent to their ambitions. The people, finding they cannot resist the nobles, also cry up the reputation of one of themselves, and make him a prince so as to be defended by his authority. He who obtains sovereignty by the assistance of the nobles maintains himself with more difficulty than he who comes to it by the aid of the people, because the former finds himself with many around him who consider themselves his equals, and because of this he can neither rule nor manage them to his liking. But he who reaches sovereignty by popular favor finds himself alone, and has none around him, or few, who are not prepared to obey him.

Besides this, one cannot by fair dealing, and without injury to others, satisfy the nobles, but you can satisfy the people, for their object is more righteous than that of the nobles, the latter wishing to oppress, while the former only desire not to be oppressed. It is to be added also that a prince can never secure himself against a hostile people, because of their being too many, whilst from the nobles he can secure himself, as they are few in number. The worst that a prince may expect from a hostile people is to be abandoned by them; but from hostile nobles he has not only to fear abandonment, but also that they will rise against him; for they, being in these affairs more far-seeing and astute, always come forward in time to save themselves, and to obtain favors from him whom they expect to prevail. Further, the prince is compelled to live always with the same people, but he can do well without the same nobles, being able to make and unmake them daily, and to give or take away authority when it pleases him.

Therefore, to make this point clearer, I say that the nobles ought to be looked at mainly in two ways: that is to say, they either shape their course in such a way as binds them entirely to your fortune, or they do not. Those who so bind themselves, and are not rapacious, ought to be honored and loved; those who do not bind themselves may be dealt with in two ways; they may fail to do this through pusillanimity and a natural want of courage, in which case you ought to make use of them, especially of those who are of good counsel; and thus, whilst in prosperity you honor them, in adversity you do not have to fear them. But when for their own ambitious ends they shun binding themselves, it is a token that they are giving more thought to themselves than to you, and a prince ought to guard against such, and to fear them as if they were open enemies, because in adversity they always help to ruin him.

Therefore, one who becomes a prince through the favor of the people ought to keep them friendly, and this he can easily do seeing they only ask not to be oppressed by him. But one who, in opposition to the people, becomes a prince by the favor of the nobles, ought, above everything, to seek to win the people over to himself, and this he may easily do if he takes them under his protection. Because men, when they receive good from him of whom they were expecting evil, are bound more closely to their benefactor; thus the people quickly become more devoted to him than if he had been raised to the principality by their favors; and the prince can win their affections in many ways, but as these vary according to

5 the circumstances one cannot give fixed rules, so I omit them; but, I repeat, it is necessary for a prince to have the people friendly, otherwise he has no security in adversity.

10 Nabis, Prince of the Spartans, sustained the attack of all Greece, and of a victorious Roman army, and against them he defended his country and his government; and for the overcoming of this peril it was only necessary for

15 him to make himself secure against a few, but this would not have been sufficient had the people been hostile. And do not let any one impugn this statement with the trite proverb that "He who builds on the people, builds on

20 the mud," for this is true when a private citizen makes a foundation there, and persuades himself that the people will free him when he is oppressed by his enemies or by the magistrates; wherein he would find himself very

25 often deceived, as happened to the Gracchi in Rome and to Messer Giorgio Scali in Florence. But granted a prince who has established himself as above, who can command, and is a man of courage, undismayed in adversity, who

30 does not fail in other qualifications, and who, by his resolution and energy, keeps the whole people encouraged--such a one will never find himself deceived in them, and it will be shown that he has laid his foundations well.

35

These principalities are liable to danger when they are passing from the civil to the absolute order of government, for such princes either rule personally or through magistrates. In the

40 latter case their government is weaker and more insecure, because it rests entirely on the goodwill of those citizens who are raised to the magistracy, and who, especially in troubled

times, can destroy the government with great
45 ease, either by intrigue or open defiance; and the prince has not the chance amid tumults to exercise absolute authority, because the citizens and subjects, accustomed to receive orders from magistrates, are not of a mind to

50 obey him amid these confusions, and there will always be in doubtful times a scarcity of men whom he can trust. For such a prince cannot rely upon what he observes in quiet times, when citizens have need of the state,

55 because then every one agrees with him; they all promise, and when death is far distant they all wish to die for him; but in troubled times, when the state has need of its citizens, then he finds but few. And so much the more is this

60 experiment dangerous, inasmuch as it can only be tried once. Therefore a wise prince ought to adopt such a course that his citizens will always in every sort and kind of circumstance have need of the state and of him, and then he

65 will always find them faithful.

CHAPTER X
CONCERNING THE WAY IN WHICH
THE STRENGTH OF ALL PRINCIPALI-
70 TIES OUGHT TO BE MEASURED

It is necessary to consider another point in examining the character of these principalities: that is, whether a prince has such power that,
75 in case of need, he can support himself with his own resources, or whether he has always need of the assistance of others. And to make this quite clear I say that I consider those who are able to support themselves by their own

80 resources who can, either by abundance of men or money, raise a sufficient army to join battle against any one who comes to attack them; and I consider those always to have need of others who cannot show themselves

85 against the enemy in the field, but are forced to defend themselves by sheltering behind

walls. The first case has been discussed, but we will speak of it again should it recur. In the second case one can say nothing except to encourage such princes to provision and forti-
5 fy their towns, and not on any account to defend the country. And whoever shall fortify his town well, and shall have managed the other concerns of his subjects in the way stated above, and to be often repeated, will never
10 be attacked without great caution, for men are always adverse to enterprises where difficulties can be seen, and it will be seen not to be an easy thing to attack one who has his town well fortified, and is not hated by his people.
15

The cities of Germany are absolutely free, they own but little country around them, and they yield obedience to the emperor when it suits them, nor do they fear this or any other power
20 they may have near them, because they are fortified in such a way that every one thinks the taking of them by assault would be tedious and difficult, seeing they have proper ditches and walls, they have sufficient artillery, and
25 they always keep in public depots enough for one year's eating, drinking, and firing. And beyond this, to keep the people quiet and without loss to the state, they always have the means of giving work to the community in
30 those labors that are the life and strength of the city, and on the pursuit of which the people are supported; they also hold military exercises in repute, and moreover have many ordinances to uphold them.
35

Therefore, a prince who has a strong city, and had not made himself odious, will not be attacked, or if any one should attack he will only be driven off with disgrace; again, because that
40 the affairs of this world are so changeable, it is almost impossible to keep an army a whole year in the field without being interfered with. And whoever should reply: If the people have

property outside the city, and see it burnt, they
45 will not remain patient, and the long siege and self-interest will make them forget their prince; to this I answer that a powerful and courageous prince will overcome all such difficulties by giving at one time hope to his sub-
50 jects that the evil will not be for long, at another time fear of the cruelty of the enemy, then preserving himself adroitly from those subjects who seem to him to be too bold.

55 Further, the enemy would naturally on his arrival at once burn and ruin the country at the time when the spirits of the people are still hot and ready for the defense; and, therefore, so much the less ought the prince to hesitate;
60 because after a time, when spirits have cooled, the damage is already done, the ills are incurred, and there is no longer any remedy; and therefore they are so much the more ready to unite with their prince, he appearing to be
65 under obligations to them now that their houses have been burnt and their possessions ruined in his defense. For it is the nature of men to be bound by the benefits they confer as much as by those they receive. Therefore, if
70 everything is well considered, it will not be difficult for a wise prince to keep the minds of his citizens steadfast from first to last, when he does not fail to support and defend them.

75 **CHAPTER XI**
CONCERNING ECCLESIASTICAL
PRINCIPALITIES

...

80 **CHAPTER XII**
HOW MANY KINDS OF SOLDIERY
THERE ARE, AND CONCERNING
MERCENARIES

85 Having discoursed particularly on the characteristics of such principalities as in the begin-

ning I proposed to discuss, and having considered in some degree the causes of their being good or bad, and having shown the methods by which many have sought to acquire them and to hold them, it now remains for me to discuss generally the means of offence and defense which belong to each of them.

We have seen above how necessary it is for a prince to have his foundations well laid, otherwise it follows of necessity he will go to ruin. The chief foundations of all states, new as well as old or composite, are good laws and good arms; and as there cannot be good laws where the state is not well armed, it follows that where they are well armed they have good laws. I shall leave the laws out of the discussion and shall speak of the arms.

I say, therefore, that the arms with which a prince defends his state are either his own, or they are mercenaries, auxiliaries, or mixed. Mercenaries and auxiliaries are useless and dangerous; and if one holds his state based on these arms, he will stand neither firm nor safe; for they are disunited, ambitious, and without discipline, unfaithful, valiant before friends, cowardly before enemies; they have neither the fear of God nor fidelity to men, and destruction is deferred only so long as the attack is; for in peace one is robbed by them, and in war by the enemy. The fact is, they have no other attraction or reason for keeping the field than a trifle of stipend, which is not sufficient to make them willing to die for you. They are ready enough to be your soldiers whilst you do not make war, but if war comes they take themselves off or run from the foe; which I should have little trouble to prove, for the ruin of Italy has been caused by nothing else than by resting all her hopes for many years on mercenaries, and although they formerly made some display and appeared valiant amongst

themselves, yet when the foreigners came they showed what they were. Thus it was that Charles, King of France, was allowed to seize Italy with chalk in hand; and he who told us that our sins were the cause of it told the truth, but they were not the sins he imagined, but those which I have related. And as they were the sins of princes, it is the princes who have also suffered the penalty.

I wish to demonstrate further the infelicity of these arms. The mercenary captains are either capable men or they are not; if they are, you cannot trust them, because they always aspire to their own greatness, either by oppressing you, who are their master, or others contrary to your intentions; but if the captain is not skillful, you are ruined in the usual way.

And if it be urged that whoever is armed will act in the same way, whether mercenary or not, I reply that when arms have to be resorted to, either by a prince or a republic, then the prince ought to go in person and perform the duty of a captain; the republic has to send its citizens, and when one is sent who does not turn out satisfactorily, it ought to recall him, and when one is worthy, to hold him by the laws so that he does not leave the command. And experience has shown princes and republics, single-handed, making the greatest progress, and mercenaries doing nothing except damage; and it is more difficult to bring a republic, armed with its own arms, under the sway of one of its citizens than it is to bring one armed with foreign arms. Rome and Sparta stood for many ages armed and free. The Swiss are completely armed and quite free.

Of ancient mercenaries, for example, there are the Carthaginians, who were oppressed by their mercenary soldiers after the first war with the Romans, although the Carthaginians had their own citizens for captains. After the death of Epaminondas, Philip of Macedon was made captain of their soldiers by the Thebans, and after victory he took away their liberty.

5   Duke Filippo being dead, the Milanese enlisted Francesco Sforza against the Venetians, and he, having overcome the enemy at Caravaggio, allied himself with them to crush the
10   Milanese, his masters. His father, Sforza, having been engaged by Queen Johanna of Naples, left her unprotected, so that she was forced to throw herself into the arms of the King of Aragon, in order to save her kingdom.
15   And if the Venetians and Florentines formerly extended their dominions by these arms, and yet their captains did not make themselves princes, but have defended them, I reply that the Florentines in this case have been favored
20   by chance, for of the able captains, of whom they might have stood in fear, some have not conquered, some have been opposed, and others have turned their ambitions elsewhere. One who did not conquer was Giovanni
25   Acuto, and since he did not conquer his fidelity cannot be proved; but every one will acknowledge that, had he conquered, the Florentines would have stood at his discretion. Sforza had the Bracceschi always against him,
30   so they watched each other. Francesco turned his ambition to Lombardy; Braccio against the Church and the kingdom of Naples. But let us come to that which happened a short while ago. The Florentines appointed as their cap-
35   tain Pagolo Vitelli, a most prudent man, who from a private position had risen to the greatest renown. If this man had taken Pisa, nobody can deny that it would have been proper for the Florentines to keep in with him, for if
40   he became the soldier of their enemies they had no means of resisting, and if they held to him they must obey him. The Venetians, if their achievements are considered, will be seen

to have acted safely and gloriously so long as
45   they sent to war their own men, when with armed gentlemen and plebeians they did valiantly. This was before they turned to enterprises on land, but when they began to fight on land they forsook this virtue and followed
50   the custom of Italy. And in the beginning of their expansion on land, through not having much territory, and because of their great reputation, they had not much to fear from their captains; but when they expanded, as under
55   Carmignuola, they had a taste of this mistake; for, having found him a most valiant man (they beat the Duke of Milan under his leadership), and, on the other hand, knowing how lukewarm he was in the war, they feared they
60   would no longer conquer under him, and for this reason they were not willing, nor were they able, to let him go; and so, not to lose again that which they had acquired, they were compelled, in order to secure themselves, to
65   murder him. They had afterwards for their captains Bartolomeo da Bergamo, Roberto da San Severino, the count of Pitigliano, and the like, under whom they had to dread loss and not gain, as happened afterwards at Vaila,
70   where in one battle they lost that which in eight hundred years they had acquired with so much trouble. Because from such arms conquests come but slowly, long delayed and inconsiderable, but the losses sudden and por-
75   tentous.

And as with these examples I have reached Italy, which has been ruled for many years by mercenaries, I wish to discuss them more seriously, in order that, having seen their rise and
80   progress, one may be better prepared to counteract them. You must understand that the empire has recently come to be repudiated in Italy, that the Pope has acquired more temporal power, and that Italy has been divided
85   up into more states, for the reason that many

of the great cities took up arms against their nobles, who, formerly favored by the emperor, were oppressing them, whilst the Church was favoring them so as to gain authority in tem-
5 poral power: in many others their citizens became princes. From this it came to pass that Italy fell partly into the hands of the Church and of republics, and, the Church consisting of priests and the republic of citizens unaccus-
10 tomed to arms, both commenced to enlist foreigners.

The first who gave renown to this soldiery was Alberigo da Conio, the Romagnian. From the
15 school of this man sprang, among others, Braccio and Sforza, who in their time were the arbiters of Italy. After these came all the other captains who till now have directed the arms of Italy; and the end of all their valor has been,
20 that she has been overrun by Charles, robbed by Louis, ravaged by Ferdinand, and insulted by the Swiss. The principle that has guided them has been, first, to lower the credit of infantry so that they might increase their own.
25 They did this because, subsisting on their pay and without territory, they were unable to support many soldiers, and a few infantry did not give them any authority; so they were led to employ cavalry, with a moderate force of
30 which they were maintained and honored; and affairs were brought to such a pass that, in an army of twenty thousand soldiers, there were not to be found two thousand foot soldiers. They had, besides this, used every art to lessen
35 fatigue and danger to themselves and their soldiers, not killing in the fray, but taking prisoners and liberating without ransom. They did not attack towns at night, nor did the garrisons of the towns attack encampments at
40 night; they did not surround the camp either with stockade or ditch, nor did they campaign in the winter. All these things were permitted by their military rules, and devised by them to

avoid, as I have said, both fatigue and dangers;
45 thus they have brought Italy to slavery and contempt.

CHAPTER XIII
CONCERNING AUXILIARIES, MIXED
50 SOLDIERY, AND ONE'S OWN

Auxiliaries, which are the other useless arm, are employed when a prince is called in with his forces to aid and defend, as was done by
55 Pope Julius in the most recent times; for he, having, in the enterprise against Ferrara, had poor proof of his mercenaries, turned to auxiliaries, and stipulated with Ferdinand, King of Spain, for his assistance with men and arms.
60 These arms may be useful and good in themselves, but for him who calls them in they are always disadvantageous; for losing, one is undone, and winning, one is their captive.

65 And although ancient histories may be full of examples, I do not wish to leave this recent one of Pope Julius the Second, the peril of which cannot fail to be perceived; for he, wishing to get Ferrara, threw himself entirely
70 into the hands of the foreigner. But his good fortune brought about a third event, so that he did not reap the fruit of his rash choice; because, having his auxiliaries routed at Ravenna, and the Swiss having risen and driven out the
75 conquerors (against all expectation, both his and others), it so came to pass that he did not become prisoner to his enemies, they having fled, nor to his auxiliaries, he having conquered by other arms than theirs.
80

The Florentines, being entirely without arms, sent ten thousand Frenchmen to take Pisa, whereby they ran more danger than at any other time of their troubles.
85

The Emperor of Constantinople, to oppose

his neighbors, sent ten thousand Turks into Greece, who, on the war being finished, were not willing to quit; this was the beginning of the servitude of Greece to the infidels.

5

Therefore, let him who has no desire to conquer make use of these arms, for they are much more hazardous than mercenaries, because with them the ruin is ready made; they

10 are all united, all yield obedience to others; but with mercenaries, when they have conquered, more time and better opportunities are needed to injure you; they are not all of one community, they are found and paid by you, and a

15 third party, which you have made their head, is not able all at once to assume enough authority to injure you. In conclusion, in mercenaries dastardy is most dangerous; in auxiliaries, valor. The wise prince, therefore, has always

20 avoided these arms and turned to his own; and has been willing rather to lose with them than to conquer with the others, not deeming that a real victory which is gained with the arms of others.

25

I shall never hesitate to cite Cesare Borgia and his actions. This duke entered the Romagna with auxiliaries, taking there only French soldiers, and with them he captured Imola and

30 Forli; but afterwards, such forces not appearing to him reliable, he turned to mercenaries, discerning less danger in them, and enlisted the Orsini and Vitelli; whom presently, on handling and finding them doubtful, unfaith-

35 ful, and dangerous, he destroyed and turned to his own men. And the difference between one and the other of these forces can easily be seen when one considers the difference there was in the reputation of the duke, when he

40 had the French, when he had the Orsini and Vitelli, and when he relied on his own soldiers, on whose fidelity he could always count and found it ever increasing; he was never es-

45 teemed more highly than when every one saw that he was complete master of his own forces.

I was not intending to go beyond Italian and recent examples, but I am unwilling to leave

50 out Hiero, the Syracusan, he being one of those I have named above. This man, as I have said, made head of the army by the Syracusans, soon found out that a mercenary soldiery, constituted like our Italian condottieri,

55 was of no use; and it appearing to him that he could neither keep them not let them go, he had them all cut to pieces, and afterwards made war with his own forces and not with aliens.

60

I wish also to recall to memory an instance from the Old Testament applicable to this subject. David offered himself to Saul to fight with Goliath, the Philistine champion, and, to

65 give him courage, Saul armed him with his own weapons; which David rejected as soon as he had them on his back, saying he could make no use of them, and that he wished to meet the enemy with his sling and his knife. In

70 conclusion, the arms of others either fall from your back, or they weigh you down, or they bind you fast.

Charles the Seventh, the father of King Louis

75 the Eleventh, having by good fortune and valor liberated France from the English, recognized the necessity of being armed with forces of his own, and he established in his kingdom ordinances concerning men-at-arms

80 and infantry. Afterwards his son, King Louis, abolished the infantry and began to enlist the Swiss, which mistake, followed by others, is, as is now seen, a source of peril to that kingdom; because, having raised the reputation of the

85 Swiss, he has entirely diminished the value of his own arms, for he has destroyed the infan-

try altogether; and his men-at-arms he has subordinated to others, for, being as they are so accustomed to fight along with Swiss, it does not appear that they can now conquer
5 without them. Hence it arises that the French cannot stand against the Swiss, and without the Swiss they do not come off well against others. The armies of the French have thus become mixed, partly mercenary and partly
10 national, both of which arms together are much better than mercenaries alone or auxiliaries alone, but much inferior to one's own forces. And this example proves it, for the kingdom of France would be unconquerable if
15 the ordinance of Charles had been enlarged or maintained.

But the scanty wisdom of man, on entering into an affair which looks well at first, cannot discern the poison that is hidden in it, as I
20 have said above of hectic fevers. Therefore, if he who rules a principality cannot recognize evils until they are upon him, he is not truly wise; and this insight is given to few. And if the first disaster to the Roman Empire should
25 be examined, it will be found to have commenced only with the enlisting of the Goths; because from that time the vigor of the Roman Empire began to decline, and all that valor which had raised it passed away to others.

30

I conclude, therefore, that no principality is secure without having its own forces; on the contrary, it is entirely dependent on good fortune, not having the valor which in adversity
35 would defend it. And it has always been the opinion and judgment of wise men that nothing can be so uncertain or unstable as fame or power not founded on its own strength. And one's own forces are those which are com-
40 posed either of subjects, citizens, or dependents; all others are mercenaries or auxiliaries. And the way to make ready one's own forces will be easily found if the rules suggested by

45 me shall be reflected upon, and if one will consider how Philip, the father of Alexander the Great, and many republics and princes have armed and organized themselves, to which rules I entirely commit myself.

50 **CHAPTER XIV**
THAT WHICH CONCERNS A PRINCE
ON THE SUBJECT OF THE ART OF
WAR

55 A prince ought to have no other aim or thought, nor select anything else for his study, than war and its rules and discipline; for this is the sole art that belongs to him who rules, and it is of such force that it not only upholds
60 those who are born princes, but it often enables men to rise from a private station to that rank. And, on the contrary, it is seen that when princes have thought more of ease than of arms they have lost their states. And the
65 first cause of your losing it is to neglect this art; and what enables you to acquire a state is to be master of the art. Francesco Sforza, through being martial, from a private person became Duke of Milan; and the sons, through
70 avoiding the hardships and troubles of arms, from dukes became private persons. For among other evils which being unarmed brings you, it causes you to be despised, and this is one of those ignominies against which a
75 prince ought to guard himself, as is shown later on. Because there is nothing proportionate between the armed and the unarmed; and it is not reasonable that he who is armed should yield obedience willingly to him who is
80 unarmed, or that the unarmed man should be secure among armed servants. Because, there being in the one disdain and in the other suspicion, it is not possible for them to work well together. And therefore a prince who does not
85 understand the art of war, over and above the other misfortunes already mentioned, cannot

be respected by his soldiers, nor can he rely on them. He ought never, therefore, to have out of his thoughts this subject of war, and in peace he should addict himself more to its 5 exercise than in war; this he can do in two ways, the one by action, the other by study.

As regards action, he ought above all things to keep his men well organized and drilled, to 10 follow incessantly the chase, by which he accustoms his body to hardships, and learns something of the nature of localities, and gets to find out how the mountains rise, how the valleys open out, how the plains lie, and to 15 understand the nature of rivers and marshes, and in all this to take the greatest care. Which knowledge is useful in two ways. Firstly, he learns to know his country, and is better able to undertake its defense; afterwards, by means 20 of the knowledge and observation of that locality, he understands with ease any other which it may be necessary for him to study hereafter; because the hills, valleys, and plains, and rivers and marshes that are, for instance, 25 in Tuscany, have a certain resemblance to those of other countries, so that with a knowledge of the aspect of one country one can easily arrive at a knowledge of others. And the prince that lacks this skill lacks the essen- 30 tial which it is desirable that a captain should possess, for it teaches him to surprise his enemy, to select quarters, to lead armies, to array the battle, to besiege towns to advantage.

35 Philopoemen, Prince of the Achaeans, among other praises which writers have bestowed on him, is commended because in time of peace he never had anything in his mind but the rules of war; and when he was in the country 40 with friends, he often stopped and reasoned with them: "If the enemy should be upon that hill, and we should find ourselves here with our army, with whom would be the ad-

vantage? How should one best advance to 45 meet him, keeping the ranks? If we should wish to retreat, how ought we to pursue?" And he would set forth to them, as he went, all the chances that could befall an army; he would listen to their opinion and state his, 50 confirming it with reasons, so that by these continual discussions there could never arise, in time of war, any unexpected circumstances that he could not deal with.

55 But to exercise the intellect the prince should read histories, and study there the actions of illustrious men, to see how they have borne themselves in war, to examine the causes of their victories and defeat, so as to avoid the 60 latter and imitate the former; and above all do as an illustrious man did, who took as an exemplar one who had been praised and famous before him, and whose achievements and deeds he always kept in his mind, as it is said 65 Alexander the Great imitated Achilles, Caesar Alexander, Scipio Cyrus. And whoever reads the life of Cyrus, written by Xenophon, will recognize afterwards in the life of Scipio how that imitation was his glory, and how in chasti- 70 ty, affability, humanity, and liberality Scipio conformed to those things which have been written of Cyrus by Xenophon. A wise prince ought to observe some such rules, and never in peaceful times stand idle, but increase his 75 resources with industry in such a way that they may be available to him in adversity, so that if fortune chances it may find him prepared to resist her blows.

80 **CHAPTER XV**
CONCERNING THINGS FOR WHICH
MEN, AND ESPECIALLY PRINCES,
ARE PRAISED OR BLAMED

85 It remains now to see what ought to be the rules of conduct for a prince towards subject

and friends. And as I know that many have written on this point, I expect I shall be considered presumptuous in mentioning it again, especially as in discussing it I shall depart from the methods of other people. But, it being my intention to write a thing which shall be useful to him who apprehends it, it appears to me more appropriate to follow up the real truth of the matter than the imagination of it; for many have pictured republics and principalities which in fact have never been known or seen, because how one lives is so far distant from how one ought to live, that he who neglects what is done for what ought to be done, sooner effects his ruin than his preservation; for a man who wishes to act entirely up to his professions of virtue soon meets with what destroys him among so much that is evil.

Hence it is necessary for a prince wishing to hold his own to know how to do wrong, and to make use of it or not according to necessity. Therefore, putting on one side imaginary things concerning a prince, and discussing those which are real, I say that all men when they are spoken of, and chiefly princes for being more highly placed, are remarkable for some of those qualities which bring them either blame or praise; and thus it is that one is reputed liberal, another miserly, using a Tuscan term (because an avaricious person in our language is still he who desires to possess by robbery, whilst we call one miserly who deprives himself too much of the use of his own); one is reputed generous, one rapacious; one cruel, one compassionate; one faithless, another faithful; one effeminate and cowardly, another bold and brave; one affable, another haughty; one lascivious, another chaste; one sincere, another cunning; one hard, another easy; one grave, another frivolous; one religious, another unbelieving, and the like. And I know that every one will confess that it would

be most praiseworthy in a prince to exhibit all the above qualities that are considered good; but because they can neither be entirely possessed nor observed, for human conditions do not permit it, it is necessary for him to be sufficiently prudent that he may know how to avoid the reproach of those vices which would lose him his state; and also to keep himself, if it be possible, from those which would not lose him it; but this not being possible, he may with less hesitation abandon himself to them. And again, he need not make himself uneasy at incurring a reproach for those vices without which the state can only be saved with difficulty, for if everything is considered carefully, it will be found that something which looks like virtue, if followed, would be his ruin; whilst something else, which looks like vice, yet followed brings him security and prosperity.

CHAPTER XVI
CONCERNING LIBERALITY AND MEANNESS

Commencing then with the first of the above-named characteristics, I say that it would be well to be reputed liberal. Nevertheless, liberality exercised in a way that does not bring you the reputation for it, injures you; for if one exercises it honestly and as it should be exercised, it may not become known, and you will not avoid the reproach of its opposite. Therefore, any one wishing to maintain among men the name of liberal is obliged to avoid no attribute of magnificence; so that a prince thus inclined will consume in such acts all his property, and will be compelled in the end, if he wish to maintain the name of liberal, to unduly weigh down his people, and tax them, and do everything he can to get money. This will soon make him odious to his subjects, and becoming poor he will be little valued by any one;

thus, with his liberality, having offended many and rewarded few, he is affected by the very first trouble and imperiled by whatever may be the first danger; recognizing this himself, and wishing to draw back from it, he runs at once into the reproach of being miserly.

Therefore, a prince, not being able to exercise this virtue of liberality in such a way that it is recognized, except to his cost, if he is wise he ought not to fear the reputation of being mean, for in time he will come to be more considered than if liberal, seeing that with his economy his revenues are enough, that he can defend himself against all attacks, and is able to engage in enterprises without burdening his people; thus it comes to pass that he exercises liberality towards all from whom he does not take, who are numberless, and meanness towards those to whom he does not give, who are few.

We have not seen great things done in our time except by those who have been considered mean; the rest have failed. Pope Julius the Second was assisted in reaching the papacy by a reputation for liberality, yet he did not strive afterwards to keep it up, when he made war on the King of France; and he made many wars without imposing any extraordinary tax on his subjects, for he supplied his additional expenses out of his long thriftiness. The present King of Spain would not have undertaken or conquered in so many enterprises if he had been reputed liberal. A prince, therefore, provided that he has not to rob his subjects, that he can defend himself, that he does not become poor and abject, that he is not forced to become rapacious, ought to hold of little account a reputation for being mean, for it is one of those vices which will enable him to govern.

And if any one should say: Caesar obtained empire by liberality, and many others have reached the highest positions by having been liberal, and by being considered so, I answer: Either you are a prince in fact, or in a way to become one. In the first case this liberality is dangerous, in the second it is very necessary to be considered liberal; and Caesar was one of those who wished to become pre-eminent in Rome; but if he had survived after becoming so, and had not moderated his expenses, he would have destroyed his government. And if any one should reply: Many have been princes, and have done great things with armies, who have been considered very liberal, I reply: Either a prince spends that which is his own or his subjects' or else that of others. In the first case he ought to be sparing, in the second he ought not to neglect any opportunity for liberality. And to the prince who goes forth with his army, supporting it by pillage, sack, and extortion, handling that which belongs to others, this liberality is necessary, otherwise he would not be followed by soldiers. And of that which is neither yours nor your subjects' you can be a ready giver, as were Cyrus, Caesar, and Alexander; because it does not take away your reputation if you squander that of others, but adds to it; it is only squandering your own that injures you.

And there is nothing wastes so rapidly as liberality, for even whilst you exercise it you lose the power to do so, and so become either poor or despised, or else, in avoiding poverty, rapacious and hated. And a prince should guard himself, above all things, against being despised and hated; and liberality leads you to both. Therefore it is wiser to have a reputation for meanness which brings reproach without hatred, than to be compelled through seeking a reputation for liberality to incur a name for rapacity which begets reproach with hatred.

CHAPTER XVII
CONCERNING CRUELTY AND CLEMENCY, AND WHETHER IT IS BETTER TO BE LOVED THAN FEARED

Coming now to the other qualities mentioned above, I say that every prince ought to desire to be considered clement and not cruel. Nevertheless he ought to take care not to misuse this clemency. Cesare Borgia was considered cruel; notwithstanding, his cruelty reconciled the Romagna, unified it, and restored it to peace and loyalty. And if this be rightly considered, he will be seen to have been much more merciful than the Florentine people, who, to avoid a reputation for cruelty, permitted Pistoia to be destroyed. Therefore a prince, so long as he keeps his subjects united and loyal, ought not to mind the reproach of cruelty; because with a few examples he will be more merciful than those who, through too much mercy, allow disorders to arise, from which follow murders or robberies; for these are wont to injure the whole people, whilst those executions which originate with a prince offend the individual only.

And of all princes, it is impossible for the new prince to avoid the imputation of cruelty, owing to new states being full of dangers. Hence Virgil, through the mouth of Dido, excuses the inhumanity of her reign owing to its being new, saying:

"Res dura, et regni novitas me talia cogunt Moliri, et late fines custode tueri."

Nevertheless he ought to be slow to believe and to act, nor should he himself show fear, but proceed in a temperate manner with prudence and humanity, so that too much confidence may not make him incautious and too much distrust render him intolerable.

Upon this a question arises: whether it be better to be loved than feared or feared than loved? It may be answered that one should wish to be both, but, because it is difficult to unite them in one person, it is much safer to be feared than loved, when, of the two, either must be dispensed with. Because this is to be asserted in general of men, that they are ungrateful, fickle, false, cowardly, covetous, and as long as you succeed they are yours entirely; they will offer you their blood, property, life, and children, as is said above, when the need is far distant; but when it approaches they turn against you. And that prince who, relying entirely on their promises, has neglected other precautions, is ruined; because friendships that are obtained by payments, and not by greatness or nobility of mind, may indeed be earned, but they are not secured, and in time of need cannot be relied upon; and men have less scruple in offending one who is beloved than one who is feared, for love is preserved by the link of obligation which, owing to the baseness of men, is broken at every opportunity for their advantage; but fear preserves you by a dread of punishment which never fails.

Nevertheless a prince ought to inspire fear in such a way that, if he does not win love, he avoids hatred; because he can endure very well being feared whilst he is not hated, which will always be as long as he abstains from the property of his citizens and subjects and from their women. But when it is necessary for him to proceed against the life of someone, he must do it on proper justification and for manifest cause, but above all things he must keep his hands off the property of others, because men more quickly forget the death of their father than the loss of their patrimony.

Besides, pretexts for taking away the property are never wanting; for he who has once begun to live by robbery will always find pretexts for seizing what belongs to others; but reasons for taking life, on the contrary, are more difficult to find and sooner lapse. But when a prince is with his army, and has under control a multitude of soldiers, then it is quite necessary for him to disregard the reputation of cruelty, for without it he would never hold his army united or disposed to its duties.

Among the wonderful deeds of Hannibal this one is enumerated: that having led an enormous army, composed of many various races of men, to fight in foreign lands, no dissensions arose either among them or against the prince, whether in his bad or in his good fortune. This arose from nothing else than his inhuman cruelty, which, with his boundless valor, made him revered and terrible in the sight of his soldiers, but without that cruelty, his other virtues were not sufficient to produce this effect. And short-sighted writers admire his deeds from one point of view and from another condemn the principal cause of them. That it is true his other virtues would not have been sufficient for him may be proved by the case of Scipio, that most excellent man, not only of his own times but within the memory of man, against whom, nevertheless, his army rebelled in Spain; this arose from nothing but his too great forbearance, which gave his soldiers more license than is consistent with military discipline. For this he was upbraided in the Senate by Fabius Maximus, and called the corrupter of the Roman soldiery. The Locrians were laid waste by a legate of Scipio, yet they were not avenged by him, nor was the insolence of the legate punished, owing entirely to his easy nature. Insomuch that someone in the Senate, wishing to excuse him, said there were many men who knew much better how not to err than to correct the errors of others. This disposition, if he had been continued in the command, would have destroyed in time the fame and glory of Scipio; but, he being under the control of the Senate, this injurious characteristic not only concealed itself, but contributed to his glory.

Returning to the question of being feared or loved, I come to the conclusion that, men loving according to their own will and fearing according to that of the prince, a wise prince should establish himself on that which is in his own control and not in that of others; he must endeavor only to avoid hatred, as is noted.

CHAPTER XVIII
CONCERNING THE WAY IN WHICH PRINCES SHOULD KEEP FAITH

Every one admits how praiseworthy it is in a prince to keep faith, and to live with integrity and not with craft. Nevertheless our experience has been that those princes who have done great things have held good faith of little account, and have known how to circumvent the intellect of men by craft, and in the end have overcome those who have relied on their word. You must know there are two ways of contesting, the one by the law, the other by force; the first method is proper to men, the second to beasts; but because the first is frequently not sufficient, it is necessary to have recourse to the second. Therefore it is necessary for a prince to understand how to avail himself of the beast and the man. This has been figuratively taught to princes by ancient writers, who describe how Achilles and many other princes of old were given to the Centaur Chiron to nurse, who brought them up in his discipline; which means solely that, as they had for a teacher one who was half beast and half man, so it is necessary for a prince to know how to make use of both natures, and that one without the other is not durable. A prince, therefore, being compelled knowingly to adopt the beast, ought to choose the fox and the lion; because the lion cannot defend himself against snares and the fox cannot defend himself against wolves. Therefore, it is necessary to be a fox to discover the snares and a lion to terrify the wolves. Those who rely simply on the lion do not understand what they are about. Therefore a wise lord cannot, nor ought he to, keep faith when such observance may be turned against him, and when the reasons that caused him to pledge it exist no longer. If men were entirely good this precept would not hold, but because they are bad, and will not keep faith with you, you too are not bound to observe it with them. Nor will there ever be wanting to a prince legitimate reasons to excuse this non-observance. Of this endless modern examples could be given, showing how many treaties and engagements have been made void and of no effect through the faithlessness of princes; and he who has known best how to employ the fox has succeeded best.

But it is necessary to know well how to disguise this characteristic, and to be a great pretender and dissembler; and men are so simple, and so subject to present necessities, that he who seeks to deceive will always find someone who will allow himself to be deceived. One recent example I cannot pass over in silence. Alexander the Sixth did nothing else but deceive men, nor ever thought of doing otherwise, and he always found victims; for there never was a man who had greater power in asserting, or who with greater oaths would affirm a thing, yet would observe it less; nevertheless his deceits always succeeded according to his wishes, because he well understood this side of mankind.

Therefore it is unnecessary for a prince to have all the good qualities I have enumerated, but it is very necessary to appear to have them. And I shall dare to say this also, that to have them and always to observe them is injurious, and that to appear to have them is useful; to appear merciful, faithful, humane, religious, upright, and to be so, but with a mind so framed that should you require not to be so, you may be able and know how to change to the opposite.

And you have to understand this, that a prince, especially a new one, cannot observe all those things for which men are esteemed, being often forced, in order to maintain the state, to act contrary to fidelity, friendship, humanity, and religion. Therefore it is necessary for him to have a mind ready to turn itself accordingly as the winds and variations of fortune force it, yet, as I have said above, not to diverge from the good if he can avoid doing so, but, if compelled, then to know how to set about it.

For this reason a prince ought to take care that he never lets anything slip from his lips that is not replete with the above-named five qualities, that he may appear to him who sees and hears him altogether merciful, faithful, humane, upright, and religious. There is nothing more necessary to appear to have than this last quality, inasmuch as men judge generally more by the eye than by the hand, because it belongs to everybody to see you, to few to come in touch with you. Every one sees what you appear to be, few really know what you are, and those few dare not oppose themselves to the opinion of the many, who have the majesty of the state to defend them; and in the actions of all men, and especially of princes, which it is not prudent to challenge, one judges by the result.

For that reason, let a prince have the credit of conquering and holding his state, the means will always be considered honest, and he will be praised by everybody; because the vulgar
5 are always taken by what a thing seems to be and by what comes of it; and in the world there are only the vulgar, for the few find a place there only when the many have no ground to rest on.
10

One prince of the present time, whom it is not well to name, never preaches anything else but peace and good faith, and to both he is most hostile, and either, if he had kept it, would
15 have deprived him of reputation and kingdom many a time.

CHAPTER XIX
THAT ONE SHOULD AVOID BEING
20 ### DESPISED AND HATED

Now, concerning the characteristics of which mention is made above, I have spoken of the more important ones, the others I wish to
25 discuss briefly under this generality, that the prince must consider, as has been in part said before, how to avoid those things which will make him hated or contemptible; and as often as he shall have succeeded he will have ful-
30 filled his part, and he need not fear any danger in other reproaches.

It makes him hated above all things, as I have said, to be rapacious, and to be a violator of
35 the property and women of his subjects, from both of which he must abstain. And when neither their property nor their honor is touched, the majority of men live content, and he has only to contend with the ambition of a
40 few, whom he can curb with ease in many ways.

It makes him contemptible to be considered fickle, frivolous, effeminate, mean-spirited,
45 irresolute, from all of which a prince should guard himself as from a rock; and he should endeavor to show in his actions greatness, courage, gravity, and fortitude; and in his private dealings with his subjects let him show
50 that his judgments are irrevocable, and maintain himself in such reputation that no one can hope either to deceive him or to get round him.

55 That prince is highly esteemed who conveys this impression of himself, and he who is highly esteemed is not easily conspired against; for, provided it is well known that he is an excellent man and revered by his people, he
60 can only be attacked with difficulty. For this reason a prince ought to have two fears, one from within, on account of his subjects, the other from without, on account of external powers. From the latter he is defended by be-
65 ing well armed and having good allies, and if he is well armed he will have good friends, and affairs will always remain quiet within when they are quiet without, unless they should have been already disturbed by conspiracy; and
70 even should affairs outside be disturbed, if he has carried out his preparations and has lived as I have said, as long as he does not despair, he will resist every attack, as I said Nabis the Spartan did.
75

But concerning his subjects, when affairs outside are disturbed he has only to fear that they will conspire secretly, from which a prince can easily secure himself by avoiding being hated
80 and despised, and by keeping the people satisfied with him, which it is most necessary for him to accomplish, as I said above at length. And one of the most efficacious remedies that a prince can have against conspiracies is not to
85 be hated and despised by the people, for he who conspires against a prince always expects

to please them by his removal; but when the conspirator can only look forward to offending them, he will not have the courage to take such a course, for the difficulties that confront a conspirator are infinite. And as experience shows, many have been the conspiracies, but few have been successful; because he who conspires cannot act alone, nor can he take a companion except from those whom he believes to be malcontents, and as soon as you have opened your mind to a malcontent you have given him the material with which to content himself, for by denouncing you he can look for every advantage; so that, seeing the gain from this course to be assured, and seeing the other to be doubtful and full of dangers, he must be a very rare friend, or a thoroughly obstinate enemy of the prince, to keep faith with you.

And, to reduce the matter into a small compass, I say that, on the side of the conspirator, there is nothing but fear, jealousy, prospect of punishment to terrify him; but on the side of the prince there is the majesty of the principality, the laws, the protection of friends and the state to defend him; so that, adding to all these things the popular goodwill, it is impossible that any one should be so rash as to conspire. For whereas in general the conspirator has to fear before the execution of his plot, in this case he has also to fear the sequel to the crime; because on account of it he has the people for an enemy, and thus cannot hope for any escape.

Endless examples could be given on this subject, but I will be content with one, brought to pass within the memory of our fathers. Messer Annibale Bentivogli, who was prince in Bologna (grandfather of the present Annibale), having been murdered by the Canneschi, who had conspired against him, not one of his family survived but Messer Giovanni, who was in childhood: immediately after his assassination the people rose and murdered all the Canneschi. This sprung from the popular goodwill which the house of Bentivogli enjoyed in those days in Bologna; which was so great that, although none remained there after the death of Annibale who was able to rule the state, the Bolognese, having information that there was one of the Bentivogli family in Florence, who up to that time had been considered the son of a blacksmith, sent to Florence for him and gave him the government of their city, and it was ruled by him until Messer Giovanni came in due course to the government.

For this reason I consider that a prince ought to reckon conspiracies of little account when his people hold him in esteem; but when it is hostile to him, and bears hatred towards him, he ought to fear everything and everybody. And well-ordered states and wise princes have taken every care not to drive the nobles to desperation, and to keep the people satisfied and contented, for this is one of the most important objects a prince can have.

Among the best ordered and governed kingdoms of our times is France, and in it are found many good institutions on which depend the liberty and security of the king; of these the first is the parliament and its authority, because he who founded the kingdom, knowing the ambition of the nobility and their boldness, considered that a bit to their mouths would be necessary to hold them in; and, on the other side, knowing the hatred of the people, founded in fear, against the nobles, he wished to protect them, yet he was not anxious for this to be the particular care of the king; therefore, to take away the reproach which he would be liable to from the nobles for favoring the people, and from the people for favoring the nobles, he set up an arbiter, who should be one who could beat down the great and favor the lesser without reproach to the king. Neither could you have a better or a more prudent arrangement, or a greater source of security to the king and kingdom. From this one can draw another important conclusion, that princes ought to leave affairs of reproach to the management of others, and keep those of grace in their own hands. And further, I consider that a prince ought to cherish the nobles, but not so as to make himself hated by the people...

CHAPTER XX
ARE FORTRESSES, AND MANY OTHER THINGS TO WHICH PRINCES OFTEN RESORT, ADVANTAGEOUS OR HURTFUL?

1. Some princes, so as to hold securely the state, have disarmed their subjects; others have kept their subject towns distracted by factions; others have fostered enmities against themselves; others have laid themselves out to gain over those whom they distrusted in the beginning of their governments; some have built fortresses; some have overthrown and destroyed them. And although one cannot give a final judgment on all of these things unless one possesses the particulars of those states in which a decision has to be made, nevertheless I will speak as comprehensively as the matter of itself will admit.

2. There never was a new prince who has disarmed his subjects; rather when he has found them disarmed he has always armed them, because, by arming them, those arms become yours, those men who were distrusted become faithful, and those who were faithful are kept so, and your subjects become your adherents. And whereas all subjects cannot be armed, yet when those whom you do arm are benefited, the others can be handled more freely, and this difference in their treatment, which they quite understand, makes the former your dependents, and the latter, considering it to be necessary that those who have the most danger and service should have the most reward, excuse you. But when you disarm them, you at once offend them by showing that you distrust them, either for cowardice or for want of loyalty, and either of these opinions breeds hatred against you. And because you cannot remain unarmed, it follows that you turn to mercenaries, which are of the character already shown; even if they should be good they would not be sufficient to defend you against powerful enemies and distrusted subjects. Therefore, as I have said, a new prince in a new principality has always distributed arms. Histories are full of examples. But when a prince acquires a new state, which he adds as a province to his old one, then it is necessary to disarm the men of that state, except those who have been his adherents in acquiring it; and these again, with time and opportunity, should be rendered soft and effeminate; and matters should be managed in such a way that all the armed men in the state shall be your own soldiers who in your old state were living near you.

3. Our forefathers, and those who were reckoned wise, were accustomed to say that it was necessary to hold Pistoia by factions and Pisa by fortresses; and with this idea they fostered quarrels in some of their tributary towns so as to keep possession of them the more easily. This may have been well enough in those times when Italy was in a way balanced, but I do not believe that it can be accepted as a precept for to-day, because I do not believe that factions can ever be of use; rather it is certain that when the enemy comes upon you in divided cities you are quickly lost, because the

weakest party will always assist the outside forces and the other will not be able to resist. The Venetians, moved, as I believe, by the above reasons, fostered the Guelph and Ghibelline factions in their tributary cities; and although they never allowed them to come to bloodshed, yet they nursed these disputes amongst them, so that the citizens, distracted by their differences, should not unite against them. Which, as we saw, did not afterwards turn out as expected, because, after the rout at Vaila, one party at once took courage and seized the state. Such methods argue, therefore, weakness in the prince, because these factions will never be permitted in a vigorous principality; such methods for enabling one the more easily to manage subjects are only useful in times of peace, but if war comes this policy proves fallacious.

4. Without doubt princes become great when they overcome the difficulties and obstacles by which they are confronted, and therefore fortune, especially when she desires to make a new prince great, who has a greater necessity to earn renown than an hereditary one, causes enemies to arise and form designs against him, in order that he may have the opportunity of overcoming them, and by them to mount higher, as by a ladder which his enemies have raised. For this reason many consider that a wise prince, when he has the opportunity, ought with craft to foster some animosity against himself, so that, having crushed it, his renown may rise higher.

5. Princes, especially new ones, have found more fidelity and assistance in those men who in the beginning of their rule were distrusted than among those who in the beginning were trusted. Pandolfo Petrucci, Prince of Siena, ruled his state more by those who had been distrusted than by others. But on this question one cannot speak generally, for it varies so much with the individual; I will only say this, that those men who at the commencement of a princedom have been hostile, if they are of a description to need assistance to support themselves, can always be gained over with the greatest ease, and they will be tightly held to serve the prince with fidelity, inasmuch as they know it to be very necessary for them to cancel by deeds the bad impression which he had formed of them; and thus the prince always extracts more profit from them than from those who, serving him in too much security, may neglect his affairs. And since the matter demands it, I must not fail to warn a prince, who by means of secret favors has acquired a new state, that he must well consider the reasons which induced those to favor him who did so; and if it be not a natural affection towards him, but only discontent with their government, then he will only keep them friendly with great trouble and difficulty, for it will be impossible to satisfy them. And weighing well the reasons for this in those examples which can be taken from ancient and modern affairs, we shall find that it is easier for the prince to make friends of those men who were contented under the former government, and are therefore his enemies, than of those who, being discontented with it, were favorable to him and encouraged him to seize it.

6. It has been a custom with princes, in order to hold their states more securely, to build fortresses that may serve as a bridle and bit to those who might design to work against them, and as a place of refuge from a first attack. I praise this system because it has been made use of formerly. Notwithstanding that, Messer Nicolo Vitelli in our times has been seen to demolish two fortresses in Citta di Castello so that he might keep that state; Guido Ubaldo, Duke of Urbino, on returning to his domin-

ion, whence he had been driven by Cesare Borgia, razed to the foundations all the fortresses in that province, and considered that without them it would be more difficult to

5 lose it; the Bentivogli returning to Bologna came to a similar decision. Fortresses, therefore, are useful or not according to circumstances; if they do you good in one way they injure you in another. And this question can

10 be reasoned thus: the prince who has more to fear from the people than from foreigners ought to build fortresses, but he who has more to fear from foreigners than from the people ought to leave them alone. The castle

15 of Milan, built by Francesco Sforza, has made, and will make, more trouble for the house of Sforza than any other disorder in the state. For this reason the best possible fortress is--not to be hated by the people, because, although you

20 may hold the fortresses, yet they will not save you if the people hate you, for there will never be wanting foreigners to assist a people who have taken arms against you. It has not been seen in our times that such fortresses have

25 been of use to any prince, unless to the Countess of Forli, when the Count Girolamo, her consort, was killed; for by that means she was able to withstand the popular attack and wait for assistance from Milan, and thus recover

30 her state; and the posture of affairs was such at that time that the foreigners could not assist the people. But fortresses were of little value to her afterwards when Cesare Borgia attacked her, and when the people, her enemy, were

35 allied with foreigners. Therefore, it would have been safer for her, both then and before, not to have been hated by the people than to have had the fortresses. All these things considered then, I shall praise him who builds fortresses

40 as well as him who does not, and I shall blame whoever, trusting in them, cares little about being hated by the people.

CHAPTER XXI

45 HOW A PRINCE SHOULD CONDUCT HIMSELF SO AS TO GAIN RENOWN

Nothing makes a prince so much esteemed as great enterprises and setting a fine example.

50 We have in our time Ferdinand of Aragon, the present King of Spain. He can almost be called a new prince, because he has risen, by fame and glory, from being an insignificant king to be the foremost king in Christendom;

55 and if you will consider his deeds you will find them all great and some of them extraordinary. In the beginning of his reign he attacked Granada, and this enterprise was the foundation of his dominions. He did this quietly at

60 first and without any fear of hindrance, for he held the minds of the barons of Castile occupied in thinking of the war and not anticipating any innovations; thus they did not perceive that by these means he was acquiring power

65 and authority over them. He was able with the money of the Church and of the people to sustain his armies, and by that long war to lay the foundation for the military skill which has since distinguished him. Further, always using

70 religion as a plea, so as to undertake greater schemes, he devoted himself with pious cruelty to driving out and clearing his kingdom of the Moors; nor could there be a more admirable example, nor one more rare. Under this

75 same cloak he assailed Africa, he came down on Italy, he has finally attacked France; and thus his achievements and designs have always been great, and have kept the minds of his people in suspense and admiration and occu-

80 pied with the issue of them. And his actions have arisen in such a way, one out of the other, that men have never been given time to work steadily against him.

85 Again, it much assists a prince to set unusual examples in internal affairs, similar to those

192

which are related of Messer Bernabo da Milano, who, when he had the opportunity, by any one in civil life doing some extraordinary thing, either good or bad, would take some method of rewarding or punishing him, which would be much spoken about. And a prince ought, above all things, always endeavor in every action to gain for himself the reputation of being a great and remarkable man.

A prince is also respected when he is either a true friend or a downright enemy, that is to say, when, without any reservation, he declares himself in favor of one party against the other; which course will always be more advantageous than standing neutral; because if two of your powerful neighbors come to blows, they are of such a character that, if one of them conquers, you have either to fear him or not. In either case it will always be more advantageous for you to declare yourself and to make war strenuously; because, in the first case, if you do not declare yourself, you will invariably fall a prey to the conqueror, to the pleasure and satisfaction of him who has been conquered, and you will have no reasons to offer, nor anything to protect or to shelter you. Because he who conquers does not want doubtful friends who will not aid him in the time of trial; and he who loses will not harbor you because you did not willingly, sword in hand, court his fate.

Antiochus went into Greece, being sent for by the Aetolians to drive out the Romans. He sent envoys to the Achaeans, who were friends of the Romans, exhorting them to remain neutral; and on the other hand the Romans urged them to take up arms. This question came to be discussed in the council of the Achaeans, where the legate of Antiochus urged them to stand neutral. To this the Roman legate answered: "As for that which has been said, that it is better and more advantageous for your state not to interfere in our war, nothing can be more erroneous; because by not interfering you will be left, without favor or consideration, the guerdon of the conqueror." Thus it will always happen that he who is not your friend will demand your neutrality, whilst he who is your friend will entreat you to declare yourself with arms. And irresolute princes, to avoid present dangers, generally follow the neutral path, and are generally ruined. But when a prince declares himself gallantly in favor of one side, if the party with whom he allies himself conquers, although the victor may be powerful and may have him at his mercy, yet he is indebted to him, and there is established a bond of amity; and men are never so shameless as to become a monument of ingratitude by oppressing you. Victories after all are never so complete that the victor must not show some regard, especially to justice. But if he with whom you ally yourself loses, you may be sheltered by him, and whilst he is able he may aid you, and you become companions on a fortune that may rise again.

In the second case, when those who fight are of such a character that you have no anxiety as to who may conquer, so much the more is it greater prudence to be allied, because you assist at the destruction of one by the aid of another who, if he had been wise, would have saved him; and conquering, as it is impossible that he should not do with your assistance, he remains at your discretion. And here it is to be noted that a prince ought to take care never to make an alliance with one more powerful than himself for the purposes of attacking others, unless necessity compels him, as is said above; because if he conquers you are at his discretion, and princes ought to avoid as much as possible being at the discretion of any one. The Venetians joined with France against the

Duke of Milan, and this alliance, which caused their ruin, could have been avoided. But when it cannot be avoided, as happened to the Florentines when the Pope and Spain sent armies to attack Lombardy, then in such a case, for the above reasons, the prince ought to favor one of the parties.

Never let any Government imagine that it can choose perfectly safe courses; rather let it expect to have to take very doubtful ones, because it is found in ordinary affairs that one never seeks to avoid one trouble without running into another; but prudence consists in knowing how to distinguish the character of troubles, and for choice to take the lesser evil.

A prince ought also to show himself a patron of ability, and to honor the proficient in every art. At the same time he should encourage his citizens to practice their callings peaceably, both in commerce and agriculture, and in every other following, so that the one should not be deterred from improving his possessions for fear lest they be taken away from him or another from opening up trade for fear of taxes; but the prince ought to offer rewards to whoever wishes to do these things and designs in any way to honor his city or state.

Further, he ought to entertain the people with festivals and spectacles at convenient seasons of the year; and as every city is divided into guilds or into societies, he ought to hold such bodies in esteem, and associate with them sometimes, and show himself an example of courtesy and liberality; nevertheless, always maintaining the majesty of his rank, for this he must never consent to abate in anything.

CHAPTER XXII
CONCERNING THE SECRETARIES OF PRINCES

...

CHAPTER XXIII
HOW FLATTERERS SHOULD BE AVOIDED

...

CHAPTER XXIV
WHY THE PRINCES OF ITALY HAVE LOST THEIR STATES

...

CHAPTER XXV
WHAT FORTUNE CAN EFFECT IN HUMAN AFFAIRS AND HOW TO WITHSTAND HER

It is not unknown to me how many men have had, and still have, the opinion that the affairs of the world are in such wise governed by fortune and by God that men with their wisdom cannot direct them and that no one can even help them; and because of this they would have us believe that it is not necessary to labor much in affairs, but to let chance govern them. This opinion has been more credited in our times because of the great changes in affairs which have been seen, and may still be seen, every day, beyond all human conjecture. Sometimes pondering over this, I am in some degree inclined to their opinion. Nevertheless, not to extinguish our free will, I hold it to be true that Fortune is the arbiter of one-half of our actions, but that she still leaves us to direct the other half, or perhaps a little less.

I compare her to one of those raging rivers, which when in flood overflows the plains, sweeping away trees and buildings, bearing away the soil from place to place; everything flies before it, all yield to its violence, without being able in any way to withstand it; and yet, though its nature be such, it does not follow therefore that men, when the weather becomes fair, shall not make provision, both with defenses and barriers, in such a manner that, rising again, the waters may pass away by canal, and their force be neither so unrestrained nor so dangerous. So it happens with fortune, who shows her power where valor has not prepared to resist her, and thither she turns her forces where she knows that barriers and defenses have not been raised to constrain her.

And if you will consider Italy, which is the seat of these changes, and which has given to them their impulse, you will see it to be an open country without barriers and without any defense. For if it had been defended by proper valor, as are Germany, Spain, and France, either this invasion would not have made the great changes it has made or it would not have come at all. And this I consider enough to say concerning resistance to fortune in general.

But confining myself more to the particular, I say that a prince may be seen happy to-day and ruined to-morrow without having shown any change of disposition or character. This, I believe, arises firstly from causes that have already been discussed at length, namely, that the prince who relies entirely on fortune is lost when it changes. I believe also that he will be successful who directs his actions according to the spirit of the times, and that he whose actions do not accord with the times will not be successful. Because men are seen, in affairs that lead to the end which every man has before him, namely, glory and riches, to get there by various methods; one with caution, another with haste; one by force, another by skill; one by patience, another by its opposite; and each one succeeds in reaching the goal by a different method. One can also see of two cautious men the one attain his end, the other fail; and

similarly, two men by different observances are equally successful, the one being cautious, the other impetuous; all this arises from nothing else than whether or not they conform in their methods to the spirit of the times. This follows from what I have said, that two men working differently bring about the same effect, and of two working similarly, one attains his object and the other does not.

Changes in estate also issue from this, for if, to one who governs himself with caution and patience, times and affairs converge in such a way that his administration is successful, his fortune is made; but if times and affairs change, he is ruined if he does not change his course of action. But a man is not often found sufficiently circumspect to know how to accommodate himself to the change, both because he cannot deviate from what nature inclines him to do, and also because, having always prospered by acting in one way, he cannot be persuaded that it is well to leave it; and, therefore, the cautious man, when it is time to turn adventurous, does not know how to do it, hence he is ruined; but had he changed his conduct with the times fortune would not have changed.

Pope Julius the Second went to work impetuously in all his affairs, and found the times and circumstances conform so well to that line of action that he always met with success. Consider his first enterprise against Bologna, Messer Giovanni Bentivogli being still alive. The Venetians were not agreeable to it, nor was the King of Spain, and he had the enterprise still under discussion with the King of France; nevertheless he personally entered upon the expedition with his accustomed boldness and energy, a move which made Spain and the Venetians stand irresolute and passive, the latter from fear, the former from desire to

recover the kingdom of Naples; on the other hand, he drew after him the King of France, because that king, having observed the movement, and desiring to make the Pope his
5 friend so as to humble the Venetians, found it impossible to refuse him. Therefore Julius with his impetuous action accomplished what no other pontiff with simple human wisdom could have done; for if he had waited in Rome
10 until he could get away, with his plans arranged and everything fixed, as any other pontiff would have done, he would never have succeeded. Because the King of France would have made a thousand excuses, and the others
15 would have raised a thousand fears.

I will leave his other actions alone, as they were all alike, and they all succeeded, for the shortness of his life did not let him experience
20 the contrary; but if circumstances had arisen which required him to go cautiously, his ruin would have followed, because he would never have deviated from those ways to which nature inclined him.

25

I conclude, therefore that, fortune being changeful and mankind steadfast in their ways, so long as the two are in agreement men are successful, but unsuccessful when they fall
30 out. For my part I consider that it is better to be adventurous than cautious, because fortune is a woman, and if you wish to keep her under it is necessary to beat and ill-use her; and it is seen that she allows herself to be mastered by
35 the adventurous rather than by those who go to work more coldly. She is, therefore, always, woman-like, a lover of young men, because they are less cautious, more violent, and with more audacity command her.
40

CHAPTER XXVI
AN EXHORTATION TO LIBERATE IT-
ALY FROM THE BARBARIANS

Having carefully considered the subject of the
45 above discourses, and wondering within myself whether the present times were propitious to a new prince, and whether there were elements that would give an opportunity to a wise and virtuous one to introduce a new or-
50 der of things which would do honor to him and good to the people of this country, it appears to me that so many things concur to favor a new prince that I never knew a time more fit than the present.
55

And if, as I said, it was necessary that the people of Israel should be captive so as to make manifest the ability of Moses; that the Persians should be oppressed by the Medes so as to
60 discover the greatness of the soul of Cyrus; and that the Athenians should be dispersed to illustrate the capabilities of Theseus: then at the present time, in order to discover the virtue of an Italian spirit, it was necessary that
65 Italy should be reduced to the extremity that she is now in, that she should be more enslaved than the Hebrews, more oppressed than the Persians, more scattered than the Athenians; without head, without order, beat-
70 en, despoiled, torn, overrun; and to have endured every kind of desolation.

Although lately some spark may have been shown by one, which made us think he was
75 ordained by God for our redemption, nevertheless it was afterwards seen, in the height of his career, that fortune rejected him; so that Italy, left as without life, waits for him who shall yet heal her wounds and put an end to
80 the ravaging and plundering of Lombardy, to the swindling and taxing of the kingdom and of Tuscany, and cleanse those sores that for long have festered. It is seen how she entreats God to send someone who shall deliver her
85 from these wrongs and barbarous insolences. It is seen also that she is ready and willing to

follow a banner if only someone will raise it.

Nor is there to be seen at present one in whom she can place more hope than in your illustrious house, with its valor and fortune, favored by God and by the Church of which it is now the chief, and which could be made the head of this redemption. This will not be difficult if you will recall to yourself the actions and lives of the men I have named. And although they were great and wonderful men, yet they were men, and each one of them had no more opportunity than the present offers, for their enterprises were neither more just nor easier than this, nor was God more their friend than He is yours.

With us there is great justice, because that war is just which is necessary, and arms are hallowed when there is no other hope but in them. Here there is the greatest willingness, and where the willingness is great the difficulties cannot be great if you will only follow those men to whom I have directed your attention. Further than this, how extraordinarily the ways of God have been manifested beyond example: the sea is divided, a cloud has led the way, the rock has poured forth water, it has rained manna, everything has contributed to your greatness; you ought to do the rest. God is not willing to do everything, and thus take away our free will and that share of glory which belongs to us.

And it is not to be wondered at if none of the above-named Italians have been able to accomplish all that is expected from your illustrious house; and if in so many revolutions in Italy, and in so many campaigns, it has always appeared as if military virtue were exhausted, this has happened because the old order of things was not good, and none of us have known how to find a new one. And nothing honors a man more than to establish new laws and new ordinances when he himself was newly risen. Such things when they are well founded and dignified will make him revered and admired, and in Italy there are not wanting opportunities to bring such into use in every form.

Here there is great valor in the limbs whilst it fails in the head. Look attentively at the duels and the hand-to-hand combats, how superior the Italians are in strength, dexterity, and subtlety. But when it comes to armies they do not bear comparison, and this springs entirely from the insufficiency of the leaders, since those who are capable are not obedient, and each one seems to himself to know, there having never been any one so distinguished above the rest, either by valor or fortune, that others would yield to him. Hence it is that for so long a time, and during so much fighting in the past twenty years, whenever there has been an army wholly Italian, it has always given a poor account of itself; the first witness to this is Il Taro, afterwards Allesandria, Capua, Genoa, Vaila, Bologna, Mestri.

If, therefore, your illustrious house wishes to follow these remarkable men who have redeemed their country, it is necessary before all things, as a true foundation for every enterprise, to be provided with your own forces, because there can be no more faithful, truer, or better soldiers. And although singly they are good, altogether they will be much better when they find themselves commanded by their prince, honored by him, and maintained at his expense. Therefore it is necessary to be prepared with such arms, so that you can be defended against foreigners by Italian valor.

And although Swiss and Spanish infantry may be considered very formidable, nevertheless there is a defect in both, by reason of which a third order would not only be able to oppose them, but might be relied upon to overthrow them. For the Spaniards cannot resist cavalry, and the Swiss are afraid of infantry whenever they encounter them in close combat. Owing to this, as has been and may again be seen, the Spaniards are unable to resist French cavalry, and the Swiss are overthrown by Spanish infantry. And although a complete proof of this latter cannot be shown, nevertheless there was some evidence of it at the battle of Ravenna, when the Spanish infantry were confronted by German battalions, who follow the same tactics as the Swiss; when the Spaniards, by agility of body and with the aid of their shields, got in under the pikes of the Germans and stood out of danger, able to attack, while the Germans stood helpless, and, if the cavalry had not dashed up, all would have been over with them. It is possible, therefore, knowing the defects of both these infantries, to invent a new one, which will resist cavalry and not be afraid of infantry; this need not create a new order of arms, but a variation upon the old. And these are the kind of improvements which confer reputation and power upon a new prince.

This opportunity, therefore, ought not to be allowed to pass for letting Italy at last see her liberator appear. Nor can one express the love with which he would be received in all those provinces which have suffered so much from these foreign scourings, with what thirst for revenge, with what stubborn faith, with what devotion, with what tears. What door would be closed to him? Who would refuse obedience to him? What envy would hinder him? What Italian would refuse him homage? To all of us this barbarous dominion stinks. Let, therefore, your illustrious house take up this charge with that courage and hope with which all just enterprises are undertaken, so that under its standard our native country may be ennobled, and under its auspices may be verified that saying of Petrarch:

> Virtu contro al Furore
> Prendera l'arme, e fia il combatter corto:
> Che l'antico valore
> Negli italici cuor non e ancor morto.

Virtue against fury shall advance the fight,
And it i' th' combat soon shall put to flight:
> For the old Roman valor is not dead,
> Nor in th' Italians' breasts extinguished.

Edward Dacre, 1640.

HOBBES

The life of Thomas Hobbes (1588-1679) was one fraught with danger. Born in the year of the Spanish Armada, he would come of age with the ascension of the Stuarts, reach middle age in the pandemonium of the English Civil War, and die following the Restoration—but only slightly before the Glorious Revolution. A brilliant individual who was truly catholic in his interests, Hobbes became attached to the Cavendish family in his early years, and so was a staunch Royalist. This became a problem was the Parliamentary side began to win the Civil Wars, and so Hobbes fled to Paris—where he briefly tutored the young Charles II. It was while in Paris that Hobbes turned his attention to politics, and produced his master-work: *Leviathan*.

Leviathan is a curious piece of philosophy. On one hand it is unquestionably liberal. It espouses an early form of 'contract theory', it demands consent by the governed, and is remarkably forward thinking on things like women's rights. However, it also one of the most conservative texts ever written, demanding absolute obedience to any established government and denying the capacity of the public to revoke their consent once given. This tension is present throughout the work, but Hobbes largely answers all questions. Ultimately, *Leviathan* is not merely an attempt at moral or political philosophy, but ultimately an attempt to silence all opposition to the traditional political order by showing them that they are factually wrong. For this, if nothing else, it is one of the most ambitious works that we will examine.

LEVIATHAN
THOMAS HOBBES

CHAPTER XIII
OF THE NATURALL CONDITION OF MANKIND, AS CONCERNING THEIR FELICITY, AND MISERY

5
Nature hath made men so equal, in the faculties of body, and mind; as that though there bee found one man sometimes manifestly stronger in body, or of quicker mind then an-

10 other; yet when all is reckoned together, the difference between man, and man, is not so considerable, as that one man can thereupon claim to himself any benefit, to which another may not pretend, as well as he. For as to the

15 strength of body, the weakest has strength enough to kill the strongest, either by secret machination, or by confederacy with others, that are in the same danger with himself.

20 And as to the faculties of the mind, (setting aside the arts grounded upon words, and especially that skill of proceeding upon general, and infallible rules, called Science; which very few have, and but in few things; as being not a

25 native faculty, born with us; nor attained, (as Prudence,) while we look after somewhat else,) I find yet a greater equality amongst men, than that of strength. For Prudence, is but Experience; which equal time, equally be-

30 stows on all men, in those things they equally apply themselves unto. That which may perhaps make such equality incredible, is but a vain conceit of ones own wisdom, which almost all men think they have in a greater de-

35 gree, than the Vulgar; that is, than all men but

Text based of the 1651 printing, with adjustments for modern spellings.

themselves, and a few others, whom by Fame, or for concurring with themselves, they approve. For such is the nature of men, that howsoever they may acknowledge many oth-

40 ers to be more witty, or more eloquent, or more learned; Yet they will hardly believe there be many so wise as themselves: For they see their own wit at hand, and other men's at a distance. But this proveth rather that men are

45 in that point equal, than unequal. For there is not ordinarily a greater sign of the equal distribution of any thing, than that every man is contented with his share.

From Equality Proceeds Diffidence
50 From this equality of ability, ariseth equality of hope in the attaining of our Ends. And therefore if any two men desire the same thing, which nevertheless they cannot both enjoy, they become enemies; and in the way to their

55 End, (which is principally their own conservation, and sometimes their delectation only,) endeavor to destroy, or subdue one an other. And from hence it comes to pass, that where an Invader hath no more to fear, than an other

60 mans single power; if one plant, sow, build, or possess a convenient Seat, others may probably be expected to come prepared with forces united, to dispossess, and deprive him, not

65 only of the fruit of his labor, but also of his life, or liberty. And the Invader again is in the like danger of another.

From Diffidence War
70 And from this diffidence of one another, there is no way for any man to secure himself, so reasonable, as Anticipation; that is, by force,

or wiles, to master the persons of all men he can, so long, till he see no other power great enough to endanger him: And this is no more than his own conservation requireth, and is generally allowed. Also because there be some, that taking pleasure in contemplating their own power in the acts of conquest, which they pursue farther than their security requires; if others, that otherwise would be glad to be at ease within modest bounds, should not by invasion increase their power, they would not be able, long time, by standing only on their defense, to subsist. And by consequence, such augmentation of dominion over men, being necessary to a mans conservation, it ought to be allowed him.

Again, men have no pleasure, (but on the contrary a great deal of grief) in keeping company, where there is no power able to over-awe them all. For every man looketh that his companion should value him, at the same rate he sets upon himself: And upon all signs of contempt, or undervaluing, naturally endeavors, as far as he dares (which amongst them that have no common power, to keep them in quiet, is far enough to make them destroy each other,) to extort a greater value from his contemners, by dommage; and from others, by the example. So that in the nature of man, we find three principal causes of quarrel. First, Competition; Secondly, Diffidence; Thirdly, Glory.

The first, maketh men invade for Gain; the second, for Safety; and the third, for Reputation. The first use Violence, to make themselves Masters of other men's persons, wives, children, and cattle; the second, to defend them; the third, for trifles, as a word, a smile, a different opinion, and any other sign of undervalue, either direct in their Persons, or by reflection in their Kindred, their Friends, their Nation, their Profession, or their Name.

Out Of Civil States,

There Is Always War Of Every One Against Every One Hereby it is manifest, that during the time men live without a common Power to keep them all in awe, they are in that condition which is called War; and such a war, as is of every man, against every man. For WAR, consisteth not in Battle only, or the act of fighting; but in a tract of time, wherein the Will to contend by Battle is sufficiently known: and therefore the notion of Time, is to be considered in the nature of War; as it is in the nature of Weather. For as the nature of Foul weather, lyeth not in a shower or two of rain; but in an inclination thereto of many days together: So the nature of War, consisteth not in actual fighting; but in the known disposition thereto, during all the time there is no assurance to the contrary. All other time is PEACE.

The Incommodities Of Such A War

Whatsoever therefore is consequent to a time of War, where every man is Enemy to every man; the same is consequent to the time, wherein men live without other security, than what their own strength, and their own invention shall furnish them withal. In such condition, there is no place for Industry; because the fruit thereof is uncertain; and consequently no Culture of the Earth; no Navigation, nor use of the commodities that may be imported by Sea; no commodious Building; no Instruments of moving, and removing such things as require much force; no Knowledge of the face of the Earth; no account of Time; no Arts; no Letters; no Society; and which is worst of all, continual fear, and danger of violent death; And the life of man, solitary, poor, nasty, brutish, and short.

It may seem strange to some man, that has not well weighed these things; that Nature should thus dissociate, and render men apt to invade, and destroy one another: and he may therefore, not trusting to this Inference, made from the Passions, desire perhaps to have the same confirmed by Experience. Let him therefore

5 consider with himself, when taking a journey, he arms himself, and seeks to go well accompanied; when going to sleep, he locks his doors; when even in his house he locks his chests; and this when he knows there bee

10 Laws, and public Officers, armed, to revenge all injuries shall bee done him; what opinion he has of his fellow subjects, when he rides armed; of his fellow Citizens, when he locks his doors; and of his children, and servants,

15 when he locks his chests. Does he not there as much accuse mankind by his actions, as I do by my words? But neither of us accuse mans nature in it. The Desires, and other Passions of man, are in themselves no Sin. No more are

20 the Actions, that proceed from those Passions, till they know a Law that forbids them; which till Laws be made they cannot know: nor can any Law be made, till they have agreed upon the Person that shall make it.

25

It may peradventure be thought, there was never such a time, nor condition of war as this; and I believe it was never generally so, over all the world: but there are many places,

30 where they live so now. For the savage people in many places of America, except the government of small Families, the concord whereof dependeth on natural lust, have no government at all; and live at this day in that

35 brutish manner, as I said before. Howsoever, it may be perceived what manner of life there would be, where there were no common Power to fear; by the manner of life, which men that have formerly lived under a peaceful gov-

40 ernment, use to degenerate into, in a civil War.

But though there had never been any time, wherein particular men were in a condition of war one against another; yet in all times,

45 Kings, and persons of Sovereign authority, because of their Independency, are in continual jealousies, and in the state and posture of Gladiators; having their weapons pointing, and their eyes fixed on one another; that is, their

50 Forts, Garrisons, and Guns upon the Frontiers of their Kingdoms; and continual Spies upon their neighbors; which is a posture of War. But because they uphold thereby, the Industry of their Subjects; there does not fol-

55 low from it, that misery, which accompanies the Liberty of particular men.

In Such A War, Nothing Is Unjust

To this war of every man against every man,

60 this also is consequent; that nothing can be Unjust. The notions of Right and Wrong, Justice and Injustice have there no place. Where there is no common Power, there is no Law: where no Law, no Injustice. Force, and Fraud,

65 are in war the two Cardinal virtues. Justice, and Injustice are none of the Faculties neither of the Body, nor Mind. If they were, they might be in a man that were alone in the world, as well as his Senses, and Passions.

70 They are Qualities, that relate to men in Society, not in Solitude. It is consequent also to the same condition, that there be no Propriety, no Dominion, no Mine and Thine distinct; but only that to be every mans that he can get; and

75 for so long, as he can keep it. And thus much for the ill condition, which man by mere Nature is actually placed in; though with a possibility to come out of it, consisting partly in the Passions, partly in his Reason.

80

The Passions That Incline Men To Peace

The Passions that incline men to Peace, are Fear of Death; Desire of such things as are necessary to commodious living; and a Hope

85 by their Industry to obtain them. And Reason suggesteth convenient Articles of Peace, upon

which men may be drawn to agreement. These Articles, are they, which otherwise are called the Laws of Nature: whereof I shall speak more particularly, in the two following Chap-

5 ters.

CHAPTER XIV
OF THE FIRST AND SECOND NATU-RALL LAWS, AND OF CONTRACTS

10

Right Of Nature What

The RIGHT OF NATURE, which Writers commonly call Jus Natural, is the Liberty each man hath, to use his own power, as he will

15 himself, for the preservation of his own Nature; that is to say, of his own Life; and consequently, of doing any thing, which in his own Judgment, and Reason, he shall conceive to be the aptest means thereunto.

20

Liberty What

By LIBERTY, is understood, according to the proper signification of the word, the absence of external Impediments: which Impediments,

25 may oft take away part of a mans power to do what he would; but cannot hinder him from using the power left him, according as his judgment, and reason shall dictate to him.

30 **A Law Of Nature What**

A LAW OF NATURE, (Lex Naturalis,) is a Precept, or general Rule, found out by Reason, by which a man is forbidden to do, that, which is destructive of his life, or taketh away the

35 means of preserving the same; and to omit, that, by which he thinketh it may be best preserved. For though they that speak of this subject, use to confound Jus, and Lex, Right and Law; yet they ought to be distinguished; be-

40 cause RIGHT, consisteth in liberty to do, or to forbear; Whereas LAW, determineth, and bindeth to one of them: so that Law, and Right, differ as much, as Obligation, and Lib-

erty; which in one and the same matter are

45 inconsistent.

Naturally Every Man Has Right To Everything

And because the condition of Man, (as hath

50 been declared in the precedent Chapter) is a condition of War of every one against every one; in which case every one is governed by his own Reason; and there is nothing he can make use of, that may not be a help unto him,

55 in preserving his life against his enemies; It followeth, that in such a condition, every man has a Right to every thing; even to one another's body. And therefore, as long as this natural Right of every man to every thing en-

60 dureth, there can be no security to any man, (how strong or wise soever he be,) of living out the time, which Nature ordinarily alloweth men to live.

65 **The Fundamental Law Of Nature**

And consequently it is a precept, or general rule of Reason, "That every man, ought to endeavor Peace, as far as he has hope of obtaining it; and when he cannot obtain it, that

70 he may seek, and use, all helps, and advantages of War." The first branch, of which Rule, containeth the first, and Fundamental Law of Nature; which is, "To seek Peace, and follow it." The Second, the sum of the Right of Nature;

75 which is, "By all means we can, to defend our selves."

The Second Law Of Nature

From this Fundamental Law of Nature, by

80 which men are commanded to endeavor Peace, is derived this second Law; "That a man be willing, when others are so too, as farforth, as for Peace, and defense of himself he shall think it necessary, to lay down this right

85 to all things; and be contented with so much liberty against other men, as he would allow

other men against himself." For as long as
every man holdeth this Right, of doing any
thing he liketh; so long are all men in the condition of War. But if other men will not lay
5 down their Right, as well as he; then there is
no Reason for any one, to divest himself of
his: For that were to expose himself to Prey,
(which no man is bound to) rather than to
dispose himself to Peace. This is that Law of
10 the Gospel; "Whatsoever you require that others should do to you, that do ye to them." And
that Law of all men, "Quod tibi feiri non vis,
alteri ne feceris."

What it is to lay down a Right

15 To Lay Down a mans Right to any thing, is to
Divest himself of the Liberty, of hindering
another of the benefit of his own Right to the
same. For he that renounceth, or passeth away
20 his Right, giveth not to any other man a Right
which he had not before; because there is
nothing to which every man had not Right by
Nature: but only standeth out of his way, that
he may enjoy his own original Right, without
25 hindrance from him; not without hindrance
from another. So that the effect which redoundeth to one man, by another mans defect
of Right, is but so much diminution of impediments to the use of his own Right original.
30

Renouncing (or) Transferring Right What; Obligation Duty Justice

Right is laid aside, either by simply Renouncing it; or by Transferring it to another. By
35 Simply RENOUNCING; when he cares not
to whom the benefit thereof redoundeth. By
TRANSFERRING; when he intendeth the
benefit thereof to some certain person, or
persons. And when a man hath in either man-
40 ner abandoned, or granted away his Right;
then is he said to be OBLIGED, or BOUND,
not to hinder those, to whom such Right is
granted, or abandoned, from the benefit of it:

and that he Ought, and it his DUTY, not to
45 make void that voluntary act of his own: and
that such hindrance is INJUSTICE, and IN-
JURY, as being Sine Jure; the Right being before renounced, or transferred. So that Injury,
or Injustice, in the controversies of the world,
50 is somewhat like to that, which in the disputations of Scholars is called Absurdity. For as it
is there called an Absurdity, to contradict what
one maintained in the Beginning: so in the
world, it is called Injustice, and Injury, volun-
55 tarily to undo that, which from the beginning
he had voluntarily done. The way by which a
man either simply Renounceth, or Transferreth his Right, is a Declaration, or Signification, by some voluntary and sufficient sign, or
60 signs, that he doth so Renounce, or Transfer;
or hath so Renounced, or Transferred the
same, to him that accepteth it. And these Signs
are either Words only, or Actions only; or (as
it happeneth most often) both Words and
65 Actions. And the same are the BONDS, by
which men are bound, and obliged: Bonds,
that have their strength, not from their own
Nature, (for nothing is more easily broken
then a mans word,) but from Fear of some
70 evil consequence upon the rupture.

Not All Rights Are Alienable

Whensoever a man Transferreth his Right, or
Renounceth it; it is either in consideration of
75 some Right reciprocally transferred to himself;
or for some other good he hopeth for thereby.
For it is a voluntary act: and of the voluntary
acts of every man, the object is some Good
To Himself. And therefore there be some
80 Rights, which no man can be understood by
any words, or other signs, to have abandoned,
or transferred. As first a man cannot lay down
the right of resisting them, that assault him by
force, to take away his life; because he cannot
85 be understood to aim thereby, at any Good to
himself. The same may be said of Wounds,

204

and Chains, and Imprisonment; both because there is no benefit consequent to such patience; as there is to the patience of suffering another to be wounded, or imprisoned: as also because a man cannot tell, when he seeth men proceed against him by violence, whether they intend his death or not. And lastly the motive, and end for which this renouncing, and transferring or Right is introduced, is nothing else but the security of a mans person, in his life, and in the means of so preserving life, as not to be weary of it. And therefore if a man by words, or other signs, seem to despoil himself of the End, for which those signs were intended; he is not to be understood as if he meant it, or that it was his will; but that he was ignorant of how such words and actions were to be interpreted.

Contract What

The mutual transferring of Right, is that which men call CONTRACT. There is difference, between transferring of Right to the Thing; and transferring, or tradition, that is, delivery of the Thing it self. For the Thing may be delivered together with the Translation of the Right; as in buying and selling with ready money; or exchange of goods, or lands: and it may be delivered some time after.

Covenant What

Again, one of the Contractors, may deliver the Thing contracted for on his part, and leave the other to perform his part at some determinate time after, and in the mean time be trusted; and then the Contract on his part, is called PACT, or COVENANT: Or both parts may contract now, to perform hereafter: in which cases, he that is to perform in time to come, being trusted, his performance is called Keeping Of Promise, or Faith; and the failing of performance (if it be voluntary) Violation Of Faith.

Free-gift

When the transferring of Right, is not mutual; but one of the parties transferreth, in hope to gain thereby friendship, or service from another, or from his friends; or in hope to gain the reputation of Charity, or Magnanimity; or to deliver his mind from the pain of compassion; or in hope of reward in heaven; This is not Contract, but GIFT, FREEGIFT, GRACE: which words signify one and the same thing.

Signs Of Contract Expressed

Signs of Contract, are either Expressed, or By Inference. Expressed, are words spoken with understanding of what they signify; And such words are either of the time Present, or Past; as, I Give, I Grant, I Have Given, I Have Granted, I Will That This Be Yours: Or of the future; as, I Will Give, I Will Grant; which words of the future, are called Promise.

Signs Of Contract By Inference

Signs by Inference, are sometimes the consequence of Words; sometimes the consequence of Silence; sometimes the consequence of Actions; sometimes the consequence of Forbearing an Action: and generally a sign by Inference, of any Contract, is whatsoever sufficiently argues the will of the Contractor.

Free Gift Passeth By Words Of The Present Or Past

Words alone, if they be of the time to come, and contain a bare promise, are an insufficient sign of a Free-gift and therefore not obligatory. For if they be of the time to Come, as, To Morrow I Will Give, they are a sign I have not given yet, and consequently that my right is not transferred, but remaineth till I transfer it by some other Act. But if the words be of the time Present, or Past, as, "I have given, or do give to be delivered to morrow," then is my to morrows Right given away to day; and that by the virtue of the words, though there were no other argument of my will. And there is a great difference in the signification of these words,

5 Volos Hoc Tuum Esse Cras, and Cros Dabo; that is between "I will that this be thine to morrow," and, "I will give it to thee to morrow:" For the word I Will, in the former manner of speech, signifies an act of the will Pre-

10 sent; but in the later, it signifies a promise of an act of the will to Come: and therefore the former words, being of the Present, transfer a future right; the later, that be of the Future, transfer nothing. But if there be other signs of

15 the Will to transfer a Right, besides Words; then, though the gift be Free, yet may the Right be understood to pass by words of the future: as if a man propound a Prize to him that comes first to the end of a race, The gift

20 is Free; and though the words be of the Future, yet the Right passeth: for if he would not have his words so be understood, he should not have let them run.

Signs Of Contract Are Words Both Of The Past, Present, and Future

In Contracts, the right passeth, not only where the words are of the time Present, or Past; but also where they are of the Future; because all

30 Contract is mutual translation, or change of Right; and therefore he that promiseth only, because he hath already received the benefit for which he promiseth, is to be understood as if he intended the Right should pass: for un-

35 less he had been content to have his words so understood, the other would not have performed his part first. And for that cause, in buying, and selling, and other acts of Contract, A Promise is equivalent to a Covenant; and

40 therefore obligatory.

Merit What

He that performeth first in the case of a Con-

tract, is said to MERIT that which he is to

45 receive by the performance of the other; and he hath it as Due. Also when a Prize is propounded to many, which is to be given to him only that winneth; or money is thrown amongst many, to be enjoyed by them that

50 catch it; though this be a Free Gift; yet so to Win, or so to Catch, is to Merit, and to have it as DUE. For the Right is transferred in the Propounding of the Prize, and in throwing down the money; though it be not determined

55 to whom, but by the Event of the contention. But there is between these two sorts of Merit, this difference, that In Contract, I Merit by virtue of my own power, and the Contractors need; but in this case of Free Gift, I am ena-

60 bled to Merit only by the benignity of the Giver; In Contract, I merit at The Contractors hand that he should depart with his right; In this case of gift, I Merit not that the giver should part with his right; but that when he

65 has parted with it, it should be mine, rather than another's. And this I think to be the meaning of that distinction of the Schools, between Meritum Congrui, and Meritum Condigni. For God Almighty, having prom-

70 ised Paradise to those men (hoodwinked with carnal desires,) that can walk through this world according to the Precepts, and Limits prescribed by him; they say, he that shall so walk, shall Merit Paradise Ex Congruo. But

75 because no man can demand a right to it, by his own Righteousness, or any other power in himself, but by the Free Grace of God only; they say, no man can Merit Paradise Ex Condigno. This I say, I think is the meaning of

80 that distinction; but because Disputers do not agree upon the signification of their own terms of Art, longer than it serves their turn; I will not affirm any thing of their meaning: only this I say; when a gift is given indefinitely,

85 as a prize to be contended for, he that winneth Meriteth, and may claim the Prize as Due.

Covenants Of Mutual Trust, When Invalid

If a Covenant be made, wherein neither of the parties perform presently, but trust one another; in the condition of mere Nature, (which is a condition of War of every man against every man,) upon any reasonable suspicion, it is Void; But if there be a common Power set over them both, with right and force sufficient to compel performance; it is not Void. For he that performeth first, has no assurance the other will perform after; because the bonds of words are too weak to bridle men's ambition, avarice, anger, and other Passions, without the fear of some coercive Power; which in the condition of mere Nature, where all men are equal, and judges of the justness of their own fears cannot possibly be supposed. And therefore he which performeth first, does but betray himself to his enemy; contrary to the Right (he can never abandon) of defending his life, and means of living.

But in a civil estate, where there is a Power set up to constrain those that would otherwise violate their faith, that fear is no more reasonable; and for that cause, he which by the Covenant is to perform first, is obliged so to do.

The cause of Fear, which maketh such a Covenant invalid, must be always something arising after the Covenant made; as some new fact, or other sign of the Will not to perform; else it cannot make the Covenant Void. For that which could not hinder a man from promising, ought not to be admitted as a hindrance of performing.

Right To The End, Containeth Right To The Means

He that transferreth any Right, transferreth the Means of enjoying it, as far as lyeth in his power. As he that selleth Land, is understood to transferre the Herbage, and whatsoever grows upon it; Nor can he that sells a Mill turn away the Stream that drives it. And they that give to a man The Right of government in Sovereignty, are understood to give him the right of levying money to maintain Soldiers; and of appointing Magistrates for the administration of Justice.

No Covenant With Beasts

To make Covenant with bruit Beasts, is impossible; because not understanding our speech, they understand not, nor accept of any translation of Right; nor can translate any Right to another; and without mutual acceptation, there is no Covenant.

Nor With God Without Special Revelation

To make Covenant with God, is impossible, but by Mediation of such as God speaketh to, either by Revelation supernatural, or by his Lieutenants that govern under him, and in his Name; For otherwise we know not whether our Covenants be accepted, or not. And therefore they that Vow any thing contrary to any law of Nature, Vow in vain; as being a thing unjust to pay such Vow. And if it be a thing commanded by the Law of Nature, it is not the Vow, but the Law that binds them.

No Covenant, But Of Possible And Future

The matter, or subject of a Covenant, is always something that falleth under deliberation; (For to Covenant, is an act of the Will; that is to say an act, and the last act, of deliberation;) and is therefore always understood to be something to come; and which is judged Possible for him that Covenanteth, to perform.

And therefore, to promise that which is known to be Impossible, is no Covenant. But if that prove impossible afterwards, which before was thought possible, the Covenant is valid, and bindeth, (though not to the thing it self,) yet to the value; or, if that also be impossible, to the unfeigned endeavor of performing as much as is possible; for to more no man can be obliged.

Covenants How Made Void

Men are freed of their Covenants two ways; by Performing; or by being Forgiven. For Performance, is the natural end of obligation; and Forgiveness, the restitution of liberty; as being a retransferring of that Right, in which the obligation consisted.

Covenants Extorted By Fear Are Valid

Covenants entered into by fear, in the condition of mere Nature, are obligatory. For example, if I Covenant to pay a ransom, or service for my life, to an enemy; I am bound by it. For it is a Contract, wherein one receiveth the benefit of life; the other is to receive money, or service for it; and consequently, where no other Law (as in the condition, of mere Nature) forbiddeth the performance, the Covenant is valid. Therefore Prisoners of War, if trusted with the payment of their Ransom, are obliged to pay it; And if a weaker Prince, make a disadvantageous peace with a stronger, for fear; he is bound to keep it; unless (as hath been said before) there ariseth some new, and just cause of fear, to renew the war. And even in Common-wealths, if I be forced to redeem my self from a Thief by promising him money, I am bound to pay it, till the Civil Law discharge me. For whatsoever I may lawfully do without Obligation, the same I may lawfully Covenant to do through fear: and what I lawfully Covenant, I cannot lawfully break.

The Former Covenant To One, Makes Void The Later To Another

A former Covenant, makes void a later. For a man that hath passed away his Right to one man to day, hath it not to pass to morrow to another: and therefore the later promise passeth no Right, but is null.

A Mans Covenant Not To Defend Himself, Is Void

A Covenant not to defend my self from force, by force, is always void. For (as I have showed before) no man can transfer, or lay down his Right to save himself from Death, Wounds, and Imprisonment, (the avoiding whereof is the only End of laying down any Right,) and therefore the promise of not resisting force, in no Covenant transferreth any right; nor is obliging. For though a man may Covenant thus, "Unless I do so, or so, kill me;" he cannot Covenant thus "Unless I do so, or so, I will not resist you, when you come to kill me." For man by nature chooseth the lesser evil, which is danger of death in resisting; rather than the greater, which is certain and present death in not resisting. And this is granted to be true by all men, in that they lead Criminals to Execution, and Prison, with armed men, notwithstanding that such Criminals have consented to the Law, by which they are condemned.

No Man Obliged To Accuse Himself

A Covenant to accuse ones Self, without assurance of pardon, is likewise invalid. For in the condition of Nature, where every man is Judge, there is no place for Accusation: and in the Civil State, the Accusation is followed with Punishment; which being Force, a man is not obliged not to resist. The same is also true, of the Accusation of those, by whose Condemnation a man falls into misery; as of a Father, Wife, or Benefactor. For the Testimony of such an Accuser, if it be not willingly given, is presumed to be corrupted by Nature; and therefore not to be received: and where a mans Testimony is not to be credited, his not bound to give it. Also Accusations upon Torture, are not to be reputed as Testimonies. For Torture is to be used but as means of conjecture, and light, in the further examination, and search of truth; and what is in that case confessed, tendeth to the ease of him that is Tortured; not to the informing of the Torturers: and therefore ought not to have the credit of a sufficient Testimony: for whether he deliver himself by true, or false Accusation, he does it by the Right of preserving his own life.

The End Of An Oath; The Form Of As Oath

The force of Words, being (as I have formerly noted) too weak to hold men to the performance of their Covenants; there are in mans nature, but two imaginable helps to strengthen it. And those are either a Fear of the consequence of breaking their word; or a Glory, or Pride in appearing not to need to break it. This later is a Generosity too rarely found to be presumed on, especially in the pursuers of Wealth, Command, or sensual Pleasure; which are the greatest part of Mankind. The Passion to be reckoned upon, is Fear; whereof there be two very general Objects: one, the Power of Spirits Invisible; the other, the Power of those men they shall therein Offend. Of these two, though the former be the greater Power, yet the fear of the later is commonly the greater Fear. The Fear of the former is in every man, his own Religion: which hath place in the nature of man before Civil Society. The later hath not so; at least not place enough, to keep men to their promises; because in the condition of mere Nature, the inequality of Power is not discerned, but by the event of Battle. So that before the time of Civil Society, or in the interruption thereof by War, there is nothing can strengthen a Covenant of Peace agreed on, against the temptations of Avarice, Ambition, Lust, or other strong desire, but the fear of that Invisible Power, which they every one

Worship as God; and Fear as a Revenger of their perfidy. All therefore that can be done between two men not subject to Civil Power, is to put one another to swear by the God he feareth: Which Swearing or OATH, is a Form Of Speech, Added To A Promise; By Which He That Promiseth, Signifieth, That Unless He Perform, He Renounceth The Mercy Of His God, Or Calleth To Him For Vengeance On Himself. Such was the Heathen Form, "Let Jupiter kill me else, as I kill this Beast." So is our Form, "I shall do thus, and thus, so help me God." And this, with the Rites and Ceremonies, which every one useth in his own Religion, that the fear of breaking faith might be the greater.

No Oath, But By God

By this it appears, that an Oath taken according to any other Form, or Rite, then his, that sweareth, is in vain; and no Oath: And there is no Swearing by any thing which the Swearer thinks not God. For though men have sometimes used to swear by their Kings, for fear, or flattery; yet they would have it thereby understood, they attributed to them Divine honor. And that Swearing unnecessarily by God, is but prophaning of his name: and Swearing by other things, as men do in common discourse, is not Swearing, but an impious Custom, gotten by too much vehemence of talking.

An Oath Adds Nothing To The Obligation

It appears also, that the Oath adds nothing to the Obligation. For a Covenant, if lawful, binds in the sight of God, without the Oath, as much as with it; if unlawful, bindeth not at all; though it be confirmed with an Oath.

CHAPTER XV
OF OTHER LAWS OF NATURE

The Third Law Of Nature, Justice

5   From that law of Nature, by which we are
obliged to transfer to another, such Rights, as
being retained, hinder the peace of Mankind,
there followeth a Third; which is this, That
Men Perform Their Covenants Made: without
10   which, Covenants are in vain, and but Empty
words; and the Right of all men to all things
remaining, wee are still in the condition of
War.

Justice And Injustice What

15   And in this law of Nature, consisteth the
Fountain and Original of JUSTICE. For
where no Covenant hath preceded, there hath
no Right been transferred, and every man has
20   right to every thing; and consequently, no action can be Unjust. But when a Covenant is
made, then to break it is Unjust: And the definition of INJUSTICE, is no other than The
Not Performance Of Covenant. And whatso-
25   ever is not Unjust, is Just.

Justice And Propriety Begin With The Constitution of Common-wealth

But because Covenants of mutual trust, where
30   there is a fear of not performance on either
part, (as hath been said in the former Chapter,) are invalid; though the Original of Justice
be the making of Covenants; yet Injustice actually there can be none, till the cause of such
35   fear be taken away; which while men are in the
natural condition of War, cannot be done.
Therefore before the names of Just, and Unjust can have place, there must be some coercive Power, to compel men equally to the per-
40   formance of their Covenants, by the terror of
some punishment, greater than the benefit
they expect by the breach of their Covenant;
and to make good that Propriety, which by

45   mutual Contract men acquire, in recompense
of the universal Right they abandon: and such
power there is none before the erection of a
Common-wealth. And this is also to be gathered out of the ordinary definition of Justice in
the Schools: For they say, that "Justice is the
50   constant Will of giving to every man his own."
And therefore where there is no Own, that is,
no Propriety, there is no Injustice; and where
there is no coercive Power erected, that is,
where there is no Common-wealth, there is no
55   Propriety; all men having Right to all things:
Therefore where there is no Common-wealth,
there nothing is Unjust. So that the nature of
Justice, consisteth in keeping of valid Covenants: but the Validity of Covenants begins
60   not but with the Constitution of a Civil Power,
sufficient to compel men to keep them: And
then it is also that Propriety begins.

Justice Not Contrary To Reason

65   The Fool hath said in his heart, there is no
such thing as Justice; and sometimes also with
his tongue; seriously alleging, that every mans
conservation, and contentment, being committed to his own care, there could be no rea-
70   son, why every man might not do what he
thought conduced thereunto; and therefore
also to make, or not make; keep, or not keep
Covenants, was not against Reason, when it
conduced to ones benefit. He does not therein
75   deny, that there be Covenants; and that they
are sometimes broken, sometimes kept; and
that such breach of them may be called Injustice, and the observance of them Justice: but
he questioneth, whether Injustice, taking away
80   the fear of God, (for the same Fool hath said
in his heart there is no God,) may not sometimes stand with that Reason, which dictateth
to every man his own good; and particularly
then, when it conduceth to such a benefit, as
85   shall put a man in a condition, to neglect not
only the dispraise, and revilings, but also the

power of other men. The Kingdome of God is gotten by violence; but what if it could be gotten by unjust violence? were it against Reason so to get it, when it is impossible to receive
5 hurt by it? and if it be not against Reason, it is not against Justice; or else Justice is not to be approved for good. From such reasoning as this, Successful wickedness hath obtained the Name of Virtue; and some that in all other
10 things have disallowed the violation of Faith; yet have allowed it, when it is for the getting of a Kingdome. And the Heathen that believed, that Saturn was deposed by his son Jupiter, believed nevertheless the same Jupiter
15 to be the avenger of Injustice: Somewhat like to a piece of Law in Cokes Commentaries on Litleton; where he says, If the right Heir of the Crown be attainted of Treason; yet the Crown shall descend to him, and Eo Instante the At-
20 tainder be void; From which instances a man will be very prone to infer; that when the Heir apparent of a Kingdome, shall kill him that is in possession, though his father; you may call it Injustice, or by what other name you will;
25 yet it can never be against Reason, seeing all the voluntary actions of men tend to the benefit of themselves; and those actions are most Reasonable, that conduce most to their ends. This specious reasoning is nevertheless false.

30

For the question is not of promises mutual, where there is no security of performance on either side; as when there is no Civil Power erected over the parties promising; for such
35 promises are no Covenants: But either where one of the parties has performed already; or where there is a Power to make him perform; there is the question whether it be against reason, that is, against the benefit of the other to
40 perform, or not. And I say it is not against reason. For the manifestation whereof, we are to consider; First, that when a man doth a thing, which notwithstanding any thing can be foreseen, and reckoned on, tendeth to his own
45 destruction, howsoever some accident which he could not expect, arriving may turn it to his benefit; yet such events do not make it reasonably or wisely done. Secondly, that in a condition of War, wherein every man to every
50 man, for want of a common Power to keep them all in awe, is an Enemy, there is no man can hope by his own strength, or wit, to defend himself from destruction, without the help of Confederates; where every one expects
55 the same defense by the Confederation, that any one else does: and therefore he which declares he thinks it reason to deceive those that help him, can in reason expect no other means of safety, than what can be had from
60 his own single Power. He therefore that breaketh his Covenant, and consequently declareth that he thinks he may with reason do so, cannot be received into any Society, that unite themselves for Peace and defense, but by
65 the error of them that receive him; nor when he is received, be retained in it, without seeing the danger of their error; which errors a man cannot reasonably reckon upon as the means of his security; and therefore if he be left, or
70 cast out of Society, he perisheth; and if he live in Society, it is by the errors of other men, which he could not foresee, nor reckon upon; and consequently against the reason of his preservation; and so, as all men that contribute
75 not to his destruction, forbear him only out of ignorance of what is good for themselves.

As for the Instance of gaining the secure and perpetual felicity of Heaven, by any way; it is
80 frivolous: there being but one way imaginable; and that is not breaking, but keeping of Covenant.

And for the other Instance of attaining Sovereignty by Rebellion; it is manifest, that though
85 the event follow, yet because it cannot reason-

ably be expected, but rather the contrary; and because by gaining it so, others are taught to gain the same in like manner, the attempt thereof is against reason. Justice therefore, that

5 is to say, Keeping of Covenant, is a Rule of Reason, by which we are forbidden to do any thing destructive to our life; and consequently a Law of Nature.

10 There be some that proceed further; and will not have the Law of Nature, to be those Rules which conduce to the preservation of mans life on earth; but to the attaining of an eternal felicity after death; to which they think the

15 breach of Covenant may conduce; and consequently be just and reasonable; (such are they that think it a work of merit to kill, or depose, or rebel against, the Sovereign Power constituted over them by their own consent.) But

20 because there is no natural knowledge of mans estate after death; much less of the reward that is then to be given to breach of Faith; but only a belief grounded upon other men's saying, that they know it supernaturally, or that they

25 know those, that knew them, that knew others, that knew it supernaturally; Breach of Faith cannot be called a Precept of Reason, or Nature.

30 **Covenants Not Discharged By The Vice Of The Person To Whom Made**

Others, that allow for a Law of Nature, the keeping of Faith, do nevertheless make exception of certain persons; as Heretics, and such

35 as use not to perform their Covenant to others: And this also is against reason. For if any fault of a man, be sufficient to discharge our Covenant made; the same ought in reason to have been sufficient to have hindered the

40 making of it.

Justice Of Men, And Justice Of Actions
45 **What**

The names of Just, and Unjust, when they are attributed to Men, signify one thing; and when they are attributed to Actions, another. When they are attributed to Men, they signify Con-

50 formity, or Inconformity of Manners, to Reason. But when they are attributed to Actions, they signify the Conformity, or Inconformity to Reason, not of Manners, or manner of life, but of particular Actions. A Just man there-

55 fore, is he that taketh all the care he can, that his Actions may be all Just: and an Unjust man, is he that neglecteth it. And such men are more often in our Language stilled by the names of Righteous, and Unrighteous; then

60 Just, and Unjust; though the meaning be the same. Therefore a Righteous man, does not lose that Title, by one, or a few unjust Actions, that proceed from sudden Passion, or mistake of Things, or Persons: nor does an Unright-

65 eous man, lose his character, for such Actions, as he does, of forbears to do, for fear: because his Will is not framed by the Justice, but by the apparent benefit of what he is to do. That which gives to humane Actions the relish of

70 Justice, is a certain Nobleness or Gallantness of courage, (rarely found,) by which a man scorns to be beholding for the contentment of his life, to fraud, or breach of promise. This Justice of the Manners, is that which is meant,

75 where Justice is called a Virtue; and Injustice a Vice.

But the Justice of Actions denominates men, not Just, but Guiltless; and the Injustice of the

80 same, (which is also called Injury,) gives them but the name of Guilty.

Justice Of Manners, And Justice Of Actions

85 Again, the Injustice of Manners, is the disposition, or aptitude to do Injury; and is Injustice

before it proceed to Act; and without supposing any individual person injured. But the Injustice of an Action, (that is to say Injury,)
supposeth an individual person Injured; name-
5 ly him, to whom the Covenant was made: And
therefore many times the injury is received by
one man, when the damage redoundeth to
another. As when The Master commandeth
his servant to give money to a stranger; if it be
10 not done, the Injury is done to the Master,
whom he had before Covenanted to obey; but
the damage redoundeth to the stranger, to
whom he had no Obligation; and therefore
could not Injure him. And so also in Com-
15 mon-wealths, private men may remit to one
another their debts; but not robberies or other
violences, whereby they are endammaged;
because the detaining of Debt, is an Injury to
themselves; but Robbery and Violence, are
20 Injuries to the Person of the Common-wealth.

Nothing Done To A Man, By His Own Consent Can Be Injury

Whatsoever is done to a man, conformable to
25 his own Will signified to the doer, is no Injury
to him. For if he that doeth it, hath not passed
away his original right to do what he please, by
some Antecedent Covenant, there is no
breach of Covenant; and therefore no Injury
30 done him. And if he have; then his Will to
have it done being signified, is a release of that
Covenant; and so again there is no Injury done
him.

Justice Commutative, And Distributive
35

Justice of Actions, is by Writers divided into
Commutative, and Distributive; and the former they say consisteth in proportion Arithmetical; the later in proportion Geometrical.
40 Commutative therefore, they place in the
equality of value of the things contracted for;
And Distributive, in the distribution of equal
benefit, to men of equal merit. As if it were

Injustice to sell dearer than we buy; or to give
45 more to a man than he merits. The value of all
things contracted for, is measured by the Appetite of the Contractors: and therefore the
just value, is that which they be contented to
give. And Merit (besides that which is by Cov-
50 enant, where the performance on one part,
meriteth the performance of the other part,
and falls under Justice Commutative, not Distributive,) is not due by Justice; but is rewarded of Grace only. And therefore this distinc-
55 tion, in the sense wherein it useth to be expounded, is not right. To speak properly,
Commutative Justice, is the Justice of a Contractor; that is, a Performance of Covenant, in
Buying, and Selling; Hiring, and Letting to
60 Hire; Lending, and Borrowing; Exchanging,
Bartering, and other acts of Contract.

And Distributive Justice, the Justice of an Arbitrator; that is to say, the act of defining what
65 is Just. Wherein, (being trusted by them that
make him Arbitrator,) if he perform his Trust,
he is said to distribute to every man his own:
and his is indeed Just Distribution, and may be
called (though improperly) Distributive Jus-
70 tice; but more properly Equity; which also is a
Law of Nature, as shall be shown in due place.

The Fourth Law Of Nature, Gratitude

As Justice dependeth on Antecedent Cove-
75 nant; so does Gratitude depend on Antecedent Grace; that is to say, Antecedent Free-gift:
and is the fourth Law of Nature; which may
be conceived in this Form, "That a man which
receiveth Benefit from another of mere Grace,
80 Endeavour that he which giveth it, have no
reasonable cause to repent him of his good
will." For no man giveth, but with intention of
Good to himself; because Gift is Voluntary;
and of all Voluntary Acts, the Object is to
85 every man his own Good; of which if men see
they shall be frustrated, there will be no be-

ginning of benevolence, or trust; nor consequently of mutual help; nor of reconciliation of one man to another; and therefore they are to remain still in the condition of War; which

5 is contrary to the first and Fundamental Law of Nature, which commandeth men to Seek Peace. The breach of this Law, is called Ingratitude; and hath the same relation to Grace, that Injustice hath to Obligation by Covenant.

The Fifth, Mutual accommodation, or Complaisance

A fifth Law of Nature, is COMPLEASANCE; that is to say, "That every man strive to ac-

15 commodate himself to the rest." For the understanding whereof, we may consider, that there is in men's aptness to Society; a diversity of Nature, rising from their diversity of Affections; not unlike to that we see in stones

20 brought together for building of an Edifice. For as that stone which by the asperity, and irregularity of Figure, takes more room from others, than it self fills; and for the hardness, cannot be easily made plain, and thereby hin-

25 dereth the building, is by the builders cast away as unprofitable, and troublesome: so also, a man that by asperity of Nature, will strive to retain those things which to himself are superfluous, and to others necessary; and

30 for the stubbornness of his Passions, cannot be corrected, is to be left, or cast out of Society, as cumbersome thereunto. For seeing every man, not only by Right, but also by necessity of Nature, is supposed to endeavor all he can,

35 to obtain that which is necessary for his conservation; He that shall oppose himself against it, for things superfluous, is guilty of the War that thereupon is to follow; and therefore doth that, which is contrary to the fundamental Law

40 of Nature, which commandeth To Seek Peace. The observers of this Law, may be called SOCIABLE, (the Latins call them Commodi;) The contrary, Stubborn, Insociable, Froward,

Intractable.

45

The Sixth, Facility To Pardon

A sixth Law of Nature is this, "That upon caution of the Future time, a man ought to pardon the offences past of them that repent-

50 ing, desire it." For PARDON, is nothing but granting of Peace; which though granted to them that persevere in their hostility, be not Peace, but Fear; yet not granted to them that give caution of the Future time, is sign of an

55 aversion to Peace; and therefore contrary to the Law of Nature.

The Seventh, That In Revenges, Men Respect Only The Future Good

60 A seventh is, " That in Revenges, (that is, retribution of evil for evil,) Men look not at the greatness of the evil past, but the greatness of the good to follow." Whereby we are forbidden to inflict punishment with any other de-

65 sign, than for correction of the offender, or direction of others. For this Law is consequent to the next before it, that commandeth Pardon, upon security of the Future Time. Besides, Revenge without respect to the Exam-

70 ple, and profit to come, is a triumph, or glorying in the hurt of another, tending to no end; (for the End is always somewhat to Come;) and glorying to no end, is vain-glory, and contrary to reason; and to hurt without reason,

75 tendeth to the introduction of War; which is against the Law of Nature; and is commonly stilled by the name of Cruelty.

The Eighth, Against Contumely

80 And because all signs of hatred, or contempt, provoke to fight; insomuch as most men choose rather to hazard their life, than not to be revenged; we may in the eighth place, for a Law of Nature set down this Precept, "That

85 no man by deed, word, countenance, or gesture, declare Hatred, or Contempt of another."

The breach of which Law, is commonly called Contumely.

The Ninth, Against Pride

5 The question who is the better man, has no place in the condition of mere Nature; where, (as has been shown before,) all men are equal. The inequality that now is, has been introduced by the Laws Civil. I know that Aristotle 10 in the first book of his Politics, for a foundation of his doctrine, maketh men by Nature, some more worthy to Command, meaning the wiser sort (such as he thought himself to be for his Philosophy;) others to Serve, (meaning 15 those that had strong bodies, but were not Philosophers as he;) as if Master and Servant were not introduced by consent of men, but by difference of Wit; which is not only against reason; but also against experience. For there 20 are very few so foolish, that had not rather govern themselves, than be governed by others: Nor when the wise in their own conceit, contend by force, with them who distrust their own wisdom, do they always, or often, or al- 25 most at any time, get the Victory. If Nature therefore have made men equal, that equality is to be acknowledged; or if Nature have made men unequal; yet because men that think themselves equal, will not enter into condi- 30 tions of Peace, but upon Equal terms, such equality must be admitted. And therefore for the ninth Law of Nature, I put this, "That every man acknowledge other for his Equal by Nature." The breach of this Precept is Pride.

35

The Tenth Against Arrogance

On this law, dependeth another, "That at the entrance into conditions of Peace, no man require to reserve to himself any Right, which 40 he is not content should be reserved to every one of the rest." As it is necessary for all men that seek peace, to lay down certain Rights of Nature; that is to say, not to have liberty to do

all they list: so is it necessary for mans life, to 45 retain some; as right to govern their own bodies; enjoy air, water, motion, ways to go from place to place; and all things else without which a man cannot live, or not live well. If in this case, at the making of Peace, men require 50 for themselves, that which they would not have to be granted to others, they do contrary to the precedent law, that commandeth the

acknowledgement of natural equality, and 55 therefore also against the law of Nature. The observers of this law, are those we call Modest, and the breakers Arrogant Men. The Greeks call the violation of this law pleonexia; that is, a desire of more than their share.

60

The Eleventh Equity

Also "If a man be trusted to judge between man and man," it is a precept of the Law of Nature, "that he deal Equally between them." 65 For without that, the Controversies of men cannot be determined but by War. He therefore that is partial in judgment, doth what in him lies, to deter men from the use of Judges, and Arbitrators; and consequently, (against the 70 fundamental Law of Nature) is the cause of War.

The observance of this law, from the equal distribution to each man, of that which in rea- 75 son belongeth to him, is called EQUITY, and (as I have said before) distributive justice: the violation, Acception Of Persons, Prosopolepsia.

The Twelfth, Equal Use Of Things Common

80

And from this followeth another law, "That such things as cannot be divided, be enjoyed in Common, if it can be; and if the quantity of 85 the thing permit, without Stint; otherwise Proportionally to the number of them that have Right." For otherwise the distribution is Unequal, and contrary to Equity.

The Thirteenth, Of Lot

But some things there be, that can neither be divided, nor enjoyed in common. Then, The Law of Nature, which prescribeth Equity, requireth, "That the Entire Right; or else, (making the use alternate,) the First Possession, be determined by Lot." For equal distribution, is of the Law of Nature; and other means of equal distribution cannot be imagined.

The Fourteenth, Of Primogeniture, And First Seizing

Of Lots there be two sorts, Arbitrary, and Natural. Arbitrary, is that which is agreed on by the Competitors; Natural, is either Primogeniture, (which the Greek calls Kleronomia, which signifies, Given by Lot;) or First Seizure.

And therefore those things which cannot be enjoyed in common, nor divided, ought to be adjudged to the First Possessor; and is some cases to the First-Borne, as acquired by Lot.

The Fifteenth, Of Mediators

It is also a Law of Nature, "That all men that mediate Peace, be allowed safe Conduct." For the Law that commandeth Peace, as the End, commandeth Intercession, as the Means; and to Intercession the Means is safe Conduct.

The Sixteenth, Of Submission To Arbitrement

And because, though men be never so willing to observe these Laws, there may nevertheless arise questions concerning a mans action; First, whether it were done, or not done; Secondly (if done) whether against the Law, or not against the Law; the former whereof, is called a question Of Fact; the later a question Of Right; therefore unless the parties to the question, Covenant mutually to stand to the sentence of another, they are as far from Peace as ever. This other, to whose Sentence they submit, is called an ARBITRATOR. And therefore it is of the Law of Nature, "That they that are at controversy, submit their Right to the judgment of an Arbitrator."

The Seventeenth, No Man Is His Own Judge

And seeing every man is presumed to do all things in order to his own benefit, no man is a fit Arbitrator in his own cause: and if he were never so fit; yet Equity allowing to each party equal benefit, if one be admitted to be Judge, the other is to be admitted also; & so the controversy, that is, the cause of War, remains, against the Law of Nature.

The Eighteenth, No Man To Be Judge, That Has In Him Cause Of Partiality

For the same reason no man in any Cause ought to be received for Arbitrator, to whom greater profit, or honor, or pleasure apparently ariseth out of the victory of one party, than of the other: for he hath taken (though an unavoidable bribe, yet) a bribe; and no man can be obliged to trust him. And thus also the controversy, and the condition of War remaineth, contrary to the Law of Nature.

The Nineteenth, Of Witness

And in a controversy of Fact, the Judge being to give no more credit to one, than to the other, (if there be no other Arguments) must give credit to a third; or to a third and fourth; or more: For else the question is undecided, and left to force, contrary to the Law of Nature.

These are the Laws of Nature, dictating Peace, for a means of the conservation of men in multitudes; and which only concern the doc-

trine of Civil Society. There be other things tending to the destruction of particular men; as Drunkenness, and all other parts of Intemperance; which may therefore also be reck-
5 oned amongst those things which the Law of Nature hath forbidden; but are not necessary to be mentioned, nor are pertinent enough to this place.

A Rule, By Which The Laws Of Nature May Easily Be Examined
10 And though this may seem too subtle a deduction of the Laws of Nature, to be taken notice of by all men; whereof the most part are too
15 busy in getting food, and the rest too negligent to understand; yet to leave all men unexcusable, they have been contracted into one easy sum, intelligible even to the meanest capacity; and that is, "Do not that to another, which
20 thou wouldest not have done to thy self;" which sheweth him, that he has no more to do in learning the Laws of Nature, but, when weighing the actions of other men with his own, they seem too heavy, to put them into
25 the other part of the balance, and his own into their place, that his own passions, and self-love, may add nothing to the weight; and then there is none of these Laws of Nature that will not appear unto him very reasonable.
30

The Laws Of Nature Oblige In Conscience Always, But In Effect Then Only When There Is Security
The Laws of Nature oblige In Foro Interno;
35 that is to say, they bind to a desire they should take place: but In Foro Externo; that is, to the putting them in act, not always. For he that should be modest, and tractable, and perform all he promises, in such time, and place, where
40 no man else should do so, should but make himself a prey to others, and procure his own certain ruin, contrary to the ground of all Laws of Nature, which tend to Natures preserva-

tion. And again, he that shall observe the same
45 Laws towards him, observes them not himself, seeketh not Peace, but War; & consequently the destruction of his Nature by Violence.

And whatsoever Laws bind In Foro Interno,
50 may be broken, not only by a fact contrary to the Law but also by a fact according to it, in case a man think it contrary. For though his Action in this case, be according to the Law; which where the Obligation is In Foro Inter-
55 no, is a breach.

The Laws Of Nature Are Eternal;
The Laws of Nature are Immutable and Eternal, For Injustice, Ingratitude, Arrogance,
60 Pride, Iniquity, Acception of persons, and the rest, can never be made lawful. For it can never be that War shall preserve life, and Peace destroy it.

65 ## And Yet Easy
The same Laws, because they oblige only to a desire, and endeavor, I mean an unfeigned and constant endeavor, are easy to be observed. For in that they require nothing but endeavor;
70 he that endeavoureth their performance, fulfilleth them; and he that fulfilleth the Law, is Just.

The Science Of These Laws, Is The True
75 ## Moral Philosophy
And the Science of them, is the true and only Moral Philosophy. For Moral Philosophy is nothing else but the Science of what is Good, and Evil, in the conversation, and Society of
80 mankind. Good, and Evil, are names that signify our Appetites, and Aversions; which in different tempers, customs, and doctrines of men, are different: And divers men, differ not only in their Judgment, on the senses of what
85 is pleasant, and unpleasant to the taste, smell, hearing, touch, and sight; but also of what is

conformable, or disagreeable to Reason, in the
actions of common life. Nay, the same man, in
divers times, differs from himself; and one
time praiseth, that is, calleth Good, what an-
5 other time he dispraiseth, and calleth Evil:
From whence arise Disputes, Controversies,
and at last War. And therefore so long as man
is in the condition of mere Nature, (which is a
condition of War,) as private Appetite is the
10 measure of Good, and Evil: and consequently
all men agree on this, that Peace is Good, and
therefore also the way, or means of Peace,
which (as I have showed before) are Justice,
Gratitude, Modesty, Equity, Mercy, & the rest
15 of the Laws of Nature, are good; that is to say,
Moral Virtues; and their contrary Vices, Evil.
Now the science of Virtue and Vice, is Moral
Philosophy; and therefore the true Doctrine of
the Laws of Nature, is the true Moral Philoso-
20 phy. But the Writers of Moral Philosophy,
though they acknowledge the same Virtues
and Vices; Yet not seeing wherein consisted
their Goodness; nor that they come to be
praised, as the means of peaceable, sociable,
25 and comfortable living; place them in a mediocrity of passions: as if not the Cause, but the
Degree of daring, made Fortitude; or not the
Cause, but the Quantity of a gift, made Liberality.
30

These dictates of Reason, men use to call by
the name of Laws; but improperly: for they are
but Conclusions, or Theorems concerning
what conduceth to the conservation and de-
35 fense of themselves; whereas Law, properly is
the word of him, that by right hath command
over others. But yet if we consider the same
Theorems, as delivered in the word of God,
that by right commandeth all things; then are
40 they properly called Laws.

CHAPTER XVII
45 ## OF THE CAUSES, GENERATION,
AND DEFINITION OF A
COMMON-WEALTH

The End Of Common-wealth, Particular
50 ### Security
The final Cause, End, or Design of men, (who
naturally love Liberty, and Dominion over
others,) in the introduction of that restraint
upon themselves, (in which we see them live
55 in Common-wealths,) is the foresight of their
own preservation, and of a more contented
life thereby; that is to say, of getting themselves out from that miserable condition of
War, which is necessarily consequent (as hath
60 been shown) to the natural Passions of men,
when there is no visible Power to keep them
in awe, and tie them by fear of punishment to
the performance of their Covenants, and observation of these Laws of Nature set down in
65 the fourteenth and fifteenth Chapters.

Which Is Not To Be Had From The Law
Of Nature:
For the Laws of Nature (as Justice, Equity,
70 Modesty, Mercy, and (in sum) Doing To Others, As We Would Be Done To,) if themselves, without the terror of some Power, to
cause them to be observed, are contrary to our
natural Passions, that carry us to Partiality,
75 Pride, Revenge, and the like. And Covenants,
without the Sword, are but Words, and of no
strength to secure a man at all. Therefore notwithstanding the Laws of Nature, (which every
one hath then kept, when he has the will to
80 keep them, when he can do it safely,) if there
be no Power erected, or not great enough for
our security; every man will and may lawfully
rely on his own strength and art, for caution
against all other men. And in all places, where
85 men have lived by small Families, to rob and
spoil one another, has been a Trade, and so far

from being reputed against the Law of Nature, that the greater spoils they gained, the greater was their honor; and men observed no other Laws therein, but the Laws of Honor; that is,

5 to abstain from cruelty, leaving to men their lives, and instruments of husbandry. And as small Families did then; so now do Cities and Kingdoms which are but greater Families (for their own security) enlarge their Dominions,

10 upon all pretenses of danger, and fear of Invasion, or assistance that may be given to Invaders, endeavor as much as they can, to subdue, or weaken their neighbors, by open force, and secret arts, for want of other Caution,

15 justly; and are remembered for it in after ages with honor.

Nor From The Conjunction Of A Few Men Or Families

20 Nor is it the joining together of a small number of men, that gives them this security; because in small numbers, small additions on the one side or the other, make the advantage of strength so great, as is sufficient to carry the

25 Victory; and therefore gives encouragement to an Invasion. The Multitude sufficient to confide in for our Security, is not determined by any certain number, but by comparison with the Enemy we fear; and is then sufficient,

30 when the odds of the Enemy is not of so visible and conspicuous moment, to determine the event of War, as to move him to attempt.

Nor From A Great Multitude, Unless Di-
35 **rected By One Judgment**

And be there never so great a Multitude; yet if their actions be directed according to their particular judgments, and particular appetites, they can expect thereby no defense, nor pro-

40 tection, neither against a Common enemy, nor against the injuries of one another. For being distracted in opinions concerning the best use and application of their strength, they do not

help, but hinder one another; and reduce their

45 strength by mutual opposition to nothing: whereby they are easily, not only subdued by a very few that agree together; but also when there is no common enemy, they make War upon each other, for their particular interests.

50 For if we could suppose a great Multitude of men to consent in the observation of Justice, and other Laws of Nature, without a common Power to keep them all in awe; we might as well suppose all Man-kind to do the same; and

55 then there neither would be nor need to be any Civil Government, or Common-wealth at all; because there would be Peace without subjection.

60 **And That Continually**

Nor is it enough for the security, which men desire should last all the time of their life, that they be governed, and directed by one judgment, for a limited time; as in one Battle, or

65 one War. For though they obtain a Victory by their unanimous endeavor against a foreign enemy; yet afterwards, when either they have no common enemy, or he that by one part is held for an enemy, is by another part held for

70 a friend, they must needs by the difference of their interests dissolve, and fall again into a War amongst themselves.

Why Certain Creatures Without Reason,
75 **Or Speech, Do Nevertheless Live In Society, Without Any Coercive Power**

It is true, that certain living creatures, as Bees, and Ants, live sociably one with another, (which are therefore by Aristotle numbered

80 amongst Political creatures;) and yet have no other direction, than their particular judgments and appetites; nor speech, whereby one of them can signify to another, what he thinks expedient for the common benefit: and there-

85 fore some man may perhaps desire to know, why Man-kind cannot do the same. To which

I answer,

First, that men are continually in competition for Honor and Dignity, which these creatures
5 are not; and consequently amongst men there ariseth on that ground, Envy and Hatred, and finally War; but amongst these not so.

Secondly, that amongst these creatures, the
10 Common good differeth not from the Private; and being by nature inclined to their private, they procure thereby the common benefit. But man, whose Joy consisteth in comparing himself with other men, can relish nothing but
15 what is eminent.

Thirdly, that these creatures, having not (as man) the use of reason, do not see, nor think they see any fault, in the administration of
20 their common business: whereas amongst men, there are very many, that think themselves wiser, and abler to govern the Public, better than the rest; and these strive to reform and innovate, one this way, another that way;
25 and thereby bring it into Distraction and Civil War.

Fourthly, that these creatures, though they have some use of voice, in making known to
30 one another their desires, and other affections; yet they want that art of words, by which some men can represent to others, that which is Good, in the likeness of Evil; and Evil, in the likeness of Good; and augment, or dimin-
35 ish the apparent greatness of Good and Evil; discontenting men, and troubling their Peace at their pleasure.

Fifthly, irrational creatures cannot distinguish
40 between Injury, and Damage; and therefore as long as they be at ease, they are not offended with their fellows: whereas Man is then most troublesome, when he is most at ease: for then

it is that he loves to show his Wisdom, and
45 control the Actions of them that govern the Common-wealth.

Lastly, the agreement of these creatures is Natural; that of men, is by Covenant only,
50 which is Artificial: and therefore it is no wonder if there be somewhat else required (besides Covenant) to make their Agreement constant and lasting; which is a Common Power, to keep them in awe, and to direct their actions
55 to the Common Benefit.

The Generation Of A Common-wealth

The only way to erect such a Common Power, as may be able to defend them from the inva-
60 sion of Foreigners, and the injuries of one another, and thereby to secure them in such sort, as that by their own industry, and by the fruits of the Earth, they may nourish themselves and live contentedly; is, to confer all
65 their power and strength upon one Man, or upon one Assembly of men, that may reduce all their Wills, by plurality of voices, unto one Will: which is as much as to say, to appoint one man, or Assembly of men, to bear their
70 Person; and every one to own, and acknowledge himself to be Author of whatsoever he that so beareth their Person, shall Act, or cause to be Acted, in those things which concern the Common Peace and Safety; and
75 therein to submit their Wills, every one to his Will, and their Judgments, to his Judgment. This is more than Consent, or Concord; it is a real Unite of them all, in one and the same Person, made by Covenant of every man with
80 every man, in such manner, as if every man should say to every man, "I Authorize and give up my Right of Governing my self, to this Man, or to this Assembly of men, on this condition, that thou give up thy Right to him, and
85 Authorize all his Actions in like manner." This done, the Multitude so united in one Person,

is called a COMMON-WEALTH, in Latin CIVITAS. This is the Generation of that great LEVIATHAN, or rather (to speak more reverently) of that Mortal God, to which we owe under the Immortal God, our peace and defense. For by this Authority, given him by every particular man in the Common-Wealth, he hath the use of so much Power and Strength conferred on him, that by terror thereof, he is enabled to form the wills of them all, to Peace at home, and mutual aid against their enemies abroad.

The Definition Of A Common-wealth

And in him consisteth the Essence of the Common-wealth; which (to define it,) is "One Person, of whose Acts a great Multitude, by mutual Covenants one with another, have made themselves every one the Author, to the end he may use the strength and means of them all, as he shall think expedient, for their Peace and Common Defense."

Sovereign, And Subject, What

And he that carryeth this Person, as called SOVEREIGN, and said to have Sovereign Power; and every one besides, his SUBJECT. The attaining to this Sovereign Power, is by two ways. One, by Natural force; as when a man maketh his children, to submit themselves, and their children to his government, as being able to destroy them if they refuse, or by War subdueth his enemies to his will, giving them their lives on that condition. The other, is when men agree amongst themselves, to submit to some Man, or Assembly of men, voluntarily, on confidence to be protected by him against all others. This later, may be called a Political Common-wealth, or Common-wealth by Institution; and the former, a Common-wealth by Acquisition. And first, I shall speak of a Common-wealth by Institution.

CHAPTER XVIII
OF THE RIGHTS OF SOVEREIGNS BY INSTITUTION

The Act Of Instituting A Common-wealth, What

A Common-wealth is said to be Instituted, when a Multitude of men do Agree, and Covenant, Every One With Every One, that to whatsoever Man, or Assembly Of Men, shall be given by the major part, the Right to Present the Person of them all, (that is to say, to be their Representative;) every one, as well he that Voted For It, as he that Voted Against It, shall Authorize all the Actions and Judgments, of that Man, or Assembly of men, in the same manner, as if they were his own, to the end, to live peaceably amongst themselves, and be protected against other men.

The Consequences To Such Institution, Are

I. The Subjects Cannot Change The Form Of Government

From this Institution of a Common-wealth are derived all the Rights, and Faculties of him, or them, on whom the Sovereign Power is conferred by the consent of the People assembled.

First, because they Covenant, it is to be understood, they are not obliged by former Covenant to any thing repugnant hereunto. And Consequently they that have already Instituted a Common-wealth, being thereby bound by Covenant, to own the Actions, and Judgments of one, cannot lawfully make a new Covenant, amongst themselves, to be obedient to any other, in any thing whatsoever, without his permission. And therefore, they that are subjects to a Monarch, cannot without his leave cast off Monarchy, and return to the confu-

sion of a disunited Multitude; nor transfer their Person from him that beareth it, to another Man, or other Assembly of men: for they are bound, every man to every man, to
5 Own, and be reputed Author of all, that he that already is their Sovereign, shall do, and judge fit to be done: so that any one man dissenting, all the rest should break their Covenant made to that man, which is injustice: and
10 they have also every man given the Sovereignty to him that beareth their Person; and therefore if they depose him, they take from him that which is his own, and so again it is injustice. Besides, if he that attempteth to depose
15 his Sovereign, be killed, or punished by him for such attempt, he is author of his own punishment, as being by the Institution, Author of all his Sovereign shall do: And because it is injustice for a man to do any thing, for which
20 he may be punished by his own authority, he is also upon that title, unjust. And whereas some men have pretended for their disobedience to their Sovereign, a new Covenant, made, not with men, but with God; this also is
25 unjust: for there is no Covenant with God, but by mediation of some body that representeth Gods Person; which none doth but Gods Lieutenant, who hath the Sovereignty under God. But this pretense of Covenant with God,
30 is so evident a lye, even in the pretenders own consciences, that it is not only an act of an unjust, but also of a vile, and unmanly disposition.

35 **2. Sovereign Power Cannot Be Forfeited**
Secondly, Because the Right of bearing the Person of them all, is given to him they make Sovereign, by Covenant only of one to another, and not of him to any of them; there can
40 happen no breach of Covenant on the part of the Sovereign; and consequently none of his Subjects, by any pretense of forfeiture, can be freed from his Subjection. That he which is

made Sovereign maketh no Covenant with his
45 Subjects beforehand, is manifest; because either he must make it with the whole multitude, as one party to the Covenant; or he must make a several Covenant with every man. With the whole, as one party, it is impossible;
50 because as yet they are not one Person: and if he make so many several Covenants as there be men, those Covenants after he hath the Sovereignty are void, because what act soever can be pretended by any one of them for
55 breach thereof, is the act both of himself, and of all the rest, because done in the Person, and by the Right of every one of them in particular. Besides, if any one, or more of them, pretend a breach of the Covenant made by the
60 Sovereign at his Institution; and others, or one other of his Subjects, or himself alone, pretend there was no such breach, there is in this case, no Judge to decide the controversy: it returns therefore to the Sword again; and every man
65 recovereth the right of Protecting himself by his own strength, contrary to the design they had in the Institution. It is therefore in vain to grant Sovereignty by way of precedent Covenant. The opinion that any Monarch receiveth
70 his Power by Covenant, that is to say on Condition, proceedeth from want of understanding this easy truth, that Covenants being but words, and breath, have no force to oblige, contain, constrain, or protect any man, but
75 what it has from the public Sword; that is, from the untied hands of that Man, or Assembly of men that hath the Sovereignty, and whose actions are avouched by them all, and performed by the strength of them all, in him
80 united. But when an Assembly of men is made Sovereign; then no man imagineth any such Covenant to have past in the Institution; for no man is so dull as to say, for example, the People of Rome, made a Covenant with the
85 Romans, to hold the Sovereignty on such or such conditions; which not performed, the

Romans might lawfully depose the Roman People. That men see not the reason to be alike in a Monarchy, and in a Popular Government, proceedeth from the ambition of

5 some, that are kinder to the government of an Assembly, whereof they may hope to participate, than of Monarchy, which they despair to enjoy.

3. No Man Can Without Injustice Protest Against The Institution Of The Sovereign Declared By The Major Part

Thirdly, because the major part hath by consenting voices declared a Sovereign; he that

15 dissented must now consent with the rest; that is, be contented to avow all the actions he shall do, or else justly be destroyed by the rest. For if he voluntarily entered into the Congregation of them that were assembled, he suffi-

20 ciently declared thereby his will (and therefore tacitly covenanted) to stand to what the major part should ordain: and therefore if he refuse to stand thereto, or make Protestation against any of their Decrees, he does contrary to his

25 Covenant, and therefore unjustly. And whether he be of the Congregation, or not; and whether his consent be asked, or not, he must either submit to their decrees, or be left in the condition of War he was in before; wherein he

30 might without injustice be destroyed by any man whatsoever.

4. The Sovereigns Actions Cannot Be Justly Accused By The Subject

35 Fourthly, because every Subject is by this Institution Author of all the Actions, and Judgments of the Sovereign Instituted; it follows, that whatsoever he doth, it can be no injury to any of his Subjects; nor ought he to be by any

40 of them accused of Injustice. For he that doth any thing by authority from another, doth therein no injury to him by whose authority he acteth: But by this Institution of a Common-

wealth, every particular man is Author of all

45 the Sovereign doth; and consequently he that complaineth of injury from his Sovereign, complaineth of that whereof he himself is Author; and therefore ought not to accuse any man but himself; no nor himself of injury;

50 because to do injury to ones self, is impossible. It is true that they that have Sovereign power, may commit Iniquity; but not Injustice, or Injury in the proper signification.

5. What Soever The Sovereign Doth, Is

55 Unpunishable By The Subject

Fifthly, and consequently to that which was said last, no man that hath Sovereign power can justly be put to death, or otherwise in any

60 manner by his Subjects punished. For seeing every Subject is author of the actions of his Sovereign; he punisheth another, for the actions committed by himself.

6. The Sovereign Is Judge Of What Is

65 Necessary For The Peace
And Defense Of His Subjects

And because the End of this Institution, is the Peace and Defense of them all; and whosoever

70 has right to the End, has right to the Means; it belongeth of Right, to whatsoever Man, or Assembly that hath the Sovereignty, to be Judge both of the means of Peace and Defense; and also of the hindrances, and disturb-

75 ances of the same; and to do whatsoever he shall think necessary to be done, both beforehand, for the preserving of Peace and Security, by prevention of discord at home and Hostility from abroad; and, when Peace and Security

80 are lost, for the recovery of the same. And therefore,

And Judge Of What Doctrines Are Fit To Be Taught Them

85 Sixthly, it is annexed to the Sovereignty, to be Judge of what Opinions and Doctrines are

averse, and what conducing to Peace; and consequently, on what occasions, how far, and what, men are to be trusted withal, in speaking to Multitudes of people; and who shall exam-
5 ine the Doctrines of all books before they be published. For the Actions of men proceed from their Opinions; and in the well governing of Opinions, consisteth the well governing of men's Actions, in order to their Peace, and
10 Concord. And though in matter of Doctrine, nothing ought to be regarded but the Truth; yet this is not repugnant to regulating of the same by Peace. For Doctrine Repugnant to Peace, can no more be True, than Peace and
15 Concord can be against the Law of Nature. It is true, that in a Common-wealth, where by the negligence, or unskillfulness of Governors, and Teachers, false Doctrines are by time generally received; the contrary Truths may be
20 generally offensive; Yet the most sudden, and rough bustling in of a new Truth, that can be, does never break the Peace, but only sometimes awake the War. For those men that are so remissely governed, that they dare take up
25 Arms, to defend, or introduce an Opinion, are still in War; and their condition not Peace, but only a Cessation of Arms for fear of one another; and they live as it were, in the precincts of battle continually. It belongeth therefore to
30 him that hath the Sovereign Power, to be Judge, or constitute all Judges of Opinions and Doctrines, as a thing necessary to Peace, thereby to prevent Discord and Civil War.

35 **7. The Right Of Making Rules, Whereby The Subject May Every Man Know What Is So His Own, As No Other Subject Can Without Injustice Take It From Him**
Seventhly, is annexed to the Sovereignty, the
40 whole power of prescribing the Rules, whereby every man may know, what Goods he may enjoy and what Actions he may do, without being molested by any of his fellow Subjects:

And this is it men Call Propriety. For before
45 constitution of Sovereign Power (as hath already been shown) all men had right to all things; which necessarily causeth War: and therefore this Propriety, being necessary to Peace, and depending on Sovereign Power, is
50 the Act of the Power, in order to the public peace. These Rules of Propriety (or Meum and Tuum) and of Good, Evil, Lawful and Unlawful in the actions of subjects, are the Civil Laws, that is to say, the Laws of each Com-
55 monwealth in particular; though the name of Civil Law be now restrained to the ancient Civil Laws of the City of Rome; which being the head of a great part of the World, her Laws at that time were in these parts the Civil
60 Law.

8. To Him Also Belongeth The Right Of All Judicature And Decision Of Controversies:
65 Eighthly, is annexed to the Sovereignty, the Right of Judicature; that is to say, of hearing and deciding all Controversies, which may arise concerning Law, either Civil, or natural, or concerning Fact. For without the decision
70 of Controversies, there is no protection of one Subject, against the injuries of another; the Laws concerning Meum and Tuum are in vain; and to every man remaineth, from the natural and necessary appetite of his own conserva-
75 tion, the right of protecting himself by his private strength, which is the condition of War; and contrary to the end for which every Common-wealth is instituted.

80 **9. And Of Making War, And Peace, As He Shall Think Best:**
Ninthly, is annexed to the Sovereignty, the Right of making War, and Peace with other Nations, and Common-wealths; that is to say,
85 of Judging when it is for the public good, and how great forces are to be assembled, armed,

and paid for that end; and to levy money upon the Subjects, to defray the expenses thereof. For the Power by which the people are to be defended, consisteth in their Armies; and the strength of an Army, in the union of their strength under one Command; which Command the Sovereign Instituted, therefore hath; because the command of the Militia, without other Institution, maketh him that hath it Sovereign. And therefore whosoever is made General of an Army, he that hath the Sovereign Power is always Generalissimo.

10. And Of Choosing All Counselors, And Ministers, Both Of Peace, And War:

Tenthly, is annexed to the Sovereignty, the choosing of all Councilors, Ministers, Magistrates, and Officers, both in peace, and War. For seeing the Sovereign is charged with the End, which is the common Peace and Defense; he is understood to have Power to use such Means, as he shall think most fit for his discharge.

11. And Of Rewarding, And Punishing, And That (Where No Former Law hath Determined The Measure Of It) Arbitrary:

Eleventhly, to the Sovereign is committed the Power of Rewarding with riches, or honor; and of Punishing with corporal, or pecuniary punishment, or with ignominy every Subject according to the Law he hath formerly made; or if there be no Law made, according as he shall judge most to conduce to the encouraging of men to serve the Common-wealth, or deterring of them from doing dis-service to the same.

12. And Of Honor And Order

Lastly, considering what values men are naturally apt to set upon themselves; what respect they look for from others; and how little they value other men; from whence continually arise amongst them, Emulation, Quarrels, Factions, and at last War, to the destroying of one another, and diminution of their strength against a Common Enemy; It is necessary that there be Laws of Honor, and a public rate of the worth of such men as have deserved, or are able to deserve well of the Commonwealth; and that there be force in the hands of some or other, to put those Laws in execution. But it hath already been shown, that not only the whole Militia, or forces of the Commonwealth; but also the Judicature of all Controversies, is annexed to the Sovereignty. To the Sovereign therefore it belongeth also to give titles of Honor; and to appoint what Order of place, and dignity, each man shall hold; and what signs of respect, in public or private meetings, they shall give to one another.

These Rights Are Indivisible

These are the Rights, which make the Essence of Sovereignty; and which are the marks, whereby a man may discern in what Man, or Assembly of men, the Sovereign Power is placed, and resideth. For these are incommunicable, and inseparable. The Power to coin Money; to dispose of the estate and persons of Infant heirs; to have preemption in Markets; and all other Statute Prerogatives, may be transferred by the Sovereign; and yet the Power to protect his Subject be retained. But if he transfer the Militia, he retains the Judicature in vain, for want of execution of the Laws; Or if he grant away the Power of raising Money; the Militia is in vain: or if he give away the government of doctrines, men will be frighted into rebellion with the fear of Spirits. And so if we consider any one of the said Rights, we shall presently see, that the holding of all the rest, will produce no effect, in the conservation of Peace and Justice, the end for which all Common-wealths are Instituted. And this division is it, whereof it is said,

"A kingdom divided in it self cannot stand:"
For unless this division precede, division into
opposite Armies can never happen. If there
had not first been an opinion received of the
5   greatest part of England, that these Powers
were divided between the King, and the
Lords, and the House of Commons, the people had never been divided, and fallen into this
Civil War; first between those that disagreed in
10   Politic; and after between the Dissenters about
the liberty of Religion; which have so instructed men in this point of Sovereign Right, that
there be few now (in England,) that do not
see, that these Rights are inseparable, and will
15   be so generally acknowledged, at the next return of Peace; and so continue, till their miseries are forgotten; and no longer, except the
vulgar be better taught than they have hether-
to been.

20

**And Can By No Grant Pass Away Without
Direct Renouncing Of The Sovereign
Power**
And because they are essential and inseparable
25   Rights, it follows necessarily, that in whatsoever, words any of them seem to be granted
away, yet if the Sovereign Power it self be not
in direct terms renounced, and the name of
Sovereign no more given by the Grantees to
30   him that Grants them, the Grant is void: for
when he has granted all he can, if we grant
back the Sovereignty, all is restored, as inseparably annexed thereunto.

35   **The Power And Honor Of Subjects Van-
isheth In The Presence Of The Power
Sovereign**
This great Authority being indivisible, and
inseparably annexed to the Sovereignty, there
40   is little ground for the opinion of them, that
say of Sovereign Kings, though they be Singu-
lis Majores, of greater Power than every one
of their Subjects, yet they be Universis Mi-

nores, of less power than them all together.
45   For if by All Together, they mean not the collective body as one person, then All Together,
and Every One, signify the same; and the
speech is absurd. But if by All Together, they
understand them as one Person (which person
50   the Sovereign bears,) then the power of all
together, is the same with the Sovereigns
power; and so again the speech is absurd;
which absurdity they see well enough, when
the Sovereignty is in an Assembly of the peo-
55   ple; but in a Monarch they see it not; and yet
the power of Sovereignty is the same in
whomsoever it be placed.

And as the Power, so also the Honor of the
60   Sovereign, ought to be greater, than that of
any, or all the Subjects. For in the Sovereignty
is the fountain of Honor. The dignities of
Lord, Earle, Duke, and Prince are his Creatures. As in the presence of the Master, the
65   Servants are equal, and without any honor at
all; So are the Subjects, in the presence of the
Sovereign. And though they shine some more,
some less, when they are out of his sight; yet
in his presence, they shine no more than the
70   Stars in presence of the Sun.

**Sovereign Power Not Hurtful As The
Want Of It, And The Hurt Proceeds For
The Greatest Part From Not Submitting
75   Readily, To A Less**
But a man may here object, that the Condition
of Subjects is very miserable; as being obnoxious to the lusts, and other irregular passions
of him, or them that have so unlimited a Pow-
80   er in their hands. And commonly they that live
under a Monarch, think it the fault of Monarchy; and they that live under the government
of Democracy, or other Sovereign Assembly,
attribute all the inconvenience to that form of
85   Common-wealth; whereas the Power in all
Forms, if they be perfect enough to protect

them, is the same; not considering that the estate of Man can never be without some in-commodity or other; and that the greatest, that in any form of Government can possibly hap-pen to the people in general, is scarce sensible, in respect of the miseries, and horrible calami-ties, that accompany a Civil War; or that disso-lute condition of masterless men, without sub-jection to Laws, and a coercive Power to tie their hands from rapine, and revenge: nor considering that the greatest pressure of Sov-ereign Governors, proceedeth not from any delight, or profit they can expect in the dam-age, or weakening of their subjects, in whose vigor, consisteth their own selves, that unwill-ingly contributing to their own defense, make it necessary for their Governors to draw from them what they can in time of Peace, that they may have means on any emergent occasion, or sudden need, to resist, or take advantage on their Enemies. For all men are by nature pro-vided of notable multiplying glasses, (that is their Passions and Self-love,) through which, every little payment appeareth a great griev-ance; but are destitute of those prospective glasses, (namely Moral and Civil Science,) to see a far off the miseries that hang over them, and cannot without such payments be avoid-ed.

CHAPTER XIX
OF THE SEVERALL KINDS OF COM-MON-WEALTH BY INSTITUTION, AND OF SUCCESSION TO THE SOV-EREIGN POWER

The Different Forms Of Common-wealths But Three
The difference of Common-wealths, con-sisteth in the difference of the Sovereign, or the Person representative of all and every one of the Multitude. And because the Sovereignty is either in one Man, or in an Assembly of more than one; and into that Assembly either Every man hath right to enter, or not every one, but Certain men distinguished from the rest; it is manifest, there can be but Three kinds of Common-wealth. For the Repre-sentative must needs be One man, or More: and if more, then it is the Assembly of All, or but of a Part. When the Representative is One man, then is the Common-wealth a MON-ARCHY: when an Assembly of All that will come together, then it is a DEMOCRACY, or Popular Common-wealth: when an Assembly of a Part only, then it is called an ARISTOC-RACY. Other kind of Common-wealth there can be none: for either One, or More, or All must have the Sovereign Power (which I have shown to be indivisible) entire.

Tyranny And Oligarchy, But Different Names Of Monarchy, And Aristocracy
There be other names of Government, in the Histories, and books of Policy; as Tyranny, and Oligarchy: But they are not the names of other Forms of Government, but of the same Forms misliked. For they that are discontented under Monarchy, call it Tyranny; and they that are displeased with Aristocracy, called it Oli-garchy: so also, they which find themselves grieved under a Democracy, call it Anarchy, (which signifies want of Government;) and yet I think no man believes, that want of Gov-ernment, is any new kind of Government: nor by the same reason ought they to believe, that the Government is of one kind, when they like it, and another, when they mislike it, or are oppressed by the Governors.

Subordinate Representatives Dangerous
It is manifest, that men who are in absolute liberty, may, if they please, give Authority to One Man, to represent them every one; as well as give such Authority to any Assembly of men whatsoever; and consequently may sub-

ject themselves, if they think good, to a Monarch, as absolutely, as to any other Representative. Therefore, where there is already erected a Sovereign Power, there can be no other Representative of the same people, but only to certain particular ends, by the Sovereign limited. For that were to erect two Sovereigns; and every man to have his person represented by two Actors, that by opposing one another, must needs divide that Power, which (if men will live in Peace) is indivisible, and thereby reduce the Multitude into the condition of War, contrary to the end for which all Sovereignty is instituted. And therefore as it is absurd, to think that a Sovereign Assembly, inviting the People of their Dominion, to send up their Deputies, with power to make known their Advise, or Desires, should therefore hold such Deputies, rather than themselves, for the absolute Representative of the people: so it is absurd also, to think the same in a Monarchy. And I know not how this so manifest a truth, should of late be so little observed; that in a Monarchy, he that had the Sovereignty from a descent of 600 years, was alone called Sovereign, had the title of Majesty from every one of his Subjects, and was unquestionably taken by them for their King; was notwithstanding never considered as their Representative; that name without contradiction passing for the title of those men, which at his command were sent up by the people to carry their Petitions, and give him (if he permitted it) their advise. Which may serve as an admonition, for those that are the true, and absolute Representative of a People, to instruct men in the nature of that Office, and to take heed how they admit of any other general Representation upon any occasion whatsoever, if they mean to discharge the truth committed to them.

Comparison Of Monarchy, With Sovereign Assemblies

The difference between these three kinds of Common-wealth, consisteth not in the difference of Power; but in the difference of Convenience, or Aptitude to produce the Peace, and Security of the people; for which end they were instituted. And to compare Monarchy with the other two, we may observe; First, that whosoever beareth the Person of the people, or is one of that Assembly that bears it, beareth also his own natural Person. And though he be careful in his political Person to procure the common interest; yet he is more, or no less careful to procure the private good of himself, his family, kindred and friends; and for the most part, if the public interest chance to cross the private, he prefers the private: for the Passions of men, are commonly more potent than their Reason. From whence it follows, that where the public and private interest are most closely united, there is the public most advanced. Now in Monarchy, the private interest is the same with the public. The riches, power, and honor of a Monarch arise only from the riches, strength and reputation of his Subjects. For no King can be rich, nor glorious, nor secure; whose Subjects are either poor, or contemptible, or too weak through want, or dissention, to maintain a war against their enemies: Whereas in a Democracy, or Aristocracy, the public prosperity confers not so much to the private fortune of one that is corrupt, or ambitious, as doth many times a perfidious advice, a treacherous action, or a Civil War.

Secondly, that a Monarch receiveth counsel of whom, when, and where he pleaseth; and consequently may hear the opinion of men versed in the matter about which he deliberates, of what rank or quality soever, and as long before the time of action, and with as much secrecy, as he will. But when a Sovereign Assembly has need of Counsel, none are admitted but such as have a Right thereto from the beginning; which for the most part are of those who have been versed more in the acquisition of Wealth than of Knowledge; and are to give their advice in long discourses, which may, and do commonly excite men to action, but not govern them in it. For the Understanding is by the flame of the Passions, never enlightened, but dazzled: Nor is there any place, or time, wherein an Assembly can receive Counsel with secrecy, because of their own Multitude.

Thirdly, that the Resolutions of a Monarch, are subject to no other Inconstancy, than that of Humane Nature; but in Assemblies, besides that of Nature, there ariseth an Inconstancy from the Number. For the absence of a few, that would have the Resolution once taken, continue firm, (which may happen by security, negligence, or private impediments,) or the diligent appearance of a few of the contrary opinion, undoes to day, all that was concluded yesterday.

Fourthly, that a Monarch cannot disagree with himself, out of envy, or interest; but an Assembly may; and that to such a height, as may produce a Civil War.

Fifthly, that in Monarchy there is this inconvenience; that any Subject, by the power of one man, for the enriching of a favorite or flatterer, may be deprived of all he possesseth; which I confess is a great and inevitable inconvenience. But the same may as well happen, where the Sovereign Power is in an Assembly: for their power is the same; and they are as subject to evil Counsel, and to be seduced by Orators, as a Monarch by Flatterers; and becoming one an others Flatterers, serve one another's Covetousness and Ambition by

turns. And whereas the Favorites of an Assembly, are many; and the Kindred much more numerous, than of any Monarch. Besides, there is no Favorite of a Monarch, which cannot as well succor his friends, as hurt his enemies: But Orators, that is to say, Favorites of Sovereign Assemblies, though they have great power to hurt, have little to save. For to accuse, requires less Eloquence (such is mans Nature) than to excuse; and condemnation, than absolution more resembles Justice.

Sixthly, that it is an inconvenience in Monarchy, that the Sovereignty may descend upon an Infant, or one that cannot discern between Good and Evil: and consisteth in this, that the use of his Power, must be in the hand of another Man, or of some Assembly of men, which are to govern by his right, and in his name; as Curators, and Protectors of his Person, and Authority. But to say there is inconvenience, in putting the use of the Sovereign Power, into the hand of a Man, or an Assembly of men; is to say that all Government is more Inconvenient, than Confusion, and Civil War. And therefore all the danger that can be pretended, must arise from the Contention of those, that for an office of so great honor, and profit, may become Competitors. To make it appear, that this inconvenience, proceedeth not from that form of Government we call Monarchy, we are to consider, that the precedent Monarch, hath appointed who shall have the Tuition of his Infant Successor, either expressly by Testament, or tacitly, by not controlling the Custom in that case received: And then such inconvenience (if it happen) is to be attributed, not to the Monarchy, but to the Ambition, and Injustice of the Subjects; which in all kinds of Government, where the people are not well instructed in their Duty, and the Rights of Sovereignty, is the same. Or else the precedent Monarch, hath not at all taken order for such Tuition; And then the Law of Nature hath provided this sufficient rule, That the Tuition shall be in him, that hath by Nature

5 most interest in the preservation of the Authority of the Infant, and to whom least benefit can accrue by his death, or diminution. For seeing every man by nature seeketh his own benefit, and promotion; to put an Infant into

10 the power of those, that can promote themselves by his destruction, or damage, is not Tuition, but Treachery. So that sufficient provision being taken, against all just quarrel, about the Government under a Child, if any

15 contention arise to the disturbance of the public Peace, it is not to be attributed to the form of Monarchy, but to the ambition of Subjects, and ignorance of their Duty. On the other side, there is no great Common-wealth, the

20 Sovereignty whereof is in a great Assembly, which is not, as to consultations of Peace, and War, and making of Laws, in the same condition, as if the Government were in a Child. For as a Child wants the judgment to dissent

25 from counsel given him, and is thereby necessitated to take the advise of them, or him, to whom he is committed: So an Assembly wanteth the liberty, to dissent from the counsel of the major part, be it good, or bad. And

30 as a Child has need of a Tutor, or Protector, to preserve his Person, and Authority: So also (in great Common-wealths,) the Sovereign Assembly, in all great dangers and troubles, have need of Custodes Libertatis; that is of Dicta-

35 tors, or Protectors of their Authority; which are as much as Temporary Monarchs; to whom for a time, they may commit the entire exercise of their Power; and have (at the end of that time) been oftener deprived thereof,

40 than Infant Kings, by their Protectors, Regents, or any other Tutors.

Though the Kinds of Sovereignty be, as I have now shown, but three; that is to say, Monar-

45 chy, where one Man has it; or Democracy, where the general Assembly of Subjects hath it; or Aristocracy, where it is in an Assembly of certain persons nominated, or otherwise distinguished from the rest: Yet he that shall

50 consider the particular Common-wealthes that have been, and are in the world, will not perhaps easily reduce them to three, and may thereby be inclined to think there be other Forms, arising from these mingled together.

55 As for example, Elective Kingdoms; where Kings have the Sovereign Power put into their hands for a time; of Kingdoms, wherein the King hath a power limited: which Governments, are nevertheless by most Writers called

60 Monarchy. Likewise if a Popular, or Aristocratical Common-wealth, subdue an Enemy's Country, and govern the same, by a President, Procurator, or other Magistrate; this may seem perhaps at first sight, to be a Democratical, or

65 Aristocratical Government. But it is not so. For Elective Kings, are not Sovereigns, but Ministers of the Sovereign; nor limited Kings Sovereigns, but Ministers of them that have the Sovereign Power: nor are those Provinces

70 which are in subjection to a Democracy, or Aristocracy of another Common-wealth, Democratically, or Aristocratically governed, but Monarchically.

75 And first, concerning an Elective King, whose power is limited to his life, as it is in many places of Christendom at this day; or to certain Years or Months, as the Dictators power amongst the Romans; If he have Right to ap-

80 point his Successor, he is no more Elective but Hereditary. But if he have no Power to elect his Successor, then there is some other Man, or Assembly known, which after his decease may elect a new, or else the Common-

85 wealth dieth, and dissolveth with him, and returneth to the condition of War. If it be

known who have the power to give the Sovereignty after his death, it is known also that the Sovereignty was in them before: For none have right to give that which they have not

5 right to possess, and keep to themselves, if they think good. But if there be none that can give the Sovereignty, after the decease of him that was first elected; then has he power, nay he is obliged by the Law of Nature, to pro-

10 vide, by establishing his Successor, to keep those that had trusted him with the Government, from relapsing into the miserable condition of Civil War. And consequently he was, when elected, a Sovereign absolute.

15

Secondly, that King whose power is limited, is not superior to him, or them that have the power to limit it; and he that is not superior, is not supreme; that is to say not Sovereign. The

20 Sovereignty therefore was always in that Assembly which had the Right to Limit him; and by consequence the government not Monarchy, but either Democracy, or Aristocracy; as of old time in Sparta; where the Kings had a

25 privileged to lead their Armies; but the Sovereignty was in the Ephori.
Thirdly, whereas heretofore the Roman People, governed the land of Judea (for example) by a President; yet was not Judea therefore a

30 Democracy; because they were not governed by any Assembly, into which, any of them, had right to enter; nor by an Aristocracy; because they were not governed by any Assembly, into which, any man could enter by their Election:

35 but they were governed by one Person, which though as to the people of Rome was an Assembly of the people, or Democracy; yet as to the people of Judea, which had no right at all of participating in the government, was a

40 Monarch. For though where the people are governed by an Assembly, chosen by themselves out of their own number, the government is called a Democracy, or Aristocracy;

yet when they are governed by an Assembly,
45 not of their own choosing, 'tis a Monarchy; not of One man, over another man; but of one people, over another people.

Of The Right Of Succession

50 Of all these Forms of Government, the matter being mortal, so that not only Monarchs, but also whole Assemblies die, it is necessary for the conservation of the peace of men, that as there was order taken for an Artificial Man, so

55 there be order also taken, for an Artificial Eternity of life; without which, men that are governed by an Assembly, should return into the condition of War in every age; and they that are governed by One man, as soon as

60 their Governor dyeth. This Artificial Eternity, is that which men call the Right of Succession.

There is no perfect form of Government, where the disposing of the Succession is not in

65 the present Sovereign. For if it be in any other particular Man, or private Assembly, it is in a person subject, and may be assumed by the Sovereign at his pleasure; and consequently the Right is in himself. And if it be in no par-

70 ticular man, but left to a new choice; then is the Common-wealth dissolved; and the Right is in him that can get it; contrary to the intention of them that did institute the Commonwealth, for their perpetual, and not temporary

75 security.

In a Democracy, the whole Assembly cannot fail, unless the Multitude that are to be governed fail. And therefore questions of the right

80 of Succession, have in that form of Government no place at all.

In an Aristocracy, when any of the Assembly dyeth, the election of another into his room

85 belongeth to the Assembly, as the Sovereign, to whom belongeth the choosing of all Coun-

selors, and Officers. For that which the Representative doth, as Actor, every one of the Subjects doth, as Author. And though the Sovereign assembly, may give Power to others, to elect new men, for supply of their Court; yet it is still by their Authority, that the Election is made; and by the same it may (when the public shall require it) be recalled.

The Present Monarch Hath Right To Dispose Of The Succession

The greatest difficulty about the right of Succession, is in Monarchy: And the difficulty ariseth from this, that at first sight, it is not manifest who is to appoint the Successor; nor many times, who it is whom he hath appointed. For in both these cases, there is required a more exact ratiocination, than every man is accustomed to use. As to the question, who shall appoint the Successor, of a Monarch that hath the Sovereign Authority; that is to say, (for Elective Kings and Princes have not the Sovereign Power in propriety, but in use only,) we are to consider, that either he that is in possession, has right to dispose of the Succession, or else that right is again in the dissolved Multitude. For the death of him that hath the Sovereign power in propriety, leaves the Multitude without any Sovereign at all; that is, without any Representative in whom they should be united, and be capable of doing any one action at all: And therefore they are incapable of Election of any new Monarch; every man having equal right to submit himself to such as he thinks best able to protect him, or if he can, protect himself by his own sword; which is a return to Confusion, and to the condition of a War of every man against every man, contrary to the end for which Monarchy had its first Institution. Therefore it is manifest, that by the Institution of Monarchy, the disposing of the Successor, is always left to the Judgment and Will of the present Possessor.

And for the question (which may arise sometimes) who it is that the Monarch in possession, hath designed to the succession and inheritance of his power; it is determined by his express Words, and Testament; or by other tacit signs sufficient.

Succession Passeth By Expressed Words;

By express Words, or Testament, when it is declared by him in his life time, viva voce, or by Writing; as the first Emperors of Rome declared who should be their Heirs. For the word Heir does not of it self imply the Children, or nearest Kindred of a man; but whomsoever a man shall any way declare, he would have to succeed him in his Estate. If therefore a Monarch declare expressly, that such a man shall be his Heir, either by Word or Writing, then is that man immediately after the decease of his Predecessor, Invested in the right of being Monarch.

Or, By Not Controlling A Custom;

But where Testament, and express Words are wanting, other natural signs of the Will are to be followed: whereof the one is Custom. And therefore where the Custom is, that the next of Kindred absolutely succeedeth, there also the next of Kindred hath right to the Succession; for that, if the will of him that was in possession had been otherwise, he might easily have declared the same in his life time. And likewise where the Custom is, that the next of the Male Kindred succeedeth, there also the right of Succession is in the next of the Kindred Male, for the same reason. And so it is if the Custom were to advance the Female. For whatsoever Custom a man may by a word control, and does not, it is a natural sign he would have that Custom stand.

Or, By Presumption Of Natural Affection

But where neither Custom, nor Testament hath preceded, there it is to be understood, First, that a Monarchs will is, that the govern-
5 ment remain Monarchical; because he hath approved that government in himself. Second-ly, that a Child of his own, Male, or Female, be preferred before any other; because men are presumed to be more inclined by nature, to
10 advance their own children, than the children of other men; and of their own, rather a Male than a Female; because men, are naturally fit-ter than women, for actions of labor and dan-ger. Thirdly, where his own Issue faileth, ra-
15 ther a Brother than a stranger; and so still the nearer in blood, rather than the more remote, because it is always presumed that the nearer of kin, is the nearer in affection; and 'tis evi-dent that a man receives always, by reflection,
20 the most honor from the greatness of his nearest kindred.

To Dispose Of The Succession, Though To A King Of Another Nation, Not Un-
25 lawful

But if it be lawful for a Monarch to dispose of the Succession by words of Contract, or Tes-tament, men may perhaps object a great in-convenience: for he may sell, or give his Right
30 of governing to a stranger; which, because strangers (that is, men not used to live under the same government, not speaking the same language) do commonly undervalue one an-other, may turn to the oppression of his Sub-
35 jects; which is indeed a great inconvenience; but it proceedeth not necessarily from the subjection to a strangers government, but from the unskillfulness of the Governors, ig-norant of the true rules of Polities. And there-
40 fore the Romans when they had subdued many Nations, to make their Government digestible, were wont to take away that griev-ance, as much as they thought necessary, by

giving sometimes to whole Nations, and
45 sometimes to Principal men of every Nation they conquered, not only the Privileges, but also the Name of Romans; and took many of them into the Senate, and Offices of charge, even in the Roman City. And this was it our
50 most wise King, King James, aimed at, in en-deavoring the Union of his two Realms of England and Scotland. Which if he could have obtained, had in all likelihood prevented the Civil Wars, which make both those Kingdoms
55 at this present, miserable. It is not therefore any injury to the people, for a Monarch to dispose of the Succession by Will; though by the fault of many Princes, it hath been some-times found inconvenient. Of the lawfulness
60 of it, this also is an argument, that whatsoever inconvenience can arrive by giving a King-dome to a stranger, may arrive also by so mar-rying with strangers, as the Right of Succes-sion may descend upon them: yet this by all
65 men is accounted lawful.

CHAPTER XX
OF DOMINION PATERNALL AND DESPOTICALL

70
A Common-wealth by Acquisition, is that, where the Sovereign Power is acquired by Force; And it is acquired by force, when men singly, or many together by plurality of voices,
75 for fear of death, or bonds, do authorize all the actions of that Man, or Assembly, that hath their lives and liberty in his Power.

Wherein Different From A Common-
80 wealth By Institution
And this kind of Dominion, or Sovereignty, differeth from Sovereignty by Institution, only in this, That men who choose their Sovereign, do it for fear of one another, and not of him
85 whom they Institute: But in this case, they subject themselves, to him they are afraid of.

233

In both cases they do it for fear: which is to be noted by them, that hold all such Covenants, as proceed from fear of death, or violence, void: which if it were true, no man, in any kind

5 of Common-wealth, could be obliged to Obedience. It is true, that in a Common-wealth once Instituted, or acquired, Promises proceeding from fear of death, or violence, are no Covenants, nor obliging, when the thing

10 promised is contrary to the Laws; But the reason is not, because it was made upon fear, but because he that promiseth, hath no right in the thing promised. Also, when he may lawfully perform, and doth not, it is not the Invalidity

15 of the Covenant, that absolveth him, but the Sentence of the Sovereign. Otherwise, whensoever a man lawfully promiseth, he unlawfully breaketh: But when the Sovereign, who is the Actor, acquitteth him, then he is acquitted

20 by him that extorted the promise, as by the Author of such absolution.

The Rights Of Sovereignty The Same In Both

25 But the Rights, and Consequences of Sovereignty, are the same in both. His Power cannot, without his consent, be Transferred to another: He cannot Forfeit it: He cannot be Accused by any of his Subjects, of Injury: He

30 cannot be Punished by them: He is Judge of what is necessary for Peace; and Judge of Doctrines: He is Sole Legislator; and Supreme Judge of Controversies; and of the Times, and Occasions of War, and Peace: to him it be-

35 longeth to choose Magistrates, Counselors, Commanders, and all other Officers, and Ministers; and to determine of Rewards, and punishments, Honor, and Order. The reasons whereof, are the same which are alleged in the

40 precedent Chapter, for the same Rights, and Consequences of Sovereignty by Institution.

Dominion Paternal How Attained Not By

45 ## Generation, But By Contract

Dominion is acquired two ways; By Generation, and by Conquest. The right of Dominion by Generation, is that, which the Parent hath over his Children; and is called PATERNALL.

50 And is not so derived from the Generation, as if therefore the Parent had Dominion over his Child because he begat him; but from the Childs Consent, either express, or by other sufficient arguments declared. For as to the

55 Generation, God hath ordained to man a helper; and there be always two that are equally Parents: the Dominion therefore over the Child, should belong equally to both; and he be equally subject to both, which is impossi-

60 ble; for no man can obey two Masters. And whereas some have attributed the Dominion to the Man only, as being of the more excellent Sex; they misreckon in it. For there is not always that difference of strength or prudence

65 between the man and the woman, as that the right can be determined without War. In Common-wealths, this controversy is decided by the Civil Law: and for the most part, (but not always) the sentence is in favor of the Fa-

70 ther; because for the most part Commonwealths have been erected by the Fathers, not by the Mothers of families. But the question lyeth now in the state of mere Nature; where there are supposed no Laws of Matrimony; no

75 Laws for the Education of Children; but the Law of Nature, and the natural inclination of the Sexes, one to another, and to their children. In this condition of mere Nature, either the Parents between themselves dispose of the

80 dominion over the Child by Contract; or do not dispose thereof at all. If they dispose thereof, the right passeth according to the Contract. We find in History that the Amazons Contracted with the Men of the neigh-

85 boring Countries, to whom they had recourse for issue, that the issue Male should be sent

back, but the Female remain with themselves: so that the dominion of the Females was in the Mother.

Or Education;

5 If there be no Contract, the Dominion is in the Mother. For in the condition of Meer Nature, where there are no Matrimonial Laws, it cannot be known who is the Father, unless it
10 be declared by the Mother: and therefore the right of Dominion over the Child dependeth on her will, and is consequently hers. Again, seeing the Infant is first in the power of the Mother; so as she may either nourish, or ex-
15 pose it, if she nourish it, it oweth its life to the Mother; and is therefore obliged to obey her, rather than any other; and by consequence the Dominion over it is hers. But if she expose it, and another find, and nourish it, the Domin-
20 ion is in him that nourisheth it. For it ought to obey him by whom it is preserved; because preservation of life being the end, for which one man becomes subject to another, every man is supposed to promise obedience, to
25 him, in whose power it is to save, or destroy him.

Or Precedent Subjection Of One Of The Parents To The Other

30 If the Mother be the Fathers subject, the Child, is in the Fathers power: and if the Father be the Mothers subject, (as when a Sovereign Queen marrieth one of her subjects,) the Child is subject to the Mother; because the
35 Father also is her subject.

If a man and a woman, Monarchies of two several Kingdoms, have a Child, and contract concerning who shall have the Dominion of
40 him, the Right of the Dominion passeth by the Contract. If they contract not, the Dominion followeth the Dominion of the place of his residence. For the Sovereign of each

Country hath Dominion over all that reside
45 therein.

He that hath the Dominion over the Child, hath Dominion also over their Children's Children. For he that hath Dominion over the
50 person of a man, hath Dominion over all that is his; without which, Dominion were but a Title, without the effect.

The Right Of Succession Followeth The
55 ## Rules Of The Rights Of Possession
The Right of Succession to Paternal dominion, proceedeth in the same manner, as doth the Right of Succession to Monarchy; of which I have already sufficiently spoken in the prece-
60 dent chapter.

Despotical Dominion, How Attained
Dominion acquired by Conquest, or Victory in war, is that which some Writers call DES-
65 POTICALL, from Despots, which signifieth a Lord, or Master; and is the Dominion of the Master over his Servant. And this Dominion is then acquired to the Victor, when the Vanquished, to avoid the present stroke of death,
70 covenanteth either in express words, or by other sufficient signs of the Will, that so long as his life, and the liberty of his body is allowed him, the Victor shall have the use thereof, at his pleasure. And after such Cove-
75 nant made, the Vanquished is a SERVANT, and not before: for by the word Servant (whether it be derived from Servire, to Serve, or from Servare, to Save, which I leave to Grammarians to dispute) is not meant a Cap-
80 tive, which is kept in prison, or bonds, till the owner of him that took him, or bought him of one that did, shall consider what to do with him: (for such men, (commonly called Slaves,) have no obligation at all; but may break their
85 bonds, or the prison; and kill, or carry away captive their Master, justly:) but one, that be-

ing taken, hath corporal liberty allowed him; and upon promise not to run away, nor to do violence to his Master, is trusted by him.

Not By The Victory, But By The Consent Of The Vanquished

It is not therefore the Victory, that giveth the right of Dominion over the Vanquished, but his own Covenant. Nor is he obliged because he is Conquered; that is to say, beaten, and taken, or put to flight; but because he commeth in, and submitteth to the Victor; Nor is the Victor obliged by an enemies rendering himself, (without promise of life,) to spare him for this his yielding to discretion; which obliges not the Victor longer, than in his own discretion he shall think fit.

And that men do, when they demand (as it is now called) Quarter, (which the Greeks called Zogria, taking alive,) is to evade the present fury of the Victor, by Submission, and to compound for their life, with Ransom, or Service: and therefore he that hath Quarter, hath not his life given, but deferred till farther deliberation; For it is not an yielding on condition of life, but to discretion. And then only is his life in security, and his service due, when the Victor hath trusted him with his corporal liberty. For Slaves that work in Prisons, or Fetters, do it not of duty, but to avoid the cruelty of their task-masters.

The Master of the Servant, is Master also of all he hath; and may exact the use thereof; that is to say, of his goods, of his labor, of his servants, and of his children, as often as he shall think fit. For he holdeth his life of his Master, by the covenant of obedience; that is, of owning, and authorizing whatsoever the Master shall do. And in case the Master, if he refuse, kill him, or cast him into bonds, or otherwise punish him for his disobedience, he is himself the author of the same; and cannot accuse him of injury.

In sum the Rights and Consequences of both Paternal and Despotically Dominion, are the very same with those of a Sovereign by Institution; and for the same reasons: which reasons are set down in the precedent chapter. So that for a man that is Monarch of divers Nations, whereof he hath, in one the Sovereignty by Institution of the people assembled, and in another by Conquest, that is by the Submission of each particular, to avoid death or bonds; to demand of one Nation more than of the other, from the title of Conquest, as being a Conquered Nation, is an act of ignorance of the Rights of Sovereignty. For the Sovereign is absolute over both alike; or else there is no Sovereignty at all; and so every man may Lawfully protect himself, if he can, with his own sword, which is the condition of war.

Difference Between A Family And A Kingdom

By this it appears, that a great Family if it be not part of some Common-wealth, is of it self, as to the Rights of Sovereignty, a little Monarchy; whether that Family consist of a man and his children; or of a man and his servants; or of a man, and his children, and servants together: wherein the Father of Master is the Sovereign. But yet a Family is not properly a Common-wealth; unless it be of that power by its own number, or by other opportunities, as not to be subdued without the hazard of war. For where a number of men are manifestly too weak to defend themselves united, every one may use his own reason in time of danger, to save his own life, either by flight, or by submission to the enemy, as he shall think best; in the same manner as a very small company of soldiers, surprised by an army, may cast down their arms, and demand quarter, or run away, rather than be put to the sword. And thus much shall suffice; concerning what I find by speculation, and deduction, of Sovereign Rights, from the nature, need, and de-

5 signs of men, in erecting of Commonwealths, and putting themselves under Monarchs, or Assemblies, entrusted with power enough for their protection.

10 **The Right Of Monarchy From Scripture**

Let us now consider what the Scripture teacheth in the same point. To Moses, the children of Israel say thus. (Exod. 20. 19) "Speak thou to us, and we will hear thee; but

15 let not God speak to us, lest we dye." This is absolute obedience to Moses. Concerning the Right of Kings, God himself by the mouth of Samuel, saith, (1 Sam. 8. 11, 12, &c.) "This shall be the Right of the King you will have to

20 reign over you. He shall take your sons, and set them to drive his Chariots, and to be his horsemen, and to run before his chariots; and gather in his harvest; and to make his engines of War, and Instruments of his chariots; and

25 shall take your daughters to make perfumes, to be his Cooks, and Bakers. He shall take your fields, your vine-yards, and your olive-yards, and give them to his servants. He shall take the tithe of your corn and wine, and give it to

30 the men of his chamber, and to his other servants. He shall take your man-servants, and your maid-servants, and the choice of your youth, and employ them in his business. He shall take the tithe of your flocks; and you

35 shall be his servants." This is absolute power, and summed up in the last words, "you shall be his servants." Again, when the people heard what power their King was to have, yet they consented thereto, and say thus, (Verse. 19

40 &c.) "We will be as all other nations, and our King shall judge our causes, and go before us, to conduct our wars." Here is confirmed the Right that Sovereigns have, both to the Militia,

45 and to all Judicature; in which is contained as absolute power, as one man can possibly transfer to another. Again, the prayer of King Salomon to God, was this. (1 Kings 3. 9) "Give to thy servant understanding, to judge thy people, and to discern between Good and

50 Evil." It belongeth therefore to the Sovereign to bee Judge, and to prescribe the Rules of Discerning Good and Evil; which Rules are Laws; and therefore in him is the Legislative Power. Saul sought the life of David; yet when

55 it was in his power to slay Saul, and his Servants would have done it, David forbad them, saying (1 Sam. 24. 9) "God forbid I should do such an act against my Lord, the anointed of God." For obedience of servants St. Paul

60 saith, (Coll. 3. 20) "Servants obey your masters in All things," and, (Verse. 22) "Children obey your Parents in All things." There is simple obedience in those that are subject to Paternal, or Despotical Dominion. Again, (Math. 23.

65 2,3) "The Scribes and Pharisees sit in Moses chair and therefore All that they shall bid you observe, that observe and do." There again is simple obedience. And St. Paul, (Tit. 3. 2) "Warn them that they subject themselves to

70 Princes, and to those that are in Authority, & obey them." This obedience is also simple. Lastly, our Savior himself acknowledges, that men ought to pay such taxes as are by Kings imposed, where he says, "Give to Caesar that

75 which is Caesars;" and paid such taxes himself. And that the Kings word, is sufficient to take any thing from any subject, when there is need; and that the King is Judge of that need: For he himself, as King of the Jews, com-

80 manded his Disciples to take the Ass, and Asses Colt to carry him into Jerusalem, saying, (Mat. 21. 2,3) "Go into the Village over against you, and you shall find a she Ass tied, and her Colt with her, untie them, and bring them to

85 me. And if any man ask you, what you mean by it, Say the Lord hath need of them: And

they will let them go." They will not ask whether his necessity be a sufficient title; nor whether he be judge of that necessity; but acquiesce in the will of the Lord.

5 To these places may be added also that of Genesis, (Gen. 3. 5) "You shall be as Gods, knowing Good and Evil." and verse 11. "Who told thee that thou wast naked? hast thou eaten of the tree, of which I commanded thee

10 thou shouldest not eat?" For the Cognizance of Judicature of Good and Evil, being forbidden by the name of the fruit of the tree of Knowledge, as a trial of Adams obedience; The Devil to enflame the Ambition of the

15 woman, to whom that fruit already seemed beautiful, told her that by tasting it, they should be as Gods, knowing Good and Evil. Whereupon having both eaten, they did indeed take upon them Gods office, which is

20 Judicature of Good and Evil; but acquired no new ability to distinguish between them aright. And whereas it is said, that having eaten, they saw they were naked; no man hath so interpreted that place, as if they had formerly blind,

25 as saw not their own skins: the meaning is plain, that it was then they first judged their nakedness (wherein it was Gods will to create them) to be uncomely; and by being ashamed, did tacitly censure God himself. And there-

30 upon God saith, "Hast thou eaten, &c." as if he should say, doest thou that owest me obedience, take upon thee to judge of my Commandments? Whereby it is clearly, (though Allegorically,) signified, that the Commands of

35 them that have the right to command, are not by their Subjects to be censured, nor disputed.

Sovereign Power Ought In All Commonwealths To Be Absolute

40 So it appeareth plainly, to my understanding, both from Reason, and Scripture, that the Sovereign Power, whether placed in One Man, as in Monarchy, or in one Assembly of men, as in Popular, and Aristocratical Common-

45 wealths, is as great, as possibly men can be imagined to make it. And though of so unlimited a Power, men may fancy many evil consequences, yet the consequences of the want of it, which is perpetual War of every man against

50 his neighbor, are much worse. The condition of man in this life shall never be without Inconveniences; but there happeneth in no Common-wealth any great Inconvenience, but what proceeds from the Subjects disobedi-

55 ence, and breach of those Covenants, from which the Common-wealth had its being. And whosoever thinking Sovereign Power too great, will seek to make it less; must subject himself, to the Power, that can limit it; that is

60 to say, to a greater.

The greatest objection is, that of the Practice; when men ask, where, and when, such Power has by Subjects been acknowledged. But one

65 may ask them again, when, or where has there been a Kingdome long free from Sedition and Civil War. In those Nations, whose Commonwealths have been long-lived, and not been destroyed, but by foreign War, the Subjects

70 never did dispute of the Sovereign Power. But howsoever, an argument for the Practice of men, that have not sifted to the bottom, and with exact reason weighed the causes, and nature of Common-wealths, and suffer daily

75 those miseries, that proceed from the ignorance thereof, is invalid. For though in all places of the world, men should lay the foundation of their houses on the sand, it could not thence be inferred, that so it ought to be.

80 The skill of making, and maintaining Common-wealths, consisteth in certain Rules, as doth Arithmetic and Geometry; not (as Tennis-play) on Practice only: which Rules, neither poor men have the leisure, nor men that have

85 had the leisure, have hitherto had the curiosity, or the method to find out.

CHAPTER XXI
OF THE LIBERTY OF SUBJECTS

Liberty What

5 Liberty, or FREEDOME, signifieth (properly) the absence of Opposition; (by Opposition, I mean external Impediments of motion;) and may be applied no less to Irrational, and Inanimate creatures, than to Rational. For whatso-
10 ever is so tied, or environed, as it cannot move, but within a certain space, which space is determined by the opposition of some external body, we say it hath not Liberty to go further. And so of all living creatures, whilst
15 they are imprisoned, or restrained, with walls, or chains; and of the water whilst it is kept in by banks, or vessels, that otherwise would spread it self into a larger space, we use to say, they are not at Liberty, to move in such man-
20 ner, as without those external impediments they would. But when the impediment of motion, is in the constitution of the thing it self, we use not to say, it wants the Liberty; but the Power to move; as when a stone lyeth still, or
25 a man is fastened to his bed by sickness.

What It Is To Be Free

And according to this proper, and generally received meaning of the word, A FREE-
30 MAN, is "he, that in those things, which by his strength and wit he is able to do, is not hindered to doe what he has a will to." But when the words Free, and Liberty, are applied to any thing but Bodies, they are abused; for
35 that which is not subject to Motion, is not subject to Impediment: And therefore, when 'tis said (for example) The way is free, no liberty of the way is signified, but of those that walk in it without stop. And when we say a
40 Gift is free, there is not meant any liberty of the Gift, but of the Giver, that was not bound by any law, or Covenant to give it. So when we Speak Freely, it is not the liberty of voice, or pronunciation, but of the man, whom no
45 law hath obliged to speak otherwise then he did. Lastly, from the use of the word Freewill, no liberty can be inferred to the will, desire, or inclination, but the liberty of the man; which consisteth in this, that he finds no stop, in
50 doing what he has the will, desire, or inclination to doe.

Fear And Liberty Consistent

Fear and Liberty are consistent; as when a
55 man throweth his goods into the Sea for Fear the ship should sink, he doth it nevertheless very willingly, and may refuse to doe it if he will: It is therefore the action, of one that was Free; so a man sometimes pays his debt, only
60 for Fear of Imprisonment, which because no body hindered him from detaining, was the action of a man at Liberty. And generally all actions which men doe in Common-wealths, for Fear of the law, or actions, which the do-
65 ers had Liberty to omit.

Liberty And Necessity Consistent

Liberty and Necessity are Consistent: As in the water, that hath not only Liberty, but a Neces-
70 sity of descending by the Channel: so likewise in the Actions which men voluntarily doe; which (because they proceed from their will) proceed from Liberty; and yet because every act of mans will, and every desire, and inclina-
75 tion proceedeth from some cause, which causes in a continual chain (whose first link in the hand of God the first of all causes) proceed from Necessity. So that to him that could see the connection of those causes, the Necessity
80 of all men's voluntary actions, would appear manifest. And therefore God, that seeth, and disposeth all things, seeth also that the Liberty of man in doing what he will, is accompanied with the Necessity of doing that which God
85 will, & no more, nor less. For though men may do many things, which God does not

239

command, nor is therefore Author of them; yet they can have no passion, nor appetite to any thing, of which appetite Gods will is not the cause. And did not his will assure the Ne-
5 cessity of mans will, and consequently of all that on mans will dependeth, the Liberty of men would be a contradiction, and impediment to the omnipotence and Liberty of God. And this shall suffice, (as to the matter in
10 hand) of that natural Liberty, which only is properly called Liberty.

Artificial Bonds, Or Covenants

But as men, for the attaining of peace, and
15 conservation of themselves thereby, have made an Artificial Man, which we call a Common-wealth; so also have they made Artificial Chains, called Civil Laws, which they themselves, by mutual covenants, have fastened at
20 one end, to the lips of that Man, or Assembly, to whom they have given the Sovereign Power; and at the other end to their own Ears. These Bonds in their own nature but weak, may nevertheless be made to hold, by the dan-
25 ger, though not by the difficulty of breaking them.

Liberty Of Subjects Consisteth In Liberty From Covenants

30 In relation to these Bonds only it is, that I am to speak now, of the Liberty of Subjects. For seeing there is no Common-wealth in the world, for the regulating of all the actions, and words of men, (as being a thing impossible:) it
35 followeth necessarily, that in all kinds of actions, by the laws pretermitted, men have the Liberty, of doing what their own reasons shall suggest, for the most profitable to themselves. For if wee take Liberty in the proper sense, for
40 corporal Liberty; that is to say, freedom from chains, and prison, it were very absurd for men to clamor as they doe, for the Liberty they so manifestly enjoy. Again, if we take

Liberty, for an exemption from Laws, it is no
45 less absurd, for men to demand as they doe, that Liberty, by which all other men may be masters of their lives. And yet as absurd as it is, this is it they demand; not knowing that the Laws are of no power to protect them, with-
50 out a Sword in the hands of a man, or men, to cause those laws to be put in execution. The Liberty of a Subject, lyeth therefore only in those things, which in regulating their actions, the Sovereign hath pretermitted; such as is the
55 Liberty to buy, and sell, and otherwise contract with one another; to choose their own abode, their own diet, their own trade of life, and institute their children as they themselves think fit; & the like.
60

Liberty Of The Subject Consistent With Unlimited Power Of The Sovereign

Nevertheless we are not to understand, that by such Liberty, the Sovereign Power of life, and
65 death, is either abolished, or limited. For it has been already shown, that nothing the Sovereign Representative can doe to a Subject, on what pretense soever, can properly be called Injustice, or Injury; because every Subject is
70 Author of every act the Sovereign doth; so that he never wanteth Right to any thing, otherwise, than as he himself is the Subject of God, and bound thereby to observe the laws of Nature. And therefore it may, and doth
75 often happen in Common-wealths, that a Subject may be put to death, by the command of the Sovereign Power; and yet neither doe the other wrong: as when Jeptha caused his daughter to be sacrificed: In which, and the
80 like cases, he that so dieth, had Liberty to doe the action, for which he is nevertheless, without Injury put to death. And the same holdeth also in a Sovereign Prince, that putteth to death an Innocent Subject. For though the
85 action be against the law of Nature, as being contrary to Equity, (as was the killing of Uriah,

by David;) yet it was not an Injury to Uriah; but to God. Not to Uriah, because the right to doe what he pleased, was given him by Uriah himself; And yet to God, because David was

5 Gods Subject; and prohibited all Iniquity by the law of Nature. Which distinction, David himself, when he repented the fact, evidently confirmed, saying, "To thee only have I sinned." In the same manner, the people of

10 Athens, when they banished the most potent of their Common-wealth for ten years, thought they committed no Injustice; and yet they never questioned what crime he had done; but what hurt he would doe: Nay they

15 commanded the banishment of they knew not whom; and every Citizen bringing his Oyster-shell into the market place, written with the name of him he desired should be banished, without actual accusing him, sometimes ban-

20 ished an Aristides, for his reputation of Justice; And sometimes a scurrilous Jester, as Hyperbolus, to make a Jest of it. And yet a man cannot say, the Sovereign People of Athens wanted right to banish them; or an Athe-

25 nian the Liberty to Jest, or to be Just.

The Liberty Which Writers Praise, Is The Liberty Of Sovereigns; Not Of Private Men

30 The Liberty, whereof there is so frequent, and honorable mention, in the Histories, and Philosophy of the Ancient Greeks, and Romans, and in the writings, and discourse of those that from them have received all their learning in

35 the Politics, is not the Liberty of Particular men; but the Liberty of the Common-wealth: which is the same with that, which every man then should have, if there were no Civil Laws, nor Common-wealth at all. And the effects of

40 it also be the same. For as amongst masterless men, there is perpetual war, of every man against his neighbor; no inheritance, to transmit to the Son, nor to expect from the Father;

no propriety of Goods, or Lands; no security;

45 but a full and absolute Liberty in every Particular man: So in States, and Common-wealths not dependent on one another, every Common-wealth, (not every man) has an absolute Liberty, to doe what it shall judge (that

50 is to say, what that Man, or Assembly that representeth it, shall judge) most conducing to their benefit. But withal, they live in the condition of a perpetual war, and upon the confines of battle, with their frontiers armed, and can-

55 ons planted against their neighbors round about. The Athenians, and Romans, were free; that is, free Common-wealths: not that any particular men had the Liberty to resist their own Representative; but that their Representa-

60 tive had the Liberty to resist, or invade other people. There is written on the Turrets of the city of Luca in great characters at this day, the word LIBERTAS; yet no man can thence infer, that a particular man has more Liberty, or

65 Immunity from the service of the Common-wealth there, than in Constantinople. Whether a Common-wealth be Monarchical, or Popular, the Freedom is still the same.

70 But it is an easy thing, for men to be deceived, by the specious name of Liberty; and for want of Judgment to distinguish, mistake that for their Private Inheritance, and Birth right, which is the right of the Public only. And

75 when the same error is confirmed by the authority of men in reputation for their writings in this subject, it is no wonder if it produce sedition, and change of Government. In these western parts of the world, we are made to

80 receive our opinions concerning the Institution, and Rights of Common-wealths, from Aristotle, Cicero, and other men, Greeks and Romans, that living under Popular States, derived those Rights, not from the Principles of

85 Nature, but transcribed them into their books, out of the Practice of their own Common-

wealths, which were Popular; as the Grammarians describe the Rules of Language, out of the Practice of the time; or the Rules of Poetry, out of the Poems of Homer and Virgil. And

5 because the Athenians were taught, (to keep them from desire of changing their Government,) that they were Freemen, and all that lived under Monarchy were slaves; therefore Aristotle puts it down in his Poli-

10 tics,(lib.6.cap.2) "In democracy, Liberty is to be supposed: for 'tis commonly held, that no man is Free in any other Government." And as Aristotle; so Cicero, and other Writers have grounded their Civil doctrine, on the opinions

15 of the Romans, who were taught to hate Monarchy, at first, by them that having deposed their Sovereign, shared amongst them the Sovereignty of Rome; and afterwards by their Successors. And by reading of these Greek,

20 and Latin Authors, men from their childhood have gotten a habit (under a false show of Liberty,) of favoring tumults, and of licentious controlling the actions of their Sovereigns; and again of controlling those controllers, with the

25 effusion of so much blood; as I think I may truly say, there was never any thing so dearly bought, as these Western parts have bought the learning of the Greek and Latin tongues.

Liberty Of The Subject How To Be Measured

30 To come now to the particulars of the true Liberty of a Subject; that is to say, what are the things, which though commanded by the Sovereign, he may nevertheless, without Injustice,

35 refuse to do; we are to consider, what Rights we pass away, when we make a Commonwealth; or (which is all one,) what Liberty we deny our selves, by owning all the Actions

40 (without exception) of the Man, or Assembly we make our Sovereign. For in the act of our Submission, consisteth both our Obligation, and our Liberty; which must therefore be in-

45 ferred by arguments taken from thence; there being no Obligation on any man, which ariseth not from some Act of his own; for all men equally, are by Nature Free. And because such arguments, must either be drawn from

50 the express words, "I Authorize all his Actions," or from the Intention of him that submitteth himself to his Power, (which Intention is to be understood by the End for which he so submitteth;) The Obligation, and Liberty of

55 the Subject, is to be derived, either from those Words, (or others equivalent;) or else from the End of the Institution of Sovereignty; namely, the Peace of the Subjects within themselves, and their Defense against a common Enemy.

Subjects Have Liberty To Defend Their Own Bodies, Even Against Them That Lawfully Invade Them

First therefore, seeing Sovereignty by Institution, is by Covenant of every one to every one;

65 and Sovereignty by Acquisition, by Covenants of the Vanquished to the Victor, or Child to the Parent; It is manifest, that every Subject has Liberty in all those things, the right whereof cannot by Covenant be transferred. I

70 have shown before in the 14. Chapter, that Covenants, not to defend a mans own body, are void. Therefore,

Are Not Bound To Hurt Themselves;

75 If the Sovereign command a man (though justly condemned,) to kill, wound, or maim himself; or not to resist those that assault him; or to abstain from the use of food, air, medicine, or any other thing, without which he

80 cannot live; yet hath that man the Liberty to disobey.

If a man be interrogated by the Sovereign, or his Authority, concerning a crime done by

85 himself, he is not bound (without assurance of Pardon) to confess it; because no man (as I

242

have shown in the same Chapter) can be obliged by Covenant to accuse himself.

Again, the Consent of a Subject to Sovereign Power, is contained in these words, "I Authorize, or take upon me, all his actions;" in which there is no restriction at all, of his own former natural Liberty: For by allowing him to Kill Me, I am not bound to Kill my self when he commands me. "'Tis one thing to say 'Kill me, or my fellow, if you please;' another thing to say, 'I will kill my self, or my fellow.'" It followeth therefore, that

No man is bound by the words themselves, either to kill himself, or any other man; And consequently, that the Obligation a man may sometimes have, upon the Command of the Sovereign to execute any dangerous, or dishonorable Office, dependeth not on the Words of our Submission; but on the Intention; which is to be understood by the End thereof. When therefore our refusal to obey, frustrates the End for which the Sovereignty was ordained; then there is no Liberty to refuse: otherwise there is.

Nor To Warfare, Unless They Voluntarily Undertake It

Upon this ground, a man that is commanded as a Soldier to fight against the enemy, though his Sovereign have Right enough to punish his refusal with death, may nevertheless in many cases refuse, without Injustice; as when he substituteth a sufficient Soldier in his place: for in this case he deserteth not the service of the Common-wealth. And there is allowance to be made for natural timorousness, not only to women, (of whom no such dangerous duty is expected,) but also to men of feminine courage. When Armies fight, there is on one side, or both, a running away; yet when they do it not out of treachery, but fear, they are

not esteemed to do it unjustly, but dishonorably. For the same reason, to avoid battle, is not Injustice, but Cowardice. But he that enrolleth himself a Soldier, or taketh imprest money, taketh away the excuse of a timorous nature; and is obliged, not only to go to the battle, but also not to run from it, without his Captains leave. And when the Defense of the Common-wealth, requireth at once the help of all that are able to bear Arms, every one is obliged; because otherwise the Institution of the Common-wealth, which they have not the purpose, or courage to preserve, was in vain.

To resist the Sword of the Common-wealth, in defense of another man, guilty, or innocent, no man hath Liberty; because such Liberty, takes away from the Sovereign, the means of Protecting us; and is therefore destructive of the very essence of Government. But in case a great many men together, have already resisted the Sovereign Power Unjustly, or committed some Capital crime, for which every one of them expecteth death, whether have they not the Liberty then to join together, and assist, and defend one another? Certainly they have: For they but defend their lives, which the guilty man may as well do, as the Innocent. There was indeed injustice in the first breach of their duty; Their bearing of Arms subsequent to it, though it be to maintain what they have done, is no new unjust act. And if it be only to defend their persons, it is not unjust at all. But the offer of Pardon taketh from them, to whom it is offered, the plea of self-defense, and maketh their perseverance in assisting, or defending the rest, unlawful.

The Greatest Liberty Of Subjects, Dependeth On The Silence Of The Law

As for other Liberties, they depend on the silence of the Law. In cases where the Sovereign has prescribed no rule, there the Subject

hath the liberty to do, or forbear, according to his own discretion. And therefore such Liberty is in some places more, and in some less; and in some times more, in other times less, ac-
5 cording as they that have the Sovereignty shall think most convenient. As for Example, there was a time, when in England a man might enter in to his own Land, (and dispossess such as wrongfully possessed it) by force. But in
10 after-times, that Liberty of Forcible entry, was taken away by a Statute made (by the King) in Parliament. And is some places of the world, men have the Liberty of many wives: in other places, such Liberty is not allowed.
15

If a Subject have a controversy with his Sovereign, of Debt, or of right of possession of lands or goods, or concerning any service required at his hands, or concerning any penalty
20 corporal, or pecuniary, grounded on a precedent Law; He hath the same Liberty to sue for his right, as if it were against a Subject; and before such Judges, as are appointed by the Sovereign. For seeing the Sovereign de-
25 mandeth by force of a former Law, and not by virtue of his Power; he declareth thereby, that he requireth no more, than shall appear to be due by that Law. The suit therefore is not contrary to the will of the Sovereign; and conse-
30 quently the Subject hath the Liberty to demand the hearing of his Cause; and sentence, according to that Law. But if he demand, or take any thing by pretense of his Power; there lyeth, in that case, no action of Law: for all
35 that is done by him in Virtue of his Power, is done by the Authority of every subject, and consequently, he that brings an action against the Sovereign, brings it against himself.

40 If a Monarch, or Sovereign Assembly, grant a Liberty to all, or any of his Subjects; which Grant standing, he is disabled to provide for their safety, the Grant is void; unless he directly renounce, or transfer the Sovereignty to
45 another. For in that he might openly, (if it had been his will,) and in plain terms, have renounced, or transferred it, and did not; it is to be understood it was not his will; but that the Grant proceeded from ignorance of the re-
50 pugnancy between such a Liberty and the Sovereign Power; and therefore the Sovereignty is still retained; and consequently all those Powers, which are necessary to the exercising thereof; such as are the Power of War, and
55 Peace, of Judicature, of appointing Officers, and Councilors, of levying Money, and the rest named in the 18th Chapter.

In What Cases Subjects Absolved Of Their
60 ## Obedience To Their Sovereign
The Obligation of Subjects to the Sovereign is understood to last as long, and no longer, than the power lasteth, by which he is able to protect them. For the right men have by Nature
65 to protect themselves, when none else can protect them, can by no Covenant be relinquished. The Sovereignty is the Soule of the Common-wealth; which once departed from the Body, the members doe no more receive
70 their motion from it. The end of Obedience is Protection; which, wheresoever a man seeth it, either in his own, or in another's sword, Nature applyeth his obedience to it, and his endeavor to maintain it. And though Sovereign-
75 ty, in the intention of them that make it, be immortal; yet is it in its own nature, not only subject to violent death, by foreign war; but also through the ignorance, and passions of men, it hath in it, from the very institution,
80 many seeds of a natural mortality, by Intestine Discord.

In Case Of Captivity
If a Subject be taken prisoner in war; or his
85 person, or his means of life be within the Guards of the enemy, and hath his life and

corporal Liberty given him, on condition to be
Subject to the Victor, he hath Liberty to accept the condition; and having accepted it, is
the subject of him that took him; because he
had no other way to preserve himself. The
case is the same, if he be detained on the same
terms, in a foreign country. But if a man be
held in prison, or bonds, or is not trusted with
the liberty of his body; he cannot be understood to be bound by Covenant to subjection;
and therefore may, if he can, make his escape
by any means whatsoever.

In Case The Sovereign Cast Off The Gov-
ernment From Himself And Heirs

If a Monarch shall relinquish the Sovereignty,
both for himself, and his heirs; His Subjects
return to the absolute Liberty of Nature; because, though Nature may declare who are his
Sons, and who are the nearest of his Kin; yet it
dependeth on his own will, (as hath been said
in the precedent chapter,) who shall be his
Heir. If therefore he will have no Heir, there is
no Sovereignty, nor Subjection. The case is the
same, if he dye without known Kindred, and
without declaration of his Heir. For then there
can no Heir be known, and consequently no
Subjection be due.

In Case Of Banishment

If the Sovereign Banish his Subject; during the
Banishment, he is not Subject. But he that is
sent on a message, or hath leave to travel, is
still Subject; but it is, by Contract between
Sovereigns, not by virtue of the covenant of
Subjection. For whosoever entreth into another's dominion, is Subject to all the Laws thereof; unless he have a privilege by the amity of
the Sovereigns, or by special license.

In Case The Sovereign Render Himself
Subject To Another

If a Monarch subdued by war, render himself

Subject to the Victor; his Subjects are delivered from their former obligation, and become
obliged to the Victor. But if he be held prisoner, or have not the liberty of his own Body; he
is not understood to have given away the
Right of Sovereignty; and therefore his Subjects are obliged to yield obedience to the
Magistrates formerly placed, governing not in
their own name, but in his. For, his Right remaining, the question is only of the Administration; that is to say, of the Magistrates and
Officers; which, if he have not means to
name, he is supposed to approve those, which
he himself had formerly appointed.

245

LOCKE

John Locke (1632-1704) is the philosopher every American knows even if they do not know they know him—as Thomas Jefferson ruthless plagiarized the opening of the Declaration of Independence from him. Born to the generation that came of age during the English Civil Wars, Locke was a staunch Whig—a supporter of the parliamentary faction. This did not preclude him from working for the monarchy, such as he did when he helped to draft the original constitution for the Colony of Carolina—but it did mean he was never a friend of the Crown. As such he and his circle of allies was frequently in danger, and Locke was forced to leave England on several occasions.

His 'whigishness' and ambivalence toward the Crown can be seen in his most famous work, *The Second Treatise on Government*. The continuation of an argument against the idea of absolute monarchy, the *Second Treatise* does not argue against any particular philosopher's take on government, but rather advances a systemic agenda detailing the origin, purpose, powers, limitations, rights, and duties of any legitimate government. Though now understood to have been written prior to the climax of this series of political crises—the Glorious Revolution—it has been taken by many and can most certainly be read, as an apology for the Whig settlement that came out of that event. Thus, rather than being a negative document, the *Second Treatise* is inherently positive—it attempts to show what makes a legitimate government, and in so doing helps to validate the government that men of Locke's political circle had helped to bring about in England.

SECOND TREATISE ON GOVERNMENT
JOHN LOCKE

CHAPTER I
AN ESSAY CONCERNING THE TRUE ORIGINAL, EXTENT AND END OF CIVIL GOVERNMENT

5

Sect. 1. It having been shown in the foregoing discourse,

(*1*). That Adam had not, either by natural right of fatherhood, or by positive donation from
10 God, any such authority over his children, or dominion over the world, as is pretended:

(*2*). That if he had, his heirs, yet, had no right to it:

15

(*3*). That if his heirs had, there being no law of nature nor positive law of God that determines which is the right heir in all cases that may arise, the right of succession, and conse-
20 quently of bearing rule, could not have been certainly determined:

(*4*). That if even that had been determined, yet the knowledge of which is the eldest line of Adam's posterity, being so long since utterly
25 lost, that in the races of mankind and families of the world, there remains not to one above another, the least pretense to be the eldest house, and to have the right of inheritance:

30 All these premises having, as I think, been clearly made out, it is impossible that the rulers now on earth should make any benefit, or derive any the least shadow of authority from that, which is held to be the fountain of all
35 power, Adam's private dominion and paternal

Text based off the 1688 printing, with adjustments for modern spelling.

jurisdiction; so that he that will not give just occasion to think that all government in the world is the product only of force and violence, and that men live together by no other
40 rules but that of beasts, where the strongest carries it, and so lay a foundation for perpetual disorder and mischief, tumult, sedition and rebellion, (things that the followers of that hypothesis so loudly cry out against) must of
45 necessity find out another rise of government, another original of political power, and another way of designing and knowing the persons that have it, than what Sir Robert Filmer hath taught us.

50

Sect. 2. To this purpose, I think it may not be amiss, to set down what I take to be political power; that the power of a MAGISTRATE over a subject may be distinguished from that
55 of a FATHER over his children, a MASTER over his servant, a HUSBAND over his wife, and a LORD over his slave. All which distinct powers happening sometimes together in the same man, if he be considered under these
60 different relations, it may help us to distinguish these powers one from wealth, a father of a family, and a captain of a galley.

Sect. 3. POLITICAL POWER, then, I take to
65 be a RIGHT of making laws with penalties of death, and consequently all less penalties, for the regulating and preserving of property, and of employing the force of the community, in the execution of such laws, and in the defense
70 of the commonwealth from foreign injury; and all this only for the public good.

CHAPTER II
OF THE STATE OF NATURE

Sect. 4. TO understand political power right,
and derive it from its original, we must consider, what state all men are naturally in, and
that is, a state of perfect freedom to order
their actions, and dispose of their possessions
and persons, as they think fit, within the
bounds of the law of nature, without asking
leave, or depending upon the will of any other
man.

A state also of equality, wherein all the power
and jurisdiction is reciprocal, no one having
more than another; there being nothing more
evident, than that creatures of the same species and rank, promiscuously born to all the
same advantages of nature, and the use of the
same faculties, should also be equal one
amongst another without subordination or
subjection, unless the lord and master of them
all should, by any manifest declaration of his
will, set one above another, and confer on
him, by an evident and clear appointment, an
undoubted right to dominion and sovereignty.

Sect. 5. This equality of men by nature, the
judicious Hooker looks upon as so evident in
itself, and beyond all question, that he makes it
the foundation of that obligation to mutual
love amongst men, on which he builds the
duties they owe one another, and from
whence he derives the great maxims of justice
and charity. His words are,

The like natural inducement hath brought men to
know that it is no less their duty, to love others than
themselves; for seeing those things which are equal,
must needs all have one measure; if I cannot but wish
to receive good, even as much at every man's hands, as
any man can wish unto his own soul, how should I
look to have any part of my desire herein satisfied,
unless myself be careful to satisfy the like desire, which
is undoubtedly in other men, being of one and the same
nature? To have any thing offered them repugnant to
this desire, must needs in all respects grieve them as
much as me; so that if I do harm, I must look to suf-
fer, there being no reason that others should show
greater measure of love to me, than they have by me
showed unto them: my desire therefore to be loved of my
equals in nature as much as possible may be, imposeth
upon me a natural duty of bearing to them-ward fully
the like affection; from which relation of equality be-
tween ourselves and them that are as ourselves, what
several rules and canons natural reason hath drawn,
for direction of life, no man is ignorant, Eccl. Pol.
Lib. 1.

Sect. 6. But though this be a state of liberty,
yet it is not a state of license: though man in
that state have an uncontrollable liberty to
dispose of his person or possessions, yet he
has not liberty to destroy himself, or so much
as any creature in his possession, but where
some nobler use than its bare preservation
calls for it. The state of nature has a law of
nature to govern it, which obliges every one:
and reason, which is that law, teaches all mankind, who will but consult it, that being all
equal and independent, no one ought to harm
another in his life, health, liberty, or possessions: for men being all the workmanship of
one omnipotent, and infinitely wise maker; all
the servants of one sovereign master, sent into
the world by his order, and about his business;
they are his property, whose workmanship
they are, made to last during his, not one another's pleasure: and being furnished with like
faculties, sharing all in one community of nature, there cannot be supposed any such subordination among us, that may authorize us to
destroy one another, as if we were made for
one another's uses, as the inferior ranks of
creatures are for our's. Every one, as he is
bound to preserve himself, and not to quit his

station willfully, so by the like reason, when his own preservation comes not in competition, ought he, as much as he can, to preserve the rest of mankind, and may not, unless it be 5 to do justice on an offender, take away, or impair the life, or what tends to the preservation of the life, the liberty, health, limb, or goods of another.

10 Sect. 7. And that all men may be restrained from invading others rights, and from doing hurt to one another, and the law of nature be observed, which willeth the peace and preservation of all mankind, the execution of the law 15 of nature is, in that state, put into every man's hands, whereby every one has a right to punish the transgressors of that law to such a degree, as may hinder its violation: for the law of nature would, as all other laws that concern 20 men in this world 'be in vain, if there were nobody that in the state of nature had a power to execute that law, and thereby preserve the innocent and restrain offenders. And if any one in the state of nature may punish another 25 for any evil he has done, every one may do so: for in that state of perfect equality, where naturally there is no superiority or jurisdiction of one over another, what any may do in prosecution of that law, every one must needs have 30 a right to do.

Sect. 8. And thus, in the state of nature, one man comes by a power over another; but yet no absolute or arbitrary power, to use a criminal, 35 when he has got him in his hands, according to the passionate heats, or boundless extravagancy of his own will; but only to retribute to him, so far as calm reason and conscience dictate, what is proportionate to his 40 transgression, which is so much as may serve for reparation and restraint: for these two are the only reasons, why one man may lawfully do harm to another, which is that we call pun-

ishment. In transgressing the law of nature, 45 the offender declares himself to live by another rule than that of reason and common equity, which is that measure God has set to the actions of men, for their mutual security; and so he becomes dangerous to mankind, the tie, 50 which is to secure them from injury and violence, being slighted and broken by him. Which being a trespass against the whole species, and the peace and safety of it, provided for by the law of nature, every man upon this 55 score, by the right he hath to preserve mankind in general, may restrain, or where it is necessary, destroy things noxious to them, and so may bring such evil on any one, who hath transgressed that law, as may make him repent 60 the doing of it, and thereby deter him, and by his example others, from doing the like mischief. And in the case, and upon this ground, EVERY MAN HATH A RIGHT TO PUNISH THE OFFENDER, AND BE EXECU-65 TIONER OF THE LAW OF NATURE.

Sect. 9. I doubt not but this will seem a very strange doctrine to some men: but before they condemn it, I desire them to resolve me, by 70 what right any prince or state can put to death, or punish an alien, for any crime he commits in their country. It is certain their laws, by virtue of any sanction they receive from the promulgated will of the legislative, reach not a 75 stranger: they speak not to him, nor, if they did, is he bound to hearken to them. The legislative authority, by which they are in force over the subjects of that commonwealth, hath no power over him. Those who have the su-80 preme power of making laws in England, France or Holland, are to an Indian, but like the rest of the world, men without authority: and therefore, if by the law of nature every man hath not a power to punish offences 85 against it, as he soberly judges the case to require, I see not how the magistrates of any community can punish an alien of another country; since, in reference to him, they can have no more power than what every man naturally may have over another.

Sect. 10. Besides the crime which consists in violating the law, and varying from the right rule of reason, whereby a man so far becomes degenerate, and declares himself to quit the principles of human nature, and to be a noxious creature, there is commonly injury done to some person or other, and some other man receives damage by his transgression: in which case he who hath received any damage, has, besides the right of punishment common to him with other men, a particular right to seek reparation from him that has done it: and any other person, who finds it just, may also join with him that is injured, and assist him in recovering from the offender so much as may make satisfaction for the harm he has suffered.

Sect. 11. From these two distinct rights, the one of punishing the crime for restraint, and preventing the like offence, which right of punishing is in every body; the other of taking reparation, which belongs only to the injured party, comes it to pass that the magistrate, who by being magistrate hath the common right of punishing put into his hands, can often, where the public good demands not the execution of the law, remit the punishment of criminal offences by his own authority, but yet cannot remit the satisfaction due to any private man for the damage he has received. That, he who has suffered the damage has a right to demand in his own name, and he alone can remit: the damnified person has this power of appropriating to himself the goods or service of the offender, by right of self-preservation, as every man has a power to punish the crime, to prevent its being committed again, by the right he has of preserving all mankind, and doing all reasonable things he can in order to that end: and thus it is, that every man, in the state of nature, has a power to kill a murderer, both to deter others from doing the like injury, which no reparation can compensate, by the example of the punishment that attends it from every body, and also to secure men from the attempts of a criminal, who having renounced reason, the common rule and measure God hath given to mankind, hath, by the unjust violence and slaughter he hath committed upon one, declared war against all mankind, and therefore may be destroyed as a lion or a tiger, one of those wild savage beasts, with whom men can have no society nor security: and upon this is grounded that great law of nature, Whoso sheddeth man's blood, by man shall his blood be shed. And Cain was so fully convinced, that every one had a right to destroy such a criminal, that after the murder of his brother, he cries out, Every one that findeth me, shall slay me; so plain was it writ in the hearts of all mankind.

Sect. 12. By the same reason may a man in the state of nature punish the lesser breaches of that law. It will perhaps be demanded, with death? I answer, each transgression may be punished to that degree, and with so much severity, as will suffice to make it an ill bargain to the offender, give him cause to repent, and terrify others from doing the like. Every offence, that can be committed in the state of nature, may in the state of nature be also punished equally, and as far forth as it may, in a commonwealth: for though it would be besides my present purpose, to enter here into the particulars of the law of nature, or its measures of punishment; yet, it is certain there is such a law, and that too, as intelligible and plain to a rational creature, and a studier of that law, as the positive laws of commonwealths; nay, possibly plainer; as much as reason is easier to be understood, than the fancies and intricate contrivances of men, following contrary and hidden interests put into words;

5 for so truly are a great part of the municipal laws of countries, which are only so far right, as they are founded on the law of nature, by which they are to be regulated and interpreted.

10 Sect. 13. To this strange doctrine, viz. That in the state of nature every one has the executive power of the law of nature, I doubt not but it will be objected, that it is unreasonable for men to be judges in their own cases, that self-

15 love will make men partial to themselves and their friends: and on the other side, that ill nature, passion and revenge will carry them too far in punishing others; and hence nothing but confusion and disorder will follow, and

20 that therefore God hath certainly appointed government to restrain the partiality and violence of men. I easily grant, that civil government is the proper remedy for the inconveniencies of the state of nature, which must cer-

25 tainly be great, where men may be judges in their own case, since it is easy to be imagined, that he who was so unjust as to do his brother an injury, will scarce be so just as to condemn himself for it: but I shall desire those who

30 make this objection, to remember, that absolute monarchs are but men; and if government is to be the remedy of those evils, which necessarily follow from men's being judges in their own cases, and the state of nature is

35 therefore not to be endured, I desire to know what kind of government that is, and how much better it is than the state of nature, where one man, commanding a multitude, has the liberty to be judge in his own case, and

40 may do to all his subjects whatever he pleases, without the least liberty to any one to question or control those who execute his pleasure? and in whatsoever he doth, whether led by reason,

mistake or passion, must be submitted to?

45 much better it is in the state of nature, wherein men are not bound to submit to the unjust will of another: and if he that judges, judges amiss in his own, or any other case, he is answerable for it to the rest of mankind.

50

Sect. 14. It is often asked as a mighty objection, where are, or ever were there any men in such a state of nature? To which it may suffice as an answer at present, that since all princes

55 and rulers of independent governments all through the world, are in a state of nature, it is plain the world never was, nor ever will be, without numbers of men in that state. I have named all governors of independent commu-

60 nities, whether they are, or are not, in league with others: for it is not every compact that puts an end to the state of nature between men, but only this one of agreeing together mutually to enter into one community, and

65 make one body politic; other promises, and compacts, men may make one with another, and yet still be in the state of nature. The promises and bargains for truck, &c. between the two men in the desert island, mentioned

70 by Garcilasso de la Vega, in his history of Peru; or between a Swiss and an Indian, in the woods of America, are binding to them, though they are perfectly in a state of nature, in reference to one another: for truth and

75 keeping of faith belongs to men, as men, and not as members of society.

Sect. 15. To those that say, there were never any men in the state of nature, I will not only

80 oppose the authority of the judicious Hooker, Eccl. Pol. lib. i. sect. 10, where he says, The laws which have been hitherto mentioned, i.e. the laws of nature, do bind men absolutely, even as they are men, although

85 they have never any settled fellowship, never any solemn agreement amongst themselves

what to do, or not to do: but forasmuch as we are not by ourselves sufficient to furnish ourselves with competent store of things, needful for such a life as our nature doth desire, a life

5 fit for the dignity of man; therefore to supply those defects and imperfections which are in us, as living single and solely by ourselves, we are naturally induced to seek communion and fellowship with others: this was the cause of

10 men's uniting themselves at first in politic societies.

But I moreover affirm, that all men are naturally in that state, and remain so, till by their

15 own consents they make themselves members of some politic society; and I doubt not in the sequel of this discourse, to make it very clear.

CHAPTER III
20 ## OF THE STATE OF WAR

Sect. 16. THE state of war is a state of enmity and destruction: and therefore declaring by word or action, not a passionate and hasty, but

25 a sedate settled design upon another man's life, puts him in a state of war with him against whom he has declared such an intention, and so has exposed his life to the other's power to be taken away by him, or any one that joins

30 with him in his defense, and espouses his quarrel; it being reasonable and just, I should have a right to destroy that which threatens me with destruction: for, by the fundamental law of nature, man being to be preserved as

35 much as possible, when all cannot be preserved, the safety of the innocent is to be preferred: and one may destroy a man who makes war upon him, or has discovered an enmity to his being, for the same reason that he may kill

40 a wolf or a lion; because such men are not under the ties of the common law of reason, have no other rule, but that of force and violence, and so may be treated as beasts of prey,

those dangerous and noxious creatures, that
45 will be sure to destroy him whenever he falls into their power.

Sect. 17. And hence it is, that he who attempts to get another man into his absolute power,
50 does thereby put himself into a state of war with him; it being to be understood as a declaration of a design upon his life: for I have reason to conclude, that he who would get me into his power without my consent, would use
55 me as he pleased when he had got me there, and destroy me too when he had a fancy to it; for no body can desire to have me in his absolute power, unless it be to compel me by force to that which is against the right of my free-
60 dom, i.e. make me a slave. To be free from such force is the only security of my preservation; and reason bids me look on him, as an enemy to my preservation, who would take away that freedom which is the fence to it; so
65 that he who makes an attempt to enslave me, thereby puts himself into a state of war with me. He that, in the state of nature, would take away the freedom that belongs to any one in that state, must necessarily be supposed to
70 have a design to take away every thing else, that freedom being the foundation of all the rest; as he that, in the state of society, would take away the freedom belonging to those of that society or commonwealth, must be sup-
75 posed to design to take away from them every thing else, and so be looked on as in a state of war.

Sect. 18. This makes it lawful for a man to kill
80 a thief, who has not in the least hurt him, nor declared any design upon his life, any farther than, by the use of force, so to get him in his power, as to take away his money, or what he pleases, from him; because using force, where
85 he has no right, to get me into his power, let his pretense be what it will, I have no reason

to suppose, that he, who would take away my liberty, would not, when he had me in his power, take away every thing else. And therefore it is lawful for me to treat him as one who
5 has put himself into a state of war with me, i.e. kill him if I can; for to that hazard does he justly expose himself, whoever introduces a state of war, and is aggressor in it.

10 Sect. 19. And here we have the plain difference between the state of nature and the state of war, which however some men have confounded, are as far distant, as a state of peace, good will, mutual assistance and preservation,
15 and a state of enmity, malice, violence and mutual destruction, are one from another. Men living together according to reason, without a common superior on earth, with authority to judge between them, is properly the state
20 of nature. But force, or a declared design of force, upon the person of another, where there is no common superior on earth to appeal to for relief, is the state of war: and it is the want of such an appeal gives a man the
25 right of war even against an aggressor, tho' he be in society and a fellow subject. Thus a thief, whom I cannot harm, but by appeal to the law, for having stolen all that I am worth, I may kill, when he sets on me to rob me but of
30 my horse or coat; because the law, which was made for my preservation, where it cannot interpose to secure my life from present force, which, if lost, is capable of no reparation, permits me my own defense, and the right of
35 war, a liberty to kill the aggressor, because the aggressor allows not time to appeal to our common judge, nor the decision of the law, for remedy in a case where the mischief may be irreparable. Want of a common judge with
40 authority, puts all men in a state of nature: force without right, upon a man's person, makes a state of war, both where there is, and is not, a common judge.

Sect. 20. But when the actual force is over, the
45 state of war ceases between those that are in society, and are equally on both sides subjected to the fair determination of the law; because then there lies open the remedy of appeal for the past injury, and to prevent future
50 harm: but where no such appeal is, as in the state of nature, for want of positive laws, and judges with authority to appeal to, the state of war once begun, continues, with a right to the innocent party to destroy the other whenever
55 he can, until the aggressor offers peace, and desires reconciliation on such terms as may repair any wrongs he has already done, and secure the innocent for the future; nay, where an appeal to the law, and constituted judges,
60 lies open, but the remedy is denied by a manifest perverting of justice, and a barefaced wresting of the laws to protect or indemnify the violence or injuries of some men, or party of men, there it is hard to imagine any thing
65 but a state of war: for wherever violence is used, and injury done, though by hands appointed to administer justice, it is still violence and injury, however colored with the name, pretenses, or forms of law, the end whereof
70 being to protect and redress the innocent, by an unbiased application of it, to all who are under it; wherever that is not bona fide done, war is made upon the sufferers, who having no appeal on earth to right them, they are left
75 to the only remedy in such cases, an appeal to heaven.

Sect. 21. To avoid this state of war (wherein there is no appeal but to heaven, and wherein
80 every the least difference is apt to end, where there is no authority to decide between the contenders) is one great reason of men's putting themselves into society, and quitting the state of nature: for where there is an authority,
85 a power on earth, from which relief can be had by appeal, there the continuance of the

state of war is excluded, and the controversy is decided by that power. Had there been any such court, any superior jurisdiction on earth, to determine the right between Jephtha and the Ammonites, they had never come to a state of war: but we see he was forced to appeal to heaven. *The Lord the Judge* (says he) *be judge this day between the children of Israel and the children of Ammon, Judg. xi. 27.* and then prosecuting, and relying on his appeal, he leads out his army to battle: and therefore in such controversies, where the question is put, who shall be judge? It cannot be meant, who shall decide the controversy; every one knows what Jephtha here tells us, that *the Lord the Judge shall judge.* Where there is no judge on earth, the appeal lies to God in heaven. That question then cannot mean, who shall judge, whether another hath put himself in a state of war with me, and whether I may, as Jephtha did, appeal to heaven in it? of that I myself can only be judge in my own conscience, as I will answer it, at the great day, to the supreme judge of all men.

CHAPTER IV
OF SLAVERY

Sect. 22. THE natural liberty of man is to be free from any superior power on earth, and not to be under the will or legislative authority of man, but to have only the law of nature for his rule. The liberty of man, in society, is to be under no other legislative power, but that established, by consent, in the commonwealth; nor under the dominion of any will, or restraint of any law, but what that legislative shall enact, according to the trust put in it. Freedom then is not what Sir Robert Filmer tells us, *Observations, A. 55. a liberty for every one to do what he lists, to live as he pleases, and not to be tied by any laws: but freedom of men under government is, to have a standing rule to live by, common to every one of that society, and made by the legislative power erected in it; a liberty to follow my own will in all things, where the rule prescribes not; and not to be subject to the inconstant, uncertain, unknown, arbitrary will of another man: as freedom of nature is, to be under no other restraint but the law of nature.*

Sect. 23. This freedom from absolute, arbitrary power, is so necessary to, and closely joined with a man's preservation, that he cannot part with it, but by what forfeits his preservation and life together: for a man, not having the power of his own life, cannot, by compact, or his own consent, enslave himself to any one, nor put himself under the absolute, arbitrary power of another, to take away his life, when he pleases. No body can give more power than he has himself; and he that cannot take away his own life, cannot give another power over it. Indeed, having by his fault forfeited his own life, by some act that deserves death; he, to whom he has forfeited it, may (when he has him in his power) delay to take it, and make use of him to his own service, and he does him no injury by it: for, whenever he finds the hardship of his slavery outweigh the value of his life, it is in his power, by resisting the will of his master, to draw on himself the death he desires.

Sect. 24. This is the perfect condition of slavery, which is nothing else, but the state of war continued, between a lawful conqueror and a captive: for, if once compact enter between them, and make an agreement for a limited power on the one side, and obedience on the other, the state of war and slavery ceases, as long as the compact endures: for, as has been said, no man can, by agreement, pass over to another that which he hath not in himself, a power over his own life.

I confess, we find among the Jews, as well as

other nations, that men did sell themselves; but, it is plain, this was only to drudgery, not to slavery: for, it is evident, the person sold was not under an absolute, arbitrary, despotical power: for the master could not have power to kill him, at any time, whom, at a certain time, he was obliged to let go free out of his service; and the master of such a servant was so far from having an arbitrary power over his life, that he could not, at pleasure, so much as maim him, but the loss of an eye, or tooth, set him free, Exod. xxi.

CHAPTER V
OF PROPERTY

Sect. 25. Whether we consider natural reason, which tells us, that men, being once born, have a right to their preservation, and consequently to meat and drink, and such other things as nature affords for their subsistence: or revelation, which gives us an account of those grants God made of the world to Adam, and to Noah, and his sons, it is very clear, that God, as king David says, Psal. cxv. 16. has given the earth to the children of men; given it to mankind in common. But this being supposed, it seems to some a very great difficulty, how any one should ever come to have a property in any thing: I will not content myself to answer, that if it be difficult to make out property, upon a supposition that God gave the world to Adam, and his posterity in common, it is impossible that any man, but one universal monarch, should have any property upon a supposition, that God gave the world to Adam, and his heirs in succession, exclusive of all the rest of his posterity. But I shall endeavor to show, how men might come to have a property in several parts of that which God gave to mankind in common, and that without any express compact of all the commoners.

Sect. 26. God, who hath given the world to men in common, hath also given them reason to make use of it to the best advantage of life, and convenience. The earth, and all that is therein, is given to men for the support and comfort of their being. And tho' all the fruits it naturally produces, and beasts it feeds, belong to mankind in common, as they are produced by the spontaneous hand of nature; and no body has originally a private dominion, exclusive of the rest of mankind, in any of them, as they are thus in their natural state: yet being given for the use of men, there must of necessity be a means to appropriate them some way or other, before they can be of any use, or at all beneficial to any particular man. The fruit, or venison, which nourishes the wild Indian, who knows no enclosure, and is still a tenant in common, must be his, and so his, i.e. a part of him, that another can no longer have any right to it, before it can do him any good for the support of his life.

Sect. 27. Though the earth, and all inferior creatures, be common to all men, yet every man has a property in his own person: this no body has any right to but himself. The labor of his body, and the work of his hands, we may say, are properly his. Whatsoever then he removes out of the state that nature hath provided, and left it in, he hath mixed his labor with, and joined to it something that is his own, and thereby makes it his property. It being by him removed from the common state nature hath placed it in, it hath by this labor something annexed to it, that excludes the common right of other men: for this labor being the unquestionable property of the laborer, no man but he can have a right to what that is once joined to, at least where there is enough, and as good, left in common for others.

Sect. 28. He that is nourished by the acorns he picked up under an oak, or the apples he gathered from the trees in the wood, has certainly appropriated them to himself. No body can deny but the nourishment is his. I ask then, when did they begin to be his? when he digested? or when he eat? or when he boiled? or when he brought them home? or when he picked them up? and it is plain, if the first gathering made them not his, nothing else could. That labor put a distinction between them and common: that added something to them more than nature, the common mother of all, had done; and so they became his private right. And will any one say, he had no right to those acorns or apples, he thus appropriated, because he had not the consent of all mankind to make them his? Was it a robbery thus to assume to himself what belonged to all in common? If such a consent as that was necessary, man had starved, notwithstanding the plenty God had given him. We see in commons, which remain so by compact, that it is the taking any part of what is common, and removing it out of the state nature leaves it in, which begins the property; without which the common is of no use. And the taking of this or that part, does not depend on the express consent of all the commoners. Thus the grass my horse has bit; the turfs my servant has cut; and the ore I have digged in any place, where I have a right to them in common with others, become my property, without the assignation or consent of any body. The labor that was mine, removing them out of that common state they were in, hath fixed my property in them.

Sect. 29. By making an explicit consent of every commoner, necessary to any one's appropriating to himself any part of what is given in common, children or servants could not cut the meat, which their father or master had provided for them in common, without assigning to every one his peculiar part. Though the water running in the fountain be every one's, yet who can doubt, but that in the pitcher is his only who drew it out? His labor hath taken it out of the hands of nature, where it was common, and belonged equally to all her children, and hath thereby appropriated it to himself.

Sect. 30. Thus this law of reason makes the deer that Indian's who hath killed it; it is allowed to be his goods, who hath bestowed his labor upon it, though before it was the common right of every one. And amongst those who are counted the civilized part of mankind, who have made and multiplied positive laws to determine property, this original law of nature, for the beginning of property, in what was before common, still takes place; and by virtue thereof, what fish any one catches in the ocean, that great and still remaining common of mankind; or what ambergris any one takes up here, is by the labor that removes it out of that common state nature left it in, made his property, who takes that pains about it. And even amongst us, the hare that any one is hunting, is thought his who pursues her during the chase: for being a beast that is still looked upon as common, and no man's private possession; whoever has employed so much labor about any of that kind, as to find and pursue her, has thereby removed her from the state of nature, wherein she was common, and hath begun a property.

Sect. 31. It will perhaps be objected to this, that if gathering the acorns, or other fruits of the earth, &c. makes a right to them, then any one may ingross as much as he will. To which I answer, Not so. The same law of nature, that does by this means give us property, does also bound that property too. God has given us all things richly, 1 Tim. vi. 12. is the voice of reason confirmed by inspiration. But how far has he given it us? To enjoy. As much as any one can make use of to any advantage of life before it spoils, so much he may by his labour fix a property in: whatever is beyond this, is more than his share, and belongs to others. Nothing was made by God for man to spoil or destroy. And thus, considering the plenty of natural provisions there was a long time in the world, and the few spenders; and to how small a part of that provision the industry of one man could extend itself, and ingross it to the prejudice of others; especially keeping within the bounds, set by reason, of what might serve for his use; there could be then little room for quarrels or contentions about property so established.

Sect. 32. But the chief matter of property being now not the fruits of the earth, and the beasts that subsist on it, but the earth itself; as that which takes in and carries with it all the rest; I think it is plain, that property in that too is acquired as the former. As much land as a man tills, plants, improves, cultivates, and can use the product of, so much is his property. He by his labor does, as it were, enclose it from the common. Nor will it invalidate his right, to say every body else has an equal title to it; and therefore he cannot appropriate, he cannot enclose, without the consent of all his fellow-commoners, all mankind. God, when he gave the world in common to all mankind, commanded man also to labor, and the penury of his condition required it of him. God and his reason commanded him to subdue the earth, i.e. improve it for the benefit of life, and therein lay out something upon it that was his own, his labor. He that in obedience to this command of God, subdued, tilled and sowed any part of it, thereby annexed to it something that was his property, which another had no title to, nor could without injury take from him.

Sect. 33. Nor was this appropriation of any parcel of land, by improving it, any prejudice to any other man, since there was still enough, and as good left; and more than the yet unprovided could use. So that, in effect, there was never the less left for others because of his enclosure for himself: for he that leaves as much as another can make use of, does as good as take nothing at all. No body could think himself injured by the drinking of another man, though he took a good draught, who had a whole river of the same water left him to quench his thirst: and the case of land and water, where there is enough of both, is perfectly the same.

Sect. 34. God gave the world to men in common; but since he gave it them for their benefit, and the greatest conveniences of life they were capable to draw from it, it cannot be supposed he meant it should always remain common and uncultivated. He gave it to the use of the industrious and rational, (and labor was to be his title to it;) not to the fancy or covetousness of the quarrelsome and contentious. He that had as good left for his improvement, as was already taken up, needed not complain, ought not to meddle with what was already improved by another's labor: if he did, it is plain he desired the benefit of another's pains, which he had no right to, and not the ground which God had given him in common with others to labor on, and whereof there was as good left, as that already possessed, and more than he knew what to do with, or his industry could reach to.

Sect. 35. It is true, in land that is common in England, or any other country, where there is plenty of people under government, who have

257

money and commerce, no one can enclose or appropriate any part, without the consent of all his fellow-commoners; because this is left common by compact, i.e. by the law of the land, which is not to be violated. And though it be common, in respect of some men, it is not so to all mankind; but is the joint property of this country, or this parish. Besides, the remainder, after such enclosure, would not be as good to the rest of the commoners, as the whole was when they could all make use of the whole; whereas in the beginning and first peopling of the great common of the world, it was quite otherwise. The law man was under, was rather for appropriating. God commanded, and his wants forced him to labor. That was his property which could not be taken from him where-ever he had fixed it. And hence subduing or cultivating the earth, and having dominion, we see are joined together. The one gave title to the other. So that God, by commanding to subdue, gave authority so far to appropriate: and the condition of human life, which requires labor and materials to work on, necessarily introduces private possessions.

Sect. 36. The measure of property nature has well set by the extent of men's labor and the conveniences of life: no man's labor could subdue, or appropriate all; nor could his enjoyment consume more than a small part; so that it was impossible for any man, this way, to intrench upon the right of another, or acquire to himself a property, to the prejudice of his neighbor, who would still have room for as good, and as large a possession (after the other had taken out his) as before it was appropriated. This measure did confine every man's possession to a very moderate proportion, and such as he might appropriate to himself, without injury to any body, in the first ages of the world, when men were more in danger to be lost, by wandering from their company, in the then vast wilderness of the earth, than to be straitened for want of room to plant in. And the same measure may be allowed still without prejudice to any body, as full as the world seems: for supposing a man, or family, in the state they were at first peopling of the world by the children of Adam, or Noah; let him plant in some inland, vacant places of America, we shall find that the possessions he could make himself, upon the measures we have given, would not be very large, nor, even to this day, prejudice the rest of mankind, or give them reason to complain, or think themselves injured by this man's encroachment, though the race of men have now spread themselves to all the corners of the world, and do infinitely exceed the small number was at the beginning. Nay, the extent of ground is of so little value, without labor, that I have heard it affirmed, that in Spain itself a man may be permitted to plough, sow and reap, without being disturbed, upon land he has no other title to, but only his making use of it. But, on the contrary, the inhabitants think themselves beholden to him, who, by his industry on neglected, and consequently waste land, has increased the stock of corn, which they wanted. But be this as it will, which I lay no stress on; this I dare boldly affirm, that the same rule of propriety, (viz.) that every man should have as much as he could make use of, would hold still in the world, without straitening any body; since there is land enough in the world to suffice double the inhabitants, had not the invention of money, and the tacit agreement of men to put a value on it, introduced (by consent) larger possessions, and a right to them; which, how it has done, I shall by and by show more at large.

Sect. 37. This is certain, that in the beginning, before the desire of having more than man needed had altered the intrinsic value of things, which depends only on their usefulness to the life of man; or had agreed, that a little piece of yellow metal, which would keep with- out wasting or decay, should be worth a great piece of flesh, or a whole heap of corn; though men had a right to appropriate, by their labor, each one of himself, as much of the things of nature, as he could use: yet this could not be much, nor to the prejudice of others, where the same plenty was still left to those who would use the same industry. To which let me add, that he who appropriates land to himself by his labor, does not lessen, but increase the common stock of mankind: for the provisions serving to the support of human life, produced by one acre of enclosed and cultivated land, are (to speak much within compass) ten times more than those which are yielded by an acre of land of an equal richness lying waste in common. And therefore he that encloses land, and has a greater plenty of the conveniences of life from ten acres, than he could have from an hundred left to nature, may truly be said to give ninety acres to man- kind: for his labor now supplies him with pro- visions out of ten acres, which were but the product of an hundred lying in common. I have here rated the improved land very low, in making its product but as ten to one, when it is much nearer an hundred to one: for I ask, whether in the wild woods and uncultivated waste of America, left to nature, without any improvement, tillage or husbandry, a thousand acres yield the needy and wretched inhabitants as many conveniences of life, as ten acres of equally fertile land do in Devonshire, where they are well cultivated?

Before the appropriation of land, he who gathered as much of the wild fruit, killed, caught, or tamed, as many of the beasts, as he could; he that so employed his pains about any of the spontaneous products of nature, as any way to alter them from the state which nature put them in, by placing any of his labor on them, did thereby acquire a propriety in them: but if they perished, in his possession, without their due use; if the fruits rotted, or the veni- son putrefied, before he could spend it, he offended against the common law of nature, and was liable to be punished; he invaded his neighbor's share, for he had no right, farther than his use called for any of them, and they might serve to afford him conveniences of life.

Sect. 38. The same measures governed the possession of land too: whatsoever he tilled and reaped, laid up and made use of, before it spoiled, that was his peculiar right; whatsoever he enclosed, and could feed, and make use of, the cattle and product was also his. But if ei- ther the grass of his enclosure rotted on the ground, or the fruit of his planting perished without gathering, and laying up, this part of the earth, notwithstanding his enclosure, was still to be looked on as waste, and might be the possession of any other. Thus, at the be- ginning, Cain might take as much ground as he could till, and make it his own land, and yet leave enough to Abel's sheep to feed on; a few acres would serve for both their possessions. But as families increased, and industry en- larged their stocks, their possessions enlarged with the need of them; but yet it was com- monly without any fixed property in the ground they made use of, till they incorpo- rated, settled themselves together, and built cities; and then, by consent, they came in time, to set out the bounds of their distinct territo- ries, and agree on limits between them and their neighbors; and by laws within them- selves, settled the properties of those of the same society: for we see, that in that part of the world which was first inhabited, and therefore like to be best peopled, even as low down as Abraham's time, they wandered with their flocks, and their herds, which was their substance, freely up and down; and this Abraham did, in a country where he was a stranger. Whence it is plain, that at least a great part of the land lay in common; that the inhabitants valued it not, nor claimed property in any more than they made use of. But when there was not room enough in the same place, for their herds to feed together, they by consent, as Abraham and Lot did, Gen. xiii. 5. separated and enlarged their pasture, where it best liked them. And for the same reason Esau went from his father, and his brother, and planted in mount Seir, Gen. xxxvi. 6.

Sect. 39. And thus, without supposing any private dominion, and property in Adam, over all the world, exclusive of all other men, which can no way be proved, nor any one's property be made out from it; but supposing the world given, as it was, to the children of men in common, we see how labor could make men distinct titles to several parcels of it, for their private uses; wherein there could be no doubt of right, no room for quarrel.

Sect. 40. Nor is it so strange, as perhaps before consideration it may appear, that the property of labor should be able to overbalance the community of land: for it is labor indeed that puts the difference of value on every thing; and let any one consider what the difference is between an acre of land planted with tobacco or sugar, sown with wheat or barley, and an acre of the same land lying in common, without any husbandry upon it, and he will find, that the improvement of labor makes the far greater part of the value. I think it will be but a very modest computation to say, that of the products of the earth useful to the life of man nine tenths are the effects of labor: nay, if we will rightly estimate things as they come to our use, and cast up the several expenses about them, what in them is purely owing to nature, and what to labor, we shall find, that in most of them ninety-nine hundredths are wholly to be put on the account of labor.

Sect. 41. There cannot be a clearer demonstration of any thing, than several nations of the Americans are of this, who are rich in land, and poor in all the comforts of life; whom nature having furnished as liberally as any other people, with the materials of plenty, i.e. a fruitful soil, apt to produce in abundance, what might serve for food, raiment, and delight; yet for want of improving it by labor, have not one hundredth part of the conveniences we enjoy: and a king of a large and fruitful territory there, feeds, lodges, and is clad worse than a day-laborer in England.

Sect. 42. To make this a little clearer, let us but trace some of the ordinary provisions of life, through their several progresses, before they come to our use, and see how much they receive of their value from human industry. Bread, wine and cloth, are things of daily use, and great plenty; yet notwithstanding, acorns, water and leaves, or skins, must be our bread, drink and clothing, did not labor furnish us with these more useful commodities: for whatever bread is more worth than acorns, wine than water, and cloth or silk, than leaves, skins or moss, that is wholly owing to labor and industry; the one of these being the food and raiment which unassisted nature furnishes us with; the other, provisions which our industry and pains prepare for us, which how much they exceed the other in value, when any one hath computed, he will then see how much labor makes the far greatest part of the value of things we enjoy in this world: and the

ground which produces the materials, is scarce to be reckoned in, as any, or at most, but a very small part of it; so little, that even amongst us, land that is left wholly to nature,
5 that hath no improvement of pasturage, tillage, or planting, is called, as indeed it is, waste; and we shall find the benefit of it amount to little more than nothing.

10 This shows how much numbers of men are to be preferred to largeness of dominions; and that the increase of lands, and the right employing of them, is the great art of government: and that prince, who shall be so wise
15 and godlike, as by established laws of liberty to secure protection and encouragement to the honest industry of mankind, against the oppression of power and narrowness of party, will quickly be too hard for his neighbors: but
20 this by the by.

To return to the argument in hand.

Sect. 43. An acre of land, that bears here twen-
25 ty bushels of wheat, and another in America, which, with the same husbandry, would do the like, are, without doubt, of the same natural intrinsic value: but yet the benefit mankind receives from the one in a year, is worth 5l.
30 and from the other possibly not worth a penny, if all the profit an Indian received from it were to be valued, and sold here; at least, I may truly say, not one thousandth. It is labor then which puts the greatest part of value up-
35 on land, without which it would scarcely be worth any thing: it is to that we owe the greatest part of all its useful products; for all that the straw, bran, bread, of that acre of wheat, is more worth than the product of an acre of as
40 good land, which lies waste, is all the effect of labor: for it is not barely the plough-man's pains, the reaper's and thresher's toil, and the baker's sweat, is to be counted into the bread

we eat; the labor of those who broke the oxen,
45 who digged and wrought the iron and stones, who felled and framed the timber employed about the plough, mill, oven, or any other utensils, which are a vast number, requisite to this corn, from its being feed to be sown to its
50 being made bread, must all be charged on the account of labor, and received as an effect of that: nature and the earth furnished only the almost worthless materials, as in themselves. It would be a strange catalogue of things, that
55 industry provided and made use of, about every loaf of bread, before it came to our use, if we could trace them; iron, wood, leather, bark, timber, stone, bricks, coals, lime, cloth, dying drugs, pitch, tar, masts, ropes, and all the ma-
60 terials made use of in the ship, that brought any of the commodities made use of by any of the workmen, to any part of the work; all which it would be almost impossible, at least too long, to reckon up.
65

Sect. 44. From all which it is evident, that though the things of nature are given in common, yet man, by being master of himself, and proprietor of his own person, and the actions
70 or labor of it, had still in himself the great foundation of property; and that, which made up the great part of what he applied to the support or comfort of his being, when invention and arts had improved the conveniences
75 of life, was perfectly his own, and did not belong in common to others.

Sect. 45. Thus labor, in the beginning, gave a right of property, wherever any one was
80 pleased to employ it upon what was common, which remained a long while the far greater part, and is yet more than mankind makes use of. Men, at first, for the most part, contented themselves with what unassisted nature of-
85 fered to their necessities: and though afterwards, in some parts of the world, (where the

increase of people and stock, with the use of money, had made land scarce, and so of some value) the several communities settled the bounds of their distinct territories, and by laws within themselves regulated the properties of the private men of their society, and so, by compact and agreement, settled the property which labor and industry began; and the leagues that have been made between several states and kingdoms, either expressly or tacitly disowning all claim and right to the land in the others possession, have, by common consent, given up their pretenses to their natural common right, which originally they had to those countries, and so have, by positive agreement, settled a property amongst themselves, in distinct parts and parcels of the earth; yet there are still great tracts of ground to be found, which (the inhabitants thereof not having joined with the rest of mankind, in the consent of the use of their common money) lie waste, and are more than the people who dwell on it do, or can make use of, and so still lie in common; tho' this can scarce happen amongst that part of mankind that have consented to the use of money.

Sect. 46. The greatest part of things really useful to the life of man, and such as the necessity of subsisting made the first commoners of the world look after, as it doth the Americans now, are generally things of short duration; such as, if they are not consumed by use, will decay and perish of themselves: gold, silver and diamonds, are things that fancy or agreement hath put the value on, more than real use, and the necessary support of life. Now of those good things which nature hath provided in common, every one had a right (as hath been said) to as much as he could use, and property in all that he could effect with his labor; all that his industry could extend to, to alter from the state nature had put it in, was

his. He that gathered a hundred bushels of acorns or apples, had thereby a property in them, they were his goods as soon as gathered. He was only to look, that he used them before they spoiled, else he took more than his share, and robbed others. And indeed it was a foolish thing, as well as dishonest, to hoard up more than he could make use of. If he gave away a part to any body else, so that it perished not uselessly in his possession, these he also made use of. And if he also bartered away plums, that would have rotted in a week, for nuts that would last good for his eating a whole year, he did no injury; he wasted not the common stock; destroyed no part of the portion of goods that belonged to others, so long as nothing perished uselessly in his hands. Again, if he would give his nuts for a piece of metal, pleased with its color; or exchange his sheep for shells, or wool for a sparkling pebble or a diamond, and keep those by him all his life he invaded not the right of others, he might heap up as much of these durable things as he pleased; the exceeding of the bounds of his just property not lying in the largeness of his possession, but the perishing of any thing uselessly in it.

Sect. 47. And thus came in the use of money, some lasting thing that men might keep without spoiling, and that by mutual consent men would take in exchange for the truly useful, but perishable supports of life.

Sect. 48. And as different degrees of industry were apt to give men possessions in different proportions, so this invention of money gave them the opportunity to continue and enlarge them: for supposing an island, separate from all possible commerce with the rest of the world, wherein there were but an hundred families, but there were sheep, horses and cows, with other useful animals, wholesome fruits, and land enough for corn for a hundred thousand times as many, but nothing in the island, either because of its commonness, or perishableness, fit to supply the place of money; what reason could any one have there to enlarge his possessions beyond the use of his family, and a plentiful supply to its consumption, either in what their own industry produced, or they could barter for like perishable, useful commodities, with others? Where there is not some thing, both lasting and scarce, and so valuable to be hoarded up, there men will not be apt to enlarge their possessions of land, were it never so rich, never so free for them to take: for I ask, what would a man value ten thousand, or an hundred thousand acres of excellent land, ready cultivated, and well stocked too with cattle, in the middle of the inland parts of America, where he had no hopes of commerce with other parts of the world, to draw money to him by the sale of the product? It would not be worth the enclosing, and we should see him give up again to the wild common of nature, whatever was more than would supply the conveniences of life to be had there for him and his family.

Sect. 49. Thus in the beginning all the world was America, and more so than that is now; for no such thing as money was any where known. Find out something that hath the use and value of money amongst his neighbors, you shall see the same man will begin presently to enlarge his possessions.

Sect. 50. But since gold and silver, being little useful to the life of man in proportion to food, raiment, and carriage, has its value only from the consent of men, whereof labor yet makes, in great part, the measure, it is plain, that men have agreed to a disproportionate and unequal possession of the earth, they having, by a tacit and voluntary consent, found out, a way how a man may fairly possess more land than he himself can use the product of, by receiving in exchange for the overplus gold and silver, which may be hoarded up without injury to any one; these metals not spoiling or decaying in the hands of the possessor. This partage of things in an inequality of private possessions, men have made practicable out of the bounds of society, and without compact, only by putting a value on gold and silver, and tacitly agreeing in the use of money: for in governments, the laws regulate the right of property, and the possession of land is determined by positive constitutions.

Sect. 51. And thus, I think, it is very easy to conceive, without any difficulty, how labor could at first begin a title of property in the common things of nature, and how the spending it upon our uses bounded it. So that there could then be no reason of quarrelling about title, nor any doubt about the largeness of possession it gave. Right and conveniency went together; for as a man had a right to all he could employ his labor upon, so he had no temptation to labor for more than he could make use of. This left no room for controversy about the title, nor for encroachment on the right of others; what portion a man carved to himself, was easily seen; and it was useless, as well as dishonest, to carve himself too much, or take more than he needed.

CHAPTER VI
OF PATERNAL POWER

Sect. 52. IT may perhaps be censured as an impertinent criticism, in a discourse of this nature, to find fault with words and names, that have obtained in the world: and yet possibly it may not be amiss to offer new ones, when the old are apt to lead men into mistakes, as this of paternal power probably has done, which seems so to place the power of parents over their children wholly in the father, as if the mother had no share in it; whereas, if we consult reason or revelation, we shall find, she hath an equal title. This may give one reason to ask, whether this might not be more properly called parental power? for whatever obligation nature and the right of generation lays on children, it must certainly bind them equal to both the concurrent causes of it. And accordingly we see the positive law of God every where joins them together, without distinction, when it commands the obedience of children, Honor thy father and thy mother, Exod. xx. 12. Whosoever curseth his father or his mother, Lev. xx. 9. Ye shall fear every man his mother and his father, Lev. xix. 3. Children, obey your parents, &c. Eph. vi. 1. is the stile of the Old and New Testament.

Sect. 53. Had but this one thing been well considered, without looking any deeper into the matter, it might perhaps have kept men from running into those gross mistakes, they have made, about this power of parents; which, however it might, without any great harshness, bear the name of absolute dominion, and regal authority, when under the title of paternal power it seemed appropriated to the father, would yet have founded but oddly, and in the very name shown the absurdity, if this supposed absolute power over children had been called parental; and thereby have discovered, that it belonged to the mother too: for it will but very ill serve the turn of those men, who contend so much for the absolute power and authority of the fatherhood, as they call it, that the mother should have any share in it; and it would have but ill supported the monarchy they contend for, when by the very name it appeared, that that fundamental authority, from whence they would derive their government of a single person only, was not placed in one, but two persons jointly. But to let this of names pass.

Sect. 54. Though I have said above, Chap. II. That all men by nature are equal, I cannot be supposed to understand all sorts of equality: age or virtue may give men a just precedency: excellency of parts and merit may place others above the common level: birth may subject some, and alliance or benefits others, to pay an observance to those to whom nature, gratitude, or other respects, may have made it due: and yet all this consists with the equality, which all men are in, in respect of jurisdiction or dominion one over another; which was the equality I there spoke of, as proper to the business in hand, being that equal right, that every man hath, to his natural freedom, without being subjected to the will or authority of any other man.

Sect. 55. Children, I confess, are not born in this full state of equality, though they are born to it. Their parents have a sort of rule and jurisdiction over them, when they come into the world, and for some time after; but it is but a temporary one. The bonds of this subjection are like the swaddling clothes they art wrapt up in, and supported by, in the weakness of their infancy: age and reason as they grow up, loosen them, till at length they drop quite off, and leave a man at his own free disposal.

Sect. 56. Adam was created a perfect man, his body and mind in full possession of their strength and reason, and so was capable, from the first instant of his being to provide for his own support and preservation, and govern his actions according to the dictates of the law of reason which God had implanted in him. From him the world is peopled with his descendants, who are all born infants, weak and helpless, without knowledge or understanding: but to supply the defects of this imperfect state, till the improvement of growth and age hath removed them, Adam and Eve, and after them all parents were, by the law of nature, under an obligation to preserve, nourish, and educate the children they had begotten; not as their own workmanship, but the workmanship of their own maker, the Almighty, to whom they were to be accountable for them.

Sect. 57. The law, that was to govern Adam, was the same that was to govern all his posterity, the law of reason. But his offspring having another way of entrance into the world, different from him, by a natural birth, that produced them ignorant and without the use of reason, they were not presently under that law; for no body can be under a law, which is not promulgated to him; and this law being promulgated or made known by reason only, he that is not come to the use of his reason, cannot be said to be under this law; and Adam's children, being not presently as soon as born under this law of reason, were not presently free: for law, in its true notion, is not so much the limitation as the direction of a free and intelligent agent to his proper interest, and prescribes no farther than is for the general good of those under that law: could they be happier without it, the law, as an useless thing, would of itself vanish; and that ill deserves the name of confinement which hedges us in only from bogs and precipices. So that, however it may be mistaken, the end of law is not to abolish or restrain, but to preserve and enlarge freedom: for in all the states of created beings capable of laws, where there is no law, there is no freedom: for liberty is, to be free from restraint and violence from others; which cannot be, where there is no law: but freedom is not, as we are told, a liberty for every man to do what he lists: (for who could be free, when every other man's humor might domineer over him?) but a liberty to dispose, and order as he lists, his person, actions, possessions, and his whole property, within the allowance of those laws under which he is, and therein not to be subject to the arbitrary will of another, but freely follow his own.

Sect. 58. The power, then, that parents have over their children, arises from that duty which is incumbent on them, to take care of their off-spring, during the imperfect state of childhood. To inform the mind, and govern the actions of their yet ignorant nonage, till reason shall take its place, and ease them of that trouble, is what the children want, and the parents are bound to: for God having given man an understanding to direct his actions, has allowed him a freedom of will, and liberty of acting, as properly belonging thereunto, within the bounds of that law he is under. But whilst he is in an estate, wherein he has not understanding of his own to direct his will, he is not to have any will of his own to follow: he that understands for him, must will for him too; he must prescribe to his will, and regulate his actions; but when he comes to the estate that made his father a freeman, the son is a freeman too.

Sect. 59. This holds in all the laws a man is under, whether natural or civil. Is a man under the law of nature? What made him free of that law? what gave him a free disposing of his property, according to his own will, within the compass of that law? I answer, a state of maturity wherein he might be supposed capable to know that law, that so he might keep his actions within the bounds of it. When he has acquired that state, he is presumed to know how far that law is to be his guide, and how far he may make use of his freedom, and so comes to have it; till then, some body else must guide him, who is presumed to know how far the law allows a liberty. If such a state of reason, such an age of discretion made him free, the same shall make his son free too. Is a man under the law of England? What made him free of that law? that is, to have the liberty to dispose of his actions and possessions according to his own will, within the permission of that law? A capacity of knowing that law; which is supposed by that law, at the age of one and twenty years, and in some cases sooner. If this made the father free, it shall make the son free too. Till then we see the law allows the son to have no will, but he is to be guided by the will of his father or guardian, who is to understand for him. And if the father die, and fail to substitute a deputy in his trust; if he hath not provided a tutor, to govern his son, during his minority, during his want of understanding, the law takes care to do it; some other must govern him, and be a will to him, till he hath attained to a state of freedom, and his understanding be fit to take the government of his will. But after that, the father and son are equally free as much as tutor and pupil after nonage; equally subjects of the same law together, without any dominion left in the father over the life, liberty, or estate of his son, whether they be only in the state and under the law of nature, or under the positive laws of an established government.

Sect. 60. But if, through defects that may happen out of the ordinary course of nature, any one comes not to such a degree of reason, wherein he might be supposed capable of knowing the law, and so living within the rules of it, he is never capable of being a free man, he is never let loose to the disposure of his own will (because he knows no bounds to it, has not understanding, its proper guide) but is continued under the tuition and government of others, all the time his own understanding is uncapable of that charge. And so lunatics and idiots are never set free from the government of their parents; children, who are not as yet come unto those years whereat they may have; and innocents which are excluded by a natural defect from ever having; thirdly, madmen, which for the present cannot possibly have the use of right reason to guide themselves, have for their guide, the reason that guided other men which are tutors over them, to seek and procure their good for them, says Hooker, Eccl. Pol. lib. i. sec. 7. All which seems no more than that duty, which God and nature has laid on man, as well as other creatures, to preserve their offspring, till they can be able to shift for themselves, and will scarce amount to an instance or proof of parents regal authority.

Sect. 61. Thus we are born free, as we are born rational; not that we have actually the exercise of either: age, that brings one, brings with it the other too. And thus we see how natural freedom and subjection to parents may consist together, and are both founded on the same principle. A child is free by his father's title, by his father's understanding, which is to govern him till he hath it of his own. The freedom of a man at years of discretion, and the subjection of a child to his parents, whilst yet short of that age, are so consistent, and so distinguishable, that the most blinded contenders for monarchy, by right of fatherhood, cannot miss this difference; the most obstinate cannot but allow their consistency: for were their doctrine all true, were the right heir of Adam now known, and by that title settled a monarch in his throne, invested with all the absolute unlimited power Sir Robert Filmer talks of; if he should die as soon as his heir were born, must not the child, notwithstanding he were never so free, never so much sovereign, be in subjection to his mother and

nurse, to tutors and governors, till age and education brought him reason and ability to govern himself and others? The necessities of his life, the health of his body, and the infor-
5 mation of his mind, would require him to be directed by the will of others, and not his own; and yet will any one think, that this restraint and subjection were inconsistent with, or spoiled him of that liberty or sovereignty he
10 had a right to, or gave away his empire to those who had the government of his nonage? This government over him only prepared him the better and sooner for it. If any body should ask me, when my son is of age to be
15 free? I shall answer, just when his monarch is of age to govern. But at what time, says the judicious Hooker, Eccl. Pol. l. i. sect. 6. a man may be said to have attained so far forth the use of reason, as sufficeth to make him capa-
20 ble of those laws whereby he is then bound to guide his actions: this is a great deal more easy for sense to discern, than for any one by skill and learning to determine.

25 Sect. 62. Common-wealths themselves take notice of, and allow, that there is a time when men are to begin to act like free men, and therefore till that time require not oaths of fealty, or allegiance, or other public owning of,
30 or submission to the government of their countries.

Sect. 63. The freedom then of man, and liberty of acting according to his own will, is ground-
35 ed on his having reason, which is able to in- struct him in that law he is to govern himself by, and make him know how far he is left to the freedom of his own will. To turn him loose to an unrestrained liberty, before he has
40 reason to guide him, is not the allowing him the privilege of his nature to be free; but to thrust him out amongst brutes, and abandon him to a state as wretched, and as much be-

neath that of a man, as their's. This is that
45 which puts the authority into the parents hands to govern the minority of their children. God hath made it their business to employ this care on their offspring, and hath placed in them suitable inclinations of tenderness and
50 concern to temper this power, to apply it, as his wisdom designed it, to the children's good, as long as they should need to be under it.

Sect. 64. But what reason can hence advance
55 this care of the parents due to their off-spring into an absolute arbitrary dominion of the father, whose power reaches no farther, than by such a discipline, as he finds most effectual, to give such strength and health to their bod-
60 ies, such vigor and rectitude to their minds, as may best fit his children to be most useful to themselves and others; and, if it be necessary to his condition, to make them work, when they are able, for their own subsistence. But in
65 this power the mother too has her share with the father.

Sect. 65. Nay, this power so little belongs to the father by any peculiar right of nature, but
70 only as he is guardian of his children, that when he quits his care of them, he loses his power over them, which goes along with their nourishment and education, to which it is in- separably annexed; and it belongs as much to
75 the foster-father of an exposed child, as to the natural father of another. So little power does the bare act of begetting give a man over his issue; if all his care ends there, and this be all the title he hath to the name and authority of a
80 father. And what will become of this paternal power in that part of the world, where one woman hath more than one husband at a time? or in those parts of America, where, when the husband and wife part, which hap-
85 pens frequently, the children are all left to the mother, follow her, and are wholly under her

care and provision? If the father die whilst the children are young, do they not naturally every where owe the same obedience to their mother, during their minority, as to their father
5 were he alive? and will any one say, that the mother hath a legislative power over her children? that she can make standing rules, which shall be of perpetual obligation, by which they ought to regulate all the concerns of their
10 property, and bound their liberty all the course of their lives? or can she enforce the observation of them with capital punishments? for this is the proper power of the magistrate, of which the father hath not so much as the
15 shadow. His command over his children is but temporary, and reaches not their life or property: it is but a help to the weakness and imperfection of their nonage, a discipline necessary to their education: and though a father
20 may dispose of his own possessions as he pleases, when his children are out of danger of perishing for want, yet his power extends not to the lives or goods, which either their own industry, or another's bounty has made their's;
25 nor to their liberty neither, when they are once arrived to the enfranchisement of the years of discretion. The father's empire then ceases, and he can from thence forwards no more dispose of the liberty of his son, than that of
30 any other man: and it must be far from an absolute or perpetual jurisdiction, from which a man may withdraw himself, having license from divine authority to leave father and mother, and cleave to his wife.
35

Sect. 66. But though there be a time when a child comes to be as free from subjection to the will and command of his father, as the father himself is free from subjection to the
40 will of any body else, and they are each under no other restraint, but that which is common to them both, whether it be the law of nature, or municipal law of their country; yet this

freedom exempts not a son from that honor
45 which he ought, by the law of God and nature, to pay his parents. God having made the parents instruments in his great design of continuing the race of mankind, and the occasions of life to their children; as he hath laid on
50 them an obligation to nourish, preserve, and bring up their offspring; so he has laid on the children a perpetual obligation of honoring their parents, which containing in it an inward esteem and reverence to be shown by all out-
55 ward expressions, ties up the child from any thing that may ever injure or affront, disturb or endanger, the happiness or life of those from whom he received his; and engages him in all actions of defense, relief, assistance and
60 comfort of those, by whose means he entered into being, and has been made capable of any enjoyments of life: from this obligation no state, no freedom can absolve children. But this is very far from giving parents a power of
65 command over their children, or an authority to make laws and dispose as they please of their lives or liberties. It is one thing to owe honor, respect, gratitude and assistance; another to require an absolute obedience and
70 submission. The honor due to parents, a monarch in his throne owes his mother; and yet this lessens not his authority, nor subjects him to her government.

75 Sect. 67. The subjection of a minor places in the father a temporary government, which terminates with the minority of the child: and the honor due from a child, places in the parents a perpetual right to respect, reverence,
80 support and compliance too, more or less, as the father's care, cost, and kindness in his education, has been more or less. This ends not with minority, but holds in all parts and conditions of a man's life. The want of distinguish-
85 ing these two powers, viz. that which the father hath in the right of tuition, during minori-

ty, and the right of honor all his life, may perhaps have caused a great part of the mistakes about this matter: for to speak properly of them, the first of these is rather the privilege of children, and duty of parents, than any prerogative of paternal power. The nourishment and education of their children is a charge so incumbent on parents for their children's good, that nothing can absolve them from taking care of it: and though the power of commanding and chastising them go along with it, yet God hath woven into the principles of human nature such a tenderness for their off-spring, that there is little fear that parents should use their power with too much rigor; the excess is seldom on the severe side, the strong byass of nature drawing the other way. And therefore God almighty when he would express his gentle dealing with the Israelites, he tells them, that though he chastened them, he chastened them as a man chastens his son, Deut. viii. 5. i.e. with tenderness and affection, and kept them under no severer discipline than what was absolutely best for them, and had been less kindness to have slackened. This is that power to which children are commanded obedience, that the pains and care of their parents may not be increased, or ill rewarded.

Sect. 68. On the other side, honor and support, all that which gratitude requires to return for the benefits received by and from them, is the indispensable duty of the child, and the proper privilege of the parents. This is intended for the parents advantage, as the other is for the child's; though education, the parents duty, seems to have most power, because the ignorance and infirmities of childhood stand in need of restraint and correction; which is a visible exercise of rule, and a kind of dominion. And that duty which is comprehended in the word honor, requires less obedience, though the obligation be stronger on grown, than younger children: for who can think the command, Children obey your parents, requires in a man, that has children of his own, the same submission to his father, as it does in his yet young children to him; and that by this precept he were bound to obey all his father's commands, if, out of a conceit of authority, he should have the indiscretion to treat him still as a boy?

Sect. 69. The first part then of paternal power, or rather duty, which is education, belongs so to the father, that it terminates at a certain season; when the business of education is over, it ceases of itself, and is also alienable before: for a man may put the tuition of his son in other hands; and he that has made his son an apprentice to another, has discharged him, during that time, of a great part of his obedience both to himself and to his mother. But all the duty of honor, the other part, remains never the less entire to them; nothing can cancel that: it is so inseparable from them both, that the father's authority cannot dispossess the mother of this right, nor can any man discharge his son from honoring her that bore him. But both these are very far from a power to make laws, and enforcing them with penalties, that may reach estate, liberty, limbs and life. The power of commanding ends with nonage; and though, after that, honor and respect, support and defense, and whatsoever gratitude can oblige a man to, for the highest benefits he is naturally capable of, be always due from a son to his parents; yet all this puts no scepter into the father's hand, no sovereign power of commanding. He has no dominion over his son's property, or actions; nor any right, that his will should prescribe to his son's in all things; however it may become his son in many things, not very inconvenient to him and his family, to pay a deference to it.

Sect. 70. A man may owe honor and respect to an ancient, or wise man; defense to his child or friend; relief and support to the distressed; and gratitude to a benefactor, to such a degree, that all he has, all he can do, cannot sufficiently pay it: but all these give no authority, no right to any one, of making laws over him from whom they are owing. And it is plain, all this is due not only to the bare title of father; not only because, as has been said, it is owing to the mother too; but because these obligations to parents, and the degrees of what is required of children, may be varied by the different care and kindness, trouble and expense, which is often employed upon one child more than another.

Sect. 71. This shows the reason how it comes to pass, that parents in societies, where they themselves are subjects, retain a power over their children, and have as much right to their subjection, as those who are in the state of nature. Which could not possibly be, if all political power were only paternal, and that in truth they were one and the same thing: for then, all paternal power being in the prince, the subject could naturally have none of it. But these two powers, political and paternal, are so perfectly distinct and separate; are built upon so different foundations, and given to so different ends, that every subject that is a father, has as much a paternal power over his children, as the prince has over his: and every prince, that has parents, owes them as much filial duty and obedience, as the meanest of his subjects do to their's; and can therefore contain not any part or degree of that kind of dominion, which a prince or magistrate has over his subject.

Sect. 72. Though the obligation on the parents to bring up their children, and the obligation on children to honor their parents, contain all the power on the one hand, and submission on the other, which are proper to this relation, yet there is another power ordinarily in the father, whereby he has a tie on the obedience of his children; which tho' it be common to him with other men, yet the occasions of showing it, almost consich tho' it be common to him with other men, yet the occasions of showing it, almost constantly happening to fathers in their private families, and the instances of it elsewhere being rare, and less taken notice of, it passes in the world for a part of paternal jurisdiction. And this is the power men generally have to bestow their estates on those who please them best; the possession of the father being the expectation and inheritance of the children, ordinarily in certain proportions, according to the law and custom of each country; yet it is commonly in the father's power to bestow it with a more sparing or liberal hand, according as the behavior of this or that child hath comported with his will and humor.

Sect. 73. This is no small tie on the obedience of children: and there being always annexed to the enjoyment of land, a submission to the government of the country, of which that land is a part; it has been commonly supposed, that a father could oblige his posterity to that government, of which he himself was a subject, and that his compact held them; whereas, it being only a necessary condition annexed to the land, and the inheritance of an estate which is under that government, reaches only those who will take it on that condition, and so is no natural tie or engagement, but a voluntary submission: for every man's children being by nature as free as himself, or any of his ancestors ever were, may, whilst they are in that freedom, choose what society they will join themselves to, what commonwealth they will put themselves under. But if they will enjoy the inheritance of their ancestors, they must take it on the same terms their ancestors had it, and submit to all the conditions annexed to such a possession. By this power

5 indeed fathers oblige their children to obedience to themselves, even when they are past minority, and most commonly too subject them to this or that political power: but neither of these by any peculiar right of father-

10 hood, but by the reward they have in their hands to enforce and recompense such a compliance; and is no more power than what a French man has over an English man, who by the hopes of an estate he will leave him, will

15 certainly have a strong tie on his obedience: and if, when it is left him, he will enjoy it, he must certainly take it upon the conditions annexed to the possession of land in that country where it lies, whether it be France or Eng-

20 land.

Sect. 74. To conclude then, tho' the father's power of commanding extends no farther than the minority of his children, and to a de-

25 gree only fit for the discipline and government of that age; and tho' that honor and respect, and all that which the Latins called piety, which they indispensably owe to their parents all their life-time, and in all estates, with all

30 that support and defense is due to them, gives the father no power of governing, i.e. making laws and enacting penalties on his children; though by all this he has no dominion over the property or actions of his son: yet it is ob-

35 vious to conceive how easy it was, in the first ages of the world, and in places still, where the thinness of people gives families leave to separate into unpossessed quarters, and they have room to remove or plant themselves in yet

40 vacant habitations, for the father of the family to become the prince of it[8]; he had been a

ruler from the beginning of the infancy of his children: and since without some government it would be hard for them to live together, it

45 was likeliest it should, by the express or tacit consent of the children when they were grown up, be in the father, where it seemed without any change barely to continue; when indeed nothing more was required to it, than the

50 permitting the father to exercise alone, in his family, that executive power of the law of nature, which every free man naturally hath, and by that permission resigning up to him a monarchical power, whilst they remained in it.

55 But that this was not by any paternal right, but only by the consent of his children, is evident from hence, that no body doubts, but if a stranger, whom chance or business had brought to his family, had there killed any of

60 his children, or committed any other fact, he might condemn and put him to death, or otherwise have punished him, as well as any of his children; which it was impossible he should do by virtue of any paternal authority

65 over one who was not his child, but by virtue of that executive power of the law of nature,

---

[8] *It is no improbable opinion therefore, which the archphilosopher was of, that the chief person in every household was always, as it were, a king: so when numbers of households joined themselves in civil societies together, kings were the first kind of governors amongst them, which is also, as it seemeth, the reason why the name of fathers continued still in them, who, of fathers, were made rulers; as also the ancient custom of governors to do as Melchizedec, and being kings, to exercise the office of priests, which fathers did at the first, grew perhaps by the same occasion. Howbeit, this is not the only kind of regiment that has been received in the world. The inconveniences of one kind have caused sundry others to be devised; so that in a word, all public regiment, of what kind soever, seemeth evidently to have risen from the deliberate advice, consultation and composition between men, judging it convenient and behoveful; there being no impossibility in nature considered by itself, but that man might have lived without any public regiment,* Hooker's Eccl. Pol. lib. i. sect. 10

which, as a man, he had a right to: and he alone could punish him in his family, where the respect of his children had laid by the exercise of such a power, to give way to the dignity and authority they were willing should remain in him, above the rest of his family.

Sect. 75. Thus it was easy, and almost natural for children, by a tacit, and scarce avoidable consent, to make way for the father's authority and government. They had been accustomed in their childhood to follow his direction, and to refer their little differences to him, and when they were men, who fitter to rule them? Their little properties, and less covetousness, seldom afforded greater controversies; and when any should arise, where could they have a fitter umpire than he, by whose care they had every one been sustained and brought up, and who had a tenderness for them all? It is no wonder that they made no distinction betwixt minority and full age; nor looked after one and twenty, or any other age that might make them the free disposers of themselves and fortunes, when they could have no desire to be out of their pupilage: the government they had been under, during it, continued still to be more their protection than restraint; and they could no where find a greater security to their peace, liberties, and fortunes, than in the rule of a father.

Sect. 76. Thus the natural fathers of families, by an insensible change, became the politic monarchs of them too: and as they chanced to live long, and leave able and worthy heirs, for several successions, or otherwise; so they laid the foundations of hereditary, or elective kingdoms, under several constitutions and mannors, according as chance, contrivance, or occasions happened to mold them. But if princes have their titles in their fathers right, and it be a sufficient proof of the natural right

of fathers to political authority, because they commonly were those in whose hands we find, de facto, the exercise of government: I say, if this argument be good, it will as strongly prove, that all princes, nay princes only, ought to be priests, since it is as certain, that in the beginning, the father of the family was priest, as that he was ruler in his own household.

CHAPTER VII
OF POLITICAL OR CIVIL SOCIETY

Sect. 77. GOD having made man such a creature, that in his own judgment, it was not good for him to be alone, put him under strong obligations of necessity, convenience, and inclination to drive him into society, as well as fitted him with understanding and language to continue and enjoy it. The first society was between man and wife, which gave beginning to that between parents and children; to which, in time, that between master and servant came to be added: and though all these might, and commonly did meet together, and make up but one family, wherein the master or mistress of it had some sort of rule proper to a family; each of these, or all together, came short of political society, as we shall see, if we consider the different ends, ties, and bounds of each of these.

Sect. 78. Conjugal society is made by a voluntary compact between man and woman; and tho' it consist chiefly in such a communion and right in one another's bodies as is necessary to its chief end, procreation; yet it draws with it mutual support and assistance, and a communion of interests too, as necessary not only to unite their care and affection, but also necessary to their common off-spring, who have a right to be nourished, and maintained by them, till they are able to provide for themselves.

Sect. 79. For the end of conjunction, between male and female, being not barely procreation, but the continuation of the species; this conjunction betwixt male and female ought to last, even after procreation, so long as is necessary to the nourishment and support of the young ones, who are to be sustained even after procreation, so long as is necessary to the nourishment and support of the young ones, who are to be sustained by those that got them, till they are able to shift and provide for themselves. This rule, which the infinite wise maker hath set to the works of his hands, we find the inferior creatures steadily obey. In those viviparous animals which feed on grass, the conjunction between male and female lasts no longer than the very act of copulation; because the teat of the dam being sufficient to nourish the young, till it be able to feed on grass, the male only begets, but concerns not himself for the female or young, to whose sustenance he can contribute nothing. But in beasts of prey the conjunction lasts longer: because the dam not being able well to subsist herself, and nourish her numerous off-spring by her own prey alone, a more laborious, as well as more dangerous way of living, than by feeding on grass, the assistance of the male is necessary to the maintenance of their common family, which cannot subsist till they are able to prey for themselves, but by the joint care of male and female. The same is to be observed in all birds, (except some domestic ones, where plenty of food excuses the cock from feeding, and taking care of the young brood) whose young needing food in the nest, the cock and hen continue mates, till the young are able to use their wing, and provide for themselves.

Sect. 80. And herein I think lies the chief, if not the only reason, why the male and female in mankind are tied to a longer conjunction than other creatures, viz. because the female is capable of conceiving, and de facto is commonly with child again, and brings forth too a new birth, long before the former is out of a dependency for support on his parents help, and able to shift for himself, and has all the assistance is due to him from his parents: whereby the father, who is bound to take care for those he hath begot, is under an obligation to continue in conjugal society with the same woman longer than other creatures, whose young being able to subsist of themselves, before the time of procreation returns again, the conjugal bond dissolves of itself, and they are at liberty, till Hymen at his usual anniversary season summons them again to chose new mates. Wherein one cannot but admire the wisdom of the great Creator, who having given to man foresight, and an ability to lay up for the future, as well as to supply the present necessity, hath made it necessary, that society of man and wife should be more lasting, than of male and female amongst other creatures; that so their industry might be encouraged, and their interest better united, to make provision and lay up goods for their common issue, which uncertain mixture, or easy and frequent solutions of conjugal society would mightily disturb.

Sect. 81. But tho' these are ties upon mankind, which make the conjugal bonds more firm and lasting in man, than the other species of animals; yet it would give one reason to enquire, why this compact, where procreation and education are secured, and inheritance taken care for, may not be made determinable, either by consent, or at a certain time, or upon certain conditions, as well as any other voluntary compacts, there being no necessity in the nature of the thing, nor to the ends of it, that it should always be for life; I mean, to such as are under no restraint of any positive law, which ordains all such contracts to be perpetual.

Sect. 82. But the husband and wife, though they have but one common concern, yet having different understandings, will unavoidably sometimes have different wills too; it therefore being necessary that the last determination, i. e. the rule, should be placed somewhere; it naturally falls to the man's share, as the abler and the stronger. But this reaching but to the things of their common interest and property, leaves the wife in the full and free possession of what by contract is her peculiar right, and gives the husband no more power over her life than she has over his; the power of the husband being so far from that of an absolute monarch, that the wife has in many cases a liberty to separate from him, where natural right, or their contract allows it; whether that contract be made by themselves in the state of nature, or by the customs or laws of the country they live in; and the children upon such separation fall to the father or mother's lot, as such contract does determine.

Sect. 83. For all the ends of marriage being to be obtained under politic government, as well as in the state of nature, the civil magistrate doth not abridge the right or power of either naturally necessary to those ends, viz. procreation and mutual support and assistance whilst they are together; but only decides any controversy that may arise between man and wife about them. If it were otherwise, and that absolute sovereignty and power of life and death naturally belonged to the husband, and were necessary to the society between man and wife, there could be no matrimony in any of those countries where the husband is allowed no such absolute authority. But the ends of matrimony requiring no such power in the husband, the condition of conjugal society put it not in him, it being not at all necessary to that state. Conjugal society could subsist and attain its ends without it; nay, community of goods, and the power over them, mutual assistance and maintenance, and other things belonging to conjugal society, might be varied and regulated by that contract which unites man and wife in that society, as far as may consist with procreation and the bringing up of children till they could shift for themselves; nothing being necessary to any society, that is not necessary to the ends for which it is made.

Sect. 84. The society betwixt parents and children, and the distinct rights and powers belonging respectively to them, I have treated of so largely, in the foregoing chapter, that I shall not here need to say any thing of it. And I think it is plain, that it is far different from a politic society.

Sect. 85. Master and servant are names as old as history, but given to those of far different condition; for a freeman makes himself a servant to another, by selling him, for a certain time, the service he undertakes to do, in exchange for wages he is to receive: and though this commonly puts him into the family of his master, and under the ordinary discipline thereof; yet it gives the master but a temporary power over him, and no greater than what is contained in the contract between them. But there is another sort of servants, which by a peculiar name we call slaves, who being captives taken in a just war, are by the right of nature subjected to the absolute dominion and arbitrary power of their masters. These men having, as I say, forfeited their lives, and with it their liberties, and lost their estates; and being in the state of slavery, not capable of any property, cannot in that state be considered as any part of civil society; the chief end whereof is the preservation of property.

Sect. 86. Let us therefore consider a master of a family with all these subordinate relations of wife, children, servants, and slaves, united under the domestic rule of a family; which, what

5 resemblance soever it may have in its order, offices, and number too, with a little commonwealth, yet is very far from it, both in its constitution, power and end: or if it must be thought a monarchy, and the paterfamilias the

10 absolute monarch in it, absolute monarchy will have but a very shattered and short power, when it is plain, by what has been said before, that the master of the family has a very distinct and differently limited power, both as to time

15 and extent, over those several persons that are in it; for excepting the slave (and the family is as much a family, and his power as paterfamilias as great, whether there be any slaves in his family or no) he has no legislative power of

20 life and death over any of them, and none too but what a mistress of a family may have as well as he. And he certainly can have no absolute power over the whole family, who has but a very limited one over every individual in it.

25 But how a family, or any other society of men, differ from that which is properly political society, we shall best see, by considering wherein political society itself consists.

30 Sect. 87. Man being born, as has been proved, with a title to perfect freedom, and an uncontrolled enjoyment of all the rights and privileges of the law of nature, equally with any other man, or number of men in the world, hath by

35 nature a power, not only to preserve his property, that is, his life, liberty and estate, against the injuries and attempts of other men; but to judge of, and punish the breaches of that law in others, as he is persuaded the offence de-

40 serves, even with death itself, in crimes where the heinousness of the fact, in his opinion, requires it. But because no political society can be, nor subsist, without having in itself the power to preserve the property, and in order

45 thereunto, punish the offences of all those of that society; there, and there only is political society, where every one of the members hath quitted this natural power, resigned it up into the hands of the community in all cases that

50 exclude him not from appealing for protection to the law established by it. And thus all private judgment of every particular member being excluded, the community comes to be umpire, by settled standing rules, indifferent,

55 and the same to all parties; and by men having authority from the community, for the execution of those rules, decides all the differences that may happen between any members of that society concerning any matter of right;

60 and punishes those offences which any member hath committed against the society, with such penalties as the law has established: whereby it is easy to discern, who are, and who are not, in political society together.

65 Those who are united into one body, and have a common established law and judicature to appeal to, with authority to decide controversies between them, and punish offenders, are in civil society one with another: but those

70 who have no such common appeal, I mean on earth, are still in the state of nature, each being, where there is no other, judge for himself, and executioner; which is, as I have before showed it, the perfect state of nature.

75

Sect. 88. And thus the commonwealth comes by a power to set down what punishment shall belong to the several transgressions which they think worthy of it, committed amongst

80 the members of that society, (which is the power of making laws) as well as it has the power to punish any injury done unto any of its members, by any one that is not of it, (which is the power of war and peace;) and all

85 this for the preservation of the property of all the members of that society, as far as is possi-

ble. But though every man who has entered into civil society, and is become a member of any commonwealth, has thereby quitted his power to punish offences, against the law of nature, in prosecution of his own private judgment, yet with the judgment of offences, which he has given up to the legislative in all cases, where he can appeal to the magistrate, he has given a right to the commonwealth to employ his force, for the execution of the judgments of the commonwealth, whenever he shall be called to it; which indeed are his own judgments, they being made by himself, or his representative. And herein we have the original of the legislative and executive power of civil society, which is to judge by standing laws, how far offences are to be punished, when committed within the commonwealth; and also to determine, by occasional judgments founded on the present circumstances of the fact, how far injuries from without are to be vindicated; and in both these to employ all the force of all the members, when there shall be need.

Sect. 89. Where-ever therefore any number of men are so united into one society, as to quit every one his executive power of the law of nature, and to resign it to the public, there and there only is a political, or civil society. And this is done, where-ever any number of men, in the state of nature, enter into society to make one people, one body politic, under one supreme government; or else when any one joins himself to, and incorporates with any government already made: for hereby he authorizes the society, or which is all one, the legislative thereof, to make laws for him, as the public good of the society shall require; to the execution whereof, his own assistance (as to his own decrees) is due. And this puts men out of a state of nature into that of a commonwealth, by setting up a judge on earth, with authority to determine all the controversies, and redress the injuries that may happen to any member of the commonwealth; which judge is the legislative, or magistrates appointed by it. And where-ever there are any number of men, however associated, that have no such decisive power to appeal to, there they are still in the state of nature.

Sect. 90. Hence it is evident, that absolute monarchy, which by some men is counted the only government in the world, is indeed inconsistent with civil society, and so can be no form of civil-government at all: for the end of civil society, being to avoid, and remedy those inconveniencies of the state of nature, which necessarily follow from every man's being judge in his own case, by setting up a known authority, to which every one of that society may appeal upon any injury received, or controversy that may arise, and which every one of the society ought to obey; where-ever any persons are, who have not such an authority to appeal to, for the decision of any difference between them, there those persons are still in the state of nature; and so is every absolute prince, in respect of those who are under his dominion.

Sect. 91. For he being supposed to have all, both legislative and executive power in himself alone, there is no judge to be found, no appeal lies open to any one, who may fairly, and indifferently, and with authority decide, and from whose decision relief and redress may be expected of any injury or inconviency, that may be suffered from the prince, or by his order: so that such a man, however intitled, Czar, or Grand Seignior, or how you please, is as much in the state of nature, with all under his dominion, as he is with the rest of mankind: for where-ever any two men are, who have no standing rule, and common judge to appeal to on earth, for the determination of controversies of right betwixt them, there they are still in the state of nature[9], and under all the inconveniencies of it, with only this woeful

5   difference to the subject, or rather slave of an absolute prince: that whereas, in the ordinary state of nature, he has a liberty to judge of his right, and according to the best of his power, to maintain it; now, whenever his property is

10 invaded by the will and order of his monarch, he has not only no appeal, as those in society ought to have, but as if he were degraded from the common state of rational creatures, is denied a liberty to judge of, or to defend his

15 right; and so is exposed to all the misery and inconveniencies, that a man can fear from one, who being in the unrestrained state of nature, is yet corrupted with flattery, and armed with power.

20

Sect. 92. For he that thinks absolute power purifies men's blood, and corrects the base-

---

[9] *To take away all such mutual grievances, injuries and wrongs, i.e. such as attend men in the state of nature, there was no way but only by growing into composition and agreement amongst themselves, by ordaining some kind of government public, and by yielding themselves subject thereunto, that unto whom they granted authority to rule and govern, by them the peace, tranquility and happy estate of the rest might be procured. Men always knew that where force and injury was offered, they might be defenders of themselves; they knew that however men may seek their own commodity, yet if this were done with injury unto others, it was not to be suffered, but by all men, and all good means to be withstood. Finally, they knew that no man might in reason take upon him to determine his own right, and according to his own deter-mination proceed in maintenance thereof, in as much as every man is towards himself, and them whom he greatly affects, partial; and therefore that strifes and troubles would be endless, except they gave their common consent, all to be ordered by some, whom they should agree upon, without which consent there would be no reason that one man should take upon him to be lord or judge over anoth-er,* Hooker's Eccl. Pol. l. i. sect. 10

ness of human nature, need read but the histo-ry of this, or any other age, to be convinced of

25 the contrary. He that would have been inso-lent and injurious in the woods of America, would not probably be much better in a throne; where perhaps learning and religion shall be found out to justify all that he shall do

30 to his subjects, and the sword presently silence all those that dare question it: for what the protection of absolute monarchy is, what kind of fathers of their countries it makes princes to be and to what a degree of happiness and

35 security it carries civil society, where this sort of government is grown to perfection, he that will look into the late relation of Ceylon, may easily see.

40 Sect. 93. In absolute monarchies indeed, as well as other governments of the world, the subjects have an appeal to the law, and judges to decide any controversies, and restrain any violence that may happen betwixt the subjects

45 themselves, one amongst another. This every one thinks necessary, and believes he deserves to be thought a declared enemy to society and mankind, who should go about to take it away. But whether this be from a true love of man-

50 kind and society, and such a charity as we owe all one to another, there is reason to doubt: for this is no more than what every man, who loves his own power, profit, or greatness, may and naturally must do, keep those animals

55 from hurting, or destroying one another, who labor and drudge only for his pleasure and advantage; and so are taken care of, not out of any love the master has for them, but love of himself, and the profit they bring him: for if it

60 be asked, what security, what fence is there, in such a state, against the violence and oppres-sion of this absolute ruler? the very question can scarce be borne. They are ready to tell you, that it deserves death only to ask after

65 safety. Betwixt subject and subject, they will

grant, there must be measures, laws and judges, for their mutual peace and security: but as for the ruler, he ought to be absolute, and is above all such circumstances; because he has power to do more hurt and wrong, it is right when he does it. To ask how you may be guarded from harm, or injury, on that side where the strongest hand is to do it, is presently the voice of faction and rebellion: as if when men quitting the state of nature entered into society, they agreed that all of them but one, should be under the restraint of laws, but that he should still retain all the liberty of the state of nature, increased with power, and made licentious by impunity. This is to think, that men are so foolish, that they take care to avoid what mischiefs may be done them by pole-cats, or foxes; but are content, nay, think it safety, to be devoured by lions.

Sect. 94. But whatever flatterers may talk to amuse people's understandings, it hinders not men from feeling; and when they perceive, that any man, in what station soever, is out of the bounds of the civil society which they are of, and that they have no appeal on earth against any harm, they may receive from him, they are apt to think themselves in the state of nature, in respect of him whom they find to be so; and to take care, as soon as they can, to have that safety and security in civil society, for which it was first instituted, and for which only they entered into it. And therefore, though perhaps at first, (as shall be showed more at large hereafter in the following part of this discourse) some one good and excellent man having got a pre-eminency amongst the rest, had this deference paid to his goodness and virtue, as to a kind of natural authority, that the chief rule, with arbitration of their differences, by a tacit consent devolved into his hands, without any other caution, but the assurance they had of his uprightness and wisdom; yet when time, giving authority, and (as some men would persuade us) sacredness of customs, which the negligent, and unforeseeing innocence of the first ages began, had brought in successors of another stamp, the people finding their properties not secure under the government, as then it was, (whereas government has no other end but the preservation of property[10]) could never be safe nor at rest, nor think themselves in civil society, till the legislature was placed in collective bodies of men, call them senate, parliament, or what you please. By which means every single person became subject, equally with other the meanest men, to those laws, which he himself, as part of the legislative, had established; nor could any one, by his own authority; avoid the force of the law, when once made; nor by any pretense of superiority plead exemption, thereby to license his own, or the miscarriages of any of his dependents.[11] No man in civil society can be exempted from the laws of it: for if any man may do what he thinks fit, and there be no appeal on earth, for redress or security against any harm he shall do; I ask, whether he be not perfectly still in the state of nature, and so can be no part or member of that civil society; unless any one will say, the

---

[10] *At the first, when some certain kind of regiment was once appointed, it may be that nothing was then farther thought upon for the manner of governing, but all permitted unto their wisdom and discretion, which were to rule, till by experience they found this for all parts very inconvenient, so as the thing which they had devised for a remedy, did indeed but increase the sore, which it should have cured. They saw, that to live by one man's will, became the cause of all men's misery. This constrained them to come unto laws, wherein all men might see their duty beforehand, and know the penalties of transgressing them.* Hooker's Eccl. Pol. l. i. sect. 10

[11] *Civil law being the act of the whole body politic, doth therefore over-rule each several part of the same body.* Hooker, ibid.

state of nature and civil society are one and the same thing, which I have never yet found any one so great a patron of anarchy as to affirm.

CHAPTER VIII
OF THE BEGINNING OF POLITICAL SOCIETIES

Sect. 95. MEN being, as has been said, by nature, all free, equal, and independent, no one can be put out of this estate, and subjected to the political power of another, without his own consent. The only way whereby any one divests himself of his natural liberty, and puts on the bonds of civil society, is by agreeing with other men to join and unite into a community for their comfortable, safe, and peaceable living one amongst another, in a secure enjoyment of their properties, and a greater security against any, that are not of it. This any number of men may do, because it injures not the freedom of the rest; they are left as they were in the liberty of the state of nature. When any number of men have so consented to make one community or government, they are thereby presently incorporated, and make one body politic, wherein the majority have a right to act and conclude the rest.

Sect. 96. For when any number of men have, by the consent of every individual, made a community, they have thereby made that community one body, with a power to act as one body, which is only by the will and determination of the majority: for that which acts any community, being only the consent of the individuals of it, and it being necessary to that which is one body to move one way; it is necessary the body should move that way whither the greater force carries it, which is the consent of the majority: or else it is impossible it should act or continue one body, one com-

munity, which the consent of every individual that united into it, agreed that it should; and so every one is bound by that consent to be concluded by the majority. And therefore we see, that in assemblies, empowered to act by positive laws, where no number is set by that positive law which empowers them, the act of the majority passes for the act of the whole, and of course determines, as having, by the law of nature and reason, the power of the whole.

Sect. 97. And thus every man, by consenting with others to make one body politic under one government, puts himself under an obligation, to every one of that society, to submit to the determination of the majority, and to be concluded by it; or else this original compact, whereby he with others incorporates into one society, would signify nothing, and be no compact, if he be left free, and under no other ties than he was in before in the state of nature. For what appearance would there be of any compact? what new engagement if he were no farther tied by any decrees of the society, than he himself thought fit, and did actually consent to? This would be still as great a liberty, as he himself had before his compact, or any one else in the state of nature hath, who may submit himself, and consent to any acts of it if he thinks fit.

Sect. 98. For if the consent of the majority shall not, in reason, be received as the act of the whole, and conclude every individual; nothing but the consent of every individual can make any thing to be the act of the whole: but such a consent is next to impossible ever to be had, if we consider the infirmities of health, and avocations of business, which in a number, though much less than that of a commonwealth, will necessarily keep many away from the public assembly. To which if we add the variety of opinions, and contrariety

of interests, which unavoidably happen in all collections of men, the coming into society upon such terms would be only like Cato's coming into the theatre, only to go out again.
5 Such a constitution as this would make the mighty Leviathan of a shorter duration, than the feeblest creatures, and not let it outlast the day it was born in: which cannot be supposed, till we can think, that rational creatures should
10 desire and constitute societies only to be dissolved: for where the majority cannot conclude the rest, there they cannot act as one body, and consequently will be immediately dissolved again.
15

Sect. 99. Whosoever therefore out of a state of nature unite into a community, must be understood to give up all the power, necessary to the ends for which they unite into society, to
20 the majority of the community, unless they expressly agreed in any number greater than the majority. And this is done by barely agreeing to unite into one political society, which is all the compact that is, or needs be, between
25 the individuals, that enter into, or make up a commonwealth. And thus that, which begins and actually constitutes any political society, is nothing but the consent of any number of freemen capable of a majority to unite and
30 incorporate into such a society. And this is that, and that only, which did, or could give beginning to any lawful government in the world.

35 Sect. 100. To this I find two objections made. First, That there are no instances to be found in story, of a company of men independent, and equal one amongst another, that met together, and in this way began and set up a
40 government.

Secondly, It is impossible of right, that men should do so, because all men being born un-

der government, they are to submit to that,
45 and are not at liberty to begin a new one.

Sect. 101. To the first there is this to answer, That it is not at all to be wondered, that history gives us but a very little account of men, that lived together in the state of nature. The
50 inconveniences of that condition, and the love and want of society, no sooner brought any number of them together, but they presently united and incorporated, if they designed to continue together. And if we may not suppose
55 men ever to have been in the state of nature, because we hear not much of them in such a state, we may as well suppose the armies of Salmanasser or Xerxes were never children, because we hear little of them, till they were
60 men, and embodied in armies. Government is every where antecedent to records, and letters seldom come in amongst a people till a long continuation of civil society has, by other more necessary arts, provided for their safety,
65 ease, and plenty: and then they begin to look after the history of their founders, and search into their original, when they have outlived the memory of it: for it is with commonwealths as with particular persons, they are commonly
70 ignorant of their own births and infancies: and if they know any thing of their original, they are beholden for it, to the accidental records that others have kept of it. And those that we have, of the beginning of any polities in the
75 world, excepting that of the Jews, where God himself immediately interposed, and which favors not at all paternal dominion, are all either plain instances of such a beginning as I
80 have mentioned, or at least have manifest footsteps of it.

Sect. 102. He must show a strange inclination to deny evident matter of fact, when it agrees
85 not with his hypothesis, who will not allow, that show a strange inclination to deny evident

matter of fact, when it agrees not with his hypothesis, who will not allow, that the beginning of Rome and Venice were by the uniting together of several men free and independent one of another, amongst whom there was no natural superiority or subjection. And if Josephus Acosta's word may be taken, he tells us, that in many parts of America there was no government at all.

There are great and apparent conjectures, says he, that these men, speaking of those of Peru, for a long time had neither kings nor commonwealths, but lived in troops, as they do this day in Florida, the Cheriquanas, those of Brazil, and many other nations, which have no certain kings, but as occasion is offered, in peace or war, they choose their captains as they please, 1. i. c. 25.

If it be said, that every man there was born subject to his father, or the head of his family; that the subjection due from a child to a father took not away his freedom of uniting into what political society he thought fit, has been already proved. But be that as it will, these men, it is evident, were actually free; and whatever superiority some politicians now would place in any of them, they themselves claimed it not, but by consent were all equal, till by the same consent they set rulers over themselves. So that their politic societies all began from a voluntary union, and the mutual agreement of men freely acting in the choice of their governors, and forms of government.

Sect. 103. And I hope those who went away from Sparta with Palantus, mentioned by Justin, 1. iii. c. 4. will be allowed to have been freemen independent one of another, and to have set up a government over themselves, by their own consent. Thus I have given several examples, out of history, of people free and in the state of nature, that being met together incorporated and began a commonwealth. And if the want of such instances be an argument to prove that government were not, nor could not be so begun, I suppose the contenders for paternal empire were better let it alone, than urge it against natural liberty: for if they can give so many instances, out of history, of governments begun upon paternal right, I think (though at best an argument from what has been, to what should of right be, has no great force) one might, without any great danger, yield them the cause. But if I might advise them in the case, they would do well not to search too much into the original of governments, as they have begun de facto, lest they should find, at the foundation of most of them, something very little favorable to the design they promote, and such a power as they contend for.

Sect. 104. But to conclude, reason being plain on our side, that men are naturally free, and the examples of history showing, that the governments of the world, that were begun in peace, had their beginning laid on that foundation, and were made by the consent of the people; there can be little room for doubt, either where the right is, or what has been the opinion, or practice of mankind, about the first erecting of governments.

Sect. 105. I will not deny, that if we look back as far as history will direct us, towards the original of commonwealths, we shall generally find them under the government and administration of one man. And I am also apt to believe, that where a family was numerous enough to subsist by itself, and continued entire together, without mixing with others, as it often happens, where there is much land, and few people, the government commonly began in the father: for the father having, by the law of nature, the same power with every man else to punish, as he thought fit, any offences against that law, might thereby punish his transgressing children, even when they were

5 men, and out of their pupilage; and they were very likely to submit to his punishment, and all join with him against the offender, in their turns, giving him thereby power to execute his sentence against any transgression, and so in

10 effect make him the law-maker, and governor over all that remained in conjunction with his family. He was fittest to be trusted; paternal affection secured their property and interest under his care; and the custom of obeying

15 him, in their childhood, made it easier to submit to him, rather than to any other. If therefore they must have one to rule them, as government is hardly to be avoided amongst men that live together; who so likely to be the man

20 as he that was their common father; unless negligence, cruelty, or any other defect of mind or body made him unfit for it? But when either the father died, and left his next heir, for want of age, wisdom, courage, or any other

25 qualities, less fit for rule; or where several families met, and consented to continue together; there, it is not to be doubted, but they used their natural freedom, to set up him, whom they judged the ablest, and most likely, to rule

30 well over them. Conformable hereunto we find the people of America, who (living out of the reach of the conquering swords, and spreading domination of the two great empires of Peru and Mexico) enjoyed their own

35 natural freedom, though, ceteris paribus, they commonly prefer the heir of their deceased king; yet if they find him any way weak, or uncapable, they pass him by, and set up the stoutest and bravest man for their ruler.

40 Sect. 106. Thus, though looking back as far as records give us any account of peopling the world, and the history of nations, we com-

monly find the government to be in one hand;

45 yet it destroys not that which I affirm, viz. that the beginning of politic society depends upon the consent of the individuals, to join into, and make one society; who, when they are thus incorporated, might set up what form of gov-

50 ernment they thought fit. But this having given occasion to men to mistake, and think, that by nature government was monarchical, and belonged to the father, it may not be amiss here to consider, why people in the beginning

55 generally pitched upon this form, which though perhaps the father's pre-eminency might, in the first institution of some commonwealths, give a rise to, and place in the beginning, the power in one hand; yet it is

60 plain that the reason, that continued the form of government in a single person, was not any regard, or respect to paternal authority; since all petty monarchies, that is, almost all monarchies, near their original, have been common-

65 ly, at least upon occasion, elective.

Sect. 107. First then, in the beginning of things, the father's government of the childhood of those sprung from him, having accus-

70 tomed them to the rule of one man, and taught them that where it was exercised with care and skill, with affection and love to those under it, it was sufficient to procure and preserve to men all the political happiness they

75 sought for in society. It was no wonder that they should pitch upon, and naturally run into that form of government, which from their infancy they had been all accustomed to; and which, by experience, they had found both

80 easy and safe. To which, if we add, that monarchy being simple, and most obvious to men, whom neither experience had instructed in forms of government, nor the ambition or insolence of empire had taught to beware of

85 the encroachments of prerogative, or the inconveniences of absolute power, which mon-

archy in succession was apt to lay claim to, and bring upon them, it was not at all strange, that they should not much trouble themselves to think of methods of restraining any exorbi-
5 tances of those to whom they had given the authority over them, and of balancing the power of government, by placing several parts of it in different hands. They had neither felt the oppression of tyrannical dominion, nor did
10 the fashion of the age, nor their possessions, or way of living, (which afforded little matter for covetousness or ambition) give them any reason to apprehend or provide against it; and therefore it is no wonder they put themselves
15 into such a frame of government, as was not only, as I said, most obvious and simple, but also best suited to their present state and condition; which stood more in need of defense against foreign invasions and injuries, than of
20 multiplicity of laws. The equality of a simple poor way of living, confining their desires within the narrow bounds of each man's small property, made few controversies, and so no need of many laws to decide them, or variety
25 of officers to superintend the process, or look after the execution of justice, where there were but few trespasses, and few offenders. Since then those, who like one another so well as to join into society, cannot but be supposed to
30 have some acquaintance and friendship together, and some trust one in another; they could not but have greater apprehensions of others, than of one another: and therefore their first care and thought cannot but be sup-
35 posed to be, how to secure themselves against foreign force. It was natural for them to put themselves under a frame of government which might best serve to that end, and chose the wisest and bravest man to conduct them in
40 their wars, and lead them out against their enemies, and in this chiefly be their ruler. Sect. 108. Thus we see, that the kings of the Indians in America, which is still a pattern of

the first ages in Asia and Europe, whilst the
45 inhabitants were too few for the country, and want of people and money gave men no temptation to enlarge their possessions of land, or contest for wider extent of ground, are little more than generals of their armies; and
50 though they command absolutely in war, yet at home and in time of peace they exercise very little dominion, and have but a very moderate sovereignty, the resolutions of peace and war being ordinarily either in the people, or in a
55 council. Tho' the war itself, which admits not of plurality of governors, naturally devolves the command into the king's sole authority.

Sect. 109. And thus in Israel itself, the chief
60 business of their judges, and first kings, seems to have been to be captains in war, and leaders of their armies; which (besides what is signified by going out and in before the people, which was, to march forth to war, and home
65 again in the heads of their forces) appears plainly in the story of Iephtha. The Ammonites making war upon Israel, the Gileadites in fear send to Iephtha, a bastard of their family whom they had cast off, and article with him,
70 if he will assist them against the Ammonites, to make him their ruler; which they do in these words, And the people made him head and captain over them, Judg. xi. ii. which was, as it seems, all one as to be judge. And he judged
75 Israel, judg. xii. 7. that is, was their captain-general six years. So when Iotham upbraids the Shechemites with the obligation they had to Gideon, who had been their judge and ruler, he tells them, He fought for you, and adven-
80 tured his life far, and delivered you out of the hands of Midian, Judg. ix. 17. Nothing mentioned of him but what he did as a general: and indeed that is all is found in his history, or in any of the rest of the judges. And
85 Abimelech particularly is called king, though at most he was but their general. And when, be-

ing weary of the ill conduct of Samuel's sons, the children of Israel desired a king, like all the nations to judge them, and to go out before them, and to fight their battles, I. Sam viii. 20.

5 God granting their desire, says to Samuel, I will send thee a man, and thou shalt anoint him to be captain over my people Israel, that he may save my people out of the hands of the Philistines, ix. 16. As if the only business

10 of a king had been to lead out their armies, and fight in their defense; and accordingly at his inauguration pouring a vial of oil upon him, declares to Saul, that the Lord had anointed him to be captain over his inher-

15 itance, x. 1. And therefore those, who after Saul's being solemnly chosen and saluted king by the tribes at Mispah, were unwilling to have him their king, made no other objection but this, How shall this man save us? v. 27. as if

20 they should have said, this man is unfit to be our king, not having skill and conduct enough in war, to be able to defend us. And when God resolved to transfer the government to David, it is in these words, But now thy king-

25 dom shall not continue: the Lord hath sought him a man after his own heart, and the Lord hath commanded him to be captain over his people, xiii. 14. As if the whole kingly authori-ty were nothing else but to be their general:

30 and therefore the tribes who had stuck to Saul's family, and opposed David's reign, when they came to Hebron with terms of submission to him, they tell him, amongst other arguments they had to submit to him as

35 to their king, that he was in effect their king in Saul's time, and therefore they had no reason but to receive him as their king now. Also (say they) in time past, when Saul was king over us, thou wast he that reddest out and broughtest

40 in Israel, and the Lord said unto thee, Thou shalt feed my people Israel, and thou shalt be a captain over Israel.

Sect. 110. Thus, whether a family by degrees
45 grew up into a commonwealth, and the father-ly authority being continued on to the elder son, every one in his turn growing up under it, tacitly submitted to it, and the easiness and equality of it not offending any one, every one
50 acquiesced, till time seemed to have confirmed it, and settled a right of succession by pre-scription: or whether several families, or the descendants of several families, whom chance, neighborhood, or business brought together,
55 uniting into society, the need of a general, whose conduct might defend them against their enemies in war, and the great confidence the innocence and sincerity of that poor but virtuous age, (such as are almost all those
60 which begin governments, that ever come to last in the world) gave men one of another, made the first beginners of commonwealths generally put the rule into one man's hand, without any other express limitation or re-
65 straint, but what the nature of the thing, and the end of government required: which ever of those it was that at first put the rule into the hands of a single person, certain it is no body was entrusted with it but for the public good
70 and safety, and to those ends, in the infancies of commonwealths, those who had it com-monly used it. And unless they had done so, young societies could not have subsisted; without such nursing fathers tender and care-
75 ful of the public weal, all governments would have sunk under the weakness and infirmities of their infancy, and the prince and the people had soon perished together.

80 Sect. 111. But though the golden age (before vain ambition, and amor sceleratus habendi, evil concupiscence, had corrupted men's minds into a mistake of true power and hon-or) had more virtue, and consequently better
85 governors, as well as less vicious subjects, and there was then no stretching prerogative on

the one side, to oppress the people; nor consequently on the other, any dispute about privilege, to lessen or restrain the power of the magistrate, and so no contest betwixt rulers and people about governors or government: yet, when ambition and luxury in future ages[12] would retain and increase the power, without doing the business for which it was given; and aided by flattery, taught princes to have distinct and separate interests from their people, men found it necessary to examine more carefully the original and rights of government; and to find out ways to restrain the exorbitances, and prevent the abuses of that power, which they having entrusted in another's hands only for their own good, they found was made use of to hurt them.

Sect. 112. Thus we may see how probable it is, that people that were naturally free, and by their own consent either submitted to the government of their father, or united together out of different families to make a government, should generally put the rule into one man's hands, and chose to be under the conduct of a single person, without so much as by express conditions limiting or regulating his power, which they thought safe enough in his honesty and prudence; though they never dreamed of monarchy being lure Divino, which we never heard of among mankind, till

it was revealed to us by the divinity of this last age; nor ever allowed paternal power to have a right to dominion, or to be the foundation of all government. And thus much may suffice to show, that as far as we have any light from history, we have reason to conclude, that all peaceful beginnings of government have been laid in the consent of the people. I say peaceful, because I shall have occasion in another place to speak of conquest, which some esteem a way of beginning of governments.

The other objection I find urged against the beginning of polities, in the way I have mentioned, is this, viz.

Sect. 113. That all men being born under government, some or other, it is impossible any of them should ever be free, and at liberty to unite together, and begin a new one, or ever be able to erect a lawful government.

If this argument be good; I ask, how came so many lawful monarchies into the world? for if any body, upon this supposition, can show me any one man in any age of the world free to begin a lawful monarchy, I will be bound to show him ten other free men at liberty, at the same time to unite and begin a new government under a regal, or any other form; it being demonstration, that if any one, born under the dominion of another, may be so free as to have a right to command others in a new and distinct empire, every one that is born under the dominion of another may be so free too, and may become a ruler, or subject, of a distinct separate government. And so by this their own principle, either all men, however born, are free, or else there is but one lawful prince, one lawful government in the world. And then they have nothing to do, but barely to show us which that is; which when they have done, I doubt not but all mankind will

---

[12] *At first, when some certain kind of regiment was once approved, it may be nothing was then farther thought upon for the manner of governing, but all permitted unto their wisdom and discretion which were to rule, till by experience they found this for all parts very inconvenient, so as the thing which they had devised for a remedy, did indeed but increase the sore which it should have cured. They saw, that to live by one man's will, became the cause of all men's misery. This constrained them to come unto laws wherein all men might see their duty before hand, and know the penalties of transgressing them.* Hooker's Eccl. Pol. l. i. sect. 10

easily agree to pay obedience to him.

Sect. 114. Though it be a sufficient answer to their objection, to show that it involves them in the same difficulties that it doth those they use it against; yet I shall endeavor to discover the weakness of this argument a little farther. All men, say they, are born under government, and therefore they cannot be at liberty to begin a new one. Every one is born a subject to his father, or his prince, and is therefore under the perpetual tie of subjection and allegiance. It is plain mankind never owned nor considered any such natural subjection that they were born in, to one or to the other that tied them, without their own consents, to a subjection to them and their heirs.

Sect. 115. For there are no examples so frequent in history, both sacred and profane, as those of men withdrawing themselves, and their obedience, from the jurisdiction they were born under, and the family or community they were bred up in, and setting up new governments in other places; from whence sprang all that number of petty commonwealths in the beginning of ages, and which always multiplied, as long as there was room enough, till the stronger, or more fortunate, swallowed the weaker; and those great ones again breaking to pieces, dissolved into lesser dominions. All which are so many testimonies against paternal sovereignty, and plainly prove, that it was not the natural right of the father descending to his heirs, that made governments in the beginning, since it was impossible, upon that ground, there should have been so many little kingdoms; all must have been but only one universal monarchy, if men had not been at liberty to separate themselves from their families, and the government, be it what it will, that was set up in it, and go and make distinct commonwealths and other governments, as they thought fit.

Sect. 116. This has been the practice of the world from its first beginning to this day; nor is it now any more hindrance to the freedom of mankind, that they are born under constituted and ancient polities, that have established laws, and set forms of government, than if they were born in the woods, amongst the unconfined inhabitants, that run loose in them: for those, who would persuade us, that by being born under any government, we are naturally subjects to it, and have no more any title or pretense to the freedom of the state of nature, have no other reason (bating that of paternal power, which we have already answered) to produce for it, but only, because our fathers or progenitors passed away their natural liberty, and thereby bound up themselves and their posterity to a perpetual subjection to the government, which they themselves submitted to. It is true, that whatever engagements or promises any one has made for himself, he is under the obligation of them, but cannot, by any compact whatsoever, bind his children or posterity: for his son, when a man, being altogether as free as the father, any act of the father can no more give away the liberty of the son, than it can of any body else: he may indeed annex such conditions to the land, he enjoyed as a subject of any commonwealth, as may oblige his son to be of that community, if he will enjoy those possessions which were his father's; because that estate being his father's property, he may dispose, or settle it, as he pleases.

Sect. 117. And this has generally given the occasion to mistake in this matter; because commonwealths not permitting any part of their dominions to be dismembered, nor to be enjoyed by any but those of their community, the son cannot ordinarily enjoy the possessions of his father, but under the same terms his father did, by becoming a member of the society; whereby he puts himself presently under the government he finds there established, as much as any other subject of that commonwealth. And thus the consent of freemen, born under government, which only makes them members of it, being given separately in their turns, as each comes to be of age, and not in a multitude together; people take no notice of it, and thinking it not done at all, or not necessary, conclude they are naturally subjects as they are men.

Sect. 118. But, it is plain, governments themselves understand it otherwise; they claim no power over the son, because of that they had over the father; nor look on children as being their subjects, by their fathers being so. If a subject of England have a child, by an English woman in France, whose subject is he? Not the king of England's; for he must have leave to be admitted to the privileges of it: nor the king of France's; for how then has his father a liberty to bring him away, and breed him as he pleases? and who ever was judged as a traytor or deserter, if he left, or warred against a country, for being barely born in it of parents that were aliens there? It is plain then, by the practice of governments themselves, as well as by the law of right reason, that a child is born a subject of no country or government. He is under his father's tuition and authority, till he comes to age of discretion; and then he is a freeman, at liberty what government he will put himself under, what body politic he will unite himself to: for if an Englishman's son, born in France, be at liberty, and may do so, it is evident there is no tie upon him by his father's being a subject of this kingdom; nor is he bound up by any compact of his ancestors. And why then hath not his son, by the same reason, the same liberty, though he be born

any where else? Since the power that a father hath naturally over his children, is the same, where-ever they be born, and the ties of natural obligations, are not bounded by the positive limits of kingdoms and commonwealths.

Sect. 119. Every man being, as has been showed, naturally free, and nothing being able to put him into subjection to any earthly power, but only his own consent; it is to be considered, what shall be understood to be a sufficient declaration of a man's consent, to make him subject to the laws of any government. There is a common distinction of an express and a tacit consent, which will concern our present case. No body doubts but an express consent, of any man entering into any society, makes him a perfect member of that society, a subject of that government. The difficulty is, what ought to be looked upon as a tacit consent, and how far it binds, i.e. how far any one shall be looked on to have consented, and thereby submitted to any government, where he has made no expressions of it at all. And to this I say, that every man, that hath any possessions, or enjoyment, of any part of the dominions of any government, doth thereby give his tacit consent, and is as far forth obliged to obedience to the laws of that government, during such enjoyment, as any one under it; whether this his possession be of land, to him and his heirs for ever, or a lodging only for a week; or whether it be barely travelling freely on the highway; and in effect, it reaches as far as the very being of any one within the territories of that government.

Sect. 120. To understand this the better, it is fit to consider, that every man, when he at first incorporates himself into any commonwealth, he, by his uniting himself thereunto, annexed also, and submits to the community, those possessions, which he has, or shall acquire, that do not already belong to any other government: for it would be a direct contradiction, for any one to enter into society with others for the securing and regulating of property; and yet to suppose his land, whose property is to be regulated by the laws of the society, should be exempt from the jurisdiction of that government, to which he himself, the proprietor of the land, is a subject. By the same act therefore, whereby any one unites his person, which was before free, to any commonwealth, by the same he unites his possessions, which were before free, to it also; and they become, both of them, person and possession, subject to the government and dominion of that commonwealth, as long as it hath a being. Whoever therefore, from thenceforth, by inheritance, purchase, permission, or otherways, enjoys any part of the land, so annexed to, and under the government of that commonwealth, must take it with the condition it is under; that is, of submitting to the government of the commonwealth, under whose jurisdiction it is, as far forth as any subject of it.

Sect. 121. But since the government has a direct jurisdiction only over the land, and reaches the possessor of it, (before he has actually incorporated himself in the society) only as he dwells upon, and enjoys that; the obligation any one is under, by virtue of such enjoyment, to submit to the government, begins and ends with the enjoyment; so that whenever the owner, who has given nothing but such a tacit consent to the government, will, by donation, sale, or otherwise, quit the said possession, he is at liberty to go and incorporate himself into any other commonwealth; or to agree with others to begin a new one, in vacuis locis, in any part of the world, they can find free and unpossessed: whereas he, that has once, by actual agreement, and any express declaration, given his consent to be of any commonwealth, is perpetually and indispensably obliged to be, and remain unalterably a subject to it, and can never be again in the liberty of the state of nature; unless, by any calamity, the government he was under comes to be dissolved; or else by some public act cuts him off from being any longer a member of it.

Sect. 122. But submitting to the laws of any country, living quietly, and enjoying privileges and protection under them, makes not a man a member of that society: this is only a local protection and homage due to and from all those, who, not being in a state of war, come within the territories belonging to any government, to all parts whereof the force of its laws extends. But this no more makes a man a member of that society, a perpetual subject of that commonwealth, than it would make a man a subject to another, in whose family he found it convenient to abide for some time; though, whilst he continued in it, he were obliged to comply with the laws, and submit to the government he found there. And thus we see, that foreigners, by living all their lives under another government, and enjoying the privileges and protection of it, though they are bound, even in conscience, to submit to its administration, as far forth as any denison; yet do not thereby come to be subjects or members of that commonwealth. Nothing can make any man so, but his actually entering into it by positive engagement, and express promise and compact. This is that, which I think, concerning the beginning of political societies, and that consent which makes any one a member of any commonwealth.

CHAPTER IX
OF THE ENDS OF POLITICAL SOCIETY AND GOVERNMENT

Sect. 123. IF man in the state of nature be so free, as has been said; if he be absolute lord of his own person and possessions, equal to the greatest, and subject to no body, why will he part with his freedom? why will he give up this empire, and subject himself to the dominion and control of any other power? To which it is obvious to answer, that though in the state of nature he hath such a right, yet the enjoyment of it is very uncertain, and constantly exposed to the invasion of others: for all being kings as much as he, every man his equal, and the greater part no strict observers of equity and justice, the enjoyment of the property he has in this state is very unsafe, very unsecure. This makes him willing to quit a condition, which, however free, is full of fears and continual dangers: and it is not without reason, that he seeks out, and is willing to join in society with others, who are already united, or have a mind to unite, for the mutual preservation of their lives, liberties and estates, which I call by the general name, property.

Sect. 124. The great and chief end, therefore, of men's uniting into commonwealths, and putting themselves under government, is the preservation of their property. To which in the state of nature there are many things wanting.

First, There wants an established, settled, known law, received and allowed by common consent to be the standard of right and wrong, and the common measure to decide all controversies between them: for though the law of nature be plain and intelligible to all rational creatures; yet men being biased by their interest, as well as ignorant for want of study of it, are not apt to allow of it as a law binding to them in the application of it to their particular cases.

Sect. 125. Secondly, In the state of nature there wants a known and indifferent judge, with authority to determine all differences according to the established law: for every one in that state being both judge and executioner of the law of nature, men being partial to themselves, passion and revenge is very apt to carry them too far, and with too much heat, in their own cases; as well as negligence, and unconcernedness, to make them too remiss in other men's.

Sect. 126. Thirdly, In the state of nature there often wants power to back and support the sentence when right, and to give it due execution, They who by any injustice offended, will seldom fail, where they are able, by force to make good their injustice; such resistance many times makes the punishment dangerous, and frequently destructive, to those who attempt it.

Sect. 127. Thus mankind, notwithstanding all the privileges of the state of nature, being but in an ill condition, while they remain in it, are quickly driven into society. Hence it comes to pass, that we seldom find any number of men live any time together in this state. The inconveniencies that they are therein exposed to, by the irregular and uncertain exercise of the power every man has of punishing the transgressions of others, make them take sanctuary under the established laws of government, and therein seek the preservation of their property. It is this makes them so willingly give up every one his single power of punishing, to be exercised by such alone, as shall be appointed to it amongst them; and by such rules as the community, or those authorized by them to that purpose, shall agree on. And in this we have the original right and rise of both the legislative and executive power, as well as of the governments and societies themselves.

Sect. 128. For in the state of nature, to omit the liberty he has of innocent delights, a man has two powers.

The first is to do whatsoever he thinks fit for the preservation of himself, and others within the permission of the law of nature: by which law, common to them all, he and all the rest of mankind are one community, make up one society, distinct from all other creatures. And were it not for the corruption and virtuousness of degenerate men, there would be no need of any other; no necessity that men should separate from this great and natural community, and by positive agreements combine into smaller and divided associations.

The other power a man has in the state of nature, is the power to punish the crimes committed against that law. Both these he gives up, when he joins in a private, if I may so call it, or particular politic society, and incorporates into any commonwealth, separate from the rest of mankind.

Sect. 129. The first power, viz. of doing whatsoever he thought for the preservation of himself, and the rest of mankind, he gives up to be regulated by laws made by the society, so far forth as the preservation of himself, and the rest of that society shall require; which laws of the society in many things confine the liberty he had by the law of nature.

Sect. 130. Secondly, The power of punishing he wholly gives up, and engages his natural force, (which he might before employ in the execution of the law of nature, by his own single authority, as he thought fit) to assist the executive power of the society, as the law

thereof shall require: for being now in a new state, wherein he is to enjoy many conveniences, from the labor, assistance, and society of others in the same community, as well as protection from its whole strength; he is to part also with as much of his natural liberty, in providing for himself, as the good, prosperity, and safety of the society shall require; which is not only necessary, but just, since the other members of the society do the like.

Sect. 131. But though men, when they enter into society, give up the equality, liberty, and executive power they had in the state of nature, into the hands of the society, to be so far disposed of by the legislative, as the good of the society shall require; yet it being only with an intention in every one the better to preserve himself, his liberty and property; (for no rational creature can be supposed to change his condition with an intention to be worse) the power of the society, or legislative constituted by them, can never be supposed to extend farther, than the common good; but is obliged to secure every one's property, by providing against those three defects above mentioned, that made the state of nature so unsafe and uneasy. And so whoever has the legislative or supreme power of any commonwealth, is bound to govern by established standing laws, promulgated and known to the people, and not by extemporary decrees; by indifferent and upright judges, who are to decide controversies by those laws; and to employ the force of the community at home, only in the execution of such laws, or abroad to prevent or redress foreign injuries, and secure the community from inroads and invasion. And all this to be directed to no other end, but the peace, safety, and public good of the people.

CHAPTER X
OF THE FORMS OF A COMMON-WEALTH

Sect. 132. THE majority having, as has been showed, upon men's first uniting into society, the whole power of the community naturally in them, may employ all that power in making laws for the community from time to time, and executing those laws by officers of their own appointing; and then the form of the government is a perfect democracy: or else may put the power of making laws into the hands of a few select men, and their heirs or successors; and then it is an oligarchy: or else into the hands of one man, and then it is a monarchy: if to him and his heirs, it is an hereditary monarchy: if to him only for life, but upon his death the power only of nominating a successor to return to them; an elective monarchy. And so accordingly of these the community may make compounded and mixed forms of government, as they think good. And if the legislative power be at first given by the majority to one or more persons only for their lives, or any limited time, and then the supreme power to revert to them again; when it is so reverted, the community may dispose of it again anew into what hands they please, and so constitute a new form of government: for the form of government depending upon the placing the supreme power, which is the legislative, it being impossible to conceive that an inferior power should prescribe to a superior, or any but the supreme make laws, according as the power of making laws is placed, such is the form of the commonwealth.

Sect. 133. By commonwealth, I must be understood all along to mean, not a democracy, or any form of government, but any independent community, which the Latins signified by the word *civitas*, to which the word which best answers in our language, is commonwealth, and most properly expresses such a society of men, which community or city in English does not; for there may be subordinate communities in a government; and city amongst us has a quite different notion from commonwealth: and therefore, to avoid ambiguity, I crave leave to use the word commonwealth in that sense, in which I find it used by king James the first; and I take it to be its genuine signification; which if any body dislike, I consent with him to change it for a better.

CHAPTER XI
OF THE EXTENT OF THE LEGISLATIVE POWER

Sect. 134. THE great end of men's entering into society, being the enjoyment of their properties in peace and safety, and the great instrument and means of that being the laws established in that society; the first and fundamental positive law of all commonwealths is the establishing of the legislative power; as the first and fundamental natural law, which is to govern even the legislative itself, is the preservation of the society, and (as far as will consist with the public good) of every person in it. This legislative is not only the supreme power of the commonwealth, but sacred and unalterable in the hands where the community have once placed it; nor can any edict of any body else, in what form soever conceived, or by what power soever backed, have the force and obligation of a law, which has not its sanction from that legislative which the public has chosen and appointed: for without this the law could not have that, which is absolutely necessary to its being a law[13], the consent of the

---

[13] *The lawful power of making laws to command whole politic societies of men, belonging so properly unto the*

society, over whom no body can have a power to make laws, but by their own consent, and by authority received from them; and therefore all the obedience, which by the most sol-
5 emn ties any one can be obliged to pay, ultimately terminates in this supreme power, and is directed by those laws which it enacts: nor can any oaths to any foreign power whatsoever, or any domestic subordinate power, dis-
10 charge any member of the society from his obedience to the legislative, acting pursuant to their trust; nor oblige him to any obedience contrary to the laws so enacted, or farther than they do allow; it being ridiculous to imagine
15 one can be tied ultimately to obey any power in the society, which is not the supreme.

Of this point therefore we are to note, that such men naturally have no full and perfect
20 power to command whole politic multitudes of men, therefore utterly without our consent, we could in such sort be at no man's commandment living. And to be commanded we do consent, when that society, whereof we be
25 a part, hath at any time before consented, without revoking the same after by the like universal agreement. Laws therefore human, of what kind so ever, are available by consent. Ibid.)
30

Sect. 135. Though the legislative, whether placed in one or more, whether it be always in being, or only by intervals, though it be the supreme power in every commonwealth; yet:
35 First, It is not, nor can possibly be absolutely

same entire societies, that for any prince or potentate of what kind soever upon earth, to exercise the same of himself, and not by express commission immediately and personally received from God, or else by authority derived at the first from their consent, upon whose persons they impose laws, it is no better than mere tyranny. Laws they are not therefore which public approbation hath not made so. Hooker's Eccl. Pol. l. i. sect. 10

arbitrary over the lives and fortunes of the people: for it being but the joint power of every member of the society given up to that person, or assembly, which is legislator; it can be
40 no more than those persons had in a state of nature before they entered into society, and gave up to the community: for no body can transfer to another more power than he has in himself; and no body has an absolute arbitrary
45 power over himself, or over any other, to destroy his own life, or take away the life or property of another. A man, as has been proved, cannot subject himself to the arbitrary power of another; and having in the state of
50 nature no arbitrary power over the life, liberty, or possession of another, but only so much as the law of nature gave him for the preservation of himself, and the rest of mankind; this is all he doth, or can give up to the common-
55 wealth, and by it to the legislative power, so that the legislative can have no more than this. Their power, in the utmost bounds of it, is limited to the public good of the society. It is a power, that hath no other end but preserva-
60 tion, and therefore can never have a right to destroy, enslave, or designedly to impoverish the subjects.[14] The obligations of the law of

14 *Two foundations there are which bear up public societies; the one a natural inclination, whereby all men desire sociable life and fellowship; the other an order, expressly or secretly agreed upon, touching the manner of their union in living together: the latter is that which we call the law of a common-weal, the very soul of a politic body, the parts whereof are by law animated, held together, and set on work in such actions as the common good requireth. Laws politic, ordained for external order and regiment amongst men, are never framed as they should be, unless presuming the will of man to be inwardly obstinate, rebellious, and averse from all obedience to the sacred laws of his nature; in a word, unless presuming man to be, in regard of his depraved mind, little better than a wild beast, they do accordingly provide, notwithstanding, so to frame his outward actions, that they be no hindrance unto the common good, for which societies are instituted. Unless they do this, they are not perfect.* Hooker's Eccl. Pol. l.

nature cease not in society, but only in many cases are drawn closer, and have by human laws known penalties annexed to them, to enforce their observation. Thus the law of nature stands as an eternal rule to all men, legislators as well as others. The rules that they make for other men's actions, must, as well as their own and other men's actions, be conformable to the law of nature, i.e. to the will of God, of which that is a declaration, and the fundamental law of nature being the preservation of mankind, no human sanction can be good, or valid against it.

Sect. 136. Secondly, The legislative, or supreme authority, cannot assume to its self a power to rule by extemporary arbitrary decrees, but is bound to dispense justice, and decide the rights of the subject by promulgated standing laws, and known authorized judges[15]:* for the law of nature being unwritten, and so no where to be found but in the minds of men, they who through passion or interest shall miscite, or misapply it, cannot so easily be convinced of their mistake where there is no established judge: and so it serves not, as it ought, to determine the rights, and fence the properties of those that live under it, especially where every one is judge, interpreter, and executioner of it too, and that in his own case: and he that has right on his side, having ordinarily but his own single strength, hath not

---

i. sect. 10

[15] *Human laws are measures in respect of men whose actions they must direct, howbeit such measures they are as have also their higher rules to be measured by, which rules are two, the law of God, and the law of nature; so that laws human must be made according to the general laws of nature, and without contradiction to any positive law of scripture, otherwise they are ill made.* Hooker's Eccl. Pol. l. iii. sect. 9. *To constrain men to any thing inconvenient doth seem unreasonable.* Ibid. l. i. sect. 10

force enough to defend himself from injuries, or to punish delinquents. To avoid these inconveniences, which disorder men's properties in the state of nature, men unite into societies, that they may have the united strength of the whole society to secure and defend their properties, and may have standing rules to bound it, by which every one may know what is his. To this end it is that men give up all their natural power to the society which they enter into, and the community put the legislative power into such hands as they think fit, with this trust, that they shall be governed by declared laws, or else their peace, quiet, and property will still be at the same uncertainty, as it was in the state of nature.

Sect. 137. Absolute arbitrary power, or governing without settled standing laws, can neither of them consist with the ends of society and government, which men would not quit the freedom of the state of nature for, and tie themselves up under, were it not to preserve their lives, liberties and fortunes, and by stated rules of right and property to secure their peace and quiet. It cannot be supposed that they should intend, had they a power so to do, to give to any one, or more, an absolute arbitrary power over their persons and estates, and put a force into the magistrate's hand to execute his unlimited will arbitrarily upon them. This were to put themselves into a worse condition than the state of nature, wherein they had a liberty to defend their right against the injuries of others, and were upon equal terms of force to maintain it, whether invaded by a single man, or many in combination. Whereas by supposing they have given up themselves to the absolute arbitrary power and will of a legislator, they have disarmed themselves, and armed him, to make a prey of them when he pleases; he being in a much worse condition, who is exposed to the arbitrary power of one man, who has the command of 100,000, than he that is exposed to the arbitrary power of 100,000 single men; no body being secure, that his will, who has such a command, is better than that of other men, though his force be 100,000 times stronger. And therefore, whatever form the commonwealth is under, the ruling power ought to govern by declared and received laws, and not by extemporary dictates and undetermined resolutions: for then mankind will be in a far worse condition than in the state of nature, if they shall have armed one, or a few men with the joint power of a multitude, to force them to obey at pleasure the exorbitant and unlimited decrees of their sudden thoughts, or unrestrained, and till that moment unknown wills, without having any measures set down which may guide and justify their actions: for all the power the government has, being only for the good of the society, as it ought not to be arbitrary and at pleasure, so it ought to be exercised by established and promulgated laws; that both the people may know their duty, and be safe and secure within the limits of the law; and the rulers too kept within their bounds, and not be tempted, by the power they have in their hands, to employ it to such purposes, and by such measures, as they would not have known, and own not willingly.

Sect. 138. Thirdly, The supreme power cannot take from any man any part of his property without his own consent: for the preservation of property being the end of government, and that for which men enter into society, it necessarily supposes and requires, that the people should have property, without which they must be supposed to lose that, by entering into society, which was the end for which they entered into it; too gross an absurdity for any man to own. Men therefore in society having property, they have such a right to the goods, which by the law of the community are their's, that no body hath a right to take their substance or any part of it from them, without their own consent: without this they have no property at all; for I have truly no property in that, which another can by right take from me, when he pleases, against my consent. Hence it is a mistake to think, that the supreme or legislative power of any commonwealth, can do what it will, and dispose of the estates of the subject arbitrarily, or take any part of them at pleasure. This is not much to be feared in governments where the legislative consists, wholly or in part, in assemblies which are variable, whose members, upon the dissolution of the assembly, are subjects under the common laws of their country, equally with the rest. But in governments, where the legislative is in one lasting assembly always in being, or in one man, as in absolute monarchies, there is danger still, that they will think themselves to have a distinct interest from the rest of the community; and so will be apt to increase their own riches and power, by taking what they think fit from the people: for a man's property is not at all secure, tho' there be good and equitable laws to set the bounds of it between him and his fellow subjects, if he who commands those subjects have power to take from any private man, what part he pleases of his property, and use and dispose of it as he thinks good.

Sect. 139. But government, into whatsoever hands it is put, being, as I have before showed, entrusted with this condition, and for this end, that men might have and secure their properties; the prince, or senate, however it may have power to make laws, for the regulating of property between the subjects one amongst another, yet can never have a power to take to themselves the whole, or any part of the subjects property, without their own consent: for this would be in effect to leave them no property at all. And to let us see, that even absolute power, where it is necessary, is not arbitrary by being absolute, but is still limited by that reason, and confined to those ends, which required it in some cases to be absolute, we need look no farther than the common practice of martial discipline: for the preservation of the army, and in it of the whole commonwealth, requires an absolute obedience to the command of every superior officer, and it is justly death to disobey or dispute the most dangerous or unreasonable of them; but yet we see, that neither the sergeant, that could command a soldier to march up to the mouth of a cannon, or stand in a breach, where he is almost sure to perish, can command that soldier to give him one penny of his money; nor the general, that can condemn him to death for deserting his post, or for not obeying the most desperate orders, can yet, with all his absolute power of life and death, dispose of one farthing of that soldier's estate, or seize one jot of his goods; whom yet he can command any thing, and hang for the least disobedience; because such a blind obedience is necessary to that end, for which the commander has his power, viz. the preservation of the rest; but the disposing of his goods has nothing to do with it.

Sect. 140. It is true, governments cannot be supported without great charge, and it is fit every one who enjoys his share of the protection, should pay out of his estate his proportion for the maintenance of it. But still it must be with his own consent, i.e. the consent of the majority, giving it either by themselves, or their representatives chosen by them: for if any one shall claim a power to lay and levy taxes on the people, by his own authority, and without such consent of the people, he thereby invades the fundamental law of property,

and subverts the end of government: for what property have I in that, which another may by right take, when he pleases, to himself?

Sect. 141. Fourthly, The legislative cannot transfer the power of making laws to any other hands: for it being but a delegated power from the people, they who have it cannot pass it over to others. The people alone can appoint the form of the commonwealth, which is by constituting the legislative, and appointing in whose hands that shall be. And when the people have said, We will submit to rules, and be governed by laws made by such men, and in such forms, no body else can say other men shall make laws for them; nor can the people be bound by any laws, but such as are enacted by those whom they have chosen, and authorized to make laws for them. The power of the legislative, being derived from the people by a positive voluntary grant and institution, can be no other than what that positive grant conveyed, which being only to make laws, and not to make legislators, the legislative can have no power to transfer their authority of making laws, and place it in other hands.

Sect. 142. These are the bounds which the trust, that is put in them by the society, and the law of God and nature, have set to the legislative power of every commonwealth, in all forms of government.

First, They are to govern by promulgated established laws, not to be varied in particular cases, but to have one rule for rich and poor, for the favorite at court, and the country man at plough.

Secondly, These laws also ought to be designed for no other end ultimately, but the good of the people.

Thirdly, They must not raise taxes on the property of the people, without the consent of the people, given by themselves, or their deputies. And this properly concerns only such governments where the legislative is always in being, or at least where the people have not reserved any part of the legislative to deputies, to be from time to time chosen by themselves.

Fourthly, The legislative neither must nor can transfer the power of making laws to any body else, or place it any where, but where the people have.

CHAPTER XII
OF THE LEGISLATIVE, EXECUTIVE, AND FEDERATIVE POWER OF THE COMMON-WEALTH

Sect. 143. THE legislative power is that, which has a right to direct how the force of the commonwealth shall be employed for preserving the community and the members of it. But because those laws which are constantly to be executed, and whose force is always to continue, may be made in a little time; therefore there is no need, that the legislative should be always in being, not having always business to do. And because it may be too great a temptation to human frailty, apt to grasp at power, for the same persons, who have the power of making laws, to have also in their hands the power to execute them, whereby they may exempt themselves from obedience to the laws they make, and suit the law, both in its making, and execution, to their own private advantage, and thereby come to have a distinct interest from the rest of the community, contrary to the end of society and government: therefore in wellordered commonwealths, where the good of the whole is so considered, as it ought, the legislative power is put into the hands of divers persons, who duly assembled, have by themselves, or jointly with others, a power to make laws, which when they have done, being separated again, they are themselves subject to the laws they have made; which is a new and near tie upon them, to take care, that they make them for the public good.

Sect. 144. But because the laws, that are at once, and in a short time made, have a constant and lasting force, and need a perpetual execution, or an attendance thereunto; therefore it is necessary there should be a power always in being, which should see to the execution of the laws that are made, and remain in force. And thus the legislative and executive power come often to be separated.

Sect. 145. There is another power in every commonwealth, which one may call natural, because it is that which answers to the power every man naturally had before he entered into society: for though in a commonwealth the members of it are distinct persons still in reference to one another, and as such as governed by the laws of the society; yet in reference to the rest of mankind, they make one body, which is, as every member of it before was, still in the state of nature with the rest of mankind. Hence it is, that the controversies that happen between any man of the society with those that are out of it, are managed by the public; and an injury done to a member of their body, engages the whole in the reparation of it. So that under this consideration, the whole community is one body in the state of nature, in respect of all other states or persons out of its community.

Sect. 146. This therefore contains the power of war and peace, leagues and alliances, and all the transactions, with all persons and communities without the commonwealth, and may be called federative, if any one pleases. So the thing be understood, I am indifferent as to the name.

Sect. 147. These two powers, executive and federative, though they be really distinct in themselves, yet one comprehending the execution of the municipal laws of the society within its self, upon all that are parts of it; the other the management of the security and interest of the public without, with all those that it may receive benefit or damage from, yet they are always almost united. And though this federative power in the well or ill management of it be of great moment to the commonwealth, yet it is much less capable to be directed by antecedent, standing, positive laws, than the executive; and so must necessarily be left to the prudence and wisdom of those, whose hands it is in, to be managed for the public good: for the laws that concern subjects one amongst another, being to direct their actions, may well enough precede them. But what is to be done in reference to foreigners, depending much upon their actions, and the variation of designs and interests, must be left in great part to the prudence of those, who have this power committed to them, to be managed by the best of their skill, for the advantage of the commonwealth.

Sect. 148. Though, as I said, the executive and federative power of every community be really distinct in themselves, yet they are hardly to be separated, and placed at the same time, in the hands of distinct persons: for both of them requiring the force of the society for their exercise, it is almost impracticable to place the force of the commonwealth in distinct, and not subordinate hands; or that the executive and federative power should be placed in persons, that might act separately, whereby the force of the public would be under different commands: which would be apt some time or other to cause disorder and ruin.

CHAPTER XIII
OF THE SUBORDINATION OF THE POWERS OF THE COMMON-WEALTH

Sect. 149. THOUGH in a constituted commonwealth, standing upon its own basis, and acting according to its own nature, that is, acting for the preservation of the community, there can be but one supreme power, which is the legislative, to which all the rest are and must be subordinate, yet the legislative being only a fiduciary power to act for certain ends, there remains still in the people a supreme power to remove or alter the legislative, when they find the legislative act contrary to the trust reposed in them: for all power given with trust for the attaining an end, being limited by that end, whenever that end is manifestly neglected, or opposed, the trust must necessarily be forfeited, and the power devolve into the hands of those that gave it, who may place it anew where they shall think best for their safety and security. And thus the community perpetually retains a supreme power of saving themselves from the attempts and designs of any body, even of their legislators, whenever they shall be so foolish, or so wicked, as to lay and carry on designs against the liberties and properties of the subject: for no man or society of men, having a power to deliver up their preservation, or consequently the means of it, to the absolute will and arbitrary dominion of another; when ever any one shall go about to bring them into such a slavish condition, they will always have a right to preserve, what they have not a power to part with; and to rid themselves of those, who invade this fundamental, sacred, and unalterable law of self-preservation, for which they entered into society. And thus the community may be said in this respect to be always the supreme power, but not as considered under any form of government, because this power of the people can never take place till the government be dissolved.

Sect. 150. In all cases, whilst the government subsists, the legislative is the supreme power: for what can give laws to another, must needs be superior to him; and since the legislative is no otherwise legislative of the society, but by the right it has to make laws for all the parts, and for every member of the society, prescribing rules to their actions, and giving power of execution, where they are transgressed, the legislative must needs be the supreme, and all other powers, in any members or parts of the society, derived from and subordinate to it.

Sect. 151. In some commonwealths, where the legislative is not always in being, and the executive is vested in a single person, who has also a share in the legislative; there that single person in a very tolerable sense may also be called supreme: not that he has in himself all the supreme power, which is that of law-making; but because he has in him the supreme execution, from whom all inferior magistrates derive all their several subordinate powers, or at least the greatest part of them: having also no legislative superior to him, there being no law to be made without his consent, which cannot be expected should ever subject him to the other part of the legislative, he is properly enough in this sense supreme. But yet it is to be observed, that tho' oaths of allegiance and fealty are taken to him, it is not to him as supreme legislator, but as supreme executor of the law, made by a joint power of him with others; allegiance being nothing but an obedience according to law, which when he violates, he has no right to obedience, nor can claim it

otherwise than as the public person vested with the power of the law, and so is to be considered as the image, phantom, or representative of the commonwealth, acted by the will of the society, declared in its laws; and thus he has no will, no power, but that of the law. But when he quits this representation, this public will, and acts by his own private will, he degrades himself, and is but a single private person without power, and without will, that has any right to obedience; the members owing no obedience but to the public will of the society.

Sect. 152. The executive power, placed any where but in a person that has also a share in the legislative, is visibly subordinate and accountable to it, and may be at pleasure changed and displaced; so that it is not the supreme executive power, that is exempt from subordination, but the supreme executive power vested in one, who having a share in the legislative, has no distinct superior legislative to be subordinate and accountable to, farther than he himself shall join and consent; so that he is no more subordinate than he himself shall think fit, which one may certainly conclude will be but very little. Of other ministerial and subordinate powers in a commonwealth, we need not speak, they being so multiplied with infinite variety, in the different customs and constitutions of distinct commonwealths, that it is impossible to give a particular account of them all. Only thus much, which is necessary to our present purpose, we may take notice of concerning them, that they have no manner of authority, any of them, beyond what is by positive grant and commission delegated to them, and are all of them accountable to some other power in the commonwealth.

Sect. 153. It is not necessary, no, nor so much as convenient, that the legislative should be always in being; but absolutely necessary that the executive power should, because there is not always need of new laws to be made, but always need of execution of the laws that are made. When the legislative hath put the execution of the laws, they make, into other hands, they have a power still to resume it out of those hands, when they find cause, and to punish for any maladministration against the laws. The same holds also in regard of the federative power, that and the executive being both ministerial and subordinate to the legislative, which, as has been showed, in a constituted commonwealth is the supreme. The legislative also in this case being supposed to consist of several persons, (for if it be a single person, it cannot but be always in being, and so will, as supreme, naturally have the supreme executive power, together with the legislative) may assemble, and exercise their legislature, at the times that either their original constitution, or their own adjournment, appoints, or when they please; if neither of these hath appointed any time, or there be no other way prescribed to convoke them: for the supreme power being placed in them by the people, it is always in them, and they may exercise it when they please, unless by their original constitution they are limited to certain seasons, or by an act of their supreme power they have adjourned to a certain time; and when that time comes, they have a right to assemble and act again.

Sect. 154. If the legislative, or any part of it, be made up of representatives chosen for that time by the people, which afterwards return into the ordinary state of subjects, and have no share in the legislature but upon a new choice, this power of choosing must also be exercised by the people, either at certain appointed seasons, or else when they are summoned to it; and in this latter case the power of convoking the legislative is ordinarily placed in the executive, and has one of these two limitations in respect of time: that either the original constitution requires their assembling and acting at certain intervals, and then the executive power does nothing but ministerially issue directions for their electing and assembling, according to due forms; or else it is left to his prudence to call them by new elections, when the occasions or exigencies of the public require the amendment of old, or making of new laws, or the redress or prevention of any inconveniencies, that lie on, or threaten the people.

Sect. 155. It may be demanded here, What if the executive power, being possessed of the force of the commonwealth, shall make use of that force to hinder the meeting and acting of the legislative, when the original constitution, or the public exigencies require it? I say, using force upon the people without authority, and contrary to the trust put in him that does so, is a state of war with the people, who have a right to reinstate their legislative in the exercise of their power: for having erected a legislative, with an intent they should exercise the power of making laws, either at certain set times, or when there is need of it, when they are hindered by any force from what is so necessary to the society, and wherein the safety and preservation of the people consists, the people have a right to remove it by force. In all states and conditions, the true remedy of force without authority, is to oppose force to it. The use of force without authority, always puts him that uses it into a state of war, as the aggressor, and renders him liable to be treated accordingly.

Sect. 156. The power of assembling and dismissing the legislative, placed in the executive, gives not the executive a superiority over it, but is a fiduciary trust placed in him, for the safety of the people, in a case where the uncertainty and variableness of human affairs could not bear a steady fixed rule: for it not being possible, that the first framers of the government should, by any foresight, be so much masters of future events, as to be able to prefix so just periods of return and duration to the assemblies of the legislative, in all times to come, that might exactly answer all the exigencies of the commonwealth; the best remedy could be found for this defect, was to trust this to the prudence of one who was always to be present, and whose business it was to watch over the public good. Constant frequent meetings of the legislative, and long continuations of their assemblies, without necessary occasion, could not but be burdensome to the people, and must necessarily in time produce more dangerous inconveniencies, and yet the quick turn of affairs might be sometimes such as to need their present help: any delay of their convening might endanger the public; and sometimes too their business might be so great, that the limited time of their sitting might be too short for their work, and rob the public of that benefit which could be had only from their mature deliberation. What then could be done in this case to prevent the community from being exposed some time or other to eminent hazard, on one side or the other, by fixed intervals and periods, set to the meeting and acting of the legislative, but to entrust it to the prudence of some, who being present, and acquainted with the state of public affairs, might make use of this prerogative for the public good? and where else could this be so well placed as in his hands, who was entrusted with the execution of the laws for the same end? Thus supposing the regulation of times for the assembling and sitting of the legislative, not settled by the original constitution, it naturally fell into the hands of the executive, not as an arbitrary power depending on his good pleasure, but with this trust always to have it exercised only for the public weal, as the occurrences of times and change of affairs might require. Whether settled periods of their convening, or a liberty left to the prince for convoking the legislative, or perhaps a mixture of both, hath the least inconvenience attending it, it is not my business here to inquire, but only to show, that though the executive power may have the prerogative of convoking and dissolving such conventions of the legislative, yet it is not thereby superior to it.

Sect. 157. Things of this world are in so constant a flux, that nothing remains long in the same state. Thus people, riches, trade, power, change their stations, flourishing mighty cities come to ruin, and prove in times neglected desolate corners, whilst other unfrequented places grow into populous countries, filled with wealth and inhabitants. But things not always changing equally, and private interest often keeping up customs and privileges, when the reasons of them are ceased, it often comes to pass, that in governments, where part of the legislative consists of representatives chosen by the people, that in tract of time this representation becomes very unequal and disproportionate to the reasons it was at first established upon. To what gross absurdities the following of custom, when reason has left it, may lead, we may be satisfied, when we see the bare name of a town, of which there remains not so much as the ruins, where scarce so much housing as a sheepcote, or more inhabitants than a shepherd is to be found, sends as many representatives to the grand assembly of law-makers, as a whole county numerous in people, and powerful in riches. This strangers stand amazed at, and every one must confess needs a remedy; tho' most think it hard to find one, because the constitution of the legislative being the original and supreme act of the society, antecedent to all positive laws in it, and depending wholly on the people, no inferior power can alter it. And therefore the people, when the legislative is once constituted, having, in such a government as we have been speaking of, no power to act as long as the government stands; this inconvenience is thought incapable of a remedy.

Sect. 158. Salus populi suprema lex, is certainly so just and fundamental a rule, that he, who sincerely follows it, cannot dangerously err. If therefore the executive, who has the power of convoking the legislative, observing rather the true proportion, than fashion of representation, regulates, not by old custom, but true reason, the number of members, in all places that have a right to be distinctly represented, which no part of the people however incorporated can pretend to, but in proportion to the assistance which it affords to the public, it cannot be judged to have set up a new legislative, but to have restored the old and true one, and to have rectified the disorders which succession of time had insensibly, as well as inevitably introduced: For it being the interest as well as intention of the people, to have a fair and equal representative; whoever brings it nearest to that, is an undoubted friend to, and establisher of the government, and cannot miss the consent and approbation of the community; prerogative being nothing but a power, in the hands of the prince, to provide for the public good, in such cases, which depending upon unforeseen and uncertain occurrences, certain and unalterable laws could not safely direct; whatsoever shall be done manifestly for the good of the people, and the establishing the government upon its true foundations, is, and always will be, just prerogative, The power of erecting new corporations, and therewith new representatives, car-

ries with it a supposition, that in time the measures of representation might vary, and those places have a just right to be represented which before had none; and by the same reason, those cease to have a right, and be too inconsiderable for such a privilege, which before had it. 'Tis not a change from the present state, which perhaps corruption or decay has introduced, that makes an inroad upon the government, but the tendency of it to injure or oppress the people, and to set up one part or party, with a distinction from, and an unequal subjection of the rest. Whatsoever cannot but be acknowledged to be of advantage to the society, and people in general, upon just and lasting measures, will always, when done, justify itself; and whenever the people shall chose their representatives upon just and undeniably equal measures, suitable to the original frame of the government, it cannot be doubted to be the will and act of the society, whoever permitted or caused them so to do.

CHAPTER XIV
OF PREROGATIVE

Sect. 159. WHERE the legislative and executive power are in distinct hands, (as they are in all moderated monarchies, and well-framed governments) there the good of the society requires, that several things should be left to the discretion of him that has the executive power: for the legislators not being able to foresee, and provide by laws, for all that may be useful to the community, the executor of the laws having the power in his hands, has by the common law of nature a right to make use of it for the good of the society, in many cases, where the municipal law has given no direction, till the legislative can conveniently be assembled to provide for it. Many things there are, which the law can by no means provide for; and those must necessarily be left to the discretion of him that has the executive power in his hands, to be ordered by him as the public good and advantage shall require: nay, it is fit that the laws themselves should in some cases give way to the executive power, or rather to this fundamental law of nature and government, viz. That as much as may be, all the members of the society are to be preserved: for since many accidents may happen, wherein a strict and rigid observation of the laws may do harm; (as not to pull down an innocent man's house to stop the fire, when the next to it is burning) and a man may come sometimes within the reach of the law, which makes no distinction of persons, by an action that may deserve reward and pardon; 'tis fit the ruler should have a power, in many cases, to mitigate the severity of the law, and pardon some offenders: for the end of government being the preservation of all, as much as may be, even the guilty are to be spared, where it can prove no prejudice to the innocent.

Sect. 160. This power to act according to discretion, for the public good, without the prescription of the law, and sometimes even against it, is that which is called prerogative: for since in some governments the lawmaking power is not always in being, and is usually too numerous, and so too slow, for the dispatch requisite to execution; and because also it is impossible to foresee, and so by laws to provide for, all accidents and necessities that may concern the public, or to make such laws as will do no harm, if they are executed with an inflexible rigor, on all occasions, and upon all persons that may come in their way; therefore there is a latitude left to the executive power, to do many things of choice which the laws do not prescribe.

Sect. 161. This power, whilst employed for the benefit of the community, and suitably to the trust and ends of the government, is undoubted prerogative, and never is questioned: for the people are very seldom or never scrupulous or nice in the point; they are far from examining prerogative, whilst it is in any tolerable degree employed for the use it was meant, that is, for the good of the people, and not manifestly against it: but if there comes to be a question between the executive power and the people, about a thing claimed as a prerogative; the tendency of the exercise of such prerogative to the good or hurt of the people, will easily decide that question.

Sect. 162. It is easy to conceive, that in the infancy of governments, when commonwealths differed little from families in number of people, they differed from them too but little in number of laws: and the governors, being as the fathers of them, watching over them for their good, the government was almost all prerogative. A few established laws served the turn, and the discretion and care of the ruler supplied the rest. But when mistake or flattery prevailed with weak princes to make use of this power for private ends of their own, and not for the public good, the people were fain by express laws to get prerogative determined in those points wherein they found disadvantage from it: and thus declared limitations of prerogative were by the people found necessary in cases which they and their ancestors had left, in the utmost latitude, to the wisdom of those princes who made no other but a right use of it, that is, for the good of their people.

Sect. 163. And therefore they have a very wrong notion of government, who say, that the people have encroached upon the prerogative, when they have got any part of it to be defined by positive laws: for in so doing they have not pulled from the prince any thing that

of right belonged to him, but only declared, that that power which they indefinitely left in his or his ancestors hands, to be exercised for their good, was not a thing which they intend-
5 ed him when he used it otherwise: for the end of government being the good of the community, whatsoever alterations are made in it, tending to that end, cannot be an encroachment upon any body, since no body in gov-
10 ernment can have a right tending to any other end: and those only are encroachments which prejudice or hinder the public good. Those who say otherwise, speak as if the prince had a distinct and separate interest from the good of
15 the community, and was not made for it; the root and source from which spring almost all those evils and disorders which happen in kingly governments. And indeed, if that be so, the people under his government are not a
20 society of rational creatures, entered into a community for their mutual good; they are not such as have set rulers over themselves, to guard, and promote that good; but are to be looked on as an herd of inferior creatures un-
25 der the dominion of a master, who keeps them and works them for his own pleasure or profit. If men were so void of reason, and brutish, as to enter into society upon such terms, prerogative might indeed be, what some men would
30 have it, an arbitrary power to do things hurtful to the people.

Sect. 164. But since a rational creature cannot be supposed, when free, to put himself into
35 subjection to another, for his own harm; (though, where he finds a good and wise ruler, he may not perhaps think it either necessary or useful to set precise bounds to his power in all things) prerogative can be nothing but the
40 people's permitting their rulers to do several things, of their own free choice, where the law was silent, and sometimes too against the direct letter of the law, for the public good; and

their acquiescing in it when so done: for as a
45 good prince, who is mindful of the trust put into his hands, and careful of the good of his people, cannot have too much prerogative, that is, power to do good; so a weak and ill prince, who would claim that power which his
50 predecessors exercised without the direction of the law, as a prerogative belonging to him by right of his office, which he may exercise at his pleasure, to make or promote an interest distinct from that of the public, gives the peo-
55 ple an occasion to claim their right, and limit that power, which, whilst it was exercised for their good, they were content should be tacitly allowed.

60 Sect. 165. And therefore he that will look into the history of England, will find, that prerogative was always largest in the hands of our wisest and best princes; because the people, observing the whole tendency of their actions
65 to be the public good, contested not what was done without law to that end: or, if any human frailty or mistake (for princes are but men, made as others) appeared in some small declinations from that end; yet 'twas visible, the
70 main of their conduct tended to nothing but the care of the public. The people therefore, finding reason to be satisfied with these princes, whenever they acted without, or contrary to the letter of the law, acquiesced in what
75 they did, and, without the least complaint, let them enlarge their prerogative as they pleased, judging rightly, that they did nothing herein to the prejudice of their laws, since they acted conformable to the foundation and end of all
80 laws, the public good.

Sect. 166. Such god-like princes indeed had some title to arbitrary power by that argument, that would prove absolute monarchy the best
85 government, as that which God himself governs the universe by; because such kings par-

take of his wisdom and goodness. Upon this is founded that saying, That the reigns of good princes have been always most dangerous to the liberties of their people: for when their successors, managing the government with different thoughts, would draw the actions of those good rulers into precedent, and make them the standard of their prerogative, as if what had been done only for the good of the people was a right in them to do, for the harm of the people, if they so pleased; it has often occasioned contest, and sometimes public disorders, before the people could recover their original right, and get that to be declared not to be prerogative, which truly was never so; since it is impossible that any body in the society should ever have a right to do the people harm; though it be very possible, and reasonable, that the people should not go about to set any bounds to the prerogative of those kings, or rulers, who themselves transgressed not the bounds of the public good: for prerogative is nothing but the power of doing public good without a rule.

Sect. 167. The power of calling parliaments in England, as to precise time, place, and duration, is certainly a prerogative of the king, but still with this trust, that it shall be made use of for the good of the nation, as the exigencies of the times, and variety of occasions, shall require: for it being impossible to foresee which should always be the fittest place for them to assemble in, and what the best season; the choice of these was left with the executive power, as might be most subservient to the public good, and best suit the ends of parliaments.

Sect. 168. The old question will be asked in this matter of prerogative, But who shall be judge when this power is made a right use of? one answer: between an executive power in being, with such a prerogative, and a legislative that depends upon his will for their convening, there can be no judge on earth; as there can be none between the legislative and the people, should either the executive, or the legislative, when they have got the power in their hands, design, or go about to enslave or destroy them. The people have no other remedy in this, as in all other cases where they have no judge on earth, but to appeal to heaven: for the rulers, in such attempts, exercising a power the people never put into their hands, (who can never be supposed to consent that any body should rule over them for their harm) do that which they have not a right to do. And where the body of the people, or any single man, is deprived of their right, or is under the exercise of a power without right, and have no appeal on earth, then they have a liberty to appeal to heaven, whenever they judge the cause of sufficient moment. And therefore, though the people cannot be judge, so as to have, by the constitution of that society, any superior power, to determine and give effective sentence in the case; yet they have, by a law antecedent and paramount to all positive laws of men, reserved that ultimate determination to themselves which belongs to all mankind, where there lies no appeal on earth, viz. to judge, whether they have just cause to make their appeal to heaven. And this judgment they cannot part with, it being out of a man's power so to submit himself to another, as to give him a liberty to destroy him; God and nature never allowing a man so to abandon himself, as to neglect his own preservation: and since he cannot take away his own life, neither can he give another power to take it. Nor let any one think, this lays a perpetual foundation for disorder; for this operates not, till the inconveniency is so great, that the majority feel it, and are weary of it, and find a necessity to have it amended. But this the executive power, or wise princes, never need come in the danger of: and it is the thing, of all others, they have most need to avoid, as of all others the most perilous…

CHAPTER XVII
OF USURPATION

Sect. 197. AS conquest may be called a foreign usurpation, so usurpation is a kind of domestic conquest, with this difference, that an usurper can never have right on his side, it being no usurpation, but where one is got into the possession of what another has right to. This, so far as it is usurpation, is a change only of persons, but not of the forms and rules of the government: for if the usurper extend his power beyond what of right belonged to the lawful princes, or governors of the commonwealth, it is tyranny added to usurpation.

Sect. 198. In all lawful governments, the designation of the persons, who are to bear rule, is as natural and necessary a part as the form of the government itself, and is that which had its establishment originally from the people; the anarchy being much alike, to have no form of government at all; or to agree, that it shall be monarchical, but to appoint no way to design the person that shall have the power, and be the monarch. Hence all commonwealths, with the form of government established, have rules also of appointing those who are to have any share in the public authority, and settled methods of conveying the right to them: for the anarchy is much alike, to have no form of government at all; or to agree that it shall be monarchical, but to appoint no way to know or design the person that shall have the power, and be the monarch. Whoever gets into the exercise of any part of the power, by other ways than what the laws of the community have prescribed, hath no right to be obeyed, though the form of the commonwealth be still preserved; since he is not the person the laws have appointed, and consequently not the person the people have consented to. Nor can such an usurper, or any deriving from him, ever have a title, till the people are both at liberty to consent, and have actually consented to allow, and confirm in him the power he hath till then usurped.

CHAPTER XVIII
OF TYRANNY

Sect. 199. AS usurpation is the exercise of power, which another hath a right to; so tyranny is the exercise of power beyond right, which no body can have a right to. And this is making use of the power any one has in his hands, not for the good of those who are under it, but for his own private separate advantage. When the governor, however intitled, makes not the law, but his will, the rule; and his commands and actions are not directed to the preservation of the properties of his people, but the satisfaction of his own ambition, revenge, covetousness, or any other irregular passion.

Sect. 200. If one can doubt this to be truth, or reason, because it comes from the obscure hand of a subject, I hope the authority of a king will make it pass with him. King James the first, in his speech to the parliament, 1603, tells them thus,

I will ever prefer the weal of the public, and of the whole commonwealth, in making of good laws and constitutions, to any particular and private ends of mine; thinking ever the wealth and weal of the commonwealth to be my greatest weal and worldly felicity; a point wherein a lawful king doth directly differ from a tyrant: for I do acknowledge, that the special

and greatest point of difference that is between a rightful king and an usurping tyrant, is
this, that whereas the proud and ambitious
tyrant doth think his kingdom and people are
5 only ordained for satisfaction of his desires
and unreasonable appetites, the righteous and
just king doth by the contrary acknowledge
himself to be ordained for the procuring of
the wealth and property of his people.
10

And again, in his speech to the parliament,
1609, he hath these words:

The king binds himself by a double oath, to
15 the observation of the fundamental laws of his
kingdom; tacitly, as by being a king, and so
bound to protect as well the people, as the
laws of his kingdom; and expressly, by his
oath at his coronation, so as every just king, in
20 a settled kingdom, is bound to observe that
paction made to his people, by his laws, in
framing his government agreeable thereunto,
according to that paction which God made
with Noah after the deluge. Hereafter, seed-
25 time and harvest, and cold and heat, and
summer and winter, and day and night, shall
not cease while the earth remaineth. And
therefore a king governing in a settled kingdom, leaves to be a king, and degenerates into
30 a tyrant, as soon as he leaves off to rule according to his laws.

And a little after,

35 Therefore all kings that are not tyrants, or per-
jured, will be glad to bound themselves within
the limits of their laws; and they that persuade
them the contrary, are vipers, and pests both
against them and the commonwealth.
40

Thus that learned king, who well understood
the notion of things, makes the difference
betwixt a king and a tyrant to consist only in

this, that one makes the laws the bounds of
45 his power, and the good of the public, the end
of his government; the other makes all give
way to his own will and appetite.

Sect. 201. It is a mistake, to think this fault is
50 proper only to monarchies; other forms of
government are liable to it, as well as that: for
wherever the power, that is put in any hands
for the government of the people, and the
preservation of their properties, is applied to
55 other ends, and made use of to impoverish,
harass, or subdue them to the arbitrary and
irregular commands of those that have it;
there it presently becomes tyranny, whether
those that thus use it are one or many. Thus
60 we read of the thirty tyrants at Athens, as well
as one at Syracuse; and the intolerable dominion of the Decemviri at Rome was nothing
better.

65 Sect. 202. Where-ever law ends, tyranny begins, if the law be transgressed to another's
harm; and whosoever in authority exceeds the
power given him by the law, and makes use of
the force he has under his command, to com-
70 pass that upon the subject, which the law allows not, ceases in that to be a magistrate; and,
acting without authority, may be opposed, as
any other man, who by force invades the right
of another. This is acknowledged in subordi-
75 nate magistrates. He that hath authority to
seize my person in the street, may be opposed
as a thief and a robber, if he endeavors to
break into my house to execute a writ, notwithstanding that I know he has such a war-
80 rant, and such a legal authority, as will empower him to arrest me abroad. And why this
should not hold in the highest, as well as in
the most inferior magistrate, I would gladly be
informed. Is it reasonable, that the eldest
85 brother, because he has the greatest part of his
father's estate, should thereby have a right to

take away any of his younger brothers portions? or that a rich man, who possessed a
whole country, should from thence have a
right to seize, when he pleased, the cottage
5 and garden of his poor neighbor? The being
rightfully possessed of great power and riches,
exceedingly beyond the greatest part of the
sons of Adam, is so far from being an excuse,
much less a reason, for rapine and oppression,
10 which the endamaging another without authority is, that it is a great aggravation of it: for
the exceeding the bounds of authority is no
more a right in a great, than in a petty officer;
no more justifiable in a king than a constable;
15 but is so much the worse in him, in that he has
more trust put in him, has already a much
greater share than the rest of his brethren, and
is supposed, from the advantages of his education, employment, and counselors, to be more
20 knowing in the measures of right and wrong.

Sect. 203. May the commands then of a prince
be opposed? may he be resisted as often as
any one shall find himself aggrieved, and but
25 imagine he has not right done him? This will
unhinge and overturn all polities, and, instead
of government and order, leave nothing but
anarchy and confusion.

30 Sect. 204. To this I answer, that force is to be
opposed to nothing, but to unjust and unlawful force; whoever makes any opposition in
any other case, draws on himself a just condemnation both from God and man; and so
35 no such danger or confusion will follow, as is
often suggested: for,

Sect. 205. First, As, in some countries, the
person of the prince by the law is sacred; and
40 so, whatever he commands or does, his person
is still free from all question or violence, not
liable to force, or any judicial censure or condemnation. But yet opposition may be made

to the illegal acts of any inferior officer, or
45 other commissioned by him; unless he will, by
actually putting himself into a state of war
with his people, dissolve the government, and
leave them to that defense which belongs to
every one in the state of nature: for of such
50 things who can tell what the end will be? and a
neighbor kingdom has showed the world an
odd example. In all other cases the sacredness
of the person exempts him from all inconveniencies, whereby he is secure, whilst the gov-
55 ernment stands, from all violence and harm
whatsoever; than which there cannot be a wiser constitution: for the harm he can do in his
own person not being likely to happen often,
nor to extend itself far; nor being able by his
60 single strength to subvert the laws, nor oppress the body of the people, should any
prince have so much weakness, and ill nature
as to be willing to do it, the inconveniency of
some particular mischiefs, that may happen
65 sometimes, when a heady prince comes to the
throne, are well recompensed by the peace of
the public, and security of the government, in
the person of the chief magistrate, thus set out
of the reach of danger: it being safer for the
70 body, that some few private men should be
sometimes in danger to suffer, than that the
head of the republic should be easily, and upon slight occasions, exposed.

75 Sect. 206. Secondly, But this privilege, belonging only to the king's person, hinders not, but
they may be questioned, opposed, and resisted, who use unjust force, though they pretend
a commission from him, which the law au-
80 thorizes not; as is plain in the case of him that
has the king's writ to arrest a man, which is a
full commission from the king; and yet he that
has it cannot break open a man's house to do
it, nor execute this command of the king upon
85 certain days, nor in certain places, though this
commission have no such exception in it; but

they are the limitations of the law, which if any one transgress, the king's commission excuses him not: for the king's authority being given him only by the law, he cannot empower any one to act against the law, or justify him, by his commission, in so doing; the commission, or command of any magistrate, where he has no authority, being as void and insignificant, as that of any private man; the difference between the one and the other, being that the magistrate has some authority so far, and to such ends, and the private man has none at all: for it is not the commission, but the authority, that gives the right of acting; and against the laws there can be no authority. But, notwithstanding such resistance, the king's person and authority are still both secured, and so no danger to governor or government.

Sect. 207. Thirdly, Supposing a government wherein the person of the chief magistrate is not thus sacred; yet this doctrine of the lawfulness of resisting all unlawful exercises of his power, will not upon every slight occasion endanger him, or embroil the government: for where the injured party may be relieved, and his damages repaired by appeal to the law, there can be no pretense for force, which is only to be used where a man is intercepted from appealing to the law: for nothing is to be accounted hostile force, but where it leaves not the remedy of such an appeal; and it is such force alone, that puts him that uses it into a state of war, and makes it lawful to resist him. A man with a sword in his hand demands my purse in the high-way, when perhaps I have not twelve pence in my pocket: this man I may lawfully kill. To another I deliver 100 pounds to hold only whilst I alight, which he refuses to restore me, when I am got up again, but draws his sword to defend the possession of it by force, if I endeavor to retake it. The mischief this man does me is a

hundred, or possibly a thousand times more than the other perhaps intended me (whom I killed before he really did me any); and yet I might lawfully kill the one, and cannot so much as hurt the other lawfully. The reason whereof is plain; because the one using force, which threatened my life, I could not have time to appeal to the law to secure it: and when it was gone, it was too late to appeal. The law could not restore life to my dead carcass: the loss was irreparable; which to prevent, the law of nature gave me a right to destroy him, who had put himself into a state of war with me, and threatened my destruction. But in the other case, my life not being in danger, I may have the benefit of appealing to the law, and have reparation for my 100 pounds that way.

Sect. 208. Fourthly, But if the unlawful acts done by the magistrate be maintained (by the power he has got), and the remedy which is due by law, be by the same power obstructed; yet the right of resisting, even in such manifest acts of tyranny, will not suddenly, or on slight occasions, disturb the government: for if it reach no farther than some private men's cases, though they have a right to defend themselves, and to recover by force what by unlawful force is taken from them; yet the right to do so will not easily engage them in a contest, wherein they are sure to perish; it being as impossible for one, or a few oppressed men to disturb the government, where the body of the people do not think themselves concerned in it, as for a raving mad-man, or heady malcontent to overturn a well settled state; the people being as little apt to follow the one, as the other.

Sect. 209. But if either these illegal acts have extended to the majority of the people; or if the mischief and oppression has lighted only

on some few, but in such cases, as the precedent, and consequences seem to threaten all;
and they are persuaded in their consciences,
that their laws, and with them their estates,
5   liberties, and lives are in danger, and perhaps
their religion too; how they will be hindered
from resisting illegal force, used against them,
I cannot tell. This is an inconvenience, I confess, that attends all governments whatsoever,
10   when the governors have brought it to this
pass, to be generally suspected of their people;
the most dangerous state which they can possibly put themselves in, wherein they are the
less to be pitied, because it is so easy to be
15   avoided; it being as impossible for a governor,
if he really means the good of his people, and
the preservation of them, and their laws together, not to make them see and feel it, as it
is for the father of a family, not to let his chil-
20   dren see he loves, and takes care of them.

Sect. 210. But if all the world shall observe
pretenses of one kind, and actions of another;
arts used to elude the law, and the trust of
25   prerogative (which is an arbitrary power in
some things left in the prince's hand to do
good, not harm to the people) employed contrary to the end for which it was given: if the
people shall find the ministers and subordinate
30   magistrates chosen suitable to such ends, and
favored, or laid by, proportionally as they
promote or oppose them: if they see several
experiments made of arbitrary power, and that
religion underhand favored, (tho' publicly pro-
35   claimed against) which is readiest to introduce
it; and the operators in it supported, as much
as may be; and when that cannot be done, yet
approved still, and liked the better: if a long
train of actions show the councils all tending
40   that way; how can a man any more hinder
himself from being persuaded in his own
mind, which way things are going; or from
casting about how to save himself, than he

could from believing the captain of the ship he
45   was in, was carrying him, and the rest of the
company, to Algiers, when he found him always steering that course, though cross winds,
leaks in his ship, and want of men and provisions did often force him to turn his course
50   another way for some time, which he steadily
returned to again, as soon as the wind, weather, and other circumstances would let him?

CHAPTER XIX
55   ## OF THE DISSOLUTION OF GOV-
ERNMENT

Sect. 211. HE that will with any clearness
speak of the dissolution of government, ought
60   in the first place to distinguish between the
dissolution of the society and the dissolution
of the government. That which makes the
community, and brings men out of the loose
state of nature, into one politic society, is the
65   agreement which every one has with the rest
to incorporate, and act as one body, and so be
one distinct commonwealth. The usual, and
almost only way whereby this union is dissolved, is the inroad of foreign force making a
70   conquest upon them: for in that case, (not
being able to maintain and support themselves, as one entire and independent body)
the union belonging to that body which consisted therein, must necessarily cease, and so
75   every one return to the state he was in before,
with a liberty to shift for himself, and provide
for his own safety, as he thinks fit, in some
other society. Whenever the society is dissolved, it is certain the government of that
80   society cannot remain. Thus conquerors
swords often cut up governments by the
roots, and mangle societies to pieces, separat-
ing the subdued or scattered multitude from
the protection of, and dependence on, that
85   society which ought to have preserved them
from violence. The world is too well instruct-

ed in, and too forward to allow of, this way of dissolving of governments, to need any more to be said of it; and there wants not much argument to prove, that where the society is dissolved, the government cannot remain; that being as impossible, as for the frame of an house to subsist when the materials of it are scattered and dissipated by a whirl-wind, or jumbled into a confused heap by an earthquake.

Sect. 212. Besides this over-turning from without, governments are dissolved from within.

First, When the legislative is altered. Civil society being a state of peace, amongst those who are of it, from whom the state of war is excluded by the umpirage, which they have provided in their legislative, for the ending all differences that may arise amongst any of them, it is in their legislative, that the members of a commonwealth are united, and combined together into one coherent living body. This is the soul that gives form, life, and unity, to the commonwealth: from hence the several members have their mutual influence, sympathy, and connection: and therefore, when the legislative is broken, or dissolved, dissolution and death follows: for the essence and union of the society consisting in having one will, the legislative, when once established by the majority, has the declaring, and as it were keeping of that will. The constitution of the legislative is the first and fundamental act of society, whereby provision is made for the continuation of their union, under the direction of persons, and bonds of laws, made by persons authorized thereunto, by the consent and appointment of the people, without which no one man, or number of men, amongst them, can have authority of making laws that shall be binding to the rest. When any one, or more, shall take upon them to make laws, whom the people have not appointed so to do, they make laws without authority, which the people are not therefore bound to obey; by which means they come again to be out of subjection, and may constitute to themselves a new legislative, as they think best, being in full liberty to resist the force of those, who without authority would impose any thing upon them. Every one is at the disposure of his own will, when those who had, by the delegation of the society, the declaring of the public will, are excluded from it, and others usurp the place, who have no such authority or delegation.

Sect. 213. This being usually brought about by such in the commonwealth who misuse the power they have; it is hard to consider it aright, and know at whose door to lay it, without knowing the form of government in which it happens. Let us suppose then the legislative placed in the concurrence of three distinct persons.

(1). A single hereditary person, having the constant, supreme, executive power, and with it the power of convoking and dissolving the other two within certain periods of time.

(2). An assembly of hereditary nobility.

(3). An assembly of representatives chosen, pro tempore, by the people. Such a form of government supposed, it is evident,

Sect. 214. First, That when such a single person, or prince, sets up his own arbitrary will in place of the laws, which are the will of the society, declared by the legislative, then the legislative is changed: for that being in effect the legislative, whose rules and laws are put in execution, and required to be obeyed; when other laws are set up, and other rules pretend-

ed, and enforced, than what the legislative, constituted by the society, have enacted, it is plain that the legislative is changed. Whoever introduces new laws, not being thereunto au-
5 thorized by the fundamental appointment of the society, or subverts the old, disowns and overturns the power by which they were made, and so sets up a new legislative.

10 Sect. 215. Secondly, When the prince hinders the legislative from assembling in its due time, or from acting freely, pursuant to those ends for which it was constituted, the legislative is altered: for it is not a certain number of men,
15 no, nor their meeting, unless they have also freedom of debating, and leisure of perfecting, what is for the good of the society, wherein the legislative consists: when these are taken away or altered, so as to deprive the society of
20 the due exercise of their power, the legislative is truly altered; for it is not names that consti-
tute governments, but the use and exercise of those powers that were intended to accompany them; so that he, who takes away the free-
25 dom, or hinders the acting of the legislative in its due seasons, in effect takes away the legislative, and puts an end to the government.

Sect. 216. Thirdly, When, by the arbitrary
30 power of the prince, the electors, or ways of election, are altered, without the consent, and contrary to the common interest of the people, there also the legislative is altered: for, if others than those whom the society hath au-
35 thorized thereunto, do chose, or in another way than what the society hath prescribed, those chosen are not the legislative appointed by the people.

40 Sect. 217. Fourthly, The delivery also of the people into the subjection of a foreign power, either by the prince, or by the legislative, is certainly a change of the legislative, and so a

dissolution of the government: for the end
45 why people entered into society being to be preserved one entire, free, independent society, to be governed by its own laws; this is lost, whenever they are given up into the power of another.
50

Sect. 218. Why, in such a constitution as this, the dissolution of the government in these cases is to be imputed to the prince, is evident; because he, having the force, treasure and of-
55 fices of the state to employ, and often per-
suading himself, or being flattered by others, that as supreme magistrate he is uncapable of control; he alone is in a condition to make great advances toward such changes, under
60 pretense of lawful authority, and has it in his hands to terrify or suppress opposers, as fac-
tious, seditious, and enemies to the govern-
ment: whereas no other part of the legislative, or people, is capable by themselves to attempt
65 any alteration of the legislative, without open and visible rebellion, apt enough to be taken notice of, which, when it prevails, produces effects very little different from foreign conquest. Besides, the prince in such a form of
70 government, having the power of dissolving the other parts of the legislative, and thereby rendering them private persons, they can never in opposition to him, or without his con-
currence, alter the legislative by a law, his con-
75 sent being necessary to give any of their de-
crees that sanction. But yet, so far as the other parts of the legislative any way contribute to any attempt upon the government, and do either promote, or not, what lies in them, hin-
80 der such designs, they are guilty, and partake in this, which is certainly the greatest crime which men can partake of one towards anoth-
er.

85 Sec. 219. There is one way more whereby such a government may be dissolved, and that is:

When he who has the supreme executive power, neglects and abandons that charge, so that the laws already made can no longer be put in execution. This is demonstratively to reduce all to anarchy, and so effectually to dissolve the government: for laws not being made for themselves, but to be, by their execution, the bonds of the society, to keep every part of the body politic in its due place and function; when that totally ceases, the government visibly ceases, and the people become a confused multitude, without order or connection. Where there is no longer the administration of justice, for the securing of men's rights, nor any remaining power within the community to direct the force, or provide for the necessities of the public, there certainly is no government left. Where the laws cannot be executed, it is all one as if there were no laws; and a government without laws is, I suppose, a mystery in politics, unconceivable to human capacity, and inconsistent with human society.

Sect. 220. In these and the like cases, when the government is dissolved, the people are at liberty to provide for themselves, by erecting a new legislative, differing from the other, by the change of persons, or form, or both, as they shall find it most for their safety and good: for the society can never, by the fault of another, lose the native and original right it has to preserve itself, which can only be done by a settled legislative, and a fair and impartial execution of the laws made by it. But the state of mankind is not so miserable that they are not capable of using this remedy, till it be too late to look for any. To tell people they may provide for themselves, by erecting a new legislative, when by oppression, artifice, or being delivered over to a foreign power, their old one is gone, is only to tell them, they may expect relief when it is too late, and the evil is past cure. This is in effect no more than to bid them first be slaves, and then to take care of their liberty; and when their chains are on, tell them, they may act like freemen. This, if barely so, is rather mockery than relief; and men can never be secure from tyranny, if there be no means to escape it till they are perfectly under it: and therefore it is, that they have not only a right to get out of it, but to prevent it.

Sect. 221. There is therefore, secondly, another way whereby governments are dissolved, and that is, when the legislative, or the prince, either of them, act contrary to their trust.

First, The legislative acts against the trust reposed in them, when they endeavor to invade the property of the subject, and to make themselves, or any part of the community, masters, or arbitrary disposers of the lives, liberties, or fortunes of the people.

Sect. 222. The reason why men enter into society, is the preservation of their property; and the end why they chose and authorize a legislative, is, that there may be laws made, and rules set, as guards and fences to the properties of all the members of the society, to limit the power, and moderate the dominion, of every part and member of the society: for since it can never be supposed to be the will of the society, that the legislative should have a power to destroy that which every one designs to secure, by entering into society, and for which the people submitted themselves to legislators of their own making; whenever the legislators endeavor to take away, and destroy the property of the people, or to reduce them to slavery under arbitrary power, they put themselves into a state of war with the people, who are thereupon absolved from any farther obedience, and are left to the common refuge, which God hath provided for all men, against force and violence. Whensoever therefore the legislative shall transgress this fundamental rule of society; and either by ambition, fear, folly or corruption, endeavor to grasp themselves, or put into the hands of any other, an absolute power over the lives, liberties, and estates of the people; by this breach of trust they forfeit the power the people had put into their hands for quite contrary ends, and it devolves to the people, who have a right to resume their original liberty, and, by the establishment of a new legislative, (such as they shall think fit) provide for their own safety and security, which is the end for which they are in society. What I have said here, concerning the legislative in general, holds true also concerning the supreme executor, who having a double trust put in him, both to have a part in the legislative, and the supreme execution of the law, acts against both, when he goes about to set up his own arbitrary will as the law of the society. He acts also contrary to his trust, when he either employs the force, treasure, and offices of the society, to corrupt the representatives, and gain them to his purposes; or openly preengages the electors, and prescribes to their choice, such, whom he has, by solicitations, threats, promises, or otherwise, won to his designs; and employs them to bring in such, who have promised before-hand what to vote, and what to enact. Thus to regulate candidates and electors, and new-model the ways of election, what is it but to cut up the government by the roots, and poison the very fountain of public security? for the people having reserved to themselves the choice of their representatives, as the fence to their properties, could do it for no other end, but that they might always be freely chosen, and so chosen, freely act, and advise, as the necessity of the commonwealth, and the public good should, upon examination, and mature debate, be judged to require. This, those who give their votes before they hear the debate, and have weighed the reasons on all sides, are not capable of doing. To prepare such an assembly as this, and endeavor to set up the declared abettors of his own will, for the true representatives of the people, and the lawmakers of the society, is certainly as great a breach of trust, and as perfect a declaration of a design to subvert the government, as is possible to be met with. To which, if one shall add rewards and punishments visibly employed to the same end, and all the arts of perverted law made use of, to take off and destroy all that stand in the way of such a design, and will not comply and consent to betray the liberties of their country, it will be past doubt what is doing. What power they ought to have in the society, who thus employ it contrary to the trust went along with it in its first institution, is easy to determine; and one cannot but see, that he, who has once attempted any such thing as this, cannot any longer be trusted.

Sect. 223. To this perhaps it will be said, that the people being ignorant, and always discontented, to lay the foundation of government in the unsteady opinion and uncertain humor of the people, is to expose it to certain ruin; and no government will be able long to subsist, if the people may set up a new legislative, whenever they take offence at the old one. To this I answer, Quite the contrary. People are not so easily got out of their old forms, as some are apt to suggest. They are hardly to be prevailed with to amend the acknowledged faults in the frame they have been accustomed to. And if there be any original defects, or adventitious ones introduced by time, or corruption; it is not an easy thing to get them changed, even when all the world sees there is an opportunity for it. This slowness and aversion in the people to quit their old constitutions, has, in the many revolutions which have been seen in this kingdom, in this and former ages, still kept us to, or, after some interval of fruitless attempts, still brought us back again to our old legislative of king, lords and commons: and whatever provocations have made the crown be taken from some of our princes heads, they never carried the people so far as to place it in another line.

Sect. 224. But it will be said, this hypothesis lays a ferment for frequent rebellion. To which I answer,

First, No more than any other hypothesis: for when the people are made miserable, and find themselves exposed to the ill usage of arbitrary power, cry up their governors, as much as you will, for sons of Jupiter; let them be sacred and divine, descended, or authorized from heaven; give them out for whom or what you please, the same will happen. The people generally ill treated, and contrary to right, will be ready upon any occasion to ease themselves of a burden that sits heavy upon them. They will wish, and seek for the opportunity, which in the change, weakness and accidents of human affairs, seldom delays long to offer itself. He must have lived but a little while in the world, who has not seen examples of this in his time; and he must have read very little, who cannot produce examples of it in all sorts of governments in the world.

Sect. 225. Secondly, I answer, such revolutions happen not upon every little mismanagement in public affairs. Great mistakes in the ruling part, many wrong and inconvenient laws, and all the slips of human frailty, will be born by the people without mutiny or murmur. But if a long train of abuses, prevarications and artifices, all tending the same way, make the design visible to the people, and they cannot but feel what they lie under, and see whither they are going; it is not to be wondered, that they should then rouse themselves, and endeavor to put the rule into such hands which may secure to them the ends for which government was at first erected; and without which, ancient names, and specious forms, are so far from being better, that they are much worse, than the state of nature, or pure anarchy; the inconveniencies being all as great and as near, but the remedy farther off and more difficult.

Sect. 226. Thirdly, I answer, that this doctrine of a power in the people of providing for their safety a-new, by a new legislative, when their legislators have acted contrary to their trust, by invading their property, is the best fence against rebellion, and the probablest means to hinder it: for rebellion being an opposition, not to persons, but authority, which is founded only in the constitutions and laws of the government; those, whoever they be, who by force break through, and by force justify their violation of them, are truly and properly rebels: for when men, by entering into society and civil-government, have excluded force, and introduced laws for the preservation of property, peace, and unity amongst themselves, those who set up force again in opposition to the laws, do rebellare, that is, bring back again the state of war, and are properly rebels: which they who are in power, (by the pretense they have to authority, the temptation of force they have in their hands, and the flattery of those about them) being likeliest to do; the properest way to prevent the evil, is to show them the danger and injustice of it, who are under the greatest temptation to run into it.

Sect. 227. In both the fore-mentioned cases, when either the legislative is changed, or the legislators act contrary to the end for which they were constituted; those who are guilty are guilty of rebellion: for if any one by force takes away the established legislative of any society, and the laws by them made, pursuant to their trust, he thereby takes away the umpirage, which every one had consented to, for a peaceable decision of all their controversies, and a bar to the state of war amongst them. They, who remove, or change the legislative, take away this decisive power, which no body can have, but by the appointment and consent of the people; and so destroying the authority which the people did, and no body else can set up, and introducing a power which the people hath not authorized, they actually introduce a state of war, which is that of force without authority: and thus, by removing the legislative established by the society, (in whose decisions the people acquiesced and united, as to that of their own will) they untie the knot, and expose the people a-new to the state of war, And if those, who by force take away the legislative, are rebels, the legislators themselves, as has been shown, can be no less esteemed so; when they, who were set up for the protection, and preservation of the people, their liberties and properties, shall by force invade and endeavor to take them away; and so they putting themselves into a state of war with those who made them the protectors and guardians of their peace, are properly, and with the greatest aggravation, rebellantes, rebels.

Sect. 228. But if they, who say it lays a foundation for rebellion, mean that it may occasion civil wars, or intestine broils, to tell the people they are absolved from obedience when illegal attempts are made upon their liberties or properties, and may oppose the unlawful violence of those who were their magistrates, when they invade their properties contrary to the trust put in them; and that therefore this doctrine is not to be allowed, being so destructive to the peace of the world: they may as well say, upon the same ground, that honest men may not oppose robbers or pirates, because this may occasion disorder or bloodshed. If any mischief come in such cases, it is not to be charged upon him who defends his own right, but on him that invades his neighbors. If the innocent honest man must quietly quit all he has, for peace sake, to him who will lay violent hands upon it, I desire it may be considered, what a kind of peace there will be in the world, which consists only in violence and rapine; and which is to be maintained only for the benefit of robbers and oppressors. Who would not think it an admirable peace betwixt the mighty and the mean, when the lamb, without resistance, yielded his throat to be torn by the imperious wolf? Polyphemus's den gives us a perfect pattern of such a peace, and such a government, wherein Ulysses and his companions had nothing to do, but quietly to suffer themselves to be devoured. And no doubt Ulysses, who was a prudent man, preached up passive obedience, and exhorted them to a quiet submission, by representing to them of what concernment peace was to mankind; and by showing the inconveniences might happen, if they should offer to resist Polyphemus, who had now the power over them.

Sect. 229. The end of government is the good of mankind; and which is best for mankind, that the people should be always exposed to the boundless will of tyranny, or that the rulers should be sometimes liable to be opposed, when they grow exorbitant in the use of their power, and employ it for the destruction, and not the preservation of the properties of their people?

Sect. 230. Nor let any one say, that mischief can arise from hence, as often as it shall please a busy head, or turbulent spirit, to desire the

alteration of the government. It is true, such men may stir, whenever they please; but it will be only to their own just ruin and perdition: for till the mischief be grown general, and the
5 ill designs of the rulers become visible, or their attempts sensible to the greater part, the people, who are more disposed to suffer than right themselves by resistance, are not apt to stir. The examples of particular injustice, or
10 oppression of here and there an unfortunate man, moves them not. But if they universally have a persuasion, grounded upon manifest evidence, that designs are carrying on against their liberties, and the general course and ten-
15 dency of things cannot but give them strong suspicions of the evil intention of their governors, who is to be blamed for it? Who can help it, if they, who might avoid it, bring themselves into this suspicion? Are the people
20 to be blamed, if they have the sense of rational creatures, and can think of things no otherwise than as they find and feel them? And is it not rather their fault, who put things into such a posture, that they would not have them
25 thought to be as they are? I grant, that the pride, ambition, and turbulency of private men have sometimes caused great disorders in commonwealths, and factions have been fatal to states and kingdoms. But whether the mis-
30 chief hath oftener begun in the peoples wantonness, and a desire to cast off the lawful authority of their rulers, or in the rulers insolence, and endeavors to get and exercise an arbitrary power over their people; whether
35 oppression, or disobedience, gave the first rise to the disorder, I leave it to impartial history to determine. This I am sure, whoever, either ruler or subject, by force goes about to invade the rights of either prince or people, and lays
40 the foundation for overturning the constitution and frame of any just government, is highly guilty of the greatest crime, I think, a man is capable of, being to answer for all

those mischiefs of blood, rapine, and desola-
45 tion, which the breaking to pieces of governments bring on a country. And he who does it, is justly to be esteemed the common enemy and pest of mankind, and is to be treated accordingly.
50

Sect. 231. That subjects or foreigners, attempting by force on the properties of any people, may be resisted with force, is agreed on all hands. But that magistrates, doing the same
55 thing, may be resisted, hath of late been denied: as if those who had the greatest privileges and advantages by the law, had thereby a power to break those laws, by which alone they were set in a better place than their breth-
60 ren: whereas their offence is thereby the greater, both as being ungrateful for the greater share they have by the law, and breaking also that trust, which is put into their hands by their brethren.
65

Sect. 232. Whosoever uses force without right, as every one does in society, who does it without law, puts himself into a state of war with those against whom he so uses it; and in that
70 state all former ties are cancelled, all other rights cease, and every one has a right to defend himself, and to resist the aggressor. This is so evident, that Barclay himself, that great assertor of the power and sacredness of kings,
75 is forced to confess, That it is lawful for the people, in some cases, to resist their king; and that too in a chapter, wherein he pretends to show, that the divine law shuts up the people from all manner of rebellion. Whereby it is
80 evident, even by his own doctrine, that, since they may in some cases resist, all resisting of princes is not rebellion...

Sect. 243. To conclude, The power that every
85 individual gave the society, when he entered into it, can never revert to the individuals

again, as long as the society lasts, but will always remain in the community; because without this there can be no community, no commonwealth, which is contrary to the original agreement: so also when the society hath placed the legislative in any assembly of men, to continue in them and their successors, with direction and authority for providing such successors, the legislative can never revert to the people whilst that government lasts; because having provided a legislative with power to continue for ever, they have given up their political power to the legislative, and cannot resume it. But if they have set limits to the duration of their legislative, and made this supreme power in any person, or assembly, only temporary; or else, when by the miscarriages of those in authority, it is forfeited; upon the forfeiture, or at the determination of the time set, it reverts to the society, and the people have a right to act as supreme, and continue the legislative in themselves; or erect a new form, or under the old form place it in new hands, as they think good.

FINIS.

ROUSSEAU

Jean Jacques Rousseau (1712-1778) is perhaps the most roguish of the canonical political theorists. Born in Geneva, Rousseau was raised by single father, then by relatives, and then by a professional proselytizer who was likely also his lover. He then moved to Paris an was both a frequent failure—as a diplomat, composer, inventor—and a rather horrible person—Rousseau had five children, all of whom he left on doorsteps. But it all turned around for him when he won a prestigious essay contest, which set the stage for his later success and a popular writer and public intellectual.

Many of Rousseau's work deal with political theory, but two standout: the *Discourse on Inequality* (or *Second Discourse*) and *Social Contract*. These two works are something of a pair, the second answer the question of the first. The *Discourse* deals with the formation of society and the birth of inequality in a world, with Rousseau controversially arguing that civilization, rather than bettering us, is the cause of man's misery. *Social Contract* picks up this thread by deal with the question of political legitimacy, arguing that the best form of government is one to which we give over everything, thus rending inequality and other social distinctions nullities. With Rousseau we can see the second branch of classical liberalism, with Locke representing the path of the Anglo-sphere and Rousseau that of the continent.

DISCOURSE ON INEQUALITY
JEAN JACQUES ROUSSEAU

A DISSERTATION ON THE ORIGIN AND FOUNDATION OF THE INEQUALITY OF MANKIND

5 It is of man that I have to speak; and the question I am investigating shows me that it is to men that I must address myself: for questions of this sort are not asked by those who are afraid to honor truth. I shall then confidently
10 uphold the cause of humanity before the wise men who invite me to do so, and shall not be dissatisfied if I acquit myself in a manner worthy of my subject and of my judges.

15 I conceive that there are two kinds of inequality among the human species; one, which I call natural or physical, because it is established by nature, and consists in a difference of age, health, bodily strength, and the qualities of the
20 mind or of the soul: and another, which may be called moral or political inequality, because it depends on a kind of convention, and is established, or at least authorized by the consent of men. This latter consists of the differ-
25 ent privileges, which some men enjoy to the prejudice of others; such as that of being more rich, more honored, more powerful or even in a position to exact obedience.

30 It is useless to ask what is the source of natural inequality, because that question is answered by the simple definition of the word. Again, it is still more useless to inquire whether there is any essential connection between
35 the two inequalities; for this would be only

Text based off the G.D.H. Cole translation, with adjustments for modern spellings.

asking, in other words, whether those who command are necessarily better than those who obey, and if strength of body or of mind, wisdom or virtue are always found in particu-
40 lar individuals, in proportion to their power or wealth: a question fit perhaps to be discussed by slaves in the hearing of their masters, but highly unbecoming to reasonable and free men in search of the truth.

45

The subject of the present discourse, therefore, is more precisely this. To mark, in the progress of things, the moment at which right took the place of violence and nature became
50 subject to law, and to explain by what sequence of miracles the strong came to submit to serve the weak, and the people to purchase imaginary repose at the expense of real felicity.

55 The philosophers, who have inquired into the foundations of society, have all felt the necessity of going back to a state of nature; but not one of them has got there. Some of them have not hesitated to ascribe to man, in such a state,
60 the idea of just and unjust, without troubling themselves to show that he must be possessed of such an idea, or that it could be of any use to him. Others have spoken of the natural right of every man to keep what belongs to
65 him, without explaining what they meant by *belongs*. Others again, beginning by giving the strong authority over the weak, proceeded directly to the birth of government, without regard to the time that must have elapsed be-
70 fore the meaning of the words authority and government could have existed among men. Every one of them, in short, constantly dwell-

ing on wants, avidity, oppression, desires and pride, has transferred to the state of nature ideas which were acquired in society; so that, in speaking of the savage, they described the social man. It has not even entered into the heads of most of our writers to doubt whether the state of nature ever existed; but it is clear from the Holy Scriptures that the first man, having received his understanding and commandments immediately from God, was not himself in such a state; and that, if we give such credit to the writings of Moses as every Christian philosopher ought to give, we must deny that, even before the deluge, men were ever in the pure state of nature; unless, indeed, they fell back into it from some very extraordinary circumstance; a paradox which it would be very embarrassing to defend, and quite impossible to prove.

Let us begin then by laying facts aside, as they do not affect the question. The investigations we may enter into, in treating this subject, must not be considered as historical truths, but only as mere conditional and hypothetical reasonings, rather calculated to explain the nature of things, than to ascertain their actual origin; just like the hypotheses which our physicists daily form respecting the formation of the world. Religion commands us to believe that, God Himself having taken men out of a state of nature immediately after the creation, they are unequal only because it is His will they should be so: but it does not forbid us to form conjectures based solely on the nature of man, and the beings around him, concerning what might have become of the human race, if it had been left to itself. This then is the question asked me, and that which I propose to discuss in the following discourse. As my subject interests mankind in general, I shall endeavor to make use of a style adapted to all nations, or rather, forgetting time and place, to attend only to men to whom I am speaking. I shall suppose myself in the Lyceum of Athens, repeating the lessons of my masters, with Plato and Xenocrates for judges, and the whole human race for audience.

O man, of whatever country you are, and whatever your opinions may be, behold your history, such as I have thought to read it, not in books written by your fellow-creatures, who are liars, but in nature, which never lies. All that comes from her will be true; nor will you meet with anything false, unless I have involuntarily put in something of my own. The times of which I am going to speak are very remote: how much are you changed from what you once were! It is so to speak, the life of your species which I am going to write, after the qualities which you have received, which your education and habits may have depraved, but cannot have entirely destroyed. There is, I feel, an age at which the individual man would wish to stop; you are about to inquire about the age at which you would have liked your whole species to stand still. Discontented with your present state, for reasons which threaten your unfortunate descendants with still greater discontent, you will perhaps wish it were in your power to go back; and this feeling should be a panegyric on your first ancestors, a criticism of your contemporaries, and a terror to the unfortunates who will come after you.

THE FIRST PART

Important as it may be, in order to judge rightly of the natural state of man, to consider him from his origin, and to examine him, as it were, in the embryo of his species; I shall not follow his organization through its successive developments, nor shall I stay to inquire what his animal system must have been at the be-

ginning, in order to become at length what it actually is. I shall not ask whether his long nails were at first, as Aristotle supposes, only crooked talons; whether his whole body, like
5 that of a bear, was not covered with hair; or whether the fact that he walked upon all fours, with his looks directed toward the earth, confined to a horizon of a few paces, did not at once point out the nature and limits of his
10 ideas. On this subject I could form none but vague and almost imaginary conjectures. Comparative anatomy has as yet made too little progress, and the observations of naturalists are too uncertain, to afford an adequate
15 basis for any solid reasoning. So that, without having recourse to the supernatural information given us on this head, or paying any regard to the changes which must have taken place in the internal, as well as the external,
20 conformation of man, as he applied his limbs to new uses, and fed himself on new kinds of food, I shall suppose his conformation to have been at all times what it appears to us at this day; that he always walked on two legs, made
25 use of his hands as we do, directed his looks over all nature, and measured with his eyes the vast expanse of Heaven.

If we strip this being, thus constituted, of all
30 the supernatural gifts he may have received, and all the artificial faculties he can have acquired only by a long process; if we consider him, in a word, just as he must have come from the hands of nature, we behold in him an
35 animal weaker than some, and less agile than others; but, taking him all round, the most advantageously organized of any. I see him satisfying his hunger at the first oak, and slaking his thirst at the first brook; finding his bed
40 at the foot of the tree which afforded him a repast; and, with that, all his wants supplied.

While the earth was left to its natural fertility

and covered with immense forests, whose
45 trees were never mutilated by the axe, it would present on every side both sustenance and shelter for every species of animal. Men dispersed up and down among the rest, would observe and imitate their industry, and thus
50 attain even to the instinct of the beasts, with the advantage that, whereas every species of brutes was confined to one particular instinct, man, who perhaps has not any one peculiar to himself, would appropriate them all, and live
55 upon most of those different foods, which other animals shared among themselves; and thus would find his subsistence much more easily than any of the rest.

60 Accustomed from their infancy to the inclemencies of the weather and the rigor of the seasons, inured to fatigue, and forced, naked and unarmed, to defend themselves and their prey from other ferocious animals, or to escape
65 them by flight, men would acquire a robust and almost unalterable constitution. The children, bringing with them into the world the excellent constitution of their parents, and fortifying it by the very exercises which first
70 produced it, would thus acquire all the vigor of which the human frame is capable. Nature in this case treats them exactly as Sparta treated the children of her citizens: those who come well formed into the world she renders
75 strong and robust, and all the rest she destroys; differing in this respect from our modern communities, in which the State, by making children a burden to their parents, kills them indiscriminately before they are born.
80

The body of a savage man being the only instrument he understands, he uses it for various purposes, of which ours, for want of practice, are incapable: for our industry deprives us of
85 that force and agility, which necessity obliges him to acquire. If he had had an axe, would he

have been able with his naked arm to break so large a branch from a tree? If he had had a sling, would he have been able to throw a stone with so great velocity? If he had had a
5 ladder, would he have been so nimble in climbing a tree? If he had had a horse, would he have been himself so swift of foot? Give civilized man time to gather all his machines about him, and he will no doubt easily beat the
10 savage; but if you would see a still more unequal contest, set them together naked and unarmed, and you will soon see the advantage of having all our forces constantly at our disposal, of being always prepared for every event,
15 and of carrying one's self, as it were, perpetually whole and entire about one.

Hobbes contends that man is naturally intrepid, and is intent only upon attacking and
20 fighting. Another illustrious philosopher holds the opposite, and Cumberland and Puffendorf also affirm that nothing is more timid and fearful than man in the state of nature; that he is always in a tremble, and ready to fly at the
25 least noise or the slightest movement. This may be true of things he does not know; and I do not doubt his being terrified by every novelty that presents itself, when he neither knows the physical good or evil he may expect
30 from it, nor can make a comparison between his own strength and the dangers he is about to encounter. Such circumstances, however, rarely occur in a state of nature, in which all things proceed in a uniform manner, and the
35 face of the earth is not subject to those sudden and continual changes which arise from the passions and caprices of bodies of men living together. But savage man, living dispersed among other animals and finding himself be-
40 times in a situation to measure his strength with theirs, soon comes to compare himself with them; and, perceiving that he surpasses them more in adroitness than they surpass him

in strength, learns to be no longer afraid of
45 them. Set a bear, or a wolf, against a robust, agile, and resolute savage, as they all are, armed with stones and a good cudgel, and you will see that the danger will be at least on both sides, and that, after a few trials of this kind,
50 wild beasts, which are not fond of attacking each other, will not be at all ready to attack man, whom they will have found to be as wild and ferocious as themselves. With regard to such animals as have really more strength than
55 man has adroitness, he is in the same situation as all weaker animals, which notwithstanding are still able to subsist; except indeed that he has the advantage that, being equally swift of foot, and finding an almost certain place of
60 refuge in every tree, he is at liberty to take or leave it at every encounter, and thus to fight or fly, as he chooses. Add to this that it does not appear that any animal naturally makes war on man, except in case of self-defense or exces-
65 sive hunger, or betrays any of those violent antipathies, which seem to indicate that one species is intended by nature for the food of another.

70 This is doubtless why negroes and savages are so little afraid of the wild beasts they may meet in the woods. The Caraibs of Venezuela among others live in this respect in absolute security and without the smallest inconven-
75 ience. Though they are almost naked, Francis Correal tells us, they expose themselves freely in the woods, armed only with bows and arrows; but no one has ever heard of one of them being devoured by wild beasts.
80

But man has other enemies more formidable, against which he is not provided with such means of defense: these are the natural infirmities of infancy, old age, and illness of every
85 kind, melancholy proofs of our weakness, of which the two first are common to all animals,

and the last belongs chiefly to man in a state of society. With regard to infancy, it is observable that the mother, carrying her child always with her, can nurse it with much greater ease than the females of many other animals, which are forced to be perpetually going and coming, with great fatigue, one way to find subsistence, and another to suckle or feed their young. It is true that if the woman happens to perish, the infant is in great danger of perishing with her; but this risk is common to many other species of animals, whose young take a long time before they are able to provide for themselves. And if our infancy is longer than theirs, our lives are longer in proportion; so that all things are in this respect fairly equal; though there are other rules to be considered regarding the duration of the first period of life, and the number of young, which do not affect the present subject. In old age, when men are less active and perspire little, the need for food diminishes with the ability to provide it. As the savage state also protects them from gout and rheumatism, and old age is, of all ills, that which human aid can least alleviate, they cease to be, without others perceiving that they are no more, and almost without perceiving it themselves.

With respect to sickness, I shall not repeat the vain and false declamations which most healthy people pronounce against medicine; but I shall ask if any solid observations have been made from which it may be justly concluded that, in the countries where the art of medicine is most neglected, the mean duration of man's life is less than in those where it is most cultivated. How indeed can this be the case, if we bring on ourselves more diseases than medicine can furnish remedies? The great inequality in manner of living, the extreme idleness of some, and the excessive labor of others, the easiness of exciting and gratifying our sensual appetites, the too exquisite foods of the wealthy which overheat and fill them with indigestion, and, on the other hand, the unwholesome food of the poor, often, bad as it is, insufficient for their needs, which induces them, when opportunity offers, to eat voraciously and overcharge their stomachs; all these, together with sitting up late, and excesses of every kind, immoderate transports of every passion, fatigue, mental exhaustion, the innumerable pains and anxieties inseparable from every condition of life, by which the mind of man is incessantly tormented; these are too fatal proofs that the greater part of our ills are of our own making, and that we might have avoided them nearly all by adhering to that simple, uniform and solitary manner of life which nature prescribed. If she destined man to be healthy, I venture to declare that a state of reflection is a state contrary to, nature, and that a thinking man is a depraved animal. When we think of the good constitution of the savages, at least of those whom we have not ruined with our spirituous liquors, and reflect that they are troubled with hardly any disorders, save wounds and old age, we are tempted to believe that, in following the history of civil society, we shall be telling also that of human sickness. Such, at least, was the opinion of Plato, who inferred from certain remedies prescribed, or approved, by Podalirius and Machaon at the siege of Troy, that several sicknesses which these remedies gave rise to in his time, were not then known to mankind: and Celsus tells us that diet, which is now so necessary, was first invented by Hippocrates.

Being subject therefore to so few causes of sickness, man, in the state of nature, can have no need of remedies, and still less of physicians: nor is the human race in this respect worse off than other animals, and it is easy to learn from hunters whether they meet with many infirm animals in the course of the chase. It is certain they frequently meet with such as carry the marks of having been considerably wounded, with many that have had bones or even limbs broken, yet have been healed without any Other surgical assistance than that of time, or any other regimen than that of their ordinary life. At the same time their cures seem not to have been less perfect, for their not having been tortured by incisions, poisoned with drugs, or wasted by fasting. In short, however useful medicine, properly administered, may be among us, it is certain that, if the savage, when he is sick and left to himself, has nothing to hope but from nature, he has, on the other hand, nothing to fear but from his disease; which renders his situation often preferable to our own.

We should beware, therefore, of confounding the savage man with the men we have daily before our eyes. Nature treats all the animals left to her care with a predilection that seems to show how jealous she is of that right. The horse, the cat, the bull, and even the ass are generally of greater stature, and always more robust, and have more vigor, strength and courage, when they run wild in the forests than when bred in the stall. By becoming domesticated, they lose half these advantages; and it seems as if all our care to feed and treat them well serves only to deprave them. It is thus with man also: as he becomes sociable and a slave, he grows weak, timid and servile; his effeminate way of life totally enervates his strength and courage. To this it may be added that there is still a greater difference between savage and civilized man, than between wild and tame beasts: for men and brutes having been treated alike by nature, the several conveniences in which men indulge themselves still more than they do their beasts, are so many additional causes of their deeper degeneracy.

It is not therefore so great a misfortune to these primitive men, nor so great an obstacle to their preservation, that they go naked, have no dwellings and lack all the superfluities which we think so necessary. If their skins are not covered with hair, they have no need of such covering in warm climates; and, in cold countries, they soon learn to appropriate the skins of the beasts they have overcome. If they have but two legs to run with, they have two arms to defend themselves with, and provide for their wants. Their children are slowly and with difficulty taught to walk; but their mothers are able to carry them with ease; advantage which other animals lack, as the mother, if pursued, is forced either to abandon her young, or to regulate her pace by theirs. Unless, in short, we suppose a singular and fortuitous concurrence of circumstances of which I shall speak later, and which would be unlikely to exist, it is plain in every state of the case, that the man who first made himself clothes or a dwelling was furnishing himself with things not at all necessary; for he had till then done without them, and there is no reason why he should not have been able to put up in manhood with the same kind of life as had been his in infancy.

Solitary, indolent, and perpetually accompanied by danger, the savage cannot but be fond of sleep; his sleep too must be light, like that of the animals, which think but little and may be said to slumber all the time they do not think. Self-preservation being his chief and almost sole concern, he must exercise most those faculties which are most concerned with attack or defense, either for overcoming his prey, or for preventing him from becoming the prey of other animals. On the other hand, those organs which are perfected only by soft-

ness and sensuality will remain in a gross and imperfect state, incompatible with any sort of delicacy; so that, his senses being divided on this head, his touch and taste will be extremely
5 coarse, his sight, hearing and smell exceedingly fine and subtle. Such in general is the animal condition, and such, according to the narratives of travellers, is that of most savage nations. It is therefore no matter for surprise
10 that the Hottentots of the Cape of Good Hope distinguish ships at sea, with the naked eye, at as great a distance as the Dutch can do with their telescopes; or that the savages of America should trace the Spaniards, by their
15 smell, as well as the best dogs could have done; or that these barbarous peoples feel no pain in going naked, or that they use large quantities of piemento with their food, and drink the strongest European liquors like wa-
20 ter.

Hitherto I have considered merely the physical man; let us now take a view of him on his metaphysical and moral side.
25

I see nothing in any animal but an ingenious machine, to which nature hath given senses to wind itself up, and to guard itself, to a certain degree, against anything that might tend to
30 disorder or destroy it. I perceive exactly the same things in the human machine, with this difference, that in the operations of the brute, nature is the sole agent, whereas man has some share in his own operations, in his char-
35 acter as a free agent. The one chooses and refuses by instinct, the other from an act of free-will: hence the brute cannot deviate from the rule prescribed to it, even when it would be advantageous for it to do so; and, on the
40 contrary, man frequently deviates from such rules to his own prejudice. Thus a pigeon would be starved to death by the side of a dish of the choicest meats, and a cat on a heap of

fruit or grain; though it is certain that either
45 might find nourishment in the foods which it thus rejects with disdain, did it think of trying them. Hence it is that dissolute men run into excesses which bring on fevers and death; because the mind depraves the senses, and the
50 will continues to speak when nature is silent.

Every animal has ideas, since it has senses; it even combines those ideas in a certain degree; and it is only in degree that man differs, in this
55 respect, from the brute. Some philosophers have even maintained that there is a greater difference between one man and another than between some men and some beasts. It is not, therefore, so much the understanding that
60 constitutes the specific difference between the man and the brute, as the human quality of free-agency. Nature lays her commands on every animal, and the brute obeys her voice. Man receives the same impulsion, but at the
65 same time knows himself at liberty to acquiesce or resist: and it is particularly in his consciousness of this liberty that the spirituality of his soul is displayed. For physics may explain, in some measure, the mechanism of the senses
70 and the formation of ideas; but in the power of willing or rather of choosing, and in the feeling of this power, nothing is to be found but acts which are purely spiritual and wholly inexplicable by the laws of mechanism.
75

However, even if the difficulties attending all these questions should still leave room for difference in this respect between men and brutes, there is another very specific quality
80 which distinguishes them, and which will admit of no dispute. This is the faculty of self-improvement, which, by the help of circumstances, gradually develops all the rest of our faculties, and is inherent in the species as in
85 the individual: whereas a brute is, at the end of a few months, all he will ever be during his

whole life, and his species, at the end of a thousand years, exactly what it was the first year of that thousand. Why is man alone liable to grow into a dotard? Is it not because he
5 returns, in this, to his primitive state; and that, while the brute, which has acquired nothing and has therefore nothing to lose, still retains the force of instinct, man, who loses, by age or accident, all that his *perfectibility* had enabled
10 him to gain, falls by this means lower than the brutes themselves? It would be melancholy, were we forced to admit that this distinctive and almost unlimited faculty is the source of all human misfortunes; that it is this which, in
15 time, draws man out of his original state, in which he would have spent his days insensibly in peace and innocence; that it is this faculty, which, successively producing in different ages his discoveries and his errors, his vices and his
20 virtues, makes him at length a tyrant both over himself and over nature. It would be shocking to be obliged to regard as a benefactor the man who first suggested to the Oroonoko Indians the use of the boards they apply to the
25 temples of their children, which secure to them some part at least of their imbecility and original happiness.

Savage man, left by nature solely to the direc-
30 tion of instinct, or rather indemnified for what he may lack by faculties capable at first of supplying its place, and afterwards of raising him much above it, must accordingly begin with purely animal functions: thus seeing and
35 feeling must be his first condition, which would be common to him and all other animals. To will, and not to will, to desire and to fear, must be the first, and almost the only operations of his soul, till new circumstances
40 occasion new developments of his faculties.

Whatever moralists may hold, the human understanding is greatly indebted to the passions, which, it is universally allowed, are also much
45 indebted to the understanding. It is by the activity of the passions that pure reason is improved; for we desire knowledge only because we wish to enjoy; and it is impossible to conceive any reason why a person who has
50 neither fears nor desires should give himself the trouble of reasoning. The passions, again, originate in our wants, and their progress depends on that of our knowledge; for we cannot desire or fear anything, except from the
55 idea we have of it, or from the simple impulse of nature. Now savage man, being destitute of every species of intelligence, can have no passions save those of the latter kind: his desires never go beyond his physical wants. The only
60 goods he recognizes in the universe are food, a female, and sleep: the only evils he fears are pain and hunger. I say pain, and not death: for no animal can know what it is to die; the knowledge of death and its terrors being one
65 of the first acquisitions made by man in departing from an animal state.

It would be easy, were it necessary, to support this opinion by facts, and to show that, in all
70 the nations of the world, the progress of the understanding has been exactly proportionate to the wants which the peoples had received from nature, or been subjected to by circumstances, and in consequence to the passions
75 that induced them to provide for those necessities. I might instance the arts, rising up in Egypt and expanding with the inundation of the Nile. I might follow their progress into Greece, where they took root afresh, grew up
80 and towered to the skies, among the rocks and sands of Attica, without being able to germinate on the fertile banks of the Eurotas: I might observe that in general, the people of the North are more industrious than those of
85 the South, because they cannot get on so well without being so: as if nature wanted to equal-

ize matters by giving their understandings the fertility she had refused to their soil.

But who does not see, without recurring to the uncertain testimony of history, that everything seems to remove from savage man both the temptation and the means of changing his condition? His imagination paints no pictures; his heart makes no demands on him. His few wants are so readily supplied, and he is so far from having the knowledge which is needful to make him want more, that he can have neither foresight nor curiosity. The face of nature becomes indifferent to him as it grows familiar. He sees in it always the same order, the same successions: he has not understanding enough to wonder at the greatest miracles; nor is it in his mind that we can expect to find that philosophy man needs, if he is to know how to notice for once what he sees every day. His soul, which nothing disturbs, is wholly wrapped up in the feeling of its present existence, without any idea of the future, however near at hand; while his projects, as limited as his views, hardly extend to the close of day. Such, even at present, is the extent of the native Caribbean's foresight: he will improvidently sell you his cotton-bed in the morning, and come crying in the evening to buy it again, not having foreseen he would want it again the next night.

The more we reflect on this subject, the greater appears the distance between pure sensation and the most simple knowledge: it is impossible indeed to conceive how a man, by his own powers alone, without the aid of communication and the spur of necessity, could have bridged so great a gap. How many ages may have elapsed before mankind were in a position to behold any other Are than that of the heavens. What a multiplicity of chances must have happened to teach them the commonest uses of that element! How often must they have let it out before they acquired the art of reproducing it? and how often may not such a secret have died with him who had discovered it? What shall we say of agriculture, an art which requires so much labor and foresight, which is so dependent on others that it is plain it could only be practiced in a society which had at least begun, and which does not serve so much to draw the means of subsistence from the earth —for these it would produce of itself—but to compel it to produce what is most to our taste? But let us suppose that men had so multiplied that the natural produce of the earth was no longer sufficient for their support; a supposition, by the way, which would prove such a life to be very advantageous for the human race; let us suppose that, without forges or workshops, the instruments of husbandry had dropped from the sky into the hands of savages; that they had overcome their natural aversion to continual labor; that they had learnt so much foresight for their needs; that they had divined how to cultivate the earth, to sow grain and plant trees; that they had discovered the arts of grinding corn, and of setting the grape to ferment—all being things that must have been taught them by the gods, since it is not to be conceived how they could discover them for themselves—yet after all this, what man among them would be so absurd as to take the trouble of cultivating a field, which might be stripped of its crop by the first comer, man or beast, that might take a liking to it; and how should each of them resolve to pass his life in wearisome labor, when, the more necessary to him the reward of his labor might be, the surer he would be of not getting it? In a word, how could such a situation induce men to cultivate the earth, till it was regularly parceled out among them; that is to say, till the state of nature had been abolished?

Were we to suppose savage man as trained in the art of thinking as philosophers make him; were we, like them, to suppose him a very philosopher capable of investigating the sublimest truths, and of forming, by highly abstract chains of reasoning, maxims of reason and justice, deduced from the love of order in general, or the known will of his Creator; in a word, were we to suppose him as intelligent and enlightened, as he must have been, and is in fact found to have been, dull and stupid, what advantage Would accrue to the species, from all such metaphysics, which could not be communicated by one to another, but must end with him who made them? What progress could be made by mankind, while dispersed in the woods among other animals? and how far could men improve or mutually enlighten one another, when, having no fixed habitation, and no need of one another's assistance, the same persons hardly met twice in their lives, and perhaps then, without knowing one another or speaking together?

Let it be considered how many ideas we owe to the use of speech; how far grammar exercises the understanding and facilitates its operations. Let us reflect on the inconceivable pains and the infinite space of time that the first invention of languages must have cost. To these reflections add what preceded, and then judge how many thousand ages must have elapsed in the successive development in the human mind of those operations of which it is capable.

I shall here take the liberty for a moment, of considering the difficulties of the origin of languages, on which subject I might content myself with a simple repetition of the Abbé Condillac's investigations, as they fully confirm my system, and perhaps even first suggested it. But it is plain, from the manner in which this philosopher solves the difficulties he himself raises, concerning the origin of arbitrary signs, that he assumes what I question, viz. that a kind of society, must already have existed among the first inventors of language. While I refer, therefore, to his observations on this head, I think it right to give my own, in order to exhibit the same difficulties in a light adapted to my subject. The first which presents itself is to conceive how language can have become necessary; for as there was no communication among men and no need for any, we can neither conceive the necessity of this invention, nor the possibility of it, if it was not somehow indispensable. I might affirm, with many others, that languages arose in the domestic intercourse between parents and their children. But this expedient would not obviate the difficulty, and would besides involve the blunder made by those who, in reasoning on the state of nature, always import into it ideas gathered in a state of society. Thus they constantly consider families as living together under one roof, and the individuals of each as observing among themselves a union as intimate and permanent as that which exists among us, where so many common interests unite them: whereas, in this primitive state, men had neither houses, nor huts, nor any kind of property whatever; every one lived where he could, seldom for more than a single night; the sexes united without design, as accident, opportunity or inclination brought them together, nor had they any great need of words to communicate their designs to each other; and they parted with the same indifference. The mother gave suck to her children at first for her own sake; and afterwards, when habit had made them dear, for theirs: but as soon as they were strong enough to go in search of their own food, they forsook her of their own accord; and, as they had hardly any other method of not losing one another than that of remaining continually within sight, they soon became quite incapable of recognizing one another when they happened to meet again. It is farther to be observed that the child, having all his wants to explain, and of course more to say to his mother than the mother could have to say to him, must have borne the brunt of the task of invention, and the language he used would be of his own device, so that the number of languages would be equal to that of the individuals speaking them, and the variety would be increased by the vagabond and roving life they led, which would not give time for any idiom to become constant. For to say that the mother dictated to her child the words he was to use in asking her for one thing or another, is an explanation of how languages already formed are taught, but by no means explains how languages were originally formed.

We will suppose, however, that this first difficulty is obviated. Let us for a moment then take ourselves as being on this side of the vast space which must lie between a pure state of nature and that in which languages had become necessary, and, admitting their necessity, let us inquire how they could first be established. Here we have a new and worse difficulty to grapple with; for if men need speech to learn to think, they must have stood in much greater need of the art of thinking, to be able to invent that of speaking. And though we might conceive how the articulate sounds of the voice came to be taken as the conventional interpreters of our ideas, it would still remain for us to inquire what could have been the interpreters of this convention for those ideas, which, answering to no sensible objects, could not be indicated either by gesture or voice; so that we can hardly form any tolerable conjectures about the origin of this art of communicating our thoughts and establishing a correspondence between minds: an art so sublime, that far distant as it is from its origin, philosophers still behold it at such an immeasurable distance from perfection, that there is none rash enough to affirm it will ever reach it, even though the revolutions time necessarily produces were suspended in its favor, though prejudice should be banished from our academies or condemned to silence, and those learned societies should devote themselves uninterruptedly for whole ages to this thorny question.

The first language of mankind, the most universal and vivid, in a word the only language man needed, before he had occasion to exert his eloquence to persuade assembled multitudes, was the simple cry of nature. But as this was excited only by a sort of instinct on urgent occasions, to implore assistance in case of danger, or relief in case of suffering, it could be of little use in the ordinary course of life, in which more moderate feelings prevail. When the ideas of men began to expand and multiply, and closer communication took place among them, they strove to invent more numerous signs and a more copious language. They multiplied the inflections of the voice, and added gestures, which are in their own nature more expressive, and depend less for their meaning on a prior determination. Visible and movable objects were therefore expressed by gestures, and audible ones by imitative sounds: but, as hardly anything can be indicated by gestures, except objects actually present or easily described, and visible actions; as they are not universally useful—for darkness or the interposition of a material object destroys their efficacy—and as besides they rather request than secure our attention; men at length bethought themselves of substituting for them the articulate sounds of the voice, which, without bearing the same relation to

any particular ideas, are better calculated to express them all, as conventional signs. Such an institution could only be made by common consent, and must have been effected in a
5　manner not very easy for men whose gross organs had not been accustomed to any such exercise. It is also in itself still more difficult to conceive, since such a common agreement must have had motives, and speech seems to
10　have been highly necessary to establish the use of it.

It is reasonable to suppose that the words first made use of by mankind had a much more extensive signification than those used in lan-
15　guages already formed, and that ignorant as they were of the division of discourse into its constituent parts, they at first gave every single word the sense of a whole proposition. When they began to distinguish subject and attribute,
20　and noun and verb, which was itself no common effort of genius, substantives were at first only so many proper names; the present infinitive was the only tense of verbs; and the very idea of adjectives must have been developed
25　with great difficulty; for every adjective is an abstract idea, and abstractions are painful and unnatural operations.

Every object at first received a particular name
30　without regard to genus or species, which these primitive originators were not in a position to distinguish; every individual presented itself to their minds in isolation, as they are in the picture of nature. If one oak was called A,
35　another was called B; for the primitive idea of two things is that they are not the same, and it often takes a long time for what they have in common to be seen: so that, the narrower the limits of their knowledge of things, the more
40　copious their dictionary must have been. The difficulty of using such a vocabulary could not be easily removed; for, to arrange beings under common and generic denominations, it

became necessary to know their distinguishing
45　properties: the need arose for observation and definition, that is to say, for natural history and metaphysics of a far more developed kind than men can at that time have possessed.

50　Add to this, that general ideas cannot be introduced into the mind without the assistance of words, nor can the understanding seize them except by means of propositions. This is one of the reasons why animals cannot form
55　such ideas, or ever acquire that capacity for self-improvement which depends on them. When a monkey goes from one nut to another, are we to conceive that he entertains any general idea of that kind of fruit, and com-
60　pares its archetype with the two individual nuts? Assuredly he does not; but the sight of one of these nuts recalls to his memory the sensations which he received from the other, and his eyes, being modified after a certain
65　manner, give information to the palate of the modification it is about to receive. Every general idea is purely intellectual; if the imagination meddles with it ever so little, the idea immediately becomes particular. If you en-
70　deavor to trace in your mind the image of a tree in general, you never attain to your end. In spite of all you can do, you will have to see it as great or little, bare or leafy, light or dark, and were you capable of seeing nothing in it
75　but what is common to all trees, it would no longer be like a tree at all. Purely abstract beings are perceivable in the same manner, or are only conceivable by the help of language. The definition of a triangle alone gives you a
80　true idea of it: the moment you imagine a triangle in your mind, it is some particular triangle and not another, and you cannot avoid giving it sensible lines and a colored area. We must then make use of propositions and of
85　language in order to form general ideas. For no sooner does the imagination cease to oper-

ate than the understanding proceeds only by the help of words. If then the first inventors of speech could give names only to ideas they already had, it follows that the first substan-

5 tives could be nothing more than proper names.

But when our new grammarians, by means of which I have no conception, began to extend

10 their ideas and generalize their terms, the ignorance of the inventors must have confined this method within very narrow limits; and, as they had at first gone too far in multiplying the names of individuals, from ignorance of their

15 genus and species, they made afterwards too few of these, from not having considered beings in all their specific differences. It would indeed have needed more knowledge and experience than they could have, and more pains

20 and inquiry than they would have bestowed, to carry these distinctions to their proper length. If, even to-day, we are continually discovering new species, which have hitherto escaped observation, let us reflect how many of them

25 must have escaped men who judged things merely from their first appearance! It is superfluous to add that the primitive classes and the most general notions must necessarily have escaped their notice also. How, for instance,

30 could they have understood or thought of the words matter, spirit, substance, mode, figure, motion, when even our philosophers, who have so long been making use of them, have themselves the greatest difficulty in under

35 standing them; and when, the ideas attached to them being purely metaphysical, there are no models of them to be found in nature?

But I stop at this point, and ask my judges to

40 suspend their reading a while, to consider, after the invention of physical substantives, which is the easiest part of language to invent, that there is still a great way to go, before the

thoughts of men will have found perfect ex-
45 pression and constant form, such as would answer the purposes of public speaking, and produce their effect on society. I beg of them to consider how much time must have been spent, and how much knowledge needed, to
50 find out numbers, abstract terms, aorists and all the tenses of verbs, particles, syntax, the method of connecting propositions, the forms of reasoning, and all the logic of speech. For myself, I am so aghast at the increasing diffi-
55 culties which present themselves, and so well convinced of the almost demonstrable impossibility that languages should owe their original institution to merely human means, that I leave, to any one who will undertake it, the
60 discussion of the difficult problem, which was most necessary, the existence of society to the invention of language, or the invention of language to the establishment of society. But be the origin of language and society what they
65 may, it may be at least inferred, from the little care which nature has taken to unite mankind by mutual wants, and to facilitate the use of speech, that she has contributed little to make them sociable, and has put little of her own
70 into all they have done to create such bonds of union. It is in fact impossible to conceive why, in a state of nature, one man should stand more in need of the assistance of another, than a monkey or a wolf of the assistance of
75 another of its kind: or, granting that he did, what motives could induce that other to assist him; or, even then, by what means they could agree about the conditions. I know it is incessantly repeated that man would in such a state
80 have been the most miserable of creatures; and indeed, if it be true, as I think I have proved, that he must have lived many ages, before he could have either desire or an opportunity of emerging from it, this would only
85 be an accusation against nature, and not against the being which she had thus unhappi-

ly constituted. But as I understand the word *miserable*, it either has no meaning at all, or else signifies only a painful privation of something, or a state of suffering either in body or soul. I should be glad to have explained to me, what kind of misery a free being, whose heart is at ease and whose body is in health, can possibly suffer. I would ask also, whether a social or a natural life is most likely to become insupportable to those who enjoy it. We see around us hardly a creature in civil society, who does not lament his existence: we even see many deprive themselves of as much of it as they can, and laws human and divine together can hardly put a stop to the disorder. I ask, if it was ever known that a savage took it into his head, when at liberty, to complain of life or to make away with himself. Let us therefore judge, with less vanity, on which side the real misery is found. On the other hand, nothing could be more unhappy than savage man, dazzled by science, tormented by his passions, and reasoning about a state different from his own. It appears that Providence most wisely determined that the faculties, which he potentially possessed, should develop themselves only as occasion offered to exercise them, in order that they might not be superfluous or perplexing to him, by appearing before their time, nor slow and useless when the need for them arose. In instinct alone, he had all he required for living in the state of nature; and with a developed understanding he has only just enough to support life in society.

It appears, at first view, that men in a state of nature, having no moral relations or determinate obligations one with another, could not be either good nor bad, virtuous or vicious; unless we take these terms in a physical sense, and call, in an individual, those qualities vices which may be injurious to his preservation, and those virtues which contribute to it; in which case, he would have to be accounted most virtuous, who put least check on the pure impulses of nature. But without deviating from the ordinary sense of the words, it will be proper to suspend the judgment we might be led to form on such a state, and be on our guard against our prejudices, till we have weighed the matter in the scales of impartiality, and seen whether virtues or vices preponderate among civilized men; and whether their virtues do them more good than their vices do harm; till we have discovered, whether the progress of the sciences sufficiently indemnifies them for the mischiefs they do one another, in proportion as they are better informed of the good they ought to do; or whether they would not be, on the whole, in a much happier condition if they had nothing to fear or to hope from any one, than as they are, subjected to universal dependence, and obliged to take everything from those who engage to give them nothing in return.

Above all, let us not conclude, with Hobbes, that because man has no idea of goodness, he must be naturally wicked; that he is vicious because he does not know virtue; that he always refuses to do his fellow-creatures services which he does not think they have a right to demand; or that by virtue of the right he truly claims to everything he needs, he foolishly imagines himself the sole proprietor of the whole universe. Hobbes had seen clearly the defects of all the modern definitions of natural right: but the consequences which he deduces from his own show that he understands it in an equally false sense. In reasoning on the principles he lays down, he ought to have said that the state of nature, being that in which the care for our own preservation is the least prejudicial to that of others, was consequently the best calculated to promote peace, and the most suitable for mankind. He does

say the exact opposite, in consequence of having improperly admitted, as a part of savage man's care for self-preservation, the gratification of a multitude of passions which are the
5 work of society, and have made laws necessary. A bad man, he says, is a robust child. But it remains to be proved whether man in a state of nature is this robust child: and, should we grant that he is, what would he infer? Why
10 truly, that if this man, when robust and strong, were dependent on others as he is when feeble, there is no extravagance he would not be guilty of; that he would beat his mother when she was too slow in giving him her breast; that
15 he would strangle one of his younger brothers, if he should be troublesome to him, or bite the arm of another, if he put him to any inconvenience. But that man in the state of nature is both strong and dependent involves
20 two contrary suppositions. Man is weak when he is dependent, and is his own master before he comes to be strong. Hobbes did not reflect that the same cause, which prevents a savage from making use of his reason, as our jurists
25 hold, prevents him also from abusing his faculties, as Hobbes himself allows: so that it may be justly said that savages are not bad merely because they do not know what it is to be good: for it is neither the development of the
30 understanding nor the restraint of law that hinders them from doing ill; but the peacefulness of their passions, and their ignorance of vice: *tanto plus in illis proficit vitiorum ignoratio, quam in his cognitio virtutis.*[17] There is another
35 principle which has escaped Hobbes; which, having been bestowed on mankind, to moderate, on certain occasions, the impetuosity of egoism, or, before its birth, the desire of self-preservation, tempers the ardor with which he

40 pursues his own welfare, by an innate repugnance at seeing a fellow-creature suffer.[18] I think I need not fear contradiction in holding man to be possessed of the only natural virtue, which could not be denied him by the most
45 violent detractor of human virtue. I am speaking of compassion which is a disposition suitable to creatures so weak and subject to so many evils as we certainly are: by so much the more universal and useful to mankind, as it
50 comes before any kind of reflection; and at the same time so natural, that the very brutes

---

[17] Justin. Hist, ii, 2. So much more does the ignorance of vice profit the one sort than the knowledge of virtue the other.

[18] Egoism must not be confused with self-respect: for they differ both in themselves and in their effects. Self-respect is a natural feeling which leads every animal to look to its own preservation, and which, guided in man by reason and modified by compassion, creates humanity and virtue. Egoism is a purely relative and factitious feeling, which arises in the state of society, leads each individual to make more of himself than of any other, causes all the mutual damage men inflict one on another, and is the real source of the "sense of honour." This being understood, I maintain that, in our primitive condition, in the true state of nature, egoism did not exist; for as each man regarded himself as the only observer of his actions, the only being in the universe who took any interest in him, and the sole judge of his deserts, no feeling arising from comparisons he could not be led to make could take root in his soul; and for the same reason, he could know neither hatred nor the desire for revenge, since these passions can spring only from a sense of injury: and as it is the contempt or the intention to hurt, and not the harm done, which constitutes the injury, men who neither valued nor compared themselves could do one another much violence, when it suited them, without feeling any sense of injury. In a word, each man, regarding his fellows almost as he regarded animals of different species, might seize the prey of a weaker or yield up his own to a stronger, and yet consider these acts of violence as mere natural occurrences, without the slightest emotion of insolence or despite, or any other feeling than the joy or grief of success or failure.

themselves sometimes give evident proofs of it. Not to mention the tenderness of mothers for their offspring and the perils they encounter to save them from danger, it is well known
5 that horses show a reluctance to trample on living bodies. One animal never passes by the dead body of another of its species: there are even some which give their fellows a sort of burial; while the mournful lowings of the cat-
10 tle when they enter the slaughter-house show the impressions made on them by the horrible spectacle which meets them. We find, with pleasure, the author of the Fable of the Bees obliged to own that man is a compassionate
15 and sensible being, and laying aside his cold subtlety of style, in the example he gives, to present us with the pathetic description of a man who, from a place of confinement, is compelled to behold a wild beast tear a child
20 from the arms of its mother, grinding its tender limbs with its murderous teeth, and tearing its palpitating entrails with its claws. What horrid agitation must not the eye-witness of such a scene experience, although he would
25 not be personally concerned! What anxiety would he not suffer at not being able to give any assistance to the fainting mother and the dying infant!

30 Such is the pure emotion of nature, prior to all kinds of reflection! Such is the force of natural compassion, which the greatest depravity of morals has as yet hardly been able to destroy! for we daily find at our theatres men affected,
35 nay shedding tears at the sufferings of a wretch who, were he in the tyrant's place, would probably even add to the torments of his enemies; like the bloodthirsty Sulla, who was so sensitive to ills he had not caused, or
40 that Alexander of Pheros who did not dare to go and see any tragedy acted, for fear of being seen weeping with Andromache and Priam, though he could listen without emotion to the

cries of all the citizens who were daily stran-
45 gled at his command.

Mollissima corda
Humano generi dare se natura fatetur,
Qua lacrimas dedit.
50 Juvenal, Satire xv, 151.[19]

Mandeville well knew that, in spite of all their morality, men would have never been better than monsters, had not nature bestowed on
55 them a sense of compassion, to aid their reason: but he did not see that from this quality alone flow all those social virtues, of which he denied man the possession. But what is generosity, clemency or humanity but compassion
60 applied to the weak, to the guilty, or to mankind in general? Even benevolence and friendship are, if we judge rightly, only the effects of compassion, constantly set upon a particular object: for how is it different to wish that an-
65 other person may not suffer pain and uneasiness and to wish him happy? Were it even true that pity is no more than a feeling, which puts us in the place of the sufferer, a feeling, obscure yet lively in a savage, developed yet fee-
70 ble in civilized man; this truth would have no other consequence than to confirm my argument. Compassion must, in fact, be the stronger, the more the animal beholding any kind of distress identifies himself with the
75 animal that suffers. Now, it is plain that such identification must have been much more perfect in a state of nature than it is in a state of reason. It is reason that engenders self-respect, and reflection that confirms it: it is reason
80 which turns man's mind back upon itself, and divides him from everything that could disturb or afflict him. It is philosophy that isolates him, and bids him say, at sight of the misfor-

---

[19] Nature avows she gave the human race the softest hearts, who gave < them tears.

tunes of others: "Perish if you will, I am secure." Nothing but such general evils as
threaten the whole community can disturb the
tranquil sleep of the philosopher, or tear him
5 from his bed. A murder may with impunity be
committed under his window; he has only to
put his hands to his ears and argue a little with
himself, to prevent nature, which is shocked
within him, from identifying itself with the
10 unfortunate sufferer. Uncivilized man has not
this admirable talent; and for want of reason
and wisdom, is always foolishly ready to obey
the first promptings of humanity. It is the
populace that flocks together at riots and
15 street-brawls, while the wise man prudently
makes off. It is the mob and the market-
women, who part the combatants, and hinder
gentle-folks from cutting one another's
throats.
20

It is then certain that compassion is a natural
feeling which, by moderating the violence of
love of self in each individual, contributes to
the preservation of the whole species. It is this
25 compassion that hurries us without reflection
to the relief of those who are in distress: it is
this which in a state of nature supplies the
place of laws, morals and virtues, with the
advantage that none are tempted to disobey its
30 gentle voice: it is this which will always prevent a sturdy savage from robbing a weak
child or a feeble old man of the sustenance
they may have with pain and difficulty acquired, if he sees a possibility of providing for
35 himself by other means: it is this which, instead of inculcating that sublime maxim of
rational justice, *Do to others as you would have
them do unto you,* inspires all men with that other maxim of natural goodness, much less per-
40 fect indeed, but perhaps more useful; *Do good
to yourself with as little evil as possible to others.* In a
word, it is rather in this natural feeling than in
any subtle arguments that we must look for

the cause of that repugnance, which every
45 man would experience in doing evil, even independently of the maxims of education. Although it might belong to Socrates and other
minds of the like craft to acquire virtue by
reason, the human race would long since have
50 ceased to be, had its preservation depended
only on the reasonings of the individuals
composing it.

With passions so little active, and so good a
55 curb, men, being rather wild than wicked, and
more intent to guard themselves against the
mischief that might be done them, than to do
mischief to others, were by no means subject
to very perilous dissensions. They maintained
60 no kind of intercourse with one another, and
were consequently strangers to vanity, deference, esteem and contempt; they had not the
least idea of *meum* and *tuum*, and no true conception of justice; they looked upon every
65 violence to which they were subjected, rather
as an injury that might easily be repaired than
as a crime that ought to be punished; and they
never thought of taking revenge, unless perhaps mechanically and on the spot, as a dog
70 will sometimes bite the stone which is thrown
at him. Their quarrels therefore would seldom
have very bloody consequences; for the subject of them would be merely the question of
subsistence. But I am aware of one greater
75 danger, which remains to be noticed.

Of the passions that stir the heart of man,
there is one which makes the sexes necessary
to each other, and is extremely ardent and
80 impetuous; a terrible passion that braves danger, surmounts all obstacles, and in its transports seems calculated to bring destruction on
the human race which it is really destined to
preserve. What must become of men who are
85 left to this brutal and boundless rage, without
modesty, without shame, and daily upholding

their amours at the price of their blood?

It must, in the first place, be allowed that, the more violent the passions are, the more are laws necessary to keep them under restraint. But, setting aside the inadequacy of laws to effect this purpose, which is evident from the crimes and disorders to which these passions daily give rise among us, we should do well to inquire if these evils did not spring up with the laws themselves; for in this case, even if the laws were capable of repressing such evils, it is the least that could be expected from them, that they should check a mischief which would not have arisen without them.

Let us begin by distinguishing between the physical and moral ingredients in the feeling of love. The physical part of love is that general desire which urges the sexes to union with each other. The moral part is that which determines and fixes this desire exclusively upon one particular object; or at least gives it a greater degree of energy toward the object thus preferred. It is easy to see that the moral part of love is a factitious feeling, born of social usage, and enhanced by the women with much care and cleverness, to establish their empire, and put in power the sex which ought to obey. This feeling, being founded on certain ideas of beauty and merit which a savage is not in a position to acquire, and on comparisons which he is incapable of making, must be for him almost non-existent; for, as his mind cannot form abstract ideas of proportion and regularity, so his heart is not susceptible of the feelings of love and admiration, which are even insensibly produced by the application of these ideas. He follows solely the character nature has implanted in him, and not tastes which he could never have acquired; so that every woman equally answers his purpose.

Men in a state of nature being confined merely to what is physical in love, and fortunate enough to be ignorant of those excellences, which whet the appetite while they increase the difficulty of gratifying it, must be subject to fewer and less violent fits of passion, and consequently fall into fewer and less violent disputes. The imagination, which causes such ravages among us, never speaks to the heart of savages, who quietly await the impulses of nature, yield to them involuntarily, with more pleasure than ardor, and, their wants once satisfied, lose the desire. It is therefore incontestable that love, as well as all other passions, must have acquired in society that glowing impetuosity, which makes it so often fatal to mankind. And it is the more absurd to represent savages as continually cutting one another's throats to indulge their brutality, because this opinion is directly contrary to experience; the Caribeans, who have as yet least of all deviated from the state of nature, being in fact the most peaceable of people in their amours, and the least subject to jealousy, though they live in a hot climate which seems always to inflame the passions.

With regard to the inferences that might be drawn, in the case of several species of animals, the males of which fill our poultry-yards with blood and slaughter, or in spring make the forests resound with their quarrels over their females; we must begin by excluding all those species, in which nature has plainly established, in the comparative power of the sexes, relations different from those which exist among us: thus we can base no conclusion about men on the habits of fighting cocks. In those species where the proportion is better observed, these battles must be entirely due to the scarcity of females in comparison with males; or, what amounts to the same thing, to the intervals during which the female

constantly refuses the advances of the male:
for if each female admits the male but during
two months in the year, it is the same as if the
number of females were five-sixths less. Now,
5 neither of these two cases is applicable to the
human species, in which the number of females usually exceeds that of males, and
among whom it has never been observed,
even among savages, that the females have,
10 like those of other animals, their stated times
of passion and indifference. Moreover, in several of these species, the individuals all take
fire at once, and there comes a fearful moment
of universal passion, tumult and disorder
15 among them; a scene which is never beheld in
the human species, whose love is not thus
seasonal. We must not then conclude from the
combats of such animals for the enjoyment of
the females, that the case would be the same
20 with mankind in a state of nature: and, even if
we drew such a conclusion, we see that such
contests do not exterminate other kinds of
animals, and we have no reason to think they
would be more fatal to ours. It is indeed clear
25 that they would do still less mischief than is
the case in a state of society; especially in
those countries in which, morals being still
held in some repute, the jealousy of lovers and
the vengeance of husbands are the daily cause
30 of duels, murders, and even worse crimes;
where the obligation of eternal fidelity only
occasions adultery, and the very laws of honour and continence necessarily increase de-
bauchery and lead to the multiplication of
35 abortions.

Let us conclude then that man in a state of
nature, wandering up and down the forests,
without industry, without speech, and without
40 home, an equal stranger to war and to all ties,
neither standing in need of his fellow-
creatures nor having any desire to hurt them,
and perhaps even not distinguishing them one

from another; let us conclude that, being self-
45 sufficient and subject to so few passions, he
could have no feelings or knowledge but such
as befitted his situation; that he felt only his
actual necessities, and disregarded everything
he did not think himself immediately con-
50 cerned to notice, and that his understanding
made no greater progress than his vanity. If by
accident he made any discovery, he was the
less able to communicate it to others, as he did
not know even his own children. Every art
55 would necessarily perish with its inventor,
where there was no kind of education among
men, and generations succeeded generations
without the least advance; when, all setting out
from the same point, centuries must have
60 elapsed in the barbarism of the first ages;
when the race was already old, and man remained a child.

If I have expatiated at such length on this
65 supposed primitive state, it is because I had so
many ancient errors and inveterate prejudices
to eradicate, and therefore thought it incumbent on me to dig down to their very root, and
show, by means of a true picture of the state
70 of nature, how far even the natural inequalities
of mankind are from having that reality and
influence which modern writers suppose.

It is in fact easy to see that many of the differ-
75 ences which distinguish men are merely the
effect of habit and the different methods of
life men adopt in society. Thus a robust or
delicate constitution, and the strength or
weakness attaching to it, are more frequently
80 the effects of a hardy or effeminate method of
education than of the original endowment of
the body. It is the same with the powers of the
mind; for education not only makes a difference between such as are cultured and such as
85 are not, but even increases the differences
which exist among the former, in proportion

to their respective degrees of culture: as the distance between a giant and a dwarf on the same road increases with every step they take. If we compare the prodigious diversity, which obtains in the education and manner of life of the various orders of men in the state of society, with the uniformity and simplicity of animal and savage life, in which every one lives on the same kind of food and in exactly the same manner, and does exactly the same things, it is easy to conceive how much less the difference between man and man must be in a state of nature than in a state of society, and how greatly the natural inequality of mankind must be increased by the inequalities of social institutions.

But even if nature really affected, in the distribution of her gifts, that partiality which is imputed to her, what advantage would the greatest of her favourites derive from it, to the detriment of others, in a state that admits of hardly any kind of relation between them? Where there is no love, of what advantage is beauty? Of what use is wit to those who do not converse, or cunning to those who have no business with others? I hear it constantly repeated that, in such a state, the strong would oppress the weak; but what is here meant by oppression? Some, it is said, would violently domineer over others, who would groan under a servile submission to their caprices. This indeed is exactly what I observe to be the case among us; but I do not see how it can be inferred of men in a state of nature, who could not easily be brought to conceive what we mean by dominion and servitude. One man, it is true, might seize the fruits which another had gathered, the game he had killed, or the cave he had chosen for shelter; but how would he ever be able to exact obedience, and what ties of dependence could there be among men without possessions? If, for instance, I am

driven from one tree, I can go to the next; if I am disturbed in one place, what hinders me from going to another? Again, should I happen to meet with a man so much stronger than myself, and at the same time so depraved, so indolent, and so barbarous, as to compel me to provide for his sustenance while he himself remains idle; he must take care not to have his eyes off me for a single moment; he must bind me fast before he goes to sleep, or I shall certainly either knock him on the head or make my escape. That is to say, he must in such a case voluntarily expose himself to much greater trouble than he seeks to avoid, or can give me. After all this, let him be off his guard ever so little; let him but turn his head aside at any sudden noise, and I shall be instantly twenty paces off, lost in the forest, and, my fetters burst asunder, he would never see me again.

Without my expatiating thus uselessly on these details, every one must see that as the bonds of servitude are formed merely by the mutual dependence of men on one another and the reciprocal needs that unite them, it is impossible to make any man a slave, unless he be first reduced to a situation in which he cannot do without the help of others: and, since such a situation does not exist in a state of nature, every one is there his own master, and the law of the strongest is of no effect.

Having proved that the inequality of mankind is hardly felt, and that its influence is next to nothing in a state of nature, I must next show its origin and trace its progress in the successive developments of the human mind. Having shown that human *perfectibility*, the social virtues, and the other faculties which natural man potentially possessed, could never develop of themselves, but must require the fortuitous concurrence of many foreign causes that might never arise, and without which he would have remained for ever in his primitive condition, I must now collect and consider the different accidents which may have improved the human understanding while depraving the species, and made man wicked while making him sociable; so as to bring him and the world from that distant period to the point at which we now behold them.

I confess that, as the events I am going to describe might have happened in various ways, I have nothing to determine my choice but conjectures: but such conjectures become reasons, when they are the most probable that can be drawn from the nature of things, and the only means of discovering the truth. The consequences, however, which I mean to deduce will not be barely conjectural; as, on the principles just laid down, it would be impossible to form any other theory that would not furnish the same results, and from which I could not draw the same conclusions.

This will be a sufficient apology for my not dwelling on the manner in which the lapse of time compensates for the little probability in the events; on the surprising power of trivial causes, when their action is constant; on the impossibility, on the one hand, of destroying certain hypotheses, though on the other we cannot give them the certainty of known matters of fact; on its being within the province of history, when two facts are given as real, and have to be connected by a series of intermediate facts, which are unknown or supposed to be so, to supply such facts as may connect them; and on its being in the province of philosophy when history is silent, to determine similar facts to serve the same end; and lastly, on the influence of similarity, which, in the case of events, reduces the facts to a much smaller number of different classes than is

commonly imagined. It is enough for me to offer these hints to the consideration of my judges, and to have so arranged that the general reader has no need to consider them at all.

THE SECOND PART

The first man who, having enclosed a piece of ground, bethought himself of saying *This is mine*, and found people simple enough to believe him, was the real founder of civil society. From how many crimes, wars and murders, from how many horrors and misfortunes might not any one have saved mankind, by pulling up the stakes, or filling up the ditch, and crying to his fellows, "Beware of listening to this impostor; you are undone if you once forget that the fruits of the earth belong to us all, and the earth itself to nobody." But there is great probability that things had then already come to such a pitch, that they could no longer continue as they were; for the idea of property depends on many prior ideas, which could only be acquired successively, and cannot have been formed all at once in the human mind.

Mankind must have made very considerable progress, and acquired considerable knowledge and industry which they must also have transmitted and increased from age to age, before they arrived at this last point of the state of nature. Let us then go farther back and endeavor to unify under a single point of view that slow succession of events and discoveries in the most natural order.

Man's first feeling was that of his own existence, and his first care that of self-preservation. The produce of the earth furnished him with all he needed, and instinct told him how to use it. Hunger and other appetites made him at various times experience various modes of existence; and among these

was one which urged him to propagate his species—a blind propensity that, having nothing to do with the heart, produced a merely animal act. The want once gratified, the two
5 sexes knew each other no more; and even the offspring was nothing to its mother, as soon as it could do without her.

Such was the condition of infant man; the life
10 of an animal limited at first to mere sensations, and hardly profiting by the gifts nature bestowed on him, much less capable of entertaining a thought of forcing anything from her. But difficulties soon presented them-
15 selves, and it became necessary to learn how to surmount them: the height of the trees, which prevented him from gathering their fruits, the competition of other animals desirous of the same fruits, and the ferocity of
20 those who needed them for their own preservation, all obliged him to apply himself to bodily exercises. He had to be active, swift of foot, and vigorous in light. Natural weapons, stones and sticks, were easily found: he learnt
25 to surmount the obstacles of nature, to contend in case of necessity with other animals, and to dispute for the means of subsistence even with other men, or to indemnify himself for what he was forced to give up to a strong-
30 er.

In proportion as the human race grew more numerous, men's cares increased. The difference of soils, climates and seasons, must have
35 introduced some differences into their manner of living. Barren years, long and sharp winters, scorching summers which parched the fruits of the earth, must have demanded a new industry. On the sea-shore and the banks of
40 rivers, they invented the hook and line, and became fishermen and eaters of fish. In the forests they made bows and arrows, and became huntsmen and warriors. In cold coun-

45 tries they clothed themselves with the skins of the beasts they had slain. The lightning, a volcano, or some lucky chance acquainted them with fire, a new resource against the rigors of winter: they next learned how to preserve this element, then how to reproduce it, and finally
50 how to prepare with it the flesh of animals which before they had eaten raw.

This repeated relevance of various beings to himself, and one to another, would naturally
55 give rise in the human mind to the perceptions of certain relations between them. Thus the relations which we denote by the terms, great, small, strong, weak, swift, slow, fearful, bold, and the like, almost insensibly compared at
60 need, must have at length produced in him a kind of reflection, or rather a mechanical prudence, which would indicate to him the precautions most necessary to his security.

65 The new intelligence which resulted from this development increased his superiority over other animals, by making him sensible of it. He would now endeavor, therefore, to ensnare them, would play them a thousand tricks, and
70 though many of them might surpass him in swiftness or in strength, would in time become the master of some and the scourge of others. Thus, the first time he looked into himself, he felt the first emotion of pride; and, at a time
75 when he scarce knew how to distinguish the different orders of beings, by looking upon his species as of the highest order, he prepared the way for assuming pre-eminence as an individual.
80

Other men, it is true, were not then to him what they now are to us, and he had no greater intercourse with them than with other animals; yet they were not neglected in his obser-
85 vations. The conformities, which he would in time discover between them, and between

himself and his female, led him to judge of others which were not then perceptible; and finding that they all behaved as he himself would have done in like circumstances, he naturally inferred that their manner of thinking and acting was altogether in conformity with his own. This important truth, once deeply impressed on his mind, must have induced him, from an intuitive feeling more certain and much more rapid than any kind of reasoning, to pursue the rules of conduct, which he had best observe towards them, for his own security and advantage.

Taught by experience that the love of wellbeing is the sole motive of human actions, he found himself in a position to distinguish the few cases, in which mutual interest might justify him in relying upon the assistance of his fellows; and also the still fewer cases in which a conflict of interests might give cause to suspect them. In the former case, he joined in the same herd with them, or at most in some kind of loose association, that laid no restraint on its members, and lasted no longer than the transitory occasion that formed it. In the latter case, every one sought his own private advantage, either by open force, if he thought himself strong enough, or by address and cunning, if he felt himself the weaker.

In this manner, men may have insensibly acquired some gross ideas of mutual undertakings, and of the advantages of fulfilling them: that is, just so far as their present and apparent interest was concerned: for they were perfect strangers to foresight, and were so far from troubling themselves about the distant future, that they hardly thought of the morrow. If a deer was to be taken, every one saw that, in order to succeed, he must abide faithfully by his post: but if a hare happened to come within the reach of any one of them, it is not to be doubted that he pursued it without scruple, and, having seized his prey, cared very little, if by so doing he caused his companions to miss theirs.

It is easy to understand that such intercourse would not require a language much more refined than that of rooks or monkeys, who associate together for much the same, purpose. Inarticulate cries, plenty of gestures and some imitative sounds, must have been for a long time the universal language; and by the addition, in every country, of some conventional articulate sounds (of which, as I have already intimated, the first institution is not too easy to explain) particular languages were produced; but these were rude and imperfect, and nearly such as now to be found among some savage nations.

Hurried on by the rapidity of time, by the abundance of things I have to say, and by the almost insensible progress of things in their beginnings, I pass over in an instant a multitude of ages; for the slower the events were in their succession, the more rapidly may they be described.

These first advances enabled men to make others with greater rapidity. In proportion as they grew enlightened, they grew industrious. They ceased to fall asleep under the first tree, or in the first cave that afforded them shelter; they invented several kinds of implements of hard and sharp stones, which they used to dig up the earth, and to cut wood; they then made huts out of branches, and afterwards learnt to plaster them over with mud and clay. This was the epoch of a first revolution, which established and distinguished families, and introduced a kind of property, in itself the source of a thousand quarrels and conflicts. As, however, the strongest were probably the first to

build themselves huts which they felt themselves able to defend, it may be concluded that the weak found it much easier and safer to imitate, than to attempt to dislodge them: and
5 of those who were once provided with huts, none could have any inducement to appropriate that of his neighbor; not indeed so much because it did not belong to him, as because it could be of no use, and he could not make
10 himself master of it without exposing himself to a desperate battle with the family which occupied it.

The first expansions of the human heart were
15 the effects of a novel situation, which united husbands and wives, fathers and children, under one roof. The habit of living together soon gave rise to the finest feelings known to humanity, conjugal love and paternal affection.
20 Every family became a little society, the more united because liberty—and reciprocal attachment were the only bonds of its union. The sexes, whose manner of life had been hitherto the same, began now to adopt differ-
25 ent ways of living. The women became more sedentary, and accustomed themselves to mind the hut and their children, while the men went abroad in search of their common subsistence. From living a softer life, both sexes
30 also began to lose something of their strength and ferocity: but, if individuals became to some extent less able to encounter wild beasts separately, they found it, on the other hand, easier to assemble and resist in common.
35
The simplicity and solitude of man's life in this new condition, the paucity of his wants, and the implements he had invented to satisfy them, left him a great deal of leisure, which he
40 employed to furnish himself with many conveniences unknown to his fathers: and this was the first yoke he inadvertently imposed on himself, and the first source of the evils he

prepared for his descendants. For, besides
45 continuing thus to enervate both body and mind, these conveniences lost with use almost all their power to please, and even degenerated into real needs, till the want of them became far more disagreeable than the possession of
50 them had been pleasant. Men would have been unhappy at the loss of them, though the possession did not make them happy.

We can here see a little better how the use of
55 speech became established, and insensibly improved in each family, and we may form a conjecture also concerning the manner in which various causes may have extended and accelerated the progress of language, by mak-
60 ing it more and more necessary. Floods or earthquakes surrounded inhabited districts with precipices or waters: revolutions of the globe tore off portions from the continent, and made them islands. It is readily seen that
65 among men thus collected and compelled to live together, a common idiom must have arisen much more easily than among those who still wandered through the forests of the continent. Thus it is very possible that after their
70 first essays in navigation the islanders brought over the use of speech to the continent: and it is at least very probable that communities and languages were first established in islands, and even came to perfection there before they
75 were known on the mainland.

Everything now begins to change its aspect. Men, who have up to now been roving in the woods, by taking to a more settled manner of
80 life, come gradually together, form separate bodies, and at length in every country arises a distinct nation, united in character and manners, not by regulations or laws, but by uniformity of life and food, and the common
85 influence of climate. Permanent neighborhood could not fail to produce, in time, some con-

nection between different families. Among young people of opposite sexes, living in neighboring huts, the transient commerce required by nature soon led, through mutual

5 intercourse, to another kind not less agreeable, and more permanent. Men began now to take the difference between objects into account, and to make comparisons; they acquired imperceptibly the ideas of beauty and merit,

10 which soon gave rise to feelings of preference. In consequence of seeing each other often, they could not do without seeing each other constantly. A tender and pleasant feeling insinuated itself into their souls, and the least

15 opposition turned it into an impetuous fury: with love arose jealousy; discord triumphed, and human blood was sacrificed to the gentlest of all passions.

20 As ideas and feelings succeeded one another, and heart and head were brought into play, men continued to lay aside their original wildness; their private connections became every day more intimate as their limits extended.

25 They accustomed themselves to assemble before their huts round a large tree; singing and dancing, the true offspring of love and leisure, became the amusement, or rather the occupation, of men and women thus assembled to-

30 gether with nothing else to do. Each one began to consider the rest, and to wish to be considered in turn; and thus a—value came to be attached to public esteem. Whoever sang or danced best, whoever was the handsomest, the

35 strongest, the most dexterous, or the most eloquent, came to be of most consideration; and this was the first step towards inequality, and at the same time towards vice. From these first distinctions arose on the one side vanity

40 and contempt and on the other shame and envy: and the fermentation caused by these new leavens ended by producing combinations fatal to innocence and happiness.

45 As soon as men began to value one another, and the idea of consideration had got a footing in the mind, every one put in his claim to it, and it became impossible to refuse it to any with impunity. Hence arose the first obliga-

50 tions of civility even among savages; and every intended injury became an affront; because, besides the hurt which might result from it, the party injured was certain to find in it a contempt for his person, which was often

55 more insupportable than the hurt itself.

Thus, as every man punished the contempt shown him by others, in proportion to his opinion of himself, revenge became terrible, and men bloody and cruel. This is precisely

60 the state reached by most of the savage nations known to us: and it is for want of having made a proper distinction in our ideas, and seen how very far they already are from the state of nature, that so many writers have hast-

65 ily concluded that man is naturally cruel, and requires civil institutions to make him more mild; whereas nothing is more gentle than man in his primitive state, as he is placed by nature at an equal distance from the stupidity

70 of brutes, and the fatal ingenuity of civilized man. Equally confined by instinct and reason to the sole care of guarding himself against the mischiefs which threaten him, he is restrained by natural compassion from doing any injury

75 to others, and is not led to do such a thing even in return for injuries received. For, according to the axiom of the wise Locke, *There can be no injury, where there is no property.*

80 But it must be remarked that the society thus formed, and the relations thus established among men, required of them qualities different from those which they possessed from their primitive constitution. Morality began to

85 appear in human actions, and every one, before the institution of law, was the only judge

and avenger of the injuries done him, so that the goodness which was suitable in the pure state of nature was no longer proper in the new-born state of society. Punishments had to
5 be made more severe, as opportunities of offending became more frequent, and the dread of vengeance had to take the place of the rigor of the law. Thus, though men had become less patient, and their natural compassion had al-
10 ready suffered some diminution, this period of expansion of the human faculties, keeping a just mean between the indolence of the primitive state and the petulant activity of our egoism, must have been the happiest and most
15 stable of epochs. The more we reflect on it, the more we shall find that this state was the least subject to revolutions, and altogether the very best man could experience; so that he can have departed from it only through some fatal
20 accident, which, for the public good, should never have happened. The example of savages, most of whom have been found in this state, seems to prove that men were meant to remain in it, that it is the real youth of the world,
25 and that all subsequent advances have been apparently so many steps towards the perfection of the individual, but in reality towards the decrepitude of the species.

30 So long as men remained content with their rustic huts, so long as they were satisfied with clothes made of the skins of animals and sewn together with thorns and fish-bones, adorned themselves only with feathers and shells, and
35 continued to paint their bodies different colors, to improve and beautify their bows and arrows and to make with sharp-edged stones fishing boats or clumsy musical instruments; in a word, so long as they undertook only
40 what a single person could accomplish, and confined themselves to such arts as did not require the joint labor of several hands, they lived free, healthy, honest and happy lives, so

long as their nature allowed, and as they con-
45 tinued to enjoy the pleasures of mutual and independent intercourse. But from the moment one man began to stand in need of the help of another; from the moment it appeared advantageous to any one man to have enough
50 provisions for two, equality disappeared, property was introduced, work became indispensable, and vast forests became smiling fields, which man had to water with the sweat of his brow, and where slavery and misery
55 were soon seen to germinate and grow up with the crops.

Metallurgy and agriculture were the two arts which produced this great revolution. The
60 poets tell us it was gold and silver, but, for the philosophers, it was iron and corn, which first civilized men, and ruined humanity. Thus both were unknown to the savages of America, who for that reason are still savage; the other na-
65 tions also seem to have continued in a state of barbarism while they practiced only one of these arts. One of the best reasons, perhaps, why Europe has been, if not longer, at least more constantly and highly civilized than the
70 rest of the world, is that it is at once the most abundant in iron and the most fertile in corn.

It is difficult to conjecture how men first came to know and use iron; for it is impossible to
75 suppose they would of themselves think of digging the ore out of the mine, and preparing it for smelting, before they knew what would be the result. On the other hand, we have the less reason to suppose this discovery the effect
80 of any accidental fire, as mines are only formed in barren places, bare of trees and plants; so that it looks as if nature had taken pains to keep the fatal secret from us. There remains, therefore, only the extraordinary ac-
85 cident of some volcano which, by ejecting metallic substances already in fusion, suggest-

ed to the spectators the idea of imitating the natural operation. And we must further conceive them as possessed of uncommon courage and foresight, to undertake so laborious a work, with so distant a prospect of drawing advantage from it; yet these qualities are united only in minds more advanced than we can suppose those of these first discoverers to have been.

With regard to agriculture, the principles of it were known long before they were put in practice; and it is indeed hardly possible that men, constantly employed in drawing their subsistence from plants and trees, should not readily acquire a knowledge of the means made use of by nature for the propagation of vegetables. It was in all probability very fang, however, before their industry took that turn, either because trees, which together with hunting and fishing afforded them food, did not require their attention; or because they were ignorant of the use of corn, or without instruments to cultivate it; or because they lacked foresight to future needs; or lastly, because they were without means of preventing others from robbing them of the fruit of their labor.

When they grew more industrious, it is natural to believe that they began, with the help of sharp stones and pointed sticks, to cultivate a few vegetables or roots around their huts; though it was long before they knew how to prepare corn, or were provided with the implements necessary for raising it in any large quantity; not to mention how essential it is, for husbandry, to consent to immediate loss, in order to reap a future gain—a precaution very foreign to the turn of a savage's mind; for, as I have said, he hardly foresees in the morning what he will need at night.

The invention of the other arts must therefore have been necessary to compel mankind to apply themselves to agriculture. No sooner were artificers wanted to smelt and forge iron, than others were required to maintain them; the more hands that were employed in manufactures, the fewer were left to provide for the common subsistence, though the number of mouths to be furnished with food remained the same: and as some required commodities in exchange for their iron, the rest at length discovered the method of making iron serve for the multiplication of commodities. By this means the arts of husbandry and agriculture were established on the one hand, and the art of working metals and multiplying their uses on the other.

The cultivation of the earth necessarily brought about its distribution; and property, once recognized, gave rise to the first rules of justice; for, to secure each man his own, it had to be possible for each to have something. Besides, as men began to look forward to the future, and all had something to lose, every one had reason to apprehend that reprisals would follow any injury he might do to another. This origin is so much the more natural, as it is impossible to conceive how property can come from anything but manual labor: for what else can a man add to things which he does not originally create, so as to make them his own property? It is the husbandman's labor alone that, giving him a title to the produce of the ground he has tilled, gives him a claim also to the land itself, at least till harvest; and so, from year to year, a constant possession which is easily transformed into property. When the ancients, says Grotius, gave to Ceres the title of Legislatrix, and to a festival celebrated in her honor the name of Thesmophoria, they meant by that that the distribution of lands had produced a new kind of right:

that is to say, the right of property, which is different from the right deducible from the law of nature.

5 In this state of affairs, equality might have been sustained, had the talents of individuals been equal, and had, for example, the use of iron and the consumption of commodities always exactly balanced each other; but, as
10 there was nothing to preserve this balance, it was soon disturbed; the strongest did most work; the most skillful turned his labor to best account; the most ingenious devised methods of diminishing his labor: the husbandman
15 wanted more iron, or the smith more corn, and, while both labored equally, the one gained a great deal by his work, while the other could hardly support himself. Thus natural inequality unfolds itself insensibly with that of
20 combination, and the difference between men, developed by their different circumstances, becomes more sensible and permanent in its effects, and begins to have an influence, in the same proportion, over the lot of individuals.
25

Matters once at this pitch, it is easy to imagine the rest. I shall not detain the reader with a description of the successive invention of other arts, the development of language, the trial
30 and utilization of talents, the inequality of fortunes, the use and abuse of riches, and all the details connected with them which the reader can easily supply for himself. I shall confine myself to a glance at mankind in this new situ-
35 ation.

Behold then all human faculties developed, memory and imagination in full play, egoism interested, reason active, and the mind almost
40 at the highest point of its perfection. Behold all the natural qualities in action, the rank and condition of every man assigned him; not merely his share of property and his power to

serve or injure others, but also his wit, beauty,
45 strength or skill, merit or talents: and these being the only qualities capable of commanding respect, it soon became necessary to possess or to affect them.

50 It now became the interest of men to appear what they really were not. To be and to seem became two totally different things; and from this distinction sprang insolent pomp and cheating trickery, with all the numerous vices
55 that go in their train. On the other hand, free and independent as men were before, they were now, in consequence of a multiplicity of new wants, brought into subjection, as it were, to all nature, and particularly to one another;
60 and each became in some degree a slave even in becoming the master of other men: if rich, they stood in need of the services of others; if poor, of their assistance; and even a middle condition did not enable them to do without
65 one another. Man must now, therefore, have been perpetually employed in getting others to interest themselves in his lot, and in making them, apparently at least, if not really, find their advantage in promoting his own. Thus
70 he must have been sly and artful in his behavior to some, and imperious and cruel to others; being under a kind of necessity to ill-use all the persons of whom he stood in need, when he could not frighten them into compli-
75 ance, and did not judge it his interest to be useful to them. Insatiable ambition, the thirst of raising their respective fortunes, not so much from real want as from the desire to surpass others, inspired all men with a vile
80 propensity to injure one another, and with a secret jealousy, which is the more dangerous, as it puts on the mask of benevolence, to carry its point with greater security. In a word, there arose rivalry and competition on the one hand,
85 and conflicting interests on the other, together with a secret desire on both of profiting at the

expense of others. All these evils were the first effects of property, and the inseparable attendants of growing inequality.

5 Before the invention of signs to represent riches, wealth could hardly consist in anything but lands and cattle, the only real possessions men can have. But, when inheritances so increased in number and extent as to occupy the 10 whole of the land, and to border on one another, one man could aggrandize himself only at the expense of another; at the same time the supernumeraries, who had been too weak or too indolent to make such acquisitions, and 15 had grown poor without sustaining any loss, because, while they saw everything change around them, they remained still the same, were obliged to receive their subsistence, or steal it, from the rich; and this soon bred, ac-20 cording to their different characters, dominion and slavery, or violence and rapine. The wealthy, on their part, had no sooner begun to taste the pleasure of command, than they disdained all others, and, using their old slaves to 25 acquire new, thought of nothing but subduing and enslaving their neighbors; like ravenous wolves, which, having once tasted human flesh, despise every other food and thenceforth seek only men to devour.

30 Thus, as the most powerful or the most miserable considered their might or misery as a kind of right to the possessions of others, equivalent, in their opinion, to that of property, the 35 destruction of equality was attended by the most terrible disorders. Usurpations by the rich, robbery by the poor, and the unbridled passions of both, suppressed the cries of natural compassion and the still feeble voice of 40 justice, and filled men with avarice, ambition and vice. Between the title of the strongest and that of the first occupier, there arose perpetual conflicts, which never ended but in

45 battles and bloodshed. The new-born state of society thus gave rise to a horrible state of war; men thus harassed and depraved were no longer capable of retracing their steps or renouncing the fatal acquisitions they had made, but, laboring by the abuse of the faculties 50 which do them honor, merely to their own confusion, brought themselves to the brink of ruin.

Attonitus novitate mali, divesque miserque,
55 *Effugere optat opes; et quæ modô voverat odit.*[20]

It is impossible that men should not at length have reflected on so wretched a situation, and on the calamities that overwhelmed them. The 60 rich, in particular, must have felt how much they suffered by a constant state of war, of which they bore all the expense; and in which, though all risked their lives, they alone risked their property. Besides, however speciously 65 they might disguise their usurpations, they knew that they were founded on precarious and false titles; so that, if others took from them by force what they themselves had gained by force, they would have no reason to 70 complain. Even those who had been enriched by their own industry, could hardly base their proprietorship on better claims. It was in vain to repeat, "I built this well; I gained this spot by my industry." Who gave you your standing, 75 it might be answered, and what right have you to demand payment of us for doing what we never asked you to do? Do you not know that numbers of your fellow-creatures are starving, for want of what you have too much of? You 80 ought to have had the express and universal consent of mankind, before appropriating

---

[20] Ovid, Metamorphoses xi, 127.
Both rich and poor, shocked at their new-found ills,
Would fly from wealth, and lose what they had sought.

more of the common subsistence than you needed for your own maintenance. Destitute of valid reasons to justify and sufficient strength to defend himself, able to crush indi-

5 viduals with ease, but easily crushed himself by a troop of bandits, one against all, and incapable, on account of mutual jealousy, of joining with his equals against numerous enemies united by the common hope of plunder, the

10 rich man, thus urged by necessity, conceived at length the profoundest plan that ever entered the mind of man: this was to employ in his favor the forces of those who attacked him, to make allies of his adversaries, to in-

15 spire them with different maxims, and to give them other institutions as favorable to himself as the law of nature was unfavorable.

With this view, after having represented to his

20 neighbors the horror of a situation which armed every man against the rest, and made their possessions as burdensome to them as their wants, and in which no safety could be expected either in riches or in poverty, he

25 readily devised plausible arguments to make them close with his design. "Let us join," said he, "to guard the weak from oppression, to restrain the ambitious, and secure to every man the possession of what belongs to him:

30 let us institute rules of justice and peace, to which all without exception may be obliged to conform; rules that may in some measure make amends for the caprices of fortune, by subjecting equally the powerful and the weak

35 to the observance of reciprocal obligations. Let us, in a word, instead of turning our forces against ourselves, collect them in a supreme power which may govern us by wise laws, protect and defend all the members of the associ-

40 ation, repulse their common enemies, and maintain eternal harmony among us."

Far fewer words to this purpose would have

45 been enough to impose on men so barbarous and easily seduced; especially as they had too many disputes among themselves to do without arbitrators, and too much ambition and avarice to go long without masters. All ran headlong to their chains, in hopes of securing

50 their liberty; for they had just wit enough to perceive the advantages of political institutions, without experience enough to enable them to foresee the dangers. The most capable of fore-seeing the dangers were the very per-

55 sons who expected to benefit by them; and even the most prudent judged it not inexpedient to sacrifice one part of their freedom to ensure the rest; as a wounded man has his arm cut off to save the rest of his body.

60

Such was, or may well have been, the origin of society and law, which bound new fetters on the poor, and gave new powers to the rich; which irretrievably destroyed natural liberty,

65 eternally fixed the law of property and inequality, converted clever usurpation into unalterable right, and, for the advantage of a few ambitious individuals, subjected all mankind to perpetual labor, slavery and wretchedness. It is

70 easy to see how the establishment of one community made that of all the rest necessary, and how, in order to make head against united forces, the rest of mankind had to unite in turn. Societies soon multiplied and spread

75 over the face of the earth, till hardly a corner of the world was left in which a man could escape the yoke, and withdraw his head from beneath the sword which he saw perpetually hanging over him by a thread. Civil right hav-

80 ing thus become the common rule among the members of each community, the law of nature maintained its place only between different communities, where, under the name of the right of nations, it was qualified by certain

85 tacit conventions, in order to make commerce practicable, and serve as a substitute for natu-

ral compassion, which lost, when applied to societies, almost all the influence it had over individuals, and survived no longer except in some great cosmopolitan spirits, who, breaking down the imaginary barriers that separate different peoples, follow the example of our Sovereign Creator, and include the whole human race in their benevolence.

But bodies politic, remaining thus in a state of nature among themselves, presently experienced the inconveniences which had obliged individuals to forsake it; for this state became still more fatal to these great bodies than it had been to the individuals of whom they were composed. Hence arose national wars, battles, murders, and reprisals, which shock nature and outrage reason; together with all those horrible prejudices which class among the virtues the honour of shedding human blood. The most distinguished men hence learned to consider cutting each other's throats a duty; at length men massacred their fellow-creatures by thousands without so much as knowing why, and committed more murders in a single day's fighting, and more violent outrages in the sack of a single town, than were committed in the state of nature during whole ages over the whole earth. Such were the first effects which we can see to have followed the division of mankind into different communities. But let us return to their institutions.

I know that some writers have given other explanations of the origin of political societies, such as the conquest of the powerful, or the association of the weak. It is, indeed, indifferent to my argument which of these causes we choose. That which I have just laid down, however, appears to me the most natural for the following reasons. First: because, in the first case, the right of conquest, being no right

in itself, could not serve as a foundation on which to build any other; the victor and the vanquished people still remained with respect to each other in the state of war, unless the vanquished, restored to the full possession of their liberty, voluntarily made choice of the victor for their chief. For till then, whatever capitulation may have been made being founded on violence, and therefore *ipso facto* void, there could not have been on this hypothesis either a real society or body politic, or any law other than that of the strongest. Secondly: because the words *strong* and *weak* are, in the second case, ambiguous; for during the interval between the establishment of a right of property, or prior occupancy, and that of political government, the meaning of these words is better expressed by the terms *rich* and *poor*: because, in fact, before the institution of laws, men had no other way of reducing their equals to submission, than by attacking their goods, or making some of their own over to them. Thirdly: because, as the poor had nothing but their freedom to lose, it would have been in the highest degree absurd for them to resign voluntarily the only good they still enjoyed, without getting anything in exchange: whereas the rich having feelings, if I may so express myself, in every part of their possessions, it was much easier to harm them, and therefore more necessary for them to take precautions against it; and, in short, because it is more reasonable to suppose a thing to have been invented by those to whom it would be of service, than by those whom it must have harmed.

Government had, in its infancy, no regular and constant form. The want of experience and philosophy prevented men from seeing any but present inconveniences, and they thought of providing against others only as they presented themselves. In spite of the endeavours

of the wisest legislators, the political state remained imperfect, because it was little more
than the work of chance; and, as it had begun
ill, though time revealed its defects and sug-
5 gested remedies, the original faults were never
repaired. It was continually being patched up,
when the first task should have been to get the
site cleared and all the old materials removed,
as was done by Lycurgus at Sparta, if a stable
10 and lasting edifice was to be erected. Society
consisted at first merely of a few general conventions, which every member bound himself
to observe; and for the performance of covenants the whole body went security to each
15 individual. Experience only could show the
weakness of such a constitution, and how easily it might be infringed with impunity, from
the difficulty of convicting men of faults,
where the public alone was to be witness and
20 judge: the laws could not but be eluded in
many ways; disorders and inconveniences
could not but multiply continually, till it became necessary to commit the dangerous trust
of public authority to private persons, and the
25 care of enforcing obedience to the deliberations of the people to the magistrate. For to
say that chiefs were chosen before the confederacy was formed, and that the administrators
of the laws were there before the laws them-
30 selves, is too absurd a supposition to consider
seriously.

It would be as unreasonable to suppose that
men at first threw themselves irretrievably and
35 unconditionally into the arms of an absolute
master, and that the first expedient which
proud and unsubdued men hit upon for their
common security was to run headlong into
slavery. For what reason, in fact, did they take
40 to themselves superiors, if it was not in order
that they might be defended from oppression,
and have protection for their lives, liberties
and properties, which are, so to speak, the

constituent elements of their being? Now, in
45 the relations between man and man, the worst
that can happen is for one to find himself at
the mercy of another, and it would have been
inconsistent with common-sense to begin by
bestowing on a chief the only things they
50 wanted his help to preserve. What equivalent
could he offer them for so great a right? And
if he had presumed to exact it under pretext of
defending them, would he not have received
the answer recorded in the fable: "What more
55 can the enemy do to us?" It is therefore beyond dispute, and indeed the fundamental
maxim of all political right, that people have
set up chiefs to protect their liberty, and not to
enslave them. *If we have a prince*, said Pliny to
60 Trajan, *it is to save ourselves from having a master.*

Politicians indulge in the same sophistry about
the love of liberty as philosophers about the
state of nature. They judge, by what they see,
65 of very different things, which they have not
seen; and attribute to man a natural propensity
to servitude, because the slaves within their
observation are seen to bear the yoke with
patience; they fail to reflect that it is with liber-
70 ty as with innocence and virtue; the value is
known only to those who possess them, and
the taste for them is forfeited when they are
forfeited themselves. "I know the charms of
your country," said Brasidas to a Satrap, who
75 was comparing the life at Sparta with that at
Persepolis, "but you cannot know the pleasures of mine."

An unbroken horse erects his mane, paws the
80 ground and starts back impetuously at the
sight of the bridle; while one which is properly
trained suffers patiently even whip and spur:
so savage man will not bend his neck to the
yoke to which civilized man submits without a
85 murmur, but prefers the most turbulent state
of liberty to the most peaceful slavery. We

cannot therefore, from the servility of nations already enslaved, judge of the natural disposition of mankind for or against slavery; we should go by the prodigious efforts of every free people to save itself from oppression. I know that the former are for ever holding forth in praise of the tranquility they enjoy in their chains, and that they call a state of wretched servitude a state of peace: *miserrimam servitutem pacem appellant*.[21] But when I observe the latter sacrificing pleasure, peace, wealth, power and life itself to the preservation of that one treasure, which is so disdained by those who have lost it; when I see free-born animals dash their brains out against the bars of their cage, from an innate impatience of captivity; when I behold numbers of naked savages, that despise European pleasures, braving hunger, fire, the sword and death, to preserve nothing but their independence, I feel that it is not for slaves to argue about liberty.

With regard to paternal authority, from which some writers have derived absolute government and all society, it is enough, without going back to the contrary arguments of Locke and Sidney, to remark that nothing on earth can be further from the ferocious spirit of despotism than the mildness of that authority which looks more to the advantage of him who obeys than to that of him who commands; that, by the law of nature, the father is the child's master no longer than his help is necessary; that from that time they are both equal, the son being perfectly independent of the father, and owing him only respect and not obedience. For gratitude is a duty which ought to be paid, but not a right to be exacted: instead of saying that civil society is derived from paternal authority, we ought to say rather

that the latter derives its principal force from the former. No individual was ever acknowledged as the father of many, till his sons and daughters remained settled around him. The goods of the father, of which he is really the master, are the ties which keep his children in dependence, and he may bestow on them, if he pleases, no share of his property, unless they merit it by constant deference to his will. But the subjects of an arbitrary despot are so far from having the like favor to expect from their chief, that they themselves and everything they possess are his property, or at least are considered by him as such; so that they are forced to receive, as a favor, the little of their own he is pleased to leave them. When he despoils them, he does but justice, and mercy in that he permits them to live.

By proceeding thus to test fact by right, we should discover as little reason as truth in the voluntary establishment of tyranny. It would also be no easy matter to prove the validity of a contract binding on only one of the parties, where all the risk is on one side, and none on the other; so that no one could suffer but he who bound himself. This hateful system is indeed, even in modern times, very far from being that of wise and good monarchs, and especially of the kings of France; as may be seen from several passages in their edicts; particularly from the following passage in a celebrated edict published in 1667 in the name and by order of Louis XIV.

"Let it not, therefore, be said that the Sovereign is not subject to the laws of his State; since the contrary is a true proposition of the right of nations, which flattery has sometimes attacked but good princes have always defended as the tutelary divinity of their dominions. How much more legitimate is it to say with the wise Plato, that the perfect felicity of a

[21] Tacitus, Hist. iv, 17. The most wretched slavery they call peace.

kingdom consists in the obedience of subjects to their prince, and of the prince to the laws, and in the laws being just and constantly directed to the public good!"[22]

I shall not stay here to inquire whether, as liberty is the noblest faculty of man, it is not degrading our very nature, reducing ourselves to the level of the brutes, which are mere slaves of instinct, and even an affront to the Author of our being, to renounce without reserve the most precious of all His gifts, and to bow to the necessity of committing all the crimes He has forbidden, merely to gratify a mad or a cruel master; or if this sublime craftsman ought not to be less angered at seeing His workmanship entirely destroyed than thus dishonored. I will waive (if my opponents please) the authority of Barbeyrac, who, following Locke, roundly declares that no man can so far sell his liberty as to submit to an arbitrary power which may use him as it likes. *For*, he adds, *this would be to sell his own life, of which he is not master*. I shall ask only what right those who were not afraid thus to debase themselves could have to subject their posterity to the same ignominy, and to renounce for them those blessings which they do not owe to the liberality of their progenitors, and without which life itself must be a burden to all who are worthy of it.

Puffendorf says that we may divest ourselves of our liberty in favor of other men, just as we transfer our property from one to another by contracts and agreements. But this seems a very weak argument. For in the first place, the property I alienate becomes quite foreign to me, nor can I suffer from the abuse of it; but it very nearly concerns me that my liberty should not be abused, and I cannot without incurring the guilt of the crimes I may be compelled to commit, expose myself to become an instrument of crime. Besides, the right of property being only a convention of human institution, men may dispose of what they possess as they please: but this is not the case with the essential gifts of nature, such as life and liberty, which every man is permitted to enjoy, and of which it is at least doubtful whether any have a right to divest themselves. By giving up the one, we degrade our being; by giving up the other, we do our best to annul it; and, as no temporal good can indemnify us for the loss of either, it would be an offence against both reason and nature to renounce them at any price whatsoever. But, even if we could transfer our liberty, as we do our property, there would be a great difference with regard to the children, who enjoy the father's substance only by the transmission of his right; whereas, liberty being a gift which they hold from nature as being men, their parents have no right whatever to deprive them of it. As then, to establish slavery, it was necessary to do violence to nature, so, in order to perpetuate such a right, nature would have to be changed. Jurists, who have gravely determined that the child of a slave comes into the world a slave, have decided, in other words, that a man shall come into the world not a man.

I regard it then as certain, that government did not begin with arbitrary power, but that this is the depravation, the extreme term, of government, and brings it back, finally, to just the law of the strongest, which it was originally designed to remedy. Supposing, however, it had begun in this manner, such power, being in itself illegitimate, could not have served as a basis for the laws of society, nor, consequently, for the inequality they instituted.

---

[22] Of the Rights of the Most Christian Queen over various States of the Monarchy of Spain, 1667.

Without entering at present upon the investigations which still remain to be made into the nature of the fundamental compact underlying all government, I content myself with adopting the common opinion concerning it, and regard the establishment of the political body as a real contract between the people and the chiefs chosen by them: a contract by which both parties bind themselves to observe the laws therein expressed, which form the ties of their union. The people having in respect of their social relations concentrated all their wills in one, the several articles, concerning which this will is explained, become so many fundamental laws, obligatory on all the members of the State without exception, and one of these articles regulates the choice and power of the magistrates appointed to watch over the execution of the rest. This power extends to everything which may maintain the constitution, without going so far as to alter it. It is accompanied by honors, in order to bring the laws and their administrators into respect. The ministers are also distinguished by personal prerogatives, in order to recompense them for the cares and labor which good administration involves. The magistrate, on his side, binds himself to use the power he is entrusted with only in conformity with the intention of his constituents, to maintain them all in the peaceable possession of what belongs to them, and to prefer on every occasion the public interest to his own.

Before experience had shown, or knowledge of the human heart enabled men to foresee, the unavoidable abuses of such a constitution, it must have appeared so much the more excellent, as those who were charged with the care of its preservation had themselves most interest in it; for magistracy and the rights attaching to it being based solely on the fundamental laws, the magistrates would cease to be legitimate as soon as these ceased to exist; the people would no longer owe them obedience; and as not the magistrates, but the laws, are essential to the being of a State, the members of it would regain the right to their natural liberty.

If we reflect with ever so little attention on this subject, we shall find new arguments to confirm this truth, and be convinced from the very nature of the contract that it cannot be irrevocable: for, if there were no superior power capable of ensuring the fidelity of the contracting parties, or compelling them to perform their reciprocal engagements, the parties would be sole judges in their own cause, and each would always have a right to renounce the contract, as soon as he found that the other had violated its terms, or that they no longer suited his convenience. It is upon this principle that the right of abdication may possibly be founded. Now, if, as here, we consider only what is human in this institution, it is certain that, if the magistrate, who has all the power in his own hands, and appropriates to himself all the advantages of the contract, has none the less a right to renounce his authority, the people, who suffer for all the faults of their chief, must have a much better right to renounce their dependence. But the terrible and innumerable quarrels and disorders that would necessarily arise from so dangerous a privilege, show, more than anything else, how much human governments stood in need of a more solid basis than mere reason, and how expedient it was for the public tranquility that the divine will should interpose to invest the sovereign authority with a sacred and inviolable character, which might deprive subjects of the fatal right of disposing of it. If the world had received no other advantages from religion, this would be enough to impose on men the duty of adopting and cultivating it, abuses and all, since it has been the means of saving more blood than fanaticism has ever spilt. But let us follow the thread of our hypothesis.

The different forms of government owe their origin to the differing degrees of inequality which existed between individuals at the time of their institution. If there happened to be any one man among them pre-eminent in power, virtue, riches or personal influence, he became sole magistrate, and the State assumed the form of monarchy. If several, nearly equal in point of eminence, stood above the rest, they were elected jointly, and formed an aristocracy. Again, among a people who had deviated less from a state of nature, and between whose fortune or talents there was less disproportion, the supreme administration was retained in common, and a democracy was formed. It was discovered in process of time which of these forms suited men the best. Some peoples remained altogether subject to the laws; others soon came to obey their magistrates. The citizens labored to preserve their liberty; the subjects, irritated at seeing others enjoying a blessing they had lost, thought only of making slaves of their neighbors. In a word, on the one side arose riches and conquests, and on the other happiness and I virtue.

In these different governments, all the offices were at first elective; and when the influence of wealth was out of the question, the preference was given to merit, which gives a natural ascendancy, and to age, which is experienced in business and deliberate in council. The Elders of the Hebrews, the Gerontes at Sparta, the Senate at Rome, and the very etymology of our word Seigneur, show how old age was once held in veneration. But the more often the choice fell upon old men, the more often elections had to be repeated, and the more

they became a nuisance; intrigues set in, factions were formed, party feeling grew—bitter, civil wars broke out; the lives of individuals were sacrificed to the pretended happiness of the State; and at length men were on the point of relapsing into their primitive anarchy. Ambitious chiefs profited by these circumstances to perpetuate their offices in their own families: at the same time the people, already used to dependence, ease, and the conveniences of life, and already incapable of breaking its fetters, agreed to an increase of its slavery, in order to secure its tranquility. Thus magistrates, having become hereditary, contracted the habit of considering their offices as a family estate, and themselves as proprietors of the communities of which they were at first only the officers, of regarding their fellow-citizens as their slaves, and numbering them, like cattle, among their belongings, and of calling themselves the equals of the gods and longs of kings.

If we follow the progress of inequality in these various revolutions, we shall find that the establishment of laws and of the right of property was its first term, the institution of magistracy the second, and the conversion of legitimate into arbitrary power the third and last; so that the condition of rich and poor was authorized by the first period; that of powerful and weak by the second; and only by the third that of master and slave, which is the last degree of inequality, and the term at which all the rest remain, when they have got so far, till the government is either entirely dissolved by new revolutions, or brought back again to legitimacy.

To understand this progress as necessary we must consider not so much the motives for the establishment of the body politic, as the forms it assumes in actuality, and the faults that necessarily attend it: for the flaws which make social institutions necessary are the same as make the abuse of them unavoidable. If we except Sparta, where the laws were mainly concerned with the education of children, and where Lycurgus established such morality as practically made laws needless—for laws as a rule, being weaker than the passions, restrain men without altering them—it would not be difficult to prove that every government, which scrupulously complied with the ends for which it was instituted, and guarded carefully against change and corruption, was set up unnecessarily. For a country, in which no one either evaded the laws or made a bad use of magisterial power, could require neither laws nor magistrates.

Political distinctions necessarily produce civil distinctions. The growing equality between the chiefs and the people is soon felt by individuals, and modified in a thousand ways according to passions, talents and circumstances. The magistrate could not usurp any illegitimate power, without giving distinction to the creatures with whom he must share it. Besides, individuals only allow themselves to be oppressed so far as they are hurried on by blind ambition, and, looking rather below than above them, come to love authority more than independence, and submit to slavery, that they may in turn enslave others. It is no easy matter to reduce to obedience a man who has no ambition to command; nor would the most adroit politician find it possible to enslave a people whose only desire was to be independent. But inequality easily makes its way among cowardly and ambitious minds, which are ever ready to run the risks of fortune, and almost indifferent whether they command or obey, as it is favorable or adverse. Thus, there must have been; a time, when the eyes of the people were so fascinated, that their rulers had only to say to the least of men, "Be great, you and all your posterity," to make him immediately appear great in the eyes of every one as well as in his own. His descendants took still more upon them, in proportion to their distance from him; the more obscure; and uncertain the cause, the greater the effect: the greater—the number of idlers one could count in a family, the more illustrious it was held to be.

If this were the place to go into details, I could readily explain how, even without the intervention of government, inequality of credit and authority became unavoidable among private persons, as soon as their union in a single society made them compare themselves one with another, and take into account the differences which they found out from the continual intercourse every man had to have with his neighbors.[23] These differences are of several

---

[23] Distributive justice would oppose this rigorous equality of the state of nature, even were it practicable in civil society; as all the members of the State owe it their services in proportion to their talents and abilities, they ought, on their side, to be distinguished and favoured in proportion to the services they have actually rendered. It is in this sense we must understand that passage of Isocrates, in which he extols the primitive Athenians, for having determined which of the two kinds of equality was the most useful, viz. that which consists in dividing the same advantages indiscriminately among all the citizens, or that which consists in distributing them to each according to his deserts. These able politicians, adds the orator, banishing that unjust inequality which makes no distinction between good and bad men, adhered inviolably to that which rewards and punishes every man according to his deserts.

But in the first place, there never existed a society, however corrupt some may have become, where no difference was made between the good and the bad; and with regard to morality, where no measures can be prescribed by law exact

kinds; but riches, nobility or rank, power and personal merit being the principal distinctions by which men form an estimate "of each other in society, I could prove that the harmony or conflict of these different forces is the surest indication of the good or bad constitution of a State. I could show that among these four kinds of inequality, personal qualities being the origin of all the others, wealth is the one to which they are all reduced in the end; for, as riches tend most immediately to the prosperity of individuals, and are easiest to communicate, they are used to purchase every other distinction. By this observation we are enabled to judge pretty exactly how far a people has departed from its primitive constitution, and of its progress towards the extreme term of corruption. I could explain how much this universal desire for reputation, honors and advancement, which inflames us all, exercises and holds up to comparison our faculties and powers; how it excites and multiplies our passions, and, by creating universal competition and rivalry, or rather enmity, among men, occasions numberless failures, successes and

disturbances of all kinds by making so many aspirants run the same course. I could show that it is to this desire of being talked about, and this unremitting rage of distinguishing ourselves, that we owe the best and the worst things we possess, both our virtues and our vices, our science and our errors, our conquerors and our philosophers; that is to say, a great many bad things, and a very few good ones. In a word, I could prove that, if we have a few rich and powerful men on the pinnacle of fortune and grandeur, while the crowd grovels in want and obscurity, it is because the former prize what they enjoy only in so far as others are destitute of it; and because, without changing their condition, they would cease to be happy the moment the people ceased to be wretched.

These details alone, however, would furnish matter for a considerable work, in which the advantages and disadvantages of every kind of government might be weighed, as they are related to man in the state of nature, and at the same time all the different aspects, under which inequality has up to the present appeared, or may appear in ages yet to come, according to the nature of the several governments, and the alterations which time must unavoidably occasion in them, might be demonstrated. We should then see the multitude oppressed from within, in consequence of the very precautions it had taken to guard against foreign tyranny. We should see oppression continually gain ground without it being possible for the oppressed to know where it would stop, or what legitimate means was left them of checking its progress. We should see the rights of citizens, and the freedom of nations slowly extinguished, and the complaints, protests and appeals of the weak treated as seditious murmurings. We should see the honor of defending the common cause

---

enough to serve as a practical rule for a magistrate, it is with great prudence that, in order not to leave the fortune or quality of the citizens to his discretion, it prohibits him from passing judgment on persons and confines his judgment to actions. Only morals such as those of the ancient Romans can bear censors, and such a tribunal among us would throw everything into confusion. The difference between good and bad men is determined by public esteem; the magistrate being strictly a judge of right alone; whereas the public is the truest judge of morals, and is of such integrity and penetration on this head, that although it may be sometimes deceived, it can never be corrupted. The rank of citizens ought, therefore, to be regulated, not according to their personal merit—for this would put it in the power of the magistrate to apply the law almost arbitrarily—but according to the actual services done to the State, which are capable of being more exactly estimated.

confined by statecraft to a mercenary part of the people. We should see taxes made necessary by such means, and the disheartened husbandman deserting his fields even in the midst of peace, and leaving the plough to gird on the sword. We should see fatal and capricious codes of honor established; and the champions of their country sooner or later becoming its enemies, and for ever holding their daggers to the breasts of their fellow-citizens. The time would come when they would be heard saying to the oppressor of their country—

Pectore si fratris gladium juguloque parentis
Condere me jubeas, gravidæque in viscera partu
Conjugis, invitâ peragam tamen omnia dextrâ.
Lucan. i, 376.

From great inequality of fortunes and conditions, from the vast variety of passions and of talents, of useless and pernicious arts, of vain sciences, would arise a multitude of prejudices equally contrary to reason, happiness and virtue. We should see the magistrates fomenting everything that might weaken men united in society, by promoting dissension among them; everything that might sow in it the seeds of actual division, while it gave society the air of harmony; everything that might inspire the different ranks of people with mutual hatred and distrust, by setting the rights and interests of one against those of another, and so strengthen the power which comprehended them all.

It is from the midst of this disorder and these revolutions, that despotism, gradually raising up its hideous head and devouring everything that remained sound and untainted in any part of the State, would at length trample on both the laws and the people, and establish itself on the ruins of the republic. The times which immediately preceded this last change would be times of trouble and calamity; but at length the monster would swallow up everything, and the people would no longer have either chiefs or laws, but only tyrants. From this moment there would be no question of virtue or morality; for despotism *cui ex honesto nulla est spes,* wherever it prevails, admits no other master; it no sooner speaks than probity and duty lose their weight and blind obedience is the only virtue which slaves can still practice.

This is the last term of inequality, the extreme points that closes the circle, and meets that from which we set out. Here all private persons return to their first equality, because they are nothing; and, subjects having no law but the will of their master, and their master no restraint but his passions, all notions of good and all principles of equity again vanish. There is here a complete return to the law of the strongest, and so to a new state of nature, differing from that we set out from; for the one was a state of nature in its first purity, while this is the consequence of excessive corruption. There is so little difference between the two states in other respects, and the contract of government is so completely dissolved by despotism, that the despot is master only so long as he remains the strongest; as soon as he can be expelled, he has no right to complain of violence. The popular insurrection that ends in the death or deposition of a Sultan is as lawful an act as those by which he disposed, the day before, of the lives and fortunes of his subjects. As he was maintained by force alone, it is force alone that overthrows him. Thus everything takes place according to the natural order; and, whatever may be the result of such frequent and precipitate revolutions, no one man has reason to complain of the injustice of another, but only of his own ill-fortune or indiscretion.

If the reader thus discovers and retraces the lost and forgotten road, by which man must have passed from the state of nature to the state of society; if he carefully restores, along
5 with the intermediate situations which I have just described, those which want of time has compelled me to suppress, or my imagination has failed to suggest, he cannot fail to be struck by the vast distance which separates the
10 two states. It is in tracing this slow succession that he will find the solution of a number of problems of politics and morals, which philosophers cannot settle. He will feel that, men being different in different ages, the reason
15 why Diogenes could not find a man was that he sought among his contemporaries a man of an earlier period. He will see that Cato died with Rome and liberty, because he did not fit the age in which he lived; the greatest of men
20 served only to astonish a world which he would certainly have ruled, had he lived five hundred years sooner. In a word, he will explain how the soul and the passions of men insensibly change their very nature; why our
25 wants and pleasures in the end seek new objects; and why, the original man having vanished by degrees, society offers to us only an assembly of artificial men and factitious passions, which are the work of all these new
30 relations, and without any real foundation in nature. We are taught nothing on this subject, by reflection, that is not entirely confirmed by observation. The savage and the civilized man differ so much in the bottom of their hearts
35 and in their inclinations, that what constitutes the supreme happiness of one would reduce the other to despair. The former breathes only peace and liberty; he desires only to live and be free from labor; even the *ataraxia* of the
40 Stoic falls far short of his profound indifference to every other object. Civilized man, on the other hand, is always moving, sweating, toiling and racking his brains to find still more

laborious occupations: he goes on in drudgery
45 to his last moment, and even seeks death to put himself in a position to live, or renounces life to acquire immortality. He pays his court to men in power, whom he hates, and to the wealthy, whom he despises; he stops at noth-
50 ing to have the honor of serving them; he is not ashamed to value himself on his own meanness and their protection; and, proud of his slavery, he speaks with disdain of those, who have not the honor of sharing it. What a
55 sight would the perplexing and envied labors of a European minister of State present to the eyes of a Caribean! How many cruel deaths would not this indolent savage prefer to the horrors of such a life, which is seldom even
60 sweetened by the pleasure of doing good! But, for him to see into the motives of all this solicitude, the words *power* and *reputation*, would have to bear some meaning in his mind; he would have to know that there are men who
65 set a value on the opinion of the rest of the world; who can be made happy and satisfied with themselves rather on the testimony of other people than on their own. In reality, the source, of all these differences is, that the sav-
70 age lives within himself, while social man lives constantly outside himself, and only knows how to live in the opinion of others, so that he seems to receive the consciousness of his own existence merely from the judgment of others
75 concerning him. It is not to my present purpose to insist on the indifference to good and evil which arises from this disposition, in spite of our many fine works on morality, or to show how, everything being reduced to ap-
80 pearances, there is but art and mummery in even honor, friendship, virtue, and often vice itself, of which we at length learn the secret of boasting; to show, in short, how, always asking others what, we are, and never daring to ask
85 ourselves, in the midst of so much philosophy, humanity and civilization, and of such sublime

codes of morality, we have nothing to show for ourselves but a frivolous and deceitful appearance, honor without virtue, reason without wisdom, and pleasure without happiness.
5 It is sufficient that I have proved that this is not by any means the original state of man, but that it is merely the spirit of society, and the inequality which society produces, that thus transform and alter all our natural inclina-
10 tions.

I have endeavored to trace the origin and progress of inequality, and the institution and abuse of political societies, as far as these are
15 capable of being deduced from the nature of man merely by the light of reason, and independently of those sacred dogmas which give the sanction of divine right to sovereign authority. It follows from this survey that, as
20 there is hardly any inequality in the state of nature, all the inequality which now prevails owes its strength and growth to the development of our faculties and the advance of the human mind, and becomes at last permanent
25 and legitimate by the establishment of property and laws. Secondly, it follows that moral inequality authorized by positive right alone, clashes with natural right, whenever it is not proportionate to physical inequality; a distinc-
30 tion which sufficiently determines what we ought to think of that species of inequality which prevails in all civilized countries; since it is plainly contrary to the law of nature, however defined, that children should command
35 old men, fools wise men, and that the privileged few should gorge themselves with superfluities, while the starving multitude are in want of the bare necessities of life.

SOCIAL CONTRACT
JEAN JACQUES ROUSSEAU

FOREWORD

This little treatise is part of a longer work which I began years ago without realizing my limitations, and long since abandoned. Of the various fragments that might have been extracted from what I wrote, this is the most considerable, and, I think, the least unworthy of being offered to the public. The rest no longer exists.

BOOK I

I mean to inquire if, in the civil order, there can be any sure and legitimate rule of administration, men being taken as they are and laws as they might be. In this inquiry I shall endeavor always to unite what right sanctions with what is prescribed by interest, in order that justice and utility may in no case be divided.

I enter upon my task without proving the importance of the subject I shall be asked if I am a prince or a legislator, to write on politics. I answer that I am neither, and that is why I do so. If I were a prince or a legislator, I should not waste time in saying what wants doing; I should do it, or hold my peace.

As I was born a citizen of a free State, and a member of the Sovereign, I feel that, however feeble the influence my voice can have on public affairs, the right of voting on them makes it my duty to study them: and I am

happy, when I reflect upon governments, to find my inquiries always furnish me with new reasons for loving that of my own country.

CHAPTER I
SUBJECT OF THE FIRST BOOK

Man is born free; and everywhere he is in chains. One thinks himself the master of others, and still remains a greater slave than they. How did this change come about? I do not know. What can make it legitimate? That question I think I can answer.

If I took into account only force, and the effects derived from it, I should say: "As long as a people is compelled to obey, and obeys, it does well; as soon as it can shake off the yoke, and shakes it off, it does still better; for, regaining its liberty by the same right as took it away, either it is justified in resuming it, or there was no justification for those who took it away." But the social order is a sacred right which is the basis of all other rights. Nevertheless, this right does not come from nature, and must therefore be founded on conventions. Before coming to that, I have to prove what I have just asserted.

CHAPTER II
THE FIRST SOCIETIES

The most ancient of all societies, and the only one that is natural is the family: and even so the children remain attached to the father only so long as they need him for their preservation. As soon as this need ceases, the natural

Text based off the G.D.H. Cole translation, with adjustments for modern spellings.

bond is dissolved. The children, released from the obedience they owed to the father, and the father, released from the care he owed his children, return equally to independence. If they remain united, they continue so no longer naturally, but voluntarily; and the family itself is then maintained only by convention.

This common liberty results from the nature of man. His first law is to provide for his own preservation, his first cares are those which he owes to himself; and, as soon as he reaches years of discretion, he is the sole judge of the proper means of preserving himself, and consequently becomes his own master.

The family then may be called the first model of political societies: the ruler corresponds to the father, and the people to the children; and all, being born free and equal, alienate their liberty only for their own advantage. The whole difference is that, in the family, the love of the father for his children repays him for the care he takes of them, while, in the State, the pleasure of commanding takes the place of the love which the chief cannot have for the peoples under him.

Grotius denies that all human power is established in favor of the governed, and quotes slavery as an example. His usual method of reasoning is constantly to establish right by fact.[25] It would be possible to employ a more logical method, but none could be more favorable to tyrants.

It is then, according to Grotius, doubtful whether the human race belongs to a hundred men, or that hundred men to the human race: and, throughout his book, he seems to incline to the former alternative, which is also the view of Hobbes. On this showing, the human species is divided into so many herds of cattle, each with its ruler, who keeps guard over them for the purpose of devouring them.

As a shepherd is of a nature superior to that of his flock, the shepherds of men, *i.e.* their rulers, are of a nature superior to that of the peoples under them. Thus, Philo tells us, the Emperor Caligula reasoned, concluding equally well either that kings were gods, or that men were beasts.

The reasoning of Caligula agrees with that of Hobbes and Grotius. Aristotle, before any of them, had said that men are by no means equal naturally, but that some are born for slavery, and others for dominion.

Aristotle was right; but he took the effect for the cause. Nothing can be more certain than that every man born in slavery is born for slavery. Slaves lose everything in their chains, even the desire of escaping from them: they love their servitude, as the comrades of Ulysses loved their brutish condition.[26] If then there are slaves by nature, it is because there have been slaves against nature. Force made the first slaves, and their cowardice perpetuated the condition.

I have said nothing of King Adam, or Emperor Noah, father of the three great monarchs who shared out the universe, like the children of Saturn, whom some scholars have recog-

---

[25] "Learned inquiries into public right are often only the history of past abuses; and troubling to study them too deeply is a profitless infatuation" (*Essay on the Interests of France in Relation to its Neighbors*, by the Marquis d'Argenson). This is exactly what Grotius has done.

---

[26] See a short treatise of Plutarch's entitled "That Animals Reason."

nized in them. I trust to getting due thanks for
my moderation; for, being a direct descendant
of one of these princes, perhaps of the eldest
branch, how do I know that a verification of
5   titles might not leave me the legitimate king of
the human race? In any case, there can be no
doubt that Adam was sovereign of the world,
as Robinson Crusoe was of his island, as long
as he was its only inhabitant; and this empire
10 had the advantage that the monarch, safe on
his throne, had no rebellions, wars, or con-
spirators to fear.

CHAPTER III
15 **THE RIGHT OF THE STRONGEST**

The strongest is never strong enough to be
always the master, unless he transforms
strength into right, and obedience into duty.
20 Hence the right of the strongest, which,
though to all seeming meant ironically, is really
laid down as a fundamental principle. But are
we never to have an explanation of this
phrase? Force is a physical power, and I fail to
25 see what moral effect it can have. To yield to
force is an act of necessity, not of will—at the
most, an act of prudence. In what sense can it
be a duty?

30 Suppose for a moment that this so-called
"right" exists. I maintain that the sole result is
a mass of inexplicable nonsense. For, if force
creates right, the effect changes with the cause:
every force that is greater than the first suc-
35 ceeds to its right. As soon as it is possible to
disobey with impunity, disobedience is legitimate; and, the strongest being always in the
right, the only thing that matters is to act so as
to become the strongest. But what kind of
40 right is that which perishes when force fails? If
we must obey perforce, there is no need to
obey because we ought; and if we are not
forced to obey, we are under no obligation to

do so. Clearly, the word "right" adds nothing
45 to force: in this connection, it means absolutely nothing.

Obey the powers that be. If this means yield
to force, it is a good precept, but superfluous:
50 I can answer for its never being violated. All
power comes from God, I admit; but so does
all sickness: does that mean that we are forbidden to call in the doctor? A brigand surprises me at the edge of a wood: must I not
55 merely surrender my purse on compulsion;
but, even if I could withhold it, am I in conscience bound to give it up? For certainly the
pistol he holds is also a power.

60 Let us then admit that force does not create
right, and that we are obliged to obey only
legitimate powers. In that case, my original
question recurs.

CHAPTER IV
65 **SLAVERY**

Since no man has a natural authority over his
fellow, and force creates no right, we must
70 conclude that conventions form the basis of
all legitimate authority among men.

If an individual, says Grotius, can alienate his
liberty and make himself the slave of a master,
75 why could not a whole people do the same
and make itself subject to a king? There are in
this passage plenty of ambiguous words which
would need explaining; but let us confine ourselves to the word *alienate*. To alienate is to
80 give or to sell. Now, a man who becomes the
slave of another does not give himself; he sells
himself, at the least for his subsistence: but for
what does a people sell itself? A king is so far
from furnishing his subjects with their subsist-
85 ence that he gets his own only from them;
and, according to Rabelais, kings do not live

on nothing. Do subjects then give their persons on condition that the king takes their goods also? I fail to see what they have left to preserve.

5 It will be said that the despot assures his subjects civil tranquility. Granted; but what do they gain, if the wars his ambition brings down upon them, his insatiable avidity, and the vexa10tious conduct of his ministers press harder on them than their own dissensions would have done? What do they gain, if the very tranquility they enjoy is one of their miseries? Tranquility is found also in dungeons; but is that 15 enough to make them desirable places to live in? The Greeks imprisoned in the cave of the Cyclops lived there very tranquilly, while they were awaiting their turn to be devoured.

20 To say that a man gives himself gratuitously, is to say what is absurd and inconceivable; such an act is null and illegitimate, from the mere fact that he who does it is out of his mind. To say the same of a whole people is to suppose a 25 people of madmen; and madness creates no right.

Even if each man could alienate himself, he could not alienate his children: they are born 30 men and free; their liberty belongs to them, and no one but they has the right to dispose of it. Before they come to years of discretion, the father can, in their name, lay down conditions for their preservation and well-being, but 35 he cannot give them, irrevocably and without conditions: such a gift is contrary to the ends of nature, and exceeds the rights of paternity. It would therefore be necessary, in order to legitimize an arbitrary government, that in 40 every generation the people should be in a position to accept or reject it; but, were this so, the government would be no longer arbitrary.

To renounce liberty is to renounce being a 45 man, to surrender the rights of humanity and even its duties. For him who renounces everything no indemnity is possible. Such a renunciation is incompatible with man's nature; to remove all liberty from his will is to remove all 50 morality from his acts. Finally, it is an empty and contradictory convention that sets up, on the one side, absolute authority, and, on the other, unlimited obedience. Is it not clear that we can be under no obligation to a person 55 from whom we have the right to exact everything? Does not this condition alone, in the absence of equivalence or exchange, in itself involve the nullity of the act? For what right can my slave have against me, when all that he 60 has belongs to me, and, his right being mine, this right of mine against myself is a phrase devoid of meaning?

Grotius and the rest find in war another origin 65 for the so-called right of slavery. The victor having, as they hold, the right of killing the vanquished, the latter can buy back his life at the price of his liberty; and this convention is the more legitimate because it is to the ad70vantage of both parties.

But it is clear that this supposed right to kill the conquered is by no means deducible from the state of war. Men, from the mere fact that, 75 while they are living in their primitive independence, they have no mutual relations stable enough to constitute either the state of peace or the state of war, cannot be naturally enemies. War is constituted by a relation between 80 things, and not between persons; and, as the state of war cannot arise out of simple personal relations, but only out of real relations, private war, or war of man with man, can exist neither in the state of nature, where there is no 85 constant property, nor in the social state, where everything is under the authority of the laws.

Individual combats, duels and encounters, are acts which cannot constitute a state; while the private wars, authorized by the Establishments of Louis IX, King of France, and suspended by the Peace of God, are abuses of feudalism, in itself an absurd system if ever there was one, and contrary to the principles of natural right and to all good polity.

War then is a relation, not between man and man, but between State and State, and individuals are enemies only accidentally, not as men, nor even as citizens,[27] but as soldiers; not as members of their country, but as its defenders. Finally, each State can have for enemies only other States, and not men; for between things disparate in nature there can be no real relation.

Furthermore, this principle is in conformity with the established rules of all times and the constant practice of all civilized peoples. Declarations of war are intimations less to powers than to their subjects. The foreigner, whether king, individual, or people, who robs, kills or detains the subjects, without declaring war on the prince, is not an enemy, but a brigand. Even in real war, a just prince, while laying hands, in the enemy's country, on all that belongs to the public, respects the lives and goods of individuals: he respects rights on which his own are founded. The object of the war being the destruction of the hostile State, the other side has a right to kill its defenders, while they are bearing arms; but as soon as they lay them down and surrender, they cease to be enemies or instruments of the enemy, and become once more merely men, whose life no one has any right to take. Sometimes it is possible to kill the State without killing a single one of its members; and war gives no right which is not necessary to the gaining of its object. These principles are not those of Grotius: they are not based on the authority of poets, but derived from the nature of reality and based on reason.

The right of conquest has no foundation other than the right of the strongest. If war does not give the conqueror the right to massacre the conquered peoples, the right to enslave them cannot be based upon a right which does not exist. No one has a right to kill an enemy except when he cannot make him a slave, and the right to enslave him cannot therefore be derived from the right to kill him. It is accordingly an unfair exchange to make him buy at the price of his liberty his life, over which the victor holds no right. Is it not clear that there is a vicious circle in founding the right of life and death on the right of slavery, and the right of slavery on the right of life and death? Even if we assume this terrible right to kill everybody, I maintain that a slave made in war, or a conquered people, is under no obli-

---

[27] The Romans, who understood and respected the right of war more than any other nation on earth, carried their scruples on this head so far that a citizen was not allowed to serve as a volunteer without engaging himself expressly against the enemy, and against such and such an enemy by name. A legion in which the younger Cato was seeing his first service under Popilius having been reconstructed, the elder Cato wrote to Popilius that, if he wished his son to continue serving under him, he must administer to him a new military oath, because, the first having been annulled, he was no longer able to bear arms against the enemy. The same Cato wrote to his son telling him to take great care not to go into battle before taking this new oath. I know that the siege of Clusium and other isolated events can be quoted against me; but I am citing laws and customs. The Romans are the people that least often transgressed its laws; and no other people has had such good ones.

gation to a master, except to obey him as far as he is compelled to do so. By taking an equivalent for his life, the victor has not done him a favor; instead of killing him without
5 profit, he has killed him usefully. So far then is he from acquiring over him any authority in addition to that of force, that the state of war continues to subsist between them: their mutual relation is the effect of it, and the usage of
10 the right of war does not imply a treaty of peace. A convention has indeed been made; but this convention, so far from destroying the state of war, presupposes its continuance.

15 So, from whatever aspect we regard the question, the right of slavery is null and void, not only as being illegitimate, but also because it is absurd and meaningless. The words *slave* and *right* contradict each other, and are mutually
20 exclusive. It will always be equally foolish for a man to say to a man or to a people: "I make with you a convention wholly at your expense and wholly to my advantage; I shall keep it as long as I like, and you will keep it as long as I
25 like."

CHAPTER V
THAT WE MUST ALWAYS GO BACK TO A FIRST CONVENTION

30
Even if I granted all that I have been refuting, the friends of despotism would be no better off. There will always be a great difference between subduing a multitude and ruling a
35 society. Even if scattered individuals were successively enslaved by one man, however numerous they might be, I still see no more than a master and his slaves, and certainly not a people and its ruler; I see what may be termed
40 an aggregation, but not an association; there is as yet neither public good nor body politic. The man in question, even if he has enslaved half the world, is still only an individual; his

interest, apart from that of others, is still a
45 purely private interest. If this same man comes to die, his empire, after him, remains scattered and without unity, as an oak falls and dissolves into a heap of ashes when the fire has consumed it.
50

A people, says Grotius, can give itself to a king. Then, according to Grotius, a people is a people before it gives itself. The gift is itself a civil act, and implies public deliberation. It
55 would be better, before examining the act by which a people gives itself to a king, to examine that by which it has become a people; for this act, being necessarily prior to the other, is the true foundation of society.
60

Indeed, if there were no prior convention, where, unless the election were unanimous, would be the obligation on the minority to submit to the choice of the majority? How
65 have a hundred men who wish for a master the right to vote on behalf of ten who do not? The law of majority voting is itself something established by convention, and presupposes unanimity, on one occasion at least.
70

CHAPTER VI
THE SOCIAL COMPACT

I suppose men to have reached the point at
75 which the obstacles in the way of their preservation in the state of nature show their power of resistance to be greater than the resources at the disposal of each individual for his maintenance in that state. That primitive con-
80 dition can then subsist no longer; and the human race would perish unless it changed its manner of existence.
But, as men cannot engender new forces, but only unite and direct existing ones, they have
85 no other means of preserving themselves than the formation, by aggregation, of a sum of

forces great enough to overcome the resistance. These they have to bring into play by means of a single motive power, and cause to act in concert.

5 This sum of forces can arise only where several persons come together: but, as the force and liberty of each man are the chief instruments of his self-preservation, how can he pledge
10 them without harming his own interests, and neglecting the care he owes to himself? This difficulty, in its bearing on my present subject, may be stated in the following terms—"
The problem is to find a form of association
15 which will defend and protect with the whole common force the person and goods of each associate, and in which each, while uniting himself with all, may still obey himself alone, and remain as free as before."
20

This is the fundamental problem of which the *Social Contract* provides the solution.

The clauses of this contract are so determined
25 by the nature of the act that the slightest modification would make them vain and ineffective; so that, although they have perhaps never been formally set forth, they are everywhere the same and everywhere tacitly admitted and
30 recognized, until, on the violation of the social compact, each regains his original rights and resumes his natural liberty, while losing the conventional liberty in favor of which he renounced it.
35

These clauses, properly understood, may be reduced to one—the total alienation of each associate, together with all his rights, to the whole community for, in the first place, as
40 each gives himself absolutely, the conditions are the same for all; and, this being so, no one has any interest in making them burdensome to others.

Moreover, the alienation being without re-
45 serve, the union is as perfect as it can be, and no associate has anything more to demand: for, if the individuals retained certain rights, as there would be no common superior to decide between them and the public, each, being on
50 one point his own judge, would ask to be so on all; the state of nature would thus continue, and the association would necessarily become inoperative or tyrannical.

55 Finally, each man, in giving himself to all, gives himself to nobody; and as there is no associate over whom he does not acquire the same right as he yields others over himself, he gains an equivalent for everything he loses,
60 and an increase of force for the preservation of what he has.

If then we discard from the social compact what is not of its essence, we shall find that it
65 reduces itself to the following terms—

"Each of us puts his person and all his power in common under the supreme direction of the general will, and, in our corporate capacity, we receive each member
70 *as an indivisible part of the whole."*

At once, in place of the individual personality of each contracting party, this act of association creates a moral and collective body, com-
75 posed of as many members as the assembly contains votes, and receiving from this act its unity, its common identity, its life and its will. This public person, so formed by the union of all other persons, formerly took the name of
80 *city*,[28] and now takes that of *Republic* or *body*

---

[28] The real meaning of this word has been almost wholly lost in modern times; most people mistake a town for a city, and a townsman for a citizen. They do not know that houses make a town, but citizens a city. The same mistake long ago cost the Carthaginians dear. I have never

politic; it is called by its members *State* when passive, *Sovereign* when active, and *Power* when compared with others like itself. Those who are associated in it take collectively the name of *people*, and severally are called *citizens*, as sharing in the sovereign power, and *subjects*, as being under the laws of the State. But these terms are often confused and taken one for another: it is enough to know how to distinguish them when they are being used with precision.

CHAPTER VII
THE SOVEREIGN

This formula shows us that the act of association comprises a mutual undertaking between the public and the individuals, and that each individual, in making a contract, as we may say, with himself, is bound in a double capacity; as a member of the Sovereign he is bound to the individuals, and as a member of the State to the Sovereign. But the maxim of civil right, that no one is bound by undertakings made to himself, does not apply in this case;

read of the title of citizens being given to the subjects of any prince, not even the ancient Macedonians or the English of to-day, though they are nearer liberty than any one else. The French alone everywhere familiarly adopt the name of citizens, because, as can be seen from their dictionaries, they have no idea of its meaning; otherwise they would be guilty in usurping it, of the crime of *lèse-majesté*: among them, the name expresses a virtue, and not a right. When Bodin spoke of our citizens and townsmen, he fell into a bad blunder in taking the one class for the other. M. d'Alembert has avoided the error, and, in his article on Geneva, has clearly distinguished the four orders of men (or even five, counting mere foreigners) who dwell in our town, of which two only compose the Republic. No other French writer, to my knowledge, has understood the real meaning of the word citizen.

for there is a great difference between incurring an obligation to yourself and incurring one to a whole of which you form a part.

Attention must further be called to the fact that public deliberation, while competent to bind all the subjects to the Sovereign, because of the two different capacities in which each of them may be regarded, cannot, for the opposite reason, bind the Sovereign to itself; and that it is consequently against the nature of the body politic for the Sovereign to impose on itself a law which it cannot infringe. Being able to regard itself in only one capacity, it is in the position of an individual who makes a contract with himself; and this makes it clear that there neither is nor can be any kind of fundamental law binding on the body of the people—not even the social contract itself. This does not mean that the body politic cannot enter into undertakings with others, provided the contract is not infringed by them; for in relation to what is external to it, it becomes a simple being, an individual.

But the body politic or the Sovereign, drawing its being wholly from the sanctity of the contract, can never bind itself, even to an outsider, to do anything derogatory to the original act, for instance, to alienate any part of itself, or to submit to another Sovereign. Violation of the act by which it exists would be self-annihilation; and that which is itself nothing can create nothing.

As soon as this multitude is so united in one body, it is impossible to offend against one of the members without attacking the body, and still more to offend against the body without the members resenting it. Duty and interest therefore equally oblige the two contracting parties to give each other help; and the same men should seek to combine, in their double capacity, all the advantages dependent upon that capacity.

Again, the Sovereign, being formed wholly of
5 the individuals who compose it, neither has
nor can have any interest contrary to theirs; and consequently the sovereign power need give no guarantee to its subjects, because it is impossible for the body to wish to hurt all its
10 members. We shall also see later on that It cannot hurt any in particular. The Sovereign, merely by virtue of what it is, is always what it should be.

15 This, however, is not the case with the relation of the subjects to the Sovereign, which, despite the common interest, would have no security that they would fulfill their undertakings, unless it found means to assure itself of
20 their fidelity.

In fact, each individual, as a man, may have a particular will contrary or dissimilar to the general will which he has as a citizen. His par-
25 ticular interest may speak to him quite differently from the common interest: his absolute and naturally independent existence may make him look upon what he owes to the common cause as a gratuitous contribution, the loss of
30 which will do less harm to others than the payment of it is burdensome to himself; and, regarding the moral person which constitutes the State as a persona ficta, because not a man, he may wish to enjoy the rights of citizenship
35 without being ready to fulfill the duties of a subject. The continuance of such an injustice could not but prove the undoing of the body politic.

In order then that the social compact may not
40 be an empty formula, it tacitly includes the undertaking, which alone can give force to the rest, that whoever refuses to obey the general will shall be compelled to do so by the whole

body. This means nothing less than that he
45 will be forced to be free; for this is the condition which, by giving each citizen to his country, secures him against all personal dependence. In this lies the key to the working of the political machine; this alone legitimizes civil
50 undertakings, which, without it, would be absurd, tyrannical, and liable to the most frightful abuses.

CHAPTER VIII
55 ## THE CIVIL STATE

The passage from the state of nature to the civil state produces a very remarkable change in man, by substituting justice, for instinct in
60 his conduct, and giving his actions the morality they had formerly lacked. Then only, when the voice of duty takes the place of physical impulses and right of appetite, does *man*, who so far had considered only himself, find that
65 he is forced to act on different principles, and to consult his reason before listening to his inclinations. Although, in this state, he deprives himself of some advantages which he got from nature, he gains in return others so
70 great, his faculties are so stimulated and developed, his ideas so extended, his feelings so ennobled, and his whole soul so uplifted, that, did not the abuses of this new condition often degrade him below that which he left, he
75 would be bound to bless continually the happy moment which took him from it for ever, and, instead of a stupid and unimaginative animal, made him an intelligent being and a man.

80 Let us draw up the whole account in terms easily commensurable. What man loses by the social contract in his natural liberty and an unlimited right to everything he tries to get and succeeds in getting; what he gains is civil
85 liberty and the proprietorship of all he possesses. If we are to avoid mistake in weighing

one against the other, we must clearly distinguish natural liberty, which is bounded only by the strength of the individual, from civil liberty, which is limited by the general will; and

5 possession, which is merely the effect of force or the right of the first occupier, from property, which can be founded only on a positive title.

10 We might, over and above all this, add, to what man acquires in the civil state, moral liberty, which alone makes him truly master of himself; for the mere impulse of appetite is slavery, while obedience to a law which we

15 prescribe to ourselves is liberty. But I have already said too much on this head, and the philosophical meaning of the word liberty does not now concern us.

20
CHAPTER IX
REAL PROPERTY

Each member of the community gives himself to it, at the moment of its foundation, just as

25 he is, with all the resources at his command, including the goods he possesses. This act does not make possession, in changing hands, change its nature, and becomes property in the hands of the Sovereign; but, as the forces of

30 the city are incomparably greater than those of an individual, public possession is also, in fact, stronger and more irrevocable, without being any more legitimate, at any rate from the point of view of foreigners. For the State, in relation

35 to its members, is master of all their goods by the social contract, which, within the State, is the basis of all rights; but, in relation to other powers, it is so only by the right of the first occupier, which it holds from its members.

40
The right of the first occupier, though more real than the right of the strongest, becomes a real right only when the right of property has

already been established. Every man has natu-
45 rally a right to everything he needs; but the positive act which makes him proprietor of one thing excludes him from everything else. Having his share, he ought to keep to it, and can have no further right against the commu-
50 nity. This is why the right of the first occupier, which in the state of nature is so weak, claims the respect of every man in civil society. In this right we are respecting not so much what belongs to another as what does not belong to
55 ourselves.

In general, to establish the right of the first occupier over a plot of ground, the following conditions are necessary: first, the land must
60 not yet be inhabited; secondly, a man must occupy only the amount he needs for his subsistence; and, in the third place, possession must be taken, not by an empty ceremony, but by labor and cultivation, the only sign of pro-
65 prietorship that should be respected by others, in default of a legal title.

In granting the right of first occupancy to necessity and labor, are we not really stretching it
70 as far as it can go? Is it possible to leave such a right unlimited? Is it to be enough to set foot on a plot of common ground, in order to be able to call yourself at once the master of it? Is it to be enough that a man has the strength to
75 expel others for a moment, in order to establish his right to prevent them from ever returning? How can a man or a people seize an immense territory and keep it from the rest of the world except by a punishable usurpation,
80 since all others are being robbed, by such an act, of the place of habitation and the means of subsistence which nature gave them in common? When Nuñez Balboa, standing on the sea-shore, took possession of the South
85 Seas and the whole of South America in the name of the crown of Castille, was that

enough to dispossess all their actual inhabitants, and to shut out from them all the princes
of the world? On such a showing, these ceremonies are idly multiplied, and the Catholic
5   King need only take possession all at once,
from his apartment, of the whole universe,
merely making a subsequent reservation about
what was already in the possession of other
princes.
10

We can imagine how the lands of individuals,
where they were contiguous and came to be
united, became the public territory, and how
the right of Sovereignty, extending from the
15   subjects over the lands they held, became at
once real and personal. The possessors were
thus made more dependent, and the forces at
their command used to guarantee their fidelity.
The advantage of this does not seem to have
20   been felt by ancient monarchs, who called
themselves King of the Persians, Scythians, or
Macedonians, and seemed to regard themselves more as rulers of men than as masters
of a country. Those of the present day more
25   cleverly call themselves Kings of France,
Spain, England, etc.: thus holding the land,
they are quite confident of holding the inhabitants.

30   The peculiar fact about this alienation is that,
in taking over the goods of individuals, the
community, so far from despoiling them, only
assures them legitimate possession, and
changes usurpation into a true right and en-
35   joyment into proprietorship. Thus the possessors, being regarded as depositaries of the
public good, and having their rights, respected
by all the members of the State and maintained against foreign aggression by all its
40   forces, have, by a cession which benefits both
the public and still more themselves, acquired,
so to speak, all that they gave up. This paradox
may easily be explained by the distinction be-

tween the rights which the Sovereign and the
45   proprietor have over the same estate, as we
shall see later on. It may also happen that men
begin to unite one with another before they
possess anything, and that, subsequently oc-
cupying a tract of country which is enough for
50   all, they enjoy it in common, or share it out
among themselves, either equally or according
to a scale fixed by they Sovereign. However
the acquisition be made, the right which each
individual has to his own estate is always sub-
55   ordinate to the right which the community has
over all: without this, there would be neither
stability in the social tie, nor real force in the
exercise of Sovereignty.

60   I shall end this chapter and this book by re-
marking on a fact on which the whole social
system should rest: *i.e.* that, instead of destroying natural inequality, the fundamental compact substitutes, for such physical inequality as
65   nature may have set up between men, an
equality that is moral and legitimate, and that
men, who may be unequal in strength or intelligence, become every one equal by convention and legal right.
70

Under bad governments, this equality is only
apparent and illusory: it serves only to keep
the pauper in his poverty and the rich man in
the position he has usurped. In fact, laws are
75   always of use to those who possess and harmful to those who have nothing: from which it
follows that the social state is advantageous to
men only when all have something and none
too much.
80

BOOK II
CHAPTER I
THAT SOVEREIGNTY IS
INALIENABLE
85

The first and most important deduction from

the principles we have so far laid down is that the general will alone can direct the State according to the object for which it was instituted, *i.e.* the common good: for if the clashing of
5 particular interests made the establishment of societies necessary, the agreement of these very interests made it possible. The common element in these different interests is what forms the social tie; and, were there no point
10 of agreement between them all, no society could exist. It is solely on the basis of this common interest that every society should be governed.

15 I hold then that Sovereignty, being nothing less than the exercise of the general will, can never be alienated, and that the Sovereign, who is no less than a collective being, cannot be represented except by himself: the power
20 indeed may be transmitted, but not the will.

In reality, if it is not impossible for a particular will to agree on some point with the general will, it is at least impossible for the agreement
25 to be lasting and constant; for the particular will tends, by its very nature, to partiality, while the general will tends to equality. It is even more impossible to have any guarantee of this agreement; for even if it should always
30 exist, it would be the effect not of art, but of chance. The Sovereign may indeed say: "I now will actually what this man wills, or at least what he says he wills"; but it cannot say: "What he wills tomorrow, I too shall will"
35 because it is absurd for the will to bind itself for the future, nor is it incumbent on any; will to consent to anything that is not for the good of the being who wills. If then the people promises simply to obey, by that very act it
40 dissolves itself and loses what makes it a people; the moment a master exists, there is no longer a Sovereign, and from that moment the body politic has ceased to exist.

This does not mean that the commands of the
45 rulers cannot pass for general wills, so long as the Sovereign, being free to oppose them, offers no opposition. In such a case, universal silence is taken to imply the consent of the people. This will be explained later on.
50

CHAPTER II
THAT SOVEREIGNTY IS
INDIVISIBLE
55

Sovereignty, for the same reason as makes it inalienable, is indivisible; for will either is, or is not, general;[29] it is the will either of the body of the people, or only of a part of it. In the
60 first case, the will, when declared, is an act of Sovereignty and constitutes law: in the second, it is merely a particular will, or act of magistracy—at the most a decree.

65 But our political theorists, unable to divide Sovereignty in principle, divide it according to its object: into force and will; into legislative power and executive power; into rights of taxation, justice and war; into internal administra-
70 tion and power of foreign treaty. Sometimes they confuse all these sections, and sometimes they distinguish them; they turn the Sovereign into a fantastic being composed of several connected pieces: it is as if they were making
75 man of several bodies, one with eyes, one with arms, another with feet, and each with nothing besides. We are told that the jugglers of Japan dismember a child before the eyes of the spectators; then they throw all the members into
80 the air one after another, and the child falls down alive and whole. The conjuring tricks of our political theorists are very like that; they

---

[29] To be general, a will need not always be unanimous; but every vote—must be counted: any exclusion is a breach of generality.

first dismember the body politic by an illusion worthy of a fair, and then join it together again we know not how.

5 This error is due to a lack of exact notions concerning the Sovereign authority, and to taking for parts of it what are only emanations from it. Thus, for example, the acts of declaring war and making peace have been regarded
10 as acts of Sovereignty; but this is not the case, as these acts do not constitute law, but merely the application of a law, a particular act which decides how the law applies, as we shall see clearly when the idea attached to the word *law*
15 has been defined.

If we examined the other divisions in the same manner, we should find that, whenever Sovereignty seems to be divided, there is an illusion:
20 the rights which are taken as being part of Sovereignty are really all subordinate, and always imply supreme wills of which they only sanction the execution.

25 It would be impossible to estimate the obscurity this lack of exactness has thrown over the decisions of writers who have dealt with political right, when they have used the principles laid down by them to pass judgment on the
30 respective rights of kings and peoples. Every one can see, in Chapters III and IV of the First Book of Grotius, how the learned man and his translator, Barbeyrac, entangle and tie themselves up in their own sophistries, for
35 fear of saying too little or too much of what they think, and so offending the interests they have to conciliate. Grotius, a refugee in France, ill-content with his own country, and desirous of paying his court to Louis XIII, to
40 whom his book is dedicated, spares no pains to rob the peoples of all their rights and invest kings with them by every conceivable artifice. This would also have been much to the taste

of Barbeyrac, who dedicated his translation to
45 George I of England. But unfortunately the expulsion of James II, which he called his "abdication," compelled him to use all reserve, to shuffle and to tergiversate, in order to avoid making William out a usurper. If these two
50 writers had adopted the true principles, all difficulties would have been removed, and they would have been always consistent; but it would have been a sad truth for them to tell, and would have paid court for them to no-one
55 save the people. Moreover, truth is no road to fortune, and the people dispenses neither ambassadorships, nor professorships, nor pensions.

60 ## CHAPTER III
WHETHER THE GENERAL WILL IS FALLIBLE

It follows from what has gone before that the
65 general will is always right and tends to the public advantage; but it does not follow that the deliberations of the people are always equally correct. Our will is always for our own good, but we do not always see what that is;
70 the people is never corrupted, but it is often deceived, and on such occasions only does it seem to will what is bad.

There is often a great deal of difference be-
75 tween the will of all and the general will; the latter considers only the common interest, while the former takes private interest into account, and is no more than a sum of particular wills: but take away from these same
80 wills the pluses and minuses that cancel one another,[30] and the general will remains as the

---

[30] "Every interest," says the Marquis d'Argenson, "has different principles. The agreement of two particular interests is formed by opposition to a third." He might have added that the agreement of all interests is formed by opposition to that of

sum of the differences.

If, when the people, being furnished with adequate information, held its deliberations, the citizens had no communication one with another, the grand total of the small differences would always give the general will, and the decision would always be good. But when factions arise, and partial associations are formed at the expense of the great association, the will of each of these associations becomes general in relation to its members, while it remains particular in relation to the State: it may then be said that there are no longer as many votes as there are men, but only as many as there are associations. The differences become less numerous and give a less general result. Lastly, when one of these associations is so great as to prevail over all the rest, the result is no longer a sum of small differences, but a single difference; in this case there is no longer a general will, and the opinion which prevails is purely particular.

It is therefore essential, if the general will is to be able to express itself, that there should be no partial society within the State, and that each citizen should think only his own thoughts:[31] which was indeed the sublime and unique system established by the great Lycur-

gus. But if there are partial societies, it is best to have as many as possible and to prevent them from being unequal, as was done by Solon, Numa and Servius. These precautions are the only ones that can guarantee that the general will shall be always enlightened, and that the people shall in no way deceive itself.

CHAPTER IV
THE LIMITS OF THE SOVEREIGN POWER

If the State is a moral person whose life is in the union of its members, and if the most important of its cares is the care for its own preservation, it must have a universal and compelling force, in order to move and dispose each part as may be most advantageous to the whole. As nature gives each man absolute power over all his members, the social compact gives the body politic absolute power over all its members also; and it is this power which, under the direction of the general will, bears, as I have said, the name of Sovereignty.

But, besides the public person, we have to consider the private persons composing it, whose life and liberty are naturally independent of it. We are bound then to distinguish clearly between the respective rights of the citizens and the Sovereign,[32] and between the duties the former have to fulfill as subjects, and the natural rights they should enjoy as men.

Each man alienates, I admit, by the social compact, only such part of his powers, goods and liberty as it is important for the community to control; but it must also be granted that

---

each. If there were no different interests, the common interest would be barely felt, as it would encounter no obstacle; all would go on of its own accord, and politics would cease to be an art.

[31] "In fact," says Machiavelli, "there are some divisions that are harmful to a Republic and some that are advantageous. Those which stir up sects and parties are harmful; those attended by neither are advantageous. Since, then, the founder of a Republic cannot help enmities arising, he ought at least to prevent them from growing into sects" (*History of Florence*, Book vii). Rousseau quotes the Italian.

---

[32] Attentive readers, do not, I pray, be in a hurry to charge me with contradicting myself. The terminology made it unavoidable, considering the poverty of the language; but wait and see.

the Sovereign is sole judge of what is important.

Every service a citizen can render the State he ought to render as soon as the Sovereign demands it; but the Sovereign, for its part, cannot impose upon its subjects any fetters that are useless to the community, nor can it even wish to do so; for no more by the law of reason than by the law of nature can anything occur without a cause.

The undertakings which bind us to the social body are obligatory only because they are mutual; and their nature is such that in fulfilling them we cannot work for others without working for ourselves. Why is it that the general will is always in the right, and that all continually will the happiness of each one, unless it is because there is not a man who does not think of "each" as meaning him, and consider himself in voting for all? This proves that equality of rights and the idea of justice which such equality creates originate in the preference each man gives to himself, and accordingly in the very nature of man. It proves that the general will, to be really such, must be general in its object as well as its essence; that it must both come from all and apply to all; and that it loses its natural rectitude when it is directed to some particular and determinate object, because in such a case we are judging of something foreign to us, and have no true principle of equity to guide us.

Indeed, as soon as a question of particular fact or right arises on a point not previously regulated by a general convention, the matter becomes contentions. It is a case in which the individuals concerned are one party, and the public the other, but in which I can see neither the law that ought to be followed nor the judge who ought to give the decision. In such a case, it would be absurd to propose to refer the question to an express decision of the general will, which can be only the conclusion reached by one of the parties and in consequence will be, for the other party, merely an external and particular will, inclined on this occasion to injustice and subject to error. Thus, just as a particular will cannot stand for the general will, the general will, in turn, changes its nature, when its object is particular, and, as general, cannot pronounce on a man or a fact. When, for instance, the people of Athens nominated or displaced its rulers, decreed honors to one, and imposed penalties on another, and, by a multitude of particular decrees, exercised all the functions of government indiscriminately, it had in such cases no longer a general will in the strict sense; it was acting no longer as Sovereign, but as magistrate. This will seem contrary to current views; but I must be given time to expound my own.

It should be seen from the foregoing that what makes the will general is less the number of voters than the common interest uniting them; for under this system, each necessarily submits to the conditions he imposes on others; and this admirable agreement between interest and justice gives to the common deliberations an equitable character which at once vanishes when any particular question is discussed, in the absence of a common interest to unite and identify the ruling of the judge with that of the party.

From whatever side we approach our principle, we reach the same conclusion, that the social compact sets up among the citizens an equality of such a kind, that they all bind themselves to observe the same conditions and should therefore all enjoy the same rights. Thus, from the very nature of the compact, every "act of Sovereignty", *i.e.* every authentic act of the general will, binds or favors all the citizens equally; so that the Sovereign recognizes only the body of the nation, and draws no distinctions between those of whom it is made up. What, then, strictly speaking is an act of Sovereignty? It is not a convention between a superior and an inferior, but a convention between the body and each of its members. It is legitimate, because based on the social contract, and, equitable, because common to all; useful, because it can have no other object than the general good, and stable, because guaranteed by the public force and the supreme power. So long as the subjects have to submit only to conventions of this sort, they obey no-one but their own will; and to ask how far the respective rights of the Sovereign and the citizens extend, is to ask up to what point the latter can enter into undertakings with themselves, each with all, and all with each.

We can see from this that the sovereign power, absolute, sacred and inviolable as it is, does not and cannot exceed the limits of general conventions, and that every man may dispose at will of such goods and liberty as these conventions leave him; so that the Sovereign never has a right to lay more charges on one subject than on another, because, in that case, the question becomes particular, and ceases to be within its competency.

When these distinctions have once been admitted, it is seen to be so untrue that there is, in the social contract, any real renunciation on the part of the individuals, that the position in which they find themselves as a result of the contract is really preferable to that in which they were before. Instead of a renunciation, they have made an advantageous exchange: instead of an uncertain and precarious way of living they have got one that is better and more secure; instead of natural independence they have got liberty, instead of the power to harm others security for themselves, and instead of their strength, which others might overcome, a right which social union makes invincible. Their very life, which they have devoted to the State, is by it constantly protected; and when they risk it in the State's defense, what more are they doing than giving back what they have received from it? What are they doing that they would not do more often and with greater danger in the state of nature, in which they would inevitably have to fight battles at the peril of their lives in defense of that which is the means of their preservation? All have indeed to fight when their country needs them; but then no one has ever to fight for himself. Do we not gain something by running, on behalf of what gives us our security, only some of the risks we should have to run for ourselves, as soon as we lost it?

CHAPTER V
THE RIGHT OF LIFE AND DEATH

The question is often asked how individuals, having no right to dispose of their own lives, can transfer to the Sovereign a right which they do not possess. The difficulty of answering this question seems to me to lie in its being wrongly stated. Every man has a right to risk his own life in order to preserve it. Has it ever, been said that a man who throws himself out of the window to escape from a fire is guilty of suicide? Has such a crime ever been laid to the charge of him who perishes in a storm because, when he went on board, he knew of the danger?

The social treaty has for its end the preservation of the contracting parties. He who wills the end wills the means also, and the means must involve some risks, and even some losses. He who wishes to preserve his life at others expense should also, when it is necessary,

5 be ready to give it up for their sake. Furthermore, the citizen is no longer the judge of the dangers to which the law desires him to expose himself; and when the prince says to him: "It is expedient for the State that you should

10 die," he ought to die, because it is only on that condition that he has been living in security up to the present, and because his life is no longer a mere bounty of nature, but a gift made conditionally by the State.

15

The death-penalty inflicted upon criminals may be looked on in much the same light: it is in order that we may not fall victims to an assassin that we consent to die if we ourselves

20 turn assassins. In this treaty, so far from disposing of our own lives, we think only of securing them, and it is not to be assumed that any of the parties then expects to get hanged.

25 Again, every malefactor, by attacking social rights, becomes on forfeit a rebel and a traitor to his country; by violating its laws he ceases to be a member of it; he even makes war upon it. In such a case the preservation of the State

30 is inconsistent with his own, and one or the other must perish; in putting the guilty to death, we slay not so much the citizen as an enemy. The trial and the judgment are the proofs that he has broken the social treaty,

35 and is in consequence no longer a member of the State. Since, then, he has recognized himself to be such by living there, he must be removed by exile as a violator of the compact, or by death as a public enemy; for such an

40 enemy is not a moral person, but merely a man; and in such a case the right of war is to kill the vanquished.

But, it will be said, the condemnation of a

45 criminal is a particular act. I admit it: but such condemnation is not a function of the Sovereign; it is a right the Sovereign can confer without being able itself to exert it. All my ideas are consistent, but I cannot expound

50 them all at once.

We may add that frequent punishments are always a sign of weakness or remissness on the part of the government. There is not a single

55 ill-doer who could not be turned to some good. The State has no right to put to death, even for the sake of making an example, any one whom it can leave alive without danger.

60 The right of pardoning or exempting the guilty from a penalty imposed by the law and pronounced by the judge belongs only to the authority which is superior to both judge and law, *i.e.* the Sovereign; even its right in this

65 matter is tar from clear, and the cases for exercising it are extremely rare. In a well-governed State, there are few punishments, not because there are many pardons, but because criminals are rare; it is when a State is in

70 decay that the multitude of crimes is a guarantee of impunity. Under the Roman Republic, neither the Senate nor the Consuls ever attempted to pardon; even the people never did so, though it sometimes revoked its own deci-

75 sion. Frequent pardons mean that crime will soon need them no longer, and no-one can help seeing whither that leads. But I feel my heart protesting and restraining my pen; let us leave these questions to the just man who has

80 never offended, and would himself stand in no-need of pardon.

CHAPTER VI
LAW

85

By the social compact we have given the body

politic existence and life: we have now by legislation to give it movement and will. For the
original act by which the body is formed and
united still in no respect determines what it
ought to do for its preservation.

What is well and in conformity with order is
so by the nature of things and independently
of human conventions. All justice comes from
God, who is its sole source; but if we knew
how to receive so high an inspiration, we
should need neither government nor laws.
Doubtless, there is a universal justice emanat-
ing from reason alone; but this justice, to be
admitted among us, must be mutual. Humanly
speaking, in default of natural sanctions, the
laws of justice are ineffective among men: they
merely make for the good of the wicked and
the undoing of the just, when the just man
observes them towards everybody and nobody
observes them towards him. Conventions and
laws are therefore needed to join rights to duties and refer justice to its object. In the state
of nature, where everything is common, I owe
nothing to him whom I nave promised nothing; I recognize as belonging to others only
what is of no use to me. In the state of society
all rights are fixed by law, and the case becomes different.

But what, after all, is a law? As long as we remain satisfied with attaching purely metaphysical ideas to the word, we shall go on arguing
without arriving at an understanding; and
when we have defined a law of nature, we
shall be no nearer the definition of a law of
the State.

I have already said that there can be no general
will directed to a particular object. Such an
object must be either within or outside the
State. If outside, a will which is alien to it cannot be, in relation to it, general; if within, it is

part of the State, and in that case there arises a
relation between whole and part which makes
them two separate beings, of which the part is
one, and the whole minus the part the other.
But the whole minus a part cannot be the
whole; and while this relation persists, there
can be no whole, but only two unequal parts;
and it follows that the will of one is no longer
in any respect general in relation to the other.

But when the whole people decrees for the
whole people, it is considering only itself; and
if a relation is then formed, it is between two
aspects of the entire object, without there being any division of the whole. In that case the
matter about which the decree is made is, like
the decreeing will general. This act is what I
call a law.

When I say that the object of laws is always
general, I mean that law considers subjects *en
masse* and actions in the abstract, and never a
particular person or action. Thus the law may
indeed decree that there shall be privileges, but
cannot confer them on anybody by name. It
may set up several classes of citizens, and even
lay down the qualifications for membership of
these classes, but it cannot nominate such and
such persons as belonging to them; it may
establish a monarchical government and hereditary succession, but it cannot choose a
king, or nominate a royal family. In a word, no
function which has a particular object belongs
to the legislative power.

On this view, we at once see that it can no
longer be asked whose business it is to make
laws, since they are acts of the general will: nor
whether the prince is above the law, since he is
a member of the State; nor whether the law
can be unjust, since no one is unjust to himself; nor how we can be both free and subject
to the laws since they are but registers of our

wills.

We see further that, as the law unites universality of will with universality of object, what a
5 man, whoever he be, commands of his own motion cannot be a law; and even what the Sovereign commands with regard to a particular matter is no nearer being a law, but is a decree, an act, not of sovereignty, but of mag-
10 istracy.

I therefore give the name 'Republic' to every State that is governed by laws, no matter what the form of its administration may be: for only
15 in such a case does the public interest govern, and the *res publica* rank as a *reality*. Every legitimate government is republican;[33] what government is I will explain later on.

20 Laws are, properly speaking, only the conditions of civil association. The people, being subject to the laws, ought to be their author: the conditions of the society ought to be regulated solely by those who come together to
25 form it. But how are they to regulate them? Is it to be by common agreement, by a sudden inspiration? Has the body politic an organ to declare its will? Who can give it the foresight to formulate and announce its acts in advance?
30 Or how is it to announce them in the hour of need? How can a blind multitude, which often does not know what it wills, because it rarely knows what is good for it, carry out for itself so great and difficult an enterprise as a system
35 of legislation? Of itself the people wills always

the good, but of itself it by no means always sees it. The general will is always in the right, but the judgment which guides it is not always enlightened. It must be got to see objects as
40 they are, and sometimes as they ought to appear to it; it must be shown the good road it is in search of, secured from the seductive influences of individual wills, taught to see times and spaces as a series, and made to weigh the
45 attractions of present and sensible advantages against the danger of distant and hidden evils. The individuals see the good they reject; the public wills the good it does not see. All stand equally in need of guidance. The former must
50 be compelled to bring their wills into conformity with their reason; the latter must be taught to know what it wills. If that is done, public enlightenment leads to the union of understanding and will in the social body: the
55 parts are made to work exactly together, and the whole is raised to its highest power. This makes a legislator necessary.

CHAPTER VII
THE LEGISLATOR

In order to discover the rules of society best suited to nations, a superior intelligence beholding all the passions of men without expe-
65 riencing any of them would be needed. This intelligence would have to be wholly unrelated to our nature, while knowing it through and through; its happiness would have to be independent of us, and yet ready to occupy itself
70 with ours; and lastly, it would have, in the march of time, to look forward to a distant glory, and, working in one century, to be able to enjoy in the next.[34] It would take gods to

---

[33] I understand by this word, not merely an aristocracy or a democracy, but generally any government directed by the general will, which is the law. To be legitimate, the government must be, not one with the Sovereign, but its minister. In such a case even a monarchy is a Republic. This will be made clearer in the following book.

---

[34] A people becomes famous only when its legislation begins to decline. We do not know for how many centuries the system of Lycurgus made the Spartans happy before the rest of Greece took any notice of it.

give men laws.

What Caligula argued from the facts, Plato, in the dialogue called the *Politicus*, argued in de-
5 fining the civil or kingly man, on the basis of right. But if great princes are rare, how much more so are great legislators? The former have only to follow the pattern which the latter have to lay down. The legislator is the engi-
10 neer who invents the machine, the prince merely the mechanic who sets it up and makes it go. "At the birth of societies," says Montes-quieu, "the rulers of Republics establish insti-tutions, and afterwards the institutions mold
15 the rulers."[35]

He who dares to undertake the making of a people's institutions ought to feel himself ca-pable, so to speak, of changing human nature, of transforming each individual, who is by
20 himself a complete and solitary whole, into part of a greater whole from which he in a manner receives his life and being; of altering man's constitution for the purpose of
25 strengthening it; and of substituting a partial and moral existence for the physical and inde-pendent existence nature has conferred on us all. He must, in a word, take away from man his own resources and give him instead new
30 ones alien to him, and incapable of being made use of without the help of other men. The more completely these natural resources are annihilated, the greater and the more last-ing are those which he acquires, and the more
35 stable and perfect the new institutions; so that if each citizen is nothing and can do nothing without the rest, and the resources acquired by the whole are equal or superior to the aggre-gate of the resources of all the individuals, it

40 may be said that legislation is at the highest possible point of perfection.

The legislator occupies in every respect an extraordinary position in the State. If he
45 should do so by reason of his genius, he does so no less by reason of his office, which is neither magistracy, nor Sovereignty. This of-fice, which sets up the Republic, nowhere en-ters into its constitution; it is an individual and
50 superior function, which has nothing in com-mon with human empire; for if he who holds command over men ought not to have com-mand over the laws, he who has command over the laws ought not any more to have it
55 over men; or else his laws would be the minis-ters of his passions and would often merely serve to perpetuate his injustices: his private aims would inevitably mar the sanctity of his work.

60

When Lycurgus gave laws to his country, he began by resigning the throne. It was the cus-tom of most Greek towns to entrust the estab-lishment of their laws to foreigners. The Re-
65 publics of modern Italy in many cases fol-lowed this example; Geneva did the same and profited by it.[36] Rome, when it was most prosperous, suffered a revival of all the crimes of tyranny, and was brought to the verge of
70 destruction, because it put the legislative au-thority and the sovereign power into the same hands.

---

[35] Montesquieu, *The Greatness and Decadence of the Romans*, ch. i.

[36] Those who know Calvin only as a theologian much underestimate the extent of his genius. The codification of our wise edicts, in which he played a large part, does him no less honor than his *Institute*. Whatever revolution time may bring in our religion, so long as the spirit of patriotism and liberty still lives among us, the memory of this great man will be for ever blessed.

Nevertheless, the decemvirs themselves never claimed the right to pass any law merely on their own authority. "Nothing we propose to you," they said to the people, "can pass into law without your consent. Romans, be yourselves the authors of the laws which are to make you happy."

He, therefore, who draws up the laws has, or should have, no right of legislation, and the people cannot, even if it wishes, deprive itself of this incommunicable right, because, according to the fundamental compact, only the general will can bind the individuals, and there can be no assurance that a particular will is in conformity with the general will, until it has been put to the free vote of the people. This I have said already; but it is worth while to repeat it.

Thus in the task of legislation we find together two things which appear to be incompatible: an enterprise too difficult for human powers, and, for its execution, an authority that is no authority.

There is a further difficulty that deserves attention. Wise men, if they try to speak their language to the common herd instead of its own, cannot possibly make themselves understood. There are a thousand kinds of ideas which it is impossible to translate into popular language. Conceptions that are too general and objects that are too remote are equally out of its range: each individual, having no taste for any other plan of government than that which suits his particular interest, finds it difficult to realize the advantages he might hope to draw from the continual privations good laws impose. For a young people to be able to relish sound principles of political theory and follow the fundamental rules of statecraft, the effect would have to become the cause; the social spirit, which should be created by these insti-

tutions, would have to preside over their very foundation; and men would have to be before law what they should become by means of law. The legislator therefore, being unable to appeal to either force or reason, must have recourse to an authority of a different order capable of constraining without violence and persuading without convincing.

This is what has, in all ages, compelled the fathers of nations to have recourse to divine intervention and credit the gods with their own wisdom, in order that the peoples, submitting to the laws of the State as to those of nature, and recognizing the same power in the formation of the city as in that of man, might obey freely, and bear with docility the yoke of the public happiness.

This sublime reason, far above the range of the common herd, is that whose decisions the legislator puts into the mouth of the immortals, in order to constrain by divine authority those whom human prudence could not move.[37] But it is not anybody who can make the gods speak, or get himself believed when he proclaims himself their interpreter. The great soul of the legislator is the only miracle that can prove his mission. Any man may grave tablets of stone, or buy an oracle; or feign secret intercourse with some divinity, or train a bird to whisper in his ear, or find other vulgar ways of imposing on the people. He whose knowledge goes no further may per-

---

[37] "In truth," says Machiavelli, "there has never been, in any country, an extraordinary legislator who has not had recourse to God; for otherwise his laws would not have been accepted: there are, in fact, many useful truths of which a wise man may have knowledge without their having in themselves such clear reasons for their being so as to be able to convince others" (*Discourses on Livy*, Bk. v, ch. xi). (Rousseau quotes the Italian.)

haps gather round him a band of fools; but he will never found an empire, and his extravagances will quickly perish with him. Idle tricks form a passing tie; only wisdom can make it lasting. The Judaic law, which still subsists, and that of the child of Ishmael, which, for ten centuries, has ruled half the world, still proclaim the great men who laid them down; and, while the pride of philosophy or the blind spirit of faction sees in them no more than lucky impostures, the true political theorist admires, in the institutions they set up, the great and powerful genius which presides over things made to endure.

We should not, with Warburton, conclude from this that politics and religion have among us a common object, but that, in the first periods of nations, the one is used as an instrument for the other.

CHAPTER VIII
THE PEOPLE

As, before putting up a large building, the architect surveys and sounds the site to see if it will bear the weight, the wise legislator does not begin by laying down laws good in themselves, but by investigating the fitness of the people, for which they are destined, to receive them. Plato refused to legislate for the Arcadians and the Cyrenæans, because he knew that both peoples were rich and could not put up with equality; and good laws and bad men were found together in Crete, because Minos had inflicted discipline on a people already burdened with vice.

A thousand nations have achieved earthly greatness, that could never have endured good laws; even such as could have endured them could have done so only for a very brief period of their long history. Most peoples, like most men, are docile only in youth; as they grow old they become incorrigible. When once customs have become established and prejudices inveterate, it is dangerous and useless to attempt their reformation; the people, like the foolish and cowardly patients who rave at sight of the doctor, can no longer bear that any one should lay hands on its faults to remedy them.

There are indeed times in the history of States when, just as some kinds of illness turn men's heads and make them forget the past, periods of violence and revolutions do to peoples what these crises do to individuals: horror of the past takes the place of forgetfulness, and the State, set on fire by civil wars, is born again, so to speak, from its ashes, and takes on anew, fresh from the jaws of death, the vigor of youth. Such were Sparta at the time of Lycurgus, Rome after the Tarquins, and, in modern times, Holland and Switzerland after the expulsion of the tyrants.

But such events are rare; they are exceptions, the cause of which is always to be found in the particular constitution of the State concerned. They cannot even happen twice to the same people, for it can make itself free as long as it remains barbarous, but not when the civic impulse has lost its vigor. Then disturbances may destroy it, but revolutions cannot mend it: it needs a master, and not a liberator. Free peoples, be mindful of maxim; "Liberty may be gained, but can never be recovered."

Youth is not infancy. There is for nations, as for men, a period of youth, or, shall we say, maturity, before which they should not be made subject to laws; but the maturity of a people is not always easily recognizable, and, if it is anticipated, the work is spoilt. One people is amenable to discipline from the beginning;

another, not after ten centuries. Russia will never be really civilized, because it was civilized too soon. Peter had a genius for imitation; but he lacked true genius, which is creative and makes all from nothing. He did some good things, but most of what he did was out of place. He saw that his people was barbarous, but did not see that it was not ripe for civilization: he wanted to civilize it when it needed only hardening. His first wish was to make Germans or Englishmen, when he ought to have been making Russians; and he prevented his subjects from ever becoming what they might have been by persuading them that they were what they are not. In this fashion too a French teacher turns out his pupil to be an infant prodigy, and for the rest of his life to be nothing whatsoever. The empire of Russia will aspire to conquer Europe, and will itself be conquered. The Tartars, its subjects or neighbors, will become its masters and ours, by a revolution which I regard as inevitable. Indeed, all the kings of Europe are working in concert to hasten its coming.

CHAPTER IX
THE PEOPLE (*continued*)

As nature has set bounds to the stature of a well-made man, and, outside those limits, makes nothing but giants or dwarfs, similarly, for the constitution of a State to be at its best, it is possible to fix limits that will make it neither too large for good government, nor too small for self-maintenance. In every body politic there is a *maximum* strength which it cannot exceed and which it only loses by increasing in size. Every extension of the social tie means its relaxation; and, generally speaking, a small State is stronger in proportion than a great one.

A thousand arguments could be advanced in favor of this principle. First, long distances make administration more difficult, just as a weight becomes heavier at the end of a longer lever. Administration therefore becomes more and more burdensome as the distance grows greater; for, in the first place, each city has its own, which is paid for by the people: each district its own, still paid for by the people: then comes each province, and then the great governments, satrapies, and vice-royalties, always costing more the higher you go, and always at the expense of the unfortunate people. Last of all comes the supreme administration, which eclipses all the rest. All these overcharges are a continual drain upon the subjects; so far from being better governed by all these different orders, they are worse governed than if there were only a single authority over them. In the meantime, there scarce remain resources enough to meet emergencies; and, when recourse must be had to these, the State is always on the eve of destruction. This is not all; not only has the government less vigor and promptitude for securing the observance of the laws, preventing nuisances, correcting abuses, and guarding against seditious undertakings begun in distant places; the people has less affection for its rulers, whom it never sees, for its country, which, to its eyes, seems like the world, and for its fellow-citizens, most of whom are unknown to it. The same laws cannot suit so many diverse provinces with different customs, situated in the most various climates, and incapable of enduring a uniform government. Different laws lead only to trouble and confusion among peoples which, living under the same rulers and in constant communication one with another, intermingle and intermarry, and, coming under the sway of new customs, never know if they can call their very patrimony their own. Talent is buried, virtue unknown and vice unpunished, among such a multitude of

men who do not know one another, gathered together in one place at the seat of the central administration. The leaders, overwhelmed with business, see nothing for themselves; the
5   State is governed by clerks. Finally, the measures which have to be taken to, maintain the general authority, which all these distant officials wish to escape or to impose upon, absorb all the energy of the public, so that
10 there is none left for the happiness of the people. There is hardly enough to defend it when need arises, and thus a body which is too big for its constitution gives way and falls crushed under its own weight.
15

Again, the State must assure itself a safe foundation, if it is to have stability, and to be able to resist the shocks it cannot help experiencing, as well as the efforts it will be forced to
20 make for its maintenance; for all peoples have a kind of centrifugal force that makes them continually act one against another, and tend to aggrandize themselves at their neighbors' expense, like the vortices of Descartes. Thus
25 the weak run the risk of being soon swallowed up; and it is almost impossible for any one to preserve itself except by putting itself in a state of equilibrium with all, so that the pressure is on all sides practically equal.
30

It may therefore be seen that there are reasons for expansion and reasons for contraction; and it is no small part of the statesman's skill to hit between them the mean that is most favorable
35 to the preservation of the State. It may be said that the reason for expansion, being merely external and relative, ought to be subordinate to the reasons for contraction, which are internal and absolute. A strong and healthy con-
40 stitution is the first thing to look for; and it is better to count on the vigor which comes of good government than on the resources a great territory furnishes.

It may be added that there have been known
45 States so constituted that the necessity of making conquests entered into their very constitution, and that, in order to maintain themselves, they were forced to expand ceaselessly. It may be that they congratulated themselves greatly
50 on this fortunate necessity, which none the less indicated to them, along with the limits of their greatness, the inevitable moment of their fall.

55   **CHAPTER X**
        THE PEOPLE (*continued*)

A body politic may be measured in two ways—either by the extent of its territory, or
60 by the number of its people; and there is, between these two measurements, a right relation which makes the State really great. The men make the State, and the territory sustains the men; the right relation therefore is that the
65 land should suffice for the maintenance of the inhabitants, and that there should be as many inhabitants as the land can maintain. In this proportion lies the *maximum* strength of a given number of people; for if there is too much
70 land, it is troublesome to guard and inadequately cultivated, produces more than is needed, and soon gives rise to wars of defense; if there is not enough, the State depends on its neighbors for what it needs over and above,
75 and this soon gives rise to wars of offence. Every people, to which its situation gives no choice save that between commerce and war, is weak in itself: it depends on its neighbors, and on circumstances; its existence can never
80 be more than short and uncertain. It either conquers others, and changes its situation, or it is conquered and becomes nothing. Only insignificance or greatness can keep it free.

85 No fixed relation can be stated between the extent of territory and the population that are

adequate one to the other, both because of the differences in the quality of land, in its fertility, in the nature of its products, and in the influence of climate, and because of the different

5 tempers of those who inhabit it; for some in a fertile country consume little, and others on an ungrateful soil much. The greater or less fecundity of women, the conditions that are more or less favorable in each country to the

10 growth of population, and the influence the legislator can hope to exercise by his institutions, must also be taken into account. The legislator therefore should not go by what he sees, but by what he foresees; he should stop

15 not so much at the state in which he actually finds the population, as at that to which it ought naturally to attain. Lastly, there are countless cases in which the particular local circumstances demand or allow the acquisition

20 of a greater territory than seems necessary. Thus, expansion will be great in a mountainous country, where the natural products, *i.e.* woods and pastures, need less labor, where we know from experience that women are more

25 fertile than in the plains, and where a great expanse of slope affords only a small level tract that can be counted on for vegetation. On the other hand, contraction is possible on the coast, even in lands of rocks and nearly

30 barren sands, because there fishing makes up to a great extent for the lack of land-produce, because the inhabitants have to congregate together more in order to repel pirates, and further because it is easier to unburden the

35 country of its superfluous inhabitants by means of colonies.

To these conditions of law-giving must be added one other which, though it cannot take

40 the place of the rest, renders them all useless when it is absent. This is the enjoyment of peace and plenty; for the moment at which a State sets its house in order is, like the mo-

ment when a battalion is forming up, that
45 when its body is least capable of offering resistance and easiest to destroy. A better resistance could be made at a time of absolute disorganization than at a moment of fermentation, when each is occupied with his own posi-
50 tion and not with the danger. If war, famine, or sedition arises at this time of crisis, the State will inevitably be overthrown.

Not that many governments have not been set
55 up during such storms; but in such cases these governments are themselves the State's destroyers. Usurpers always bring about or select troublous times to get passed, under cover of the public terror, destructive laws, which the
60 people would never adopt in cold blood. The moment chosen is one of the surest means of distinguishing the work of the legislator from that of the tyrant.

65 What people, then, is a fit subject for legislation? One which, already bound by some unity of origin, interest, or convention, has never yet felt the real yoke of law; one that has neither customs nor superstitions deeply ingrained,
70 one which stands in no fear of being overwhelmed by sudden invasion; one which, without entering into its neighbors' quarrels, can resist each of them single-handed, or get the help of one to repel another; one in which
75 every member may be known by every other, and there is no need to lay on any man burdens too heavy for a man to bear; one which can do without other peoples, and without which all others can do;[38] one which is neither

---

[38] If there were two neighboring peoples, one of which could not do without the other, it would be very hard on the former, and very dangerous for the latter. Every wise nation, in such a case, would make haste to free the other from dependence. The Republic of Thlascala, enclosed by the Mexican Empire, preferred doing without

rich nor poor, but self-sufficient; and, lastly, one which unites the consistency of an ancient people with the docility of a new one. Legislation is made difficult less by what it is necessary to build up than by what has to be destroyed; and what makes success so rare is the impossibility of finding natural simplicity together with social requirements. All these conditions are indeed rarely found united, and therefore few States have good constitutions.

There is still in Europe one country capable of being given laws—Corsica. The valor and persistency with which that brave people has regained and defended its liberty well deserves that some wise man should teach it how to preserve what it has won. I have a feeling that some day that little island will astonish Europe.

CHAPTER XI
THE VARIOUS SYSTEMS OF
LEGISLATION

If we ask in what precisely consists the greatest good of all, which should be the end of every system of legislation, we shall find it reduce itself to two main objects, liberty and equality—liberty, because all particular dependence means so much force taken from the body of the State, and equality, because liberty cannot exist without it.

I have already defined civil liberty; by equality, we should understand, not that the degrees of power and riches are to be absolutely identical for everybody; but that power shall never be great enough for violence, and shall always be exercised by virtue of rank and law; and that, in respect of riches, no citizen shall ever be wealthy enough to buy another, and none poor enough to be forced to sell himself:[39] which implies, on the part of the great, moderation in goods and position, and, on the side of the common sort, moderation in avarice and covetousness.

Such equality, we are told, is an unpractical ideal that cannot actually exist. But if its abuse is inevitable, does it follow that we should not at least make regulations concerning it? It is precisely because the force of circumstances tends continually to destroy equality that the force of legislation should always tend to its maintenance.

But these general objects of every good legislative system need modifying in every country in accordance with the local situation and the temper of the inhabitants; and these circumstances should determine, in each case, the particular system of institutions which is best, not perhaps in itself, but for the State for which it is destined. If, for instance, the soil is barren and unproductive, or the land too crowded for its inhabitants, the people should turn to industry and the crafts, and exchange what they produce for the commodities they lack. If, on the other hand, a people dwells in rich plains and fertile slopes, or, in a good

---

salt to buying from the Mexicans, or even getting it from them as a gift The Thlascalans were wise enough to see the snare hidden under such liberality. They kept their freedom, and that little State, shut up in that great Empire, was finally the instrument of its ruin.

[39] If the object is to give the State consistency, bring the two extremes as near to each other as possible; allow neither rich men nor beggars. These two estates, which are naturally inseparable, are equally fatal to the common good; from the one come the friends of tyranny, and from the other tyrants. It is always between them that public liberty is put up to auction; the one buys, and the other sells.

land, lacks inhabitants, it should give all its attention to agriculture, which causes men to multiply, and should drive out the crafts, which would only result in depopulation, by grouping in a few localities the few inhabitants there are.[40] If a nation dwells on an extensive and convenient coast-line, let it cover the sea with ships and foster commerce and navigation. It will have a life that will be short and glorious. If, on its coasts, the sea washes nothing but almost inaccessible rocks, let it remain barbarous and ichthyophagous: it will have a quieter, perhaps a better, and certainly a happier life. In a word, besides the principles that are common to all, every nation has in itself something that gives them a particular application, and makes its legislation peculiarly its own. Thus, among the Jews long ago and more recently among the Arabs, the chief object was religion, among the Athenians letters, at Carthage and Tyre commerce, at Rhodes shipping, at Sparta war, at Rome virtue. The author of *The Spirit of the Laws* has shown with many examples by what art the legislator directs the constitution towards each of these objects.

What makes the constitution of a State really solid and lasting is the due observance of what is proper, so that the natural relations are always in agreement with the laws on every point, and law only serves, so to speak, to assure, accompany and rectify them. But if the legislator mistakes his object and adopts a principle other than circumstances naturally direct; if his principle makes for servitude while they make for liberty, or if it makes for

riches, while they make for populousness, or if it makes for peace, while they make for conquest—the laws will insensibly lose their influence, the constitution will alter, and the State will have no rest from trouble till it is either destroyed or changed, and nature has resumed her invincible sway.

CHAPTER XII
THE DIVISION OF THE LAWS

If the whole is to be set in order, and the commonwealth put into the best possible shape, there are various relations to be considered. First, there is the action of the complete body upon itself, the relation of the whole to the whole, of the Sovereign to the State; and this relation, as we shall see, is made up of the relations of the intermediate terms.

The laws which regulate this relation bear the name of political laws, and are also called fundamental laws, not without reason if they are wise. For, if there is, in each State, only one good system, the people that is in possession of it should hold fast to this; but if the established order is bad, why should laws that prevent men from being good be regarded as fundamental? Besides, in any case, a people is always in a position to change its laws, however good; for, if it choose to do itself harm, who can have a right to stop it?

The second relation is that of the members one to another, or to the body as a whole; and this relation should be in the first respect as unimportant, and in the second as important, as possible. Each citizen would then be perfectly independent of all the rest, and at the same time very dependent on the city; which is brought about always by the same means, as the strength of the State can alone secure the liberty of its members. From this second rela-

---

[40] "Any branch of foreign commerce," says M. d'Argenson, "creates on the whole only apparent advantage for the kingdom in general; it may enrich some individuals, or even some towns; but the nation as a whole gains nothing by it, and the people is no better off."

tion arise civil laws.

We may consider also a third kind of relation between the individual and the law, a relation of disobedience to its penalty. This gives rise to the setting up of criminal laws, which, at bottom, are less a particular class of law than the sanction behind all the rest.

Along with these three kinds of law goes a fourth, most important of all, which is not graven on tablets of marble or brass, but on the hearts of the citizens. This forms the real constitution of the State, takes on every day new powers, when other laws decay or die out, restores them or takes their place, keeps a people in the ways in which it was meant to go, and insensibly replaces authority by the force of habit. I am speaking of morality, of custom, above all of public opinion; a power unknown to political thinkers, on which none the less success in everything else depends. With this the great legislator concerns himself in secret, though he seems to confine himself to particular regulations; for these are only the arc of the arch, while manners and morals, slower to arise, form in the end its immovable keystone.

Among the different classes of laws, the political, which determine the form of the government, are alone relevant to my subject.

TOCQUEVILLE

Alexis de Tocqueville (1805-1859) was born in Normandy to a family of French nobles during the midst of the Napoleonic Wars. Coming of age under the restored Bourbon monarchy, Tocqueville became of liberal lawyer imbued with a strong sense of noblesse oblige. As an adult he would see the abdication of one king and the forced dissolution of the monarchy—but also rise of Louis Napoleon, aka Emperor Napoleon III. Thus he lived through time of political and social tumult, in which, while generally a liberal, one can clearly see that Tocqueville is a man with liberalism rooted in a strong sense of *noblesse oblige*, rather than love of democracy.

Indeed, it was his fascination with democracy and its functioning in the United States that led Tocqueville to travel to the new nation in the 1830's—though e did so under the guide of studying the American penal system. The result of his travels is perhaps the definitive analysis of American social and political structure: *Democracy in America*. Written both about his travels (Part I) and about his reflections (Part II), this work remains an amazingly insightful commentary on American life. From the work there are two large take always that bear on us today as they did on him then. First, Tocqueville believed that we did not have a political science well formulated to modern democracy and democratic society, and thus lacked the tools to effectively understand and manage the new form of government. Second, he also believed that democracy and equality were not entirely good things, and he worried about the long wrong impacts of their presence in the world—particularly in the European world which he did not feel was necessarily prepared to handle them.

DEMOCRACY IN AMERICA
ALEXIS DE TOCQUEVILLE

Book Four: Influence Of Democratic Opinions On Political Society

Chapter I:
That Equality Naturally Gives Men A Taste For Free Institutions

I should imperfectly fulfill the purpose of this book, if, after having shown what opinions and sentiments are suggested by the principle of equality, I did not point out, ere I conclude, the general influence which these same opinions and sentiments may exercise upon the government of human societies. To succeed in this object I shall frequently have to retrace my steps; but I trust the reader will not refuse to follow me through paths already known to him, which may lead to some new truth.

The principle of equality, which makes men independent of each other, gives them a habit and a taste for following, in their private actions, no other guide but their own will. This complete independence, which they constantly enjoy towards their equals and in the intercourse of private life, tends to make them look upon all authority with a jealous eye, and speedily suggests to them the notion and the love of political freedom. Men living at such times have a natural bias to free institutions. Take any one of them at a venture, and search if you can his most deep-seated instincts; you will find that of all governments he will soonest conceive and most highly value that government, whose head he has himself elected,

and whose administration he may control. Of all the political effects produced by the equality of conditions, this love of independence is the first to strike the observing, and to alarm the timid; nor can it be said that their alarm is wholly misplaced, for anarchy has a more formidable aspect in democratic countries than elsewhere. As the citizens have no direct influence on each other, as soon as the supreme power of the nation fails, which kept them all in their several stations, it would seem that disorder must instantly reach its utmost pitch, and that, every man drawing aside in a different direction, the fabric of society must at once crumble away.

I am, however, persuaded that anarchy is not the principal evil which democratic ages have to fear, but the least. For the principle of equality begets two tendencies; the one leads men straight to independence, and may suddenly drive them into anarchy; the other conducts them by a longer, more secret, but more certain road, to servitude. Nations readily discern the former tendency, and are prepared to resist it; they are led away by the latter, without perceiving its drift; hence it is peculiarly important to point it out. For myself, I am so far from urging as a reproach to the principle of equality that it renders men untractable, that this very circumstance principally calls forth my approbation. I admire to see how it deposits in the mind and heart of man the dim conception and instinctive love of political independence, thus preparing the remedy for the evil which it engenders; it is on this very account that I am attached to it.

Text based off the Henry Reeve translation, with adjustments for modern spellings.

Chapter II:
That The Notions Of Democratic Nations On Government Are Naturally Favorable To The Concentration Of Power

The notion of secondary powers, placed between the sovereign and his subjects, occurred naturally to the imagination of aristocratic nations, because those communities contained individuals or families raised above the common level, and apparently destined to command by their birth, their education, and their wealth. This same notion is naturally wanting in the minds of men in democratic ages, for converse reasons: it can only be introduced artificially, it can only be kept there with difficulty; whereas they conceive, as it were, without thinking upon the subject, the notion of a sole and central power which governs the whole community by its direct influence. Moreover in politics, as well as in philosophy and in religion, the intellect of democratic nations is peculiarly open to simple and general notions. Complicated systems are repugnant to it, and its favorite conception is that of a great nation composed of citizens all resembling the same pattern, and all governed by a single power.

The very next notion to that of a sole and central power, which presents itself to the minds of men in the ages of equality, is the notion of uniformity of legislation. As every man sees that he differs but little from those about him, he cannot understand why a rule which is applicable to one man should not be equally applicable to all others. Hence the slightest privileges are repugnant to his reason; the faintest dissimilarities in the political institutions of the same people offend him, and uniformity of legislation appears to him to be the first condition of good government. I find, on the contrary, that this same notion of a uniform rule, equally binding on all the members of the community, was almost unknown to the human mind in aristocratic ages; it was either never entertained, or it was rejected. These contrary tendencies of opinion ultimately turn on either side to such blind instincts and such ungovernable habits that they still direct the actions of men, in spite of particular exceptions. Notwithstanding the immense variety of conditions in the Middle Ages, a certain number of persons existed at that period in precisely similar circumstances; but this did not prevent the laws then in force from assigning to each of them distinct duties and different rights. On the contrary, at the present time all the powers of government are exerted to impose the same customs and the same laws on populations which have as yet but few points of resemblance. As the conditions of men become equal amongst a people, individuals seem of less importance, and society of greater dimensions; or rather, every citizen, being assimilated to all the rest, is lost in the crowd, and nothing stands conspicuous but the great and imposing image of the people at large.

This naturally gives the men of democratic periods a lofty opinion of the privileges of society, and a very humble notion of the rights of individuals; they are ready to admit that the interests of the former are everything, and those of the latter nothing. They are willing to acknowledge that the power which represents the community has far more information and wisdom than any of the members of that community; and that it is the duty, as well as the right, of that power to guide as well as govern each private citizen.

If we closely scrutinize our contemporaries, and penetrate to the root of their political opinions, we shall detect some of the notions which I have just pointed out, and we shall perhaps be surprised to find so much accordance between men who are so often at variance. The Americans hold, that in every State the supreme power ought to emanate from the people; but when once that power is constituted, they can conceive, as it were, no limits to it, and they are ready to admit that it has the right to do whatever it pleases. They have not the slightest notion of peculiar privileges granted to cities, families, or persons: their minds appear never to have foreseen that it might be possible not to apply with strict uniformity the same laws to every part, and to all the inhabitants. These same opinions are more and more diffused in Europe; they even insinuate themselves amongst those nations which most vehemently reject the principle of the sovereignty of the people. Such nations assign a different origin to the supreme power, but they ascribe to that power the same characteristics. Amongst them all, the idea of intermediate powers is weakened and obliterated: the idea of rights inherent in certain individuals is rapidly disappearing from the minds of men; the idea of the omnipotence and sole authority of society at large rises to fill its place. These ideas take root and spread in proportion as social conditions become more equal, and men more alike; they are engendered by equality, and in turn they hasten the progress of equality.

In France, where the revolution of which I am speaking has gone further than in any other European country, these opinions have got complete hold of the public mind. If we listen attentively to the language of the various parties in France, we shall find that there is not one which has not adopted them. Most of these parties censure the conduct of the government, but they all hold that the government ought perpetually to act and interfere in everything that is done. Even those which are most at variance are nevertheless agreed upon this head. The unity, the ubiquity, the omnipotence of the supreme power, and the uniformity of its rules, constitute the principal characteristics of all the political systems which have been put forward in our age. They recur even in the wildest visions of political regeneration: the human mind pursues them in its dreams. If these notions spontaneously arise in the minds of private individuals, they suggest themselves still more forcibly to the minds of princes. Whilst the ancient fabric of European society is altered and dissolved, sovereigns acquire new conceptions of their opportunities and their duties; they learn for the first time that the central power which they represent may and ought to administer by its own agency, and on a uniform plan, all the concerns of the whole community. This opinion, which, I will venture to say, was never conceived before our time by the monarchs of Europe, now sinks deeply into the minds of kings, and abides there amidst all the agitation of more unsettled thoughts.

Our contemporaries are therefore much less divided than is commonly supposed; they are constantly disputing as to the hands in which supremacy is to be vested, but they readily agree upon the duties and the rights of that supremacy. The notion they all form of government is that of a sole, simple, providential, and creative power. All secondary opinions in politics are unsettled; this one remains fixed, invariable, and consistent. It is adopted by statesmen and political philosophers; it is eagerly laid hold of by the multitude; those who govern and those who are governed agree to pursue it with equal ardor: it is the foremost notion of their minds, it seems inborn. It originates therefore in no caprice of the human intellect, but it is a necessary condition of the present state of mankind.

Chapter III:
That The Sentiments Of Democratic Nations Accord With Their Opinions In Leading Them To Concentrate Political Power

If it be true that, in ages of equality, men readily adopt the notion of a great central power, it cannot be doubted on the other hand that their habits and sentiments predispose them to recognize such a power and to give it their support. This may be demonstrated in a few words, as the greater part of the reasons, to which the fact may be attributed, have been previously stated. As the men who inhabit democratic countries have no superiors, no inferiors, and no habitual or necessary partners in their undertakings, they readily fall back upon themselves and consider themselves as beings apart. I had occasion to point this out at considerable length in treating of individualism. Hence such men can never, without an effort, tear themselves from their private affairs to engage in public business; their natural bias leads them to abandon the latter to the sole visible and permanent representative of the interests of the community, that is to say, to the State. Not only are they naturally wanting in a taste for public business, but they have frequently no time to attend to it. Private life is so busy in democratic periods, so excited, so full of wishes and of work, that hardly any energy or leisure remains to each individual for public life. I am the last man to contend that these propensities are unconquerable, since my chief object in writing this book has been to combat them. I only maintain that at the present day a secret power is fostering them in the human heart, and that if they are not checked they will wholly overgrow it.

I have also had occasion to show how the increasing love of well-being, and the fluctuating character of property, cause democratic nations to dread all violent disturbance. The love of public tranquility is frequently the only passion which these nations retain, and it becomes more active and powerful amongst them in proportion as all other passions droop and die. This naturally disposes the members of the community constantly to give or to surrender additional rights to the central power, which alone seems to be interested in defending them by the same means that it uses to defend itself. As in ages of equality no man is compelled to lend his assistance to his fellow-men, and none has any right to expect much support from them, everyone is at once independent and powerless. These two conditions, which must never be either separately considered or confounded together, inspire the citizen of a democratic country with very contrary propensities. His independence fills him with self-reliance and pride amongst his equals; his debility makes him feel from time to time the want of some outward assistance, which he cannot expect from any of them, because they are all impotent and unsympathizing. In this predicament he naturally turns his eyes to that imposing power which alone rises above the level of universal depression. Of that power his wants and especially his desires continually remind him, until he ultimately views it as the sole and necessary support of his own weakness.[42] This may more

---

[42] In democratic communities nothing but the central power has any stability in its position or any permanence in its undertakings. All the members of society are in ceaseless stir and transformation. Now it is in the nature of all governments to seek constantly to enlarge their sphere of action; hence it is almost impossible that such a government should not ultimately succeed, because it acts with a fixed principle and a constant will, upon men, whose position, whose notions, and whose desires are in contin-

completely explain what frequently takes place in democratic countries, where the very men who are so impatient of superiors patiently submit to a master, exhibiting at once their pride and their servility.

The hatred which men bear to privilege increases in proportion as privileges become more scarce and less considerable, so that democratic passions would seem to burn most fiercely at the very time when they have least fuel. I have already given the reason of this phenomenon. When all conditions are unequal, no inequality is so great as to offend the eye; whereas the slightest dissimilarity is odious in the midst of general uniformity: the more complete is this uniformity, the more insupportable does the sight of such a difference become. Hence it is natural that the love of equality should constantly increase together

---

ual vacillation. It frequently happens that the members of the community promote the influence of the central power without intending it. Democratic ages are periods of experiment, innovation, and adventure. At such times there are always a multitude of men engaged in difficult or novel undertakings, which they follow alone, without caring for their fellowmen. Such persons may be ready to admit, as a general principle, that the public authority ought not to interfere in private concerns; but, by an exception to that rule, each of them craves for its assistance in the particular concern on which he is engaged, and seeks to draw upon the influence of the government for his own benefit, though he would restrict it on all other occasions. If a large number of men apply this particular exception to a great variety of different purposes, the sphere of the central power extends insensibly in all directions, although each of them wishes it to be circumscribed. Thus a democratic government increases its power simply by the fact of its permanence. Time is on its side; every incident befriends it; the passions of individuals unconsciously promote it; and it may be asserted, that the older a democratic community is, the more centralized will its government become.

with equality itself, and that it should grow by what it feeds upon. This never-dying, ever-kindling hatred, which sets a democratic people against the smallest privileges, is peculiarly favorable to the gradual concentration of all political rights in the hands of the representative of the State alone. The sovereign, being necessarily and incontestably above all the citizens, excites not their envy, and each of them thinks that he strips his equals of the prerogative which he concedes to the crown. The man of a democratic age is extremely reluctant to obey his neighbor who is his equal; he refuses to acknowledge in such a person ability superior to his own; he mistrusts his justice, and is jealous of his power; he fears and he contemns him; and he loves continually to remind him of the common dependence in which both of them stand to the same master. Every central power which follows its natural tendencies courts and encourages the principle of equality; for equality singularly facilitates, extends, and secures the influence of a central power.

In like manner it may be said that every central government worships uniformity: uniformity relieves it from inquiry into an infinite number of small details which must be attended to if rules were to be adapted to men, instead of indiscriminately subjecting men to rules: thus the government likes what the citizens like, and naturally hates what they hate. These common sentiments, which, in democratic nations, constantly unite the sovereign and every member of the community in one and the same conviction, establish a secret and lasting sympathy between them. The faults of the government are pardoned for the sake of its tastes; public confidence is only reluctantly withdrawn in the midst even of its excesses and its errors, and it is restored at the first call. Democratic nations often hate those in whose hands the central power is vested; but they always love that power itself.

Thus, by two separate paths, I have reached the same conclusion. I have shown that the principle of equality suggests to men the notion of a sole, uniform, and strong government: I have now shown that the principle of equality imparts to them a taste for it. To governments of this kind the nations of our age are therefore tending. They are drawn thither by the natural inclination of mind and heart; and in order to reach that result, it is enough that they do not check themselves in their course. I am of opinion, that, in the democratic ages which are opening upon us, individual independence and local liberties will ever be the produce of artificial contrivance; that centralization will be the natural form of government.

Chapter IV:
Of Certain Peculiar And Accidental Causes Which Either Lead A People To Complete Centralization Of Government, Or Which Divert Them From It

If all democratic nations are instinctively led to the centralization of government, they tend to this result in an unequal manner. This depends on the particular circumstances which may promote or prevent the natural consequences of that state of society—circumstances which are exceedingly numerous; but I shall only advert to a few of them. Amongst men who have lived free long before they became equal, the tendencies derived from free institutions combat, to a certain extent, the propensities superinduced by the principle of equality; and although the central power may increase its privileges amongst such a people, the private members of such a community will never entirely forfeit their independence. But when the equality of conditions grows up amongst a people which has never known, or has long ceased to know, what freedom is (and such is the case upon the Continent of Europe), as the former habits of the nation are suddenly combined, by some sort of natural attraction, with the novel habits and principles engendered by the state of society, all powers seem spontaneously to rush to the center. These powers accumulate there with astonishing rapidity, and the State instantly attains the utmost limits of its strength, whilst private persons allow themselves to sink as suddenly to the lowest degree of weakness.

The English who emigrated three hundred years ago to found a democratic commonwealth on the shores of the New World, had all learned to take a part in public affairs in their mother-country; they were conversant with trial by jury; they were accustomed to liberty of speech and of the press—to personal freedom, to the notion of rights and the practice of asserting them. They carried with them to America these free institutions and manly customs, and these institutions preserved them against the encroachments of the State. Thus amongst the Americans it is freedom which is old—equality is of comparatively modern date. The reverse is occurring in Europe, where equality, introduced by absolute power and under the rule of kings, was already infused into the habits of nations long before freedom had entered into their conceptions.

I have said that amongst democratic nations the notion of government naturally presents itself to the mind under the form of a sole and central power, and that the notion of intermediate powers is not familiar to them. This is peculiarly applicable to the democratic nations which have witnessed the triumph of the principle of equality by means of a violent revolution. As the classes which managed local affairs have been suddenly swept away by the storm, and as the confused mass which remains has as yet neither the organization nor the habits which fit it to assume the administration of these same affairs, the State alone seems capable of taking upon itself all the details of government, and centralization becomes, as it were, the unavoidable state of the country. Napoleon deserves neither praise nor censure for having centered in his own hands almost all the administrative power of France; for, after the abrupt disappearance of the nobility and the higher rank of the middle classes, these powers devolved on him of course: it would have been almost as difficult for him to reject as to assume them. But no necessity of this kind has ever been felt by the Americans, who, having passed through no revolution, and having governed themselves from the first, never had to call upon the State to act for a time as their guardian. Thus the progress of centralization amongst a democratic people depends not only on the progress of equality, but on the manner in which this equality has been established.

At the commencement of a great democratic revolution, when hostilities have but just broken out between the different classes of society, the people endeavors to centralize the public administration in the hands of the government, in order to wrest the management of local affairs from the aristocracy. Towards the close of such a revolution, on the contrary, it is usually the conquered aristocracy that endeavors to make over the management of all affairs to the State, because such an aristocracy dreads the tyranny of a people which has become its equal, and not unfrequently its master. Thus it is not always the same class of the community which strives to increase the prerogative of the government; but as long as the democratic revolution lasts there is always one class in the nation, powerful in numbers or in wealth, which is induced, by peculiar passions or interests, to centralize the public administration, independently of that hatred of being governed by one's neighbor, which is a general and permanent feeling amongst democratic nations. It may be remarked, that at the present day the lower orders in England are striving with all their might to destroy local independence, and to transfer the administration from all points of the circumference to the center; whereas the higher classes are endeavoring to retain this administration within its ancient boundaries. I venture to predict that a time will come when the very reverse will happen.

These observations explain why the supreme power is always stronger, and private individuals weaker, amongst a democratic people which has passed through a long and arduous struggle to reach a state of equality than amongst a democratic community in which the citizens have been equal from the first. The example of the Americans completely demonstrates the fact. The inhabitants of the United States were never divided by any privileges; they have never known the mutual relation of master and inferior, and as they neither dread nor hate each other, they have never known the necessity of calling in the supreme power to manage their affairs. The lot of the Americans is singular: they have derived from the aristocracy of England the notion of private rights and the taste for local freedom; and they have been able to retain both the one and the other, because they have had no aristocracy to combat.

If at all times education enables men to defend their independence, this is most especially true in democratic ages. When all men are alike, it is easy to found a sole and all-powerful government, by the aid of mere instinct. But men require much intelligence, knowledge, and art to organize and to maintain secondary powers under similar circumstances, and to create amidst the independence and individual weakness of the citizens such free associations as may be in a condition to struggle against tyranny without destroying public order.

Hence the concentration of power and the subjection of individuals will increase amongst democratic nations, not only in the same proportion as their equality, but in the same proportion as their ignorance. It is true, that in ages of imperfect civilization the government is frequently as wanting in the knowledge required to impose a despotism upon the people as the people are wanting in the knowledge required to shake it off; but the effect is not the same on both sides. However rude a democratic people may be, the central power which rules it is never completely devoid of cultivation, because it readily draws to its own uses what little cultivation is to be found in the country, and, if necessary, may seek assistance elsewhere. Hence, amongst a nation which is ignorant as well as democratic, an amazing difference cannot fail speedily to arise between the intellectual capacity of the ruler and that of each of his subjects. This completes the easy concentration of all power in his hands: the administrative function of the State is perpetually extended, because the State alone is competent to administer the affairs of the country. Aristocratic nations, however unenlightened they may be, never afford the same spectacle, because in them instruction is nearly equally diffused between the monarch and the leading members of the community.

The pasha who now rules in Egypt found the population of that country composed of men exceedingly ignorant and equal, and he has borrowed the science and ability of Europe to govern that people. As the personal attainments of the sovereign are thus combined with the ignorance and democratic weakness of his subjects, the utmost centralization has been established without impediment, and the pasha has made the country his manufactory, and the inhabitants his workmen.

I think that extreme centralization of government ultimately enervates society, and thus after a length of time weakens the government itself; but I do not deny that a centralized social power may be able to execute great undertakings with facility in a given time and on a particular point. This is more especially true of war, in which success depends much more on the means of transferring all the resources of a nation to one single point, than on the extent of those resources. Hence it is chiefly in war that nations desire and frequently require to increase the powers of the central government. All men of military genius are fond of centralization, which increases their strength; and all men of centralizing genius are fond of war, which compels nations to combine all their powers in the hands of the government. Thus the democratic tendency which leads men unceasingly to multiply the privileges of the State, and to circumscribe the rights of private persons, is much more rapid and constant amongst those democratic nations which are exposed by their position to great and frequent wars, than amongst all others.

I have shown how the dread of disturbance and the love of well-being insensibly lead democratic nations to increase the functions of central government, as the only power which appears to be intrinsically sufficiently strong, enlightened, and secure, to protect

them from anarchy. I would now add, that all
the particular circumstances which tend to
make the state of a democratic community
agitated and precarious, enhance this general
5 propensity, and lead private persons more and
more to sacrifice their rights to their tranquility. A people is therefore never so disposed to
increase the functions of central government
as at the close of a long and bloody revolution,
10 which, after having wrested property from the
hands of its former possessors, has shaken all
belief, and filled the nation with fierce hatreds,
conflicting interests, and contending factions.
The love of public tranquility becomes at such
15 times an indiscriminating passion, and the
members of the community are apt to conceive a most inordinate devotion to order.

I have already examined several of the inci-
20 dents which may concur to promote the centralization of power, but the principal cause
still remains to be noticed. The foremost of
the incidental causes which may draw the
management of all affairs into the hands of the
25 ruler in democratic countries, is the origin of
that ruler himself, and his own propensities.
Men who live in the ages of equality are naturally fond of central power, and are willing to
extend its privileges; but if it happens that this
30 same power faithfully represents their own
interests, and exactly copies their own inclinations, the confidence they place in it knows no
bounds, and they think that whatever they
bestow upon it is bestowed upon themselves.
35

The attraction of administrative powers to the
center will always be less easy and less rapid
under the reign of kings who are still in some
way connected with the old aristocratic order,
40 than under new princes, the children of their
own achievements, whose birth, prejudices,
propensities, and habits appear to bind them
indissolubly to the cause of equality. I do not

mean that princes of aristocratic origin who
45 live in democratic ages do not attempt to centralize; I believe they apply themselves to that
object as diligently as any others. For them,
the sole advantages of equality lie in that direction; but their opportunities are less great,
50 because the community, instead of volunteer-
ing compliance with their desires, frequently
obeys them with reluctance. In democratic
communities the rule is that centralization
must increase in proportion as the sovereign is
55 less aristocratic. When an ancient race of kings
stands at the head of an aristocracy, as the
natural prejudices of the sovereign perfectly
accord with the natural prejudices of the nobility, the vices inherent in aristocratic com-
60 munities have a free course, and meet with no
corrective. The reverse is the case when the
scion of a feudal stock is placed at the head of
a democratic people. The sovereign is constantly led, by his education, his habits, and his
65 associations, to adopt sentiments suggested by
the inequality of conditions, and the people
tend as constantly, by their social condition, to
those manners which are engendered by equality. At such times it often happens that the
70 citizens seek to control the central power far
less as a tyrannical than as an aristocratical
power, and that they persist in the firm defense of their independence, not only because
they would remain free, but especially because
75 they are determined to remain equal. A revolution which overthrows an ancient regal family,
in order to place men of more recent growth
at the head of a democratic people, may temporarily weaken the central power; but howev-
80 er anarchical such a revolution may appear at
first, we need not hesitate to predict that its
final and certain consequence will be to extend
and to secure the prerogatives of that power.
The foremost or indeed the sole condition
85 which is required in order to succeed in centralizing the supreme power in a democratic

community, is to love equality, or to get men to believe you love it. Thus the science of despotism, which was once so complex, is simplified, and reduced as it were to a single principle.

Chapter V:
That Amongst The European Nations Of Our Time The Power Of Governments Is Increasing, Although The Persons Who Govern Are Less Stable

On reflecting upon what has already been said, the reader will be startled and alarmed to find that in Europe everything seems to conduce to the indefinite extension of the prerogatives of government, and to render all that enjoyed the rights of private independence more weak, more subordinate, and more precarious. The democratic nations of Europe have all the general and permanent tendencies which urge the Americans to the centralization of government, and they are moreover exposed to a number of secondary and incidental causes with which the Americans are unacquainted. It would seem as if every step they make towards equality brings them nearer to despotism. And indeed if we do but cast our looks around, we shall be convinced that such is the fact. During the aristocratic ages which preceded the present time, the sovereigns of Europe had been deprived of, or had relinquished, many of the rights inherent in their power. Not a hundred years ago, amongst the greater part of European nations, numerous private persons and corporations were sufficiently independent to administer justice, to raise and maintain troops, to levy taxes, and frequently even to make or interpret the law. The State has everywhere resumed to itself alone these natural attributes of sovereign power; in all matters of government the State tolerates no intermediate agent between itself and the people, and in general business it directs the people by its own immediate influence. I am far from blaming this concentration of power, I simply point it out.

At the same period a great number of secondary powers existed in Europe, which represented local interests and administered local affairs. Most of these local authorities have already disappeared; all are speedily tending to disappear, or to fall into the most complete dependence. From one end of Europe to the other the privileges of the nobility, the liberties of cities, and the powers of provincial bodies, are either destroyed or upon the verge of destruction. Europe has endured, in the course of the last half-century, many revolutions and counter-revolutions which have agitated it in opposite directions: but all these perturbations resemble each other in one respect—they have all shaken or destroyed the secondary powers of government. The local privileges which the French did not abolish in the countries they conquered, have finally succumbed to the policy of the princes who conquered the French. Those princes rejected all the innovations of the French Revolution except centralization: that is the only principle they consented to receive from such a source. My object is to remark, that all these various rights, which have been successively wrested, in our time, from classes, corporations, and individuals, have not served to raise new secondary powers on a more democratic basis, but have uniformly been concentrated in the hands of the sovereign. Everywhere the State acquires more and more direct control over the humblest members of the community, and a more exclusive power of governing each of them in his smallest concerns.[43] Almost all the chari-

---

[43] This gradual weakening of individuals in relation to society at large may be traced in a thou-

table establishments of Europe were formerly in the hands of private persons or of corporations; they are now almost all dependent on the supreme government, and in many coun-
5   tries are actually administered by that power. The State almost exclusively undertakes to supply bread to the hungry, assistance and shelter to the sick, work to the idle, and to act as the sole reliever of all kinds of misery. Edu-
10 cation, as well as charity, is become in most countries at the present day a national concern. The State receives, and often takes, the child from the arms of the mother, to hand it over to official agents: the State undertakes to
15 train the heart and to instruct the mind of each generation. Uniformity prevails in the courses of public instruction as in everything else; diversity, as well as freedom, is disappearing day by day. Nor do I hesitate to affirm,
20 that amongst almost all the Christian nations of our days, Catholic as well as Protestant, religion is in danger of falling into the hands of the government. Not that rulers are overjealous of the right of settling points of doc-
25 trine, but they get more and more hold upon

----

sand ways. I shall select from amongst these examples one derived from the law of wills. In aristocracies it is common to profess the greatest reverence for the last testamentary dispositions of a man; this feeling sometimes even became superstitious amongst the older nations of Europe: the power of the State, far from interfering with the caprices of a dying man, gave full force to the very least of them, and insured to him a perpetual power. When all living men are enfeebled, the will of the dead is less respected: it is circumscribed within a narrow range, beyond which it is annulled or checked by the supreme power of the laws. In the Middle Ages, testamentary power had, so to speak, no limits: amongst the French at the present day, a man cannot distribute his fortune amongst his children without the interference of the State; after having domineered over a whole life, the law insists upon regulating the very last act of it.

the will of those by whom doctrines are expounded; they deprive the clergy of their property, and pay them by salaries; they divert to their own use the influence of the priest-
30 hood, they make them their own ministers—often their own servants—and by this alliance with religion they reach the inner depths of the soul of man.[44]

35 But this is as yet only one side of the picture. The authority of government has not only spread, as we have just seen, throughout the sphere of all existing powers, till that sphere can no longer contain it, but it goes further,
40 and invades the domain heretofore reserved to private independence. A multitude of actions, which were formerly entirely beyond the control of the public administration, have been subjected to that control in our time, and the
45 number of them is constantly increasing. Amongst aristocratic nations the supreme government usually contented itself with managing and superintending the community in whatever directly and ostensibly concerned the
50 national honor; but in all other respects the people were left to work out their own free will. Amongst these nations the government often seemed to forget that there is a point at which the faults and the sufferings of private
55 persons involve the general prosperity, and

----

[44] In proportion as the duties of the central power are augmented, the number of public officers by whom that power is represented must increase also. They form a nation in each nation; and as they share the stability of the government, they more and more fill up the place of an aristocracy.

In almost every part of Europe the government rules in two ways; it rules one portion of the community by the fear which they entertain of its agents, and the other by the hope they have of becoming its agents.

that to prevent the ruin of a private individual must sometimes be a matter of public importance. The democratic nations of our time lean to the opposite extreme. It is evident that
5 most of our rulers will not content themselves with governing the people collectively: it would seem as if they thought themselves responsible for the actions and private condition of their subjects—as if they had undertaken to
10 guide and to instruct each of them in the various incidents of life, and to secure their happiness quite independently of their own consent. On the other hand private individuals grow more and more apt to look upon the
15 supreme power in the same light; they invoke its assistance in all their necessities, and they fix their eyes upon the administration as their mentor or their guide.

20 I assert that there is no country in Europe in which the public administration has not become, not only more centralized, but more inquisitive and more minute it everywhere interferes in private concerns more than it did;
25 it regulates more undertakings, and undertakings of a lesser kind; and it gains a firmer footing every day about, above, and around all private persons, to assist, to advise, and to coerce them. Formerly a sovereign lived upon
30 the income of his lands, or the revenue of his taxes; this is no longer the case now that his wants have increased as well as his power. Under the same circumstances which formerly compelled a prince to put on a new tax, he
35 now has recourse to a loan. Thus the State gradually becomes the debtor of most of the wealthier members of the community, and centralizes the largest amounts of capital in its own hands. Small capital is drawn into its
40 keeping by another method. As men are intermingled and conditions become more equal, the poor have more resources, more education, and more desires; they conceive the

notion of bettering their condition, and this
45 teaches them to save. These savings are daily producing an infinite number of small capitals, the slow and gradual produce of labor, which are always increasing. But the greater part of this money would be unproductive if it re-
50 mained scattered in the hands of its owners. This circumstance has given rise to a philanthropic institution, which will soon become, if I am not mistaken, one of our most important political institutions. Some charitable persons
55 conceived the notion of collecting the savings of the poor and placing them out at interest. In some countries these benevolent associations are still completely distinct from the State; but in almost all they manifestly tend to
60 identify themselves with the government; and in some of them the government has superseded them, taking upon itself the enormous task of centralizing in one place, and putting out at interest on its own responsibility, the
65 daily savings of many millions of the working classes. Thus the State draws to itself the wealth of the rich by loans, and has the poor man's mite at its disposal in the savings banks. The wealth of the country is perpetually flow-
70 ing around the government and passing through its hands; the accumulation increases in the same proportion as the equality of conditions; for in a democratic country the State alone inspires private individuals with confi-
75 dence, because the State alone appears to be endowed with strength and durability.[45] *c
Thus the sovereign does not confine himself

---

[45] On the one hand the taste for worldly welfare is perpetually increasing, and on the other the government gets more and more complete possession of the sources of that welfare. Thus men are following two separate roads to servitude: the taste for their own welfare withholds them from taking a part in the government, and their love of that welfare places them in closer dependence upon those who govern.]

to the management of the public treasury; he interferes in private money matters; he is the superior, and often the master, of all the members of the community; and, in addition

5 to this, he assumes the part of their steward and paymaster.

The central power not only fulfills of itself the whole of the duties formerly discharged by

10 various authorities—extending those duties, and surpassing those authorities—but it performs them with more alertness, strength, and independence than it displayed before. All the governments of Europe have in our time sin-

15 gularly improved the science of administration: they do more things, and they do everything with more order, more celerity, and at less expense; they seem to be constantly enriched by all the experience of which they

20 have stripped private persons. From day to day the princes of Europe hold their subordinate officers under stricter control, and they invent new methods for guiding them more closely, and inspecting them with less trouble.

25 Not content with managing everything by their agents, they undertake to manage the conduct of their agents in everything; so that the public administration not only depends upon one and the same power, but it is more

30 and more confined to one spot and concentrated in the same hands. The government centralizes its agency whilst it increases its prerogative—hence a twofold increase of strength.

35

In examining the ancient constitution of the judicial power, amongst most European nations, two things strike the mind—the independence of that power, and the extent of its

40 functions. Not only did the courts of justice decide almost all differences between private persons, but in very many cases they acted as arbiters between private persons and the State.

I do not here allude to the political and admin-

45 istrative offices which courts of judicature had in some countries usurped, but the judicial office common to them all. In most of the countries of Europe, there were, and there still are, many private rights, connected for the

50 most part with the general right of property, which stood under the protection of the courts of justice, and which the State could not violate without their sanction. It was this semi-political power which mainly distin-

55 guished the European courts of judicature from all others; for all nations have had judges, but all have not invested their judges with the same privileges. Upon examining what is now occurring amongst the democratic na-

60 tions of Europe which are called free, as well as amongst the others, it will be observed that new and more dependent courts are everywhere springing up by the side of the old ones, for the express purpose of deciding, by

65 an extraordinary jurisdiction, such litigated matters as may arise between the government and private persons. The elder judicial power retains its independence, but its jurisdiction is narrowed; and there is a growing tendency to

70 reduce it to be exclusively the arbiter between private interests. The number of these special courts of justice is continually increasing, and their functions increase likewise. Thus the government is more and more absolved from

75 the necessity of subjecting its policy and its rights to the sanction of another power. As judges cannot be dispensed with, at least the State is to select them, and always to hold them under its control; so that, between the

80 government and private individuals, they place the effigy of justice rather than justice itself. The State is not satisfied with drawing all concerns to itself, but it acquires an ever-increasing power of deciding on them all

without restriction and without appeal.[46]

There exists amongst the modern nations of Europe one great cause, independent of all those which have already been pointed out, which perpetually contributes to extend the agency or to strengthen the prerogative of the supreme power, though it has not been sufficiently attended to: I mean the growth of manufactures, which is fostered by the progress of social equality. Manufactures generally collect a multitude of men of the same spot, amongst whom new and complex relations spring up. These men are exposed by their calling to great and sudden alternations of plenty and want, during which public tranquility is endangered. It may also happen that these employments sacrifice the health, and even the life, of those who gain by them, or of those who live by them. Thus the manufacturing classes require more regulation, superintendence, and restraint than the other classes of society, and it is natural that the powers of government should increase in the same proportion as those classes.

This is a truth of general application; what follows more especially concerns the nations of Europe. In the centuries which preceded that in which we live, the aristocracy was in possession of the soil, and was competent to defend it: landed property was therefore surrounded by ample securities, and its possessors enjoyed great independence. This gave rise to laws and customs which have been perpetuated, notwithstanding the subdivision of lands and the ruin of the nobility; and, at the present time, landowners and agriculturists are still those amongst the community who must easily escape from the control of the supreme power. In these same aristocratic ages, in which all the sources of our history are to be traced, personal property was of small importance, and those who possessed it were despised and weak: the manufacturing class formed an exception in the midst of those aristocratic communities; as it had no certain patronage, it was not outwardly protected, and was often unable to protect itself.

Hence a habit sprung up of considering manufacturing property as something of a peculiar nature, not entitled to the same deference, and not worthy of the same securities as property in general; and manufacturers were looked upon as a small class in the bulk of the people, whose independence was of small importance, and who might with propriety be abandoned to the disciplinary passions of princes. On glancing over the codes of the middle ages, one is surprised to see, in those periods of personal independence, with what incessant royal regulations manufactures were hampered, even in their smallest details: on this point centralization was as active and as minute as it can ever be. Since that time a great revolution has taken place in the world; manufacturing property, which was then only in the germ, has spread till it covers Europe: the manufacturing class has been multiplied and enriched by the remnants of all other ranks; it has grown and is still perpetually growing in number, in importance, in wealth. Almost all those who do not belong to it are connected with it at least on some one point; after having been an exception in society, it threatens to become the chief, if not the only, class; never-

---

[46] A strange sophism has been made on this head in France. When a suit arises between the government and a private person, it is not to be tried before an ordinary judge—in order, they say, not to mix the administrative and the judicial powers; as if it were not to mix those powers, and to mix them in the most dangerous and oppressive manner, to invest the government with the office of judging and administering at the same time.

theless the notions and political precedents engendered by it of old still cling about it. These notions and these precedents remain unchanged, because they are old, and also be-
5 cause they happen to be in perfect accordance with the new notions and general habits of our contemporaries. Manufacturing property then does not extend its rights in the same ratio as its importance. The manufacturing classes do
10 not become less dependent, whilst they become more numerous; but, on the contrary, it would seem as if despotism lurked within them, and naturally grew with their growth.[47]
As a nation becomes more engaged in manu-
15 factures, the want of roads, canals, harbors,

---

[47] I shall quote a few facts in corroboration of this remark. Mines are the natural sources of manufacturing wealth: as manufactures have grown up in Europe, as the produce of mines has become of more general importance, and good mining more difficult from the subdivision of property which is a consequence of the equality of conditions, most governments have asserted a right of owning the soil in which the mines lie, and of inspecting the works; which has never been the case with any other kind of property. Thus mines, which were private property, liable to the same obligations and sheltered by the same guarantees as all other landed property, have fallen under the control of the State. The State either works them or farms them; the owners of them are mere tenants, deriving their rights from the State; and, moreover, the State almost everywhere claims the power of directing their operations: it lays down rules, enforces the adoption of particular methods, subjects the mining adventurers to constant superintendence, and, if refractory, they are ousted by a government court of justice, and the government transfers their contract to other hands; so that the government not only possesses the mines, but has all the adventurers in its power. Nevertheless, as manufactures increase, the working of old mines increases also; new ones are opened, the mining population extends and grows up; day by day governments augment their subterranean dominions, and people them with their agents.

and other works of a semi-public nature, which facilitate the acquisition of wealth, is more strongly felt; and as a nation becomes more democratic, private individuals are less
20 able, and the State more able, to execute works of such magnitude. I do not hesitate to assert that the manifest tendency of all governments at the present time is to take upon themselves alone the execution of these un-
25 dertakings; by which means they daily hold in closer dependence the population which they govern.

On the other hand, in proportion as the power
30 of a State increases, and its necessities are augmented, the State consumption of manufactured produce is always growing larger, and these commodities are generally made in the arsenals or establishments of the government.
35 Thus, in every kingdom, the ruler becomes the principal manufacturer; he collects and retains in his service a vast number of engineers, architects, mechanics, and handicraftsmen. Not only is he the principal manufacturer, but he
40 tends more and more to become the chief, or rather the master of all other manufacturers. As private persons become more powerless by becoming more equal, they can effect nothing in manufactures without combination; but the
45 government naturally seeks to place these combinations under its own control.

It must be admitted that these collective beings, which are called combinations, are
50 stronger and more formidable than a private individual can ever be, and that they have less of the responsibility of their own actions; whence it seems reasonable that they should not be allowed to retain so great an independ-
55 ence of the supreme government as might be conceded to a private individual.

Rulers are the more apt to follow this line of

policy, as their own inclinations invite them to it. Amongst democratic nations it is only by association that the resistance of the people to the government can ever display itself: hence the latter always looks with ill-favor on those associations which are not in its own power; and it is well worthy of remark, that amongst democratic nations, the people themselves often entertain a secret feeling of fear and jealousy against these very associations, which prevents the citizens from defending the institutions of which they stand so much in need. The power and the duration of these small private bodies, in the midst of the weakness and instability of the whole community, astonish and alarm the people; and the free use which each association makes of its natural powers is almost regarded as a dangerous privilege. All the associations which spring up in our age are, moreover, new corporate powers, whose rights have not been sanctioned by time; they come into existence at a time when the notion of private rights is weak, and when the power of government is unbounded; hence it is not surprising that they lose their freedom at their birth. Amongst all European nations there are some kinds of associations which cannot be formed until the State has examined their by-laws, and authorized their existence. In several others, attempts are made to extend this rule to all associations; the consequences of such a policy, if it were successful, may easily be foreseen. If once the sovereign had a general right of authorizing associations of all kinds upon certain conditions, he would not be long without claiming the right of superintending and managing them, in order to prevent them from departing from the rules laid down by himself. In this manner, the State, after having reduced all who are desirous of forming associations into dependence, would proceed to reduce into the same condition all who belong to associations already

formed—that is to say, almost all the men who are now in existence. Governments thus appropriate to themselves, and convert to their own purposes, the greater part of this new power which manufacturing interests have in our time brought into the world. Manufacturers govern us—they govern manufactures.

I attach so much importance to all that I have just been saying, that I am tormented by the fear of having impaired my meaning in seeking to render it more clear. If the reader thinks that the examples I have adduced to support my observations are insufficient or ill-chosen—if he imagines that I have anywhere exaggerated the encroachments of the supreme power, and, on the other hand, that I have underrated the extent of the sphere which still remains open to the exertions of individual independence, I entreat him to lay down the book for a moment, and to turn his mind to reflect for himself upon the subjects I have attempted to explain. Let him attentively examine what is taking place in France and in other countries—let him inquire of those about him—let him search himself, and I am much mistaken if he does not arrive, without my guidance, and by other paths, at the point to which I have sought to lead him. He will perceive that for the last half-century, centralization has everywhere been growing up in a thousand different ways. Wars, revolutions, conquests, have served to promote it: all men have labored to increase it. In the course of the same period, during which men have succeeded each other with singular rapidity at the head of affairs, their notions, interests, and passions have been infinitely diversified; but all have by some means or other sought to centralize. This instinctive centralization has been the only settled point amidst the extreme mutability of their lives and of their thoughts.

If the reader, after having investigated these details of human affairs, will seek to survey the wide prospect as a whole, he will be struck by the result. On the one hand the most settled dynasties shaken or overthrown—the people everywhere escaping by violence from the sway of their laws—abolishing or limiting the authority of their rulers or their princes—the nations, which are not in open revolution, restless at least, and excited—all of them animated by the same spirit of revolt: and on the other hand, at this very period of anarchy, and amongst these untractable nations, the incessant increase of the prerogative of the supreme government, becoming more centralized, more adventurous, more absolute, more extensive—the people perpetually falling under the control of the public administration—led insensibly to surrender to it some further portion of their individual independence, till the very men, who from time to time upset a throne and trample on a race of kings, bend more and more obsequiously to the slightest dictate of a clerk. Thus two contrary revolutions appear in our days to be going on; the one continually weakening the supreme power, the other as continually strengthening it: at no other period in our history has it appeared so weak or so strong. But upon a more attentive examination of the state of the world, it appears that these two revolutions are intimately connected together, that they originate in the same source, and that after having followed a separate course, they lead men at last to the same result. I may venture once more to repeat what I have already said or implied in several parts of this book: great care must be taken not to confound the principle of equality itself with the revolution which finally establishes that principle in the social condition and the laws of a nation: here lies the reason of almost all the phenomena which occasion our astonishment. All the old political powers of Europe, the greatest as well as the least, were founded in ages of aristocracy, and they more or less represented or defended the principles of inequality and of privilege. To make the novel wants and interests, which the growing principle of equality introduced, preponderate in government, our contemporaries had to overturn or to coerce the established powers. This led them to make revolutions, and breathed into many of them, that fierce love of disturbance and independence, which all revolutions, whatever be their object, always engender. I do not believe that there is a single country in Europe in which the progress of equality has not been preceded or followed by some violent changes in the state of property and persons; and almost all these changes have been attended with much anarchy and license, because they have been made by the least civilized portion of the nation against that which is most civilized. Hence proceeded the two-fold contrary tendencies which I have just pointed out. As long as the democratic revolution was glowing with heat, the men who were bent upon the destruction of old aristocratic powers hostile to that revolution, displayed a strong spirit of independence; but as the victory or the principle of equality became more complete, they gradually surrendered themselves to the propensities natural to that condition of equality, and they strengthened and centralized their governments. They had sought to be free in order to make themselves equal; but in proportion as equality was more established by the aid of freedom, freedom itself was thereby rendered of more difficult attainment.

These two states of a nation have sometimes been contemporaneous: the last generation in France showed how a people might organize a stupendous tyranny in the community, at the very time when they were baffling the authori-

ty of the nobility and braving the power of all kings—at once teaching the world the way to win freedom, and the way to lose it. In our days men see that constituted powers are di-
5 lapidated on every side—they see all ancient authority gasping away, all ancient barriers tottering to their fall, and the judgment of the wisest is troubled at the sight: they attend only to the amazing revolution which is taking
10 place before their eyes, and they imagine that mankind is about to fall into perpetual anarchy: if they looked to the final consequences of this revolution, their fears would perhaps assume a different shape. For myself, I con-
15 fess that I put no trust in the spirit of freedom which appears to animate my contemporaries. I see well enough that the nations of this age are turbulent, but I do not clearly perceive that they are liberal; and I fear lest, at the close of
20 those perturbations which rock the base of thrones, the domination of sovereigns may prove more powerful than it ever was before.

Chapter VI:
25 **What Sort Of Despotism Democratic Nations Have To Fear**

I had remarked during my stay in the United States, that a democratic state of society, simi-
30 lar to that of the Americans, might offer singular facilities for the establishment of despotism; and I perceived, upon my return to Europe, how much use had already been made by most of our rulers, of the notions, the senti-
35 ments, and the wants engendered by this same social condition, for the purpose of extending the circle of their power. This led me to think that the nations of Christendom would perhaps eventually undergo some sort of oppres-
40 sion like that which hung over several of the nations of the ancient world. A more accurate examination of the subject, and five years of further meditations, have not diminished my

apprehensions, but they have changed the
45 object of them. No sovereign ever lived in former ages so absolute or so powerful as to undertake to administer by his own agency, and without the assistance of intermediate powers, all the parts of a great empire: none
50 ever attempted to subject all his subjects indiscriminately to strict uniformity of regulation, and personally to tutor and direct every member of the community. The notion of such an undertaking never occurred to the human
55 mind; and if any man had conceived it, the want of information, the imperfection of the administrative system, and above all, the natural obstacles caused by the inequality of conditions, would speedily have checked the execu-
60 tion of so vast a design. When the Roman emperors were at the height of their power, the different nations of the empire still preserved manners and customs of great diversity; although they were subject to the same mon-
65 arch, most of the provinces were separately administered; they abounded in powerful and active municipalities; and although the whole government of the empire was centered in the hands of the emperor alone, and he always
70 remained, upon occasions, the supreme arbiter in all matters, yet the details of social life and private occupations lay for the most part beyond his control. The emperors possessed, it is true, an immense and unchecked power,
75 which allowed them to gratify all their whimsical tastes, and to employ for that purpose the whole strength of the State. They frequently abused that power arbitrarily to deprive their subjects of property or of life: their tyranny
80 was extremely onerous to the few, but it did not reach the greater number; it was fixed to some few main objects, and neglected the rest; it was violent, but its range was limited.

85 But it would seem that if despotism were to be established amongst the democratic nations of

406

our days, it might assume a different character; it would be more extensive and more mild; it would degrade men without tormenting them. I do not question, that in an age of instruction

5 and equality like our own, sovereigns might more easily succeed in collecting all political power into their own hands, and might interfere more habitually and decidedly within the circle of private interests, than any sovereign

10 of antiquity could ever do. But this same principle of equality which facilitates despotism, tempers its rigor. We have seen how the manners of society become more humane and gentle in proportion as men become more

15 equal and alike. When no member of the community has much power or much wealth, tyranny is, as it were, without opportunities and a field of action. As all fortunes are scanty, the passions of men are naturally circum-

20 scribed—their imagination limited, their pleasures simple. This universal moderation moderates the sovereign himself, and checks within certain limits the inordinate extent of his desires.

25

Independently of these reasons drawn from the nature of the state of society itself, I might add many others arising from causes beyond my subject; but I shall keep within the limits I

30 have laid down to myself. Democratic governments may become violent and even cruel at certain periods of extreme effervescence or of great danger: but these crises will be rare and brief. When I consider the petty passions

35 of our contemporaries, the mildness of their manners, the extent of their education, the purity of their religion, the gentleness of their morality, their regular and industrious habits, and the restraint which they almost all observe

40 in their vices no less than in their virtues, I have no fear that they will meet with tyrants in their rulers, but rather guardians. I think then that the species of oppression by which dem-

ocratic nations are menaced is unlike anything

45 which ever before existed in the world: our contemporaries will find no prototype of it in their memories. I am trying myself to choose an expression which will accurately convey the whole of the idea I have formed of it, but in

50 vain; the old words "despotism" and "tyranny" are inappropriate: the thing itself is new; and since I cannot name it, I must attempt to define it.

55 I seek to trace the novel features under which despotism may appear in the world. The first thing that strikes the observation is an innumerable multitude of men all equal and alike, incessantly endeavoring to procure the petty

60 and paltry pleasures with which they glut their lives. Each of them, living apart, is as a stranger to the fate of all the rest—his children and his private friends constitute to him the whole of mankind; as for the rest of his fel-

65 low-citizens, he is close to them, but he sees them not—he touches them, but he feels them not; he exists but in himself and for himself alone; and if his kindred still remain to him, he may be said at any rate to have lost his

70 country. Above this race of men stands an immense and tutelary power, which takes upon itself alone to secure their gratifications, and to watch over their fate. That power is absolute, minute, regular, provident, and mild.

75 It would be like the authority of a parent, if, like that authority, its object was to prepare men for manhood; but it seeks on the contrary to keep them in perpetual childhood: it is well content that the people should rejoice, provid-

80 ed they think of nothing but rejoicing. For their happiness such a government willingly labors, but it chooses to be the sole agent and the only arbiter of that happiness: it provides for their security, foresees and supplies their

85 necessities, facilitates their pleasures, manages their principal concerns, directs their industry,

407

regulates the descent of property, and subdivides their inheritances—what remains, but to spare them all the care of thinking and all the trouble of living? Thus it every day renders the
5 exercise of the free agency of man less useful and less frequent; it circumscribes the will within a narrower range, and gradually robs a man of all the uses of himself. The principle of equality has prepared men for these things:
10 it has predisposed men to endure them, and oftentimes to look on them as benefits.

After having thus successively taken each member of the community in its powerful
15 grasp, and fashioned them at will, the supreme power then extends its arm over the whole community. It covers the surface of society with a net-work of small complicated rules, minute and uniform, through which the most
20 original minds and the most energetic characters cannot penetrate, to rise above the crowd. The will of man is not shattered, but softened, bent, and guided: men are seldom forced by it to act, but they are constantly restrained from
25 acting: such a power does not destroy, but it prevents existence; it does not tyrannize, but it compresses, enervates, extinguishes, and stupefies a people, till each nation is reduced to be nothing better than a flock of timid and
30 industrious animals, of which the government is the shepherd. I have always thought that servitude of the regular, quiet, and gentle kind which I have just described, might be combined more easily than is commonly believed
35 with some of the outward forms of freedom; and that it might even establish itself under the wing of the sovereignty of the people. Our contemporaries are constantly excited by two conflicting passions; they want to be led, and
40 they wish to remain free: as they cannot destroy either one or the other of these contrary propensities, they strive to satisfy them both at once. They devise a sole, tutelary, and all-

powerful form of government, but elected by
45 the people. They combine the principle of centralization and that of popular sovereignty; this gives them a respite; they console themselves for being in tutelage by the reflection that they have chosen their own guardians.
50 Every man allows himself to be put in leading-strings, because he sees that it is not a person or a class of persons, but the people at large that holds the end of his chain. By this system the people shake off their state of dependence
55 just long enough to select their master, and then relapse into it again. A great many persons at the present day are quite contented with this sort of compromise between administrative despotism and the sovereignty of the
60 people; and they think they have done enough for the protection of individual freedom when they have surrendered it to the power of the nation at large. This does not satisfy me: the nature of him I am to obey signifies less to me
65 than the fact of extorted obedience.

I do not however deny that a constitution of this kind appears to me to be infinitely preferable to one, which, after having concentrated
70 all the powers of government, should vest them in the hands of an irresponsible person or body of persons. Of all the forms which democratic despotism could assume, the latter would assuredly be the worst. When the sov-
75 ereign is elective, or narrowly watched by a legislature which is really elective and independent, the oppression which he exercises over individuals is sometimes greater, but it is always less degrading; because every man,
80 when he is oppressed and disarmed, may still imagine, that whilst he yields obedience it is to himself he yields it, and that it is to one of his own inclinations that all the rest give way. In like manner I can understand that when the
85 sovereign represents the nation, and is dependent upon the people, the rights and the

power of which every citizen is deprived, not only serve the head of the State, but the State itself; and that private persons derive some return from the sacrifice of their independence which they have made to the public. To create a representation of the people in every centralized country, is therefore, to diminish the evil which extreme centralization may produce, but not to get rid of it. I admit that by this means room is left for the intervention of individuals in the more important affairs; but it is not the less suppressed in the smaller and more private ones. It must not be forgotten that it is especially dangerous to enslave men in the minor details of life. For my own part, I should be inclined to think freedom less necessary in great things than in little ones, if it were possible to be secure of the one without possessing the other. Subjection in minor affairs breaks out every day, and is felt by the whole community indiscriminately. It does not drive men to resistance, but it crosses them at every turn, till they are led to surrender the exercise of their will. Thus their spirit is gradually broken and their character enervated; whereas that obedience, which is exacted on a few important but rare occasions, only exhibits servitude at certain intervals, and throws the burden of it upon a small number of men. It is in vain to summon a people, which has been rendered so dependent on the central power, to choose from time to time the representatives of that power; this rare and brief exercise of their free choice, however important it may be, will not prevent them from gradually losing the faculties of thinking, feeling, and acting for themselves, and thus gradually falling below the level of humanity. I add that they will soon become incapable of exercising the great and only privilege which remains to them. The democratic nations which have introduced freedom into their political constitution, at the very time when they were augmenting the despotism of their administrative constitution, have been led into strange paradoxes. To manage those minor affairs in which good sense is all that is wanted—the people are held to be unequal to the task, but when the government of the country is at stake, the people are invested with immense powers; they are alternately made the playthings of their ruler, and his masters—more than kings, and less than men. After having exhausted all the different modes of election, without finding one to suit their purpose, they are still amazed, and still bent on seeking further; as if the evil they remark did not originate in the constitution of the country far more than in that of the electoral body. It is, indeed, difficult to conceive how men who have entirely given up the habit of self-government should succeed in making a proper choice of those by whom they are to be governed; and no one will ever believe that a liberal, wise, and energetic government can spring from the suffrages of a subservient people. A constitution, which should be republican in its head and ultra-monarchical in all its other parts, has ever appeared to me to be a short-lived monster. The vices of rulers and the ineptitude of the people would speedily bring about its ruin; and the nation, weary of its representatives and of itself, would create freer institutions, or soon return to stretch itself at the feet of a single master.

Chapter VII:
Continuation Of The Preceding Chapters

I believe that it is easier to establish an absolute and despotic government amongst a people in which the conditions of society are equal, than amongst any other; and I think that if such a government were once established amongst such a people, it would not only oppress men, but would eventually strip

each of them of several of the highest qualities of humanity. Despotism therefore appears to me peculiarly to be dreaded in democratic ages. I should have loved freedom, I believe,
5 at all times, but in the time in which we live I am ready to worship it. On the other hand, I am persuaded that all who shall attempt, in the ages upon which we are entering, to base freedom upon aristocratic privilege, will fail—that
10 all who shall attempt to draw and to retain authority within a single class, will fail. At the present day no ruler is skillful or strong enough to found a despotism, by re-establishing permanent distinctions of rank
15 amongst his subjects: no legislator is wise or powerful enough to preserve free institutions, if he does not take equality for his first principle and his watchword. All those of our contemporaries who would establish or secure the
20 independence and the dignity of their fellow-men, must show themselves the friends of equality; and the only worthy means of showing themselves as such, is to be so: upon this depends the success of their holy enterprise.
25 Thus the question is not how to reconstruct aristocratic society, but how to make liberty proceed out of that democratic state of society in which God has placed us.

30 These two truths appear to me simple, clear, and fertile in consequences; and they naturally lead me to consider what kind of free government can be established amongst a people in which social conditions are equal. It results
35 from the very constitution of democratic nations and from their necessities, that the power of government amongst them must be more uniform, more centralized, more extensive, more searching, and more efficient than
40 in other countries. Society at large is naturally stronger and more active, individuals more subordinate and weak; the former does more, the latter less; and this is inevitably the case. It

is not therefore to be expected that the range
45 of private independence will ever be as extensive in democratic as in aristocratic countries—nor is this to be desired; for, amongst aristocratic nations, the mass is often sacrificed to the individual, and the prosperity of
50 the greater number to the greatness of the few. It is both necessary and desirable that the government of a democratic people should be active and powerful: and our object should not be to render it weak or indolent, but solely to
55 prevent it from abusing its aptitude and its strength.

The circumstance which most contributed to secure the independence of private persons in
60 aristocratic ages, was, that the supreme power did not affect to take upon itself alone the government and administration of the community; those functions were necessarily partially left to the members of the aristocracy: so
65 that as the supreme power was always divided, it never weighed with its whole weight and in the same manner on each individual. Not only did the government not perform everything by its immediate agency; but as most of the
70 agents who discharged its duties derived their power not from the State, but from the circumstance of their birth, they were not perpetually under its control. The government could not make or unmake them in an instant,
75 at pleasure, nor bend them in strict uniformity to its slightest caprice—this was an additional guarantee of private independence. I readily admit that recourse cannot be had to the same means at the present time: but I discover certain
80 tain democratic expedients which may be substituted for them. Instead of vesting in the government alone all the administrative powers of which corporations and nobles have been deprived, a portion of them may be en-
85 trusted to secondary public bodies, temporarily composed of private citizens: thus the liber-

410

ty of private persons will be more secure, and their equality will not be diminished.

The Americans, who care less for words than the French, still designate by the name of "county" the largest of their administrative districts: but the duties of the count or lord-lieutenant are in part performed by a provincial assembly. At a period of equality like our own it would be unjust and unreasonable to institute hereditary officers; but there is nothing to prevent us from substituting elective public officers to a certain extent. Election is a democratic expedient which insures the independence of the public officer in relation to the government, as much and even more than hereditary rank can insure it amongst aristocratic nations. Aristocratic countries abound in wealthy and influential persons who are competent to provide for themselves, and who cannot be easily or secretly oppressed: such persons restrain a government within general habits of moderation and reserve. I am very well aware that democratic countries contain no such persons naturally; but something analogous to them may be created by artificial means. I firmly believe that an aristocracy cannot again be founded in the world; but I think that private citizens, by combining together, may constitute bodies of great wealth, influence, and strength, corresponding to the persons of an aristocracy. By this means many of the greatest political advantages of aristocracy would be obtained without its injustice or its dangers. An association for political, commercial, or manufacturing purposes, or even for those of science and literature, is a powerful and enlightened member of the community, which cannot be disposed of at pleasure, or oppressed without remonstrance; and which, by defending its own rights against the encroachments of the government, saves the common liberties of the country.

In periods of aristocracy every man is always bound so closely to many of his fellow-citizens, that he cannot be assailed without their coming to his assistance. In ages of equality every man naturally stands alone; he has no hereditary friends whose co-operation he may demand—no class upon whose sympathy he may rely: he is easily got rid of, and he is trampled on with impunity. At the present time, an oppressed member of the community has therefore only one method of self-defense—he may appeal to the whole nation; and if the whole nation is deaf to his complaint, he may appeal to mankind: the only means he has of making this appeal is by the press. Thus the liberty of the press is infinitely more valuable amongst democratic nations than amongst all others; it is the only cure for the evils which equality may produce. Equality sets men apart and weakens them; but the press places a powerful weapon within every man's reach, which the weakest and loneliest of them all may use. Equality deprives a man of the support of his connections; but the press enables him to summon all his fellow-countrymen and all his fellow-men to his assistance. Printing has accelerated the progress of equality, and it is also one of its best correctives.

I think that men living in aristocracies may, strictly speaking, do without the liberty of the press: but such is not the case with those who live in democratic countries. To protect their personal independence I trust not to great political assemblies, to parliamentary privilege, or to the assertion of popular sovereignty. All these things may, to a certain extent, be reconciled with personal servitude—but that servitude cannot be complete if the press is free: the press is the chiefest democratic instrument of freedom.

Something analogous may be said of the judicial power. It is a part of the essence of judicial power to attend to private interests, and to fix itself with predilection on minute objects submitted to its observation; another essential quality of judicial power is never to volunteer its assistance to the oppressed, but always to be at the disposal of the humblest of those who solicit it; their complaint, however feeble they may themselves be, will force itself upon the ear of justice and claim redress, for this is inherent in the very constitution of the courts of justice. A power of this kind is therefore peculiarly adapted to the wants of freedom, at a time when the eye and finger of the government are constantly intruding into the minutest details of human actions, and when private persons are at once too weak to protect themselves, and too much isolated for them to reckon upon the assistance of their fellows. The strength of the courts of law has ever been the greatest security which can be offered to personal independence; but this is more especially the case in democratic ages: private rights and interests are in constant danger, if the judicial power does not grow more extensive and more strong to keep pace with the growing equality of conditions.

Equality awakens in men several propensities extremely dangerous to freedom, to which the attention of the legislator ought constantly to be directed. I shall only remind the reader of the most important amongst them. Men living in democratic ages do not readily comprehend the utility of forms: they feel an instinctive contempt for them—I have elsewhere shown for what reasons. Forms excite their contempt and often their hatred; as they commonly aspire to none but easy and present gratifications, they rush onwards to the object of their desires, and the slightest delay exasperates them. This same temper, carried with them into political life, renders them hostile to forms, which perpetually retard or arrest them in some of their projects. Yet this objection which the men of democracies make to forms is the very thing which renders forms so useful to freedom; for their chief merit is to serve as a barrier between the strong and the weak, the ruler and the people, to retard the one, and give the other time to look about him. Forms become more necessary in proportion as the government becomes more active and more powerful, whilst private persons are becoming more indolent and more feeble. Thus democratic nations naturally stand more in need of forms than other nations, and they naturally respect them less. This deserves most serious attention. Nothing is more pitiful than the arrogant disdain of most of our contemporaries for questions of form; for the smallest questions of form have acquired in our time an importance which they never had before: many of the greatest interests of mankind depend upon them. I think that if the statesmen of aristocratic ages could sometimes contemn forms with impunity, and frequently rise above them, the statesmen to whom the government of nations is now confided ought to treat the very least among them with respect, and not neglect them without imperious necessity. In aristocracies the observance of forms was superstitious; amongst us they ought to be kept with a deliberate and enlightened deference.

Another tendency, which is extremely natural to democratic nations and extremely dangerous, is that which leads them ta despise and undervalue the rights of private persons. The attachment which men feel to a right, and the respect which they display for it, is generally proportioned to its importance, or to the length of time during which they have enjoyed it. The rights of private persons amongst democratic nations are commonly of small importance, of recent growth, and extremely precarious—the consequence is that they are often sacrificed without regret, and almost

5 always violated without remorse. But it happens that at the same period and amongst the same nations in which men conceive a natural contempt for the rights of private persons, the rights of society at large are naturally extended

10 and consolidated: in other words, men become less attached to private rights at the very time at which it would be most necessary to retain and to defend what little remains of them. It is therefore most especially in the

15 present democratic ages, that the true friends of the liberty and the greatness of man ought constantly to be on the alert to prevent the power of government from lightly sacrificing the private rights of individuals to the general

20 execution of its designs. At such times no citizen is so obscure that it is not very dangerous to allow him to be oppressed—no private rights are so unimportant that they can be surrendered with impunity to the caprices of a

25 government. The reason is plain:—if the private right of an individual is violated at a time when the human mind is fully impressed with the importance and the sanctity of such rights, the injury done is confined to the individual

30 whose right is infringed; but to violate such a right, at the present day, is deeply to corrupt the manners of the nation and to put the whole community in jeopardy, because the very notion of this kind of right constantly

35 tends amongst us to be impaired and lost. There are certain habits, certain notions, and certain vices which are peculiar to a state of revolution, and which a protracted revolution cannot fail to engender and to propagate,

40 whatever be, in other respects, its character, its purpose, and the scene on which it takes place. When any nation has, within a short space of time, repeatedly varied its rulers, its opinions,

and its laws, the men of whom it is composed
45 eventually contract a taste for change, and grow accustomed to see all changes effected by sudden violence. Thus they naturally conceive a contempt for forms which daily prove ineffectual; and they do not support without

50 impatience the dominion of rules which they have so often seen infringed. As the ordinary notions of equity and morality no longer suffice to explain and justify all the innovations daily begotten by a revolution, the principle of

55 public utility is called in, the doctrine of political necessity is conjured up, and men accustom themselves to sacrifice private interests without scruple, and to trample on the rights of individuals in order more speedily to ac-

60 complish any public purpose.

These habits and notions, which I shall call revolutionary, because all revolutions produce them, occur in aristocracies just as much as
65 amongst democratic nations; but amongst the former they are often less powerful and always less lasting, because there they meet with habits, notions, defects, and impediments, which counteract them: they consequently disappear

70 as soon as the revolution is terminated, and the nation reverts to its former political courses. This is not always the case in democratic countries, in which it is ever to be feared that revolutionary tendencies, becoming more gen-

75 tle and more regular, without entirely disappearing from society, will be gradually transformed into habits of subjection to the administrative authority of the government. I know of no countries in which revolutions re more

80 dangerous than in democratic countries; because, independently of the accidental and transient evils which must always attend them, they may always create some evils which are permanent and unending. I believe that there

85 are such things as justifiable resistance and legitimate rebellion: I do not therefore assert,

as an absolute proposition, that the men of democratic ages ought never to make revolutions; but I think that they have especial reason to hesitate before they embark in them, and that it is far better to endure many grievances in their present condition than to have recourse to so perilous a remedy.

I shall conclude by one general idea, which comprises not only all the particular ideas which have been expressed in the present chapter, but also most of those which it is the object of this book to treat of. In the ages of aristocracy which preceded our own, there were private persons of great power, and a social authority of extreme weakness. The outline of society itself was not easily discernible, and constantly confounded with the different powers by which the community was ruled. The principal efforts of the men of those times were required to strengthen, aggrandize, and secure the supreme power; and on the other hand, to circumscribe individual independence within narrower limits, and to subject private interests to the interests of the public. Other perils and other cares await the men of our age. Amongst the greater part of modern nations, the government, whatever may be its origin, its constitution, or its name, has become almost omnipotent, and private persons are falling, more and more, into the lowest stage of weakness and dependence. In olden society everything was different; unity and uniformity were nowhere to be met with. In modern society everything threatens to become so much alike, that the peculiar characteristics of each individual will soon be entirely lost in the general aspect of the world. Our forefathers were ever prone to make an improper use of the notion, that private rights ought to be respected; and we are naturally prone on the other hand to exaggerate the idea that the interest of a private individual ought always to bend to the interest of the many. The political world is metamorphosed: new remedies must henceforth be sought for new disorders. To lay down extensive, but distinct and settled limits, to the action of the government; to confer certain rights on private persons, and to secure to them the undisputed enjoyment of those rights; to enable individual man to maintain whatever independence, strength, and original power he still possesses; to raise him by the side of society at large, and uphold him in that position—these appear to me the main objects of legislators in the ages upon which we are now entering. It would seem as if the rulers of our time sought only to use men in order to make things great; I wish that they would try a little more to make great men; that they would set less value on the work, and more upon the workman; that they would never forget that a nation cannot long remain strong when every man belonging to it is individually weak, and that no form or combination of social polity has yet been devised, to make an energetic people out of a community of pusillanimous and enfeebled citizens.

I trace amongst our contemporaries two contrary notions which are equally injurious. One set of men can perceive nothing in the principle of equality but the anarchical tendencies which it engenders: they dread their own free agency—they fear themselves. Other thinkers, less numerous but more enlightened, take a different view: besides that track which starts from the principle of equality to terminate in anarchy, they have at last discovered the road which seems to lead men to inevitable servitude. They shape their souls beforehand to this necessary condition; and, despairing of remaining free, they already do obeisance in their hearts to the master who is soon to appear. The former abandon freedom, because they think it dangerous; the latter, because they hold it to be impossible. If I had entertained the latter conviction, I should not have written this book, but I should have confined myself to deploring in secret the destiny of

5 mankind. I have sought to point out the dangers to which the principle of equality exposes the independence of man, because I firmly believe that these dangers are the most formidable, as well as the least foreseen, of all those

10 which futurity holds in store: but I do not think that they are insurmountable. The men who live in the democratic ages upon which we are entering have naturally a taste for independence: they are naturally impatient of regu-

15 lation, and they are wearied by the permanence even of the condition they themselves prefer. They are fond of power; but they are prone to despise and hate those who wield it, and they easily elude its grasp by their own

20 mobility and insignificance. These propensities will always manifest themselves, because they originate in the groundwork of society, which will undergo no change: for a long time they will prevent the establishment of any despot-

25 ism, and they will furnish fresh weapons to each succeeding generation which shall struggle in favor of the liberty of mankind. Let us then look forward to the future with that salutary fear which makes men keep watch and

30 ward for freedom, not with that faint and idle terror which depresses and enervates the heart.

Chapter VIII:
35 ### General Survey Of The Subject

Before I close forever the theme that has detained me so long, I would fain take a parting survey of all the various characteristics of

40 modern society, and appreciate at last the general influence to be exercised by the principle of equality upon the fate of mankind; but I am stopped by the difficulty of the task, and in

presence of so great an object my sight is
45 troubled, and my reason fails. The society of the modern world which I have sought to delineate, and which I seek to judge, has but just come into existence. Time has not yet shaped it into perfect form: the great revolution by
50 which it has been created is not yet over: and amidst the occurrences of our time, it is almost impossible to discern what will pass away with the revolution itself, and what will survive its close. The world which is rising
55 into existence is still half encumbered by the remains of the world which is waning into decay; and amidst the vast perplexity of human affairs, none can say how much of ancient institutions and former manners will
60 remain, or how much will completely disappear. Although the revolution which is taking place in the social condition, the laws, the opinions, and the feelings of men, is still very far from being terminated, yet its results al-
65 ready admit of no comparison with anything that the world has ever before witnessed. I go back from age to age up to the remotest antiquity; but I find no parallel to what is occurring before my eyes: as the past has ceased to
70 throw its light upon the future, the mind of man wanders in obscurity. Nevertheless, in the midst of a prospect so wide, so novel and so confused, some of the more prominent characteristics may already be discerned and point-
75 ed out. The good things and the evils of life are more equally distributed in the world: great wealth tends to disappear, the number of small fortunes to increase; desires and gratifications are multiplied, but extraordinary prosperity
80 and irremediable penury are alike unknown. The sentiment of ambition is universal, but the scope of ambition is seldom vast. Each individual stands apart in solitary weakness; but society at large is active, provident, and
85 powerful: the performances of private persons are insignificant, those of the State immense.

There is little energy of character; but manners are mild, and laws humane. If there be few instances of exalted heroism or of virtues of the highest, brightest, and purest temper,
5 men's habits are regular, violence is rare, and cruelty almost unknown. Human existence becomes longer, and property more secure: life is not adorned with brilliant trophies, but it is extremely easy and tranquil. Few pleasures
10 are either very refined or very coarse; and highly polished manners are as uncommon as great brutality of tastes. Neither men of great learning, nor extremely ignorant communities, are to be met with; genius becomes more rare,
15 information more diffused. The human mind is impelled by the small efforts of all mankind combined together, not by the strenuous activity of certain men. There is less perfection, but more abundance, in all the productions of
20 the arts. The ties of race, of rank, and of country are relaxed; the great bond of humanity is strengthened. If I endeavor to find out the most general and the most prominent of all these different characteristics, I shall have oc-
25 casion to perceive, that what is taking place in men's fortunes manifests itself under a thousand other forms. Almost all extremes are softened or blunted: all that was most prominent is superseded by some mean term, at
30 once less lofty and less low, less brilliant and less obscure, than what before existed in the world.

When I survey this countless multitude of
35 beings, shaped in each other's likeness, amidst whom nothing rises and nothing falls, the sight of such universal uniformity saddens and chills me, and I am tempted to regret that state of society which has ceased to be. When the
40 world was full of men of great importance and extreme insignificance, of great wealth and extreme poverty, of great learning and extreme ignorance, I turned aside from the latter to fix

my observation on the former alone, who
45 gratified my sympathies. But I admit that this gratification arose from my own weakness: it is because I am unable to see at once all that is around me, that I am allowed thus to select and separate the objects of my predilection
50 from among so many others. Such is not the case with that almighty and eternal Being whose gaze necessarily includes the whole of created things, and who surveys distinctly, though at once, mankind and man. We may
55 naturally believe that it is not the singular prosperity of the few, but the greater wellbeing of all, which is most pleasing in the sight of the Creator and Preserver of men. What appears to me to be man's decline, is to His
60 eye advancement; what afflicts me is acceptable to Him. A state of equality is perhaps less elevated, but it is more just; and its justice constitutes its greatness and its beauty. I would strive then to raise myself to this point
65 of the divine contemplation, and thence to view and to judge the concerns of men.

No man, upon the earth, can as yet affirm absolutely and generally, that the new state of
70 the world is better than its former one; but it is already easy to perceive that this state is different. Some vices and some virtues were so inherent in the constitution of an aristocratic nation, and are so opposite to the character
75 of a modern people, that they can never be infused into it; some good tendencies and some bad propensities which were unknown to the former, are natural to the latter; some ideas suggest themselves spontaneously to the
80 imagination of the one, which are utterly repugnant to the mind of the other. They are like two distinct orders of human beings, each of which has its own merits and defects, its own advantages and its own evils. Care must
85 therefore be taken not to judge the state of society, which is now coming into existence,

by notions derived from a state of society which no longer exists; for as these states of society are exceedingly different in their structure, they cannot be submitted to a just or fair comparison. It would be scarcely more reasonable to require of our own contemporaries the peculiar virtues which originated in the social condition of their forefathers, since that social condition is itself fallen, and has drawn into one promiscuous ruin the good and evil which belonged to it.

But as yet these things are imperfectly understood. I find that a great number of my contemporaries undertake to make a certain selection from amongst the institutions, the opinions, and the ideas which originated in the aristocratic constitution of society as it was: a portion of these elements they would willingly relinquish, but they would keep the remainder and transplant them into their new world. I apprehend that such men are wasting their time and their strength in virtuous but unprofitable efforts. The object is not to retain the peculiar advantages which the inequality of conditions bestows upon mankind, but to secure the new benefits which equality may supply. We have not to seek to make ourselves like our progenitors, but to strive to work out that species of greatness and happiness which is our own. For myself, who now look back from this extreme limit of my task, and discover from afar, but at once, the various objects which have attracted my more attentive investigation upon my way, I am full of apprehensions and of hopes. I perceive mighty dangers which it is possible to ward off— mighty evils which may be avoided or alleviated; and I cling with a firmer hold to the belief, that for democratic nations to be virtuous and prosperous they require but to will it. I am aware that many of my contemporaries maintain that nations are never their own masters here below, and that they necessarily obey some insurmountable and unintelligent power, arising from anterior events, from their race, or from the soil and climate of their country. Such principles are false and cowardly; such principles can never produce aught but feeble men and pusillanimous nations. Providence has not created mankind entirely independent or entirely free. It is true that around every man a fatal circle is traced, beyond which he cannot pass; but within the wide verge of that circle he is powerful and free: as it is with man, so with communities. The nations of our time cannot prevent the conditions of men from becoming equal; but it depends upon themselves whether the principle of equality is to lead them to servitude or freedom, to knowledge or barbarism, to prosperity or to wretchedness.

MILL

John Stuart Mill (1806-1879) was born to an already famous Mill—his father James, a noted British intellectual. Home-schooled in a unique fashion, John was reading Greek by three and wrapped up his (highly advanced) schooling by the age of fourteen. He then went to work for the British East India Company, which governed colonial India on behalf of the Crown until the mid-19th century. A radical liberal in all sorts off ways, the younger Mill was actively involved in projects for women's rights, the expansion of suffrage, and the abolition of slavery. He was the quintessential liberal, born in the era of democratic 'rebirth' across Europe.

Mill, however, was not entirely comfortable with the rise of democracy in the 19th century, and attempts to tackle its excesses in two of his most famous political works, *On Liberty* and *Representative Government*. Much like the ancients he feared the power of democratic government and wanted it strictly controlled—through constitutional and representative structures. He deals with this concern in *Representative Government*, where he argues that not only is democracy not only not for all nations, but not for all people within those nations.

But more than the power of democratic government, Mill feared the impact of democratization on the relationship between society and the individual. He handles this in his classic work, *On Liberty*, which stands as the foundation of libertarianism. Mill puts forth a powerful (though frequently flawed) vision of a world of near absolute individual liberty—not merely from government, but for the coercive power of society as well.

ON LIBERTY
JOHN STUART MILL

CHAPTER I
INTRODUCTORY

The subject of this Essay is not the so-called
Liberty of the Will, so unfortunately opposed
to the misnamed doctrine of PhilosophicalNe-
cessity; but Civil, or Social Liberty: the nature
and limits of the power which can be legitimately exercised by society over the individual.
A question seldom stated, and hardly ever
discussed, in general terms, but which pro-
foundly influences the practical controversies
of the age by its latent presence, and is likely
soon to make itself recognized as the vital
question of the future. It is so far from being
new, that in a certain sense, it has divided
mankind, almost from the remotest ages; but
in the stage of progress into which the more
civilized portions of the species have now entered, it presents itself under new conditions,
and requires a different and more fundamental
treatment.

The struggle between Liberty and Authority is
the most conspicuous feature in the portions
of history with which we are earliest familiar,
particularly in that of Greece, Rome, and England. But in old times this contest was between subjects, or some classes of subjects,
and the government. By liberty, was meant
protection against the tyranny of the political
rulers. The rulers were conceived (except in
some of the popular governments of Greece)
as in a necessarily antagonistic position to the
people whom they ruled. They consisted of a

governing One, or a governing tribe or caste,
who derived their authority from inheritance
or conquest, who, at all events, did not hold it
at the pleasure of the governed, and whose
supremacy men did not venture, perhaps did
not desire, to contest, whatever precautions
might be taken against its oppressive exercise.
Their power was regarded as necessary, but
also as highly dangerous; as a weapon which
they would attempt to use against their subjects, no less than against external enemies. To
prevent the weaker members of the community from being preyed upon by innumerable
vultures, it was needful that there should be an
animal of prey stronger than the rest, commissioned to keep them down. But as the king of
the vultures would be no less bent upon preying on the flock than any of the minor harpies,
it was indispensable to be in a perpetual atti-
tude of defense against his beak and claws.
The aim, therefore, of patriots, was to set limits to the power which the ruler should be
suffered to exercise over the community; and
this limitation was what they meant by liberty.
It was attempted in two ways. First, by obtaining a recognition of certain immunities, called
political liberties or rights, which it was to be
regarded as a breach of duty in the ruler to
infringe, and which if he did infringe, specific
resistance, or general rebellion, was held to be
justifiable. A second, and generally a later expedient, was the establishment of constitutional checks; by which the consent of the
community, or of a body of some sort, supposed to represent its interests, was made a
necessary condition to some of the more important acts of the governing power. To the

---

Text based off original printing, with adjustments for modern spellings.

first of these modes of limitation, the ruling power, in most European countries, was compelled, more or less, to submit. It was not so with the second; and to attain this, or when already in some degree possessed, to attain it more completely, became everywhere the principal object of the lovers of liberty. And so long as mankind were content to combat one enemy by another, and to be ruled by a master, on condition of being guaranteed more or less efficaciously against his tyranny, they did not carry their aspirations beyond this point.

A time, however, came, in the progress of human affairs, when men ceased to think it a necessity of nature that their governors should be an independent power, opposed in interest to themselves. It appeared to them much better that the various magistrates of the State should be their tenants or delegates, revocable at their pleasure. In that way alone, it seemed, could they have complete security that the powers of government would never be abused to their disadvantage. By degrees, this new demand for elective and temporary rulers became the prominent object of the exertions of the popular party, wherever any such party existed; and superseded, to a considerable extent, the previous efforts to limit the power of rulers. As the struggle proceeded for making the ruling power emanate from the periodical choice of the ruled, some persons began to think that too much importance had been attached to the limitation of the power itself. *That* (it might seem) was a resource against rulers whose interests were habitually opposed to those of the people. What was now wanted was, that the rulers should be identified with the people; that their interest and will should be the interest and will of the nation. The nation did not need to be protected against its own will. There was no fear of its tyrannizing over itself. Let the rulers be effectually responsible to it, promptly removable by it, and it could afford to trust them with power of which it could itself dictate the use to be made. Their power was but the nation's own power, concentrated, and in a form convenient for exercise. This mode of thought, or rather perhaps of feeling, was common among the last generation of European liberalism, in the Continental section of which it still apparently predominates. Those who admit any limit to what a government may do, except in the case of such governments as they think ought not to exist, stand out as brilliant exceptions among the political thinkers of the Continent. A similar tone of sentiment might by this time have been prevalent in our own country, if the circumstances which for a time encouraged it, had continued unaltered.

But, in political and philosophical theories, as well as in persons, success discloses faults and infirmities which failure might have concealed from observation. The notion, that the people have no need to limit their power over themselves, might seem axiomatic, when popular government was a thing only dreamed about, or read of as having existed at some distant period of the past. Neither was that notion necessarily disturbed by such temporary aberrations as those of the French Revolution, the worst of which were the work of a usurping few, and which, in any case, belonged, not to the permanent working of popular institutions, but to a sudden and convulsive outbreak against monarchical and aristocratic despotism. In time, however, a democratic republic came to occupy a large portion of the earth's surface, and made itself felt as one of the most powerful members of the community of nations; and elective and responsible government became subject to the observations and criticisms which wait upon a great existing fact. It was now perceived that such phrases as "self-government," and "the power of the people over themselves," do not express the true state of the case. The "people" who exercise the power are not always the same people with those over whom it is exercised; and the "self-government" spoken of is not the government of each by himself, but of each by all the rest. The will of the people, moreover, practically means, the will of the most numerous or the most active *part* of the people; the majority, or those who succeed in making themselves accepted as the majority: the people, consequently, *may* desire to oppress a part of their number; and precautions are as much needed against this, as against any other abuse of power. The limitation, therefore, of the power of government over individuals, loses none of its importance when the holders of power are regularly accountable to the community, that is, to the strongest party therein. This view of things, recommending itself equally to the intelligence of thinkers and to the inclination of those important classes in European society to whose real or supposed interests democracy is adverse, has had no difficulty in establishing itself; and in political speculations "the tyranny of the majority" is now generally included among the evils against which society requires to be on its guard.

Like other tyrannies, the tyranny of the majority was at first, and is still vulgarly, held in dread, chiefly as operating through the acts of the public authorities. But reflecting persons perceived that when society is itself the tyrant—society collectively, over the separate individuals who compose it—its means of tyrannizing are not restricted to the acts which it may do by the hands of its political functionaries. Society can and does execute its own mandates: and if it issues wrong mandates instead of right, or any mandates at all in things with which it ought not to meddle, it practices a social tyranny more formidable than many kinds of political oppression, since, though not usually upheld by such extreme penalties, it leaves fewer means of escape, penetrating much more deeply into the details of life, and enslaving the soul itself. Protection, therefore, against the tyranny of the magistrate is not enough: there needs protection also against the tyranny of the prevailing opinion and feeling; against the tendency of society to impose, by other means than civil penalties, its own ideas and practices as rules of conduct on those who dissent from them; to fetter the development, and, if possible, prevent the formation, of any individuality not in harmony with its ways, and compel all characters to fashion themselves upon the model of its own. There is a limit to the legitimate interference of collective opinion with individual independence: and to find that limit, and maintain it against encroachment, is as indispensable to a good condition of human affairs, as protection against political despotism.

But though this proposition is not likely to be contested in general terms, the practical question, where to place the limit—how to make the fitting adjustment between individual independence and social control—is a subject on which nearly everything remains to be done. All that makes existence valuable to any one, depends on the enforcement of restraints upon the actions of other people. Some rules of conduct, therefore, must be imposed, by law in the first place, and by opinion on many things which are not fit subjects for the operation of law. What these rules should be, is the principal question in human affairs; but if we except a few of the most obvious cases, it is one of those which least progress has been made in resolving. No two ages, and scarcely any two countries, have decided it alike; and

the decision of one age or country is a wonder to another. Yet the people of any given age and country no more suspect any difficulty in it, than if it were a subject on which mankind
5 had always been agreed. The rules which obtain among themselves appear to them self-evident and self-justifying. This all but universal illusion is one of the examples of the magical influence of custom, which is not only, as
10 the proverb says, a second nature, but is continually mistaken for the first. The effect of custom, in preventing any misgiving respecting the rules of conduct which mankind impose on one another, is all the more complete
15 because the subject is one on which it is not generally considered necessary that reasons should be given, either by one person to others, or by each to himself. People are accustomed to believe, and have been encouraged
20 in the belief by some who aspire to the character of philosophers, that their feelings, on subjects of this nature, are better than reasons, and render reasons unnecessary. The practical principle which guides them to their opinions
25 on the regulation of human conduct, is the feeling in each person's mind that everybody should be required to act as he, and those with whom he sympathizes, would like them to act. No one, indeed, acknowledges to himself that
30 his standard of judgment is his own liking; but an opinion on a point of conduct, not supported by reasons, can only count as one person's preference; and if the reasons, when given, are a mere appeal to a similar preference
35 felt by other people, it is still only many people's liking instead of one. To an ordinary man, however, his own preference, thus supported, is not only a perfectly satisfactory reason, but the only one he generally has for any
40 of his notions of morality, taste, or propriety, which are not expressly written in his religious creed; and his chief guide in the interpretation even of that. Men's opinions, accordingly, on

what is laudable or blamable, are affected by
45 all the multifarious causes which influence their wishes in regard to the conduct of others, and which are as numerous as those which determine their wishes on any other subject. Sometimes their reason—at other times their
50 prejudices or superstitions: often their social affections, not seldom their anti-social ones, their envy or jealousy, their arrogance or contemptuousness: but most commonly, their desires or fears for themselves—their legiti-
55 mate or illegitimate self-interest. Wherever there is an ascendant class, a large portion of the morality of the country emanates from its class interests, and its feelings of class superiority. The morality between Spartans and Hel-
60 ots, between planters and negroes, between princes and subjects, between nobles and roturiers, between men and women, has been for the most part the creation of these class interests and feelings: and the sentiments thus
65 generated, react in turn upon the moral feelings of the members of the ascendant class, in their relations among themselves. Where, on the other hand, a class, formerly ascendant, has lost its ascendancy, or where its ascendan-
70 cy is unpopular, the prevailing moral sentiments frequently bear the impress of an impatient dislike of superiority. Another grand determining principle of the rules of conduct, both in act and forbearance, which have been
75 enforced by law or opinion, has been the servility of mankind towards the supposed preferences or aversions of their temporal masters, or of their gods. This servility, though essentially selfish, is not hypocrisy; it gives rise to
80 perfectly genuine sentiments of abhorrence; it made men burn magicians and heretics. Among so many baser influences, the general and obvious interests of society have of course had a share, and a large one, in the direction of
85 the moral sentiments: less, however, as a matter of reason, and on their own account, than

as a consequence of the sympathies and antipathies which grew out of them: and sympathies and antipathies which had little or nothing to do with the interests of society, have
5 made themselves felt in the establishment of
moralities with quite as great force.

The likings and dislikings of society, or of
some powerful portion of it, are thus the main
10 thing which has practically determined the
rules laid down for general observance, under
the penalties of law or opinion. And in general, those who have been in advance of society in thought and feeling have left this condi-
15 tion of things unassailed in principle, however
they may have come into conflict with it in
some of its details. They have occupied themselves rather in inquiring what things society
ought to like or dislike, than in questioning
20 whether its likings or dislikings should be a
law to individuals. They preferred endeavoring
to alter the feelings of mankind on the particular points on which they were themselves heretical, rather than make common cause in
25 defense of freedom, with heretics generally.
The only case in which the higher ground has
been taken on principle and maintained with
consistency, by any but an individual here and
there, is that of religious belief: a case instruc-
30 tive in many ways, and not least so as forming
a most striking instance of the fallibility of
what is called the moral sense: for the *odium
theologicum*, in a sincere bigot, is one of the
most unequivocal cases of moral feeling.
35 Those who first broke the yoke of what called
itself the Universal Church, were in general as
little willing to permit difference of religious
opinion as that church itself. But when the
heat of the conflict was over, without giving a
40 complete victory to any party, and each church
or sect was reduced to limit its hopes to retaining possession of the ground it already
occupied; minorities, seeing that they had no

chance of becoming majorities, were under the
45 necessity of pleading to those whom they
could not convert, for permission to differ. It
is accordingly on this battle-field, almost solely, that the rights of the individual against society have been asserted on broad grounds of
50 principle, and the claim of society to exercise
authority over dissentients, openly controverted. The great writers to whom the world owes
what religious liberty it possesses, have mostly
asserted freedom of conscience as an indefea-
55 sible right, and denied absolutely that a human
being is accountable to others for his religious
belief. Yet so natural to mankind is intolerance
in whatever they really care about, that religious freedom has hardly anywhere been prac-
60 tically realized, except where religious indifference, which dislikes to have its peace disturbed by theological quarrels, has added its
weight to the scale. In the minds of almost all
religious persons, even in the most tolerant
65 countries, the duty of toleration is admitted
with tacit reserves. One person will bear with
dissent in matters of church government, but
not of dogma; another can tolerate everybody,
short of a Papist or a Unitarian; another, every
70 one who believes in revealed religion; a few
extend their charity a little further, but stop at
the belief in a God and in a future state.
Wherever the sentiment of the majority is still
genuine and intense, it is found to have abated
75 little of its claim to be obeyed.

In England, from the peculiar circumstances
of our political history, though the yoke of
opinion is perhaps heavier, that of law is light-
80 er, than in most other countries of Europe;
and there is considerable jealousy of direct
interference, by the legislative or the executive
power, with private conduct; not so much
from any just regard for the independence of
85 the individual, as from the still subsisting habit
of looking on the government as representing

an opposite interest to the public. The majority have not yet learnt to feel the power of the government their power, or its opinions their opinions. When they do so, individual liberty will probably be as much exposed to invasion from the government, as it already is from public opinion. But, as yet, there is a considerable amount of feeling ready to be called forth against any attempt of the law to control individuals in things in which they have not hitherto been accustomed to be controlled by it; and this with very little discrimination as to whether the matter is, or is not, within the legitimate sphere of legal control; insomuch that the feeling, highly salutary on the whole, is perhaps quite as often misplaced as well grounded in the particular instances of its application. There is, in fact, no recognized principle by which the propriety or impropriety of government interference is customarily tested. People decide according to their personal preferences. Some, whenever they see any good to be done, or evil to be remedied, would willingly instigate the government to undertake the business; while others prefer to bear almost any amount of social evil, rather than add one to the departments of human interests amenable to governmental control. And men range themselves on one or the other side in any particular case, according to this general direction of their sentiments; or according to the degree of interest which they feel in the particular thing which it is proposed that the government should do, or according to the belief they entertain that the government would, or would not, do it in the manner they prefer; but very rarely on account of any opinion to which they consistently adhere, as to what things are fit to be done by a government. And it seems to me that in consequence of this absence of rule or principle, one side is at present as often wrong as the other; the interference of government is, with about equal frequency, improperly invoked and improperly condemned.

The object of this Essay is to assert one very simple principle, as entitled to govern absolutely the dealings of society with the individual in the way of compulsion and control, whether the means used be physical force in the form of legal penalties, or the moral coercion of public opinion. That principle is, that the sole end for which mankind are warranted, individually or collectively, in interfering with the liberty of action of any of their number, is self-protection. That the only purpose for which power can be rightfully exercised over any member of a civilized community, against his will, is to prevent harm to others. His own good, either physical or moral, is not a sufficient warrant. He cannot rightfully be compelled to do or forbear because it will be better for him to do so, because it will make him happier, because, in the opinions of others, to do so would be wise, or even right. These are good reasons for remonstrating with him, or reasoning with him, or persuading him, or entreating him, but not for compelling him, or visiting him with any evil in case he do otherwise. To justify that, the conduct from which it is desired to deter him must be calculated to produce evil to some one else. The only part of the conduct of any one, for which he is amenable to society, is that which concerns others. In the part which merely concerns himself, his independence is, of right, absolute. Over himself, over his own body and mind, the individual is sovereign.

It is, perhaps, hardly necessary to say that this doctrine is meant to apply only to human beings in the maturity of their faculties. We are not speaking of children, or of young persons below the age which the law may fix as that of manhood or womanhood. Those who are still in a state to require being taken care of by others, must be protected against their own actions as well as against external injury. For the same reason, we may leave out of consideration those backward states of society in which the race itself may be considered as in its nonage. The early difficulties in the way of spontaneous progress are so great, that there is seldom any choice of means for overcoming them; and a ruler full of the spirit of improvement is warranted in the use of any expedients that will attain an end, perhaps otherwise unattainable. Despotism is a legitimate mode of government in dealing with barbarians, provided the end be their improvement, and the means justified by actually effecting that end. Liberty, as a principle, has no application to any state of things anterior to the time when mankind have become capable of being improved by free and equal discussion. Until then, there is nothing for them but implicit obedience to an Akbar or a Charlemagne, if they are so fortunate as to find one. But as soon as mankind have attained the capacity of being guided to their own improvement by conviction or persuasion (a period long since reached in all nations with whom we need here concern ourselves), compulsion, either in the direct form or in that of pains and penalties for non-compliance, is no longer admissible as a means to their own good, and justifiable only for the security of others.

It is proper to state that I forego any advantage which could be derived to my argument from the idea of abstract right, as a thing independent of utility. I regard utility as the ultimate appeal on all ethical questions; but it must be utility in the largest sense, grounded on the permanent interests of man as a progressive being. Those interests, I contend, authorize the subjection of individual spontaneity to external control, only in respect to those actions of each, which concern the interest of other people. If any one does an act hurtful to others, there is a *primâ facie* case for punishing him, by law, or, where legal penalties are not safely applicable, by general disapprobation. There are also many positive acts for the benefit of others, which he may rightfully be compelled to perform; such as, to give evidence in a court of justice; to bear his fair share in the common defense, or in any other joint work necessary to the interest of the society of which he enjoys the protection; and to perform certain acts of individual beneficence, such as saving a fellow-creature's life, or interposing to protect the defenseless against ill-usage, things which whenever it is obviously a man's duty to do, he may rightfully be made responsible to society for not doing. A person may cause evil to others not only by his actions but by his inaction, and in either case he is justly accountable to them for the injury. The latter case, it is true, requires a much more cautious exercise of compulsion than the former. To make any one answerable for doing evil to others, is the rule; to make him answerable for not preventing evil, is, comparatively speaking, the exception. Yet there are many cases clear enough and grave enough to justify that exception. In all things which regard the external relations of the individual, he is *de jure* amenable to those whose interests are concerned, and if need be, to society as their protector. There are often good reasons for not holding him to the responsibility; but these reasons must arise from the special expediencies of the case: either because it is a kind of case in which he is on the whole likely to act better, when left to his own discretion, than when controlled in any way in which society have it in their power to control him; or because the attempt to exercise control would produce other evils, greater than those which it would prevent. When such reasons as these

preclude the enforcement of responsibility, the conscience of the agent himself should step into the vacant judgment seat, and protect those interests of others which have no exter-
5 nal protection; judging himself all the more rigidly, because the case does not admit of his being made accountable to the judgment of his fellow-creatures.

10 But there is a sphere of action in which socie-ty, as distinguished from the individual, has, if any, only an indirect interest; comprehending all that portion of a person's life and conduct which affects only himself, or if it also affects
15 others, only with their free, voluntary, and undeceived consent and participation. When I say only himself, I mean directly, and in the first instance: for whatever affects himself, may affect others *through* himself; and the ob-
20 jection which may be grounded on this con-tingency, will receive consideration in the se-quel. This, then, is the appropriate region of human liberty. It comprises, first, the inward domain of consciousness; demanding liberty
25 of conscience, in the most comprehensive sense; liberty of thought and feeling; absolute freedom of opinion and sentiment on all sub-jects, practical or speculative, scientific, moral, or theological. The liberty of expressing and
30 publishing opinions may seem to fall under a different principle, since it belongs to that part of the conduct of an individual which con-cerns other people; but, being almost of as much importance as the liberty of thought
35 itself, and resting in great part on the same reasons, is practically inseparable from it. Sec-ondly, the principle requires liberty of tastes and pursuits; of framing the plan of our life to suit our own character; of doing as we like,
40 subject to such consequences as may follow: without impediment from our fellow-creatures, so long as what we do does not harm them, even though they should think our

conduct foolish, perverse, or wrong. Thirdly,
45 from this liberty of each individual, follows the liberty, within the same limits, of combina-tion among individuals; freedom to unite, for any purpose not involving harm to others: the persons combining being supposed to be of
50 full age, and not forced or deceived.

No society in which these liberties are not, on the whole, respected, is free, whatever may be its form of government; and none is complete-
55 ly free in which they do not exist absolute and unqualified. The only freedom which deserves the name, is that of pursuing our own good in our own way, so long as we do not attempt to deprive others of theirs, or impede their ef-
60 forts to obtain it. Each is the proper guardian of his own health, whether bodily, or mental and spiritual. Mankind are greater gainers by suffering each other to live as seems good to themselves, than by compelling each to live as
65 seems good to the rest.

Though this doctrine is anything but new, and, to some persons, may have the air of a truism, there is no doctrine which stands more direct-
70 ly opposed to the general tendency of existing opinion and practice. Society has expended fully as much effort in the attempt (according to its lights) to compel people to conform to its notions of personal, as of social excellence.
75 The ancient commonwealths thought them-selves entitled to practice, and the ancient phi-losophers countenanced, the regulation of every part of private conduct by public author-ity, on the ground that the State had a deep
80 interest in the whole bodily and mental disci-pline of every one of its citizens; a mode of thinking which may have been admissible in small republics surrounded by powerful ene-mies, in constant peril of being subverted by
85 foreign attack or internal commotion, and to which even a short interval of relaxed energy

and self-command might so easily be fatal, that they could not afford to wait for the salutary permanent effects of freedom. In the modern world, the greater size of political

5 communities, and above all, the separation between spiritual and temporal authority (which placed the direction of men's consciences in other hands than those which controlled their worldly affairs), prevented so

10 great an interference by law in the details of private life; but the engines of moral repression have been wielded more strenuously against divergence from the reigning opinion in self-regarding, than even in social matters;

15 religion, the most powerful of the elements which have entered into the formation of moral feeling, having almost always been governed either by the ambition of a hierarchy, seeking control over every department of hu-

20 man conduct, or by the spirit of Puritanism. And some of those modern reformers who have placed themselves in strongest opposition to the religions of the past, have been noway behind either churches or sects in their

25 assertion of the right of spiritual domination: M. Comte, in particular, whose social system, as unfolded in his *Traité de Politique Positive*, aims at establishing (though by moral more than by legal appliances) a despotism of socie-

30 ty over the individual, surpassing anything contemplated in the political ideal of the most rigid disciplinarian among the ancient philosophers...

35 **CHAPTER II**
OF THE LIBERTY OF THOUGHT
AND DISCUSSION

The time, it is to be hoped, is gone by, when

40 any defense would be necessary of the "liberty of the press" as one of the securities against corrupt or tyrannical government. No argument, we may suppose, can now be needed,

against permitting a legislature or an executive,

45 not identified in interest with the people, to prescribe opinions to them, and determine what doctrines or what arguments they shall be allowed to hear. This aspect of the question, besides, has been so often and so trium-

50 phantly enforced by preceding writers, that it need not be specially insisted on in this place. Though the law of England, on the subject of the press, is as servile to this day as it was in the time of the Tudors, there is little danger of

55 its being actually put in force against political discussion, except during some temporary panic, when fear of insurrection drives ministers and judges from their propriety[49]; and,

---

[49] These words had scarcely been written, when, as if to give them an emphatic contradiction, occurred the Government Press Prosecutions of 1858. That ill-judged interference with the liberty of public discussion has not, however, induced me to alter a single word in the text, nor has it at all weakened my conviction that, moments of panic excepted, the era of pains and penalties for political discussion has, in our own country, passed away. For, in the first place, the prosecutions were not persisted in; and, in the second, they were never, properly speaking, political prosecutions. The offence charged was not that of criticizing institutions, or the acts or persons of rulers, but of circulating what was deemed an immoral doctrine, the lawfulness of Tyrannicide.

If the arguments of the present chapter are of any validity, there ought to exist the fullest liberty of professing and discussing, as a matter of ethical conviction, any doctrine, however immoral it may be considered. It would, therefore, be irrelevant and out of place to examine here, whether the doctrine of Tyrannicide deserves that title. I shall content myself with saying, that the subject has been at all times one of the open questions of morals; that the act of a private citizen in striking down a criminal, who, by raising himself above the law, has placed himself beyond the reach of legal punishment or control, has been accounted by whole nations, and by some of the best and wisest of men, not a crime,

speaking generally, it is not, in constitutional countries, to be apprehended that the government, whether completely responsible to the people or not, will often attempt to con-

5 trol the expression of opinion, except when in doing so it makes itself the organ of the general intolerance of the public. Let us suppose, therefore, that the government is entirely at one with the people, and never thinks of ex-

10 erting any power of coercion unless in agreement with what it conceives to be their voice. But I deny the right of the people to exercise such coercion, either by themselves or by their government. The power itself is illegitimate.

15 The best government has no more title to it than the worst. It is as noxious, or more noxious, when exerted in accordance with public opinion, than when in or opposition to it. If all mankind minus one, were of one opinion,

20 and only one person were of the contrary opinion, mankind would be no more justified in silencing that one person, than he, if he had the power, would be justified in silencing mankind. Were an opinion a personal posses-

25 sion of no value except to the owner; if to be obstructed in the enjoyment of it were simply a private injury, it would make some difference whether the injury was inflicted only on a few persons or on many. But the peculiar evil

30 of silencing the expression of an opinion is, that it is robbing the human race; posterity as

---

but an act of exalted virtue; and that, right or wrong, it is not of the nature of assassination, but of civil war. As such, I hold that the instigation to it, in a specific case, may be a proper subject of punishment, but only if an overt act has followed, and at least a probable connection can be established between the act and the instigation. Even then, it is not a foreign government, but the very government assailed, which alone, in the exercise of self-defence, can legitimately punish attacks directed against its own existence.

well as the existing generation; those who dissent from the opinion, still more than those who hold it. If the opinion is right, they are

35 deprived of the opportunity of exchanging error for truth: if wrong, they lose, what is almost as great a benefit, the clearer perception and livelier impression of truth, produced by its collision with error.

40

It is necessary to consider separately these two hypotheses, each of which has a distinct branch of the argument corresponding to it. We can never be sure that the opinion we are

45 endeavoring to stifle is a false opinion; and if we were sure, stifling it would be an evil still.

First: the opinion which it is attempted to suppress by authority may possibly be true.

50 Those who desire to suppress it, of course deny its truth; but they are not infallible. They have no authority to decide the question for all mankind, and exclude every other person from the means of judging. To refuse a hear-

55 ing to an opinion, because they are sure that it is false, is to assume that *their* certainty is the same thing as *absolute* certainty. All silencing of discussion is an assumption of infallibility. Its condemnation may be allowed to rest on this

60 common argument, not the worse for being common.

Unfortunately for the good sense of mankind, the fact of their fallibility is far from carrying

65 the weight in their practical judgment, which is always allowed to it in theory; for while every one well knows himself to be fallible, few think it necessary to take any precautions against their own fallibility, or admit the sup-

70 position that any opinion, of which they feel very certain, may be one of the examples of the error to which they acknowledge themselves to be liable. Absolute princes, or others who are accustomed to unlimited deference,

usually feel this complete confidence in their own opinions on nearly all subjects. People more happily situated, who sometimes hear their opinions disputed, and are not wholly

5 unused to be set right when they are wrong, place the same unbounded reliance only on such of their opinions as are shared by all who surround them, or to whom they habitually defer: for in proportion to a man's want of

10 confidence in his own solitary judgment, does he usually repose, with implicit trust, on the infallibility of "the world" in general. And the world, to each individual, means the part of it with which he comes in contact; his party, his

15 sect, his church, his class of society: the man may be called, by comparison, almost liberal and large-minded to whom it means anything so comprehensive as his own country or his own age. Nor is his faith in this collective au-

20 thority at all shaken by his being aware that other ages, countries, sects, churches, classes, and parties have thought, and even now think, the exact reverse. He devolves upon his own world the responsibility of being in the right

25 against the dissentient worlds of other people; and it never troubles him that mere accident has decided which of these numerous worlds is the object of his reliance, and that the same causes which make him a Churchman in Lon-

30 don, would have made him a Buddhist or a Confucian in Pekin. Yet it is as evident in itself as any amount of argument can make it, that ages are no more infallible than individuals; every age having held many opinions which

35 subsequent ages have deemed not only false but absurd; and it is as certain that many opinions, now general, will be rejected by future ages, as it is that many, once general, are rejected by the present.

40

The objection likely to be made to this argument, would probably take some such form as the following. There is no greater assumption of infallibility in forbidding the propagation of

45 error, than in any other thing which is done by public authority on its own judgment and responsibility. Judgment is given to men that they may use it. Because it may be used erroneously, are men to be told that they ought

50 not to use it at all? To prohibit what they think pernicious, is not claiming exemption from error, but fulfilling the duty incumbent on them, although fallible, of acting on their conscientious conviction. If we were never to act

55 on our opinions, because those opinions may be wrong, we should leave all our interests uncared for, and all our duties unperformed. An objection which applies to all conduct, can be no valid objection to any conduct in partic-

60 ular. It is the duty of governments, and of individuals, to form the truest opinions they can; to form them carefully, and never impose them upon others unless they are quite sure of being right. But when they are sure (such rea-

65 soners may say), it is not conscientiousness but cowardice to shrink from acting on their opinions, and allow doctrines which they honestly think dangerous to the welfare of mankind, either in this life or in another, to be

70 scattered abroad without restraint, because other people, in less enlightened times, have persecuted opinions now believed to be true. Let us take care, it may be said, not to make the same mistake: but governments and na-

75 tions have made mistakes in other things, which are not denied to be fit subjects for the exercise of authority: they have laid on bad taxes, made unjust wars. Ought we therefore to lay on no taxes, and, under whatever prov-

80 ocation, make no wars? Men, and governments, must act to the best of their ability. There is no such thing as absolute certainty, but there is assurance sufficient for the purposes of human life. We may, and must, as-

85 sume our opinion to be true for the guidance of our own conduct: and it is assuming no

more when we forbid bad men to pervert society by the propagation of opinions which we regard as false and pernicious.

5 I answer that it is assuming very much more. There is the greatest difference between presuming an opinion to be true, because, with every opportunity for contesting it, it has not been refuted, and assuming its truth for the
10 purpose of not permitting its refutation. Complete liberty of contradicting and disproving our opinion, is the very condition which justifies us in assuming its truth for purposes of action; and on no other terms can a being
15 with human faculties have any rational assurance of being right.

When we consider either the history of opinion, or the ordinary conduct of human life, to what is it to be ascribed that the one and the
20 other are no worse than they are? Not certainly to the inherent force of the human understanding; for, on any matter not self-evident, there are ninety-nine persons totally incapable of judging of it, for one who is capable; and
25 the capacity of the hundredth person is only comparative; for the majority of the eminent men of every past generation held many opinions now known to be erroneous, and did or approved numerous things which no one will
30 now justify. Why is it, then, that there is on the whole a preponderance among mankind of rational opinions and rational conduct? If there really is this preponderance—which there must be, unless human affairs are, and
35 have always been, in an almost desperate state—it is owing to a quality of the human mind, the source of everything respectable in man either as an intellectual or as a moral being, namely, that his errors are corrigible. He is
40 capable of rectifying his mistakes, by discussion and experience. Not by experience alone. There must be discussion, to show how experience is to be interpreted. Wrong opinions

45 and practices gradually yield to fact and argument: but facts and arguments, to produce any effect on the mind, must be brought before it. Very few facts are able to tell their own story, without comments to bring out their meaning.
50 The whole strength and value, then, of human judgment, depending on the one property, that it can be set right when it is wrong, reliance can be placed on it only when the means of setting it right are kept constantly at hand. In
55 the case of any person whose judgment is really deserving of confidence, how has it become so? Because he has kept his mind open to criticism of his opinions and conduct. Because it has been his practice to listen to all that could be said against him; to profit by as much of it
60 as was just, and expound to himself, and upon occasion to others, the fallacy of what was fallacious. Because he has felt, that the only way in which a human being can make some approach to knowing the whole of a subject, is
65 by hearing what can be said about it by persons of every variety of opinion, and studying all modes in which it can be looked at by every character of mind. No wise man ever acquired his wisdom in any mode but this; nor is it in
70 the nature of human intellect to become wise in any other manner. The steady habit of correcting and completing his own opinion by collating it with those of others, so far from causing doubt and hesitation in carrying it into
75 practice, is the only stable foundation for a just reliance on it: for, being cognizant of all that can, at least obviously, be said against him, and having taken up his position against all gainsayers—knowing that he has sought for
80 objections and difficulties, instead of avoiding them, and has shut out no light which can be thrown upon the subject from any quarter— he has a right to think his judgment better than that of any person, or any multitude, who
85 have not gone through a similar process.

It is not too much to require that what the wisest of mankind, those who are best entitled to trust their own judgment, find necessary to warrant their relying on it, should be submitted to by that miscellaneous collection of a few wise and many foolish individuals, called the public. The most intolerant of churches, the Roman Catholic Church, even at the canonization of a saint, admits, and listens patiently to, a "devil's advocate." The holiest of men, it appears, cannot be admitted to posthumous honors, until all that the devil could say against him is known and weighed. If even the Newtonian philosophy were not permitted to be questioned, mankind could not feel as complete assurance of its truth as they now do. The beliefs which we have most warrant for, have no safeguard to rest on, but a standing invitation to the whole world to prove them unfounded. If the challenge is not accepted, or is accepted and the attempt fails, we are far enough from certainty still; but we have done the best that the existing state of human reason admits of; we have neglected nothing that could give the truth a chance of reaching us: if the lists are kept open, we may hope that if there be a better truth, it will be found when the human mind is capable of receiving it; and in the meantime we may rely on having attained such approach to truth, as is possible in our own day. This is the amount of certainty attainable by a fallible being, and this the sole way of attaining it.

Strange it is, that men should admit the validity of the arguments for free discussion, but object to their being "pushed to an extreme;" not seeing that unless the reasons are good for an extreme case, they are not good for any case. Strange that they should imagine that they are not assuming infallibility, when they acknowledge that there should be free discussion on all subjects which can possibly be *doubtful*, but think that some particular principle or doctrine should be forbidden to be questioned because it is *so certain*, that is, because *they are certain* that it is certain. To call any proposition certain, while there is any one who would deny its certainty if permitted, but who is not permitted, is to assume that we ourselves, and those who agree with us, are the judges of certainty, and judges without hearing the other side.

In the present age—which has been described as "destitute of faith, but terrified at skepticism"—in which people feel sure, not so much that their opinions are true, as that they should not know what to do without them— the claims of an opinion to be protected from public attack are rested not so much on its truth, as on its importance to society. There are, it is alleged, certain beliefs, so useful, not to say indispensable to well-being, that it is as much the duty of governments to uphold those beliefs, as to protect any other of the interests of society. In a case of such necessity, and so directly in the line of their duty, something less than infallibility may, it is maintained, warrant, and even bind, governments, to act on their own opinion, confirmed by the general opinion of mankind. It is also often argued, and still oftener thought, that none but bad men would desire to weaken these salutary beliefs; and there can be nothing wrong, it is thought, in restraining bad men, and prohibiting what only such men would wish to practice. This mode of thinking makes the justification of restraints on discussion not a question of the truth of doctrines, but of their usefulness; and flatters itself by that means to escape the responsibility of claiming to be an infallible judge of opinions. But those who thus satisfy themselves, do not perceive that the assumption of infallibility is merely shifted from one point to another. The usefulness of an opinion is itself matter of opinion: as disputable, as open to discussion, and requiring discussion as much, as the opinion itself. There is the same need of an infallible judge of opinions to decide an opinion to be noxious, as to decide it to be false, unless the opinion condemned has full opportunity of defending itself. And it will not do to say that the heretic may be allowed to maintain the utility or harmlessness of his opinion, though forbidden to maintain its truth. The truth of an opinion is part of its utility. If we would know whether or not it is desirable that a proposition should be believed, is it possible to exclude the consideration of whether or not it is true? In the opinion, not of bad men, but of the best men, no belief which is contrary to truth can be really useful: and can you prevent such men from urging that plea, when they are charged with culpability for denying some doctrine which they are told is useful, but which they believe to be false? Those who are on the side of received opinions, never fail to take all possible advantage of this plea; you do not find *them* handling the question of utility as if it could be completely abstracted from that of truth: on the contrary, it is, above all, because their doctrine is "the truth," that the knowledge or the belief of it is held to be so indispensable. There can be no fair discussion of the question of usefulness, when an argument so vital may be employed on one side, but not on the other. And in point of fact, when law or public feeling do not permit the truth of an opinion to be disputed, they are just as little tolerant of a denial of its usefulness. The utmost they allow is an extenuation of its absolute necessity, or of the positive guilt of rejecting it.

In order more fully to illustrate the mischief of denying a hearing to opinions because we, in our own judgment, have condemned them, it will be desirable to fix down the discussion to a concrete case; and I choose, by preference, the cases which are least favorable to me—in which the argument against freedom of opinion, both on the score of truth and on that of utility, is considered the strongest. Let the opinions impugned be the belief in a God and in a future state, or any of the commonly received doctrines of morality. To fight the battle on such ground, gives a great advantage to an unfair antagonist; since he will be sure to say (and many who have no desire to be unfair will say it internally), Are these the doctrines which you do not deem sufficiently certain to be taken under the protection of law? Is the belief in a God one of the opinions, to feel sure of which, you hold to be assuming infallibility? But I must be permitted to observe, that it is not the feeling sure of a doctrine (be it what it may) which I call an assumption of infallibility. It is the undertaking to decide that question *for others*, without allowing them to hear what can be said on the contrary side. And I denounce and reprobate this pretension not the less, if put forth on the side of my most solemn convictions. However positive any one's persuasion may be, not only of the falsity, but of the pernicious consequences— not only of the pernicious consequences, but (to adopt expressions which I altogether condemn) the immorality and impiety of an opinion; yet if, in pursuance of that private judgment, though backed by the public judgment of his country or his contemporaries, he prevents the opinion from being heard in its defense, he assumes infallibility. And so far from the assumption being less objectionable or less dangerous because the opinion is called immoral or impious, this is the case of all others in which it is most fatal. These are exactly the occasions on which the men of one generation commit those dreadful mistakes, which excite the astonishment and horror of posterity. It is among such that we find the instances memorable in history, when the arm of the law has been employed to root out the best men and the noblest doctrines; with deplorable success as to the men, though some of the doctrines have survived to be (as if in mockery) invoked, in defense of similar conduct towards those who dissent from *them*, or from their received interpretation.

Mankind can hardly be too often reminded that there was once a man named Socrates, between whom and the legal authorities and public opinion of his time, there took place a memorable collision. Born in an age and country abounding in individual greatness, this man has been handed down to us by those who best knew both him and the age, as the most virtuous man in it; while *we* know him as the head and prototype of all subsequent teachers of virtue, the source equally of the lofty inspiration of Plato and the judicious utilitarianism of Aristotle, "*i maëstri di color che sanno*," the two headsprings of ethical as of all other philosophy. This acknowledged master of all the eminent thinkers who have since lived—whose fame, still growing after more than two thousand years, all but outweighs the whole remainder of the names which make his native city illustrious—was put to death by his countrymen, after a judicial conviction, for impiety and immorality. Impiety, in denying the gods recognized by the State; indeed his accuser asserted (see the "Apologia") that he believed in no gods at all. Immorality, in being, by his doctrines and instructions, a "corruptor of youth." Of these charges the tribunal, there is every ground for believing, honestly found him guilty, and condemned the man who probably of all then born had deserved best of mankind, to be put to death as a criminal.

To pass from this to the only other instance of judicial iniquity, the mention of which, after the condemnation of Socrates, would not be an anticlimax: the event which took place on Calvary rather more than eighteen hundred years ago. The man who left on the memory of those who witnessed his life and conversation, such an impression of his moral grandeur, that eighteen subsequent centuries have done homage to him as the Almighty in person, was ignominiously put to death, as what? As a blasphemer. Men did not merely mistake their benefactor; they mistook him for the exact contrary of what he was, and treated him as that prodigy of impiety, which they themselves are now held to be, for their treatment of him. The feelings with which mankind now regard these lamentable transactions, especially the later of the two, render them extremely unjust in their judgment of the unhappy actors. These were, to all appearance, not bad men—not worse than men commonly are, but rather the contrary; men who possessed in a full, or somewhat more than a full measure, the religious, moral, and patriotic feelings of their time and people: the very kind of men who, in all times, our own included, have every chance of passing through life blameless and respected. The high-priest who rent his garments when the words were pronounced, which, according to all the ideas of his country, constituted the blackest guilt, was in all probability quite as sincere in his horror and indignation, as the generality of respectable and pious men now are in the religious and moral sentiments they profess; and most of those who now shudder at his conduct, if they had lived in his time, and been born Jews, would have acted precisely as he did. Orthodox Christians who are tempted to think that those who stoned to death the first martyrs must have been worse men than they themselves are, ought to remember that one of those persecutors was Saint Paul.

Let us add one more example, the most striking of all, if the impressiveness of an error is measured by the wisdom and virtue of him who falls into it. If ever any one, possessed of power, had grounds for thinking himself the best and most enlightened among his cotemporaries, it was the Emperor Marcus Aurelius. Absolute monarch of the whole civilized world, he preserved through life not only the most unblemished justice, but what was less to be expected from his Stoical breeding, the tenderest heart. The few failings which are attributed to him, were all on the side of indulgence: while his writings, the highest ethical product of the ancient mind, differ scarcely perceptibly, if they differ at all, from the most characteristic teachings of Christ. This man, a better Christian in all but the dogmatic sense of the word, than almost any of the ostensibly Christian sovereigns who have since reigned, persecuted Christianity. Placed at the summit of all the previous attainments of humanity, with an open, unfettered intellect, and a character which led him of himself to embody in his moral writings the Christian ideal, he yet failed to see that Christianity was to be a good and not an evil to the world, with his duties to which he was so deeply penetrated. Existing society he knew to be in a deplorable state. But such as it was, he saw, or thought he saw, that it was held together, and prevented from being worse, by belief and reverence of the received divinities. As a ruler of mankind, he deemed it his duty not to suffer society to fall in pieces; and saw not how, if its existing ties were removed, any others could be formed which could again knit it together. The new religion openly aimed at dissolving these ties: unless, therefore, it was his duty to adopt that religion, it seemed to be his duty to put it down. Inasmuch then as the theology of Christianity did not appear to him true or of divine origin; inasmuch as this strange history of a crucified God was not credible to him, and a system which purported to rest entirely upon a foundation to him so wholly unbelievable, could not be foreseen by him to be that renovating agency which, after all abatements, it has in fact proved to be; the gentlest and most amiable of philosophers and rulers, under a solemn sense of duty, authorized the persecution of Christianity. To my mind this is one of the most tragical facts in all history. It is a bitter thought, how different a thing the Christianity of the world might have been, if the Christian faith had been adopted as the religion of the empire under the auspices of Marcus Aurelius instead of those of Constantine. But it would be equally unjust to him and false to truth, to deny, that no one plea which can be urged for punishing anti-Christian teaching, was wanting to Marcus Aurelius for punishing, as he did, the propagation of Christianity. No Christian more firmly believes that Atheism is false, and tends to the dissolution of society, than Marcus Aurelius believed the same things of Christianity; he who, of all men then living, might have been thought the most capable of appreciating it. Unless any one who approves of punishment for the promulgation of opinions, flatters himself that he is a wiser and better man than Marcus Aurelius—more deeply versed in the wisdom of his time, more elevated in his intellect above it—more earnest in his search for truth, or more single-minded in his devotion to it when found;—let him abstain from that assumption of the joint infallibility of himself and the multitude, which the great Antoninus made with so unfortunate a result.

Aware of the impossibility of defending the use of punishment for restraining irreligious opinions, by any argument which will not justify Marcus Antoninus, the enemies of religious freedom, when hard pressed, occasionally accept this consequence, and say, with Dr. Johnson, that the persecutors of Christianity were in the right; that persecution is an ordeal through which truth ought to pass, and always passes successfully, legal penalties being, in the end, powerless against truth, though sometimes beneficially effective against mischievous errors. This is a form of the argument for religious intolerance, sufficiently remarkable not to be passed without notice.

A theory which maintains that truth may justifiably be persecuted because persecution cannot possibly do it any harm, cannot be charged with being intentionally hostile to the reception of new truths; but we cannot commend the generosity of its dealing with the persons to whom mankind are indebted for them. To discover to the world something which deeply concerns it, and of which it was previously ignorant; to prove to it that it had been mistaken on some vital point of temporal or spiritual interest, is as important a service as a human being can render to his fellow-creatures, and in certain cases, as in those of the early Christians and of the Reformers, those who think with Dr. Johnson believe it to have been the most precious gift which could be bestowed on mankind. That the authors of such splendid benefits should be requited by martyrdom; that their reward should be to be dealt with as the vilest of criminals, is not, upon this theory, a deplorable error and misfortune, for which humanity should mourn in sackcloth and ashes, but the normal and justifiable state of things. The propounder of a new truth, according to this doctrine, should stand, as stood, in the legislation of the Locrians, the proposer of a new law, with a halter round his neck, to be instantly tightened if the public assembly did not, on hearing his reasons, then and there adopt his proposition. People who defend this mode of treating ben-

efactors, cannot be supposed to set much value on the benefit; and I believe this view of the subject is mostly confined to the sort of persons who think that new truths may have been desirable once, but that we have had enough of them now.

But, indeed, the dictum that truth always triumphs over persecution, is one of those pleasant falsehoods which men repeat after one another till they pass into commonplaces, but which all experience refutes. History teems with instances of truth put down by persecution. If not suppressed for ever, it may be thrown back for centuries. To speak only of religious opinions: the Reformation broke out at least twenty times before Luther, and was put down. Arnold of Brescia was put down. Fra Dolcino was put down. Savonarola was put down. The Albigeois were put down. The Vaudois were put down. The Lollards were put down. The Hussites were put down. Even after the era of Luther, wherever persecution was persisted in, it was successful. In Spain, Italy, Flanders, the Austrian empire, Protestantism was rooted out; and, most likely, would have been so in England, had Queen Mary lived, or Queen Elizabeth died. Persecution has always succeeded, save where the heretics were too strong a party to be effectually persecuted. No reasonable person can doubt that Christianity might have been extirpated in the Roman Empire. It spread, and became predominant, because the persecutions were only occasional, lasting but a short time, and separated by long intervals of almost undisturbed propagandism. It is a piece of idle sentimentality that truth, merely as truth, has any inherent power denied to error, of prevailing against the dungeon and the stake. Men are not more zealous for truth than they often are for error, and a sufficient application of legal or even of social penalties will generally succeed in stopping the propagation of either. The real advantage which truth has, consists in this, that when an opinion is true, it may be extinguished once, twice, or many times, but

5 in the course of ages there will generally be found persons to rediscover it, until some one of its reappearances falls on a time when from favorable circumstances it escapes persecution until it has made such head as to withstand all

10 subsequent attempts to suppress it.

It will be said, that we do not now put to death the introducers of new opinions: we are not like our fathers who slew the prophets, we

15 even build sepulchers to them. It is true we no longer put heretics to death; and the amount of penal infliction which modern feeling would probably tolerate, even against the most obnoxious opinions, is not sufficient to extir-

20 pate them. But let us not flatter ourselves that we are yet free from the stain even of legal persecution. Penalties for opinion, or at least for its expression, still exist by law; and their enforcement is not, even in these times, so

25 unexampled as to make it at all incredible that they may some day be revived in full force. In the year 1857, at the summer assizes of the county of Cornwall, an unfortunate man[50], said to be of unexceptionable conduct in all

30 relations of life, was sentenced to twenty-one months' imprisonment, for uttering, and writing on a gate, some offensive words concerning Christianity. Within a month of the same time, at the Old Bailey, two persons, on two

35 separate occasions[51], were rejected as jurymen, and one of them grossly insulted by the judge and by one of the counsel, because they honestly declared that they had no theological

belief; and a third, a foreigner[52], for the same

40 reason, was denied justice against a thief. This refusal of redress took place in virtue of the legal doctrine, that no person can be allowed to give evidence in a court of justice, who does not profess belief in a God (any god is

45 sufficient) and in a future state; which is equivalent to declaring such persons to be outlaws, excluded from the protection of the tribunals; who may not only be robbed or assaulted with impunity, if no one but them-

50 selves, or persons of similar opinions, be present, but any one else may be robbed or assaulted with impunity, if the proof of the fact depends on their evidence. The assumption on which this is grounded, is that the oath is

55 worthless, of a person who does not believe in a future state; a proposition which betokens much ignorance of history in those who assent to it (since it is historically true that a large proportion of infidels in all ages have been

60 persons of distinguished integrity and honor); and would be maintained by no one who had the smallest conception how many of the persons in greatest repute with the world, both for virtues and for attainments, are well

65 known, at least to their intimates, to be unbelievers. The rule, besides, is suicidal, and cuts away its own foundation. Under pretense that atheists must be liars, it admits the testimony of all atheists who are willing to lie, and rejects

70 only those who brave the obloquy of publicly confessing a detested creed rather than affirm a falsehood. A rule thus self-convicted of absurdity so far as regards its professed purpose, can be kept in force only as a badge of hatred,

75 a relic of persecution; a persecution, too, having the peculiarity, that the qualification for undergoing it, is the being clearly proved not to deserve it. The rule, and the theory it im-

---

[50] Thomas Pooley, Bodmin Assizes, July 31, 1857. In December following, he received a free pardon from the Crown.
[51] George Jacob Holyoake, August 17, 1857; Edward Truelove, July, 1857.

---

[52] Baron de Gleichen, Marlborough-Street Police Court, August 4, 1857.

plies, are hardly less insulting to believers than to infidels. For if he who does not believe in a future state, necessarily lies, it follows that they who do believe are only prevented from lying, if prevented they are, by the fear of hell. We will not do the authors and abettors of the rule the injury of supposing, that the conception which they have formed of Christian virtue is drawn from their own consciousness.

These, indeed, are but rags and remnants of persecution, and may be thought to be not so much an indication of the wish to persecute, as an example of that very frequent infirmity of English minds, which makes them take a preposterous pleasure in the assertion of a bad principle, when they are no longer bad enough to desire to carry it really into practice. But unhappily there is no security in the state of the public mind, that the suspension of worse forms of legal persecution, which has lasted for about the space of a generation, will continue. In this age the quiet surface of routine is as often ruffled by attempts to resuscitate past evils, as to introduce new benefits. What is boasted of at the present time as the revival of religion, is always, in narrow and uncultivated minds, at least as much the revival of bigotry; and where there is the strong permanent leaven of intolerance in the feelings of a people, which at all times abides in the middle classes of this country, it needs but little to provoke them into actively persecuting those whom they have never ceased to think proper objects of persecution.[53] For it is this—it is the opinions men entertain, and the feelings they cherish, respecting those who disown the beliefs they deem important, which makes this country not a place of mental freedom. For a long time past, the chief mischief of the legal penalties is that they strengthen the social stigma.

It is that stigma which is really effective, and so effective is it that the profession of opinions which are under the ban of society is much less common in England, than is, in many other countries, the avowal of those which incur risk of judicial punishment. In respect to all persons but those whose pecuniary circumstances make them independent of the good will of other people, opinion, on this subject, is as efficacious as law; men might as

---

[53] Ample warning may be drawn from the large infusion of the passions of a persecutor, which mingled with the general display of the worst parts of our national character on the occasion of the Sepoy insurrection. The ravings of fanatics or charlatans from the pulpit may be unworthy of notice; but the heads of the Evangelical party have announced as their principle, for the government of Hindoos and Mahomedans, that no schools be supported by public money in which the Bible is not taught, and by necessary consequence that no public employment be given to any but real or pretended Christians. An Under-Secretary of State, in a speech delivered to his constituents on the 12th of November, 1857, is reported to have said: "Toleration of their faith" (the faith of a hundred millions of British subjects), "the superstition which they called religion, by the British Government, had had the effect of retarding the ascendency of the British name, and preventing the salutary growth of Christianity.... Toleration was the great corner-stone of the religious liberties of this country; but do not let them abuse that precious word toleration. As he understood it, it meant the complete liberty to all, freedom of worship, *among Christians, who worshipped upon the same foundation*. It meant toleration of all sects and denominations of *Christians who believed in the one mediation*." I desire to call attention to the fact, that a man who has been deemed fit to fill a high office in the government of this country, under a liberal Ministry, maintains the doctrine that all who do not believe in the divinity of Christ are beyond the pale of toleration. Who, after this imbecile display, can indulge the illusion that religious persecution has passed away, never to return?

well be imprisoned, as excluded from the means of earning their bread. Those whose bread is already secured, and who desire no favors from men in power, or from bodies of men, or from the public, have nothing to fear from the open avowal of any opinions, but to be ill-thought of and ill-spoken of, and this it ought not to require a very heroic mold to enable them to bear. There is no room for any appeal *ad misericordiam* in behalf of such persons. But though we do not now inflict so much evil on those who think differently from us, as it was formerly our custom to do, it may be that we do ourselves as much evil as ever by our treatment of them. Socrates was put to death, but the Socratic philosophy rose like the sun in heaven, and spread its illumination over the whole intellectual firmament. Christians were cast to the lions, but the Christian church grew up a stately and spreading tree, overtopping the older and less vigorous growths, and stifling them by its shade. Our merely social intolerance kills no one, roots out no opinions, but induces men to disguise them, or to abstain from any active effort for their diffusion. With us, heretical opinions do not perceptibly gain, or even lose, ground in each decade or generation; they never blaze out far and wide, but continue to smolder in the narrow circles of thinking and studious persons among whom they originate, without ever lighting up the general affairs of mankind with either a true or a deceptive light. And thus is kept up a state of things very satisfactory to some minds, because, without the unpleasant process of fining or imprisoning anybody, it maintains all prevailing opinions outwardly undisturbed, while it does not absolutely interdict the exercise of reason by dissentients afflicted with the malady of thought. A convenient plan for having peace in the intellectual world, and keeping all things going on therein very much as they do already. But the price paid for this sort of intellectual pacification, is the sacrifice of the entire moral courage of the human mind. A state of things in which a large portion of the most active and inquiring intellects find it advisable to keep the genuine principles and grounds of their convictions within their own breasts, and attempt, in what they address to the public, to fit as much as they can of their own conclusions to premises which they have internally renounced, cannot send forth the open, fearless characters, and logical, consistent intellects who once adorned the thinking world. The sort of men who can be looked for under it, are either mere conformers to commonplace, or time-servers for truth, whose arguments on all great subjects are meant for their hearers, and are not those which have convinced themselves. Those who avoid this alternative, do so by narrowing their thoughts and interest to things which can be spoken of without venturing within the region of principles, that is, to small practical matters, which would come right of themselves, if but the minds of mankind were strengthened and enlarged, and which will never be made effectually right until then: while that which would strengthen and enlarge men's minds, free and daring speculation on the highest subjects, is abandoned.

Those in whose eyes this reticence on the part of heretics is no evil, should consider in the first place, that in consequence of it there is never any fair and thorough discussion of heretical opinions; and that such of them as could not stand such a discussion, though they may be prevented from spreading, do not disappear. But it is not the minds of heretics that are deteriorated most, by the ban placed on all inquiry which does not end in the orthodox conclusions. The greatest harm done is to those who are not heretics, and whose whole mental development is cramped, and their reason cowed, by the fear of heresy. Who can compute what the world loses in the multitude of promising intellects combined with timid characters, who dare not follow out any bold, vigorous, independent train of thought, lest it should land them in something which would admit of being considered irreligious or immoral? Among them we may occasionally see some man of deep conscientiousness, and subtle and refined understanding, who spends a life in sophisticating with an intellect which he cannot silence, and exhausts the resources of ingenuity in attempting to reconcile the promptings of his conscience and reason with orthodoxy, which yet he does not, perhaps, to the end succeed in doing. No one can be a great thinker who does not recognize, that as a thinker it is his first duty to follow his intellect to whatever conclusions it may lead. Truth gains more even by the errors of one who, with due study and preparation, thinks for himself, than by the true opinions of those who only hold them because they do not suffer themselves to think. Not that it is solely, or chiefly, to form great thinkers, that freedom of thinking is required. On the contrary, it is as much, and even more indispensable, to enable average human beings to attain the mental stature which they are capable of. There have been, and may again be, great individual thinkers, in a general atmosphere of mental slavery. But there never has been, nor ever will be, in that atmosphere, an intellectually active people. Where any people has made a temporary approach to such a character, it has been because the dread of heterodox speculation was for a time suspended. Where there is a tacit convention that principles are not to be disputed; where the discussion of the greatest questions which can occupy humanity is considered to be closed, we cannot hope to find that generally high scale of mental activity which has made some periods of history so remarkable. Never when controversy avoided the subjects which are large and important enough to kindle enthusiasm, was the mind of a people stirred up from its foundations, and the impulse given which raised even persons of the most ordinary intellect to something of the dignity of thinking beings. Of such we have had an example in the condition of Europe during the times immediately following the Reformation; another, though limited to the Continent and to a more cultivated class, in the speculative movement of the latter half of the eighteenth century; and a third, of still briefer duration, in the intellectual fermentation of Germany during the Goethian and Fichtean period. These periods differed widely in the particular opinions which they developed; but were alike in this, that during all three the yoke of authority was broken. In each, an old mental despotism had been thrown off, and no new one had yet taken its place. The impulse given at these three periods has made Europe what it now is. Every single improvement which has taken place either in the human mind or in institutions, may be traced distinctly to one or other of them. Appearances have for some time indicated that all three impulses are well-nigh spent; and we can expect no fresh start, until we again assert our mental freedom.

Let us now pass to the second division of the argument, and dismissing the supposition that any of the received opinions may be false, let us assume them to be true, and examine into the worth of the manner in which they are likely to be held, when their truth is not freely and openly canvassed. However unwillingly a person who has a strong opinion may admit the possibility that his opinion may be false, he ought to be moved by the consideration that however true it may be, if it is not fully, frequently, and fearlessly discussed, it will be held as a dead dogma, not a living truth.

There is a class of persons (happily not quite so numerous as formerly) who think it enough if a person assents undoubtingly to what they think true, though he has no knowledge whatever of the grounds of the opinion, and could not make a tenable defense of it against the most superficial objections. Such persons, if they can once get their creed taught from authority, naturally think that no good, and some harm, comes of its being allowed to be questioned. Where their influence prevails, they make it nearly impossible for the received opinion to be rejected wisely and considerately, though it may still be rejected rashly and ignorantly; for to shut out discussion entirely is seldom possible, and when it once gets in, beliefs not grounded on conviction are apt to give way before the slightest semblance of an argument. Waiving, however, this possibility—assuming that the true opinion abides in the mind, but abides as a prejudice, a belief independent of, and proof against, argument—this is not the way in which truth ought to be held by a rational being. This is not knowing the truth. Truth, thus held, is but one superstition the more, accidentally clinging to the words which enunciate a truth.

If the intellect and judgment of mankind ought to be cultivated, a thing which Protestants at least do not deny, on what can these faculties be more appropriately exercised by any one, than on the things which concern him so much that it is considered necessary for him to hold opinions on them? If the cultivation of the understanding consists in one thing more than in another, it is surely in learning the grounds of one's own opinions. Whatever people believe, on subjects on which it is of the first importance to believe rightly, they ought to be able to defend against at least the common objections. But, some one may say, "Let them be *taught* the grounds of their opinions. It does not follow that opinions must be merely parroted because they are never heard controverted. Persons who learn geometry do not simply commit the theorems to memory, but understand and learn likewise the demonstrations; and it would be absurd to say that they remain ignorant of the grounds of geometrical truths, because they never hear any one deny, and attempt to disprove them." Undoubtedly: and such teaching suffices on a subject like mathematics, where there is nothing at all to be said on the wrong side of the question. The peculiarity of the evidence of mathematical truths is, that all the argument is on one side. There are no objections, and no answers to objections. But on every subject on which difference of opinion is possible, the truth depends on a balance to be struck between two sets of conflicting reasons. Even in natural philosophy, there is always some other explanation possible of the same facts; some geocentric theory instead of heliocentric, some phlogiston instead of oxygen; and it has to be shown why that other theory cannot be the true one: and until this is shown, and until we know how it is shown, we do not understand the grounds of our opinion. But when we turn to subjects infinitely more complicated, to morals, religion, politics, social relations, and the business of life, three-fourths of the arguments for every disputed opinion consist in dispelling the appearances which favor some opinion different from it. The greatest orator, save one, of antiquity, has left it on record that he always studied his adversary's case with as great, if not with still greater, intensity than even his own. What Cicero practiced as the means of forensic success, requires to be imitated by all who study any subject in order to arrive at the truth. He who knows only his own side of the case, knows little of that. His reasons may be good, and no one may have been able to refute them. But if he is equally unable to refute the reasons on the opposite side; if he does not so much as know what they are, he has no ground for preferring either opinion. The rational position for him would be suspension of judgment, and unless he contents himself with that, he is either led by authority, or adopts, like the generality of the world, the side to which he feels most inclination. Nor is it enough that he should hear the arguments of adversaries from his own teachers, presented as they state them, and accompanied by what they offer as refutations. That is not the way to do justice to the arguments, or bring them into real contact with his own mind. He must be able to hear them from persons who actually believe them; who defend them in earnest, and do their very utmost for them. He must know them in their most plausible and persuasive form; he must feel the whole force of the difficulty which the true view of the subject has to encounter and dispose of; else he will never really possess himself of the portion of truth which meets and removes that difficulty. Ninety-nine in a hundred of what are called educated men are in this condition; even of those who can argue fluently for their opinions. Their conclusion may be true, but it might be false for anything they know: they have never thrown themselves into the mental position of those who think differently from them, and considered what such persons may have to say; and consequently they do not, in any proper sense of the word, know the doctrine which they themselves profess. They do not know those parts of it which explain and justify the remainder; the considerations which show that a fact which seemingly conflicts with another is reconcilable with it, or that, of two apparently strong reasons, one and not the other ought to be preferred. All that part of the truth which turns the scale, and decides the judgment of a completely informed mind, they are strangers to; nor is it ever really known, but to those who have attended equally and impartially to both sides, and endeavored to see the reasons of both in the strongest light. So essential is this discipline to a real understanding of moral and human subjects, that if opponents of all important truths do not exist, it is indispensable to imagine them, and supply them with the strongest arguments which the most skillful devil's advocate can conjure up.

To abate the force of these considerations, an enemy of free discussion may be supposed to say, that there is no necessity for mankind in general to know and understand all that can be said against or for their opinions by philosophers and theologians. That it is not needful for common men to be able to expose all the misstatements or fallacies of an ingenious opponent. That it is enough if there is always somebody capable of answering them, so that nothing likely to mislead uninstructed persons remains unrefuted. That simple minds, having been taught the obvious grounds of the truths inculcated on them, may trust to authority for the rest, and being aware that they have neither knowledge nor talent to resolve every difficulty which can be raised, may repose in the assurance that all those which have been raised have been or can be answered, by those who are specially trained to the task.

Conceding to this view of the subject the utmost that can be claimed for it by those most easily satisfied with the amount of understanding of truth which ought to accompany the belief of it; even so, the argument for free discussion is no way weakened. For even this doctrine acknowledges that mankind ought to have a rational assurance that all objections have been satisfactorily answered; and how are they to be answered if that which requires to be answered is not spoken? or how can the answer be known to be satisfactory, if the objectors have no opportunity of showing that it is unsatisfactory? If not the public, at least the philosophers and theologians who are to resolve the difficulties, must make themselves familiar with those difficulties in their most puzzling form; and this cannot be accomplished unless they are freely stated, and placed in the most advantageous light which they admit of. The Catholic Church has its own way of dealing with this embarrassing problem. It makes a broad separation between those who can be permitted to receive its doctrines on conviction, and those who must accept them on trust. Neither, indeed, are allowed any choice as to what they will accept; but the clergy, such at least as can be fully confided in, may admissibly and meritoriously make themselves acquainted with the arguments of opponents, in order to answer them, and may, therefore, read heretical books; the laity, not unless by special permission, hard to be obtained. This discipline recognizes a knowledge of the enemy's case as beneficial to the teachers, but finds means, consistent with this, of denying it to the rest of the world: thus giving to the *élite* more mental culture, though not more mental freedom, than it allows to the mass. By this device it succeeds in obtaining the kind of mental superiority which its purposes require; for though culture without freedom never made a large and liberal mind, it can make a clever *nisi prius* advocate of a cause. But in countries professing Protestantism, this resource is denied; since Protestants hold, at least in theory, that the responsibility for the choice of a religion must be borne by each for himself, and cannot be thrown off upon teachers. Besides, in the present state of the world, it is practically impossible that writings which are read by the instructed can be kept from the uninstructed. If the teachers of mankind are to be cognizant of all that they ought to know, everything must be free to be written and published without restraint.

If, however, the mischievous operation of the absence of free discussion, when the received opinions are true, were confined to leaving men ignorant of the grounds of those opinions, it might be thought that this, if an intellectual, is no moral evil, and does not affect the worth of the opinions, regarded in their influence on the character. The fact, however, is, that not only the grounds of the opinion are forgotten in the absence of discussion, but too often the meaning of the opinion itself. The words which convey it, cease to suggest ideas, or suggest only a small portion of those they were originally employed to communicate. Instead of a vivid conception and a living belief, there remain only a few phrases retained by rote; or, if any part, the shell and husk only of the meaning is retained, the finer essence being lost. The great chapter in human history which this fact occupies and fills, cannot be too earnestly studied and meditated on.

It is illustrated in the experience of almost all ethical doctrines and religious creeds. They are all full of meaning and vitality to those who originate them, and to the direct disciples of the originators. Their meaning continues to be felt in undiminished strength, and is perhaps brought out into even fuller consciousness, so long as the struggle lasts to give the doctrine or creed an ascendency over other creeds. At last it either prevails, and becomes the general opinion, or its progress stops; it keeps possession of the ground it has gained, but ceases to spread further. When either of these results has become apparent, controversy on the subject flags, and gradually dies away. The doctrine has taken its place, if not as a received opinion, as one of the admitted sects or divisions of opinion: those who hold it have generally inherited, not adopted it; and conversion from one of these doctrines to another, being now an exceptional fact, occupies little place in the thoughts of their professors. Instead of being, as at first, constantly on the alert either to defend themselves against the world, or to bring the world over to them, they have subsided into acquiescence, and neither listen, when they can help it, to arguments against their creed, nor trouble dissentients (if there be such) with arguments in its favor. From this time may usually be dated the decline in the living power of the doctrine. We often hear the teachers of all creeds lamenting the difficulty of keeping up in the minds of believers a lively apprehension of the truth which they nominally recognize, so that it may penetrate the feelings, and acquire a real mastery over the conduct. No such difficulty is complained of while the creed is still fighting for its existence: even the weaker combatants then know and feel what they are fighting for, and the difference between it and other doctrines; and in that period of every creed's existence, not a few persons may be found, who have realized its fundamental principles in all the forms of thought, have weighed and considered them in all their important bearings, and have experienced the full effect on the character, which belief in that creed ought to produce in a mind thoroughly imbued with it. But when it has come to be a hereditary creed, and to be received passively, not actively—when the mind is no longer compelled, in the same degree as at first, to exercise its vital powers on the questions which its belief presents to it, there is a progressive tendency to forget all of the belief except the formularies, or to give it a dull and torpid assent, as if accepting it on trust dispensed with the necessity of realizing it in consciousness, or testing it by personal experience; until it almost ceases to connect itself at all with the inner life of the human being. Then are seen the cases, so frequent in this age of the world as almost to form the majority, in which the creed remains as it were outside the mind, encrusting and petrifying it against all other influences addressed to the higher parts of our nature; manifesting its power by not suffering any fresh and living conviction to get in, but itself doing nothing for the mind or heart, except standing sentinel over them to keep them vacant.

To what an extent doctrines intrinsically fitted to make the deepest impression upon the mind may remain in it as dead beliefs, without being ever realized in the imagination, the feelings, or the understanding, is exemplified by the manner in which the majority of believers hold the doctrines of Christianity. By Christianity I here mean what is accounted such by all churches and sects—the maxims and precepts contained in the New Testament. These are considered sacred, and accepted as laws, by all professing Christians. Yet it is scarcely too much to say that not one Christian in a thousand guides or tests his individual conduct by reference to those laws. The standard to which he does refer it, is the custom of his nation, his class, or his religious profession. He has thus, on the one hand, a collection of ethical maxims, which he believes to have been vouchsafed to him by infallible wisdom as rules for his government; and on the other, a set of every-day judgments and practices, which go a certain length with some of those maxims, not so great a length with others, stand in direct opposition to some, and are, on the whole, a compromise between the Christian creed and the interests and suggestions of worldly life. To the first of these standards he gives his homage; to the other his real allegiance. All Christians believe that the blessed

are the poor and humble, and those who are ill-used by the world; that it is easier for a camel to pass through the eye of a needle than for a rich man to enter the kingdom of heav-
5 en; that they should judge not, lest they be judged; that they should swear not at all; that they should love their neighbor as themselves; that if one take their cloak, they should give him their coat also; that they should take no
10 thought for the morrow; that if they would be perfect, they should sell all that they have and give it to the poor. They are not insincere when they say that they believe these things. They do believe them, as people believe what
15 they have always heard lauded and never dis-cussed. But in the sense of that living belief which regulates conduct, they believe these doctrines just up to the point to which it is usual to act upon them. The doctrines in their
20 integrity are serviceable to pelt adversaries with; and it is understood that they are to be put forward (when possible) as the reasons for whatever people do that they think laudable. But any one who reminded them that the
25 maxims require an infinity of things which they never even think of doing, would gain nothing but to be classed among those very unpopular characters who affect to be better than other people. The doctrines have no hold
30 on ordinary believers—are not a power in their minds. They have a habitual respect for the sound of them, but no feeling which spreads from the words to the things signified, and forces the mind to take *them* in, and make
35 them conform to the formula. Whenever con-duct is concerned, they look round for Mr. A and B to direct them how far to go in obeying Christ.

40 Now we may be well assured that the case was not thus, but far otherwise, with the early Christians. Had it been thus, Christianity never would have expanded from an obscure sect of the despised Hebrews into the religion of the
45 Roman empire. When their enemies said, "See how these Christians love one another" (a remark not likely to be made by anybody now), they assuredly had a much livelier feel-ing of the meaning of their creed than they
50 have ever had since. And to this cause, proba-bly, it is chiefly owing that Christianity now makes so little progress in extending its do-main, and after eighteen centuries, is still near-ly confined to Europeans and the descendants
55 of Europeans. Even with the strictly religious, who are much in earnest about their doctrines, and attach a greater amount of meaning to many of them than people in general, it com-monly happens that the part which is thus
60 comparatively active in their minds is that which was made by Calvin, or Knox, or some such person much nearer in character to themselves. The sayings of Christ coexist pas-sively in their minds, producing hardly any
65 effect beyond what is caused by mere listening to words so amiable and bland. There are many reasons, doubtless, why doctrines which are the badge of a sect retain more of their vitality than those common to all recognized
70 sects, and why more pains are taken by teach-ers to keep their meaning alive; but one reason certainly is, that the peculiar doctrines are more questioned, and have to be oftener de-fended against open gainsayers. Both teachers
75 and learners go to sleep at their post, as soon as there is no enemy in the field.

The same thing holds true, generally speaking, of all traditional doctrines—those of prudence
80 and knowledge of life, as well as of morals or religion. All languages and literatures are full of general observations on life, both as to what it is, and how to conduct oneself in it; observations which everybody knows, which
85 everybody repeats, or hears with acquiescence, which are received as truisms, yet of which

most people first truly learn the meaning, when experience, generally of a painful kind, has made it a reality to them. How often, when smarting under some unforeseen mis-
5 fortune or disappointment, does a person call to mind some proverb or common saying, familiar to him all his life, the meaning of which, if he had ever before felt it as he does now, would have saved him from the calamity.
10 There are indeed reasons for this, other than the absence of discussion: there are many truths of which the full meaning *cannot* be realized, until personal experience has brought it home. But much more of the meaning even of
15 these would have been understood, and what was understood would have been far more deeply impressed on the mind, if the man had been accustomed to hear it argued *pro* and *con* by people who did understand it. The fatal
20 tendency of mankind to leave off thinking about a thing when it is no longer doubtful, is the cause of half their errors. A contemporary author has well spoken of "the deep slumber of a decided opinion."
25
But what! (it may be asked) Is the absence of unanimity an indispensable condition of true knowledge? Is it necessary that some part of mankind should persist in error, to enable any
30 to realize the truth? Does a belief cease to be real and vital as soon as it is generally received—and is a proposition never thoroughly understood and felt unless some doubt of it remains? As soon as mankind have unani-
35 mously accepted a truth, does the truth perish within them? The highest aim and best result of improved intelligence, it has hitherto been thought, is to unite mankind more and more in the acknowledgment of all important truths:
40 and does the intelligence only last as long as it has not achieved its object? Do the fruits of conquest perish by the very completeness of the victory?

I affirm no such thing. As mankind improve,
45 the number of doctrines which are no longer disputed or doubted will be constantly on the increase: and the well-being of mankind may almost be measured by the number and gravity of the truths which have reached the point of
50 being uncontested. The cessation, on one question after another, of serious controversy, is one of the necessary incidents of the consolidation of opinion; a consolidation as salutary in the case of true opinions, as it is dangerous
55 and noxious when the opinions are erroneous. But though this gradual narrowing of the bounds of diversity of opinion is necessary in both senses of the term, being at once inevitable and indispensable, we are not therefore
60 obliged to conclude that all its consequences must be beneficial. The loss of so important an aid to the intelligent and living apprehension of a truth, as is afforded by the necessity of explaining it to, or defending it against, op-
65 ponents, though not sufficient to outweigh, is no trifling drawback from, the benefit of its universal recognition. Where this advantage can no longer be had, I confess I should like to see the teachers of mankind endeavoring to
70 provide a substitute for it; some contrivance for making the difficulties of the question as present to the learner's consciousness, as if they were pressed upon him by a dissentient champion, eager for his conversion.
75
But instead of seeking contrivances for this purpose, they have lost those they formerly had. The Socratic dialectics, so magnificently exemplified in the dialogues of Plato, were a
80 contrivance of this description. They were essentially a negative discussion of the great questions of philosophy and life, directed with consummate skill to the purpose of convincing any one who had merely adopted the
85 commonplaces of received opinion, that he did not understand the subject—that he as yet

attached no definite meaning to the doctrines he professed; in order that, becoming aware of his ignorance, he might be put in the way to attain a stable belief, resting on a clear appre-

5 hension both of the meaning of doctrines and of their evidence. The school disputations of the middle ages had a somewhat similar object. They were intended to make sure that the pupil understood his own opinion, and (by

10 necessary correlation) the opinion opposed to it, and could enforce the grounds of the one and confute those of the other. These last-mentioned contests had indeed the incurable defect, that the premises appealed to were

15 taken from authority, not from reason; and, as a discipline to the mind, they were in every respect inferior to the powerful dialectics which formed the intellects of the "Socratici viri": but the modern mind owes far more to

20 both than it is generally willing to admit, and the present modes of education contain nothing which in the smallest degree supplies the place either of the one or of the other. A person who derives all his instruction from teach-

25 ers or books, even if he escape the besetting temptation of contenting himself with cram, is under no compulsion to hear both sides; accordingly it is far from a frequent accomplishment, even among thinkers, to know both

30 sides; and the weakest part of what everybody says in defense of his opinion, is what he intends as a reply to antagonists. It is the fashion of the present time to disparage negative logic—that which points out weaknesses in theo-

35 ry or errors in practice, without establishing positive truths. Such negative criticism would indeed be poor enough as an ultimate result; but as a means to attaining any positive knowledge or conviction worthy the name, it

40 cannot be valued too highly; and until people are again systematically trained to it, there will be few great thinkers, and a low general average of intellect, in any but the mathematical

and physical departments of speculation. On
45 any other subject no one's opinions deserve the name of knowledge, except so far as he has either had forced upon him by others, or gone through of himself, the same mental process which would have been required of
50 him in carrying on an active controversy with opponents. That, therefore, which when absent, it is so indispensable, but so difficult, to create, how worse than absurd is it to forego, when spontaneously offering itself! If there are
55 any persons who contest a received opinion, or who will do so if law or opinion will let them, let us thank them for it, open our minds to listen to them, and rejoice that there is some one to do for us what we otherwise
60 ought, if we have any regard for either the certainty or the vitality of our convictions, to do with much greater labor for ourselves.

It still remains to speak of one of the principal
65 causes which make diversity of opinion advantageous, and will continue to do so until mankind shall have entered a stage of intellectual advancement which at present seems at an incalculable distance. We have hitherto con-
70 sidered only two possibilities: that the received opinion may be false, and some other opinion, consequently, true; or that, the received opinion being true, a conflict with the opposite error is essential to a clear apprehension and
75 deep feeling of its truth. But there is a commoner case than either of these; when the conflicting doctrines, instead of being one true and the other false, share the truth between them; and the nonconforming opinion is
80 needed to supply the remainder of the truth, of which the received doctrine embodies only a part. Popular opinions, on subjects not palpable to sense, are often true, but seldom or never the whole truth. They are a part of the
85 truth; sometimes a greater, sometimes a smaller part, but exaggerated, distorted, and dis-

joined from the truths by which they ought to be accompanied and limited. Heretical opinions, on the other hand, are generally some of these suppressed and neglected truths, bursting the bonds which kept them down, and either seeking reconciliation with the truth contained in the common opinion, or fronting it as enemies, and setting themselves up, with similar exclusiveness, as the whole truth. The latter case is hitherto the most frequent, as, in the human mind, one-sidedness has always been the rule, and many-sidedness the exception. Hence, even in revolutions of opinion, one part of the truth usually sets while another rises. Even progress, which ought to superadd, for the most part only substitutes one partial and incomplete truth for another; improvement consisting chiefly in this, that the new fragment of truth is more wanted, more adapted to the needs of the time, than that which it displaces. Such being the partial character of prevailing opinions, even when resting on a true foundation; every opinion which embodies somewhat of the portion of truth which the common opinion omits, ought to be considered precious, with whatever amount of error and confusion that truth may be blended. No sober judge of human affairs will feel bound to be indignant because those who force on our notice truths which we should otherwise have overlooked, overlook some of those which we see. Rather, he will think that so long as popular truth is one-sided, it is more desirable than otherwise that unpopular truth should have one-sided asserters too; such being usually the most energetic, and the most likely to compel reluctant attention to the fragment of wisdom which they proclaim as if it were the whole.

Thus, in the eighteenth century, when nearly all the instructed, and all those of the uninstructed who were led by them, were lost in admiration of what is called civilization, and of the marvels of modern science, literature, and philosophy, and while greatly overrating the amount of unlikeness between the men of modern and those of ancient times, indulged the belief that the whole of the difference was in their own favor; with what a salutary shock did the paradoxes of Rousseau explode like bombshells in the midst, dislocating the compact mass of one-sided opinion, and forcing its elements to recombine in a better form and with additional ingredients. Not that the current opinions were on the whole farther from the truth than Rousseau's were; on the contrary, they were nearer to it; they contained more of positive truth, and very much less of error. Nevertheless there lay in Rousseau's doctrine, and has floated down the stream of opinion along with it, a considerable amount of exactly those truths which the popular opinion wanted; and these are the deposit which was left behind when the flood subsided. The superior worth of simplicity of life, the enervating and demoralizing effect of the trammels and hypocrisies of artificial society, are ideas which have never been entirely absent from cultivated minds since Rousseau wrote; and they will in time produce their due effect, though at present needing to be asserted as much as ever, and to be asserted by deeds, for words, on this subject, have nearly exhausted their power.

In politics, again, it is almost a commonplace, that a party of order or stability, and a party of progress or reform, are both necessary elements of a healthy state of political life; until the one or the other shall have so enlarged its mental grasp as to be a party equally of order and of progress, knowing and distinguishing what is fit to be preserved from what ought to be swept away. Each of these modes of thinking derives its utility from the deficiencies of the other; but it is in a great measure the opposition of the other that keeps each within the limits of reason and sanity. Unless opinions favorable to democracy and to aristocracy, to property and to equality, to co-operation and to competition, to luxury and to abstinence, to sociality and individuality, to liberty and discipline, and all the other standing antagonisms of practical life, are expressed with equal freedom, and enforced and defended with equal talent and energy, there is no chance of both elements obtaining their due; one scale is sure to go up and the other down. Truth, in the great practical concerns of life, is so much a question of the reconciling and combining of opposites, that very few have minds sufficiently capacious and impartial to make the adjustment with an approach to correctness, and it has to be made by the rough process of a struggle between combatants fighting under hostile banners. On any of the great open questions just enumerated, if either of the two opinions has a better claim than the other, not merely to be tolerated, but to be encouraged and countenanced, it is the one which happens at the particular time and place to be in a minority. That is the opinion which, for the time being, represents the neglected interests, the side of human well-being which is in danger of obtaining less than its share. I am aware that there is not, in this country, any intolerance of differences of opinion on most of these topics. They are adduced to show, by admitted and multiplied examples, the universality of the fact, that only through diversity of opinion is there, in the existing state of human intellect, a chance of fair-play to all sides of the truth. When there are persons to be found, who form an exception to the apparent unanimity of the world on any subject, even if the world is in the right, it is always probable that dissentients have something worth hearing to say for themselves, and that truth would lose something by their silence...

We have now recognized the necessity to the mental well-being of mankind (on which all their other well-being depends) of freedom of opinion, and freedom of the expression of opinion, on four distinct grounds; which we will now briefly recapitulate.

First, if any opinion is compelled to silence, that opinion may, for aught we can certainly know, be true. To deny this is to assume our own infallibility. Secondly, though the silenced opinion be an error, it may, and very commonly does, contain a portion of truth; and since the general or prevailing opinion on any subject is rarely or never the whole truth, it is only by the collision of adverse opinions, that the remainder of the truth has any chance of being supplied.

Thirdly, even if the received opinion be not only true, but the whole truth; unless it is suffered to be, and actually is, vigorously and earnestly contested, it will, by most of those who receive it, be held in the manner of a prejudice, with little comprehension or feeling of its rational grounds. And not only this, but, fourthly, the meaning of the doctrine itself will be in danger of being lost, or enfeebled, and deprived of its vital effect on the character and conduct: the dogma becoming a mere formal profession, inefficacious for good, but cumbering the ground, and preventing the growth of any real and heartfelt conviction, from reason or personal experience.

Before quitting the subject of freedom of opinion, it is fit to take some notice of those who say, that the free expression of all opinions should be permitted, on condition that the manner be temperate, and do not pass the bounds of fair discussion. Much might be said

on the impossibility of fixing where these supposed bounds are to be placed; for if the test
be offence to those whose opinion is attacked,
I think experience testifies that this offence is
given whenever the attack is telling and powerful, and that every opponent who pushes
them hard, and whom they find it difficult to
answer, appears to them, if he shows any
strong feeling on the subject, an intemperate
opponent. But this, though an important consideration in a practical point of view, merges
in a more fundamental objection. Undoubtedly the manner of asserting an opinion, even
though it be a true one, may be very objectionable, and may justly incur severe censure.
But the principal offences of the kind are such
as it is mostly impossible, unless by accidental
self-betrayal, to bring home to conviction. The
gravest of them is, to argue sophistically, to
suppress facts or arguments, to misstate the
elements of the case, or misrepresent the opposite opinion. But all this, even to the most
aggravated degree, is so continually done in
perfect good faith, by persons who are not
considered, and in many other respects may
not deserve to be considered, ignorant or in-
competent, that it is rarely possible on adequate grounds conscientiously to stamp the
misrepresentation as morally culpable; and still
less could law presume to interfere with this
kind of controversial misconduct. With regard
to what is commonly meant by intemperate
discussion, namely invective, sarcasm, personality, and the like, the denunciation of these
weapons would deserve more sympathy if it
were ever proposed to interdict them equally
to both sides; but it is only desired to restrain
the employment of them against the prevailing
opinion: against the unprevailing they may not
only be used without general disapproval, but
will be likely to obtain for him who uses them
the praise of honest zeal and righteous indignation. Yet whatever mischief arises from
their use, is greatest when they are employed
against the comparatively defenseless; and
whatever unfair advantage can be derived by
any opinion from this mode of asserting it,
accrues almost exclusively to received opinions. The worst offence of this kind which can
be committed by a polemic, is to stigmatize
those who hold the contrary opinion as bad
and immoral men. To calumny of this sort,
those who hold any unpopular opinion are
peculiarly exposed, because they are in general
few and uninfluential, and nobody but themselves feel much interest in seeing justice done
them; but this weapon is, from the nature of
the case, denied to those who attack a prevailing opinion: they can neither use it with safety
to themselves, nor, if they could, would it do
anything but recoil on their own cause. In
general, opinions contrary to those commonly
received can only obtain a hearing by studied
moderation of language, and the most cautious avoidance of unnecessary offence, from
which they hardly ever deviate even in a slight
degree without losing ground: while unmeas-
ured vituperation employed on the side of the
prevailing opinion, really does deter people
from professing contrary opinions, and from
listening to those who profess them. For the
interest, therefore, of truth and justice, it is far
more important to restrain this employment
of vituperative language than the other; and,
for example, if it were necessary to choose,
there would be much more need to discourage
offensive attacks on infidelity, than on religion. It is, however, obvious that law and authority have no business with restraining either, while opinion ought, in every instance, to
determine its verdict by the circumstances of
the individual case; condemning every one, on
whichever side of the argument he places himself, in whose mode of advocacy either want
of candor, or malignity, bigotry, or intolerance
of feeling manifest themselves; but not infer-

ring these vices from the side which a person takes, though it be the contrary side of the question to our own: and giving merited honor to every one, whatever opinion he may hold, who has calmness to see and honesty to state what his opponents and their opinions really are, exaggerating nothing to their discredit, keeping nothing back which tells, or can be supposed to tell, in their favor. This is the real morality of public discussion; and if often violated, I am happy to think that there are many controversialists who to a great extent observe it, and a still greater number who conscientiously strive towards it.

CHAPTER III
OF INDIVIDUALITY, AS ONE OF
THE ELEMENTS OF WELL-BEING

Such being the reasons which make it imperative that human beings should be free to form opinions, and to express their opinions without reserve; and such the baneful consequences to the intellectual, and through that to the moral nature of man, unless this liberty is either conceded, or asserted in spite of prohibition; let us next examine whether the same reasons do not require that men should be free to act upon their opinions—to carry these out in their lives, without hindrance, either physical or moral, from their fellow-men, so long as it is at their own risk and peril. This last proviso is of course indispensable. No one pretends that actions should be as free as opinions. On the contrary, even opinions lose their immunity, when the circumstances in which they are expressed are such as to constitute their expression a positive instigation to some mischievous act. An opinion that corn-dealers are starvers of the poor, or that private property is robbery, ought to be unmolested when simply circulated through the press, but may justly incur punishment when delivered orally to an excited mob assembled before the house of a corn-dealer, or when handed about among the same mob in the form of a placard. Acts, of whatever kind, which, without justifiable cause, do harm to others, may be, and in the more important cases absolutely require to be, controlled by the unfavorable sentiments, and, when needful, by the active interference of mankind. The liberty of the individual must be thus far limited; he must not make himself a nuisance to other people. But if he refrains from molesting others in what concerns them, and merely acts according to his own inclination and judgment in things which concern himself, the same reasons which show that opinion should be free, prove also that he should be allowed, without molestation, to carry his opinions into practice at his own cost. That mankind are not infallible; that their truths, for the most part, are only half-truths; that unity of opinion, unless resulting from the fullest and freest comparison of opposite opinions, is not desirable, and diversity not an evil, but a good, until mankind are much more capable than at present of recognizing all sides of the truth, are principles applicable to men's modes of action, not less than to their opinions. As it is useful that while mankind are imperfect there should be different opinions, so is it that there should be different experiments of living; that free scope should be given to varieties of character, short of injury to others; and that the worth of different modes of life should be proved practically, when any one thinks fit to try them. It is desirable, in short, that in things which do not primarily concern others, individuality should assert itself. Where, not the person's own character, but the traditions or customs of other people are the rule of conduct, there is wanting one of the principal ingredients of human happiness, and quite the chief ingredient of individual and social progress.

In maintaining this principle, the greatest difficulty to be encountered does not lie in the appreciation of means towards an acknowledged end, but in the indifference of persons in general to the end itself. If it were felt that the free development of individuality is one of the leading essentials of well-being; that it is not only a co-ordinate element with all that is designated by the terms civilization, instruction, education, culture, but is itself a necessary part and condition of all those things; there would be no danger that liberty should be under-valued, and the adjustment of the boundaries between it and social control would present no extraordinary difficulty. But the evil is, that individual spontaneity is hardly recognized by the common modes of thinking, as having any intrinsic worth, or deserving any regard on its own account. The majority, being satisfied with the ways of mankind as they now are (for it is they who make them what they are), cannot comprehend why those ways should not be good enough for everybody; and what is more, spontaneity forms no part of the ideal of the majority of moral and social reformers, but is rather looked on with jealousy, as a troublesome and perhaps rebellious obstruction to the general acceptance of what these reformers, in their own judgment, think would be best for mankind. Few persons, out of Germany, even comprehend the meaning of the doctrine which Wilhelm von Humboldt, so eminent both as a *savant* and as a politician, made the text of a treatise—that "the end of man, or that which is prescribed by the eternal or immutable dictates of reason, and not suggested by vague and transient desires, is the highest and most harmonious development of his powers to a complete and consistent whole;" that, therefore, the object "towards which every human being must ceaselessly direct his efforts, and on which especially those who design to influence their fellow-men must ever keep their eyes, is the individuality of power and development;" that for this there are two requisites, "freedom, and a variety of situations;" and that from the union of these arise "individual vigor and manifold diversity," which combine themselves in "originality."[54]

Little, however, as people are accustomed to a doctrine like that of Von Humboldt, and surprising as it may be to them to find so high a value attached to individuality, the question, one must nevertheless think, can only be one of degree. No one's idea of excellence in conduct is that people should do absolutely nothing but copy one another. No one would assert that people ought not to put into their mode of life, and into the conduct of their concerns, any impress whatever of their own judgment, or of their own individual character. On the other hand, it would be absurd to pretend that people ought to live as if nothing whatever had been known in the world before they came into it; as if experience had as yet done nothing towards showing that one mode of existence, or of conduct, is preferable to another. Nobody denies that people should be so taught and trained in youth, as to know and benefit by the ascertained results of human experience. But it is the privilege and proper condition of a human being, arrived at the maturity of his faculties, to use and interpret experience in his own way. It is for him to find out what part of recorded experience is properly applicable to his own circumstances and character. The traditions and customs of other people are, to a certain extent, evidence of what their experience has taught *them*; presumptive evidence, and as such, have a claim

---

[54] *The Sphere and Duties of Government*, from the German of Baron Wilhelm von Humboldt, pp. 11-13.

to his deference: but, in the first place, their experience may be too narrow; or they may not have interpreted it rightly. Secondly, their interpretation of experience may be correct,

5 but unsuitable to him. Customs are made for customary circumstances, and customary characters: and his circumstances or his character may be uncustomary. Thirdly, though the customs be both good as customs, and suitable to

10 him, yet to conform to custom, merely *as* custom, does not educate or develop in him any of the qualities which are the distinctive endowment of a human being. The human faculties of perception, judgment, discriminative

15 feeling, mental activity, and even moral preference, are exercised only in making a choice. He who does anything because it is the custom, makes no choice. He gains no practice either in discerning or in desiring what is best.

20 The mental and moral, like the muscular powers, are improved only by being used. The faculties are called into no exercise by doing a thing merely because others do it, no more than by believing a thing only because others

25 believe it. If the grounds of an opinion are not conclusive to the person's own reason, his reason cannot be strengthened, but is likely to be weakened by his adopting it: and if the inducements to an act are not such as are con-

30 sentaneous to his own feelings and character (where affection, or the rights of others, are not concerned), it is so much done towards rendering his feelings and character inert and torpid, instead of active and energetic.

35

He who lets the world, or his own portion of it, choose his plan of life for him, has no need of any other faculty than the ape-like one of imitation. He who chooses his plan for him-

40 self, employs all his faculties. He must use observation to see, reasoning and judgment to foresee, activity to gather materials for decision, discrimination to decide, and when he

has decided, firmness and self-control to hold

45 to his deliberate decision. And these qualities he requires and exercises exactly in proportion as the part of his conduct which he determines according to his own judgment and feelings is a large one. It is possible that he might be

50 guided in some good path, and kept out of harm's way, without any of these things. But what will be his comparative worth as a human being? It really is of importance, not only what men do, but also what manner of men

55 they are that do it. Among the works of man, which human life is rightly employed in perfecting and beautifying, the first in importance surely is man himself. Supposing it were possible to get houses built, corn grown, battles

60 fought, causes tried, and even churches erected and prayers said, by machinery—by automatons in human form—it would be a considerable loss to exchange for these automatons even the men and women who at present in-

65 habit the more civilized parts of the world, and who assuredly are but starved specimens of what nature can and will produce. Human nature is not a machine to be built after a model, and set to do exactly the work pre-

70 scribed for it, but a tree, which requires to grow and develop itself on all sides, according to the tendency of the inward forces which make it a living thing.

75 It will probably be conceded that it is desirable people should exercise their understandings, and that an intelligent following of custom, or even occasionally an intelligent deviation from custom, is better than a blind and simply me-

80 chanical adhesion to it. To a certain extent it is admitted, that our understanding should be our own: but there is not the same willingness to admit that our desires and impulses should be our own likewise; or that to possess im-

85 pulses of our own, and of any strength, is anything but a peril and a snare. Yet desires and

impulses are as much a part of a perfect human being, as beliefs and restraints: and strong impulses are only perilous when not properly balanced; when one set of aims and inclinations is developed into strength, while others, which ought to co-exist with them, remain weak and inactive. It is not because men's desires are strong that they act ill; it is because their consciences are weak. There is no natural connection between strong impulses and a weak conscience. The natural connection is the other way. To say that one person's desires and feelings are stronger and more various than those of another, is merely to say that he has more of the raw material of human nature, and is therefore capable, perhaps of more evil, but certainly of more good. Strong impulses are but another name for energy. Energy may be turned to bad uses; but more good may always be made of an energetic nature, than of an indolent and impassive one. Those who have most natural feeling, are always those whose cultivated feelings may be made the strongest. The same strong susceptibilities which make the personal impulses vivid and powerful, are also the source from whence are generated the most passionate love of virtue, and the sternest self-control. It is through the cultivation of these, that society both does its duty and protects its interests: not by rejecting the stuff of which heroes are made, because it knows not how to make them. A person whose desires and impulses are his own—are the expression of his own nature, as it has been developed and modified by his own culture—is said to have a character. One whose desires and impulses are not his own, has no character, no more than a steam-engine has a character. If, in addition to being his own, his impulses are strong, and are under the government of a strong will, he has an energetic character. Whoever thinks that individuality of desires and impulses should not be encouraged to unfold itself, must maintain that society has no need of strong natures—is not the better for containing many persons who have much character—and that a high general average of energy is not desirable.

In some early states of society, these forces might be, and were, too much ahead of the power which society then possessed of disciplining and controlling them. There has been a time when the element of spontaneity and individuality was in excess, and the social principle had a hard struggle with it. The difficulty then was, to induce men of strong bodies or minds to pay obedience to any rules which required them to control their impulses. To overcome this difficulty, law and discipline, like the Popes struggling against the Emperors, asserted a power over the whole man, claiming to control all his life in order to control his character—which society had not found any other sufficient means of binding. But society has now fairly got the better of individuality; and the danger which threatens human nature is not the excess, but the deficiency, of personal impulses and preferences. Things are vastly changed, since the passions of those who were strong by station or by personal endowments were in a state of habitual rebellion against laws and ordinances, and required to be rigorously chained up to enable the persons within their reach to enjoy any particle of security. In our times, from the highest class of society down to the lowest, every one lives as under the eye of a hostile and dreaded censorship. Not only in what concerns others, but in what concerns only themselves, the individual, or the family, do not ask themselves—what do I prefer? or, what would suit my character and disposition? or, what would allow the best and highest in me to have fair-play, and enable it to grow and thrive? They ask themselves, what is suitable to my position? what is usually done by persons of my station and pecuniary circumstances? or (worse still) what is usually done by persons of a station and circumstances superior to mine? I do not mean that they choose what is customary, in preference to what suits their own inclination. It does not occur to them to have any inclination, except for what is customary. Thus the mind itself is bowed to the yoke: even in what people do for pleasure, conformity is the first thing thought of; they like in crowds; they exercise choice only among things commonly done: peculiarity of taste, eccentricity of conduct, are shunned equally with crimes: until by dint of not following their own nature, they have no nature to follow: their human capacities are withered and starved: they become incapable of any strong wishes or native pleasures, and are generally without either opinions or feelings of home growth, or properly their own. Now is this, or is it not, the desirable condition of human nature?

It is so, on the Calvinistic theory. According to that, the one great offence of man is Self-will. All the good of which humanity is capable, is comprised in Obedience. You have no choice; thus you must do, and no otherwise: "whatever is not a duty, is a sin." Human nature being radically corrupt, there is no redemption for any one until human nature is killed within him. To one holding this theory of life, crushing out any of the human faculties, capacities, and susceptibilities, is no evil: man needs no capacity, but that of surrendering himself to the will of God: and if he uses any of his faculties for any other purpose but to do that supposed will more effectually, he is better without them. That is the theory of Calvinism; and it is held, in a mitigated form, by many who do not consider themselves Calvinists; the mitigation consisting in giving a less ascetic interpretation to the alleged will of God; asserting it to be his will that mankind should gratify some of their inclinations; of course not in the manner they themselves prefer, but in the way of obedience, that is, in a way prescribed to them by authority; and, therefore, by the necessary conditions of the case, the same for all.

In some such insidious form there is at present a strong tendency to this narrow theory of life, and to the pinched and hidebound type of human character which it patronizes. Many persons, no doubt, sincerely think that human beings thus cramped and dwarfed, are as their Maker designed them to be; just as many have thought that trees are a much finer thing when clipped into pollards, or cut out into figures of animals, than as nature made them. But if it be any part of religion to believe that man was made by a good being, it is more consistent with that faith to believe, that this Being gave all human faculties that they might be cultivated and unfolded, not rooted out and consumed, and that he takes delight in every nearer approach made by his creatures to the ideal conception embodied in them, every increase in any of their capabilities of comprehension, of action, or of enjoyment. There is a different type of human excellence from the Calvinistic; a conception of humanity as having its nature bestowed on it for other purposes than merely to be abnegated. "Pagan self-assertion" is one of the elements of human worth, as well as "Christian self-denial."[55][12] There is a Greek ideal of self-development, which the Platonic and Christian ideal of self-government blends with, but does not supersede. It may be better to be a John Knox than an Alcibiades, but it is better to be a Pericles than either; nor would a Pericles, if we had one in these days, be without anything good which belonged to John

---

[55] Sterling's *Essays.*

Knox.

It is not by wearing down into uniformity all that is individual in themselves, but by culti-
5 vating it and calling it forth, within the limits imposed by the rights and interests of others, that human beings become a noble and beautiful object of contemplation; and as the works partake the character of those who do them,
10 by the same process human life also becomes rich, diversified, and animating, furnishing more abundant aliment to high thoughts and elevating feelings, and strengthening the tie which binds every individual to the race, by
15 making the race infinitely better worth belonging to. In proportion to the development of his individuality, each person becomes more valuable to himself, and is therefore capable of being more valuable to others. There is a
20 greater fullness of life about his own existence, and when there is more life in the units there is more in the mass which is composed of them. As much compression as is necessary to prevent the stronger specimens of human na-
25 ture from encroaching on the rights of others, cannot be dispensed with; but for this there is ample compensation even in the point of view of human development. The means of development which the individual loses by being
30 prevented from gratifying his inclinations to the injury of others, are chiefly obtained at the expense of the development of other people. And even to himself there is a full equivalent in the better development of the social part of
35 his nature, rendered possible by the restraint put upon the selfish part. To be held to rigid rules of justice for the sake of others, develops the feelings and capacities which have the good of others for their object. But to be re-
40 strained in things not affecting their good, by their mere displeasure, develops nothing valuable, except such force of character as may unfold itself in resisting the restraint. If acqui-

esced in, it dulls and blunts the whole nature.
45 To give any fair-play to the nature of each, it is essential that different persons should be allowed to lead different lives. In proportion as this latitude has been exercised in any age, has that age been noteworthy to posterity. Even
50 despotism does not produce its worst effects, so long as Individuality exists under it; and whatever crushes individuality is despotism, by whatever name it may be called, and whether it professes to be enforcing the will of God or
55 the injunctions of men.

Having said that Individuality is the same thing with development, and that it is only the cultivation of individuality which produces, or
60 can produce, well-developed human beings, I might here close the argument: for what more or better can be said of any condition of human affairs, than that it brings human beings themselves nearer to the best thing they can
65 be? or what worse can be said of any obstruction to good, than that it prevents this? Doubtless, however, these considerations will not suffice to convince those who most need convincing; and it is necessary further to
70 show, that these developed human beings are of some use to the undeveloped—to point out to those who do not desire liberty, and would not avail themselves of it, that they may be in some intelligible manner rewarded for allow-
75 ing other people to make use of it without hindrance.

In the first place, then, I would suggest that they might possibly learn something from
80 them. It will not be denied by anybody, that originality is a valuable element in human affairs. There is always need of persons not only to discover new truths, and point out when what were once truths are true no longer, but
85 also to commence new practices, and set the example of more enlightened conduct, and

better taste and sense in human life. This cannot well be gainsaid by anybody who does not believe that the world has already attained perfection in all its ways and practices. It is true that this benefit is not capable of being rendered by everybody alike: there are but few persons, in comparison with the whole of mankind, whose experiments, if adopted by others, would be likely to be any improvement on established practice. But these few are the salt of the earth; without them, human life would become a stagnant pool. Not only is it they who introduce good things which did not before exist; it is they who keep the life in those which already existed. If there were nothing new to be done, would human intellect cease to be necessary? Would it be a reason why those who do the old things should forget why they are done, and do them like cattle, not like human beings? There is only too great a tendency in the best beliefs and practices to degenerate into the mechanical; and unless there were a succession of persons whose ever-recurring originality prevents the grounds of those beliefs and practices from becoming merely traditional, such dead matter would not resist the smallest shock from anything really alive, and there would be no reason why civilization should not die out, as in the Byzantine Empire. Persons of genius, it is true, are, and are always likely to be, a small minority; but in order to have them, it is necessary to preserve the soil in which they grow. Genius can only breathe freely in an *atmosphere* of freedom. Persons of genius are, *ex vi termini*, *more* individual than any other people—less capable, consequently, of fitting themselves, without hurtful compression, into any of the small number of molds which society provides in order to save its members the trouble of forming their own character. If from timidity they consent to be forced into one of these molds, and to let all that part of themselves which cannot expand under the pressure remain unexpanded, society will be little the better for their genius. If they are of a strong character, and break their fetters, they become a mark for the society which has not succeeded in reducing them to commonplace, to point at with solemn warning as "wild," "erratic," and the like; much as if one should complain of the Niagara river for not flowing smoothly between its banks like a Dutch canal.

I insist thus emphatically on the importance of genius, and the necessity of allowing it to unfold itself freely both in thought and in practice, being well aware that no one will deny the position in theory, but knowing also that almost every one, in reality, is totally indifferent to it. People think genius a fine thing if it enables a man to write an exciting poem, or paint a picture. But in its true sense, that of originality in thought and action, though no one says that it is not a thing to be admired, nearly all, at heart, think that they can do very well without it. Unhappily this is too natural to be wondered at. Originality is the one thing which unoriginal minds cannot feel the use of. They cannot see what it is to do for them: how should they? If they could see what it would do for them, it would not be originality. The first service which originality has to render them, is that of opening their eyes: which being once fully done, they would have a chance of being themselves original. Meanwhile, recollecting that nothing was ever yet done which some one was not the first to do, and that all good things which exist are the fruits of originality, let them be modest enough to believe that there is something still left for it to accomplish, and assure themselves that they are more in need of originality, the less they are conscious of the want.

In sober truth, whatever homage may be pro-

fessed, or even paid, to real or supposed mental superiority, the general tendency of things throughout the world is to render mediocrity the ascendant power among mankind. In an-
5 cient history, in the middle ages, and in a diminishing degree through the long transition from feudality to the present time, the individual was a power in himself; and if he had either great talents or a high social position, he
10 was a considerable power. At present individuals are lost in the crowd. In politics it is almost a triviality to say that public opinion now rules the world. The only power deserving the name is that of masses, and of governments
15 while they make themselves the organ of the tendencies and instincts of masses. This is as true in the moral and social relations of private life as in public transactions. Those whose opinions go by the name of public opinion,
20 are not always the same sort of public: in America they are the whole white population; in England, chiefly the middle class. But they are always a mass, that is to say, collective mediocrity. And what is a still greater novelty, the
25 mass do not now take their opinions from dignitaries in Church or State, from ostensible leaders, or from books. Their thinking is done for them by men much like themselves, addressing them or speaking in their name, on
30 the spur of the moment, through the newspapers. I am not complaining of all this. I do not assert that anything better is compatible, as a general rule, with the present low state of the human mind. But that does not hinder the
35 government of mediocrity from being mediocre government. No government by a democracy or a numerous aristocracy, either in its political acts or in the opinions, qualities, and tone of mind which it fosters, ever did or
40 could rise above mediocrity, except in so far as the sovereign Many have let themselves be guided (which in their best times they always have done) by the counsels and influence of a

more highly gifted and instructed One or Few.
45 The initiation of all wise or noble things, comes and must come from individuals; generally at first from some one individual. The honor and glory of the average man is that he is capable of following that initiative; that he
50 can respond internally to wise and noble things, and be led to them with his eyes open. I am not countenancing the sort of "hero-worship" which applauds the strong man of genius for forcibly seizing on the government
55 of the world and making it do his bidding in spite of itself. All he can claim is, freedom to point out the way. The power of compelling others into it, is not only inconsistent with the freedom and development of all the rest, but
60 corrupting to the strong man himself. It does seem, however, that when the opinions of masses of merely average men are everywhere become or becoming the dominant power, the counterpoise and corrective to that tendency
65 would be, the more and more pronounced individuality of those who stand on the higher eminences of thought. It is in these circumstances most especially, that exceptional individuals, instead of being deterred, should be
70 encouraged in acting differently from the mass. In other times there was no advantage in their doing so, unless they acted not only differently, but better. In this age the mere example of nonconformity, the mere refusal to
75 bend the knee to custom, is itself a service. Precisely because the tyranny of opinion is such as to make eccentricity a reproach, it is desirable, in order to break through that tyranny, that people should be eccentric. Eccen-
80 tricity has always abounded when and where strength of character has abounded; and the amount of eccentricity in a society has generally been proportional to the amount of genius, mental vigor, and moral courage which it con-
85 tained. That so few now dare to be eccentric, marks the chief danger of the time.

I have said that it is important to give the freest scope possible to uncustomary things, in order that it may in time appear which of these are fit to be converted into customs. But independence of action, and disregard of custom are not solely deserving of encouragement for the chance they afford that better modes of action, and customs more worthy of general adoption, may be struck out; nor is it only persons of decided mental superiority who have a just claim to carry on their lives in their own way. There is no reason that all human existences should be constructed on some one, or some small number of patterns. If a person possesses any tolerable amount of common-sense and experience, his own mode of laying out his existence is the best, not because it is the best in itself, but because it is his own mode. Human beings are not like sheep; and even sheep are not undistinguishably alike. A man cannot get a coat or a pair of boots to fit him, unless they are either made to his measure, or he has a whole warehouseful to choose from: and is it easier to fit him with a life than with a coat, or are human beings more like one another in their whole physical and spiritual conformation than in the shape of their feet? If it were only that people have diversities of taste, that is reason enough for not attempting to shape them all after one model. But different persons also require different conditions for their spiritual development; and can no more exist healthily in the same moral, than all the variety of plants can in the same physical, atmosphere and climate. The same things which are helps to one person towards the cultivation of his higher nature, are hindrances to another. The same mode of life is a healthy excitement to one, keeping all his faculties of action and enjoyment in their best order, while to another it is a distracting burthen, which suspends or crushes all internal life. Such are the differences among human beings in their sources of pleasure, their susceptibilities of pain, and the operation on them of different physical and moral agencies, that unless there is a corresponding diversity in their modes of life, they neither obtain their fair share of happiness, nor grow up to the mental, moral, and aesthetic stature of which their nature is capable. Why then should tolerance, as far as the public sentiment is concerned, extend only to tastes and modes of life which extort acquiescence by the multitude of their adherents? Nowhere (except in some monastic institutions) is diversity of taste entirely unrecognized; a person may, without blame, either like or dislike rowing, or smoking, or music, or athletic exercises, or chess, or cards, or study, because both those who like each of these things, and those who dislike them, are too numerous to be put down. But the man, and still more the woman, who can be accused either of doing "what nobody does," or of not doing "what everybody does," is the subject of as much depreciatory remark as if he or she had committed some grave moral delinquency. Persons require to possess a title, or some other badge of rank, or of the consideration of people of rank, to be able to indulge somewhat in the luxury of doing as they like without detriment to their estimation. To indulge somewhat, I repeat: for whoever allow themselves much of that indulgence, incur the risk of something worse than disparaging speeches—they are in peril of a commission *de lunatico*, and of having their property taken from them and given to their relations.[56]

---

[56] There is something both contemptible and frightful in the sort of evidence on which, of late years, any person can be judicially declared unfit for the management of his affairs; and after his death, his disposal of his property can be set aside, if there is enough of it to pay the expenses of litigation—which are charged on the property

There is one characteristic of the present direction of public opinion, peculiarly calculated to make it intolerant of any marked demonstration of individuality. The general average of mankind are not only moderate in intellect, but also moderate in inclinations: they have no tastes or wishes strong enough to incline them to do anything unusual, and they consequently do not understand those who have, and class all such with the wild and intemperate whom they are accustomed to look down upon. Now, in addition to this fact which is general, we have only to suppose that a strong movement has set in towards the improvement of morals, and it is evident what we have to expect. In these days such a movement has set in; much has actually been effected in the way of increased regularity of conduct, and discouragement of excesses; and there is a philanthropic spirit abroad, for the exercise of which there is no more inviting field than the moral and prudential improvement of our fellow-creatures. These tendencies of the times cause the public to be more disposed than at most former periods to prescribe general rules of conduct, and endeavor to make every one conform to the approved standard. And that standard, express or tacit, is to desire nothing strongly. Its ideal of character is to be without any marked character; to maim by compression, like a Chinese lady's foot, every part of human nature which stands out prominently, and tends to make the person markedly dissimilar in outline to commonplace humanity. As is usually the case with ideals which exclude one-half of what is desirable, the present standard of approbation produces only an inferior imitation of the other half. Instead of great energies guided by vigorous reason, and strong feelings strongly controlled by a conscientious will, its result is weak feelings and weak energies, which therefore can be kept in outward conformity to rule without any strength either of will or of reason. Already energetic characters on any large scale are becoming merely traditional. There is now scarcely any outlet for energy in this country except business. The energy expended in that may still be regarded as considerable. What little is left from that employment, is expended on some hobby; which may be a useful, even a philanthropic hobby, but is always some one thing, and generally a thing of small dimensions. The greatness of England is now all collective: individually small, we only appear capable of anything great by our habit of combining; and with this our moral and religious philanthropists are perfectly contented. But it was men of another stamp than this that made England what it has been; and men of

---

itself. All the minute details of his daily life are pried into, and whatever is found which, seen through the medium of the perceiving and describing faculties of the lowest of the low, bears an appearance unlike absolute commonplace, is laid before the jury as evidence of insanity, and often with success; the jurors being little, if at all, less vulgar and ignorant than the witnesses; while the judges, with that extraordinary want of knowledge of human nature and life which continually astonishes us in English lawyers, often help to mislead them. These trials speak volumes as to the state of feeling and opinion among the vulgar with regard to human liberty. So far from setting any value on individuality—so far from respecting the rights of each individual to act, in things indifferent, as seems good to his own judgment and inclinations, judges and juries cannot even conceive that a person in a state of sanity can desire such freedom. In former days, when it was proposed to burn atheists, charitable people used to suggest putting them in a madhouse instead: it would be nothing surprising nowadays were we to see this done, and the doers applauding themselves, because, instead of persecuting for religion, they had adopted so humane and Christian a mode of treating these unfortunates, not without a silent satisfaction at their having thereby obtained their deserts.

another stamp will be needed to prevent its decline.

The despotism of custom is everywhere the standing hindrance to human advancement, being in unceasing antagonism to that disposition to aim at something better than customary, which is called, according to circumstances, the spirit of liberty, or that of progress or improvement. The spirit of improvement is not always a spirit of liberty, for it may aim at forcing improvements on an unwilling people; and the spirit of liberty, in so far as it resists such attempts, may ally itself locally and temporarily with the opponents of improvement; but the only unfailing and permanent source of improvement is liberty, since by it there are as many possible independent centers of improvement as there are individuals. The progressive principle, however, in either shape, whether as the love of liberty or of improvement, is antagonistic to the sway of Custom, involving at least emancipation from that yoke; and the contest between the two constitutes the chief interest of the history of mankind. The greater part of the world has, properly speaking, no history, because the despotism of Custom is complete. This is the case over the whole East. Custom is there, in all things, the final appeal; justice and right mean conformity to custom; the argument of custom no one, unless some tyrant intoxicated with power, thinks of resisting. And we see the result. Those nations must once have had originality; they did not start out of the ground populous, lettered, and versed in many of the arts of life; they made themselves all this, and were then the greatest and most powerful nations in the world. What are they now? The subjects or dependents of tribes whose forefathers wandered in the forests when theirs had magnificent palaces and gorgeous temples, but over whom custom exercised only a divided rule with liberty and progress. A people, it appears, may be progressive for a certain length of time, and then stop: when does it stop? When it ceases to possess individuality. If a similar change should befall the nations of Europe, it will not be in exactly the same shape: the despotism of custom with which these nations are threatened is not precisely stationariness. It proscribes singularity, but it does not preclude change, provided all change together. We have discarded the fixed costumes of our forefathers; every one must still dress like other people, but the fashion may change once or twice a year. We thus take care that when there is change, it shall be for change's sake, and not from any idea of beauty or convenience; for the same idea of beauty or convenience would not strike all the world at the same moment, and be simultaneously thrown aside by all at another moment. But we are progressive as well as changeable: we continually make new inventions in mechanical things, and keep them until they are again superseded by better; we are eager for improvement in politics, in education, even in morals, though in this last our idea of improvement chiefly consists in persuading or forcing other people to be as good as ourselves. It is not progress that we object to; on the contrary, we flatter ourselves that we are the most progressive people who ever lived. It is individuality that we war against: we should think we had done wonders if we had made ourselves all alike; forgetting that the unlikeness of one person to another is generally the first thing which draws the attention of either to the imperfection of his own type, and the superiority of another, or the possibility, by combining the advantages of both, of producing something better than either. We have a warning example in China—a nation of much talent, and, in some respects, even wisdom, owing to the rare good fortune of having been

provided at an early period with a particularly good set of customs, the work, in some measure, of men to whom even the most enlightened European must accord, under certain
5 limitations, the title of sages and philosophers. They are remarkable, too, in the excellence of their apparatus for impressing, as far as possible, the best wisdom they possess upon every mind in the community, and securing that
10 those who have appropriated most of it shall occupy the posts of honor and power. Surely the people who did this have discovered the secret of human progressiveness, and must have kept themselves steadily at the head of
15 the movement of the world. On the contrary, they have become stationary—have remained so for thousands of years; and if they are ever to be farther improved, it must be by foreigners. They have succeeded beyond all hope in
20 what English philanthropists are so industriously working at—in making a people all alike, all governing their thoughts and conduct by the same maxims and rules; and these are the fruits. The modern *régime* of public opinion is,
25 in an unorganized form, what the Chinese educational and political systems are in an organized; and unless individuality shall be able successfully to assert itself against this yoke, Europe, notwithstanding its noble ante-
30 cedents and its professed Christianity, will tend to become another China.

What is it that has hitherto preserved Europe from this lot? What has made the European
35 family of nations an improving, instead of a stationary portion of mankind? Not any superior excellence in them, which, when it exists, exists as the effect, not as the cause; but their remarkable diversity of character and culture.
40 Individuals, classes, nations, have been extremely unlike one another: they have struck out a great variety of paths, each leading to something valuable; and although at every

period those who travelled in different paths
45 have been intolerant of one another, and each would have thought it an excellent thing if all the rest could have been compelled to travel his road, their attempts to thwart each other's development have rarely had any permanent
50 success, and each has in time endured to receive the good which the others have offered. Europe is, in my judgment, wholly indebted to this plurality of paths for its progressive and many-sided development. But it already begins
55 to possess this benefit in a considerably less degree. It is decidedly advancing towards the Chinese ideal of making all people alike. M. de Tocqueville, in his last important work, remarks how much more the Frenchmen of the
60 present day resemble one another, than did those even of the last generation. The same remark might be made of Englishmen in a far greater degree. In a passage already quoted from Wilhelm von Humboldt, he points out
65 two things as necessary conditions of human development, because necessary to render people unlike one another; namely, freedom, and variety of situations. The second of these two conditions is in this country every day
70 diminishing. The circumstances which surround different classes and individuals, and shape their characters, are daily becoming more assimilated. Formerly, different ranks, different neighborhoods, different trades and
75 professions, lived in what might be called different worlds; at present, to a great degree in the same. Comparatively speaking, they now read the same things, listen to the same things, see the same things, go to the same places,
80 have their hopes and fears directed to the same objects, have the same rights and liberties, and the same means of asserting them. Great as are the differences of position which remain, they are nothing to those which have
85 ceased. And the assimilation is still proceeding. All the political changes of the age promote it,

since they all tend to raise the low and to lower the high. Every extension of education promotes it, because education brings people under common influences, and gives them access to the general stock of facts and sentiments. Improvements in the means of communication promote it, by bringing the inhabitants of distant places into personal contact, and keeping up a rapid flow of changes of residence between one place and another. The increase of commerce and manufactures promotes it, by diffusing more widely the advantages of easy circumstances, and opening all objects of ambition, even the highest, to general competition, whereby the desire of rising becomes no longer the character of a particular class, but of all classes. A more powerful agency than even all these, in bringing about a general similarity among mankind, is the complete establishment, in this and other free countries, of the ascendency of public opinion in the State. As the various social eminences which enabled persons entrenched on them to disregard the opinion of the multitude, gradually become leveled; as the very idea of resisting the will of the public, when it is positively known that they have a will, disappears more and more from the minds of practical politicians; there ceases to be any social support for non-conformity—any substantive power in society, which, itself opposed to the ascendency of numbers, is interested in taking under its protection opinions and tendencies at variance with those of the public.

The combination of all these causes forms so great a mass of influences hostile to Individuality, that it is not easy to see how it can stand its ground. It will do so with increasing difficulty, unless the intelligent part of the public can be made to feel its value—to see that it is good there should be differences, even though not for the better, even though, as it may appear to them, some should be for the worse. If the claims of Individuality are ever to be asserted, the time is now, while much is still wanting to complete the enforced assimilation. It is only in the earlier stages that any stand can be successfully made against the encroachment. The demand that all other people shall resemble ourselves, grows by what it feeds on. If resistance waits till life is reduced *nearly* to one uniform type, all deviations from that type will come to be considered impious, immoral, even monstrous and contrary to nature. Mankind speedily become unable to conceive diversity, when they have been for some time unaccustomed to see it.

CHAPTER IV
OF THE LIMITS TO THE AUTHORITY OF SOCIETY OVER THE INDIVIDUAL

What, then, is the rightful limit to the sovereignty of the individual over himself? Where does the authority of society begin? How much of human life should be assigned to individuality, and how much to society?

Each will receive its proper share, if each has that which more particularly concerns it. To individuality should belong the part of life in which it is chiefly the individual that is interested; to society, the part which chiefly interests society.

Though society is not founded on a contract, and though no good purpose is answered by inventing a contract in order to deduce social obligations from it, every one who receives the protection of society owes a return for the benefit, and the fact of living in society renders it indispensable that each should be bound to observe a certain line of conduct towards the rest. This conduct consists, first, in not injuring the interests of one another; or rather certain interests which, either by express legal provision or by tacit understanding, ought to be considered as rights; and secondly, in each person's bearing his share (to be fixed on some equitable principle) of the labors and sacrifices incurred for defending the society or its members from injury and molestation.

These conditions society is justified in enforcing, at all costs to those who endeavor to withhold fulfillment. Nor is this all that society may do. The acts of an individual may be hurtful to others, or wanting in due consideration for their welfare, without going the length of violating any of their constituted rights. The offender may then be justly punished by opinion though not by law. As soon as any part of a person's conduct affects prejudicially the interests of others, society has jurisdiction over it, and the question whether the general welfare will or will not be promoted by interfering with it, becomes open to discussion. But there is no room for entertaining any such question when a person's conduct affects the interests of no persons besides himself, or needs not affect them unless they like (all the persons concerned being of full age, and the ordinary amount of understanding). In all such cases there should be perfect freedom, legal and social, to do the action and stand the consequences.

It would be a great misunderstanding of this doctrine, to suppose that it is one of selfish indifference, which pretends that human beings have no business with each other's conduct in life, and that they should not concern themselves about the well-doing or well-being of one another, unless their own interest is involved. Instead of any diminution, there is need of a great increase of disinterested exertion to promote the good of others. But disinterested benevolence can find other instruments to persuade people to their good, than whips and scourges, either of the literal or the metaphorical sort. I am the last person to undervalue the self-regarding virtues; they are only second in importance, if even second, to the social. It is equally the business of education to cultivate both. But even education works by conviction and persuasion as well as by compulsion, and it is by the former only that, when the period of education is past, the self-regarding virtues should be inculcated. Human beings owe to each other help to distinguish the better from the worse, and encouragement to choose the former and avoid the latter. They should be for ever stimulating each other to increased exercise of their higher faculties, and increased direction of their feelings and aims towards wise instead of foolish, elevating instead of degrading, objects and contemplations. But neither one person, nor any number of persons, is warranted in saying to another human creature of ripe years, that he shall not do with his life for his own benefit what he chooses to do with it. He is the person most interested in his own well-being: the interest which any other person, except in cases of strong personal attachment, can have in it, is trifling, compared with that which he himself has; the interest which society has in him individually (except as to his conduct to others) is fractional, and altogether indirect: while, with respect to his own feelings and circumstances, the most ordinary man or woman has means of knowledge immeasurably surpassing those that can be possessed by any one else. The interference of society to overrule his judgment and purposes in what only regards himself, must be grounded on general presumptions; which may be altogether wrong, and even if right, are as likely as not to be misapplied to individual cases, by persons no better acquainted with the circumstances of such cases than those are who look at them merely from without. In this department, therefore, of human affairs, Individuality has its proper field of action. In the conduct of human beings towards one another, it is necessary that general rules should for the most part be observed, in order that people may know what they have to expect; but in each person's own concerns, his individual spontaneity is entitled to free exercise. Considerations to aid his judgment, exhortations to strengthen his will, may be offered to him, even obtruded on him, by others; but he himself is the final judge. All errors which he is likely to commit against advice and warning, are far outweighed by the evil of allowing others to constrain him to what they deem his good.

I do not mean that the feelings with which a person is regarded by others, ought not to be in any way affected by his self-regarding qualities or deficiencies. This is neither possible nor desirable. If he is eminent in any of the qualities which conduce to his own good, he is, so far, a proper object of admiration. He is so much the nearer to the ideal perfection of human nature. If he is grossly deficient in those qualities, a sentiment the opposite of admiration will follow. There is a degree of folly, and a degree of what may be called (though the phrase is not unobjectionable) lowness or depravation of taste, which, though it cannot justify doing harm to the person who manifests it, renders him necessarily and properly a subject of distaste, or, in extreme cases, even of contempt: a person could not have the opposite qualities in due strength without entertaining these feelings. Though doing no wrong to any one, a person may so act as to compel us to judge him, and feel to him, as a fool, or as a being of an inferior order: and since this judgment and feeling are a

fact which he would prefer to avoid, it is doing him a service to warn him of it beforehand, as of any other disagreeable consequence to which he exposes himself. It would be well, indeed, if this good office were much more freely rendered than the common notions of politeness at present permit, and if one person could honestly point out to another that he thinks him in fault, without being considered unmannerly or presuming. We have a right, also, in various ways, to act upon our unfavorable opinion of any one, not to the oppression of his individuality, but in the exercise of ours. We are not bound, for example, to seek his society; we have a right to avoid it (though not to parade the avoidance), for we have a right to choose the society most acceptable to us. We have a right, and it may be our duty, to caution others against him, if we think his example or conversation likely to have a pernicious effect on those with whom he associates. We may give others a preference over him in optional good offices, except those which tend to his improvement. In these various modes a person may suffer very severe penalties at the hands of others, for faults which directly concern only himself; but he suffers these penalties only in so far as they are the natural, and, as it were, the spontaneous consequences of the faults themselves, not because they are purposely inflicted on him for the sake of punishment. A person who shows rashness, obstinacy, self-conceit—who cannot live within moderate means—who cannot restrain himself from hurtful indulgences—who pursues animal pleasures at the expense of those of feeling and intellect—must expect to be lowered in the opinion of others, and to have a less share of their favorable sentiments; but of this he has no right to complain, unless he has merited their favor by special excellence in his social relations, and has thus established a title to their good offices, which is not affected by his demerits towards himself.

What I contend for is, that the inconveniences which are strictly inseparable from the unfavorable judgment of others, are the only ones to which a person should ever be subjected for that portion of his conduct and character which concerns his own good, but which does not affect the interests of others in their relations with him. Acts injurious to others require a totally different treatment. Encroachment on their rights; infliction on them of any loss or damage not justified by his own rights; falsehood or duplicity in dealing with them; unfair or ungenerous use of advantages over them; even selfish abstinence from defending them against injury—these are fit objects of moral reprobation, and, in grave cases, of moral retribution and punishment. And not only these acts, but the dispositions which lead to them, are properly immoral, and fit subjects of disapprobation which may rise to abhorrence. Cruelty of disposition; malice and ill-nature; that most anti-social and odious of all passions, envy; dissimulation and insincerity; irascibility on insufficient cause, and resentment disproportioned to the provocation; the love of domineering over others; the desire to engross more than one's share of advantages (the πλεονεξία [Greek: pleonexia] of the Greeks); the pride which derives gratification from the abasement of others; the egotism which thinks self and its concerns more important than everything else, and decides all doubtful questions in its own favor;—these are moral vices, and constitute a bad and odious moral character: unlike the self-regarding faults previously mentioned, which are not properly immoralities, and to whatever pitch they may be carried, do not constitute wickedness. They may be proofs of any amount of folly, or want of personal dignity and self-respect; but they are only a subject of moral reprobation when they involve a breach of duty to others, for whose sake the individual is bound to have care for himself. What are called duties to ourselves are not socially obligatory, unless circumstances render them at the same time duties to others. The term duty to oneself, when it means anything more than prudence, means self-respect or self-development; and for none of these is any one accountable to his fellow-creatures, because for none of them is it for the good of mankind that he be held accountable to them.

The distinction between the loss of consideration which a person may rightly incur by defect of prudence or of personal dignity, and the reprobation which is due to him for an offence against the rights of others, is not a merely nominal distinction. It makes a vast difference both in our feelings and in our conduct towards him, whether he displeases us in things in which we think we have a right to control him, or in things in which we know that we have not. If he displeases us, we may express our distaste, and we may stand aloof from a person as well as from a thing that displeases us; but we shall not therefore feel called on to make his life uncomfortable. We shall reflect that he already bears, or will bear, the whole penalty of his error; if he spoils his life by mismanagement, we shall not, for that reason, desire to spoil it still further: instead of wishing to punish him, we shall rather endeavor to alleviate his punishment, by showing him how he may avoid or cure the evils his conduct tends to bring upon him. He may be to us an object of pity, perhaps of dislike, but not of anger or resentment; we shall not treat him like an enemy of society: the worst we shall think ourselves justified in doing is leaving him to himself, if we do not interfere benevolently by showing interest or concern for him. It is far otherwise if he has infringed the rules necessary for the protection of his fellow-creatures, individually or collectively. The evil consequences of his acts do not then fall on himself, but on others; and society, as the

5 protector of all its members, must retaliate on him; must inflict pain on him for the express purpose of punishment, and must take care that it be sufficiently severe. In the one case, he is an offender at our bar, and we are called

10 on not only to sit in judgment on him, but, in one shape or another, to execute our own sentence: in the other case, it is not our part to inflict any suffering on him, except what may incidentally follow from our using the same

15 liberty in the regulation of our own affairs, which we allow to him in his.

The distinction here pointed out between the part of a person's life which concerns only

20 himself, and that which concerns others, many persons will refuse to admit. How (it may be asked) can any part of the conduct of a member of society be a matter of indifference to the other members? No person is an entirely

25 isolated being; it is impossible for a person to do anything seriously or permanently hurtful to himself, without mischief reaching at least to his near connections, and often far beyond them. If he injures his property, he does harm

30 to those who directly or indirectly derived support from it, and usually diminishes, by a greater or less amount, the general resources of the community. If he deteriorates his bodily or mental faculties, he not only brings evil

35 upon all who depended on him for any portion of their happiness, but disqualifies himself for rendering the services which he owes to his fellow-creatures generally; perhaps becomes a burthen on their affection or benevo-

40 lence; and if such conduct were very frequent, hardly any offence that is committed would detract more from the general sum of good. Finally, if by his vices or follies a person does

no direct harm to others, he is nevertheless (it

45 may be said) injurious by his example; and ought to be compelled to control himself, for the sake of those whom the sight or knowledge of his conduct might corrupt or mislead.

50

And even (it will be added) if the consequences of misconduct could be confined to the vicious or thoughtless individual, ought society to abandon to their own guidance those who

55 are manifestly unfit for it? If protection against themselves is confessedly due to children and persons under age, is not society equally bound to afford it to persons of mature years who are equally incapable of self-government?

60 If gambling, or drunkenness, or incontinence, or idleness, or uncleanliness, are as injurious to happiness, and as great a hindrance to improvement, as many or most of the acts prohibited by law, why (it may be asked) should

65 not law, so far as is consistent with practicability and social convenience, endeavor to repress these also? And as a supplement to the unavoidable imperfections of law, ought not opinion at least to organize a powerful police

70 against these vices, and visit rigidly with social penalties those who are known to practice them? There is no question here (it may be said) about restricting individuality, or impeding the trial of new and original experiments in

75 living. The only things it is sought to prevent are things which have been tried and condemned from the beginning of the world until now; things which experience has shown not to be useful or suitable to any person's indi-

80 viduality. There must be some length of time and amount of experience, after which a moral or prudential truth may be regarded as established: and it is merely desired to prevent generation after generation from falling over the

85 same precipice which has been fatal to their predecessors.

I fully admit that the mischief which a person does to himself, may seriously affect, both through their sympathies and their interests, those nearly connected with him, and in a minor degree, society at large. When, by conduct of this sort, a person is led to violate a distinct and assignable obligation to any other person or persons, the case is taken out of the self-regarding class, and becomes amenable to moral disapprobation in the proper sense of the term. If, for example, a man, through intemperance or extravagance, becomes unable to pay his debts, or, having undertaken the moral responsibility of a family, becomes from the same cause incapable of supporting or educating them, he is deservedly reprobated, and might be justly punished; but it is for the breach of duty to his family or creditors, not for the extravagance. If the resources which ought to have been devoted to them, had been diverted from them for the most prudent investment, the moral culpability would have been the same. George Barnwell murdered his uncle to get money for his mistress, but if he had done it to set himself up in business, he would equally have been hanged. Again, in the frequent case of a man who causes grief to his family by addiction to bad habits, he deserves reproach for his unkindness or ingratitude; but so he may for cultivating habits not in themselves vicious, if they are painful to those with whom he passes his life, or who from personal ties are dependent on him for their comfort. Whoever fails in the consideration generally due to the interests and feelings of others, not being compelled by some more imperative duty, or justified by allowable self-preference, is a subject of moral disapprobation for that failure, but not for the cause of it, nor for the errors, merely personal to himself, which may have remotely led to it. In like manner, when a person disables himself, by conduct purely self-regarding, from the performance of some definite duty incumbent on him to the public, he is guilty of a social offence. No person ought to be punished simply for being drunk; but a soldier or a policeman should be punished for being drunk on duty. Whenever, in short, there is a definite damage, or a definite risk of damage, either to an individual or to the public, the case is taken out of the province of liberty, and placed in that of morality or law.

But with regard to the merely contingent, or, as it may be called, constructive injury which a person causes to society, by conduct which neither violates any specific duty to the public, nor occasions perceptible hurt to any assignable individual except himself; the inconvenience is one which society can afford to bear, for the sake of the greater good of human freedom. If grown persons are to be punished for not taking proper care of themselves, I would rather it were for their own sake, than under pretense of preventing them from impairing their capacity of rendering to society benefits which society does not pretend it has a right to exact. But I cannot consent to argue the point as if society had no means of bringing its weaker members up to its ordinary standard of rational conduct, except waiting till they do something irrational, and then punishing them, legally or morally, for it. Society has had absolute power over them during all the early portion of their existence: it has had the whole period of childhood and nonage in which to try whether it could make them capable of rational conduct in life. The existing generation is master both of the training and the entire circumstances of the generation to come; it cannot indeed make them perfectly wise and good, because it is itself so lamentably deficient in goodness and wisdom; and its best efforts are not always, in individual cases, its most successful ones; but it is perfectly well able to make the rising generation, as a whole, as good as, and a little better than, itself. If society lets any considerable number of its members grow up mere children, incapable of being acted on by rational consideration of distant motives, society has itself to blame for the consequences. Armed not only with all the powers of education, but with the ascendency which the authority of a received opinion always exercises over the minds who are least fitted to judge for themselves; and aided by the *natural* penalties which cannot be prevented from falling on those who incur the distaste or the contempt of those who know them; let not society pretend that it needs, besides all this, the power to issue commands and enforce obedience in the personal concerns of individuals, in which, on all principles of justice and policy, the decision ought to rest with those who are to abide the consequences. Nor is there anything which tends more to discredit and frustrate the better means of influencing conduct, than a resort to the worse. If there be among those whom it is attempted to coerce into prudence or temperance, any of the material of which vigorous and independent characters are made, they will infallibly rebel against the yoke. No such person will ever feel that others have a right to control him in his concerns, such as they have to prevent him from injuring them in theirs; and it easily comes to be considered a mark of spirit and courage to fly in the face of such usurped authority, and do with ostentation the exact opposite of what it enjoins; as in the fashion of grossness which succeeded, in the time of Charles II., to the fanatical moral intolerance of the Puritans. With respect to what is said of the necessity of protecting society from the bad example set to others by the vicious or the self-indulgent; it is true that bad example may have a pernicious effect, especially the example of doing wrong to others with impunity to the wrong-doer. But we are now speaking of conduct which, while it does no wrong to others, is supposed to do great harm to the agent himself: and I do not see how those who believe this, can think otherwise than that the example, on the whole, must be more salutary than hurtful, since, if it displays the misconduct, it displays also the painful or degrading consequences which, if the conduct is justly censured, must be supposed to be in all or most cases attendant on it.

But the strongest of all the arguments against the interference of the public with purely personal conduct, is that when it does interfere, the odds are that it interferes wrongly, and in the wrong place. On questions of social morality, of duty to others, the opinion of the public, that is, of an overruling majority, though often wrong, is likely to be still oftener right; because on such questions they are only required to judge of their own interests; of the manner in which some mode of conduct, if allowed to be practiced, would affect themselves. But the opinion of a similar majority, imposed as a law on the minority, on questions of self-regarding conduct, is quite as likely to be wrong as right; for in these cases public opinion means, at the best, some people's opinion of what is good or bad for other people; while very often it does not even mean that; the public, with the most perfect indifference, passing over the pleasure or convenience of those whose conduct they censure, and considering only their own preference. There are many who consider as an injury to themselves any conduct which they have a distaste for, and resent it as an outrage to their feelings; as a religious bigot, when charged with disregarding the religious feelings of others, has been known to retort that they disregard his feelings, by persisting in their abominable worship or creed. But there is no parity between the feeling of a person for his own opinion, and the feeling of another who is offended at his holding it; no more than between the desire of a thief to take a purse, and

5 the desire of the right owner to keep it. And a person's taste is as much his own peculiar concern as his opinion or his purse. It is easy for any one to imagine an ideal public, which leaves the freedom and choice of individuals

10 in all uncertain matters undisturbed, and only requires them to abstain from modes of conduct which universal experience has condemned. But where has there been seen a public which set any such limit to its censorship?

15 or when does the public trouble itself about universal experience? In its interferences with personal conduct it is seldom thinking of anything but the enormity of acting or feeling differently from itself; and this standard of

20 judgment, thinly disguised, is held up to mankind as the dictate of religion and philosophy, by nine-tenths of all moralists and speculative writers. These teach that things are right because they are right; because we feel them to

25 be so. They tell us to search in our own minds and hearts for laws of conduct binding on ourselves and on all others. What can the poor public do but apply these instructions, and make their own personal feelings of good and

30 evil, if they are tolerably unanimous in them, obligatory on all the world?

The evil here pointed out is not one which exists only in theory; and it may perhaps be

35 expected that I should specify the instances in which the public of this age and country improperly invests its own preferences with the character of moral laws. I am not writing an essay on the aberrations of existing moral feel-

40 ing. That is too weighty a subject to be discussed parenthetically, and by way of illustration. Yet examples are necessary, to show that the principle I maintain is of serious and prac-

tical moment, and that I am not endeavoring

45 to erect a barrier against imaginary evils. And it is not difficult to show, by abundant instances, that to extend the bounds of what may be called moral police, until it encroaches on the most unquestionably legitimate liberty

50 of the individual, is one of the most universal of all human propensities...

CHAPTER V
APPLICATIONS

55

The principles asserted in these pages must be more generally admitted as the basis for discussion of details, before a consistent application of them to all the various departments of

60 government and morals can be attempted with any prospect of advantage. The few observations I propose to make on questions of detail, are designed to illustrate the principles, rather than to follow them out to their consequenc-

65 es. I offer, not so much applications, as specimens of application; which may serve to bring into greater clearness the meaning and limits of the two maxims which together form the entire doctrine of this Essay, and to assist the

70 judgment in holding the balance between them, in the cases where it appears doubtful which of them is applicable to the case.

The maxims are, first, that the individual is not

75 accountable to society for his actions, in so far as these concern the interests of no person but himself. Advice, instruction, persuasion, and avoidance by other people if thought necessary by them for their own good, are the only

80 measures by which society can justifiably express its dislike or disapprobation of his conduct. Secondly, that for such actions as are prejudicial to the interests of others, the individual is accountable and may be subjected

85 either to social or to legal punishments, if society is of opinion that the one or the other is

requisite for its protection.

In the first place, it must by no means be supposed, because damage, or probability of damage, to the interests of others, can alone justify the interference of society, that therefore it always does justify such interference. In many cases, an individual, in pursuing a legitimate object, necessarily and therefore legitimately causes pain or loss to others, or intercepts a good which they had a reasonable hope of obtaining. Such oppositions of interest between individuals often arise from bad social institutions, but are unavoidable while those institutions last; and some would be unavoidable under any institutions. Whoever succeeds in an overcrowded profession, or in a competitive examination; whoever is preferred to another in any contest for an object which both desire, reaps benefit from the loss of others, from their wasted exertion and their disappointment. But it is, by common admission, better for the general interest of mankind, that persons should pursue their objects undeterred by this sort of consequences. In other words, society admits no rights, either legal or moral, in the disappointed competitors, to immunity from this kind of suffering; and feels called on to interfere, only when means of success have been employed which it is contrary to the general interest to permit—namely, fraud or treachery, and force.

Again, trade is a social act. Whoever undertakes to sell any description of goods to the public, does what affects the interest of other persons, and of society in general; and thus his conduct, in principle, comes within the jurisdiction of society: accordingly, it was once held to be the duty of governments, in all cases which were considered of importance, to fix prices, and regulate the processes of manufacture. But it is now recognized, though not till after a long struggle, that both the cheapness and the good quality of commodities are most effectually provided for by leaving the producers and sellers perfectly free, under the sole check of equal freedom to the buyers for supplying themselves elsewhere. This is the so-called doctrine of Free Trade, which rests on grounds different from, though equally solid with, the principle of individual liberty asserted in this Essay. Restrictions on trade, or on production for purposes of trade, are indeed restraints; and all restraint, *quâ* restraint, is an evil: but the restraints in question affect only that part of conduct which society is competent to restrain, and are wrong solely because they do not really produce the results which it is desired to produce by them. As the principle of individual liberty is not involved in the doctrine of Free Trade, so neither is it in most of the questions which arise respecting the limits of that doctrine: as for example, what amount of public control is admissible for the prevention of fraud by adulteration; how far sanitary precautions, or arrangements to protect work-people employed in dangerous occupations, should be enforced on employers. Such questions involve considerations of liberty, only in so far as leaving people to themselves is always better, *cæteris paribus*, than controlling them: but that they may be legitimately controlled for these ends, is in principle undeniable. On the other hand, there are questions relating to interference with trade, which are essentially questions of liberty; such as the Maine Law, already touched upon; the prohibition of the importation of opium into China; the restriction of the sale of poisons; all cases, in short, where the object of the interference is to make it impossible or difficult to obtain a particular commodity. These interferences are objectionable, not as infringements on the liberty of the producer or seller, but on that of the buyer.

One of these examples, that of the sale of poisons, opens a new question; the proper limits of what may be called the functions of police; how far liberty may legitimately be invaded for the prevention of crime, or of accident. It is one of the undisputed functions of government to take precautions against crime before it has been committed, as well as to detect and punish it afterwards. The preventive function of government, however, is far more liable to be abused, to the prejudice of liberty, than the punitory function; for there is hardly any part of the legitimate freedom of action of a human being which would not admit of being represented, and fairly too, as increasing the facilities for some form or other of delinquency. Nevertheless, if a public authority, or even a private person, sees any one evidently preparing to commit a crime, they are not bound to look on inactive until the crime is committed, but may interfere to prevent it. If poisons were never bought or used for any purpose except the commission of murder, it would be right to prohibit their manufacture and sale. They may, however, be wanted not only for innocent but for useful purposes, and restrictions cannot be imposed in the one case without operating in the other. Again, it is a proper office of public authority to guard against accidents. If either a public officer or any one else saw a person attempting to cross a bridge which had been ascertained to be unsafe, and there were no time to warn him of his danger, they might seize him and turn him back, without any real infringement of his liberty; for liberty consists in doing what one desires, and he does not desire to fall into the river. Nevertheless, when there is not a certainty, but only a danger of mischief, no one but the person himself can judge of the sufficiency of the motive which may prompt him to incur the risk: in this case, therefore (unless he is a child, or delirious, or in some state of excitement or absorption incompatible with the full use of the reflecting faculty), he ought, I conceive, to be only warned of the danger; not forcibly prevented from exposing himself to it. Similar considerations, applied to such a question as the sale of poisons, may enable us to decide which among the possible modes of regulation are or are not contrary to principle. Such a precaution, for example, as that of labeling the drug with some word expressive of its dangerous character, may be enforced without violation of liberty: the buyer cannot wish not to know that the thing he possesses has poisonous qualities. But to require in all cases the certificate of a medical practitioner, would make it sometimes impossible, always expensive, to obtain the article for legitimate uses. The only mode apparent to me, in which difficulties may be thrown in the way of crime committed through this means, without any infringement, worth taking into account, upon the liberty of those who desire the poisonous substance for other purposes, consists in providing what, in the apt language of Bentham, is called "preappointed evidence." This provision is familiar to every one in the case of contracts. It is usual and right that the law, when a contract is entered into, should require as the condition of its enforcing performance, that certain formalities should be observed, such as signatures, attestation of witnesses, and the like, in order that in case of subsequent dispute, there may be evidence to prove that the contract was really entered into, and that there was nothing in the circumstances to render it legally invalid: the effect being, to throw great obstacles in the way of fictitious contracts, or contracts made in circumstances which, if known, would destroy their validity. Precautions of a similar nature might be enforced in the sale of articles adapted to be instruments of crime. The seller, for example, might be required to enter into a register the exact time of the transaction, the name and address of the buyer, the precise quality and quantity sold; to ask the purpose for which it was wanted, and record the answer he received. When there was no medical prescription, the presence of some third person might be required, to bring home the fact to the purchaser, in case there should afterwards be reason to believe that the article had been applied to criminal purposes. Such regulations would in general be no material impediment to obtaining the article, but a very considerable one to making an improper use of it without detection.

The right inherent in society, to ward off crimes against itself by antecedent precautions, suggests the obvious limitations to the maxim, that purely self-regarding misconduct cannot properly be meddled with in the way of prevention or punishment. Drunkenness, for example, in ordinary cases, is not a fit subject for legislative interference; but I should deem it perfectly legitimate that a person, who had once been convicted of any act of violence to others under the influence of drink, should be placed under a special legal restriction, personal to himself; that if he were afterwards found drunk, he should be liable to a penalty, and that if when in that state he committed another offence, the punishment to which he would be liable for that other offence should be increased in severity. The making himself drunk, in a person whom drunkenness excites to do harm to others, is a crime against others. So, again, idleness, except in a person receiving support from the public, or except when it constitutes a breach of contract, cannot without tyranny be made a subject of legal punishment; but if either from idleness or from any other avoidable cause, a man fails to perform his legal duties to others, as for instance to support his children, it is no tyranny to force him to fulfill that obligation, by compulsory labor, if no other means are available.

Again, there are many acts which, being directly injurious only to the agents themselves, ought not to be legally interdicted, but which, if done publicly, are a violation of good manners and coming thus within the category of offences against others may rightfully be prohibited. Of this kind are offences against decency; on which it is unnecessary to dwell, the rather as they are only connected indirectly with our subject, the objection to publicity being equally strong in the case of many actions not in themselves condemnable, nor supposed to be so.

There is another question to which an answer must be found, consistent with the principles which have been laid down. In cases of personal conduct supposed to be blamable, but which respect for liberty precludes society from preventing or punishing, because the evil directly resulting falls wholly on the agent; what the agent is free to do, ought other persons to be equally free to counsel or instigate? This question is not free from difficulty. The case of a person who solicits another to do an act, is not strictly a case of self-regarding conduct. To give advice or offer inducements to any one, is a social act, and may therefore, like actions in general which affect others, be supposed amenable to social control. But a little reflection corrects the first impression, by showing that if the case is not strictly within the definition of individual liberty, yet the reasons on which the principle of individual liberty is grounded, are applicable to it. If people must be allowed, in whatever concerns only themselves, to act as seems best to themselves at their own peril, they must equally be free to consult with one another about what is fit to be so done; to exchange opinions, and give and receive suggestions. Whatever it is permitted to do, it must be permitted to advise to do. The question is doubtful, only when the instigator derives a personal benefit from his advice; when he makes it his occupation, for subsistence or pecuniary gain, to promote what society and the state consider to be an evil. Then, indeed, a new element of complication is introduced; namely, the existence of classes of persons with an interest opposed to what is considered as the public weal, and whose mode of living is grounded on the counteraction of it. Ought this to be interfered with, or not? Fornication, for example, must be tolerated, and so must gambling; but should a person be free to be a pimp, or to keep a gambling-house? The case is one of those which lie on the exact boundary line between two principles, and it is not at once apparent to which of the two it properly belongs. There are arguments on both sides. On the side of toleration it may be said, that the fact of following anything as an occupation, and living or profiting by the practice of it, cannot make that criminal which would otherwise be admissible; that the act should either be consistently permitted or consistently prohibited; that if the principles which we have hitherto defended are true, society has no business, *as* society, to decide anything to be wrong which concerns only the individual; that it cannot go beyond dissuasion, and that one person should be as free to persuade, as another to dissuade. In opposition to this it may be contended, that although the public, or the State, are not warranted in authoritatively deciding, for purposes of repression or punishment, that such or such conduct affecting only the interests of the individual is good or bad, they are fully justified in assuming, if they regard it as bad, that its being so or not is at least a disputable question: That, this being supposed, they cannot be acting wrongly in

endeavoring to exclude the influence of solicitations which are not disinterested, of instigators who cannot possibly be impartial—who have a direct personal interest on one side, and that side the one which the State believes to be wrong, and who confessedly promote it for personal objects only. There can surely, it may be urged, be nothing lost, no sacrifice of good, by so ordering matters that persons shall make their election, either wisely or foolishly, on their own prompting, as free as possible from the arts of persons who stimulate their inclinations for interested purposes of their own. Thus (it may be said) though the statutes respecting unlawful games are utterly indefensible—though all persons should be free to gamble in their own or each other's houses, or in any place of meeting established by their own subscriptions, and open only to the members and their visitors—yet public gambling-houses should not be permitted. It is true that the prohibition is never effectual, and that whatever amount of tyrannical power is given to the police, gambling-houses can always be maintained under other pretenses; but they may be compelled to conduct their operations with a certain degree of secrecy and mystery, so that nobody knows anything about them but those who seek them; and more than this, society ought not to aim at. There is considerable force in these arguments; I will not venture to decide whether they are sufficient to justify the moral anomaly of punishing the accessary, when the principal is (and must be) allowed to go free; or fining or imprisoning the procurer, but not the fornicator, the gambling-house keeper, but not the gambler.

Still less ought the common operations of buying and selling to be interfered with on analogous grounds. Almost every article which is bought and sold may be used in excess, and the sellers have a pecuniary interest in encouraging that excess; but no argument can be founded on this, in favor, for instance, of the Maine Law; because the class of dealers in strong drinks, though interested in their abuse, are indispensably required for the sake of their legitimate use. The interest, however, of these dealers in promoting intemperance is a real evil, and justifies the State in imposing restrictions and requiring guarantees, which but for that justification would be infringements of legitimate liberty.

A further question is, whether the State, while it permits, should nevertheless indirectly discourage conduct which it deems contrary to the best interests of the agent; whether, for example, it should take measures to render the means of drunkenness more costly, or add to the difficulty of procuring them, by limiting the number of the places of sale. On this as on most other practical questions, many distinctions require to be made. To tax stimulants for the sole purpose of making them more difficult to be obtained, is a measure differing only in degree from their entire prohibition; and would be justifiable only if that were justifiable. Every increase of cost is a prohibition, to those whose means do not come up to the augmented price; and to those who do, it is a penalty laid on them for gratifying a particular taste. Their choice of pleasures, and their mode of expending their income, after satisfying their legal and moral obligations to the State and to individuals, are their own concern, and must rest with their own judgment. These considerations may seem at first sight to condemn the selection of stimulants as special subjects of taxation for purposes of revenue. But it must be remembered that taxation for fiscal purposes is absolutely inevitable; that in most countries it is necessary that a considerable part of that taxation should be indirect; that the State, therefore, cannot help imposing penalties, which to some persons may be prohibitory, on the use of some articles of consumption. It is hence the duty of the State to consider, in the imposition of taxes, what commodities the consumers can best spare; and *à fortiori*, to select in preference those of which it deems the use, beyond a very moderate quantity, to be positively injurious. Taxation, therefore, of stimulants, up to the point which produces the largest amount of revenue (supposing that the State needs all the revenue which it yields) is not only admissible, but to be approved of.

The question of making the sale of these commodities a more or less exclusive privilege, must be answered differently, according to the purposes to which the restriction is intended to be subservient. All places of public resort require the restraint of a police, and places of this kind peculiarly, because offences against society are especially apt to originate there. It is, therefore, fit to confine the power of selling these commodities (at least for consumption on the spot) to persons of known or vouched-for respectability of conduct; to make such regulations respecting hours of opening and closing as may be requisite for public surveillance, and to withdraw the licence if breaches of the peace repeatedly take place through the connivance or incapacity of the keeper of the house, or if it becomes a rendezvous for concocting and preparing offences against the law. Any further restriction I do not conceive to be, in principle, justifiable. The limitation in number, for instance, of beer and spirit-houses, for the express purpose of rendering them more difficult of access, and diminishing the occasions of temptation, not only exposes all to an inconvenience because there are some by whom the facility would be abused, but is suited only to a state of society in which the laboring classes are

avowedly treated as children or savages, and placed under an education of restraint, to fit them for future admission to the privileges of freedom. This is not the principle on which
5 the laboring classes are professedly governed in any free country; and no person who sets due value on freedom will give his adhesion to their being so governed, unless after all efforts have been exhausted to educate them for
10 freedom and govern them as freemen, and it has been definitively proved that they can only be governed as children. The bare statement of the alternative shows the absurdity of supposing that such efforts have been made in
15 any case which needs be considered here. It is only because the institutions of this country are a mass of inconsistencies, that things find admittance into our practice which belong to the system of despotic, or what is called pater-
20 nal, government, while the general freedom of our institutions precludes the exercise of the amount of control necessary to render the restraint of any real efficacy as a moral education…
25

I have already observed that, owing to the absence of any recognized general principles, liberty is often granted where it should be withheld, as well as withheld where it should
30 be granted; and one of the cases in which, in the modern European world, the sentiment of liberty is the strongest, is a case where, in my view, it is altogether misplaced. A person should be free to do as he likes in his own
35 concerns; but he ought not to be free to do as he likes in acting for another, under the pretext that the affairs of another are his own affairs. The State, while it respects the liberty of each in what specially regards himself, is
40 bound to maintain a vigilant control over his exercise of any power which it allows him to possess over others. This obligation is almost entirely disregarded in the case of the family

relations, a case, in its direct influence on hu-
45 man happiness, more important than all others taken together. The almost despotic power of husbands over wives need not be enlarged upon here because nothing more is needed for the complete removal of the evil, than that
50 wives should have the same rights, and should receive the protection of law in the same manner, as all other persons; and because, on this subject, the defenders of established injustice do not avail themselves of the plea of lib-
55 erty, but stand forth openly as the champions of power. It is in the case of children, that misapplied notions of liberty are a real obstacle to the fulfillment by the State of its duties. One would almost think that a man's children
60 were supposed to be literally, and not metaphorically, a part of himself, so jealous is opinion of the smallest interference of law with his absolute and exclusive control over them; more jealous than of almost any interference
65 with his own freedom of action: so much less do the generality of mankind value liberty than power. Consider, for example, the case of education. Is it not almost a self-evident axiom, that the State should require and compel the
70 education, up to a certain standard, of every human being who is born its citizen? Yet who is there that is not afraid to recognize and assert this truth? Hardly any one indeed will deny that it is one of the most sacred duties of
75 the parents (or, as law and usage now stand, the father), after summoning a human being into the world, to give to that being an education fitting him to perform his part well in life towards others and towards himself. But while
80 this is unanimously declared to be the father's duty, scarcely anybody, in this country, will bear to hear of obliging him to perform it. Instead of his being required to make any exertion or sacrifice for securing education to
85 the child, it is left to his choice to accept it or not when it is provided gratis! It still remains

unrecognized, that to bring a child into existence without a fair prospect of being able, not
only to provide food for its body, but instruction and training for its mind, is a moral crime,
5   both against the unfortunate offspring and
against society; and that if the parent does not
fulfill this obligation, the State ought to see it
fulfilled, at the charge, as far as possible, of the
parent.
10

Were the duty of enforcing universal education once admitted, there would be an end to
the difficulties about what the State should
teach, and how it should teach, which now
15   convert the subject into a mere battle-field for
sects and parties, causing the time and labor
which should have been spent in educating, to
be wasted in quarrelling about education. If
the government would make up its mind to
20   *require* for every child a good education, it
might save itself the trouble of *providing* one. It
might leave to parents to obtain the education
where and how they pleased, and content itself
with helping to pay the school fees of the
25   poorer class of children, and defraying the
entire school expenses of those who have no
one else to pay for them. The objections
which are urged with reason against State education, do not apply to the enforcement of
30   education by the State, but to the State's taking
upon itself to direct that education; which is a
totally different thing. That the whole or any
large part of the education of the people
should be in State hands, I go as far as any one
35   in deprecating. All that has been said of the
importance of individuality of character, and
diversity in opinions and modes of conduct,
involves, as of the same unspeakable importance, diversity of education. A general
40   State education is a mere contrivance for
molding people to be exactly like one another;
and as the mold in which it casts them is that
which pleases the predominant power in the

government, whether this be a monarch, a
45   priesthood, an aristocracy, or the majority of
the existing generation, in proportion as it is
efficient and successful, it establishes a despotism over the mind, leading by natural tendency
to one over the body. An education estab-
50   lished and controlled by the State, should only
exist, if it exist at all, as one among many
competing experiments, carried on for the
purpose of example and stimulus, to keep the
others up to a certain standard of excellence.
55   Unless, indeed, when society in general is in so
backward a state that it could not or would
not provide for itself any proper institutions
of education, unless the government undertook the task; then, indeed, the government
60   may, as the less of two great evils, take upon
itself the business of schools and universities,
as it may that of joint stock companies, when
private enterprise, in a shape fitted for undertaking great works of industry, does not exist
65   in the country. But in general, if the country
contains a sufficient number of persons qualified to provide education under government
auspices, the same persons would be able and
willing to give an equally good education on
70   the voluntary principle, under the assurance of
remuneration afforded by a law rendering education compulsory, combined with State aid
to those unable to defray the expense.

75   The instrument for enforcing the law could be
no other than public examinations, extending
to all children, and beginning at an early age.
An age might be fixed at which every child
must be examined, to ascertain if he (or she) is
80   able to read. If a child proves unable, the father, unless he has some sufficient ground of
excuse, might be subjected to a moderate fine,
to be worked out, if necessary, by his labor,
and the child might be put to school at his
85   expense. Once in every year the examination
should be renewed, with a gradually extending

range of subjects, so as to make the universal acquisition, and what is more, retention, of a certain minimum of general knowledge, virtually compulsory. Beyond that minimum, there should be voluntary examinations on all subjects, at which all who come up to a certain standard of proficiency might claim a certificate. To prevent the State from exercising, through these arrangements, an improper influence over opinion, the knowledge required for passing an examination (beyond the merely instrumental parts of knowledge, such as languages and their use) should, even in the higher class of examinations, be confined to facts and positive science exclusively. The examinations on religion, politics, or other disputed topics, should not turn on the truth or falsehood of opinions, but on the matter of fact that such and such an opinion is held, on such grounds, by such authors, or schools, or churches. Under this system, the rising generation would be no worse off in regard to all disputed truths, than they are at present; they would be brought up either churchmen or dissenters as they now are, the state merely taking care that they should be instructed churchmen, or instructed dissenters. There would be nothing to hinder them from being taught religion, if their parents chose, at the same schools where they were taught other things. All attempts by the state to bias the conclusions of its citizens on disputed subjects, are evil; but it may very properly offer to ascertain and certify that a person possesses the knowledge, requisite to make his conclusions, on any given subject, worth attending to. A student of philosophy would be the better for being able to stand an examination both in Locke and in Kant, whichever of the two he takes up with, or even if with neither: and there is no reasonable objection to examining an atheist in the evidences of Christianity, provided he is not required to profess a belief in them. The examinations, however, in the higher branches of knowledge should, I conceive, be entirely voluntary. It would be giving too dangerous a power to governments, were they allowed to exclude any one from professions, even from the profession of teacher, for alleged deficiency of qualifications: and I think, with Wilhelm von Humboldt, that degrees, or other public certificates of scientific or professional acquirements, should be given to all who present themselves for examination, and stand the test; but that such certificates should confer no advantage over competitors, other than the weight which may be attached to their testimony by public opinion.

It is not in the matter of education only, that misplaced notions of liberty prevent moral obligations on the part of parents from being recognized, and legal obligations from being imposed, where there are the strongest grounds for the former always, and in many cases for the latter also. The fact itself, of causing the existence of a human being, is one of the most responsible actions in the range of human life. To undertake this responsibility— to bestow a life which may be either a curse or a blessing—unless the being on whom it is to be bestowed will have at least the ordinary chances of a desirable existence, is a crime against that being. And in a country either over-peopled, or threatened with being so, to produce children, beyond a very small number, with the effect of reducing the reward of labor by their competition, is a serious offence against all who live by the remuneration of their labor. The laws which, in many countries on the Continent, forbid marriage unless the parties can show that they have the means of supporting a family, do not exceed the legitimate powers of the state: and whether such laws be expedient or not (a question mainly dependent on local circumstances and feelings), they are not objectionable as violations of liberty. Such laws are interferences of the state to prohibit a mischievous act—an act injurious to others, which ought to be a sub-ject of reprobation, and social stigma, even when it is not deemed expedient to superadd legal punishment. Yet the current ideas of liberty, which bend so easily to real infringe-ments of the freedom of the individual, in things which concern only himself, would re-pel the attempt to put any restraint upon his inclinations when the consequence of their indulgence is a life, or lives, of wretchedness and depravity to the offspring, with manifold evils to those sufficiently within reach to be in any way affected by their actions. When we compare the strange respect of mankind for liberty, with their strange want of respect for it, we might imagine that a man had an indis-pensable right to do harm to others, and no right at all to please himself without giving pain to any one.

I have reserved for the last place a large class of questions respecting the limits of govern-ment interference, which, though closely con-nected with the subject of this Essay, do not, in strictness, belong to it. These are cases in which the reasons against interference do not turn upon the principle of liberty: the question is not about restraining the actions of individ-uals, but about helping them: it is asked whether the government should do, or cause to be done, something for their benefit, in-stead of leaving it to be done by themselves, individually, or in voluntary combination.

The objections to government interference, when it is not such as to involve infringement of liberty, may be of three kinds.

The first is, when the thing to be done is likely to be better done by individuals than by the government. Speaking generally, there is no one so fit to conduct any business, or to de-termine how or by whom it shall be conduct-ed, as those who are personally interested in it. This principle condemns the interferences, once so common, of the legislature, or the officers of government, with the ordinary pro-cesses of industry. But this part of the subject has been sufficiently enlarged upon by political economists, and is not particularly related to the principles of this Essay.

The second objection is more nearly allied to our subject. In many cases, though individuals may not do the particular thing so well, on the average, as the officers of government, it is nevertheless desirable that it should be done by them, rather than by the government, as a means to their own mental education—a mode of strengthening their active faculties, exercising their judgment, and giving them a familiar knowledge of the subjects with which they are thus left to deal. This is a principal, though not the sole, recommendation of jury trial (in cases not political); of free and popular local and municipal institutions; of the con-duct of industrial and philanthropic enterpris-es by voluntary associations. These are not questions of liberty, and are connected with that subject only by remote tendencies; but they are questions of development. It belongs to a different occasion from the present to dwell on these things as parts of national edu-cation; as being, in truth, the peculiar training of a citizen, the practical part of the political education of a free people, taking them out of the narrow circle of personal and family self-ishness, and accustoming them to the com-prehension of joint interests, the management of joint concerns—habituating them to act from public or semi-public motives, and guide their conduct by aims which unite instead of isolating them from one another. Without these habits and powers, a free constitution can neither be worked nor preserved, as is exemplified by the too-often transitory nature of political freedom in countries where it does not rest upon a sufficient basis of local liberties. The management of purely local business by the localities, and of the great enterprises of industry by the union of those who voluntarily supply the pecuniary means, is further recommended by all the advantages which have been set forth in this Essay as belonging to individuality of development, and diversity of modes of action. Government operations tend to be everywhere alike. With individuals and voluntary associations, on the contrary, there are varied experiments, and endless diversity of experience. What the State can usefully do, is to make itself a central depository, and active circulator and diffuser, of the experience resulting from many trials. Its business is to enable each experimentalist to benefit by the experiments of others, instead of tolerating no experiments but its own.

The third, and most cogent reason for restricting the interference of government, is the great evil of adding unnecessarily to its power. Every function superadded to those already exercised by the government, causes its influence over hopes and fears to be more widely diffused, and converts, more and more, the active and ambitious part of the public into hangers-on of the government, or of some party which aims at becoming the government. If the roads, the railways, the banks, the insurance offices, the great joint-stock companies, the universities, and the public charities, were all of them branches of the government; if, in addition, the municipal corporations and local boards, with all that now devolves on them, became departments of the central administration; if the employees of all these different enterprises were appointed and paid by the government, and looked to the government for every rise in life; not all the freedom of the press and popular constitution of the legislature would make this or any other country free otherwise than in name. And the evil would be greater, the more efficiently and scientifically the administrative machinery was constructed—the more skillful the arrangements for obtaining the best qualified hands and heads with which to work it. In England it has of late been proposed that all the members of the civil service of government should be selected by competitive examination, to obtain for those employments the most intelligent and instructed persons procurable; and much has been said and written for and against this proposal. One of the arguments most insisted on by its opponents, is that the occupation of a permanent official servant of the State does not hold out sufficient prospects of emolument and importance to attract the highest talents, which will always be able to find a more inviting career in the professions, or in the service of companies and other public bodies. One would not have been surprised if this argument had been used by the friends of the proposition, as an answer to its principal difficulty. Coming from the opponents it is strange enough. What is urged as an objection is the safety-valve of the proposed system. If indeed all the high talent of the country *could* be drawn into the service of the government, a proposal tending to bring about that result might well inspire uneasiness. If every part of the business of society which required organized concert, or large and comprehensive views, were in the hands of the government, and if government offices were universally filled by the ablest men, all the enlarged culture and practiced intelligence in the country, except the purely speculative, would be concentrated in a numerous bureaucracy, to whom alone the rest of the community would look for all things: the multitude for direction and dictation in all they had to do; the able and aspiring for personal advancement. To be admitted into the ranks of this bureaucracy, and when admitted, to rise therein, would be the sole objects of ambition. Under this régime, not only is the outside public ill-qualified, for want of practical experience, to criticize or check the mode of operation of the bureaucracy, but even if the accidents of despotic or the natural working of popular institutions occasionally raise to the summit a ruler or rulers of reforming inclinations, no reform can be effected which is contrary to the interest of the bureaucracy. Such is the melancholy condition of the Russian empire, as is shown in the accounts of those who have had sufficient opportunity of observation. The Czar himself is powerless against the bureaucratic body; he can send any one of them to Siberia, but he cannot govern without them, or against their will. On every decree of his they have a tacit veto, by merely refraining from carrying it into effect. In countries of more advanced civilization and of a more insurrectionary spirit, the public, accustomed to expect everything to be done for them by the State, or at least to do nothing for themselves without asking from the State not only leave to do it, but even how it is to be done, naturally hold the State responsible for all evil which befalls them, and when the evil exceeds their amount of patience, they rise against the government and make what is called a revolution; whereupon somebody else, with or without legitimate authority from the nation, vaults into the seat, issues his orders to the bureaucracy, and everything goes on much as it did before; the bureaucracy being unchanged, and nobody else being capable of taking their place.

A very different spectacle is exhibited among a people accustomed to transact their own business. In France, a large part of the people having been engaged in military service, many of whom have held at least the rank of non-commissioned officers, there are in every popular insurrection several persons competent to take the lead, and improvise some tolerable plan of action. What the French are in military affairs, the Americans are in every kind of civil business; let them be left without a government, every body of Americans is able to improvise one, and to carry on that or any other public business with a sufficient amount of intelligence, order, and decision. This is what every free people ought to be: and a people capable of this is certain to be free; it will never let itself be enslaved by any man or body of men because these are able to seize and pull the reins of the central administration. No bureaucracy can hope to make such a people as this do or undergo anything that they do not like. But where everything is done through the bureaucracy, nothing to which the bureaucracy is really adverse can be done at all. The constitution of such countries is an organization of the experience and practical ability of the nation, into a disciplined body for the purpose of governing the rest; and the more perfect that organization is in itself, the more successful in drawing to itself and educating for itself the persons of greatest capacity from all ranks of the community, the more complete is the bondage of all, the members of the bureaucracy included. For the governors are as much the slaves of their organization and discipline, as the governed are of the governors. A Chinese mandarin is as much the tool and creature of a despotism as the humblest cultivator. An individual Jesuit is to the utmost degree of abasement the slave of his order, though the order itself exists for the collective power and importance of its members.

It is not, also, to be forgotten, that the absorption of all the principal ability of the country into the governing body is fatal, sooner or later, to the mental activity and progressiveness of the body itself. Banded together as they are—working a system which, like all systems, necessarily proceeds in a great measure by fixed rules—the official body are under the constant temptation of sinking into indolent routine, or, if they now and then desert that mill-horse round, of rushing into some half-examined crudity which has struck the fancy of some leading member of the corps: and the sole check to these closely allied, though seemingly opposite, tendencies, the only stimulus which can keep the ability of the body itself up to a high standard, is liability to the watchful criticism of equal ability outside the body. It is indispensable, therefore, that the means should exist, independently of the government, of forming such ability, and furnishing it with the opportunities and experience necessary for a correct judgment of great practical affairs. If we would possess permanently a skillful and efficient body of functionaries—above all, a body able to originate and willing to adopt improvements; if we would not have our bureaucracy degenerate into a pedantocracy, this body must not engross all the occupations which form and cultivate the faculties required for the government of mankind.

To determine the point at which evils, so formidable to human freedom and advancement, begin, or rather at which they begin to predominate over the benefits attending the collective application of the force of society, under its recognized chiefs, for the removal of the obstacles which stand in the way of its well-being; to secure as much of the advantages of centralized power and intelligence, as can be had without turning into governmental channels too great a proportion of the general activity, is one of the most difficult and complicated questions in the art of government. It is, in a great measure, a question of detail, in which many and various considerations must be kept in view, and no absolute rule can be laid down. But I believe that the practical principle in which safety resides, the ideal to be kept in view, the standard by which to test all arrangements intended for overcoming the difficulty, may be conveyed in these words: the greatest dissemination of power consistent with efficiency; but the greatest possible centralization of information, and diffusion of it from the center. Thus, in municipal administration, there would be, as in the New England States, a very minute division among separate officers, chosen by the localities, of all business which is not better left to the persons directly interested; but besides this, there would be, in each department of local affairs, a central superintendence, forming a branch of the general government. The organ of this superintendence would concentrate, as in a focus, the variety of information and experience derived from the conduct of that branch of public business in all the localities, from everything analogous which is done in foreign countries, and from the general principles of political science. This central organ should have a right to know all that is done, and its special duty should be that of making the knowledge acquired in one place available for others. Emancipated from the petty prejudices and narrow views of a locality by its elevated position and comprehensive sphere of observation, its advice would naturally carry much authority; but its actual power, as a permanent institution, should, I conceive, be limited to compelling the local officers to obey the laws laid down for their guidance. In all things not provided for by general rules, those officers should be left to their own judgment, under responsibility to their constituents. For the violation of rules, they should be responsible to law, and the rules themselves should be laid down by the legislature; the central administrative authority only watching over their execution, and if they were not properly carried into effect, appealing, according to the nature of the case, to the tribunal to enforce the law, or to the constituencies to dismiss the functionaries who had not executed it according to its spirit. Such, in its general conception, is the central superintendence which the Poor Law Board is intended to exercise over the administrators of the Poor Rate throughout the country. Whatever powers the Board exercises beyond this limit, were right and necessary in that peculiar case, for the cure of rooted habits of maladministration in matters deeply affecting not the localities merely, but the whole community; since no locality has a moral right to make itself by mismanagement a nest of pauperism, necessarily overflowing into other localities, and impairing the moral and physical condition of the whole laboring community. The powers of administrative coercion and subordinate legislation possessed by the Poor Law Board (but which, owing to the state of opinion on the subject, are very scantily exercised by them), though perfectly justifiable in a case of first-rate national interest, would be wholly out of place in the superintendence of interests purely local. But a central organ of information and instruction for all the localities, would be equally valuable in all departments of administration. A government cannot have too much of the kind of activity which does not impede, but aids and stimulates, individual exertion and development. The mischief begins when, instead of calling forth the activity and powers of individuals and bodies, it substitutes its own activity for theirs; when, instead of informing, advising, and, upon occasion, denouncing, it makes them work in fetters, or bids them stand aside and does their work instead of them. The worth of a State, in the long run, is the worth of the individuals composing it; and a State which postpones the interests of *their* mental expansion and elevation, to a little more of administrative skill, or of that semblance of it which practice gives, in the details of business; a State which dwarfs its men, in order that they may be more docile instruments in its hands even for beneficial purposes, will find that with small men no great thing can really be accomplished; and that the perfection of machinery to which it has sacrificed everything, will in the end avail it nothing, for want of the vital power which, in order that the machine might work more smoothly, it has preferred to banish.

NIETZSCHE

Friedrich Nietzsche (1844-1900) is one the most important modern political thinkers, and yet he may very well not have thought of himself as such—he was a philologist by training and occupation. Born to a middle class family in what was then Prussia, Nietzsche was a bright child who took up philology to help in a ministerial career, before losing his faith and sticking with philology. His mentor at the University of Leipzig believed him to be the greatest mind he had even seen, and so at the age of 24 Nietzsche was given the Chair of Classical Philology at the University of Basel—without any experience or a Ph.D. However, it was after his time at Basel that he was most productive, publishing a mountain of incredible work in the 1880's, before suffering a complete mental and physical breakdown that left him in the care of his family for the remainder of his life.

Nietzsche's work is largely concerned with what he sees as a crisis in Western civilization, a nihilism that threatens to destroy the world. He sees at the root of this nihilism the dominance of 'slave-morality'—in modern times epitomized by popular democracy—which emphasizes meek qualities like equality and fairness, at the expense of the master-morality that would emphasize individuality and power. Thus, Nietzsche sits at the 'end' of the theoretical cannon—the questions have been answered, so to speak, and the only one left if what to do now? Nietzsche sees this as deeply problematic, and yearns for the coming of the *Ubermensch*. Not shockingly, Nietzschian thought is closely associated with some of the more unsavory parts of the 20th century.

THE GENEALOGY OF MORALS
FRIEDRICH NIETZSCHE

First Essay
"Good and Evil," "Good and Bad."

1

5 Those English psychologists, who up to the
present are the only philosophers who are to
be thanked for any endeavor to get as far as a
history of the origin of morality—these men, I
say, offer us in their own personalities no pal-
10 try problem;—tthey even have, if I am to be
quite frank about it, in their capacity of living
riddles, an advantage over their books—*they
themselves are interesting*! These English psychologists—what do they really mean? We
15 always find them voluntarily or involuntarily at
the same task of pushing to the front the *partie
honteuse*[58] of our inner world, and looking for
the efficient, governing, and decisive principle
in that precise quarter where the intellectual
20 self-respect of the race would be the most
reluctant to find it (for example, in the *vis iner-
ti*[59] of habit, or in forgetfulness, or in a blind
and fortuitous mechanism and association of
ideas, or in some factor that is purely passive,
25 reflex, molecular, or fundamentally stupid)—
what is the real motive power which always
impels these psychologists in precisely this
direction? Is it an instinct for human dispar-
agement somewhat sinister, vulgar, and malig-
30 nant, or perhaps incomprehensible even to
itself? or perhaps a touch of pessimistic jealousy, the mistrust of disillusioned idealists
who have become gloomy, poisoned, and bit-

Adapted from the translation of Horace B. Samuel
[58] [Shameful part]
[59] [Strength of inertia]

ter? or a petty subconscious enmity and rancor
35 against Christianity (and Plato), that has con-
ceivably never crossed the threshold of consciousness? or just a vicious taste for those
elements of life which are bizarre, painfully
paradoxical, mystical, and illogical? or, as a
40 final alternative, a dash of each of these motives—a little vulgarity, a little gloominess, a
little anti-Christianity, a little craving for the
necessary piquancy?

45 But I am told that it is simply a case of old
frigid and tedious frogs crawling and hopping
around men and inside men, as if they were as
thoroughly at home there, as they would be in
a swamp.
50

I am opposed to this statement, nay, I do not
believe it; and if, in the impossibility of
knowledge, one is permitted to wish, so do I
wish from my heart that just the converse
55 metaphor should apply, and that these analysts
with their psychological microscopes should
be, at bottom, brave, proud, and magnanimous animals who know how to bridle both
their hearts and their smarts, and have specifi-
60 cally trained themselves to sacrifice what is
desirable to what is true, *any* truth in fact, even
the simple, bitter, ugly, repulsive, unchristian,
and immoral truths—for there are truths of
that description.
65

2

All honor, then, to the noble spirits who
would fain dominate these historians of morality. But it is certainly a pity that they lack the
70 historical sense itself, that they themselves are

quite deserted by all the beneficent spirits of history. The whole train of their thought runs, as was always the way of old-fashioned philosophers, on *thoroughly* unhistorical lines: there is no doubt on this point. The crass ineptitude of their genealogy of morals is immediately apparent when the question arises of ascertaining the origin of the idea and judgment of "good." "Man had originally" so speaks their decree, "praised and called 'good' altruistic acts from the standpoint of those on whom they were conferred, that is, those to whom they were *useful*; subsequently the origin of this praise was *forgotten*, and altruistic acts, simply because, as a sheer matter of habit, they were praised as good, came also to be felt as good—as though they contained in themselves some intrinsic goodness." The thing is obvious:—this initial derivation contains already all the typical and idiosyncratic traits of the English psychologists—we have "utility," "forgetting," "habit," and finally "error," the whole assemblage forming the basis of a system of values, on which the higher man has up to the present prided himself as though it were a kind of privilege of man in general. This pride *must* be brought low, this system of values *must* lose its values: is that attained?

Now the first argument that comes ready to my hand is that the real homestead of the concept "good" is sought and located in the wrong place: the judgment "good" did not originate among those to whom goodness was shown. Much rather has it been the good themselves, that is, the aristocratic, the powerful, the high-stationed, the high-minded, who have felt that they themselves were good, and that their actions were good, that is to say of the first order, in contradistinction to all the low, the low-minded, the vulgar, and the plebeian. It was out of this pathos of distance that they first arrogated the right to create values for their own profit, and to coin the names of such values: what had they to do with utility? The standpoint of utility is as alien and as inapplicable as it could possibly be, when we have to deal with so volcanic an effervescence of supreme values, creating and demarcating as they do a hierarchy within themselves: it is at this juncture that one arrives at an appreciation of the contrast to that tepid temperature, which is the presupposition on which every combination of worldly wisdom and every calculation of practical expediency is always based—and not for one occasional, not for one exceptional instance, but chronically. The pathos of nobility and distance, as I have said, the chronic and despotic *esprit de corps* and fundamental instinct of a higher dominant race coming into association with a meaner race, an "under race," this is the origin of the antithesis of good and bad.

(The masters' right of giving names goes so far that it is permissible to look upon language itself as the expression of the power of the masters: they say "this *is* that, and that," they seal finally every object and every event with a sound, and thereby at the same time take possession of it.) It is because of this origin that the word "good" is far from having any necessary connection with altruistic acts, in accordance with the superstitious belief of these moral philosophers. On the contrary, it is on the occasion of the *decay* of aristocratic values, that the antitheses between "egoistic" and "altruistic" presses more and more heavily on the human conscience—it is, to use my own language, the *herd instinct* which finds in this antithesis an expression in many ways. And even then it takes a considerable time for this instinct to become sufficiently dominant, for the valuation to be inextricably dependent on this antithesis (as is the case in contemporary Europe); for to-day that prejudice is predominant, which, acting even now with all the intensity of an obsession and brain disease, holds that "moral," "altruistic," and "désintréssé"[60] are concepts of equal value.

3

In the second place, quite apart from the fact that this hypothesis as to the genesis of the value "good" cannot be historically upheld, it suffers from an inherent psychological contradiction. The utility of altruistic conduct has presumably been the origin of its being praised, and this origin has become *forgotten:*— But in what conceivable way is this forgetting *possible*! Has perchance the utility of such conduct ceased at some given moment? The contrary is the case. This utility has rather been experienced every day at all times, and is consequently a feature that obtains a new and regular emphasis with every fresh day; it follows that, so far from vanishing from the consciousness, so far indeed from being forgotten, it must necessarily become impressed on the consciousness with ever-increasing distinctness. How much more logical is that contrary theory (it is not the truer for that) which is represented, for instance, by Herbert Spencer, who places the concept "good" as essentially similar to the concept "useful," "purposive," so that in the judgments "good" and "bad" mankind is simply summarizing and investing with a sanction its *unforgotten* and *unforgettable* experiences concerning the "useful-purposive" and the "mischievous-non-purposive." According to this theory, "good" is the attribute of that which has previously shown itself useful; and so is able to claim to be considered "valuable in the highest degree," "valuable in itself." This method of explanation is also, as I have said, wrong, but

at any rate the explanation itself is coherent, and psychologically tenable.

4

The guide-post which first put me on the right track was this question—what is the true etymological significance of the various symbols for the idea "good" which have been coined in the various languages? I then found that they all led back to *the same evolution of the same idea*—that everywhere "aristocrat," "noble" (in the social sense), is the root idea, out of which have necessarily developed "good" in the sense of "with aristocratic soul," "noble," in the sense of "with a soul of high caliber," "with a privileged soul"—a development which invariably runs parallel with that other evolution by which "vulgar," "plebeian," "low," are made to change finally into "bad." The most eloquent proof of this last contention is the German word "*schlecht*" itself: this word is identical with "*schlicht*"—(compare "*schlechtweg*" and "*schlechterdings*")[61]—which, originally and as yet without any sinister innuendo, simply denoted the plebeian man in contrast to the aristocratic man. It is at the sufficiently late period of the Thirty Years' War that this sense becomes changed to the sense now current. From the standpoint of the Genealogy of Morals this discovery seems to be substantial: the lateness of it is to be attributed to the retarding influence exercised in the modern world by democratic prejudice in the sphere of all questions of origin. This extends, as will shortly be shown, even to the province of natural science and physiology, which, *prima facie* is the most objective. The extent of the mischief which is caused by this prejudice (once it is free of all trammels except those of its own malice), particularly to Ethics and History, is shown by the notorious case of

---

[60] [Disinterested]

[61] [Bad]; [simple]; [simply]

Buckle: it was in Buckle that that *plebeianism* of
the modern spirit, which is of English origin,
broke out once again from its malignant soil
with all the violence of a slimy volcano, and
5 with that salted, rampant, and vulgar eloquence with which up to the present time all
volcanoes have spoken.

5

10 With regard to our problem, which can justly
be called an intimate problem, and which
elects to appeal to only a limited number of
ears: it is of no small interest to ascertain that
in those words and roots which denote
15 "good" we catch glimpses of that arch-trait,
on the strength of which the aristocrats feel
themselves to be beings of a higher order than
their fellows. Indeed, they call themselves in
perhaps the most frequent instances simply
20 after their superiority in power (*e.g.* "the powerful," "the lords," "the commanders"), or
after the most obvious sign of their superiority, as for example "the rich," "the possessors"
(that is the meaning of *arya*; and the Iranian
25 and Slav languages correspond). But they also
call themselves after some *characteristic idiosyncrasy*; and this is the case which now concerns
us. They name themselves, for instance, "the
truthful": this is first done by the Greek nobil-
30 ity whose mouthpiece is found in Theognis,
the Megarian poet. The word εσθος, which is
coined for the purpose, signifies etymological-
ly "one who *is*," who has reality, who is real,
who is true; and then with a subjective twist,
35 the "true," as the "truthful": at this stage in
the evolution of the idea, it becomes the motto and party cry of the nobility, and quite
completes the transition to the meaning "noble," so as to place outside the pale the lying,
40 vulgar man, as Theognis conceives and portrays him—till finally the word after the decay
of the nobility is left to delineate psychological
noblesse, and becomes as it were ripe and mel-

low. In the word κακος[62] as in δειλος[63] (the
45 plebeian in contrast to the αγανος[64]) the cowardice is emphasized. This affords perhaps an
inkling on what lines the etymological origin
of the very ambiguous αγανος is to be investigated. In the Latin *malus* (which I place side by
50 side with μελας)[65] the vulgar man can be distinguished as the dark-colored, and above all
as the black-haired ("*hic niger est*")[66], as the pre-
Aryan inhabitants of the Italian soil, whose
complexion formed the clearest feature of
55 distinction from the dominant blondes, namely, the Aryan conquering race:—at any rate
Gaelic has afforded me the exact analogue—
Fin (for instance, in the name Fin-Gal), the
distinctive word of the nobility, finally—good,
60 noble, clean, but originally the blonde-haired
man in contrast to the dark black-haired abo-
riginals. The Celts, if I may make a parenthetic
statement, were throughout a blonde race; and
it is wrong to connect, as Virchow still con-
65 nects, those traces of an essentially dark-haired
population which are to be seen on the more
elaborate ethnographical maps of Germany
with any Celtic ancestry or with any admixture
of Celtic blood: in this context it is rather the
70 *pre-Aryan* population of Germany which surg-
es up to these districts. (The same is true sub-
stantially of the whole of Europe: in point of
fact, the subject race has finally again obtained
the upper hand, in complexion and the short-
75 ness of the skull, and perhaps in the intellectual and social qualities. Who can guarantee that
modern democracy, still more modern anarchy, and indeed that tendency to the "Com-
mune," the most primitive form of society,
80 which is now common to all the Socialists in

---

[62] [Bad]
[63] [Timid]
[64] [Good]
[65] [Bad]; [Black]
[66] [He is of black heart/character]; literally: He is
black/dark (from Horace)

Europe, does not in its real essence signify a monstrous reversion—and that the conquering and *master* race—the Aryan race, is not also becoming inferior physiologically?) I believe

5 that I can explain the Latin *bonus* as the "warrior": my hypothesis is that I am right in deriving *bonus*[67] from an older *duonus* (compare *bellum = duellum = duen-lum*, in which the word *duonus* appears to me to be contained). Bonus

10 accordingly as the man of discord, of variance, "entzweiung" (*duo*), as the warrior: one sees what in ancient Rome "the good" meant for a man. Must not our actual German word *gut*[68] mean "*the godlike*, the man of godlike race"?

15 and be identical with the national name (originally the nobles' name) of the *Goths*?

The grounds for this supposition do not appertain to this work.

20

6

Above all, there is no exception (though there are opportunities for exceptions) to this rule, that the idea of political superiority always

25 resolves itself into the idea of psychological superiority, in those cases where the highest caste is at the same time the *priestly* caste, and in accordance with its general characteristics confers on itself the privilege of a title which

30 alludes specifically to its priestly function. It is in these cases, for instance, that "clean" and "unclean" confront each other for the first time as badges of class distinction; here again there develops a "good" and a "bad," in a

35 sense which has ceased to be merely social. Moreover, care should be taken not to take these ideas of "clean" and "unclean" too seriously, too broadly, or too symbolically: all the ideas of ancient man have, on the contrary,

40 got to be understood in their initial stages, in a

---

[67] [Good]
[68] [Good]

sense which is, to an almost inconceivable extent, crude, coarse, physical, and narrow, and above all essentially unsymbolical. The "clean man" is originally only a man who

45 washes himself, who abstains from certain foods which are conducive to skin diseases, who does not sleep with the unclean women of the lower classes, who has a horror of blood—not more, not much more! On the

50 other hand, the very nature of a priestly aristocracy shows the reasons why just at such an early juncture there should ensue a really dangerous sharpening and intensification of opposed values: it is, in fact, through these op-

55 posed values that gulfs are cleft in the social plane, which a veritable Achilles of free thought would shudder to cross. There is from the outset a certain *diseased taint* in such sacerdotal aristocracies, and in the habits

60 which prevail in such societies—habits which, *averse* as they are to action, constitute a compound of introspection and explosive emotionalism, as a result of which there appears that introspective morbidity and neurasthenia,

65 which adheres almost inevitably to all priests at all times: with regard, however, to the remedy which they themselves have invented for this disease—the philosopher has no option but to state, that it has proved itself in its ef-

70 fects a hundred times more dangerous than the disease, from which it should have been the deliverer. Humanity itself is still diseased from the effects of the naïvetés of this priestly cure. Take, for instance, certain kinds of diet

75 (abstention from flesh), fasts, sexual continence, flight into the wilderness (a kind of Weir-Mitchell isolation, though of course without that system of excessive feeding and fattening which is the most efficient antidote

80 to all the hysteria of the ascetic ideal); consider too the whole metaphysic of the priests, with its war on the senses, its enervation, its hairsplitting; consider its self-hypnotism on the

fakir and Brahman principles (it uses Brahman as a glass disc and obsession), and that climax which we can understand only too well of an unusual satiety with its panacea of *nothingness*
5 (or God:—the demand for a *unio mystica*[69] with God is the demand of the Buddhist for nothingness, Nirvana—and nothing else!). In sacerdotal societies *every* element is on a more dangerous scale, not merely cures and reme-
10 dies, but also pride, revenge, cunning, exaltation, love, ambition, virtue, morbidity:— further, it can fairly be stated that it is on the soil of this *essentially dangerous* form of human society, the sacerdotal form, that man really
15 becomes for the first time an *interesting animal,* that it is in this form that the soul of man has in a higher sense attained *depths* and become *evil*—and those are the two fundamental forms of the superiority which up to the present man
20 has exhibited over every other animal.

7

The reader will have already surmised with what ease the priestly mode of valuation can
25 branch off from the knightly aristocratic mode, and then develop into the very antithesis of the latter: special impetus is given to this opposition, by every occasion when the castes of the priests and warriors confront each other
30 with mutual jealousy and cannot agree over the prize. The knightly-aristocratic "values" are based on a careful cult of the physical, on a flowering, rich, and even effervescing healthiness, that goes considerably beyond what is
35 necessary for maintaining life, on war, adventure, the chase, the dance, the tourney—on everything, in fact, which is contained in strong, free, and joyous action. The priestly-aristocratic mode of valuation is—we have
40 seen—based on other hypotheses: it is bad enough for this class when it is a question of

---

[69] [Mystical union/marriage]

war! Yet the priests are, as is notorious, *the worst enemies*—why? Because they are the weakest. Their weakness causes their hate to
45 expand into a monstrous and sinister shape, a shape which is most crafty and most poisonous. The really great haters in the history of the world have always been priests, who are also the cleverest haters—in comparison with
50 the cleverness of priestly revenge, every other piece of cleverness is practically negligible. Human history would be too fatuous for anything were it not for the cleverness imported into it by the weak—take at once the most
55 important instance. All the world's efforts against the "aristocrats," the "mighty," the "masters," the "holders of power," are negligible by comparison with what has been accomplished against those classes by *the Jews*—
60 the Jews, that priestly nation which eventually realized that the one method of effecting satisfaction on its enemies and tyrants was by means of a radical transvaluation of values, which was at the same time an act of the *clever-*
65 *est revenge.* Yet the method was only appropriate to a nation of priests, to a nation of the most jealously nursed priestly revengefulness. It was the Jews who, in opposition to the aristocratic equation (good = aristocratic = beau-
70 tiful = happy = loved by the gods), dared with a terrifying logic to suggest the contrary equation, and indeed to maintain with the teeth of the most profound hatred (the hatred of weakness) this contrary equation, namely, "the
75 wretched are alone the good; the poor, the weak, the lowly, are alone the good; the suffering, the needy, the sick, the loathsome, are the only ones who are pious, the only ones who are blessed, for them alone is salvation—but
80 you, on the other hand, you aristocrats, you men of power, you are to all eternity the evil, the horrible, the covetous, the insatiate, the godless; eternally also shall you be the unblessed, the cursed, the damned!" We know

who it was who reaped the heritage of this Jewish transvaluation. In the context of the monstrous and inordinately fateful initiative which the Jews have exhibited in connection 5 with this most fundamental of all declarations of war, I remember the passage which came to my pen on another occasion (*Beyond Good and Evil*, Aph. 195)—that it was, in fact, with the Jews that the *revolt of the slaves* begins in the 10 sphere *of morals*; that revolt which has behind it a history of two millennia, and which at the present day has only moved out of our sight, because it—has achieved victory.

8

But you understand this not? You have no eyes for a force which has taken two thousand years to achieve victory?—There is nothing wonderful in this: all *lengthy* processes are hard 20 to see and to realize. But *this* is what took place: from the trunk of that tree of revenge and hate, Jewish hate,—that most profound and sublime hate, which creates ideals and changes old values to new creations, the like 25 of which has never been on earth,—there grew a phenomenon which was equally incomparable, *a new love*, the most profound and sublime of all kinds of love;—and from what other trunk could it have grown? But beware 30 of supposing that this love has soared on its upward growth, as in any way a real negation of that thirst for revenge, as an antithesis to the Jewish hate! No, the contrary is the truth! This love grew out of that hate, as its crown, 35 as its triumphant crown, circling wider and wider amid the clarity and fullness of the sun, and pursuing in the very kingdom of light and height its goal of hatred, its victory, its spoil, its strategy, with the same intensity with which 40 the roots of that tree of hate sank into everything which was deep and evil with increasing stability and increasing desire. This Jesus of Nazareth, the incarnate gospel of love, this

45 "Redeemer" bringing salvation and victory to the poor, the sick, the sinful—was he not really temptation in its most sinister and irresistible form, temptation to take the tortuous path to those very *Jewish* values and those very Jewish ideals? Has not Israel really obtained the 50 final goal of its sublime revenge, by the tortuous paths of this "Redeemer," for all that he might pose as Israel's adversary and Israel's destroyer? Is it not due to the black magic of a really *great* policy of revenge, of a far-seeing, 55 burrowing revenge, both acting and calculating with slowness, that Israel himself must repudiate before all the world the actual instrument of his own revenge and nail it to the cross, so that all the world—that is, all the enemies of 60 Israel—could nibble without suspicion at this very bait? Could, moreover, any human mind with all its elaborate ingenuity invent a bait that was more truly *dangerous*? Anything that was even equivalent in the power of its seduc- 65 tive, intoxicating, defiling, and corrupting influence to that symbol of the holy cross, to that awful paradox of a "god on the cross," to that mystery of the unthinkable, supreme, and utter horror of the self-crucifixion of a god for 70 the *salvation of man*? It is at least certain that *sub hoc signo*[70] Israel, with its revenge and transvaluation of all values, has up to the present always triumphed again over all other ideals, over all more aristocratic ideals.

75

9

"But why do you talk of nobler ideals? Let us submit to the facts; that the people have triumphed—or the slaves, or the populace, or 80 the herd, or whatever name you care to give them—if this has happened through the Jews, so be it! In that case no nation ever had a greater mission in the world's history. The

---

[70] [Under this sign]; references Constantine's vision prior to Battle at the Milvian Bridge

'masters' have been done away with; the morality of the vulgar man has triumphed. This triumph may also be called a blood-poisoning (it has mutually fused the races)—I do not

5 dispute it; but there is no doubt but that this intoxication has succeeded. The 'redemption' of the human race (that is, from the masters) is progressing swimmingly; everything is obviously becoming Judaized, or Christianized, or

10 vulgarized (what is there in the words?). It seems impossible to stop the course of this poisoning through the whole body politic of mankind—but its *tempo* and pace may from the present time be slower, more delicate, qui-

15 eter, more discreet—there is time enough. In view of this context has the Church nowadays any necessary purpose? has it, in fact, a right to live? Or could man get on without it? *Quæritur*[71]. It seems that it fetters and retards

20 this tendency, instead of accelerating it. Well, even that might be its utility. The Church certainly is a crude and boorish institution, that is repugnant to an intelligence with any pretense at delicacy, to a really modern taste. Should it

25 not at any rate learn to be somewhat more subtle? It alienates nowadays, more than it allures. Which of us would, forsooth, be a freethinker if there were no Church? It is the Church which repels us, not its poison—apart

30 from the Church we like the poison." This is the epilogue of a freethinker to my discourse, of an honorable animal (as he has given abundant proof), and a democrat to boot; he had up to that time listened to me, and could not

35 endure my silence, but for me, indeed, with regard to this topic there is much on which to be silent.

10

40 The revolt of the slaves in morals begins in the very principle of *resentment* becoming creative

---

[71] [The question is raised]

and giving birth to values—a resentment experienced by creatures who, deprived as they are of the proper outlet of action, are forced

45 to find their compensation in an imaginary revenge. While every aristocratic morality springs from a triumphant affirmation of its own demands, the slave morality says "no" from the very outset to what is "outside it-

50 self," "different from itself," and "not itself": and this "no" is its creative deed. This volte-face of the valuing standpoint—this *inevitable* gravitation to the objective instead of back to the subjective—is typical of "resentment": the

55 slave-morality requires as the condition of its existence an external and objective world, to employ physiological terminology, it requires objective stimuli to be capable of action at all—its action is fundamentally a reaction. The

60 contrary is the case when we come to the aristocrat's system of values: it acts and grows spontaneously, it merely seeks its antithesis in order to pronounce a more grateful and exultant "yes" to its own self;—its negative con-

65 ception, "low," "vulgar," "bad," is merely a pale late-born foil in comparison with its positive and fundamental conception (saturated as it is with life and passion), of "we aristocrats, we good ones, we beautiful ones, we happy

70 ones."

When the aristocratic morality goes astray and commits sacrilege on reality, this is limited to that particular sphere with which it is *not* suffi-

75 ciently acquainted—a sphere, in fact, from the real knowledge of which it disdainfully defends itself. It misjudges, in some cases, the sphere which it despises, the sphere of the common vulgar man and the low people: on

80 the other hand, due weight should be given to the consideration that in any case the mood of contempt, of disdain, of superciliousness, even on the supposition that it *falsely* portrays the object of its contempt, will always be far re-

moved from that degree of falsity which will always characterize the attacks—in effigy, of course—of the vindictive hatred and revengefulness of the weak in onslaughts on their enemies. In point of fact, there is in contempt too strong an admixture of nonchalance, of casualness, of boredom, of impatience, even of personal exultation, for it to be capable of distorting its victim into a real caricature or a real monstrosity. Attention again should be paid to the almost benevolent *nuances* which, for instance, the Greek nobility imports into all the words by which it distinguishes the common people from itself; note how continuously a kind of pity, care, and consideration imparts its honeyed *flavor*, until at last almost all the words which are applied to the vulgar man survive finally as expressions for "unhappy," "worthy of pity" (compare δειλος, δειλαιος, πονηρος, νοχνηρος[72]; the latter two names really denoting the vulgar man as labour-slave and beast of burden)—and how, conversely, "bad," "low," "unhappy" have never ceased to ring in the Greek ear with a tone in which "unhappy" is the predominant note: this is a heritage of the old noble aristocratic morality, which remains true to itself even in contempt (let philologists remember the sense in which ὄϊζυρός, ἄνολβος, τλήμων, δυστυχεῖν, ξυμφορά[73] used to be employed). The "well-born" simply *felt* themselves the "happy"; they did not have to manufacture their happiness artificially through looking at their enemies, or in cases to talk and *lie themselves* into happiness (as is the custom with all resentful men); and similarly, complete men as they were, exuberant with strength, and consequently *necessarily* energetic, they were too wise to dissociate happiness from action— activity becomes in their minds necessarily

counted as happiness (that is the etymology of εὖ πράττειν[74])—all in sharp contrast to the "happiness" of the weak and the oppressed, with their festering venom and malignity, among whom happiness appears essentially as a narcotic, a deadening, a quietude, a peace, a "Sabbath," an enervation of the mind and relaxation of the limbs,—in short, a purely *passive* phenomenon. While the aristocratic man lived in confidence and openness with himself (γενναῖος[75], "noble-born," emphasizes the nuance "sincere," and perhaps also "naïf"), the resentful man, on the other hand, is neither sincere nor naïf, nor honest and candid with himself. His soul *squints*; his mind loves hidden crannies, tortuous paths and backdoors, everything secret appeals to him as *his* world, *his* safety, *his* balm; he is past master in silence, in not forgetting, in waiting, in provisional self-depreciation and self-abasement. A race of such *resentful* men will of necessity eventually prove more *prudent* than any aristocratic race, it will honor prudence on quite a distinct scale, as, in fact, a paramount condition of existence, while prudence among aristocratic men is apt to be tinged with a delicate flavor of luxury and refinement; so among them it plays nothing like so integral a part as that complete certainty of function of the governing *unconscious* instincts, or as indeed a certain lack of prudence, such as a vehement and valiant charge, whether against danger or the enemy, or as those ecstatic bursts of rage, love, reverence, gratitude, by which at all times noble souls have recognized each other. When the resentment of the aristocratic man manifests itself, it fulfills and exhausts itself in an immediate reaction, and consequently instills no *venom*: on the other hand, it never manifests itself at all in countless instances, when in the

---

[72] [Cowardly, mean, base, struggling]
[73] [Sad, unlucky, base, sorrowful, misfortune]

[74] [Do rightly]
[75] [Brave]

case of the feeble and weak it would be inevitable. An inability to take seriously for any length of time their enemies, their disasters, their *misdeeds*—that is the sign of the full
5　strong natures who possess a superfluity of molding plastic force, that heals completely and produces forgetfulness: a good example of this in the modern world is Mirabeau, who had no memory for any insults and mean-
10　nesses which were practiced on him, and who was only incapable of forgiving because he forgot. Such a man indeed shakes off with a shrug many a worm which would have buried itself in another; it is only in characters like
15　these that we see the possibility (supposing, of course, that there is such a possibility in the world) of the real "*love of one's enemies.*" What respect for his enemies is found, forsooth, in an aristocratic man—and such a rev-
20　erence is already a bridge to love! He insists on having his enemy to himself as his distinction. He tolerates no other enemy but a man in whose character there is nothing to despise and much to honor! On the other hand, imag-
25　ine the "enemy" as the resentful man conceives him—and it is here exactly that we see his work, his creativeness; he has conceived "the evil enemy," the "evil one," and indeed that is the root idea from which he now
30　evolves as a contrasting and corresponding figure a "good one," himself—his very self!

11

The method of this man is quite contrary to
35　that of the aristocratic man, who conceives the root idea "good" spontaneously and straight away, that is to say, out of himself, and from that material then creates for himself a concept of "bad"! This "bad" of aristocratic origin
40　and that "evil" out of the cauldron of unsatisfied hatred—the former an imitation, an "extra," an additional nuance; the latter, on the other hand, the original, the beginning, the

essential act in the conception of a slave-
45　morality—these two words "bad" and "evil," how great a difference do they mark, in spite of the fact that they have an identical contrary in the idea "good." But the idea "good" is not the same: much rather let the question be
50　asked, "Who is really evil according to the meaning of the morality of resentment?" In all sternness let it be answered thus:—*just* the good man of the other morality, just the aristocrat, the powerful one, the one who rules,
55　but who is distorted by the venomous eye of resentfulness, into a new color, a new signification, a new appearance. This particular point we would be the last to deny: the man who learnt to know those "good" ones only as en-
60　emies, learnt at the same time not to know them only as "*evil enemies*" and the same men who *inter pares* were kept so rigorously in bounds through convention, respect, custom, and gratitude, though much more through
65　mutual vigilance and jealousy *inter pares*, these men who in their relations with each other find so many new ways of manifesting consideration, self-control, delicacy, loyalty, pride, and friendship, these men are in reference to
70　what is outside their circle (where the foreign element, a *foreign* country, begins), not much better than beasts of prey, which have been let loose. They enjoy there freedom from all social control, they feel that in the wilderness
75　they can give vent with impunity to that tension which is produced by enclosure and imprisonment in the peace of society, they *revert* to the innocence of the beast-of-prey conscience, like jubilant monsters, who perhaps
80　come from a ghastly bout of murder, arson, rape, and torture, with bravado and a moral equanimity, as though merely some wild student's prank had been played, perfectly convinced that the poets have now an ample
85　theme to sing and celebrate. It is impossible not to recognize at the core of all these aristo-

cratic races the beast of prey; the magnificent *blonde brute*, avidly rampant for spoil and victory; this hidden core needed an outlet from time to time, the beast must get loose again,
5 must return into the wilderness—the Roman, Arabic, German, and Japanese nobility, the Homeric heroes, the Scandinavian Vikings, are all alike in this need. It is the aristocratic races who have left the idea "Barbarian" on all the
10 tracks in which they have marched; nay, a consciousness of this very barbarianism, and even a pride in it, manifests itself even in their highest civilization (for example, when Pericles says to his Athenians in that celebrated funeral
15 oration, "Our audacity has forced a way over every land and sea, rearing everywhere imperishable memorials of itself for *good* and for *evil*"). This audacity of aristocratic races, mad, absurd, and spasmodic as may be its expres-
20 sion; the incalculable and fantastic nature of their enterprises, Pericles sets in special relief and glory the ραθυμία⁷⁶ of the Athenians, their nonchalance and contempt for safety, body, life, and comfort, their awful joy and
25 intense delight in all destruction, in all the ecstasies of victory and cruelty,—all these features become crystallized, for those who suffered thereby in the picture of the "barbarian," of the "evil enemy," perhaps of the "Goth"
30 and of the "Vandal." The profound, icy mistrust which the German provokes, as soon as he arrives at power,—even at the present time,—is always still an aftermath of that inextinguishable horror with which for whole cen-
35 turies Europe has regarded the wrath of the blonde Teuton beast (although between the old Germans and ourselves there exists scarcely a psychological, let alone a physical, relationship). I have once called attention to the
40 embarrassment of Hesiod, when he conceived the series of social ages, and endeavored to

---

⁷⁶ [Indolence]

express them in gold, silver, and bronze. He could only dispose of the contradiction, with which he was confronted, by the Homeric
45 world, an age magnificent indeed, but at the same time so awful and so violent, by making two ages out of one, which he henceforth placed one behind each other—first, the age of the heroes and demigods, as that world had
50 remained in the memories of the aristocratic families, who found therein their own ancestors; secondly, the bronze age, as that corresponding age appeared to the descendants of the oppressed, spoiled, ill-treated, exiled, en-
55 slaved; namely, as an age of bronze, as I have said, hard, cold, terrible, without feelings and without conscience, crushing everything, and bespattering everything with blood. Granted the truth of the theory now believed to be
60 true, that the very *essence of all civilization* is to *train* out of man, the beast of prey, a tame and civilized animal, a domesticated animal, it follows indubitably that we must regard as the real *tools of civilization* all those instincts of reac-
65 tion and resentment, by the help of which the aristocratic races, together with their ideals, were finally degraded and overpowered; though that has not yet come to be synonymous with saying that the bearers of those
70 tools also *represented* the civilization. It is rather the contrary that is not only probable—nay, it is *palpable* to-day; these bearers of vindictive instincts that have to be bottled up, these descendants of all European and non-European
75 slavery, especially of the pre-Aryan population—these people, I say, represent the *decline* of humanity! These "tools of civilization" are a disgrace to humanity, and constitute in reality more of an argument against civilization, more
80 of a reason why civilization should be suspected. One may be perfectly justified in being always afraid of the blonde beast that lies at the core of all aristocratic races, and in being on one's guard: but who would not a hundred

times prefer to be afraid, when one at the same time admires, than to be immune from fear, at the cost of being perpetually obsessed with the loathsome spectacle of the distorted,
5 the dwarfed, the stunted, the envenomed? And is that not our fate? What produces to-day our repulsion towards "man"?—for we *suffer* from "man," there is no doubt about it. It is not fear; it is rather that we have nothing
10 more to fear from men; it is that the worm "man" is in the foreground and pullulates; it is that the "tame man," the wretched mediocre and unedifying creature, has learnt to consider himself a goal and a pinnacle, an inner mean-
15 ing, an historic principle, a "higher man"; yes, it is that he has a certain right so to consider himself, in so far as he feels that in contrast to that excess of deformity, disease, exhaustion, and effeteness whose odor is beginning to
20 pollute present-day Europe, he at any rate has achieved a relative success, he at any rate still says "yes" to life.

12

25 I cannot refrain at this juncture from uttering a sigh and one last hope. What is it precisely which I find intolerable? That which I alone cannot get rid of, which makes me choke and faint? Bad air! bad air! That something misbe-
30 gotten comes near me; that I must inhale the odor of the entrails of a misbegotten soul!— That excepted, what can one not endure in the way of need, privation, bad weather, sickness, toil, solitude? In point of fact, one manages to
35 get over everything, born as one is to a bur-rowing and battling existence; one always re-turns once again to the light, one always lives again one's golden hour of victory—and then one stands as one was born, unbreakable,
40 tense, ready for something more difficult, for something more distant, like a bow stretched but the tauter by every strain. But from time to time do ye grant me—assuming that "be-

yond good and evil" there are goddesses who
45 can grant—one glimpse, grant me but one glimpse only, of something perfect, fully real-ized, happy, mighty, triumphant, of something that still gives cause for fear! A glimpse of a man that justifies the existence of man, a
50 glimpse of an incarnate human happiness that realizes and redeems, for the sake of which one may hold fast to *the belief in man*! For the position is this: in the dwarfing and leveling of the European man lurks *our* greatest peril, for
55 it is this outlook which fatigues—we see to-day nothing which wishes to be greater, we surmise that the process is always still back-wards, still backwards towards something more attenuated, more inoffensive, more cun-
60 ning, more comfortable, more mediocre, more indifferent, more Chinese, more Christian— man, there is no doubt about it, grows always "better"—the destiny of Europe lies even in this—that in losing the fear of man, we have
65 also lost the hope in man, yea, the will to be man. The sight of man now fatigues.—What is present-day Nihilism if it is not *that*?—We are tired of *man*.

13

70 But let us come back to it; the problem of another origin of the *good*—of the good, as the resentful man has thought it out—demands its solution. It is not surprising that the lambs
75 should bear a grudge against the great birds of prey, but that is no reason for blaming the great birds of prey for taking the little lambs. And when the lambs say among themselves, "These birds of prey are evil, and he who is as
80 far removed from being a bird of prey, who is rather its opposite, a lamb,—is he not good?" then there is nothing to cavil at in the setting up of this ideal, though it may also be that the birds of prey will regard it a little sneeringly,
85 and perchance say to themselves, "*We* bear no grudge against them, these good lambs, we

even like them: nothing is tastier than a tender lamb." To require of strength that it should not express itself as strength, that it should not be a wish to overpower, a wish to overthrow, a wish to become master, a thirst for enemies and antagonisms and triumphs, is just as absurd as to require of weakness that it should express itself as strength. A quantum of force is just such a quantum of movement, will, action—rather it is nothing else than just those very phenomena of moving, willing, acting, and can only appear otherwise in the misleading errors of language (and the fundamental fallacies of reason which have become petrified therein), which understands, and understands wrongly, all working as conditioned by a worker, by a "subject." And just exactly as the people separate the lightning from its flash, and interpret the latter as a thing done, as the working of a subject which is called lightning, so also does the popular morality separate strength from the expression of strength, as though behind the strong man there existed some indifferent neutral *substratum*, which enjoyed a *caprice and option* as to whether or not it should express strength. But there is no such *substratum*, there is no "being" behind doing, working, becoming; "the doer" is a mere appanage to the action. The action is everything. In point of fact, the people duplicate the doing, when they make the lightning lighten, that is a "doing-doing": they make the same phenomenon first a cause, and then, secondly, the effect of that cause. The scientists fail to improve matters when they say, "Force moves, force causes," and so on. Our whole science is still, in spite of all its coldness, of all its freedom from passion, a dupe of the tricks of language, and has never succeeded in getting rid of that superstitious changeling "the subject" (the atom, to give another instance, is such a changeling, just as the Kantian "Thing-in-itself"). What wonder, if the suppressed and stealthily simmering passions of revenge and hatred exploit for their own advantage this belief, and indeed hold no belief with a more steadfast enthusiasm than this—"that the strong has the *option* of being weak, and the bird of prey of being a lamb." Thereby do they win for themselves the right of attributing to the birds of prey the *responsibility* for being birds of prey: when the oppressed, down-trodden, and overpowered say to themselves with the vindictive guile of weakness, "Let us be otherwise than the evil, namely, good! and good is every one who does not oppress, who hurts no one, who does not attack, who does not pay back, who hands over revenge to God, who holds himself, as we do, in hiding; who goes out of the way of evil, and demands, in short, little from life; like ourselves the patient, the meek, the just,"—yet all this, in its cold and unprejudiced interpretation, means nothing more than "once for all, the weak are weak; it is good to do *nothing for which we are not strong enough*"; but this dismal state of affairs, this prudence of the lowest order, which even insects possess (which in a great danger are fain to sham death so as to avoid doing "too much"), has, thanks to the counterfeiting and self-deception of weakness, come to masquerade in the pomp of an ascetic, mute, and expectant virtue, just as though the *very* weakness of the weak—that is, forsooth, its *being*, its working, its whole unique inevitable inseparable reality—were a voluntary result, something wished, chosen, a deed, an act of *merit*. This kind of man finds the belief in a neutral, free-choosing "subject" *necessary* from an instinct of self-preservation, of self-assertion, in which every lie is fain to sanctify itself. The subject (or, to use popular language, the *soul*) has perhaps proved itself the best dogma in the world simply because it rendered possible to the horde of mortal, weak, and oppressed individuals of every kind, that most sublime specimen of self-deception, the interpretation of weakness as freedom, of being this, or being that, as *merit*.

14

Will any one look a little into—right into—the mystery of how *ideals are manufactured* in this world? Who has the courage to do it? Come! Here we have a vista opened into these grimy workshops. Wait just a moment, dear Mr. Inquisitive and Foolhardy; your eye must first grow accustomed to this false changing light—Yes! Enough! Now speak! What is happening below down yonder? Speak out that what you see, man of the most dangerous curiosity—for now *I* am the listener.

"I see nothing, I hear the more. It is a cautious, spiteful, gentle whispering and muttering together in all the corners and crannies. It seems to me that they are lying; a sugary softness adheres to every sound. Weakness is turned to *merit*, there is no doubt about it—it is just as you say."

Further!

"And the impotence which requites not, is turned to 'goodness,' craven baseness to meekness, submission to those whom one hates, to obedience (namely, obedience to one of whom they say that he ordered this submission—they call him God). The inoffensive character of the weak, the very cowardice in which he is rich, his standing at the door, his forced necessity of waiting, gain here fine names, such as 'patience,' which is also called 'virtue'; not being able to avenge one's self, is called not wishing to avenge one's self, perhaps even forgiveness (for *they* know not what they do—we alone know what *they* do). They also talk of the 'love of their enemies' and sweat thereby."

Further!

"They are miserable, there is no doubt about it, all these whisperers and counterfeiters in the corners, although they try to get warm by crouching close to each other, but they tell me that their misery is a favour and distinction given to them by God, just as one beats the dogs one likes best; that perhaps this misery is also a preparation, a probation, a training; that perhaps it is still more something which will one day be compensated and paid back with a tremendous interest in gold, nay in happiness. This they call 'Blessedness.'"

Further!

"They are now giving me to understand, that not only are they better men than the mighty, the lords of the earth, whose spittle they have got to lick (not out of fear, not at all out of fear! But because God ordains that one should honour all authority)—not only are they better men, but that they also have a 'better time,' at any rate, will one day have a 'better time.' But enough! Enough! I can endure it no longer. Bad air! Bad air! These workshops *where ideals are manufactured*—verily they reek with the crassest lies."

Nay. Just one minute! You are saying nothing about the masterpieces of these virtuosos of black magic, who can produce whiteness, milk, and innocence out of any black you like: have you not noticed what a pitch of refinement is attained by their *chef d'≈iuvre*, their most audacious, subtle, ingenious, and lying artist-trick? Take care! These cellar-beasts, full of revenge and hate—what do they make, forsooth, out of their revenge and hate? Do you hear these words? Would you suspect, if you trusted only their words, that you are among men of resentment and nothing else?

"I understand, I prick my ears up again (ah! ah! ah! and I hold my nose). Now do I hear for the first time that which they have said so often: 'We good, *we are the righteous*'—what they demand they call not revenge but 'the triumph of *righteousness*'; what they hate is not their enemy, no, they hate 'unrighteousness,' 'godlessness'; what they believe in and hope is not the hope of revenge, the intoxication of sweet revenge ("sweeter than honey," did Homer call it?), but the victory of God, of the *righteous God* over the 'godless'; what is left for them to love in this world is not *their* brothers in hate, but their 'brothers in love,' as they say, all the good and righteous on the earth."

And how do they name that which serves them as a solace against all the troubles of life—their phantasmagoria of their anticipated future blessedness?

"How? Do I hear right? They call it 'the last judgment,' the advent of their kingdom, 'the kingdom of God'—but *in the meanwhile* they live 'in faith,' 'in love,' 'in hope.'"

Enough! Enough!

15

In the faith in what? In the love for what? In the hope of what? These weaklings!—they also, forsooth, wish to be the strong some time; there is no doubt about it, some time *their* kingdom also must come—"the kingdom of God" is their name for it, as has been mentioned: they are so meek in everything! Yet in order to experience *that* kingdom it is necessary to live long, to live beyond death,—yes, *eternal* life is necessary so that one can make up for ever for that earthly life "in faith," "in love," "in hope." Make up for what? Make up by what? Dante, as it seems to me, made a crass mistake when with awe-inspiring ingenuity he placed that inscription over the gate of his hell, "Me too made eternal love": at any rate the following inscription would have a much better right to stand over the gate of the Christian Paradise and its "eternal blessedness"—"Me too made eternal hate"—granted of course that a truth may rightly stand over the gate to a lie! For what is the blessedness of that Paradise? Possibly we could quickly surmise it; but it is better that it should be explicitly attested by an authority who in such matters is not to be disparaged, Thomas of Aquinas, the great teacher and saint. "*Beati in regno celesti*" says he, as gently as a lamb, "*videbunt pœnas damnatorum, ut beatitudo illis magis complaceat.*[77]" Or if we wish to hear a stronger tone, a word from the mouth of a triumphant father of the Church, who warned his disciples against the cruel ecstasies of the public spectacles—But why? Faith offers us much more,—says he, *de Spectac.*, c. 29 ss.,—something much stronger; thanks to the redemption, joys of quite another kind stand at our disposal; instead of athletes we have our martyrs; we wish for blood, well, we have the blood of Christ—but what then awaits us on the day of his return, of his triumph. And then does he proceed, does this enraptured visionary: "*at enim supersunt alia spectacula, ille ultimas et perpetuus judicii dies, ille nationibus insperatus, ille derisus, cum tanta sæculi vetustas et tot ejus nativitates uno igne haurientur. Quæ tunc spectaculi latitudo! Quid admirer! quid rideam! Ubi gaudeam! Ubi exultem, spectans tot et tantos reges, qui in cælum recepti nuntiabantur, cum ipso Jove et ipsis suis testibus in imis tenebris congemescentes! Item præsides*" (the provincial governors) "*persecutores dominici nominis sævioribus quam ipsi flammis sævierunt insultantibus contra Christianos liquescentes! Quos præterea sapientes illos*

---

[77] [The blessed in the kingdom of heaven will see the suffering of the damned, so that their blessedness is more pleasing.]

philosophos coram discipulis suis una conflagrantibus
erubescentes, quibus nihil ad deum pertinere
suadebant, quibus animas aut nullas aut non in
pristina corpora redituras affirmabant! Etiam poetas
5 *non ad Rhadamanti nec ad Minois, sed ad inopinati*
Christi tribunal palpitantes! Tunc magis tragœidi
audiendi, magis scilicet vocales" (with louder tones
and more violent shrieks) *"in sua propria*
calamitate; tunc histriones cognoscendi, solutiores multo
10 *per ignem; tunc spectandus auriga in flammea rota*
totus rubens, tunc xystici contemplandi non in gymna-
siis, sed in igne jaculati, nisi quod ne tunc quidem illos
velim vivos, ut qui malim ad eos potius conspectum
insatiabilem conferre, qui in dominum scevierunt. Hic
15 *est ille, dicam fabri aut quæstuariæ filius"* (as is
shown by the whole of the following, and in
particular by this well-known description of
the mother of Jesus from the Talmud, Tertullian is henceforth referring to the Jews), *"sab-*
20 *bati destructor, Samarites et dæmonium habens. Hic*
est quem a Juda redemistis, hic est ille arundine et
colaphis diverberatus, sputamentis de decoratus, felle et
acete potatus. Hic est, quem clam discentes
subripuerunt, ut resurrexisse dicatur vel hortulanus
25 *detraxit, ne lactucæ suæ frequentia commeantium*
laderentur. Ut talia species, ut talibus exultes, quis
tibi prætor aut consul aut sacerdos de sua liberalitate
prastabit? Et tamen hæc jam habemus quodammodo
per fidem spiritu imaginante repræsentata. Ceterum
30 *qualia illa sunt, quæ nec oculus vidit nec auris audivit*
nec in cor hominis ascenderunt?" (I Cor. ii. 9.) *"Cre-*
do circo et utraque caveâ" (first and fourth row,
or, according to others, the comic and the
tragic stage) *"et omni studio gratiora.*[78]*" Per*

---

[78] From Tertullian's De Spectaculis (Of Public
Shows). Here is a translation by C. Dodgson
(1842): And yet there remain other shows: that
last and eternal Day of Judgment, the unlooked
for, the scorned of the Nations, when all the
ancient things of the world, and all that are rising
into life, shall be consumed in one fire? what
shall then be the expanse of the show? whereat
shall I wonder? whereat laugh? whereat rejoice?
whereat exult? beholding so many kings, who

35 *fidem*[79]: so stands it written.

16

Let us come to a conclusion. The two *opposing*

---

were declared to be admitted into Heaven, with
Jupiter himself and all that testify of him, groaning together in the lowest darkness? those rulers
too, the persecutors of the Name of the Lord,
melting amid insulting fires more raging than
those wherewith themselves raged against the
Christians: those wise philosophers moreover
reddening before their own disciples, now burning together with them, whom they persuaded
that there was nothing which appertained to
God, before whom they affirmed that there were
either no souls, or that they should not return
again to their former bodies: poets too trembling
before the judgment-seat, not of Rhadamanthus,
not of Minos, but of the unlooked-for Christ.
Then will the tragic actors be the more to be
heard, because more loud in their cries amidst
real affliction of their own: then the players to be
recognized, more dissolute by far when dissolved
by fire: then the charioteer to be gazed on, all red
upon his fiery wheel: then the wrestlers to be
viewed tossing about, not in the theatre, but in
the fire----unless perchance I may even then not
desire to see them, as wishing rather to fix my
gaze, never to be satisfied, on those who have
furiously raged against the Lord. This, I shall say,
is He, the son of the carpenter or the harlot, the
destroyer of the Sabbath, the Samaritan and
Who had a devil. This is He, Whom ye bought
of Judas: this is He, Who was smitten with a reed
and with bufferings, dishonored with spittings,
drugged with gall and vinegar. This is He, Whom
the disciples stole secretly away, that it might be
said that He had risen again, or Whom the gar-
dener removed, lest his lettuces should be injured by the crowds of visitors. Such shows as
these, such triumphs as these, what praetor, or
consul, or quaestor, or priest, shall of his own
bounty bestow upon thee? and yet we have them
even now in some sort present to us, through
Faith, in the imagination of the spirit. But what
are those things which eye hath not seen, nor ear
heard, neither have entered into the heart of
man? Greater joys, methinks, than the circus,
and both the theatres, and any race-course.
[79] [From faith]

values, "good and bad," "good and evil," have fought a dreadful, thousand-year fight in the world, and though indubitably the second value has been for a long time in the preponderance, there are not wanting places where the fortune of the fight is still undecisive. It can almost be said that in the meanwhile the fight reaches a higher and higher level, and that in the meanwhile it has become more and more intense, and always more and more psychological; so that nowadays there is perhaps no more decisive mark of the *higher nature*, of the more psychological nature, than to be in that sense self-contradictory, and to be actually still a battleground for those two opposites. The symbol of this fight, written in a writing which has remained worthy of perusal throughout the course of history up to the present time, is called "Rome against Judæa, Judæa against Rome." Hitherto there has been no greater event than *that* fight, the putting of *that* question, *that* deadly antagonism. Rome found in the Jew the incarnation of the unnatural, as though it were its diametrically opposed monstrosity, and in Rome the Jew was held to be *convicted of hatred* of the whole human race: and rightly so, in so far as it is right to link the well-being and the future of the human race to the unconditional mastery of the aristocratic values, of the Roman values. What, conversely, did the Jews feel against Rome? One can surmise it from a thousand symptoms, but it is sufficient to carry one's mind back to the Johannian Apocalypse, that most obscene of all the written outbursts, which has revenge on its conscience. (One should also appraise at its full value the profound logic of the Christian instinct, when over this very book of hate it wrote the name of the Disciple of Love, that self-same disciple to whom it attributed that impassioned and ecstatic Gospel—therein lurks a portion of truth, however much literary forging may have been necessary for this pur-

pose.) The Romans were the strong and aristocratic; a nation stronger and more aristocratic has never existed in the world, has never even been dreamed of; every relic of them, every inscription enraptures, granted that one can divine *what* it is that writes the inscription. The Jews, conversely, were that priestly nation of resentment par excellence, possessed by a unique genius for popular morals: just compare with the Jews the nations with analogous gifts, such as the Chinese or the Germans, so as to realize afterwards what is first rate, and what is fifth rate.

Which of them has been provisionally victorious, Rome or Judæa? but there is not a shadow of doubt; just consider to whom in Rome itself nowadays you bow down, as though before the quintessence of all the highest values—and not only in Rome, but almost over half the world, everywhere where man has been tamed or is about to be tamed—to *three Jews*, as we know, and *one Jewess* (to Jesus of Nazareth, to Peter the fisher, to Paul the tentmaker, and to the mother of the aforesaid Jesus, named Mary). This is very remarkable: Rome is undoubtedly defeated. At any rate there took place in the Renaissance a brilliantly sinister revival of the classical ideal, of the aristocratic valuation of all things: Rome herself, like a man waking up from a trance, stirred beneath the burden of the new Judaised Rome that had been built over her, which presented the appearance of an œcumenical synagogue and was called the "Church": but immediately Judæa triumphed again, thanks to that fundamentally popular (German and English) movement of revenge, which is called the Reformation, and taking also into account its inevitable corollary, the restoration of the Church—the restoration also of the ancient graveyard peace of classical Rome. Judæa proved yet once more victorious over the clas-

sical ideal in the French Revolution, and in a sense which was even more crucial and even more profound: the last political aristocracy that existed in Europe, that of the *French* sev-
5 enteenth and eighteenth centuries, broke into pieces beneath the instincts of a resentful populace—never had the world heard a greater jubilation, a more uproarious enthusiasm: indeed, there took place in the midst of it the
10 most monstrous and unexpected phenomenon; the ancient ideal *itself* swept before the eyes and conscience of humanity with all its life and with unheard-of splendor, and in opposition to resentment's lying war-cry of *the*
15 *prerogative of the most*, in opposition to the will to lowliness, abasement, and equalization, the will to a retrogression and twilight of humanity, there rang out once again, stronger, simpler, more penetrating than ever, the terrible
20 and enchanting counter-warcry of *the prerogative of the few*! Like a final signpost to other ways, there appeared Napoleon, the most unique and violent anachronism that ever existed, and in him the incarnate problem *of the aristocratic*
25 *ideal in itself*—consider well what a problem it is:—Napoleon, that synthesis of Monster and Superman.

17

30 Was it therewith over? Was that greatest of all antitheses of ideals thereby relegated *ad acta*[80] for all time? Or only postponed, postponed for a long time? May there not take place at some time or other a much more awful, much
35 more carefully prepared flaring up of the old conflagration? Further! Should not one wish *that* consummation with all one's strength?— will it one's self? demand it one's self? He who at this juncture begins, like my readers, to re-
40 flect, to think further, will have difficulty in coming quickly to a conclusion,—ground

---

80 [To the record]

enough for me to come myself to a conclusion, taking it for granted that for some time past what I mean has been sufficiently clear,
45 what I exactly *mean* by that dangerous motto which is inscribed on the body of my last book: *Beyond Good and Evil*—at any rate that is not the same as "Beyond Good and Bad."

50 Note.—I avail myself of the opportunity offered by this treatise to express, openly and formally, a wish which up to the present has only been expressed in occasional conversations with scholars, namely, that some Faculty
55 of philosophy should, by means of a series of prize essays, gain the glory of having promoted the further study of the *history of morals*— perhaps this book may serve to give forcible impetus in such a direction. With regard to a
60 possibility of this character, the following question deserves consideration. It merits quite as much the attention of philologists and historians as of actual professional philosophers.

65

"What indication of the history of the evolution of the moral ideas is afforded by philology, and especially by etymological investigation?"

70 On the other hand, it is of course equally necessary to induce physiologists and doctors to be interested in these problems (*of the value of the valuations* which have prevailed up to the present): in this connection the professional
75 philosophers may be trusted to act as the spokesmen and intermediaries in these particular instances, after, of course, they have quite succeeded in transforming the relationship between philosophy and physiology and
80 medicine, which is originally one of coldness and suspicion, into the most friendly and fruitful reciprocity. In point of fact, all tables of values, all the "thou shalts" known to history and ethnology, need primarily a *physiological*, at

any rate in preference to a psychological, elucidation and interpretation; all equally require a critique from medical science. The question, "What is the *value* of this or that table of 'values' and morality?" will be asked from the most varied standpoints. For instance, the question of "valuable *for what*" can never be analyzed with sufficient nicety. That, for instance, which would evidently have value with regard to promoting in a race the greatest possible powers of endurance (or with regard to increasing its adaptability to a specific climate, or with regard to the preservation of the greatest number) would have nothing like the same value, if it were a question of evolving a stronger species. In gauging values, the good of the majority and the good of the minority are opposed standpoints: we leave it to the naïveté of English biologists to regard the former standpoint as *intrinsically* superior. *All the sciences have now to pave the way for the future task of the philosopher; this task being understood to mean, that he must solve the problem of value, that he has to fix the hierarchy of values.*

SECOND ESSAY.
"GUILT," "BAD CONSCIENCE," AND THE LIKE.

1

The breeding of an animal that *can promise*—is not this just that very paradox of a task which nature has set itself in regard to man? Is not this the very problem of man? The fact that this problem has been to a great extent solved, must appear all the more phenomenal to one who can estimate at its full value that force of *forgetfulness* which works in opposition to it. Forgetfulness is no mere *vis inertiæ*, as the superficial believe, rather is it a power of obstruction, active and, in the strictest sense of the word, positive—a power responsible for the fact that what we have lived, experienced, taken into ourselves, no more enters into consciousness during the process of digestion (it might be called psychic absorption) than all the whole manifold process by which our physical nutrition, the so-called "incorporation," is carried on. The temporary shutting of the doors and windows of consciousness, the relief from the clamant alarums and excursions, with which our subconscious world of servant organs works in mutual co-operation and antagonism; a little quietude, a little *tabula rasa* of the consciousness, so as to make room again for the new, and above all for the more noble functions and functionaries, room for government, foresight, predetermination (for our organism is on an oligarchic model)—this is the utility, as I have said, of the active forgetfulness, which is a very sentinel and nurse of psychic order, repose, etiquette; and this shows at once why it is that there can exist no happiness, no gladness, no hope, no pride, no real *present*, without forgetfulness. The man in whom this preventative apparatus is damaged and discarded, is to be compared to a dyspeptic, and it is something more than a comparison—he can "get rid of" nothing. But this very animal who finds it necessary to be forgetful, in whom, in fact, forgetfulness represents a force and a form of *robust* health, has reared for himself an opposition-power, a memory, with whose help forgetfulness is, in certain instances, kept in check—in the cases, namely, where promises have to be made;—so that it is by no means a mere passive inability to get rid of a once indented impression, not merely the indigestion occasioned by a once pledged word, which one cannot dispose of, but an *active* refusal to get rid of it, a continuing and a wish to continue what has once been willed, an actual *memory of the will*; so that between the original "I will," "I shall do," and the actual discharge of the will, its act, we can easily interpose a world of new strange phenomena, circumstances, veritable volitions, without the snapping of this long chain of the will. But what is the underlying hypothesis of all this? How thoroughly, in order to be able to regulate the future in this way, must man have first learnt to distinguish between necessitated and accidental phenomena, to think causally, to see the distant as present and to anticipate it, to fix with certainty what is the end, and what is the means to that end; above all, to reckon, to have power to calculate—how thoroughly must man have first become *calculable, disciplined, necessitated* even for himself and his own conception of himself, that, like a man entering into a promise, he could guarantee himself *as a future*.

2

This is simply the long history of the origin of *responsibility*. That task of breeding an animal which can make promises, includes, as we have already grasped, as its condition and preliminary, the more immediate task of first *making* man to a certain extent, necessitated, uniform, like among his like, regular, and consequently calculable. The immense work of what I have called, "morality of custom"[81] (cp. *Dawn of Day*, Aphs. 9, 14, and 16), the actual work of man on himself during the longest period of the human race, his whole prehistoric work, finds its meaning, its great justification (in spite of all its innate hardness, despotism, stupidity, and idiocy) in this fact: man, with the help of the morality of customs and of social strait-waistcoats, was *made* genuinely calculable. If, however, we place ourselves at the end of this colossal process, at the point where the tree finally matures its fruits, when society and its morality of custom finally bring to light that to which it was only the means,

then do we find as the ripest fruit on its tree the *sovereign individual*, that resembles only himself, that has got loose from the morality of custom, the autonomous "super-moral" individual (for "autonomous" and "moral" are mutually-exclusive terms),—in short, the man of the personal, long, and independent will, *competent to promise*, and we find in him a proud consciousness (vibrating in every fiber), of *what* has been at last achieved and become vivified in him, a genuine consciousness of power and freedom, a feeling of human perfection in general. And this man who has grown to freedom, who is really *competent* to promise, this lord of the *free* will, this sovereign—how is it possible for him not to know how great is his superiority over everything incapable of binding itself by promises, or of being its own security, how great is the trust, the awe, the reverence that he awakes—he "deserves" all three—not to know that with this mastery over himself he is necessarily also given the mastery over circumstances, over nature, over all creatures with shorter wills, less reliable characters? The "free" man, the owner of a long unbreakable will, finds in this possession his *standard of value*: looking out from himself upon the others, he honors or he despises, and just as necessarily as he honors his peers, the strong and the reliable (those who can bind themselves by promises),—that is, every one who promises like a sovereign, with difficulty, rarely and slowly, who is sparing with his trusts but confers *honor* by the very fact of trusting, who gives his word as something that can be relied on, because he knows himself strong enough to keep it even in the teeth of disasters, even in the "teeth of fate,"—so with equal necessity will he have the heel of his foot ready for the lean and empty jackasses, who promise when they have no business to do so, and his rod of chastisement ready for the liar, who already breaks his

---

[81] The German is: "*Sittlichkeit der Sitte.*" H. B. S.

word at the very minute when it is on his lips. The proud knowledge of the extraordinary privilege of *responsibility*, the consciousness of this rare freedom, of this power over himself

5 and over fate, has sunk right down to his innermost depths, and has become an instinct, a dominating instinct—what name will he give to it, to this dominating instinct, if he needs to have a word for it? But there is no doubt

10 about it—the sovereign man calls it his *conscience*.

3

His conscience?—One apprehends at once

15 that the idea "conscience," which is here seen in its supreme manifestation, supreme in fact to almost the point of strangeness, should already have behind it a long history and evolution. The ability to guarantee one's self with

20 all due pride, and also at the same time to *say yes* to one's self—that is, as has been said, a ripe fruit, but also a *late* fruit:—How long must needs this fruit hang sour and bitter on the tree! And for an even longer period there

25 was not a glimpse of such a fruit to be had—no one had taken it on himself to promise it, although everything on the tree was quite ready for it, and everything was maturing for that very consummation. "How is a memory

30 to be made for the man-animal? How is an impression to be so deeply fixed upon this ephemeral understanding, half dense, and half silly, upon this incarnate forgetfulness, that it will be permanently present?" As one may

35 imagine, this primeval problem was not solved by exactly gentle answers and gentle means; perhaps there is nothing more awful and more sinister in the early history of man than his *system of mnemonics*. "Something is burnt in so

40 as to remain in his memory: only that which never stops *hurting* remains in his memory." This is an axiom of the oldest (unfortunately also the longest) psychology in the world. It

might even be said that wherever solemnity,

45 seriousness, mystery, and gloomy colors are now found in the life of the men and of nations of the world, there is some *survival* of that horror which was once the universal concomitant of all promises, pledges, and obliga-

50 tions. The past, the past with all its length, depth, and hardness, wafts to us its breath, and bubbles up in us again, when we become "serious." When man thinks it necessary to make for himself a memory, he never accom-

55 plishes it without blood, tortures, and sacrifice; the most dreadful sacrifices and forfeitures (among them the sacrifice of the first-born), the most loathsome mutilation (for instance, castration), the most cruel rituals of all the

60 religious cults (for all religions are really at bottom systems of cruelty)—all these things originate from that instinct which found in pain its most potent mnemonic. In a certain sense the whole of asceticism is to be ascribed

65 to this: certain ideas have got to be made inextinguishable, omnipresent, "fixed," with the object of hypnotizing the whole nervous and intellectual system through these "fixed ideas"—and the ascetic methods and modes of

70 life are the means of freeing those ideas from the competition of all other ideas so as to make them "unforgettable." The worse memory man had, the ghastlier the signs presented by his customs; the severity of the pe-

75 nal laws affords in particular a gauge of the extent of man's difficulty in conquering forgetfulness, and in keeping a few primal postulates of social intercourse ever present to the minds of those who were the slaves of every

80 momentary emotion and every momentary desire. We Germans do certainly not regard ourselves as an especially cruel and hardhearted nation, still less as an especially casual and happy-go-lucky one; but one has only to

85 look at our old penal ordinances in order to realize what a lot of trouble it takes in the

world to evolve a "nation of thinkers" (I mean: *the* European nation which exhibits at this very day the maximum of reliability, seriousness, bad taste, and positiveness, which has on the strength of these qualities a right to train every kind of European mandarin). These Germans employed terrible means to make for themselves a memory, to enable them to master their rooted plebeian instincts and the brutal crudity of those instincts: think of the old German punishments, for instance, stoning (as far back as the legend, the millstone falls on the head of the guilty man), breaking on the wheel (the most original invention and speciality of the German genius in the sphere of punishment), dart-throwing, tearing, or trampling by horses ("quartering"), boiling the criminal in oil or wine (still prevalent in the fourteenth and fifteenth centuries), the highly popular flaying ("slicing into strips"), cutting the flesh out of the breast; think also of the evil-doer being besmeared with honey, and then exposed to the flies in a blazing sun. It was by the help of such images and precedents that man eventually kept in his memory five or six "I will nots" with regard to which he had already given his *promise*, so as to be able to enjoy the advantages of society—and verily with the help of this kind of memory man eventually attained "reason"! Alas! reason, seriousness, mastery over the emotions, all these gloomy, dismal things which are called reflection, all these privileges and pageantries of humanity: how dear is the price that they have exacted! How much blood and cruelty is the foundation of all "good things"!

4

But how is it that that other melancholy object, the consciousness of sin, the whole "bad conscience," came into the world? And it is here that we turn back to our genealogists of morals. For the second time I say—or have I not said it yet?—that they are worth nothing. Just their own five-spans-long limited modern experience; no knowledge of the past, and no wish to know it; still less a historic instinct, a power of "second sight" (which is what is really required in this case)—and despite this to go in for the history of morals. It stands to reason that this must needs produce results which are removed from the truth by something more than a respectful distance.

Have these current genealogists of morals ever allowed themselves to have even the vaguest notion, for instance, that the cardinal moral idea of "ought"[82] originates from the very material idea of "owe"? Or that punishment developed as a retaliation absolutely independently of any preliminary hypothesis of the freedom or determination of the will?—And this to such an extent, that a high degree of civilization was always first necessary for the animal man to begin to make those much more primitive distinctions of "intentional," "negligent," "accidental," "responsible," and their contraries, and apply them in the assessing of punishment. That idea—"the wrong-doer deserves punishment *because* he might have acted otherwise," in spite of the fact that it is nowadays so cheap, obvious, natural, and inevitable, and that it has had to serve as an illustration of the way in which the sentiment of justice appeared on earth, is in point of fact an exceedingly late, and even refined form of human judgment and inference; the placing of this idea back at the beginning of the world is simply a clumsy violation of the principles of primitive psychology. Throughout the longest period of human history punishment was *never* based on the re-

---

[82] The German world "*schuld*" means both debt and guilt. Cp. the English "owe" and "ought," by which I occasionally render the double meaning.—H. B. S.

sponsibility of the evil-doer for his action, and was consequently not based on the hypothesis that only the guilty should be punished;—on the contrary, punishment was inflicted in those days for the same reason that parents punish their children even nowadays, out of anger at an injury that they have suffered, an anger which vents itself mechanically on the author of the injury—but this anger is kept in bounds and modified through the idea that every injury has somewhere or other its *equivalent* price, and can really be paid off, even though it be by means of pain to the author. Whence is it that this ancient deep-rooted and now perhaps ineradicable idea has drawn its strength, this idea of an equivalency between injury and pain? I have already revealed its origin, in the contractual relationship between *creditor* and *ower*, that is as old as the existence of legal rights at all, and in its turn points back to the primary forms of purchase, sale, barter, and trade.

5

The realization of these contractual relations excites, of course (as would be already expected from our previous observations), a great deal of suspicion and opposition towards the primitive society which made or sanctioned them. In this society promises will be made; in this society the object is to provide the promiser with a memory; in this society, so may we suspect, there will be full scope for hardness, cruelty, and pain: the "ower," in order to induce credit in his promise of repayment, in order to give a guarantee of the earnestness and sanctity of his promise, in order to drill into his own conscience the duty, the solemn duty, of repayment, will, by virtue of a contract with his creditor to meet the contingency of his not paying, pledge something that he still possesses, something that he still has in his power, for instance, his life or his wife, or his freedom or his body (or under certain religious conditions even his salvation, his soul's welfare, even his peace in the grave; so in Egypt, where the corpse of the ower found even in the grave no rest from the creditor—of course, from the Egyptian standpoint, this peace was a matter of particular importance). But especially has the creditor the power of inflicting on the body of the ower all kinds of pain and torture—the power, for instance, of cutting off from it an amount that appeared proportionate to the greatness of the debt;—this point of view resulted in the universal prevalence at an early date of precise schemes of valuation, frequently horrible in the minuteness and meticulosity of their application, *legally* sanctioned schemes of valuation for individual limbs and parts of the body. I consider it as already a progress, as a proof of a freer, less petty, and more Roman conception of law, when the Roman Code of the Twelve Tables decreed that it was immaterial how much or how little the creditors in such a contingency cut off, "*si plus minusve secuerunt, ne fraude esto.*[83]" Let us make the logic of the whole of this equalization process clear; it is strange enough. The equivalence consists in this: instead of an advantage directly compensatory of his injury (that is, instead of an equalization in money, lands, or some kind of chattel), the creditor is granted by way of repayment and compensation a certain *sensation of satisfaction*—the satisfaction of being able to vent, without any trouble, his power on one who is powerless, the delight "*de faire le mal pour le plaisir de le faire*[84]," the joy in sheer violence: and this joy will be relished in proportion to the lowness and humbleness of the creditor in the social scale, and is quite apt to

---

[83] [If they have removed more or less, it is not a crime]
[84] [Doing bad for the pleasure of it]

have the effect of the most delicious dainty, and even seem the foretaste of a higher social position. Thanks to the punishment of the "ower," the creditor participates in the rights

5 of the masters. At last he too, for once in a way, attains the edifying consciousness of being able to despise and ill-treat a creature—as an "inferior"—or at any rate of *seeing* him being despised and ill-treated, in case the actual

10 power of punishment, the administration of punishment, has already become transferred to the "authorities." The compensation consequently consists in a claim on cruelty and a right to draw thereon.

15

6

It is then in *this* sphere of the law of contract that we find the cradle of the whole moral world of the ideas of "guilt," "conscience,"

20 "duty," the "sacredness of duty,"—their commencement, like the commencement of all great things in the world, is thoroughly and continuously saturated with blood. And should we not add that this world has never

25 really lost a certain savor of blood and torture (not even in old Kant; the categorical imperative reeks of cruelty). It was in this sphere likewise that there first became formed that sinister and perhaps now indissoluble associa-

30 tion of the ideas of "guilt" and "suffering." To put the question yet again, why can suffering be a compensation for "owing"?—Because the *infliction* of suffering produces the highest degree of happiness, because the injured party

35 will get in exchange for his loss (including his vexation at his loss) an extraordinary counter-pleasure: the *infliction* of suffering—a real *feast*, something that, as I have said, was all the more appreciated the greater the paradox cre-

40 ated by the rank and social status of the credi-tor. These observations are purely conjectural; for, apart from the painful nature of the task, it is hard to plumb such profound depths: the

clumsy introduction of the idea of "revenge"

45 as a connecting-link simply hides and obscures the view instead of rendering it clearer (re-venge itself simply leads back again to the identical problem—"How can the infliction of suffering be a satisfaction?"). In my opinion it

50 is repugnant to the delicacy, and still more to the hypocrisy of tame domestic animals (that is, modern men; that is, ourselves), to realize with all their energy the extent to which *cruelty* constituted the great joy and delight of ancient

55 man, was an ingredient which seasoned nearly all his pleasures, and conversely the extent of the naïveté and innocence with which he man-ifested his need for cruelty, when he actually made as a matter of principle "disinterested

60 malice" (or, to use Spinoza's expression, the *sympathia malevolens*) into a *normal* characteristic of man—as consequently something to which the conscience says a hearty yes. The more profound observer has perhaps already had

65 sufficient opportunity for noticing this most ancient and radical joy and delight of mankind; in *Beyond Good and Evil*, Aph. 188 (and even earlier, in *The Dawn of Day*, Aphs. 18, 77, 113), I have cautiously indicated the continually

70 growing spiritualization and "deification" of cruelty, which pervades the whole history of the higher civilization (and in the larger sense even constitutes it). At any rate the time is not so long past when it was impossible to con-

75 ceive of royal weddings and national festivals on a grand scale, without executions, tortures, or perhaps an *auto-da-fé*", or similarly to conceive of an aristocratic household, without a creature to serve as a butt for the cruel and

80 malicious baiting of the inmates. (The reader will perhaps remember Don Quixote at the court of the Duchess: we read nowadays the whole of *Don Quixote* with a bitter taste in the mouth, almost with a sensation of torture, a

85 fact which would appear very strange and very incomprehensible to the author and his con-

temporaries—they read it with the best conscience in the world as the gayest of books;
they almost died with laughing at it.) The sight
of suffering does one good, the infliction of
5   suffering does one more good—this is a hard
maxim, but none the less a fundamental maxim, old, powerful, and "human, all-too-
human"; one, moreover, to which perhaps
even the apes as well would subscribe: for it is
10 said that in inventing bizarre cruelties they are
giving abundant proof of their future humanity, to which, as it were, they are playing the
prelude. Without cruelty, no feast: so teaches
the oldest and longest history of man—and in
15 punishment too is there so much of the festive.

7

Entertaining, as I do, these thoughts, I am, let
20 me say in parenthesis, fundamentally opposed
to helping our pessimists to new water for the
discordant and groaning mills of their disgust
with life; on the contrary, it should be shown
specifically that, at the time when mankind
25 was not yet ashamed of its cruelty, life in the
world was brighter than it is nowadays when
there are pessimists. The darkening of the
heavens over man has always increased in
proportion to the growth of man's shame *be-*
30 *fore man*. The tired pessimistic outlook, the
mistrust of the riddle of life, the icy negation
of disgusted ennui, all those are not the signs
of the *most evil* age of the human race: much
rather do they come first to the light of day, as
35 the swamp-flowers, which they are, when the
swamp to which they belong, comes into existence—I mean the diseased refinement and
moralization, thanks to which the "animal
man" has at last learnt to be ashamed of all his
40 instincts. On the road to angelhood (not to
use in this context a harder word) man has
developed that dyspeptic stomach and coated
tongue, which have made not only the joy and

innocence of the animal repulsive to him, but
45 also life itself:—so that sometimes he stands
with stopped nostrils before his own self, and,
like Pope Innocent the Third, makes a black
list of his own horrors ("unclean generation,
loathsome nutrition when in the maternal
50 body, badness of the matter out of which man
develops, awful stench, secretion of saliva,
urine, and excrement"). Nowadays, when suffering is always trotted out as the first argument *against* existence, as its most sinister que-
55 ry, it is well to remember the times when men
judged on converse principles because they
could not dispense with the *infliction* of suffering, and saw therein a magic of the first order,
a veritable bait of seduction to life.

60

Perhaps in those days (this is to solace the
weaklings) pain did not hurt so much as it
does nowadays: any physician who has treated
negroes (granted that these are taken as repre-
65 sentative of the prehistoric man) suffering
from severe internal inflammations which
would bring a European, even though he had
the soundest constitution, almost to despair,
would be in a position to come to this conclu-
70 sion. Pain has *not* the same effect with negroes.
(The curve of human sensibilities to pain
seems indeed to sink in an extraordinary and
almost sudden fashion, as soon as one has
passed the upper ten thousand or ten millions
75 of over-civilized humanity, and I personally
have no doubt that, by comparison with one
painful night passed by one single hysterical
chit of a cultured woman, the suffering of all
the animals taken together who have been put
80 to the question of the knife, so as to give scientific answers, are simply negligible.) We may
perhaps be allowed to admit the possibility of
the craving for cruelty not necessarily having
become really extinct: it only requires, in view
85 of the fact that pain hurts more nowadays, a
certain sublimation and subtilization, it must

especially be translated to the imaginative and psychic plane, and be adorned with such smug euphemisms, that even the most fastidious and hypocritical conscience could never grow

5 suspicious of their real nature ("Tragic pity" is one of these euphemisms: another is "*les nostalgies de la croix*[85]"). What really raises one's indignation against suffering is not suffering intrinsically, but the senselessness of suffering;

10 such a *senselessness*, however, existed neither in Christianity, which interpreted suffering into a whole mysterious salvation-apparatus, nor in the beliefs of the naïve ancient man, who only knew how to find a meaning in suffering from

15 the standpoint of the spectator, or the inflictor of the suffering. In order to get the secret, undiscovered, and unwitnessed suffering out of the world it was almost compulsory to invent gods and a hierarchy of intermediate be-

20 ings, in short, something which wanders even among secret places, sees even in the dark, and makes a point of never missing an interesting and painful spectacle. It was with the help of such inventions that life got to learn the *tour de*

25 *force*, which has become part of its stock-in-trade, the *tour de force* of self-justification, of the justification of evil; nowadays this would perhaps require other auxiliary devices (for instance, life as a riddle, life as a problem of

30 knowledge). "Every evil is justified in the sight of which a god finds edification," so rang the logic of primitive sentiment—and, indeed, was it only of primitive? The gods conceived as friends of spectacles of cruelty—oh how far

35 does this primeval conception extend even nowadays into our European civilization! One would perhaps like in this context to consult Luther and Calvin. It is at any rate certain that even the Greeks knew no more piquant sea-

40 soning for the happiness of their gods than the joys of cruelty. What, do you think, was the mood with which Homer makes his gods look down upon the fates of men? What final meaning have at bottom the Trojan War and

45 similar tragic horrors? It is impossible to entertain any doubt on the point: they were intended as festival games for the gods, and, in so far as the poet is of a more godlike breed than other men, as festival games also for the

50 poets. It was in just this spirit and no other, that at a later date the moral philosophers of Greece conceived the eyes of God as still looking down on the moral struggle, the heroism, and the self-torture of the virtuous; the

55 Heracles of duty was on a stage, and was conscious of the fact; virtue without witnesses was something quite unthinkable for this nation of actors. Must not that philosophic invention, so audacious and so fatal, which was then abso-

60 lutely new to Europe, the invention of "free will," of the absolute spontaneity of man in good and evil, simply have been made for the specific purpose of justifying the idea, that the interest of the gods in humanity and human

65 virtue was *inexhaustible*?

There would never on the stage of this free-will world be a dearth of really new, really novel and exciting situations, plots, catastro-

70 phes. A world thought out on completely deterministic lines would be easily guessed by the gods, and would consequently soon bore them—sufficient reason for these *friends of the gods*, the philosophers, not to ascribe to their

75 gods such a deterministic world. The whole of ancient humanity is full of delicate consideration for the spectator, being as it is a world of thorough publicity and theatricality, which could not conceive of happiness without spec-

80 tacles and festivals.—And, as has already been said, even in great punishment there is so much which is festive.

---

[85] [Desire for the cross]

8

The feeling of "ought," of personal obligation (to take up again the train of our inquiry), has had, as we saw, its origin in the oldest and most original personal relationship that there is, the relationship between buyer and seller, creditor and ower: here it was that individual confronted individual, and that individual *matched himself against* individual. There has not yet been found a grade of civilization so low, as not to manifest some trace of this relationship. Making prices, assessing values, thinking out equivalents, exchanging—all this preoccupied the primal thoughts of man to such an extent that in a certain sense it constituted *thinking* itself: it was here that was trained the oldest form of sagacity, it was here in this sphere that we can perhaps trace the first commencement of man's pride, of his feeling of superiority over other animals. Perhaps our word "Mensch" (*manas*) still expresses just something of *this* self-pride: man denoted himself as the being who measures values, who values and measures, as the "assessing" animal *par excellence*. Sale and purchase, together with their psychological concomitants, are older than the origins of any form of social organization and union: it is rather from the most rudimentary form of individual right that the budding consciousness of exchange, commerce, debt, right, obligation, compensation was first transferred to the rudest and most elementary of the social complexes (in their relation to similar complexes), the habit of comparing force with force, together with that of measuring, of calculating. His eye was now focused to this perspective; and with that ponderous consistency characteristic of ancient thought, which, though set in motion with difficulty, yet proceeds inflexibly along the line on which it has started, man soon arrived at the great generalization, "everything has its price, *all* can be paid for," the oldest and most naive moral canon of *justice*, the be-

ginning of all "kindness," of all "equity," of all "goodwill," of all "objectivity" in the world. Justice in this initial phase is the goodwill among people of about equal power to come to terms with each other, to come to an understanding again by means of a settlement, and with regard to the less powerful, to *compel* them to agree among themselves to a settlement.

9

Measured always by the standard of antiquity (this antiquity, moreover, is present or again possible at all periods), the community stands to its members in that important and radical relationship of creditor to his "owers." Man lives in a community, man enjoys the advantages of a community (and what advantages! we occasionally underestimate them nowadays), man lives protected, spared, in peace and trust, secure from certain injuries and enmities, to which the man outside the community, the "peaceless" man, is exposed,—a German understands the original meaning of "Elend" (*elend*),—secure because he has entered into pledges and obligations to the community in respect of these very injuries and enmities. What happens *when this is not the case*? The community, the defrauded creditor, will get itself paid, as well as it can, one can reckon on that. In this case the question of the direct damage done by the offender is quite subsidiary: quite apart from this the nal[86][3] is above all a breaker, a breaker of word and covenant *to the whole*, as regards all the advantages and amenities of the communal life in which up to that time he had participated. The criminal is an "ower" who not only fails to repay the advances and advantages that have been given to him, but even sets out to attack his creditor: conse-

---

[86] German: "*Verbrecher*."—H.B.S.

quently he is in the future not only, as is fair, deprived of all these advantages and amenities—he is in addition reminded of the *importance* of those advantages. The wrath of the injured creditor, of the community, puts him back in the wild and outlawed status from which he was previously protected: the community repudiates him—and now every kind of enmity can vent itself on him. Punishment is in this stage of civilization simply the copy, the mimic, of the normal treatment of the hated, disdained, and conquered enemy, who is not only deprived of every right and protection but of every mercy; so we have the martial law and triumphant festival of the *væ victis*[87] in all its mercilessness and cruelty. This shows why war itself (counting the sacrificial cult of war) has produced all the forms under which punishment has manifested itself in history.

10

As it grows more powerful, the community tends to take the offences of the individual less seriously, because they are now regarded as being much less revolutionary and dangerous to the corporate existence: the evil-doer is no more outlawed and put outside the pale, the common wrath can no longer vent itself upon him with its old license,—on the contrary, from this very time it is against this wrath, and particularly against the wrath of those directly injured, that the evil-doer is carefully shielded and protected by the community. As, in fact, the penal law develops, the following characteristics become more and more clearly marked: compromise with the wrath of those directly affected by the misdeed; a consequent endeavor to localize the matter and to prevent a further, or indeed a general spread of the disturbance; attempts to find equivalents and

to settle the whole matter (*compositio*); above all, the will, which manifests itself with increasing definiteness, to treat every offence as in a certain degree capable of *being paid off*, and consequently, at any rate up to a certain point, to *isolate* the offender from his act. As the power and the self-consciousness of a community increases, so proportionately does the penal law become mitigated; conversely every weakening and jeopardizing of the community revives the harshest forms of that law. The creditor has always grown more humane proportionately as he has grown more rich; finally the amount of injury he can endure without really suffering becomes the criterion of his wealth. It is possible to conceive of a society blessed with so great a *consciousness of its own power* as to indulge in the most aristocratic luxury of letting its wrong-doers go *scot-free.*— "What do my parasites matter to me?" might society say. "Let them live and flourish! I am strong enough for it."—The justice which began with the maxim, "Everything can be paid off, everything must be paid off," ends with connivance at the escape of those who cannot pay to escape—it ends, like every good thing on earth, by *destroying itself.*—The self-destruction of Justice! We know the pretty name it calls itself—*Grace!* it remains, as is obvious, the privilege of the strongest, better still, their super-law.

11

A deprecatory word here against the attempts, that have lately been made, to find the origin of justice on quite another basis—namely, on that of *resentment.* Let me whisper a word in the ear of the psychologists, if they would fain study revenge itself at close quarters: this plant blooms its prettiest at present among Anarchists and anti-Semites, a hidden flower, as it has ever been, like the violet, though, forsooth, with another perfume. And as like must

---

[87] [Woe to vanquished/conquered]

necessarily emanate from like, it will not be a matter for surprise that it is just in such circles that we see the birth of endeavors (it is their old birthplace—compare above, First Essay, paragraph 14), to sanctify *revenge* under the name of *justice* (as though Justice were at bottom merely a *development* of the consciousness of injury), and thus with the rehabilitation of revenge to reinstate generally and collectively all the *reactive* emotions. I object to this last point least of all. It even seems *meritorious* when regarded from the standpoint of the whole problem of biology (from which standpoint the value of these emotions has up to the present been underestimated). And that to which I alone call attention, is the circumstance that it is the spirit of revenge itself, from which develops this new nuance of scientific equity (for the benefit of hate, envy, mistrust, jealousy, suspicion, rancour, revenge). This scientific "equity" stops immediately and makes way for the accents of deadly enmity and prejudice, so soon as another group of emotions comes on the scene, which in my opinion are of a much higher biological value than these reactions, and consequently have a paramount claim to the valuation and appreciation of science: I mean the really *active* emotions, such as personal and material ambition, and so forth. (E. Dühring, *Value of Life; Course of Philosophy*, and *passim*.) So much against this tendency in general: but as for the particular maxim of Dühring's, that the home of Justice is to be found in the sphere of the reactive feelings, our love of truth compels us drastically to invert his own proposition and to oppose to him this other maxim: the *last* sphere conquered by the spirit of justice is the sphere of the feeling of reaction! When it really comes about that the just man remains just even as regards his injurer (and not merely cold, moderate, reserved, indifferent: being just is always a *positive* state); when, in spite of the strong provocation of personal insult, contempt, and calumny, the lofty and clear objectivity of the just and judging eye (whose glance is as profound as it is gentle) is untroubled, why then we have a piece of perfection, a past master of the world—something, in fact, which it would not be wise to expect, and which should not at any rate be too easily *believed*. Speaking generally, there is no doubt but that even the justest individual only requires a little dose of hostility, malice, or innuendo to drive the blood into his brain and the fairness *from* it. The active man, the attacking, aggressive man is always a hundred degrees nearer to justice than the man who merely reacts; he certainly has no need to adopt the tactics, necessary in the case of the reacting man, of making false and biased valuations of his object. It is, in point of fact, for this reason that the aggressive man has at all times enjoyed the stronger, bolder, more aristocratic, and also *freer* outlook, the *better* conscience. On the other hand, we already surmise who it really is that has on his conscience the invention of the "bad conscience,"—the resentful man! Finally, let man look at himself in history. In what sphere up to the present has the whole administration of law, the actual need of law, found its earthly home? Perchance in the sphere of the reacting man? Not for a minute: rather in that of the active, strong, spontaneous, aggressive man? I deliberately defy the above-mentioned agitator (who himself makes this self-confession, "the creed of revenge has run through all my works and endeavors like the red thread of Justice"), and say, that judged historically law in the world represents the very war *against* the reactive feelings, the very war waged on those feelings by the powers of activity and aggression, which devote some of their strength to damming and keeping within bounds this effervescence of hysterical reactivity, and to forcing it to some compromise.

Everywhere where justice is practiced and justice is maintained, it is to be observed that the stronger power, when confronted with the weaker powers which are inferior to it (whether they be groups, or individuals), searches for weapons to put an end to the senseless fury of resentment, while it carries on its object, partly by taking the victim of resentment out of the clutches of revenge, partly by substituting for revenge a campaign of its own against the enemies of peace and order, partly by finding, suggesting, and occasionally enforcing settlements, partly by standardizing certain equivalents for injuries, to which equivalents the element of resentment is henceforth finally referred. The most drastic measure, however, taken and effectuated by the supreme power, to combat the preponderance of the feelings of spite and vindictiveness—it takes this measure as soon as it is at all strong enough to do so—is the foundation of *law*, the imperative declaration of what in its eyes is to be regarded as just and lawful, and what unjust and unlawful: and while, after the foundation of law, the supreme power treats the aggressive and arbitrary acts of individuals, or of whole groups, as a violation of law, and a revolt against itself, it distracts the feelings of its subjects from the immediate injury inflicted by such a violation, and thus eventually attains the very opposite result to that always desired by revenge, which sees and recognizes nothing but the standpoint of the injured party. From henceforth the eye becomes trained to a more and more *impersonal* valuation of the deed, even the eye of the injured party himself (though this is in the final stage of all, as has been previously remarked)—on this principle "right" and "wrong" first manifest themselves after the foundation of law (and not, as Dühring maintains, only after the act of violation). To talk of intrinsic right and intrinsic wrong is absolutely non-sensical; intrinsically, an injury, an oppression, an exploitation, an annihilation can be nothing wrong, inasmuch as life is *essentially* (that is, in its cardinal functions) something which functions by injuring, oppressing, exploiting, and annihilating, and is absolutely inconceivable without such a character. It is necessary to make an even more serious confession:—viewed from the most advanced biological standpoint, conditions of legality can be only *exceptional conditions*, in that they are partial restrictions of the real life-will, which makes for power, and in that they are subordinated to the life-will's general end as particular means, that is, as means to create *larger* units of strength. A legal organization, conceived of as sovereign and universal, not as a weapon in a fight of complexes of power, but as a weapon *against* fighting, generally something after the style of Dühring's communistic model of treating every will as equal with every other will, would be a principle *hostile to life*, a destroyer and dissolver of man, an outrage on the future of man, a symptom of fatigue, a secret cut to Nothingness.—

12

A word more on the origin and end of punishment—two problems which are or ought to be kept distinct, but which unfortunately are usually lumped into one. And what tactics have our moral genealogists employed up to the present in these cases? Their inveterate naïveté. They find out some "end" in the punishment, for instance, revenge and deterrence, and then in all their innocence set this end at the beginning, as the *causa fiendi*[88] of the punishment, and—they have done the trick. But the patching up of a history of the origin of law is the last use to which the "End in Law"[89]

---

[88] [Basis of existence]
[89] An allusion to *Der Zweck im Recht*, by the great German jurist, Professor Ihering. –H.B.S.

ought to be put. Perhaps there is no more pregnant principle for any kind of history than the following, which, difficult though it is to master, *should* none the less be *mastered* in every detail.—The origin of the existence of a thing and its final utility, its practical application and incorporation in a system of ends, are *toto cœlo*[90] opposed to each other—everything, anything, which exists and which prevails anywhere, will always be put to new purposes by a force superior to itself, will be commandeered afresh, will be turned and transformed to new uses; all "happening" in the organic world consists of *overpowering* and dominating, and again all overpowering and domination is a new interpretation and adjustment, which must necessarily obscure or absolutely extinguish the subsisting "meaning" and "end." The most perfect comprehension of the utility of any physiological organ (or also of a legal institution, social custom, political habit, form in art or in religious worship) does not for a minute imply any simultaneous comprehension of its origin: this may seem uncomfortable and unpalatable to the older men,—for it has been the immemorial belief that understanding the final cause or the utility of a thing, a form, an institution, means also understanding the reason for its origin: to give an example of this logic, the eye was made to see, the hand was made to grasp. So even punishment was conceived as invented with a view to punishing. But all ends and all utilities are only *signs* that a Will to Power has mastered a less powerful force, has impressed thereon out of its own self the meaning of a function; and the whole history of a "Thing," an organ, a custom, can on the same principle be regarded as a continuous "sign-chain" of perpetually new interpretations and adjustments, whose causes, so far from needing to have even a mutual connection, sometimes follow and alternate with each other absolutely haphazard. Similarly, the evolution of a "thing," of a custom, is anything but its *progressus* to an end, still less a logical and direct *progressus* attained with the minimum expenditure of energy and cost: it is rather the succession of processes of subjugation, more or less profound, more or less mutually independent, which operate on the thing itself; it is, further, the resistance which in each case invariably displayed this subjugation, the Protean wriggles by way of defense and reaction, and, further, the results of successful counter-efforts. The form is fluid, but the meaning is even more so—even inside every individual organism the case is the same: with every genuine growth of the whole, the "function" of the individual organs becomes shifted,—in certain cases a partial perishing of these organs, a diminution of their numbers (for instance, through annihilation of the connecting members), can be a symptom of growing strength and perfection. What I mean is this: even partial *loss of utility*, decay, and degeneration, loss of function and purpose, in a word, death, appertain to the conditions of the genuine *progressus*; which always appears in the shape of a will and way to *greater* power, and is always realized at the expense of innumerable smaller powers. The magnitude of a "progress" is gauged by the greatness of the sacrifice that it requires: humanity as a mass sacrificed to the prosperity of the one *stronger* species of Man—that *would be* a progress. I emphasize all the more this cardinal characteristic of the historic method, for the reason that in its essence it runs counter to predominant instincts and prevailing taste, which much prefer to put up with absolute casualness, even with the mechanical senselessness of all phenomena, than with the theory of a power-will, in exhaustive play throughout all phenomena. The democratic idiosyncrasy against every-

---

[90] [Entirety of the heavens]

thing which rules and wishes to rule, the modern *misarchism* (to coin a bad word for a bad thing), has gradually but so thoroughly transformed itself into the guise of intellectualism,
5 the most abstract intellectualism, that even nowadays it penetrates and *has the right* to penetrate step by step into the most exact and apparently the most objective sciences: this tendency has, in fact, in my view already dom-
10 inated the whole of physiology and biology, and to their detriment, as is obvious, in so far as it has spirited away a radical idea, the idea of true *activity*. The tyranny of this idiosyncrasy, however, results in the theory of "adapta-
15 tion" being pushed forward into the van of the argument, exploited; adaptation—that means to say, a second-class activity, a mere capacity for "reacting"; in fact, life itself has been defined (by Herbert Spencer) as an in-
20 creasingly effective internal adaptation to external circumstances. This definition, however, fails to realize the real essence of life, its will to power. It fails to appreciate the paramount superiority enjoyed by those plastic forces of
25 spontaneity, aggression, and encroachment with their new interpretations and tendencies, to the operation of which adaptation is only a natural corollary: consequently the sovereign office of the highest functionaries in the or-
30 ganism itself (among which the life-will appears as an active and formative principle) is repudiated. One remembers Huxley's reproach to Spencer of his "administrative Nihilism": but it is a case of something much
35 *more* than "administration."

13

To return to our subject, namely *punishment*, we must make consequently a double distinction: first, the relatively permanent *element*, the
40 custom, the act, the "drama," a certain rigid sequence of methods of procedure; on the other hand, the fluid element, the meaning, the end, the expectation which is attached to

the operation of such procedure. At this point
45 we immediately assume, *per analogiam* (in accordance with the theory of the historic method, which we have elaborated above), that the procedure itself is something older and earlier than its utilization in punishment, that this
50 utilization was *introduced* and interpreted into the procedure (which had existed for a long time, but whose employment had another meaning), in short, that the case is *different* from that hitherto supposed by our *naif* gene-
55 alogists of morals and of law, who thought that the procedure was *invented* for the purpose of punishment, in the same way that the hand had been previously thought to have been invented for the purpose of grasping. With
60 regard to the other element in *punishment*, its fluid element, its meaning, the idea of punishment in a very late stage of civilization (for instance, contemporary Europe) is not content with manifesting merely one meaning, but
65 manifests a whole synthesis "of meanings." The past general history of punishment, the history of its employment for the most diverse ends, crystallizes eventually into a kind of unity, which is difficult to analyze into its parts,
70 and which, it is necessary to emphasize, absolutely defies definition. (It is nowadays impossible to say definitely *the precise reason* for punishment: all ideas, in which a whole process is promiscuously comprehended, elude defini-
75 tion; it is only that which has no history, which can be defined.) At an earlier stage, on the contrary, that synthesis of meanings appears much less rigid and much more elastic; we can realize how in each individual case the ele-
80 ments of the synthesis change their value and their position, so that now one element and now another stands out and predominates over the others, nay, in certain cases one element (perhaps the end of deterrence) seems to
85 eliminate all the rest. At any rate, so as to give some idea of the uncertain, supplementary,

and accidental nature of the meaning of punishment and of the manner in which one identical procedure can be employed and adapted
for the most diametrically opposed objects, I
will at this point give a scheme that has suggested itself to me, a scheme itself based on
comparatively small and accidental material.—
Punishment, as rendering the criminal harmless and incapable of further injury.—
Punishment, as compensation for the injury
sustained by the injured party, in any form
whatsoever (including the form of sentimental
compensation).—Punishment, as an isolation
of that which disturbs the equilibrium, so as to
prevent the further spreading of the disturbance.—Punishment as a means of inspiring
fear of those who determine and execute the
punishment.—Punishment as a kind of compensation for advantages which the wrong-
doer has up to that time enjoyed (for example,
when he is utilized as a slave in the mines).—
Punishment, as the elimination of an element
of decay (sometimes of a whole branch, as
according to the Chinese laws, consequently as
a means to the purification of the race, or the
preservation of a social type).—Punishment as
a festival, as the violent oppression and humil-
iation of an enemy that has at last been subdued.—Punishment as a mnemonic, whether
for him who suffers the punishment—the so-
called "correction," or for the witnesses of its
administration. Punishment, as the payment of
a fee stipulated for by the power which protects the evil-doer from the excesses of revenge.—Punishment, as a compromise with
the natural phenomenon of revenge, in so far
as revenge is still maintained and claimed as a
privilege by the stronger races.—Punishment
as a declaration and measure of war against an
enemy of peace, of law, of order of authority,
who is fought by society with the weapons
which war provides, as a spirit dangerous to
the community, as a breaker of the contract
on which the community is based, as a rebel, a
traitor, and a breaker of the peace.

14

This list is certainly not complete; it is obvious
that punishment is overloaded with utilities of
all kinds. This makes it all the more permissible to eliminate one supposed utility, which
passes, at any rate in the popular mind, for its
most essential utility, and which is just what
even now provides the strongest support for
that faith in punishment which is nowadays
for many reasons tottering. Punishment is
supposed to have the value of exciting in the
guilty the consciousness of guilt; in punishment is sought the proper instrumentum of
that psychic reaction which becomes known
as a "bad conscience," "remorse." But this
theory is even, from the point of view of the
present, a violation of reality and psychology:
and how much more so is the case when we
have to deal with the longest period of man's
history, his primitive history! Genuine remorse
is certainly extremely rare among wrong-doers
and the victims of punishment; prisons and
houses of correction are not *the* soil on which
this worm of remorse pullulates for choice—
this is the unanimous opinion of all conscientious observers, who in many cases arrive at
such a judgment with enough reluctance and
against their own personal wishes. Speaking
generally, punishment hardens and numbs, it
produces concentration, it sharpens the consciousness of alienation, it strengthens the
power of resistance. When it happens that it
breaks the man's energy and brings about a
piteous prostration and abjectness, such a result is certainly even less salutary than the average effect of punishment, which is character-
ized by a harsh and sinister doggedness. The
thought of those *prehistoric* millennia brings us
to the unhesitating conclusion, that it was
simply through punishment that the evolution

of the consciousness of guilt was most forcibly retarded—at any rate in the victims of the punishing power. In particular, let us not underestimate the extent to which, by the very sight of the judicial and executive procedure, the wrong-doer is himself prevented from feeling that his deed, the character of his act, is *intrinsically* reprehensible: for he sees clearly the same kind of acts practiced in the service of justice, and then called good, and practiced with a good conscience; acts such as espionage, trickery, bribery, trapping, the whole intriguing and insidious art of the policeman and the informer—the whole system, in fact, manifested in the different kinds of punishment (a system not excused by passion, but based on principle), of robbing, oppressing, insulting, imprisoning, racking, murdering.— All this he sees treated by his judges, not as acts meriting censure and condemnation *in themselves*, but only in a particular context and application. It was not on this soil that grew the "bad conscience," that most sinister and interesting plant of our earthly vegetation—in point of fact, throughout a most lengthy period, no suggestion of having to do with a "guilty man" manifested itself in the consciousness of the man who judged and punished. One had merely to deal with an author of an injury, an irresponsible piece of fate. And the man himself, on whom the punishment subsequently fell like a piece of fate, was occasioned no more of an "inner pain" than would be occasioned by the sudden approach of some uncalculated event, some terrible natural catastrophe, a rushing, crushing avalanche against which there is no resistance.

15

This truth came insidiously enough to the consciousness of Spinoza (to the disgust of his commentators, who (like Kuno Fischer, for instance) give themselves no end of *trouble* to misunderstand him on this point), when one afternoon (as he sat raking up who knows what memory) he indulged in the question of what was really left for him personally of the celebrated *morsus conscientiæ*[91]—Spinoza, who had relegated "good and evil" to the sphere of human imagination, and indignantly defended the honor of his "free" God against those blasphemers who affirmed that God did everything *sub ratione boni*[92] ("but this was tantamount to subordinating God to fate, and would really be the greatest of all absurdities"). For Spinoza the world had returned again to that innocence in which it lay before the discovery of the bad conscience: what, then, had happened to the *morsus conscientiæ*? "The antithesis of *gaudium*[93]," said he at last to himself,— "A sadness accompanied by the recollection of a past event which has turned out contrary to all expectation" (*Eth.* III., Propos. XVIII. Schol. i. ii.). Evil-doers have throughout thousands of years felt when overtaken by punishment *exactly like Spinoza*, on the subject of their "offence": "here is something which went wrong contrary to my anticipation," not "I ought not to have done this."—They submitted themselves to punishment, just as one submits one's self to a disease, to a misfortune, or to death, with that stubborn and resigned fatalism which gives the Russians, for instance, even nowadays, the advantage over us Westerners, in the handling of life. If at that period there was a critique of action, the criterion was prudence: the real *effect* of punishment is unquestionably chiefly to be found in a sharpening of the sense of prudence, in a lengthening of the memory, in a will to adopt more of a policy of caution, suspicion, and secrecy; in the recognition that there are many

91 [Troubled conscience]
92 [With good reasons]
93 [Joy]

things which are unquestionably beyond one's capacity; in a kind of improvement in self-criticism. The broad effects which can be obtained by punishment in man and beast, are the increase of fear, the sharpening of the sense of cunning, the mastery of the desires: so it is that punishment *tames* man, but does not make him "better"—it would be more correct even to go so far as to assert the contrary ("Injury makes a man cunning," says a popular proverb: so far as it makes him cunning, it makes him also bad. Fortunately, it often enough makes him stupid).

16

At this juncture I cannot avoid trying to give a tentative and provisional expression to my own hypothesis concerning the origin of the bad conscience: it is difficult to make it fully appreciated, and it requires continuous meditation, attention, and digestion. I regard the bad conscience as the serious illness which man was bound to contract under the stress of the most radical change which he has ever experienced—that change, when he found himself finally imprisoned within the pale of society and of peace.

Just like the plight of the water-animals, when they were compelled either to become land-animals or to perish, so was the plight of these half-animals, perfectly adapted as they were to the savage life of war, prowling, and adventure—suddenly all their instincts were rendered worthless and "switched off." Henceforward they had to walk on their feet—"carry themselves," whereas heretofore they had been carried by the water: a terrible heaviness oppressed them. They found themselves clumsy in obeying the simplest directions, confronted with this new and unknown world they had no longer their old guide—the regulative instincts that had led them unconsciously to safety—they were reduced, were those unhappy creatures, to thinking, inferring, calculating, putting together causes and results, reduced to that poorest and most erratic organ of theirs, their "consciousness." I do not believe there was ever in the world such a feeling of misery, such a leaden discomfort—further, those old instincts had not immediately ceased their demands! Only it was difficult and rarely possible to gratify them: speaking broadly, they were compelled to satisfy themselves by new and, as it were, hole-and-corner methods. All instincts which do not find a vent without, *turn inwards*—this is what I mean by the growing "internalization" of man: consequently we have the first growth in man, of what subsequently was called his soul. The whole inner world, originally as thin as if it had been stretched between two layers of skin, burst apart and expanded proportionately, and obtained depth, breadth, and height, when man's external outlet became *obstructed*. These terrible bulwarks, with which the social organization protected itself against the old instincts of freedom (punishments belong pre-eminently to these bulwarks), brought it about that all those instincts of wild, free, prowling man became turned backwards against man himself. Enmity, cruelty, the delight in persecution, in surprises, change, destruction—the turning all these instincts against their own possessors: this is the origin of the "bad conscience." It was man, who, lacking external enemies and obstacles, and imprisoned as he was in the oppressive narrowness and monotony of custom, in his own impatience lacerated, persecuted, gnawed, frightened, and ill-treated himself; it was this animal in the hands of the tamer, which beat itself against the bars of its cage; it was this being who, pining and yearning for that desert home of which it had been deprived, was compelled to create out of its own self, an adventure, a torture-chamber, a hazardous and perilous desert—it was this fool, this homesick and desperate prisoner—who invented the "bad conscience." But thereby he introduced that most grave and sinister illness, from which mankind has not yet recovered, the suffering of man from the disease called man, as the result of a violent breaking from his animal past, the result, as it were, of a spasmodic plunge into a new environment and new conditions of existence, the result of a declaration of war against the old instincts, which up to that time had been the staple of his power, his joy, his formidableness. Let us immediately add that this fact of an animal ego turning against itself, taking part against itself, produced in the world so novel, profound, unheard-of, problematic, inconsistent, and *pregnant* a phenomenon, that the aspect of the world was radically altered thereby. In sooth, only divine spectators could have appreciated the drama that then began, and whose end baffles conjecture as yet—a drama too subtle, too wonderful, too paradoxical to warrant its undergoing a non-sensical and unheeded performance on some random grotesque planet! Henceforth man is to be counted as one of the most unexpected and sensational lucky shots in the game of the "big baby" of Heracleitus, whether he be called Zeus or Chance—he awakens on his behalf the interest, excitement, hope, almost the confidence, of his being the harbinger and forerunner of something, of man being no end, but only a stage, an interlude, a bridge, a great promise.

17

It is primarily involved in this hypothesis of the origin of the bad conscience, that that alteration was no gradual and no voluntary alteration, and that it did not manifest itself as an organic adaptation to new conditions, but as a break, a jump, a necessity, an inevitable fate, against which there was no resistance and never a spark of resentment. And secondarily, that the fitting of a hitherto unchecked and amorphous population into a fixed form, starting as it had done in an act of violence, could only be accomplished by acts of violence and nothing else—that the oldest "State" appeared consequently as a ghastly tyranny, a grinding ruthless piece of machinery, which went on working, till this raw material of a semi-animal populace was not only thoroughly kneaded and elastic, but also *moulded*. I used the word "State": my meaning is self-evident, namely, a herd of blonde beasts of prey, a race of conquerors and masters, which with all its warlike organization and all its organizing power pounces with its terrible claws on a population, in numbers possibly tremendously superior, but as yet formless, as yet nomad. Such is the origin of the "State." That fantastic theory that makes it begin with a contract is, I think, disposed of. He who can command, he who is a master by "nature," he who comes on the scene forceful in deed and gesture—what has he to do with contracts? Such beings defy calculation, they come like fate, without cause, reason, notice, excuse, they are there like the lightning is there, too terrible, too sudden, too convincing, too "different," to be personally even hated. Their work is an instinctive creating and impressing of forms, they are the most involuntary, unconscious artists that there are:—their appearance produces instantaneously a scheme of sovereignty which is live, in which the functions are partitioned and apportioned, in which above all no part is received or finds a place, until pregnant with a "meaning" in regard to the whole. They are ignorant of the meaning of guilt, responsibility, consideration, are these born organisers; in them predominates that terrible artist-egoism, that gleams like brass, and that knows itself justified to all eternity, in its work, even as a mother in her child. It is not in *them* that there grew the bad conscience, that is elementary—but it would not have grown *without* them, repulsive growth as it was, it would be missing, had not a tremendous quantity of freedom been expelled from the world by the stress of their hammer-strokes, their artist violence, or been at any rate made invisible and, as it were, *latent*. This *instinct of freedom* forced into being latent—it is already clear—this instinct of freedom forced back, trodden back, imprisoned within itself, and finally only able to find vent and relief in itself; this, only this, is the beginning of the "bad conscience."

18

Beware of thinking lightly of this phenomenon, by reason of its initial painful ugliness. At bottom it is the same active force which is at work on a more grandiose scale in those potent artists and organizers, and builds states, which here, internally, on a smaller and pettier scale and with a retrogressive tendency, makes itself a bad science in the "labyrinth of the breast," to use Goethe's phrase, and which builds negative ideals; it is, I repeat, that identical *instinct of freedom* (to use my own language, the will to power): only the material, on which this force with all its constructive and tyrannous nature is let loose, is here man himself, his whole old animal self—and not as in the case of that more grandiose and sensational phenomenon, the *other* man, *other* men. This secret self-tyranny, this cruelty of the artist, this delight in giving a form to one's self as a piece of difficult, refractory, and suffering material, in burning in a will, a critique, a contradiction, a contempt, a negation; this sinister and ghastly labour of love on the part of a soul, whose will is cloven in two within itself, which makes itself suffer from delight in the infliction of suffering; this wholly *active* bad conscience has finally (as one already anticipates)—true fountainhead as it is of idealism and imagination—produced an abundance of novel and amazing beauty and affirmation, and perhaps has really been the first to give birth to beauty at all. What would beauty be, forsooth, if its contradiction had not first been presented to consciousness, if the ugly had not first said to itself, "I am ugly"? At any rate, after this hint the problem of how far idealism and beauty can be traced in such opposite ideas as "*selflessness*," *self-denial, self-sacrifice*, becomes less problematical; and indubitably in future we shall certainly know the real and original character of the *delight* experienced by the self-less, the self-denying, the self-sacrificing: this delight is a phase of cruelty.— So much provisionally for the origin of "altruism" as a *moral* value, and the marking out the ground from which this value has grown: it is only the bad conscience, only the will for self-abuse, that provides the necessary conditions for the existence of altruism as a *value*.

19

Undoubtedly the bad conscience is an illness, but an illness like pregnancy is an illness. If we search out the conditions under which this illness reaches its most terrible and sublime zenith, we shall see what really first brought about its entry into the world. But to do this we must take a long breath, and we must first of all go back once again to an earlier point of view. The relation at civil law of the ower to his creditor (which has already been discussed in detail), has been interpreted once again (and indeed in a manner which historically is exceedingly remarkable and suspicious) into a relationship, which is perhaps more incomprehensible to us moderns than to any other era; that is, into the relationship of the *existing* generation to its *ancestors*. Within the original tribal association—we are talking of primitive times—each living generation recognises a

legal obligation towards the earlier generation, and particularly towards the earliest, which founded the family (and this is something much more than a mere sentimental obliga-
5 tion, the existence of which, during the longest period of man's history, is by no means indisputable). There prevails in them the conviction that it is only thanks to sacrifices and efforts of their ancestors, that the race *persists* at
10 all—and that this has to be *paid back* to them by sacrifices and services. Thus is recognized the *owing* of a debt, which accumulates continually by reason of these ancestors never ceasing in their subsequent life as potent spirits to
15 secure by their power new privileges and advantages to the race. Gratis, perchance? But there is no gratis for that raw and "meansouled" age. What return can be made?— Sacrifice (at first, nourishment, in its crudest
20 sense), festivals, temples, tributes of veneration, above all, obedience—since all customs are, *quae* works of the ancestors, equally their precepts and commands—are the ancestors ever given enough? This suspicion remains
25 and grows: from time to time it extorts a great wholesale ransom, something monstrous in the way of repayment of the creditor (the notorious sacrifice of the first-born, for example, blood, human blood in any case). The *fear* of
30 ancestors and their power, the consciousness of owing debts to them, necessarily increases, according to this kind of logic, in the exact proportion that the race itself increases, that the race itself becomes more victorious, more
35 independent, more honored, more feared. This, and not the contrary, is the fact. Each step towards race decay, all disastrous events, all symptoms of degeneration, of approaching disintegration, always *diminish* the fear of the
40 founders' spirit, and whittle away the idea of his sagacity, providence, and potent presence. Conceive this crude kind of logic carried to its climax: it follows that the ancestors of the *most*

powerful races must, through the growing fear
45 that they exercise on the imaginations, grow themselves into monstrous dimensions, and become relegated to the gloom of a divine mystery that transcends imagination—the ancestor becomes at last necessarily transfigured
50 into a *god*. Perhaps this is the very origin of the gods, that is, an origin from *fear*! And those who feel bound to add, "but from piety also," will have difficulty in maintaining this theory, with regard to the primeval and longest period
55 of the human race. And of course this is even more the case as regards the *middle* period, the formative period of the aristocratic races—the aristocratic races which have given back with interest to their founders, the ancestors (he-
60 roes, gods), all those qualities which in the meanwhile have appeared in themselves, that is, the aristocratic qualities. We will later on glance again at the ennobling and promotion of the gods (which of course is totally distinct
65 from their "sanctification"): let us now provisionally follow to its end the course of the whole of this development of the consciousness of "owing."

20

70 According to the teaching of history, the consciousness of owing debts to the deity by no means came to an end with the decay of the clan organization of society; just as mankind
75 has inherited the ideas of "good" and "bad" from the race-nobility (together with its fundamental tendency towards establishing social distinctions), so with the heritage of the racial and tribal gods it has also inherited the incu-
80 bus of debts as yet unpaid and the desire to discharge them. The transition is effected by those large populations of slaves and bondsmen, who, whether through compulsion or through submission and "*mimicry*," have ac-
85 commodated themselves to the religion of their masters; through this channel these in-

herited tendencies inundate the world. The feeling of owing a debt to the deity has grown continuously for several centuries, always in the same proportion in which the idea of God
5 and the consciousness of God have grown and become exalted among mankind. (The whole history of ethnic fights, victories, reconciliations, amalgamations, everything, in fact, which precedes the eventual classing of
10 all the social elements in each great race-synthesis, are mirrored in the hotch-potch genealogy of their gods, in the legends of their fights, victories, and reconciliations. Progress towards universal empires invariably means
15 progress towards universal deities; despotism, with its subjugation of the independent nobility, always paves the way for some system or other of monotheism.) The appearance of the Christian god, as the record god up to this
20 time, has for that very reason brought equally into the world the record amount of guilt consciousness. Granted that we have gradually started on the *reverse* movement, there is no little probability in the deduction, based on the
25 continuous decay in the belief in the Christian god, to the effect that there also already exists a considerable decay in the human consciousness of owing (ought); in fact, we cannot shut our eyes to the prospect of the complete and
30 eventual triumph of atheism freeing mankind from all this feeling of obligation to their origin, their *causa prima*. Atheism and a kind of second innocence complement and supplement each other.
35

21

So much for my rough and preliminary sketch of the interrelation of the ideas "ought" (owe) and "duty" with the postulates of religion. I
40 have intentionally shelved up to the present the actual moralization of these ideas (their being pushed back into the conscience, or more precisely the interweaving of the *bad*

conscience with the idea of God), and at the
45 end of the last paragraph used language to the effect that this moralization did not exist, and that consequently these ideas had necessarily come to an end, by reason of what had happened to their hypothesis, the credence in our
50 "creditor," in God. The actual facts differ terribly from this theory. It is with the moralization of the ideas "ought" and "duty," and with their being pushed back into the *bad* conscience, that comes the first actual attempt to
55 *reverse* the direction of the development we have just described, or at any rate to arrest its evolution; it is just at this juncture that the very hope of an eventual redemption *has to* put itself once for all into the prison of pessimism,
60 it is at this juncture that the eye *has to* recoil and rebound in despair from off an adamantine impossibility, it is at this juncture that the ideas "guilt" and "duty" have to turn backwards—turn backwards against *whom*? There is
65 no doubt about it; primarily against the "ower," in whom the bad conscience now establishes itself, eats, extends, and grows like a polypus throughout its length and breadth, all with such virulence, that at last, with the im-
70 possibility of paying the debt, there becomes conceived the idea of the impossibility of paying the penalty, the thought of its inexplicability (the idea of "eternal punishment")—finally, too, it turns against the "creditor," whether
75 found in the *causa prima* of man, the origin of the human race, its sire, who henceforth becomes burdened with a curse ("Adam," "original sin," "determination of the will"), or in Nature from whose womb man springs, and
80 on whom the responsibility for the principle of evil is now cast ("Diabolisation of Nature"), or in existence generally, on this logic an absolute *white elephant*, with which mankind is landed (the Nihilistic flight from life, the demand
85 for Nothingness, or for the opposite of existence, for some other existence, Buddhism and

the like)—till suddenly we stand before that paradoxical and awful expedient, through which a tortured humanity has found a temporary alleviation, that stroke of genius called
5 Christianity:—God personally immolating himself for the debt of man, God paying himself personally out of a pound of his own flesh, God as the one being who can deliver man from what man had become unable to
10 deliver himself—the creditor playing scapegoat for his debtor, from *love* (can you believe it?), from love of his debtor!...

22

15 The reader will already have conjectured what took place on the stage and behind the scenes of this drama. That will for self-torture, that inverted cruelty of the animal man, who, turned subjective and scared into introspec-
20 tion (encaged as he was in "the State," as part of his taming process), invented the bad conscience so as to hurt himself, after the *natural* outlet for this will to hurt, became blocked— in other words, this man of the bad con-
25 science exploited the religious hypothesis so as to carry his martyrdom to the ghastliest pitch of agonized intensity. Owing something to *God*: this thought becomes his instrument of torture. He apprehends in God the most ex-
30 treme antitheses that he can find to his own characteristic and ineradicable animal instincts, he himself gives a new interpretation to these animal instincts as being against what he "owes" to God (as enmity, rebellion, and re-
35 volt against the "Lord," the "Father," the "Sire," the "Beginning of the world"), he places himself between the horns of the dilemma, "God" and "Devil." Every negation which he is inclined to utter to himself, to the nature,
40 naturalness, and reality of his being, he whips into an ejaculation of "yes," uttering it as something existing, living, efficient, as being God, as the holiness of God, the judgment of

God, as the hangmanship of God, as tran-
45 scendence, as eternity, as unending torment, as hell, as infinity of punishment and guilt. This is a kind of madness of the will in the sphere of psychological cruelty which is absolutely unparalleled:—man's *will* to find himself guilty
50 and blameworthy to the point of inexpiability, his *will* to think of himself as punished, without the punishment ever being able to balance the guilt, his *will* to infect and to poison the fundamental basis of the universe with the
55 problem of punishment and guilt, in order to cut off once and for all any escape out of this labyrinth of "fixed ideas," his will for rearing an ideal—that of the "holy God"—face to face with which he can have tangible proof of
60 his own un-worthiness. Alas for this mad melancholy beast man! What phantasies invade it, what paroxysms of perversity, hysterical sense-lessness, and *mental bestiality* break out immediately, at the very slightest check on its being
65 the beast of action. All this is excessively interesting, but at the same time tainted with a black, gloomy, enervating melancholy, so that a forcible veto must be invoked against looking too long into these abysses. Here is *disease*,
70 undubitably, the most ghastly disease that has as yet played havoc among men: and he who can still hear (but man turns now deaf ears to such sounds), how in this night of torment and nonsense there has rung out the cry of
75 *love*, the cry of the most passionate ecstasy, of redemption in *love*, he turns away gripped by an invincible horror—in man there is so much that is ghastly—too long has the world been a mad-house.
80

23

Let this suffice once for all concerning the origin of the "holy God." The fact that *in itself* the conception of gods is not bound to lead
85 necessarily to this degradation of the imagination (a temporary representation of whose

vagaries we felt bound give), the fact that there exist nobler methods of utilizing the invention of gods than in this self-crucifixion and self-degradation of man, in which the last two thousand years of Europe have been past masters—these facts can fortunately be still perceived from every glance that we cast at the Grecian gods, these mirrors of noble and grandiose men, in which the *animal* in man felt itself deified, and did *not* devour itself in subjective frenzy. These Greeks long utilised their gods as simple buffers against the "bad conscience"—so that they could continue to enjoy their freedom of soul: this, of course, is diametrically opposed to Christianity's theory of its god. They went *very far* on this principle, did these splendid and lion-hearted children; and there is no lesser authority than that of the Homeric Zeus for making them realise occasionally that they are taking life too casually. "Wonderful," says he on one occasion—it has to do with the case of Ægistheus, a *very* bad case indeed—

"Wonderful how they grumble, the mortals against the immortals, *Only from us*, they presume, *comes evil*, but in their folly,
Fashion they, spite of fate, the doom of their own disaster."

Yet the reader will note and observe that this Olympian spectator and judge is far from being angry with them and thinking evil of them on this score. "How *foolish* they are," so thinks he of the misdeeds of mortals—and "folly," "imprudence," "a little brain disturbance," and nothing more, are what the Greeks, even of the strongest, bravest period, have admitted to be the ground of much that is evil and fatal.— Folly, *not* sin, do you understand?... But even this brain disturbance was a problem— "Come, how is it even possible? How could it have really got in brains like ours, the brains of men of aristocratic ancestry, of men of fortune, of men of good natural endowments, of men of the best society, of men of nobility and virtue?" This was the question that for century on century the aristocratic Greek put to himself when confronted with every (to him incomprehensible) outrage and sacrilege with which one of his peers had polluted himself. "It must be that a god had infatuated him," he would say at last, nodding his head.—This solution is *typical* of the Greeks, ... accordingly the gods in those times subserved the functions of justifying man to a certain extent even in evil—in those days they took upon themselves not the punishment, but, what is more noble, the guilt.

24

I conclude with three queries, as you will see. "Is an ideal actually set up here, or is one pulled down?" I am perhaps asked.... But have ye sufficiently asked yourselves how dear a payment has the setting up of every ideal in the world exacted? To achieve that consummation how much truth must always be traduced and misunderstood, how many lies must be sanctified, how much conscience has got to be disturbed, how many pounds of "God" have got to be sacrificed every time? To enable a sanctuary to be set up *a sanctuary has got to be destroyed*: that is a law—show me an instance where it has not been fulfilled!... We modern men, we inherit the immemorial tradition of vivisecting the conscience, and practicing cruelty to our animal selves. That is the sphere of our most protracted training, perhaps of our artistic prowess, at any rate of our dilettantism and our perverted taste. Man has for too long regarded his natural proclivities with an "evil eye," so that eventually they have become in his system affiliated to a bad conscience. A converse endeavor would be intrinsically feasible—but who is strong enough to attempt it?—namely, to affiliate to the "bad conscience" all those *unnatural* proclivities, all those transcendental aspirations, contrary to sense, instinct, nature, and animalism—in

5 short, all past and present ideals, which are all ideals opposed to life, and traducing the world. To whom is one to turn nowadays with *such* hopes and pretensions?—It is just the *good* men that we should thus bring about our ears;

10 and in addition, as stands to reason, the indolent, the hedgers, the vain, the hysterical, the tired.... What is more offensive or more thoroughly calculated to alienate, than giving any hint of the exalted severity with which we treat

15 ourselves? And again how conciliatory, how full of love does all the world show itself towards us so soon as we do as all the world docs, and "let ourselves go" like all the world. For such a consummation we need spirits of

20 *different* caliber than seems really feasible in this age; spirits rendered potent through wars and victories, to whom conquest, adventure, danger, even pain, have become a need; for such a consummation we need habituation to sharp,

25 rare air, to winter wanderings, to literal and metaphorical ice and mountains; we even need a kind of sublime malice, a supreme and most self-conscious insolence of knowledge, which is the appanage of great health; we need (to

30 summarize the awful truth) just this *great health*!

Is this even feasible to-day?... But some day, in a stronger age than this rotting and introspective present, must he in sooth come to us,

35 even the *redeemer* of great love and scorn, the creative spirit, rebounding by the impetus of his own force back again away from every transcendental plane and dimension, he whose solitude is misunderstanded (sic) of the peo-

40 ple, as though it were a flight *from* reality;— while actually it is only his diving, burrowing, and penetrating *into* reality, so that when he comes again to the light he can at once bring

about by these means the *redemption* of this

45 reality; its redemption from the curse which the old ideal has laid upon it. This man of the future, who in this wise will redeem us from the old ideal, as he will from that ideal's necessary corollary of great nausea, will to nothing-

50 ness, and Nihilism; this tocsin of noon and of the great verdict, which renders the will again free, who gives back to the world its goal and to man his hope, this Antichrist and Antinihilist, this conqueror of God and of Nothing-

55 ness—*he must one day come.*

25

But what am I talking of? Enough! Enough? At this juncture I have only one proper

60 course, silence: otherwise trespass on a domain open alone to one who is younger than I, one stronger, more "future" than I—open alone to Zarathustra, Zarathustra the godless.

ABOUT THE AUTHOR

The editor of this text is Michael Julius. Dr. Julius received his Ph.D. from the University of Minnesota in 2013.

Made in the USA
Middletown, DE
20 May 2017